LG DEm

INTRODUCTION TO
PSYCHOLOGY

VOLUME 1

Introduction to Psychology Course Team

Steve Best   *Graphic Artist*
Gillian Cohen   *Senior Lecturer in Psychology, Faculty of Social Sciences*
Rudi Dallos   *Staff Tutor, Faculty of Social Sciences*
Ann Davey   *Print Production Co-ordinator*
Harry Dodd   *Print Production Controller*
Judith Greene   *Professor of Psychology, Faculty of Social Sciences*
Fiona Harris   *Editor*
Siân Lewis   *Graphic Designer*
Paul Light   *Professor of Psychology, School of Education*
Vic Lockwood   *Senior BBC Producer*
Dorothy Miell   *Lecturer in Psychology, Faculty of Social Sciences*
John Oates   *Lecturer in Education, School of Education*
Hugh Phillips   *BBC Producer*
Ortenz Rose   *Secretary*
Ilona Roth   *Lecturer in Psychology, Faculty of Social Sciences (Course Team Chair)*
Ingrid Slack   *Course Manager, Faculty of Social Sciences*
Jon Slack   *Lecturer in Psychology, Faculty of Social Sciences*
Richard Stevens   *Senior Lecturer in Psychology, Faculty of Social Sciences*
Kerry Thomas   *Senior Lecturer in Psychology, Faculty of Social Sciences*
Frederick Toates   *Senior Lecturer in Biology, Faculty of Science*
Pat Vasiliou   *Secretary*
Margaret Wetherell   *Lecturer in Psychology, Faculty of Social Sciences*
David Wilson   *Editor*

Consultants

Andrew M. Colman   *Reader in Psychology, Department of Psychology, University of Leicester*
Chris Cullen   *Professor of Learning Difficulties, Department of Psychology, University of St Andrews*

External assessor

Antony J. Chapman   *Professor of Psychology, University of Leeds*

The Open University's

INTRODUCTION TO

PSYCHOLOGY

VOLUME 1

Psychology Press in association with The Open University

Edited by Ilona Roth

Psychology Press Ltd.
(an imprint of Taylor & Francis)
27 Church Road, Hove, East Sussex BN3 2FA
in association with
The Open University
Walton Hall
Milton Keynes MK7 6AB

First published 1990 - reprinted 1991, 1992, 1997, 1998, 1999, 2000 (twice)
Copyright © 1990 The Open University

British Library Cataloguing in Publication Data
Introduction to psychology.
  Vol. 1.
  1. Psychology
  I. Roth, Ilona   II. Open University
  150

  ISBN 0 86377 136 X (Hardback)
  ISBN 0 86377 138 6 (Paperback)

Designed by the Graphic Design Group of the Open University
Typeset by Phoenix Photosetting, Chatham, Kent
Printed in Great Britain by Bath Press Colourbooks, Glasgow

Introduction to Psychology Volumes 1 and 2 form part of the Open University course
DSE202 *Introduction to Psychology*. If you would like a copy of *Studying with The
Open University*, please write to the Course Enquiries Data Service, PO Box 625, Dane
Road, Milton Keynes MK1 1TY.

Contents

Preface   vii

Part I   Introduction   **1**

Chapter 1
What is Psychology?   *Ilona Roth*   2

Part II   The Developing Person   **27**

Introduction to Part II   28

Chapter 2
The Self and the Social World   *Dorothy Miell*   30

Chapter 3
The Development of Children's Understanding   *Paul Light and
John Oates*   79

Chapter 4
Psychodynamics: The Freudian Approach   *Kerry Thomas*   131

Overview of Part II   185

Part III   The Foundations of Behaviour   **189**

Introduction to Part III   190

Chapter 5
Biological Perspectives   *Frederick Toates*   191

Chapter 6
Behaviourism and its Consequences   *Frederick Toates and Ingrid Slack*   250

Overview of Part III   314

Part IV   Individual Diversity   **319**

Introduction to Part IV   320

Chapter 7
Aspects of Intelligence   *Andrew M. Colman*   322

Chapter 8
Dimensions of Personality   *Kerry Thomas*   373

Chapter 9
Humanistic Psychology   *Richard Stevens*   417

Overview of Part IV   470

Acknowledgements for Volume 1   ix

Name index for Volume 1   x

Concept index for Volume 1   xiv

Contents of Volume 2

Part V Cognitive Processes

Introduction to Part V

Chapter 10
Perception   *Judith Greene*

Chapter 11
Attention   *Jon Slack*

Chapter 12
Memory   *Gillian Cohen*

Overview of Part V

Part VI The Social Dimension

Introduction to Part VI

Chapter 13
Topics in Language and Communication   *Judith Greene*

Chapter 14
Issues in Social Psychology   *Dorothy Miell*

Overview of Part VI

Part VII Applications to Problems

Introduction to Part VII

Chapter 15
Clinical Psychology   *Rudi Dallos and Chris Cullen*

Chapter 16
Autism   *Ilona Roth*

Overview of Part VII

Part VIII Review

Chapter 17
Understanding Psychology   *Judith Greene and Kerry Thomas*

Acknowledgements for Volume 2

Name index for Volumes 1 and 2

Concept index for Volumes 1 and 2

Preface

As their title indicates, the two volumes of this *Introduction to psychology* provide an introduction to the subject. They have been written and designed to suit the reader or student who has no prior knowledge of psychology.

The two books form part of the Open University course also called Introduction to Psychology. Open University courses are put together by a course team which includes academics, editors, designers, BBC producers, course managers and course secretaries. The full course team responsible for producing this Introduction to Psychology course is listed on page ii.

Open University courses are the result of a long collaborative process, a central feature of which is detailed discussion about the topics which should be included and how they should be presented. The individual chapters in these two books have been prepared by their authors in several drafts, each commented on by all members of the course team. Careful consideration has been given to the integration of these chapters into a coherent and organized whole. The end product provides a wide-ranging introduction to many psychological topics, presented in considerable depth.

While these two volumes are free-standing and self-contained, they are complemented by other materials and activities for students studying them as part of the Open University Introduction to Psychology course. These students will carry out research projects, learn statistics, view television programmes and listen to audiocassettes, attend day schools and summer schools, prepare assignments and sit a final examination. If you are interested in extending your own studies with any of these course components, you should write, enquiring about availability, to: Open University Educational Enterprises Limited, 12 Cofferidge Close, Stony Stratford, Milton Keynes MK11 1BY, Great Britain.

The preparation of the main texts of the course in book form has two purposes. Open University students will have the textual materials for their course in a convenient format. All readers will, we hope, be able to benefit from an introductory textbook on psychology, carefully designed, with the long experience of Open University course teams, to provide teaching materials tailored to the needs of students working with a fair degree of independence. Particular emphasis is placed on a style of presentation which encourages active participation on the part of the reader.

How to use this book

In each chapter in these volumes you will find various teaching aids:

SAQs

These are Self Assessment Questions which are designed so that you can test your knowledge as you study. The only real way to benefit from these is to try and answer each SAQ *before* looking up the answers at the end of each chapter. You will also sometimes find other more general questions posed in the text which you should think about before reading on.

Activities

Various types of activity appear throughout each chapter to give you the opportunity to try out a variety of psychological techniques for yourselves. In the spirit of 'active' learning, you will find that quite complex approaches will be much easier to grasp if you get a feel for the kind of work undertaken by psychologists.

Boxes

These are mainly used to present details of experiments and other kinds of research, in a form to which you can easily refer whenever you wish.

Summaries of Sections

Most students find these 'summings up' of the content of the main sections invaluable. They are useful to look at immediately after finishing a section to help consolidate what you have read. They are also particularly helpful as a revision device. When you refer back to a summary, you should find it revives your memory of essential points. If you are puzzled by any statements, you may need to re-read part of the preceding text to clarify your understanding.

Index of Concepts

You will notice that many of the key psychological terms used in the text are indicated in bold print when they are first defined. This will draw your attention to crucial terms used in psychology. These words are also listed in an Index of Concepts at the back of each volume. There you will find references to the pages on which the terms were first introduced and defined.

Further Reading and References

At the end of each chapter there is a brief list of books suggested for further reading, either because they provide more details about certain topics or because they provide readable accounts of the work of important psychologists. There are also references to all the books and articles cited in the chapter.

Introductions and Overviews

At the beginning of each major Part there is a brief introduction to the topics covered in the chapters. At the end of each major Part there is an overview which is intended to focus on issues common to the chapters in the Part. These overviews are not meant to be summaries. Their aim is to point out interesting links between chapters and to develop general theoretical issues. They should also provide a thread linking the controversial points raised in Chapter 1 in the first volume to the concluding Chapter 17 at the end of the second volume.

PART I
INTRODUCTION

1 WHAT IS PSYCHOLOGY?

Ilona Roth

Contents

1	**Psychology and everyday life**	**3**
1.1	Some everyday misconceptions	3
1.2	The impact of psychology	4
1.3	Psychology as a resource	6
	Summary of Section 1	6
2	**Psychology and common sense**	**7**
2.1	People are psychologists; psychologists are people	7
2.2	Some pitfalls of common sense	9
	Summary of Section 2	10
3	**Theory and method in psychology**	**10**
3.1	Formulating a theory	10
3.2	Designing a study	11
3.3	The experimental method	14
3.4	Drawing conclusions	15
3.5	The whole story?	15
	Summary of Section 3	16
4	**Special problems for psychology**	**16**
4.1	The problems of studying people	16
4.2	Is psychology a science?	17
4.3	Ethics	18
	Summary of Section 4	21
5	**This *Introduction to psychology***	**21**
5.1	A common objective?	24
	References	24
	Answers to SAQs	24

1 | Psychology and everyday life

As you start this *Introduction to psychology*, you probably have your own idea of what psychology is. Perhaps you know a psychologist, or have met one through your job, your child's school, or in some other context. Perhaps you have read some of the works of a famous figure of psychology such as Freud, Eysenck, Piaget or Skinner. Some of you will have studied courses with psychological content. If so, you will be aware that psychology is a very diverse field—psychologists do a wide variety of things. Yet the everyday image of psychology is sometimes narrow and over-simplified.

1.1 Some everyday misconceptions

There is a common caricature of the psychologist as a somewhat learned and intimidating person who can 'read one's mind'. I am sure that I am not the only psychologist who has been asked what I do in casual conversation, only to be met with the horrified response of, 'Oh dear, perhaps you are reading my mind!'. I can assure you that psychologists feel as uncomfortable with this suggestion as the people who make it.

What is it that psychologists do which has earned them this reputation? I can think of no branch of psychology which *literally* involves reading other people's minds. What goes on in a person's mind is not available for direct scrutiny like the pages of a book. Only those people who believe in telepathy might claim that the mind is accessible in this way. However, many psychologists believe that it is possible to gain *indirect* access to the mind, and thus to arrive at an understanding of how it works. For although the mind cannot be directly observed, we can observe other people's **behaviour**, that is, all the things they do and say.

A key assumption in psychology is that the way people behave bears a relationship to what is going on in their minds. To take a simple example, if someone is observed to be smiling, this is more likely to reflect an internal state of happiness rather than one of sadness. It is possible to *infer* with some confidence that the person is happy. So while psychology does not involve literally reading minds, the goal, for many psychologists, is to provide insight into how the mind works and what experiences people are having, based on observations of human behaviour.

Some psychologists reject even these indirect forms of 'mind reading'. One notable group of psychologists, called **behaviourists**, regards attempts to 'go beyond' observable behaviour in this way as little more than crystal ball gazing. Behaviourists argue that anything which cannot be *directly* observed is beyond the scope of psychology. For them, behaviour is the central subject-matter of psychology, not a means to discover what people are thinking and feeling.

Another common misconception about psychologists is that their interests are narrowly focused on topics such as how you feel—**emotion**—and what provides the driving force for behaviour—**motivation**. But these are just small corners of the field. All aspects of how the mind and behaviour function interest psychologists, ranging from **mental processes** such as thinking, memory and attention, to complex **social behaviour** such as speaking a language, making friends or helping someone across the road.

It may also be thought that psychologists are mainly interested in the thoughts, feelings, experiences and behaviour of the *individual*. Again, there are psychologists who believe that each individual is unique. But many psychologists are more interested in the characteristics which are common to people in general: they seek to establish the *general* principles governing how all minds work and why all people display certain patterns of behaviour.

A different kind of misconception is that the work of psychologists is especially or exclusively concerned with 'abnormal' minds and 'abnormal' behaviour. But this is the domain of just one kind of specialist psychologist called a **clinical psychologist**. The work of clinical psychologists typically involves helping people with mental or behavioural problems. There are many other kinds of psychologist, most of whom are more concerned with 'normal' than 'abnormal' psychological functioning. Some of these work in practical fields, such as education and industry; others do academic work, particularly research and teaching.

To summarize, psychology seeks to *understand*, rather than actually to read minds; it is broad rather than narrow in scope; it is concerned with characteristics common to people in general as well as with the experiences of unique individuals; and it deals with both normal and abnormal functioning. This may none the less leave you thinking that psychology is a somewhat remote and mysterious subject. Although there *are* topics and methods in psychology which you may find unfamiliar, there are many ways in which psychology pervades and is part of everyday life. Let us take the demystification of psychology one step further by describing some of them.

1.2 The impact of psychology

Over the years, some important ideas from psychology have had such an impact on our thoughts and behaviour that we are barely aware of their origin.

The psychologist whose impact on everyday thinking has probably been greatest is Sigmund Freud (1856–1939). At the heart of his theory is the idea that people's behaviour is driven by unconscious mental forces which are beyond their awareness and control. The strength of these forces and the precise ways in which they affect a person's behaviour are largely determined by experiences in early childhood. Neither of these ideas seems particularly remarkable to us, because they have become so much part of the way in which we make sense of other people's behaviour. For instance, if someone makes a tactless remark to you and then immediately apologizes, you may still think that 'deep down' the person had intended to hurt your feelings. Yet the notion that we are unconsciously motivated to behave in ways which seem, consciously, unacceptable to us, originated with Freud.

The approach pioneered by Freud has penetrated everyday thinking at many different levels. Our everyday language contains many expressions and phrases which Freud originated—the Oedipus complex, phallic symbol and wish fulfilment, for example. And his theory has provided a fertile source of ideas for novelists and literary critics, because it offers a framework within which meaning can be given to the strange and frequently destructive ways in which people behave towards one another.

Freud is by no means the only psychologist whose ideas have affected our lives. For example, the behaviourist B. F. Skinner (born 1904) has had both positive and negative effects on the way children are educated. His work has drawn attention to the fact that children are more likely to learn if they are encouraged or rewarded for the right kind of behaviour, than if they are punished for the wrong kind of behaviour. His claim that learning involves little more than this kind of encouragement has been less useful. The work of the developmental psychologist Jean Piaget (1896–1980) has done much to promote the view that children will only learn when they are ready. According to Piaget, when children's mental faculties have reached a certain stage of maturity, they will discover things for themselves. As a result of this insight, teachers these days are much less likely to impose a rigid learning regime on their pupils. Instead, teaching is tuned to the needs of individual children.

You may wonder whether psychology has had too much of an impact on our outlook and everyday behaviour. Perhaps some of the ideas which have come from psychology are too 'permissive'. Some may think, for instance, that people should be held responsible for their actions at all times, rather than, as Freud has led us to believe, being driven by forces beyond their control. Both parents and teachers are sometimes heard to claim that there is too little discipline in the classroom—that 'sparing the rod and spoiling the child' has led to a decline in standards of behaviour and education.

Psychological ideas can also be seen as reinforcing 'reactionary' attitudes within society. The psychologist Sir Cyril Burt argued that a child's intelligence, as measured by an IQ test, was a relatively fixed quantity, which could be determined at an early age. This stimulated the policy, reflected in the eleven-plus examination, that children's schooling opportunities should be finally decided on the basis of their performance at this age. Children who performed well in the eleven-plus benefited from entry to grammar schools, but the academic provision for the remaining children was inadequate, particularly for bright 'late developers'.

The point is that the impact of psychology on everyday life is not necessarily experienced as beneficial, or even neutral, by everyone. This is because attitudes and values vary from one individual to another and from one era and society to another. For instance, although some people deplore the more relaxed atmosphere which prevails in today's schools, others regard it as infinitely preferable to what they regard as the rigid authoritarian regime of earlier years. And, of course, psychologists, as individuals within a particular society, have their own beliefs and values. These inevitably influence the type of problem they choose to work on, and the nature of the solutions they put forward.

1.3 Psychology as a resource

There are many areas in which psychology provides a practical resource, the beneficial effects of which few would deny. A pioneer in this field is the psychologist Donald Broadbent who has argued that the starting point for psychology should be practical problems in the real world (Open University, 1981). He became particularly interested in the problems air traffic controllers experience when dealing with several important messages reaching their ears at the same time. Other psychologists have devised tests to ensure that pilots are selected with the right kind of personality characteristics as well as intellectual and motor skills. They have worked on the safe design of aircraft instrument panels to ensure that pilots can cope with all the important signals that come in when flying a plane. They have looked at how efficiently pilots fly under conditions of jet lag or sleep deprivation. They have even provided aircraft staff with expert advice on how to handle hijackers and terrorists, and have counselled victims of both hijacking and air crashes. Psychologists have made similar contributions to safety standards on roads and in factories. In these areas, at least, we can see psychology as a resource which has had beneficial effects on our everyday lives.

In this section I have tried to give some idea of what psychologists do and how their work has affected our lives. But there is an even closer and more subtle link between the work of psychologists and what people do every day of their lives. This is the subject of the next section.

Summary of Section 1

- Contrary to common misconception, psychologists do not literally read people's minds. They attempt to understand how the mind works by studying behaviour.

- Psychologists are interested in many topics besides feelings and emotions. They also study mental processes such as memory and thinking, and complex social behaviour such as communicating with and helping other people.

- Psychologists are interested in the characteristics common to people in general as well as in understanding unique individuals.

- Clinical psychologists seek to help people with psychological problems. Many psychologists are more concerned with 'normal' psychological functioning.

- Psychology has had a profound influence on our everyday lives, particularly on ideas about what motivates behaviour and the best methods of educating children.

- Psychology has provided an important practical resource in fields such as aircraft and road safety.

2 | Psychology and common sense

The psychologist Robert Farr once observed that 'the man in the street was successfully a psychologist long before there was ever a separate study of psychology' (Open University, 1981). What he meant was that we are constantly engaged in trying to understand what is going on in other people's minds and why they behave as they do. If we were not, we would not be able to interact with each other because other people's intentions would be constantly misunderstood. In short, Farr's claim is that our commonsense understanding of other people is itself a form of psychology. Let us look more closely at the basis for this claim.

2.1 People are psychologists; psychologists are people

Suppose you see a crying child walking up and down the pavement and casting searching glances in all directions. You are likely to assume that the child is worried about something she has lost—her bus-fare or a favourite toy perhaps. Why do you make this assumption? The chances are that you have observed similar events happening before, with similar consequences. Previous experience has led you to associate a particular set of circumstances (a child losing something) with a particular type of behaviour (crying and searching for the lost object) and even a particular state of mind (sadness and anxiety). You can be said to have formulated a **theory**, based on your previous observations, about how children will react to one kind of situation. This general theory provides you with a potential **explanation** of the behaviour of one particular child. Of course, you do not know for sure that this explanation is correct.

SAQ 1   (*SAQ answers are given at the end of the chapter*)
   (a) What further observations would help you to find out whether your explanation is correct?
   (b) What kind of behaviour on the part of the child might suggest to you that your explanation is incorrect?

Notice that in taking steps to investigate and observe the child's behaviour further, you are seeking **evidence** for or against your explanation about why she is behaving as she is. If you see her pick something up from the pavement and stop crying, this suggests that your original explanation was correct. On the other hand, if you discover after a few minutes' observation that the child is participating in a 'pretend' game with friends, this provides you with evidence against your explanation. Either way, you can be said to be **testing** your explanation against the evidence provided by your observations.

It may perhaps strike you as odd to analyse such a commonplace, everyday situation in terms of concepts such as 'theory', 'explanation', and 'testing of evidence'. Our understanding of everyday behaviour seems spontaneous and automatic. We are not aware of drawing on theories to explain this behaviour, nor of seeking evidence to test our explanations. Another objection to this analysis is that it makes us sound like bystanders, people who simply observe what other people are doing, rather than interacting with them. If you saw a child apparently searching for something on the pavement, it is unlikely that you would have *only* stood and watched. You would probably have offered to help.

It is true that people's theories about why other people behave as they do are rarely consciously articulated or openly expressed. This is why they are sometimes known as **implicit theories**. But they are theories none the less. Otherwise, we would not find ourselves considering alternative explanations for the behaviour of the child in the street. It is also true that we interact with, rather than simply observe, other people. But our implicit theories about their behaviour are critical in ensuring that our interactions are appropriate. It is *because* we think that the child in the street has lost something that we are moved to offer to help.

The process of formulating and testing theories is, then, very much part of our everyday, commonsense approach to making sense of other people's behaviour. But it is also the means psychologists use to understand their subject-matter—other people. So, in one sense, people function as psychologists all the time.

Not only do people act like psychologists, but it is important to remember that psychologists are people too! They have the same characteristics and function in the same way as their subject-matter. In fact some of the most famous figures in the history of psychology have based their theories on observations of themselves. The founder of psychoanalysis, Sigmund Freud, derived a significant body of evidence from his own memories of his childhood, and from dreams and events in his everyday life. Hermann Ebbinghaus (1850–1909), the first psychologist to make systematic studies of memory, constructed long lists, sometimes of numbers and sometimes of letters, which he gave himself to remember. These psychologists saw themselves as no different from the people about whom they formulated their theories, and therefore saw nothing problematic in using themselves as the testing ground for their theories.

You may have noticed something of a paradox in the discussion so far. I started out by arguing that the work of professional psychologists has had powerful and frequently beneficial effects on our lives. I went on to argue that we are all, in a sense, psychologists in our everyday approach to understanding other people. But, if we all have a commonsense understanding of human behaviour and experience, why do we need the specialized work of professional psychologists at all? Is there perhaps more to psychology than common sense? To answer this we will first consider some of the limitations of common sense.

2.2 Some pitfalls of common sense

Consider an issue about which many people, particularly parents, have very definite views: what causes aggression in young people? One strongly held commonsense theory is that children who watch violent television programmes are more likely to be aggressive themselves.

The first thing to ask is where does an everyday theory like this come from? There are probably a variety of sources, including articles in the newspapers, television news items and views expressed by friends, as well as parents' observations of their own and other children. Notice that these sources are not necessarily reliable. Newspapers and television frequently exaggerate or slant an argument in one direction in order to influence their audience. Also, the theory is rather vague—it is not clear whether it is meant to apply to all children, or just particular groups of children. It is not clear what is meant by a violent television programme, nor what 'being aggressive' means.

Even so, parents may feel that their own observations provide evidence to support this theory. A father may have noticed that Tom, the boy next door, is always watching programmes like *Action Force* and *The A Team*, and that his favourite pastime is fighting other children in the street. He may have noticed that his own child, John, who watches programmes like *Blue Peter*, spends much less time fighting. But although these observations appear to support the theory, it is easy to show that they do not really argue either for or against it.

SAQ 2   Can you think of any reasons, apart from the effect of violent television programmes, why Tom might engage in more fighting than John?

There may be other problems with the parent's conclusion. There could be children who watch as many violent television programmes as Tom, but who show no particular signs of aggressiveness. It could even be that watching violent programmes serves a 'cathartic' function for Tom: that is, the programmes could serve as a release for aggressive tendencies which would be even greater if he did not watch them. So evidence which seems intuitively convincing does not necessarily stand up to critical scrutiny.

This example shows that people's commonsense intuitions about other people's behaviour and experience are sometimes unreliable. Yet earlier I argued that 'implicit theories' provide the basis for people's interactions with one another. The implication is that some of these interactions are based on misunderstandings!

In the hypothetical example of the crying child, it would not matter too much if one's implicit theory led one to adopt the wrong explanation of the child's behaviour, and to take inappropriate action based on this explanation. But a parent who acted on the assumption that exposure to television violence is the main cause of aggressive behaviour in children, *might* be overlooking more important factors. He might, for instance, fail to notice that his own child's aggressive behaviour towards friends is partly due to the bullying he is receiving at school.

Can the psychologist do any better? In the next section, we will consider some of the ways in which the approach of psychologists differs from everyday thinking, and what implications these differences have for their explanations of behaviour and experience.

Summary of Section 2

- People act like psychologists in formulating theories (albeit implicit ones) to explain other people's behaviour.

- Psychologists are people themselves; this may give them special insights into their subject-matter.

- Commonsense theories are sometimes imprecise and based on inadequate evidence. This may have important implications for any actions which are based on the theory.

3 | Theory and method in psychology

To highlight some of the special features of the psychologist's approach, we will use the same example of explanations for aggression in young people. Many psychologists are interested in this topic, and, like parents, some psychologists have come to adopt the theory that violent television programmes have an effect on children's aggressive behaviour. However, the route to adopting and evaluating this theory would typically be rather different from the commonsense approach.

3.1 Formulating a theory

A psychologist would probably start by considering a range of factors which could be responsible for aggression among young people. Here are just a few of the factors which might be considered:

- *Heredity*: the aggressive tendencies displayed by some children are **inherited** (passed on via the genes) from parents.
- *Learning*: children learn patterns of aggressive behaviour, for example, by copying the aggressive behaviour of people around them.
- *Media influence*: children's aggressive behaviour is influenced by watching violence on television.

One thing to notice about this list is that it consists of possible **causes** for aggressive behaviour; that is, the influences which might result in aggressive behaviour. Psychologists are often interested in causes of behaviour. Notice too that these causes are not necessarily mutually exclusive; more than one of them may play a part in producing aggression. For instance, a child might inherit aggressive tendencies *and* as a result be more susceptible to the effects of television violence. Alternatively, television violence might have an effect *because* the child is learning behaviour seen in a programme. In each case, two or more causes are interacting with one another.

Even if more than one item on the list is a possible cause of aggression, the psychologist would initially need to narrow the focus in order to proceed further. She would need to decide which of the possible causes is most worthy of investigation. To some extent this is a matter of personal choice: one psychologist might be particularly interested in genetic factors while another might be particularly interested in learning, or in the effects of television. But the psychologist's choice would also be influenced by any reliable sources of information already in existence, that is, by research carried out by psychologists, sociologists and other experts in the field. If research pointed particularly strongly to one of the causes on the list, it would be logical for the psychologist to start there.

At this point, the psychologist would need to ensure that her theory about the cause(s) of aggression provided a coherent summary of existing work and its implications. An important aspect of this involves indicating what consequences should follow if the theory is correct. Suppose a psychologist decides that exposure to television violence is indeed a likely cause of aggression in children. A reasonable assumption, if this is the case, is that the *more* television violence to which children are exposed the more likely they are to be aggressive. This can be thought of as a **prediction** about what the psychologist will discover if she observes the behaviour of children exposed to television violence. By making observations, the psychologist can find out whether or not her prediction is correct; that is, she can test the prediction against the evidence. In psychology a prediction which can be tested in this way is often referred to as a **hypothesis**.

Next, the psychologist would design a study to test whether the hypothesis is correct or not. There are many different methods which could be used. We will start by examining one which illustrates the design problems many psychologists would face in this area.

3.2 Designing a study

The psychologist would need to decide where and how to make the observations which would provide evidence for or against the hypothesis. She might decide to observe children in the natural settings of their own homes. But which children and which homes should she choose?

SAQ 3   (a) Which children were observed by the parent described in Section 2.2?

(b) What criticism could be made of the conclusion the parent drew from his observations?

It is obviously impractical to make observations of every child to whom the theory might apply. On the other hand if, like the parent, one observes a handful of children selected in an arbitrary way, any conclusions are likely to be limited or even invalid. The solution is to make observations of a reasonably sized and representative **sample** of children. This means that the psychologist would avoid selecting children of one particular age, sex, social background and so on. Instead she would ensure that there is an even mix of these factors among the children selected for observation. In practice this is by no means easy to achieve. The psychologist needs to be explicit about any biases present in the sample of children observed, because this affects the extent to which any conclusions can be generalized to a wider group of children.

The psychologist would also need to establish some kind of **criterion** of the violent content of television programmes. It is not enough to appeal to one's intuition that *The A Team* is a violent programme whereas *The Muppets* is not. It could be that what seems violent to one person does not seem violent to another. On a recent trip to the cinema, my 8-year-old son was terrified by the implicit violence of the cartoon characters, and yet he has *seemed* unperturbed by programmes which to me appeared more violent.

The problem of what counts as a violent television programme is by no means easy for the psychologist to solve. However, one possible criterion would be whether it included acts such as kicking, punching and firing a gun, since these represent what many people would agree are manifestations of violence. With this kind of criterion it is also possible to **measure** the extent of violence in a particular programme, that is, one can count the number of times each act of violence occurs. This kind of measure is known as an **objective measure** because it does not depend on the intuitions of the particular person doing the measuring. It should produce the same result regardless of who makes the measurement.

The psychologist would then need to observe, for each of the children in the sample, how many violent programmes were watched, what level of violent content they contained, and how often they were seen over a period of time. She would also need to make observations of each child's behaviour after watching such programmes—is a child, for instance, more likely to thump a younger sibling after watching an episode of *The A Team*? Again the problem of defining what counts as an act of aggression arises. A mother may feel she has a fair idea of when her children are being aggressive to one another, but another mother may regard the same behaviour as just boisterous. The psychologist needs to devise a measure of aggressive acts which would be accepted as such by others and which would produce the same result if used by others, in other words, an objective measure.

SAQ 4   What behaviour on the part of the children could be used to obtain an objective measure of aggression?

The psychologist would also need to decide how to interpret the results of her observations, the source of the evidence or **data** for her hypothesis. Suppose her observations contained a greater number of aggressive acts from children who had been exposed to high levels of television violence, than from children who were exposed to low levels of television violence. Common sense might tell us that this supports the hypothesis about violent television programmes. But it is also possible that the difference in the numbers of aggressive acts occurred by chance.

When you toss a coin a number of times, it does not necessarily land heads up or tails up on an exactly equal number of occasions. But you cannot conclude from this that the coin is biased; it might be a matter of chance. Similarly, numerical differences in the psychologist's observations do not automatically tell her that there are genuine differences between the behaviour of children exposed to high and low levels of violence. However, the psychologist can draw upon **statistical analysis** which is a powerful tool for deciding whether a particular result is due to chance or to the cause being investigated. In this case, the psychologist would use a statistical test to tell her whether a difference in the number of aggressive acts displayed by the different children was likely to be related to the amount of television violence they had watched.

The method used in the study outlined above is known as the **observational method** because it involves making observations of the children's behaviour as it occurs in their natural environment. However, there are difficulties with this method.

One problem is that the psychologist might fail to find enough children who chose to watch either the violent or the non-violent programmes. Also, the opportunities for children to display their aggression might vary among the homes the psychologist visited. One child might have several brothers and sisters around while another's brothers and sisters were all out playing. These problems would make it more difficult to collect the evidence needed to test the hypothesis.

Another kind of problem is that, in addition to watching more violent programmes, children who displayed high levels of aggression might live in more 'violent' homes. Perhaps these children were frequently exposed to acts of violence committed by other members of the family. It could be this environment, rather than the television violence as such, which encouraged the children to commit acts of aggression.

In order to overcome these difficulties, the psychologist would need to extend the range and duration of her observations. She might need to wait until children turned on the 'right kind' of television programmes or until brothers and sisters came home. She would need to make extended observations of the way all members of the family treated one another. The business of observing behaviour in this way can become very complex indeed. Many psychologists feel that the complexities of human behaviour are so great that it is necessary to simplify and structure the situation by the use of experiments.

3.3 **The experimental method**

The **experiment** often provides the best way of collecting suitable evidence to test a hypothesis. It also maximizes the chance that an observed result (e.g. that some children perform more acts of aggression than others) can be attributed to the hypothesis being investigated (i.e. that exposure to television violence affects children's behaviour) rather than to some other influence (e.g. that one group of children is exposed to more violence in daily life than another). This is because, in an experiment, the psychologist sets out to **control** the situation of interest, rather than just observe it.

One way to control the setting would be to watch the children not in their homes, but in a laboratory specially adapted for observing children. This would ensure that each child is observed in exactly the same setting. The psychologist might also arrange for a whole series of children to see a particular sequence preselected for its violent content. This ensures that the whole group of children is exposed to exactly the same material with exactly the same level of violence. The psychologist might then arrange for each child to play with a preselected range of toys, such as dolls, animals and action figures, and observe whether the child 'acts out' aggressive feelings in play. Again the point is that each child is exposed to exactly the same *opportunities* for displaying aggression.

In order to draw any conclusions about the effects of television violence on this group of children, the psychologist would need to compare their behaviour with that of children in another group exposed to little or no television violence. In the experiment, the children in this second group would be preselected to match those in the first group in terms of age, sex, social background and so on. This second group would also be treated *identically* to the first group except that they would watch a different television sequence preselected to have a low level of violence. This kind of comparison group is called a **control group**. Since the only difference between the first group of children and this control group should be the level of television violence to which they have been exposed, any differences in their subsequent behaviour should be due to this influence.

To conclude, the most important difference between the observational method and the experimental method is that in the first no deliberate attempt is made to influence the situation being observed. In the second, the psychologist structures or manipulates the situation in order to achieve better control over the influences which affect how the children behave.

You will learn more about these two methods (and others) as you work through this *Introduction to psychology*. What is common to these different approaches, and what differentiates them from the approach of the 'person in the street', is that they rely on clear, explicitly formulated theories. These theories are tested using systematic methods and the results are analysed using statistical tests, to avoid subjective or intuitive judgements about the behaviour in question. But what sort of difference does this make to the psychologist's insights into human behaviour and experience?

3.4 Drawing conclusions

For one thing, the psychologist's theory will probably have a wider or clearer range of application than the commonsense view. The parent who bases his observations of aggression on just his own child and the child next door cannot legitimately make assumptions about other children. The psychologist who has made observations of a sample of children can fairly assume that her conclusions apply to this group. And if this sample has been selected with care (drawing on a group of children who are representative of a wider population), the psychologist can legitimately argue that the theory applies to this wider group. That is, she can argue with some confidence that the conclusion drawn about the sample of children tested will apply to the population which they have been chosen to represent.

Another important point is that the psychologist's explanation will seek to specify precisely the way in which a particular cause has its effect on human behaviour. For instance, the psychologist studying children's aggressive behaviour might want to consider whether the children are imitating the behaviour of characters portrayed in the television programmes. If so, what type of characters are they most likely to imitate: cartoon figures or real people? Another possibility might be that children become excited while watching the programmes, and need to find an 'outlet' for this excitement. A psychologist could design experiments to investigate such alternatives.

Sometimes psychological findings do not just elaborate on common sense— they actually contradict it. The theory that television violence affects children's behaviour certainly has intuitive appeal. But psychological studies of this phenomenon have come up with a mixture of findings. Not all of them provide clear support for the theory. The importance of psychological research is that it has helped to establish some of the conditions under which the commonsense view is true or not.

Finally, some branches of psychology provide insights which no amount of common sense could achieve. For instance, physiological psychologists have studied the kind of changes which take place in the brain, and in the hormone levels in the body, during aggressive behaviour. They have also studied which parts of the brain are especially involved in aggressive behaviour.

3.5 The whole story?

The discussion in this section has described psychological research as proceeding in a systematic and rigorous fashion to produce insights far beyond what common sense can achieve. However, this could be seen as presenting an excessively unified and optimistic picture of what psychology is and what it can do! In practice, there are fundamental disagreements among different psychologists about what form theories should take, how one should set about investigating them, and what conclusions can be drawn. Many psychologists would question whether the complexities of a real-life emotion, such as aggression, can ever be captured by following the kind of systematic procedures I have outlined. Some have argued that, in terms of human insight, psychologists still have a great deal to learn from the commonsense judgements of the person in the street.

These and other controversies stem from the rather special nature of the subject-matter: humans and other animals rather than, say, chemical particles or cloud formations. In the next section we will consider some of the special problems which this subject-matter poses for psychologists.

Summary of Section 3

- Psychologists may consider many alternative causes for a problem like aggression.

- In formulating a theory, psychologists draw on and try to extend the implications of existing work. Often, this involves making predictions about what should happen if the theory is correct or incorrect.

- In designing a study to test a prediction (e.g. about aggression), psychologists need to ensure that their observations are representative and objective, and that the results are not due to chance alone.

- Psychologists use the experimental method to control the situation under study. This reduces the possibility that causes other than the one being investigated are affecting the results.

- Psychological theories and methods may provide more powerful explanations for people's behaviour than common sense.

4 | Special problems for psychology

As noted earlier, some psychologists have made good use of the fact that both they and their subject-matter are people. But in some ways this may operate to the psychologist's disadvantage.

4.1 The problems of studying people

All people, including psychologists, have beliefs and expectations about how others will behave. And, it has been argued, these may bias psychologists' observations of how people are actually behaving. For instance, if a psychologist is expecting that children who watch violent television programmes will display more aggression, she might be disposed to interpret certain types of behaviour as aggressive even if they are not. Even if the psychologist takes pains to avoid the kind of subjective assumptions parents might make about their own children's aggressive behaviour, her judgements may be affected by more subtle assumptions of her own. One problem, then, is that psychologists may find it difficult to be **objective** about their subject-matter, other people.

Another problem is that a psychologist observing other people's behaviour may change the behaviour being observed. If a psychologist is observing children in their own homes, the children may be reluctant to turn on the television, or they may be much more restrained in their behaviour than they would normally be. On the other hand, the children may deliberately try to produce the behaviour they think the psychologist is hoping to observe. The use of an experimental laboratory may make the psychologist less obtrusive, but it does not really solve the problem. Since the children are in an artificial environment, they may behave differently from the way they would normally behave.

A third difficulty about the subject-matter of psychology is that much of it goes on in people's minds and so cannot be directly observed. An emotion like aggression is not just a way of behaving towards other people, it is also a mental (and physical) experience. The psychologist has to find ways of assessing what this experience is like and when it is occurring. In the example described in Section 3, the psychologist took measurements of the children's observable behaviour; for example, whether the children punched or kicked one another. But does this really tell her what the children are *feeling*?

Compare these difficulties with those of a physicist using an electron microscope to observe minute sub-atomic particles; it might seem that none of the same problems arise. This has led some people to argue that psychology will never attain the scientific status of a subject like chemistry or physics—that there is an unbridgeable gulf between the study of people and what some people see as proper science.

4.2 Is psychology a science?

Many psychologists do see psychology as modelling itself on the natural sciences, such as chemistry and physics. These psychologists, by and large, see systematic methods, particularly experiments, as appropriate to psychology. They would argue that any difference between psychology and the natural sciences is a matter of degree rather than of kind. As the psychologist Jeffrey Gray has put it, psychology is much younger than other sciences; it is only a matter of time before it 'catches up' (Open University, 1981).

In support of this argument, the kind of difficulties I have outlined are not, in fact, unique to psychology. They also arise in some of the 'purest' of the natural sciences. Just as psychologists may observe those behaviours they are hoping or expecting to observe, so physicists may interpret the activity of particles in terms of particular patterns they are hoping or expecting will be present. Just as the presence of psychologists may affect the behaviour of the subject-matter, so, believe it or not, may the presence of physicists! The very act of measurement disturbs what is being measured. And, finally, psychologists are not alone in contending with inaccessible subject-matter. After all, physicists cannot *see* sub-microscopic particles with the naked eye. The electron microscope is a tool which provides an indirect representation of these particles.

Some psychologists give a different answer to the question, 'is psychology a science?'. They argue that psychology is a quite different *kind* of science from chemistry and physics, and therefore calls for different methods. These psychologists argue that the special nature of the subject-matter, and the psychologist's relationship to it, must be acknowledged and allowed for. For instance, if studying aggression in children, the psychologist should not even *try* to detach herself from the situation in order to avoid affecting the children's behaviour. She should participate fully, and treat her effect on the situation as one of the things to be observed. This technique is known as **participant observation**. Another implication might be that the psychologist should try to establish what the children's experiences are by asking them. Instead of taking behaviour as the criterion of aggression, she should ask the children to *describe* how they are feeling. This calls for the children to introspect about their feelings and the method is known as **introspection**.

The point about these methods is that they produce data which cannot easily be measured. If a child produces a complex account of how he feels after seeing a violent television programme, the psychologist will have to use her judgement in deciding how much aggression the child has experienced. But the data may also give a much *richer* picture of what the child is feeling. Many psychologists, then, place higher priority on the richness of insights which comes from methods like these, than on the opportunities for control and measurement provided by experiments and other systematic methods.

This gives just a flavour of a very complex debate about whether psychology is a science, and if so in what sense. As you work through this *Introduction to psychology*, you will come across this debate frequently, and you will become aware of the many different arguments and solutions which psychologists have proposed. Whatever their approach, however, psychologists have to contend with a further set of problems posed by their subject-matter.

4.3 Ethics

The subject-matter of psychology poses a number of **ethical problems**, that is, problems about what it is acceptable to do to other people or animals in the course of psychological research. There are many situations in which the observations that a psychologist might want to make would have undesirable consequences. For example, psychologists studying aggressive behaviour in children might want to question them about the violence in the television programmes they watch. But this might encourage the children to pay attention to implicit violence which would otherwise have gone unnoticed. In the interest of their observations of aggression, psychologists might feel constrained to sit by and watch while one child inflicted pain on another child, although it would be normal to intervene to avoid harm to the child.

Ethical considerations apply particularly strongly to research on the brain. Supposing a psychologist wished to investigate the brain mechanisms involved in aggressive behaviour. With one or two exceptions (e.g. when someone is having a brain operation for medical reasons), it would be quite unacceptable to interfere with the anatomy or physiology of the human brain. But the solution of using animals as a substitute also poses problems. Some people would see this kind of intervention as equally unacceptable— particularly because animals have no choice in the matter.

Another ethical problem is that experiments and other research methods sometimes involve deceiving the participants (known as **subjects**) about the part they are playing. Frequently this deception is of a minor nature. In a memory experiment, people might be given a list of numbers to add up in the belief that the psychologist wants to study how they carry out addition. Without any prior warning the subjects are later asked to recall the results of their additions. The psychologist's real interest may lie in finding out how many of these results subjects memorize incidentally (without making a conscious effort) while doing the sums. Obviously the deception is necessary, most people would regard it as innocuous, and a full explanation can be given immediately the experiment is over.

However, there have been some psychological experiments in which the need to deceive subjects has raised serious ethical issues. In a study of obedience to authority, Milgram (1963) instructed each member of one group of subjects to administer shocks of an increasingly powerful force to another 'subject'. This person was not really a subject at all. He was secretly told by Milgram to utter groans and shrieks as if he was receiving real electric shocks. Thus, although the real subjects were not actually inflicting any pain, they were made to believe they were doing so. Some of these subjects went on to administer 'shocks' which, had they been real, would have severely injured or even killed the recipient.

This experiment suggests the important insight that quite ordinary people may behave quite unacceptably when under authoritative command to do so. Milgram made the obvious analogy with Nazi guards in concentration camps. But did this important insight justify the experiment? Although subjects were told after the experiments that they had inflicted no pain, many of them, given the chance to reflect outside the experimental situation, became extremely disturbed at what they *might* have been doing. Some even required psychiatric treatment. This experiment has raised some complex issues, and ethical controversy about it has continued for a long time.

There are no easy solutions to ethical problems, but psychologists have become increasingly aware of them. These days there is an active and continuing debate among psychologists about attaining acceptable standards of ethics. There are also clear guidelines provided by bodies such as the British Psychological Society (BPS), setting out what is currently regarded as acceptable practice, and there are strong sanctions against any psychologist who is found to be breaking these guidelines. Box A provides an extract taken from a recent version of the BPS's ethical principles for work with human subjects. Another association, the Experimental Psychology Society, has laid down guidelines for work with animals.

BOX A   Extract from the BPS's ethical guidelines, 1978

(At the time this book went to press these guidelines were being further modified.)

1 Whenever possible the researcher should inform subjects of the objectives and eventually the results of the study.

2 The researcher should consider the ethical implications of the work and the psychological consequences for the subjects.

3 The researcher should consult with experienced and impartial colleagues about any proposed deceptions and the likelihood of stress or encroachments on privacy.

4 Deception or withholding information from subjects should only occur when other means are completely impractical.

5 The researcher should consider the risks of stress or encroachments on privacy, and should emphasize subjects' right to withdraw from the study should they so wish.

6 Data obtained from psychological research about subjects must be treated as confidential.

7 Studies on non-volunteers (e.g. in an observational study) must respect the privacy and the psychological well-being of subjects.

8 The researcher should maintain the highest standards of safety.

9 Research on children should only be carried out with informed parental consent.

10 If a subject asks advice on psychological problems, extreme caution must be exercised in giving answers and if necessary the subject should be referred to professional advice.

11 The researcher must ensure that all associates, employees or students involved in a research study comply with these standards.

12 Any psychologist who believes that research conducted by another psychologist fails to comply with these rules should try to make the other rethink his or her approach.

(Adapted from British Psychological Society, 1978)

SAQ 5   Do you think that Milgram's experiment would be judged to be acceptable by today's standards? To help you to answer this you may find it useful to work through the list of guidelines in Box A, writing beside each one: 'yes' if you think that Milgram took the principle into account; 'no' if you think he did not; '?' if you are uncertain or it is impossible to tell; or 'N/A' if the guideline is not applicable to his experiment.

Generally speaking, these days there is much greater awareness of ethical problems, and much greater control over what psychologists can do to both human and animal subjects. Many of the early experiments carried out on animals would be prohibited today. However, animals are still used in a number of studies. Some people find this unacceptable, even though more effort is now made to minimize the animals' discomfort and to ensure that the objectives of the research are sufficiently important to justify their use.

Finally, psychological work poses the problem that it may carry implications about how people should live their lives. It may even suggest ways of controlling people's lives. Thus, a therapist or clinical psychologist may be in a position to help a patient overcome difficulties in acting sociably, but who is to say that this change is in the best interests of the patient? These are, perhaps, the most difficult problems of all, since their solutions depend on society's values and priorities. Psychologists must be aware of the implications of their work. They must articulate the ethical problems, and enter into debate about them. As you work through this *Introduction to psychology*, you too should consider the ethical issues which are raised by the subject-matter, and whether there is room for improvement in the ways psychologists handle them.

Summary of Section 4

- The fact that psychologists are people studying other people may affect the observations they make, and it may affect the behaviour they are studying.

- Psychologists interested in what people think or feel cannot make direct observations of their subject-matter.

- Some psychologists model their approach on the natural sciences and favour systematic methods of research, such as experiments.

- Other psychologists argue that psychology is a special kind of science, which calls for methods suited to the richness of the subject-matter.

- Psychological research poses ethical problems, such as the harmful effects of observations on humans or animals, and the need for deception.

- Ethical debate and ethical guidelines represent current attempts to confront these problems.

5 | This *Introduction to psychology*

By now you will have gained some impression of what a diverse subject psychology is. This impression will be confirmed if you look at the contents page of the two volumes that make up this *Introduction to psychology*. You will see that there are six main parts each dealing with a different general theme or perspective. Within each part there are two or three chapters dealing with a different aspect of the theme.

You may wonder what is the rationale for organizing the material in this way. There is no *simple* answer to this question because there is no single obvious criterion by which to divide up the subject-matter. The best way to understand the organization of the material is to start working on it! However, to help you, I shall identify some of the main themes which play a part in the organization of the material.

Part II The developing person

As we have seen, psychologists are interested in almost all areas of psychological functioning. These include emotions such as aggression and pain, mental processes such as perception and memory, and complex social behaviour such as speaking a language or making friends. Although these are characteristics of all humans, they are not fully developed in the new-born infant. They are subject to a process of change and development. Thus the thoughts, feelings and behaviour of the adult are different from, and yet rooted in, those of the child. This process of childhood change, and the way in which it accounts for the psychology of the adult, is the theme of Part II. The three chapters in this part present three somewhat contrasting perspectives on this theme.

Part III The foundations of behaviour

When discussing theories of aggression in Section 3 above, I suggested that psychologists may consider alternative explanations for a particular type of behaviour. Frequently these explanations are not mutually exclusive. Rather they represent different **levels of analysis** of the same problem. While one psychologist asks questions about the effects of television violence on aggression, another is interested in whether some of children's aggressive tendencies are inherited so that they are biologically predisposed to aggression. A third psychologist may be interested in the role played by learning.

Part III of this book deals with these latter two levels of analysis. One chapter considers how far all of the behaviour of humans and other organisms can be explained in biological terms; that is, in terms of evolution, genetics and physiology. The other chapter considers learning as one of the basic phenomena underlying the behaviour of both humans and other animals. The title of this section reflects the view that studies of both biology and learning can be seen as fundamental to understanding all kinds of behaviour.

Part IV Individual diversity

Although processes such as learning are characteristic of the behaviour of all individuals, there are quite large variations in the way people behave. Not only do children differ from adults, as discussed in Part II, but adults display enormous diversity in their intellectual skills, personality and the whole way in which they approach the world. This is the theme of Part IV. Two chapters deal with diversity along specific dimensions—the first with how and why people vary in intelligence and the way they think; the second with variations in personality, from introvert to extravert, from stable to unstable and so on. The third chapter deals with the approach known as humanistic psychology in which the opportunity for people to explore and express their own individuality is seen as fundamental for their ability to thrive in their world.

Part V Cognitive processes

At the very beginning of this introductory chapter I suggested that an understanding of how the mind works is the central goal for many psychologists. Despite the difficulties of gaining access to this subject-matter, an understanding of the workings of the mind is central to explaining how we make sense of the world around us. It is difficult to imagine a world in which we could not see and feel objects, pay close attention to a conversation, or remember information from one day to the next. The study of these so-called cognitive processes, using a combination of experimental and other methods, is the theme of Part V. The chapters in this part deal in turn with perception, selective attention and memory.

Part VI The social dimension

Studies of cognitive processes such as perception, attention and memory play an important part in explaining complex behaviour such as speaking a language. But equally central to an understanding of this behaviour is an appreciation of its social function. Language is an inherently social phenomenon; the very word 'language' implies one person in communication with another. It follows that an explanation of the capacity to communicate with language must take into account its social aspects. This is the theme of the first chapter. The second chapter deals with another phenomenon which is by definition social, that of aggression. The chapter takes up the point, made earlier in this introduction, that several different levels may play a part in a comprehensive account of aggression. The chapter discusses the interplay of these different levels, and shows how the theories and methods of social psychology are especially tailored to an exploration of the social level of analysis.

Part VII Applications to problems

By now you will be aware that there are many psychologists whose goal is to put their ideas to practical use in fields such as education, industry and clinical work. Taking aggression as an example, these psychologists would be less concerned with theoretical explanations of why aggression occurs than with treating or helping people for whom aggression is a problem.

This style of approach is sometimes described as 'applied' psychology (aimed at putting understanding to practical use) to contrast it with 'pure' psychology (aimed at providing theoretical understanding). There is no hard and fast distinction between the two approaches. Most psychologists with a theoretical interest in aggression will also have a commitment to help solve problems of aggressive behaviour. And many psychologists combine both theoretical and practical elements in their work.

Despite this overlap, Part VII is devoted to a special survey of some areas in which psychological principles are put to use. Chapter 15 deals with the broad field of clinical psychology, describing how clinical psychologists help people with psychological problems. Chapter 16 deals with one specific psychological problem—autism. It describes how psychological research has helped provide an understanding of this condition.

Part VIII Review

The chapter which makes up this final part looks back on the many different approaches, theories and methods discussed in this *Introduction to psychology*, and seeks to integrate the material from the point of view of the many psychological perspectives that have been introduced.

5.1 A common objective?

I would like to leave you with one final thought: do psychologists in all their diversity share a common goal? A good answer to this question was given by Derek Blackman, who commented that 'all psychologists would like to understand a little better what makes people tick' (Open University, 1981). This remark encapsulates, by implication, both the unity and diversity of psychologists' goals. All psychologists seek a better understanding of human behaviour and experience, but there are many ways to go about it. At one extreme, Blackman's remark could be taken to imply an analogy with the mechanism of a clock. The pathway to understanding, in this case, would be analogous to understanding the components which make the clock function. At the other extreme, his remark could be interpreted as referring to all the complex thoughts and feelings which differentiate humans from other organisms. In this case, understanding may require an appreciation of people as wholes, in all their complexity, rather than an analysis of their component processes or mechanisms. As you work through this *Introduction to psychology*, you will find that psychologists occupy all possible variations of approach between these two extremes.

References

BRITISH PSYCHOLOGICAL SOCIETY (1978) 'Ethical principles for research with human subjects', *Bulletin of the British Psychological Society*, vol. 31, pp. 48–9.

MILGRAM, S. (1963) 'Behavioural study of obedience', *Journal of Abnormal and Social Psychology*, vol. 67, pp. 371–8.

OPEN UNIVERSITY (1981) 'Four psychologists on psychology', DS262 *Introduction to psychology*, Audio-cassette 1, Milton Keynes: The Open University.

Answers to SAQs

SAQ 1

(a) You would try to see if the child's behaviour was *consistent* with your explanation, for instance by observing whether the child continued to search the pavement and cry. You would try to observe whether she picked something up and stopped crying. You might *ask* her if she had lost something. The answer 'yes' would obviously be consistent with your explanation.

(b) If the child started to giggle and then ran off to join a group of previously unnoticed friends, you might conclude that your explanation was wrong.

SAQ 2

Tom may be a 'naturally' more aggressive child, or he may act aggressively because his parents have encouraged him to 'stand up for himself'.

SAQ 3

(a) The parent made observations of his own child and the child next door.

(b) Because the parent's observations were so limited, they led him to jump to the conclusion that watching violence on television was the only reason for Tom's aggressiveness.

SAQ 4

Behaviour such as kicking, punching and slapping could reasonably be chosen to provide an objective measure of aggression.

SAQ 5

Milgram probably believed that deception was essential for his experiment to be effective. Indeed it is hard to see how his study could have been carried out without deception. So, technically, he can be said to have taken guideline 4 into account. For the same reason he would have been unable to inform subjects of the objectives of the study (guideline 1) although he did explain the real purpose of the experiment afterwards. Therefore he just merits a 'yes' on guideline 1. It seems unlikely that he took into account guidelines 2, 3, 5, or 8, so he is marked 'no' on these. It is difficult to know whether he followed guideline 6. His work became so widely known and so closely scrutinized that details of how particular individuals behaved may have become known. Guideline 7 was also, in a sense, contravened. Although Milgram's subjects volunteered for his experiment, they might not have volunteered if they had known what stressful experiences it entailed. Guidelines 9–12 are not applicable. Overall it seems unlikely that Milgram's experiment would be acceptable by today's standards. Obviously the moral issues here are complex. You will read more about this experiment in Chapter 14.

PART II
THE DEVELOPING PERSON

Introduction to Part II

Many people who come to study psychology expect to find insights into why they behave, think and feel as they do. A large part of psychology is concerned with just these issues and offers a wealth of theory and research evidence about the way the adult mind 'works'. But just looking at the psychology of adults is only part of the story, for each of us has a life history. If someone asks us about ourselves, we are quite likely at some point to start talking about our background; in other words, the sort of childhood we had and what were our formative experiences. Even though it is difficult for us to recall the very early years of our lives, we can all think back to our childhoods and see in those years the gradual emergence of the person we are now. For some of us, those memories will be predominantly happy ones, for others they will evoke painful feelings. But, whether seen as good or bad, the experience of our own childhood is seen as a central part of what has made us what we are. To put it in a nutshell, the person that we are now did not suddenly step on to life's stage fully formed, but rather *developed* through the years of childhood. The three chapters in Part II are dedicated to showing you how psychologists have tried to come to grips with early experiences that relate to the way we function as adults.

Chapter 2 focuses on the central question of how we come to develop a sense of *self*, a sense of our identity as individuals, separate from others and with our own thoughts and feelings. This chapter explores the idea that this comes about as a consequence of growing up in a social world, a world of other people. Through our interactions with others, we gradually come to form a self-concept that is the core of our psychological being. This chapter uses as an organizing framework the ideas of George Herbert Mead, who believed that we all go through recognizable stages in developing the ability to relate to other people. He argued that an essential part of being able to enter fully into relationships is not just seeing ourselves as individuals but also seeing other people as individuals, with their own thoughts and feelings. For Mead, the development of these two abilities goes hand-in-hand: it is from a growing awareness of other people that our own self-awareness grows.

Another central figure in developmental psychology is Jean Piaget. Chapter 3 introduces Piaget's ideas and shows how influential these have been in determining the basic framework for studying intellectual development. Piaget was the first person to offer a highly detailed account of how the child's mind appears to change in fundamental ways during development, passing through a regular set of stages. Taking Piaget's ideas as a starting point, many later studies have been carried out to put these to the test, and the results have led to a reappraisal of some aspects of Piaget's theory. In this chapter we trace these developments and discuss various views of how a child's mind develops.

Chapter 4 is devoted to another very well-known psychologist, Sigmund Freud. Freud was a firm believer in the existence of instincts, such as the instinct to seek sexual pleasure. His theory is developmental in that he saw adult personality as arising from the way these instincts are coped with during childhood. Like Mead and Piaget, he saw childhood as being composed of a series of stages through which all children pass. Freud's focus was on the emotional aspects of development and the effects of unconscious motivations on adult personality, a focus that is usually termed *psychodynamic*. Since Freud, many psychodynamic theorists have stressed the importance of the child's earliest social experiences, particularly with the mother, for emotional development.

Debates about child development, such as those in which we hope to engage you in the following pages, have a crucial importance for the way children are treated. On the basis of Piagetian ideas, schools have changed the way they teach. Psychodynamic theories are influential in much therapeutic work with children. The importance of a child's self-concept, as proposed by Mead, is being stressed increasingly in the process of helping children to develop socially. The way parents view and treat their own children is affected by the theories that they themselves hold, and these are in turn influenced by what they believe are the established 'facts' of child development.

In the following chapters, we have tried to encourage you to take a critical stance, to evaluate what you read, not to take it as established 'fact', but to examine the evidence we put forward and consider how far it supports the theories being presented. Above all, we want to stress that the study of development opens up many questions and tackles some basic assumptions underlying commonsense views of childhood.

chapter 2

THE SELF AND THE SOCIAL WORLD

Dorothy Miell

Contents

1	**Introduction**	**31**
2	**In the beginning**	**32**
2.1	The sociable newborn	33
2.2	The beginnings of self-recognition	37
	Summary of Section 2	44
3	**The social self: symbolic interactionism**	**44**
3.1	The 'I' and the 'me'	46
3.2	'Taking the role of the other'	47
	Summary of Section 3	50
4	**Interacting with others**	**51**
4.1	Learning through play	52
4.2	Friendships	54
	Summary of Section 4	61
5	**Gaining information about the self**	**61**
5.1	Social feedback	62
5.2	Social comparison theory	64
	Summary of Section 5	66
6	**Many selves?**	**67**
6.1	Roles	67
6.2	Managing our 'masks'	70
6.3	A core self?	72
	Summary of Section 6	73
7	**Reflection**	**73**
	Further reading	75
	References	75
	Answers to SAQs	78

1 | Introduction

From babyhood, all humans are both social *and* individual beings. At first sight, this might appear to be a contradiction. How can we be separate from our social world and yet fully integrated into it? How do babies begin to develop a sense of being individuals whilst also learning how to fit into the complex social world into which they arrive? The contradiction, however, is not a real one. Becoming *integrated into* the social world and *differentiated from* it are *complementary* processes, and the growing child develops sociability and individuality in parallel.

The first of these two complementary processes of social development is usually called **socialization**, which includes all the influences that make us accepted members of society and help us to establish and maintain relationships with others. As such, socialization is the *integrating* process which allows the child to become a full member of society. There are many ways in which the growing child is given incentives to conform, from the direct instructions of parents (e.g. to the toddler during potty training) to the more subtle influences of images in the media (e.g. about 'appropriate' behaviour for men and women).

The second process of social development is the development of the individual's personal identity, or **self**. Children need to develop a sense of their own personal characteristics, abilities and attitudes and, at the same time, they need to reconcile their individuality with the many requirements of the social world, such as those of status, gender and occupation. This process is the *differentiating* role of social development, whereby individuals distinguish themselves from others and find a personal position within the social network. The differentiating process, like the integrating process of socialization, begins early in life and continues throughout development: babies have to see themselves as distinct from their mothers; toddlers have to establish their new found autonomy by saying 'no' (so often that this period is called the 'terrible twos'); and, in adolescence, there is often a struggle to establish an individual identity apart from the family.

Both the integrating and differentiating processes in social development are equally essential to an individual's ability to operate successfully in the world, and they are deeply interconnected. In this chapter, we will examine the links between people's sense of self and their adaptation to the social world. We will look both at how these links begin to develop during childhood and at how the adult balances what may seem to be the conflicting demands of the self and the social world.

2 | In the beginning

Imagine a bird's egg: the tiny bird inside is physically complete and it has developed all the functions and structures necessary for survival, but before the shell begins to crack it has no awareness of, or need for, the external world. This image of the bird shut off within its egg was first introduced by Margaret Mahler, a follower of Sigmund Freud, as a metaphor to describe the state of the newborn human infant. According to Mahler (1968), the human baby, even when it is born, is still shut off from the outside world by an exclusive focus on its own needs and feelings. Among other things, this means that the newborn baby is only aware of physical sensations—such as those of tiredness, hunger and cold—and of physical tensions being relieved, but is not aware of *how* this relief is achieved. Mahler suggests that babies do not distinguish between their carers' attentions (e.g. rocking or changing) and their own tension-reducing behaviours (e.g. urinating or vomiting); between their mothers' nipples and their own mouths. As Winnicott puts it: 'Psychologically, the infant takes from a breast that is part infant, and the mother gives milk to an infant that is part of herself' (1960, p. 589).

Mahler sees this intense self-absorption as a 'shell' around the newborn, and she claims that at first the 'shell' is both physical *and* psychological. Babies do not seem to know that an external world exists, let alone where their own bodies end and the rest of the world begins, or that feelings exist other than those they are currently experiencing. According to Mahler, babies soon begin to become aware of their mothers or carers but still believe that 'carer' and 'self' share a common boundary and are not differentiated. She claims that, at around 2 months old, the advent of smiling more at familiar people is an indication of a budding ability to differentiate between self and other. The slow process of establishing a sense of being a separate physical and psychological self continues, suggests Mahler, into at least the third year.

Mahler believes that self-awareness develops slowly as babies recognize the distinction between self and not-self, between their bodies and everything else in their physical environment. Only afterwards, and very gradually in Mahler's view, do they learn to recognize and sort out the parts of their bodies, their feelings, their names and their behaviour as integral parts of a single '*me*'. Mahler's account of the baby's struggle to see him or herself as a separate entity is an interesting one, and it is useful in suggesting just how formidable a task this must be. It is not easy, though, to imagine how one would be able to obtain concrete evidence for her theory.

It is worth pausing here for a cautionary aside. You have already come across phrases such as, ' . . . babies become aware . . .' and, '. . . infants recognize they are physically and emotionally separate . . .', and there are similar statements in the following pages. What can they mean? Can infants have such sophisticated knowledge about their own state of knowledge (often called 'metacognition')? There is no simple answer, since before children begin to talk it is very difficult to have any idea of what they know, let alone what they know or think *about* this knowledge. Instead, we have to observe their behaviour and infer what they know about themselves and their world from this. Thus, when children do something for the first time (like recognize themselves in a mirror), we can infer that they know what they look like, although we are not claiming that they *know* that they are able to do this or that they realize the *implications* of this knowledge. The ability to *perform* a particular action may be labelled by psychologists as evidence of a 'self-concept,' but this does not mean that the psychologist believes that the child is *aware* of something as intangible as this 'self-concept'. The following discussion, then, is concerned with the abilities children display; we are not suggesting that they are necessarily aware of possessing them.

2.1 The sociable newborn

Mahler's view that the process of separation from the mother can take up to three years is not completely shared by other writers. Whilst they do not challenge the idea that newborn infants may be psychologically 'merged' with their mothers and carers, research has suggested that, within just a few weeks, infants are responding to other objects around them, and especially to other people. The infants are *not* so caught up in their own sensations that they do not make every effort to interact with those around them, within their physical limitations.

This view indicates that infants can be seen as active, competent organisms interacting with their environment and initiating social contact, rather than inward-looking, passive recipients of stimulation. Babies are very effective in getting attention from their carers and in stimulating interaction. They do this primarily by crying and smiling. Wolff (1969) distinguished three cries; those of hunger, anger and pain, which all have identifiable characteristics. These cries signal to the carer to come nearer to the baby and engage in interaction. Moss (1967) conducted an observational study of infants and their mothers and showed clearly that crying bouts in the first months of life are successful, as cries were very likely to be followed by maternal contact. Similarly, as Darwin noticed as long ago as 1872, the infant's smile acts as a strong social signal for maintaining contact with his or her carers. Facial expressions that are interpreted as smiles begin early and are initially endogenous (i.e. due to internal stimulation, such as wind), but the baby very quickly moves into a phase of exogenous smiling (where external stimulation, especially the human face, elicits the smile). The baby becomes more selective about which faces trigger most smiling, preferring familiar ones. Even as early as 2 months old, babies seem to smile more at familiar people and objects than at unfamiliar ones.

Infants not only initiate and maintain social contact with their carers, they also seem to be 'tuned in' to certain stimuli, selecting and attending most readily to the *social* cues in their environment. It is difficult to know whether this is an **innate** preference (i.e. something the baby is born with) or whether it is learned soon after birth. But it is obviously a useful biological tool, since the result is that the baby is particularly sensitized and attracted to cues given off by the adults it needs. Furthermore, the baby's predisposition to look at faces leads caregivers to develop nurturant feelings toward the baby and to want to care for it.

Work by Fantz (1961) uncovered clear preferences for looking at complex patterns amongst very young infants. Babies were shown two patterns and an observer recorded the amount of time the baby looked at each pattern, with this measure of 'time spent looking' used as an indicator of the infant's preference. Fantz found that even 2-day-old babies could discriminate between patterned and unpatterned shapes and preferred to look at the patterned ones. He also found that infants between 1 and 6 months old preferred face-like patterns and patterns with scrambled facial features to patterns with the same amount of light and shade, but with less complexity (see Figure 2.1).

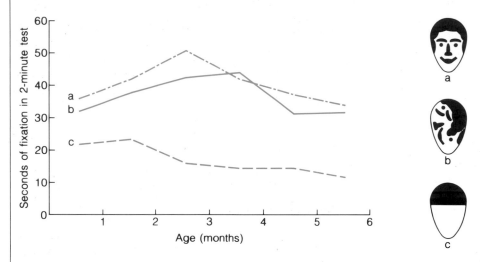

Figure 2.1 Average length of time each face-shaped object was looked at by infants up to 6 months old.
(Source: adapted from Fantz, 1961)

Fantz suggested that this preference was innate. However, later researchers (e.g. Hershenson, 1967), have suggested that it is a learned preference which emerges in the first three or four months. Whichever view we accept, it seems that young infants prefer to look at patterns in general and face-like patterns in particular. This can be seen as important for development since it focuses the children's attention on stimuli (i.e. human faces) that help them to adapt to their social world.

Another example of this kind of selection is the preference of infants for speech-like sounds (Brazelton, 1976); babies seem to prefer to attend to, and turn towards, human speech (which, incidentally, makes them more likely to see human faces). There is also evidence that even newborn babies can discriminate their mothers' voices and prefer to hear them. Box A describes the research of DeCasper and Fifer (1980) on this subject.

DeCasper and Fifer's results show that, as early as 3 days old, babies can discriminate their mothers' voices and learn to change their behaviour in order to hear the mother, thus showing a preference for her voice. These listening skills are further evidence for very early abilities to discriminate social cues in the baby's environment.

BOX A   Newborns' preferences for their mothers' voices

DeCasper and Fifer (1980) investigated the voice preference of ten babies less than 3 days old. These babies had been looked after in nursery-based maternity wards and, since birth, had only had a few hours contact with their mothers, during feeding periods. The researchers wanted to establish whether or not such babies could discriminate their mothers' voices from those of other women. To do this, they recorded the voices of each mother reading a passage of a children's story shortly after the babies were delivered. Then each baby was fitted with earphones and given a 'non-nutritive nipple' to suck. This nipple was connected to a pressure monitor which allowed the researchers to gauge the rate at which the baby normally sucked (the baseline rate). Once each baby's baseline rate of sucking was recorded, the voice of the mother or another woman was played through the headphones. The babies were divided into two groups. For one group (A), the babies could switch on the mother's voice by pausing for *longer* between bursts of sucking than they had done when their baseline rates were established. Pausing for less time produced the voice of another woman. For the other group (B), the babies had to pause for *less* time between bursts of sucking than in the baseline period to hear the mother's voice. Group (B) babies who paused for longer produced the voice of another woman.

The results were interesting. Eight (i.e. 80 per cent) of the infants changed the length of their pauses between bursts of sucking to hear their mothers' voices. If the infants really were working to gain access to their mothers' voices, then, the researchers reasoned, reversing the requirements for groups (A) and (B) should result in the babies changing their pause lengths again. Thus, babies in group (A) now had to pause for *less* time between bursts of sucking than their baseline rates and babies in group (B) now had to pause for *longer* in order to hear the mother rather than another woman. This was tried out with two of the infants from each of the groups twenty-four hours after the first test, and all four infants did indeed reverse their responses in order to get access to their mothers' voices.

True interaction involves both speaking and listening in a meaningful sequence, in other words, turn-taking. Both partners need to have a chance to express themselves, and both, while speaking, need to feel their partner is attending and listening. This may seem a rather more sophisticated skill than those we have already suggested young babies are capable of. It is a skill which you might reasonably expect would require speech, but within weeks of birth it is possible to see the beginnings of such turn-taking (see Figure 2.2).

The social process is there long before the baby learns to talk or understands the meaning of words. An adult and baby interacting take turns to make sounds, look and smile at each other. After the first few weeks, the interaction sequences become more and more complex. As Richards observed in one of his studies of videotapes of mothers with their children:

After eight weeks or so when social smiling is well established, the mother may spend long periods eliciting smiling in her infant . . . The mother smiles and vocalizes to the infant and moves her head rhythmically towards and away from his face. The infant first responds with rapt attention, with a widening of the eyes and a stilling of his body movements. Then his excitement increases, body movements begin again, he

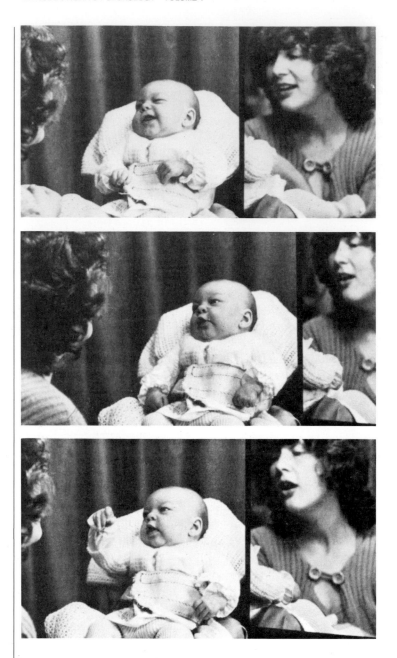

Figure 2.2 The earliest form of interpersonal expression. A girl, 6 weeks old, smiles at her mother's face, then responds to gentle baby talk with cooing vocalization and a conspicuous hand movement. In the third picture, the mother is imitating the preceding vocalization of her baby.
(Source: Olsen, 1980, p. 319)

may vocalize and eventually a smile spreads over his face. At this point he turns away from the mother before beginning the whole cycle once again. Throughout this sequence the mother's actions are carefully phased with those of the infant. During the infant's attention phase the mother's behaviour is restrained but as his excitement increases she vocalizes more rapidly and the pitch of her voice rises. At the point where he is about to smile her movements are suddenly reduced, as if she were allowing him time to reply.

(Richards, 1971, p 35)

It is through these initial preferences for social stimuli, during these preverbal yet complex interactions, that children begin to cope with the demands of a social world and become integrated into it. However, these social encounters are also instrumental in developing children's sense of themselves as individuals. How, you may wonder, can interaction with another person lead to an increasing sense of self? It has been suggested (Brazelton *et al.*, 1974; Schaffer, 1977) that babies gradually acquire an understanding of their effects on the world and of their feelings and expressions, because adults behave towards them *as if* the babies have intentions and beliefs about their behaviour. Most adults are unwilling or unable to see their baby's behaviour as random or unintentional, and so they constantly seek to interpret the baby's actions and attribute meanings to them. For example, in the earliest endogenous smiles and random movements, the mother will 'see' her baby smiling, waving, pointing to things and 'saying' hello. The adult carer behaves towards babies *as if* they fully understand the process of social interaction and communication, and as a result the babies see the effects of their actions on the adult and gradually acquire an understanding of themselves as individual agents. Furthermore, by giving social meanings to the babies' actions, the adults help to link and integrate the babies into their culture.

The suggestion here is that children develop an understanding of themselves as separate from their carers, as individuals with their own thoughts, feelings and activities *through* social interaction with their carers. Recognizing this, many writers on child development (e.g. Bowlby, 1969) do not talk about studying the infant alone at all. Winnicott, for example, says that 'if you set out to describe a baby, you will find you are describing a baby and someone. A baby cannot exist alone, but is essentially part of a relationship' (1964, p. 4). This argument proposes that the baby and carer cannot be seen as separate, and that their *interaction* should form the basic unit of analysis.

2.2 The beginnings of self-recognition

To achieve a sense of self, one of the first things we need to be able to do is to perceive ourselves as having a stable, permanent identity. This begins with recognizing our own physical appearance—perceiving a stable *physical* identity—but this is not a straightforward process for a young child.

We constantly see others' faces but we rarely see our own, except in mirrors and photographs. How are young children to understand that the image of themselves in a mirror is not that of another child? Before the age of about 2 years, a child may not answer correctly when given a mirror and asked: 'who is that?'. But this mistake may be due to problems with understanding what the adult means, rather than not recognizing him or herself, so how are we to know when a child *can* recognize his or her image in a mirror?

Research work has explored the origins of a self-concept through inventive non-verbal techniques. Here we will consider one very comprehensive research programme carried out by Lewis and Brooks-Gunn (1979) on visual self-recognition in infants; Box B outlines their work using a one-way mirror.

BOX B   Visual self-recognition in infants

In the first of their studies, Lewis and Brooks-Gunn examined how infants reacted to seeing mirror-images of themselves. Infants aged between 9 and 24 months were each observed individually as they played in a room equipped with a **one-way mirror**. This looks and acts like a mirror on one side (the side the infants saw), but it can be seen through like a window from the other side. A video camera behind the mirror allowed the experimenters to observe and record the infants' behaviour and responses to their reflected images. Later analysis of the videotape involved counting the number of times each infant made various responses, including mirror-directed behaviours (looking at, pointing at, touching the mirror), imitation (making faces, acting coy) and self-directed behaviours (touching, pointing at self). Altogether they tested ninety-six infants, divided equally between the age groups of 9 to 12 months, 15 to 18 months, and 21 to 24 months.

Most of the infants responded to their mirror-image, and seemed to take both pleasure and interest in it. However, we cannot conclude from this that they recognized the image as themselves, since infants may find mirror-images interesting for other reasons. Indeed, other research has shown that even very young babies like to look at faces, and especially other babies' faces, so these infants may have thought the image in the mirror was just another infant. To test convincingly for self-recognition, the experimenters had to elicit from the babies a particular kind of response: explicitly self-directed behaviour shown only when viewing their *own* image; see Box C.

BOX C   The red mark condition

Lewis and Brooks-Gunn set up a further condition in their experiment in which they surreptitiously marked the infants' noses red. (This was done by the mothers wiping their children's noses—a very common piece of maternal behaviour—using a cloth with rouge on it.) They then observed the infants in the same play situation in front of the one-way mirror and analysed their behaviour to see whether or not they responded to the reflection of themselves by touching their own (red) noses more than usual. The rationale for this was that they would only touch their *own* noses if they realized that the image in the mirror was of themselves (looking different because of the red mark) rather than another infant. If they thought the image was of another infant, they were expected to engage in other-directed behaviour, such as touching the mirror-image.

The data from the play session in the first condition (described in Box B) gave the experimenters a baseline measurement of the number of times each particular infant normally responded to the mirror in a variety of ways, including touching their noses. Having subsequently been given red noses, a second play session was held. Both videotapes were analysed to see if there was any difference in the types or numbers of the various responses between the two sessions. The findings suggested that some form of self-recognition was found across all the age ranges. Infants from 9 months of age displayed some self-directed behaviour by touching their bodies more in the red mark condition than in the normal image, or control, condition. However, it was not until 15 months of age that the infants began to direct their behaviour specifically to the red mark by touching their noses (see Figure 2.3). The observation of some self-directed behaviour across the age range suggests that infants as young as 9 months show some, albeit slight, self-recognition, with a steady development from this age in their ability to recognize their own images in detail.

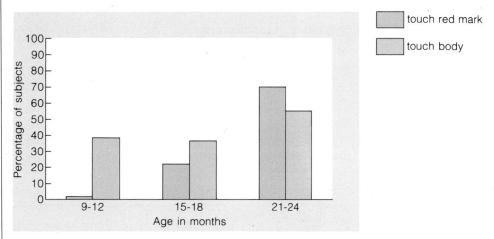

Figure 2.3 Percentage of children who exhibited the self-directed behaviours of touching the red mark specifically, or their bodies generally (from the Lewis and Brooks-Gunn mirror study)
(Source: adapted from Lewis and Brooks-Gunn, 1979)

SAQ 1   (*SAQ answers are given at the end of the chapter*) Look at Figure 2.3 and jot down answers to the following questions.

(a) What percentage of children aged 9 to 12 months touched (i) their bodies and (ii) their red noses?

(b) What are the implications of these results?

From this study by Lewis and Brooks-Gunn, it is clear that children as young as 9 months of age are able to recognize themselves in mirrors to some degree. Although virtually none of the children younger than 15 months showed *explicit* self-recognition by touching the red mark, they did show *some* self-directed behaviour by touching themselves (their bodies) more in the red mark condition than in the control condition.

What is it about the image in a mirror that leads a child to recognize it as him or herself? The reflected image not only looks like the child—that is, it has the same physical appearance—but it also makes movements which have a one-to-one correspondence with his or her own movements, or, to put it another way, it makes movements which are *contingent* upon the child's own movements. When the child waves, for example, the image waves at precisely the same time. Perhaps the younger children in Lewis and Brooks-Gunn's study were relying on these powerful **movement contingency cues** to recognize themselves, rather than really recognizing their own physical appearance.

Lewis and Brooks-Gunn designed another study which would test this possible explanation and find out just how the children recognized their images. By using video technology, Lewis and Brooks-Gunn could look separately at the two different types of cue to self-recognition: contingency of movements and the particular physical appearance of each infant. The children's responses to three types of video image were observed under three conditions:

1   live video of themselves;

2   video of themselves made one week earlier; and

3   video of another child.

SAQ 2   To clarify Lewis and Brooks-Gunn's reasoning in devising this video condition of their study, try to identify which of the cues for self-recognition (*contingent movement* or *same physical appearance*) were present in each of the three conditions. Lay out your answers in the form of a table:

	contingent movement	same physical appearance
(a) live video of themselves		
(b) one-week-old video of themselves		
(c) video of another child		

BOX D   The video condition

Ninety-six children aged from 9 to 24 months old were observed. In this study, each child was placed in a high chair in front of a video monitor and his or her responses to the images on the screen were coded under a number of categories of response (eg. facial expression, vocalization, imitation, attention). The children were shown video images from the three conditions listed above. The results of the study suggested that the 9-month-old infants could distinguish their own live image from the other images—they were generally more positive towards it and played with it more than with the images in the other two conditions. The 9-month-old infants appeared less interested in the images where they could not see contingent movements (i.e. the videos of themselves made a week earlier and of another child), and they did not react differently to the videos in these two conditions.

If the youngest children had been able to recognize their own features like the colour of their hair or eyes, they would have responded more to their own images, *even though* videoed one week before, and have been less interested in the images of another child. In fact they made few responses to either. It was not until 15 months of age that there was a difference in the responses made to the other infant and to their own image filmed a week earlier, with more behaviour directed to their own week-old image (classified as imitation of and playing with their own image) and more smiling at the other infant (other-directed behaviour). These differences between the responses to the two images increased when the behaviour of the older children was analysed. Thus the self-recognition shown by the youngest, 9-month-old children seems to be explained by their reliance on movement contingency cues, rather than by their familiarity with their own individual physical appearance. These results tie in with the mirror studies, since it was at 15 months of age that the children in that study began to show specifically self-directed behaviour, by touching the marks on their noses, indicating that they recognized their own appearance and changes in that appearance (see Figure 2.3).

It seems, then, that children younger than 15 months can recognize themselves only by noticing when their own movements coincide with those of their reflected image in the mirror. At about 15 months, they gradually become able to recognize their own physical appearance and distinguish it from other children. However, we should note that it is possible that the younger children *could* in fact recognize themselves without the movement contingency cues, because the observational techniques may not be sophisticated enough to pick up, for example, very subtle differences between their reactions to the other infant and towards their own images videoed at the earlier session. This is always a problem with research on preverbal children, where the researchers can only base their conclusions on what can be observed 'from the outside'. They cannot ask the infant participants in the research for their own versions of what they saw, or why they acted as they did.

The same problem, of relying on observation only, exists when studying animals. Gallup (1977), who first developed the red mark mirror recognition technique, examined the beginnings of self-recognition in primates. He wanted to know whether self-recognition was a uniquely human ability and, if not, under what conditions it would be found in animals. Working with a number of pre-adolescent chimpanzees who were born in the wild, he began by putting a full length mirror in each chimp's cage. At first, they reacted as if another chimp had appeared in the cage and either threatened the image or made conciliatory gestures to it. However, by the third day they had begun to use the mirrors to explore themselves and to watch themselves do things, like blow bubbles or roll over. After ten days exposure to the mirror, red marks were placed on each chimp, on one ear and one eyebrow. They were then all returned to their cages and observed playing, with no mirror present, in order to get a baseline measurement of how often they touched their ears and eyebrows.

When the mirror was put back in each chimp's cage, they were again observed and their behaviour analysed. The results were clear. Each chimp immediately began to explore the red marks when the mirror was returned, and touched their red ears and eyebrows, twenty-five times as often as they did during the same observation period without the mirror in their cages. When a new set of chimps, who had never previously seen themselves in a mirror, had the red marks put on them, they reacted to the mirror-image of themselves with red marks much as the other chimps had done when they first saw the mirror, that is, with gestures of hostility or conciliation toward what they seemed to believe was another animal in the cage. They did not touch the red marks in particular. It therefore seemed that the first set of chimps had *learned* to recognize themselves during the first ten days with the mirror.

Other animals which were tested did not seem able to recognize themselves in a mirror, even after considerable periods of learning. A macaque monkey, for example, did not show any signs of self-recognition, even after five months of exposure to a mirror. What is interesting, however, is that this monkey did seem to understand many other things about the mirror, using it, for example, to locate food it could not see directly. Gallup suggested that what makes the great apes (including chimpanzees and orang-utans) different from other animals is that they have developed a concept of self-identity, on to which they can 'map' the mirror-image of themselves, and this allows them to make sense of the image and thus recognize themselves. The other animals had not developed a concept of self and so, even after repeated exposure, could not ascribe that meaning to the mirror-image of themselves. Gallup believed that the ability to consider the self as an object of one's own attention is a skill confined to human beings and their closest relatives in the animal world.

In trying to explain this, Gallup drew upon the works of Cooley (1902) and Mead (1934), both of whom were social philosophers who speculated on the origins of the self, and whom we will discuss further in Section 3. These writers referred to the 'looking-glass self', meaning that a person's understanding of his or her own identity represents a reflection of how he or she is regarded by others. Thus the self, according to this view, is the internalization of others' viewpoints. As Cooley put it:

As we see our face, figure and dress in the glass (mirror), and are interested in them because they are ours, and pleased or otherwise with them according as they do or do not answer to what we should like them to be; so in imagination we see in another's mind some thought of our appearance, manners, aims, deeds, character, friends, and so on, and are variously affected by it.

(1902, p. 35)

Without these abilities, children would never be able to develop a view of themselves as individuals, represented as a **self-concept**. This is the notion that each of us exists as an individual with a personal history and unique qualities, characteristics and roles. But how do infants come to develop self-concepts? The research described in this section has indicated that it is a gradual process evolving through interactions with initial carers.

Gallup suggested that, if chimps were raised in isolation, away from social interactions with other chimps, one of the results of such social deprivation would be the failure to develop the concept of self which would allow them to recognize themselves. Gallup (1977) tested chimps reared in isolation using exactly the same procedure as with the first set of chimps; that is, by giving them mirror experience, marking their faces red, and then observing them with and without the mirror. He found that the chimps reared in isolation always reacted to the mirror-image as if it were another animal rather than an image of themselves. Even after an opportunity for learning, they did not touch the red marks more often than they had touched their ears and eyebrows before they were marked, unlike the socially reared chimps in the first test (see Figure 2.4). This is evidence that the development of a concept of self depends on being exposed to the reactions of other members of the species.

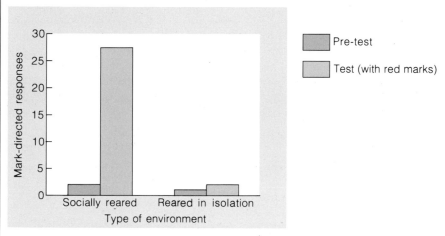

Figure 2.4 Self-recognition in chimpanzees. The number of times chimps raised normally and chimps raised in isolation touched red marks on their faces when they looked in a mirror
(Source: Maccoby, 1980)

However, it is important to note that this is only one of a number of effects on animals of being reared in isolation. Work by Harlow and Harlow (1962) showed that chimps reared in this way became very withdrawn and were unable to rear their own offspring properly if they later became mothers. The failure to learn to recognize themselves is thus only one of a number of results of this impoverished upbringing. Whilst the effects on human infants of rearing them in isolation cannot be tested, the observations of mother–baby interactions discussed earlier suggest that they also need social interaction to develop a sense of self. Furthermore, there have been cases of children being abandoned or kept socially isolated in lofts or cellars. In most of these cases, the children have responded quite well to human contact once it has been re-established, but they seem to be irretrievably damaged by their earlier lack of normal social contact and some do not develop language. (You can read more about such children in MacLean, 1979.)

Summary of Section 2

- Mahler suggested that newborn infants are unable to distinguish between themselves and the people and things around them.

- From very early on, however, infants can be seen to be responsive to some of the social cues in their environment—such as human speech and faces—and they are active in interactions with their carers.

- Infants are socialized and come to understand the rules of the culture they are born into by adults treating them *as if* they already understand these rules.

- Adults play an important part in giving children a sense of themselves as agents and of their individuality by responding to their earliest actions *as if* the children fully understand the actions and their implications.

- Studies by Lewis and Brooks-Gunn, which observed how young children reacted to seeing their reflection in a mirror, suggested that some self-recognition is present at 9 months of age, but that it becomes more specific and accurate at around 15 months.

- Studies using video techniques suggest that the self-recognition in children around 9 months old results from their use of movement contingency cues, and that only by 15 months do children really recognize their own physical appearance.

- Chimps also show the capacity for visual self-recognition, but only if they have been reared socially. If they have not experienced interaction with other chimps, they are unable to learn to recognize themselves in a mirror. Animals other than great apes are unable to learn to recognize themselves in mirrors at all.

3 | The social self: symbolic interactionism

Having introduced the idea of the interplay between the development of individuality and sociability, and given some concrete examples of this in the mirror studies with children and chimps, it is worth pausing to consider the theoretical position which underlies much of this chapter. The position is broadly based on **symbolic interactionism**, which stresses the importance of *social interaction* in human life, and of *symbols* or meanings which exist between people in their interactions. Symbolic interactionism views the development of the self as inextricably bound up with the development of the person as a social being.

It has been argued (Bryson, 1945; Stryker and Statham, 1985) that some of the concerns of symbolic interactionism were foreshadowed by the work of the

Scottish moral philosophers of the eighteenth century, in particular Adam Smith and David Hume. Although these writers developed views very different from those held by later symbolic interactionists, they emphasized a similar point in their analysis of the interplay between the individual and society; in the concept of 'sympathy'. Sympathy can be seen as similar to the more modern notion of 'empathy'; it allows people to put themselves in the place of others and experience the world as these others do. It also makes communication between people possible. The moral philosophers viewed communication of meanings as important because it is the means through which people can seek each other's approval for their actions.

Bring him into society, and he is immediately provided with a mirror which he wanted [lacked] before. It is placed in the countenance and behaviour of those he lives with. This is the only looking glass by which we can, in some measure, with the eyes of other people, scrutinize the propriety of our own conduct.

(Smith, 1759; quoted in Stryker and Statham, 1985, p.316)

Symbolic interactionism was linked to these early philosophical ideas by the work of William James, a north American philosopher and one of the earliest psychologists. James (1890) elaborated the idea of the link between the person and society, and he developed an important view of the self in suggesting that it was the product of the many different relationships a person has with other people, and that the self was, therefore, multifaceted.

Symbolic interactionism became widely acknowledged as a school of social psychological thought in the 1930s through the posthumous publications of its foremost proponent, George Herbert Mead (e.g. Mead, 1934). It is with Mead's contribution and his developments of social interactionism that we will mainly be dealing in this chapter. Mead's position on the interrelationship between the self and the social world was unequivocal:

The self is something which has a development; it is not initially there, at birth, but arises in the process of social experience and activity, that is, develops in a given individual as a result of his relations to that process as a whole and to other individuals within that process. . . . The self . . . is essentially a social structure, and it arises in social experience.

(1934, p.135)

This view is very much the one that was put forward in the previous section. The research on young infants and their interactions with their carers emphasized the importance of interaction with adults for the development of both individuality and sociability. Gallup's work with chimps further stressed the importance of interaction with others of the same species for the development of a concept of self. Mead's theory is known as *symbolic* interactionism because he believed that the self is not so much a physical reality, but depends on the symbols people use to express themselves. It is through interaction that symbols, like words and gestures, come to have a shared meaning.

Mead's view of the pre-eminence of the social process contrasts strongly with the views of some other psychologists who suggest that the self is a *non-social* concept. Views of the self as a 'personality', for example, suggest that a person is born with certain traits and later acquires others which determine his or her behaviour. In this view (which is considered in greater detail in Chapter 8) these traits have more influence upon a person than the context surrounding the person, and thus personality tests are developed to measure individual differences in the various traits such as introversion and extraversion. The trait theory approach assumes that these traits provide all the motive and explanation necessary to explain behaviour, whatever the situation a person is in. Thus, it is an *asocial* approach, paying little if any attention to the ways in which people may be affected by their social context. In this section, however, we will examine how Mead envisaged the social process and the development of the self and the implications of his, strongly social, view of the self.

3.1 The 'I' and the 'me'

As we have seen, Mead viewed the self as a social product. Since we have relationships with a wide variety of other people, this implies that we develop rather distinct aspects of ourselves through the different relationships in which we are involved. As James had suggested earlier, 'A man has as many social selves as there are individuals who recognize him and carry an image of him in their minds' (1892, p. 46). However, in contrast to this, it is also clear, as Damon notes, that:

Although a person's self-knowledge is socially influenced, nevertheless self-knowledge is not totally dependent, at least from moment to moment, upon the views and opinions of others. Although self-knowledge is diverse and multifaceted, there is also coherence and stability in a person's identity over time and context.

(1983, p. 12)

How can we resolve this apparent contradiction? On the one hand, we have the almost chameleon quality of the self described by James. On the other hand, there is the stability of the self which we all feel and which Damon described. One possible solution lies in an important distinction first made by James and later followed up by Mead. This is to split the self-concept into what James (1892) called the **I** and the **me**. The 'I' is the 'self-as-subject' and the 'me' is the 'self-as-object'. James suggested that the 'me' consists of what can be known about the self, such as physical descriptions of one's body, clothes, possessions, one's manner of thinking, moral and religious values, roles, social identity, reputation and behaviour. Some of these physical characteristics are given, such as height and gender, but the importance placed on them is influenced by other people's attitudes. As regards other characteristics, such as reputation and social identity, the attitudes and judgements of others are the major defining factor. Thus, we can suggest that the influence of the social context upon the self-concept is felt mainly on the 'me' part of the self-concept, the part which comprises what is generally known about an individual.

The 'I' or the 'self-as-subject' is the active process of experiencing, as opposed to the content of that experiencing, the 'me'. The 'I' represents the basic capacity for awareness, or as Descartes put it in his well-known saying, 'I think therefore I am' ('cogito ergo sum'). This part of the self-concept enables individuals to be free from relying absolutely on others' views for their sense of self. Whilst the 'me' represents the perceived attitudes and perspectives of other people which have become internalized, the 'I' is free to reject or change these views and it acts independently. The 'I' is the self-as-subject, the part which acts and reacts to circumstances creatively and spontaneously.

Through this view of the two distinct parts of the self-concept we can perhaps resolve the apparent contradiction between our sense of unique individuality—of distinctness from other people (through the 'I')—and our awareness of the influence of others and of our multifaceted personality when with other people (reflected in the 'me'). Whilst the 'me' reflects social influence, the 'I' ensures our individuality. Their combination results, as Damon suggests, in people's ability 'to construct and organize their own self-knowledge, even though this is always done within a context of multiple social influences' (1983, p. 12).

3.2 'Taking the role of the other'

Mead believed that the essential quality of the self is its *reflexive* nature. We experience and reflect on ourselves in the same way that we experience and reflect on other people around us. We see ourselves through the perceived reactions of others and this leads us to react to and appraise ourselves in the same way as we appraise other people. In the words of Cooley, a philosopher-sociologist who was also very influential in the early development of symbolic interactionism, we have a 'reflected or looking-glass self'. As he commented:

A self-idea of this sort seems to have three principle elements: the imagination of our appearance to the other person; the imagination of his judgement of that appearance; and some sort of self-feeling, such as pride or mortification. The comparison with a looking glass hardly suggests the second element, the imagined judgement, which is quite essential. The thing that moves us to pride or shame is not the mere mechanical reflection of ourselves, but an imputed sentiment, the imagined effect of this imagination upon another's mind. . . . We always imagine, and in imagining, share the judgements of the other mind.

(1902, pp. 184–5)

Thus people can be viewed as acting socially towards themselves, just as they do towards other people, praising or blaming themselves. These are the hallmarks of **self-reflexiveness**.

In order to achieve this, however, we have to be able to **role-take**, to put ourselves 'in the role of' the other person, to anticipate their responses, imagine how we appear to them and then adjust our responses to come into line with theirs.

Taking the role of the other in interaction is not an easy task, and we only gradually master it, beginning in childhood but *continuing* to learn and adapt to new relationships throughout life. Some people never master it. In particular, many autistic children seem unable to conceive of another point of view different from their own, or to reflect on their own behaviour from another person's perspective. Mead argued that it is not until we gain an understanding of other's reactions to ourselves that we can reach an understanding of ourselves. He proposed that there are three stages to the initial development of the ability to take the role of the other in order to internalize it as the 'me' part of the self-concept. These are the 'preparatory', 'play' and 'game' stages. He called these first three stages of initial development **primary socialization**. Later developments occurring throughout adulthood were termed **secondary socialization**.

Mead's stages were not associated with specific chronological ages. He did not believe that the chronological age of a child was of paramount importance in determining his or her ability to take the role of the other. This view would suggest that social meaning arose from chronological, time-released, cognitive capacities within each individual. Instead, Mead wanted to stress that social meaning arose in interactions with other people. Thus, a very young child who had experience in many varied interactions might show greater role-taking ability than an older, but less experienced, child. As a result, the term **interactional age** rather than chronological age is sometimes used to distinguish children of different role-taking abilities.

Preparatory stage

In Mead's preparatory stage, infants and young children are believed to imitate the behaviour of others around them in a rather primitive way, such as the young child 'reading' a newspaper as an adult does. However, with the acquisition of language, children internalize the symbols (through the words) of the adult world around them. Mead places a great stress on language as being of prime importance in the development of the social self, and Cooley nicely expresses this in his account of what is involved in learning a word:

A word is a vehicle, a boat floating down from the past, laden with the thoughts of men we never saw; and in coming to understand it we enter into the minds not only of our contemporaries, but into the general mind of humanity continuous through time. . . . Such words, for instance, as good, right, truth, love, home, justice, beauty, freedom, are powerful makers of what they stand for. 'This way,' says the word, 'is an interesting thought: come and find it.' And so we are led on to rediscover old knowledge.

(1902, p. 69)

Where spoken language is absent or slow to develop, such as in deaf or mute children, the symbolism may take longer to develop, although it does emerge at some point. However, it seems that in many autistic children the ability to use such symbols and to take the role of the other is severely impaired. As we will explore further in Chapter 16, although they have some sense of self (they can recognize themselves in a mirror) autistic children do not seem to develop a 'social self' as most other children do.

Play stage

Mead's play stage is characterized by children playing at various imagined roles, such as mother, engine driver, nurse or teacher. In doing this, the children are in a position to be able to view the world, and so themselves, from a different perspective, that of the (pretend) other person. Mead's idea of the self emerges from this ability to reflect on and act toward the self in the same way as other people are reflected on and acted towards. Whilst the play stage represents an important step along the road of development, children need to build up a more complex and unified self-concept, taking into account more than one other perspective on themselves at a time.

Game stage

In the game stage, Mead points out that organized games, like football or Monopoly, require individuals to take into account the different perspectives of a number of other people. The processes that are needed for successful participation in such games include anticipating the intentions of others, planning our own actions accordingly, and assessing their view of our actions, being aware that the others are also observing us to plan their actions. Mead suggests that these are the same processes necessary for successful participation in all forms of social interaction. Using the analogy of the game, he suggests that children come to cope with social interaction by becoming able to take the composite role of groups of others, of society at large, or, as Mead calls it, the role of the **generalized other**.

Internalizing the 'generalized other' into the 'me' of the self-concept allows children to participate competently in social interaction. However, Mead does not believe that the self ceases to develop after the game stage. He suggests that adults continue to adapt to new roles and new relationships as they encounter them throughout their lives in what he calls secondary socialization. New perspectives on the self are encountered through relationships with a variety of other people, and this changes the self by adding to and changing the 'me'.

BOX E   Mead's theory as a developmental theory

Whilst Mead discusses the development of the ability to take the role of the other, it has been argued (Flavell et al., 1968) that this falls rather short of being a truly developmental theory. Flavell and his colleagues note that a developmental theory should outline the difficulties that children might have in acquiring a skill like role-taking, and that it should analyse how children overcome these difficulties. Mead does neither of these, being less interested in the mechanics of the development of role-taking abilities than in discussing the significance of this ability for self-development through social interaction. Other workers since Mead have, however, addressed these developmental points more fully, as we will see with the work of Selman in Section 4.

Let us summarize Mead's view on the related developments of the self and of perspective-taking. Through their use of language, their games and their play, young children begin to take the perspective of other persons towards themselves, and in so doing, become capable of reflecting on themselves.

(Note, however, the critique of Mead's theory in Box E.) As a result of the process of taking the role of the other, the reactions of a 'generalized other' are internalized into the 'me' aspect of an individual's self-concept to allow him or her to make comparisons and judgements about how other people would react, even when no other people are actually present.

Another important result of the ability to take the role of the other is that individuals are able to find agreement between the meanings that they and others place on various actions and events; in other words, they establish shared meanings. For Mead, human society rests upon shared meanings between people, upon shared understandings about each other's intentions and upon being able to interpret each other's behaviour. In order to be a social being, therefore, we must be capable of putting ourselves in the position of the other person. In order to understand their meanings we have to be able to take on their role *symbolically*, to imagine how they might react to us. We acquire a sense of self by being able to see ourselves from the perspective of another person. By being able to anticipate the interpretation that the other will place on something, the individual can adjust his or her actions or speech to ensure that the intended meaning is conveyed, and thus that communication is effective. This is what Mead meant by **symbolic dialogue**, which is, in his view, the basis of all social interaction.

In the rest of this chapter, we will use many of the concepts introduced by the symbolic interactionists to examine the relationship between a person's developing individuality and sociability. In the next section we will look at children's play and friendships and examine in more detail the development of role-taking abilities and the emergence of symbolic behaviour. Then we will take Mead's point about the continuing interplay throughout life between the self and the social world and, leaving childhood behind, look in more detail at adults. In particular, we will examine how adults gain information about themselves from other people, and how they cope with the many roles they have to play in a complex social world. We will conclude the chapter with a critical appraisal of this theoretical approach to analysing the individual in his or her social context.

Summary of Section 3

- Symbolic interactionism emerged as a school of thought in sociology and social psychology in the 1930s, primarily as a result of Mead's writings. It has early roots in the writings of the eighteenth century Scottish moral philosophers (Smith and Hume), in early psychology (James) and in sociology (Cooley).

- According to the symbolic interactionist view, the self-concept develops out of social experience and symbolic interactions.

- The self-concept is divided into two parts, the 'I' and the 'me'. The 'I' (self-as-subject) is the unique, personal aspect which can act independently. The 'me' (self-as-object) is made up of the internalized views and opinions of other people.

- The self is reflexive in that we can think about ourselves in the same way as we think about other people. This is achieved by taking the role of the other person to view ourselves.

- According to Mead, the ability to take the role of other people develops through the preparatory, play and game stages. Particularly with the acquisition of symbolic language, children become able to take the role, first, of one other person at a time and subsequently, of the collective or 'generalized other'. This 'generalized other' is then internalized into the 'me'. This early development is termed 'primary socialization'.

- The self continues to evolve and change throughout life as different relationships, and therefore different perspectives on the self, are encountered. This continuing development is termed 'secondary socialization'.

4 | Interacting with others

In Section 3 we stepped aside from examples of research to look more closely at a theoretical perspective on the self and the social world. We return now to more concrete examples of research concentrating on the interplay between the development of individuality and sociability. As Mead suggested, children begin to adopt the perspective of others towards themselves through their use of language, games and play, and this allows them to reflect on themselves. To illustrate this process, we will examine some aspects of play and friendship in more detail. In playing with siblings and other playmates, children can be something or someone other than themselves. Through play and friendships, they learn more about themselves, other people and how the social world operates, and they learn about status, fairness and relationships. We will consider how play helps children to acquire a firmer understanding of the roles they can adopt and see how their developing understanding of the rules of the social world enable them to take the role of the other, as reflected by the changing nature of their friendships. As you probably realize, the processes of becoming integrated into the social world and of becoming an individual are not separable: play and friendships promote both individuality and sociality.

Extract A is from an observation of two children at play, and a number of the important features of play are evident. The girl and boy create a reality between them. They are like actors and playwrights in the shared story, and they are conscious of one another's aims. The children can also be seen to be taking on roles—the girl, of a baby boy; the boy, of a mother or father. It is fascinating that even at around 3 years old they are so aware of a number of rules about how they should behave in those roles. When the boy (as the parent) attempts to punish the girl (as the baby) and to explain his reasons, the girl helps him along, stepping out of her role as a baby.

4.1 Learning through play

Extract A

Girl (39 months)   *Boy* (33 months)

  (1) Say, 'Go to sleep now!'   (2) Go sleep now.

  (3) Why? (*whining*)   (4) Baby . . .

  (5) Why?   (6) Because.

  (7) No, say 'Because'. (*emphatically*)   (8) Because! (*emphatically*)

  (9) Why? Because why?   (10) Not good. You bad.

(11) Why?   (12) 'Cause you spill your milk.

(13) No, 'cause I bit somebody.   (14) Yes, you did.

(15) Say, 'Go to sleep. Put your head down'. (*sternly*)   (16) Put your head down. (*sternly*)

(17) No.   (18) Yes

(19) No.   (20) Yes, okay, I will spank you. Bad boy. (*spanks her*)

(21) My head's up. (*giggles*)

(22) I want my teddy bear. (*petulant voice*)   (23) No, your teddy bear go away. (*sternly*)

(24) Why?   (25) 'Cause he does. (*walks off with teddy bear*)

(Garvey, 1977; quoted in Damon, pp. 102–3)

In a study by Denzin (1977) in which he observed preschool children at play in their nursery, 3 year olds assigned roles to each other, and engaged in very complex, joint action to negotiate these roles and play together. In Extract B, three girls came over to the big doll's house.

Extract B

A   'Come on M and J. Here baby, someone's been in our doll's house.'

M   'I know who it was. I know it was T, and that's a bad thing.'

They then go upstairs into the doll's house, and the following observations were noted.

P   'I want to be the baby.'

M   'I'm going to be the mother.'

T   'I want to be the baby, too.'

M   'You be the big baby.'

P   'I have to be the little baby because I have the high-chair.'

Another girl comes up.

M   'She has to be the daddy. Little girl you have to put your shoes on in the morning.'

A boy, W, comes up.

M   'W, what do you want to be?'

W   'I'll be the daddy.'

M   'We'll have two daddies, then. Where do you sit?'

In this exchange, each child was assigned a role, and M, in particular, was aware of a number of constraints on the play sequence, assigning some to be babies, inventing the extra roles of 'big baby' and 'second daddy' when necessary, and taking account of the other children's preferences for particular roles. She (M) was acting reflexively in symbolic interactionist terms, since she was adopting a role herself (mother at home), fitting it to the situation in which she found herself, and acting on it in assigning appropriate roles to the others she was playing with.

In most play situations, children are not bound by the normal rules of interaction, but experiment with them. In their pretend world, the meanings of words, objects and actions used as symbols are not as strictly defined as they are in the 'real' world. Cardboard boxes can symbolize ships or cars, rugs can be islands, and children can become adults or animals. Meanings, rituals and roles are more important than reality (Shotter, 1974). As a result, play allows children to learn about roles and interaction by experimenting with them. What is done in a conscious, deliberate and exaggerated form in play is often taken for granted in real life.

A good example of this was given by the Soviet psychologist, Vygotsky. As reported by Damon (1983), Vygotsky observed two young sisters aged 5 and 7, who decided to 'play at' being sisters. As they did so, their behaviour changed dramatically from their normal sisterly conduct. For example, it became stylized and self-conscious as they acted out stereotypes of sisterhood roles by dressing alike and always holding hands. Vygotsky commented that the 'vital difference in play is that the child in playing tried to be a sister' (1983; in Damon p. 107). Instead of behaving as real sisters, they are *intending* to be sisters and are conscious of each other's aims.

In life the child behaves without thinking that she is her sister's sister . . . except perhaps in those cases where her mother says, 'Give in to her'. In the game of sisters playing at 'sisters', however, they are both concerned with displaying their sisterhood; the fact that the two sisters decided to play sisters makes them both acquire rules of behaviour. . . . Only actions which will fit these rules are acceptable to the play situation.

(Vygotsky, 1933; quoted in Damon, 1983, p. 107)

According to Vygotsky, play affords children unique opportunities to manipulate and test out rules of social interaction. He also makes the important point that in play children are able to substitute *symbols* for the real world. When a box is used as a ship, it is a symbol for the ship. In the same way, the exaggerated sisterly behaviour is a symbol for real sisterly behaviour. Symbols are in fact **representations** of what is going on in the real world. As we saw in Section 3, it is only through the shared meanings of symbols that concepts about the self, personal roles and the behaviour of others can develop. Language provides the most potent symbols, as can be seen in the above extracts of children's conversation. It allows children to think symbolically, to reason about what is possible rather than what is real, and to examine the underlying meaning of their own social behaviour.

Through increasingly complex social relations, children gain an awareness of other people's points of view. They learn that these may be at variance with their own and must be taken into account in planning their own course of action. By imitating the roles of adults during their pretend games, children acquire an ability to see objects, other people and themselves from a different perspective. They thus become more socially aware, and also begin to form and clarify their own self-concepts.

4.2 Friendships

ACTIVITY 1

If you have the opportunity, ask one or more children some questions about friendship. Ideally, you should ask children of different ages, but any child between about 4 and 14 years of age would be fine. You should ask about their own friends (i.e. who are their 'best friends', what do they like to do with their friends?). Also ask about their more general ideas of friendship (e.g. what is a friend; how do you make friends; how do you know you can trust someone; how would you be kind or unkind to someone; what would make you not want to be friends with someone anymore?). Keep brief notes of their responses, and of any problems you found when asking the questions.

These questions are like those asked by a number of researchers who have examined the changing nature of children's friendships. Did you find any problems in asking the children these questions? You may well have found it easier to ask the more specific questions about particular friends and events than to ask the more abstract, general ones about defining friendship. Researchers have tried to get round this problem of abstract definitions in a number of ways; see Box F.

The results of the study described in Box F showed that younger children saw kindness as sharing material goods, like toys, and that they showed friendship by playing with another child. Older children saw kindness as being a comfort to another person and providing psychological support, and they saw friendship as responding to each other's needs. If you asked children about their views on kindness in Activity 1, did the responses you elicited fit in with those Youniss obtained?

BOX F   Stories about friendship

In a study by Youniss (1975) some 6 to 13 year olds were asked to tell short one or two sentence stories about how they would tell someone that they liked them or that they are friends with them. They were also asked to write down sentences that described how they would be kind or unkind to someone. Later, other children were shown some of these stories and asked to pick out stories which described kind or unkind actions and to say *why* they were kind or unkind. By using stories that other children had told, Youniss could be sure that he was not imposing his own ideas of friendship on the children, but was genuinely eliciting their own views. He wanted to see whether the same types of actions would be judged as either kind or unkind by children of different ages, and also whether their ways of showing friendship with someone would change with age.

A different method for accessing views of friendship was used by Selman (1980). In his study, he asked children in the United States aged between 7 and 12 to read and respond to dilemmas about typical problems and conflicts encountered between friends. An example of these dilemmas is given in Box G. This particular dilemma naturally leads into a discussion of the different relationships between the three girls but also allows the researcher to ask in a fairly natural way for the children's views on the formation of their own friendships, and on trust, jealousy and conflict.

BOX G   Friendship dilemmas

Kathy and Becky have been best friends since they were 5 years old. They went to the same kindergarten and have been in the same class ever since.

One day a new girl, Jeanette, moved into their neighbourhood and soon introduced herself to Kathy and Becky. Right away Jeanette and Kathy seemed to hit it off very well. Becky, on the other hand, didn't seem to like Jeanette. She thought Jeanette was a showoff, but was also jealous of all the attention Kathy was giving Jeanette.

When Jeanette left the other two alone, Becky told Kathy how she felt about Jeanette. 'What did you think of her, Kathy? I thought she was kind of pushy, butting in on us like that.'

'Come on, Becky. She's new in town and just trying to make friends. The least we can do is to be nice to her.'

'Yeah, but that doesn't mean we have to be friends with her', replied Becky. 'Anyway, what would you like to do this Saturday? You know those old puppets of mine, I thought we could fix them up and make our own puppet show.'

'Sure, Becky, that sounds great', said Kathy. 'I'll be over after lunch.'

Later that evening, Jeanette called Kathy and surprised her with an invitation to the circus, the last show before it left town. The only problem was that the circus happened to be at the same time that Kathy had promised to go to Becky's. Kathy didn't know what to do, go to the circus and leave her best friend alone, or stick with her best friend and miss a good time.

(Selman, 1980, pp. 321–2)

Selman presented his findings on friendship development in terms of a broader model which he had constructed from other studies of the development of social perspective taking. As was discussed in Section 3, this is consistent with the symbolic interactionist's stress on the importance of the ability to take the role of another person.

Selman was conscious of the symbolic interactionist's view that attaching chronological ages is not appropriate in the study of the development of social processes. Nevertheless, he was also influenced by those developmental psychologists (especially Jean Piaget whose work will be discussed in the next chapter) who proposed chronological ages in development. Selman took a position midway between these two positions, and provided some very general age-trends. These are included in the following descriptions of the stages of friendship development and the corresponding levels in the development of social perspective taking.

Stage 0 of friendship development

The preschool child is at the lowest level of social perspective taking and cannot distinguish his or her own perspective from that of someone else. At the corresponding stage in the development of friendship, children regard everyone they play with as a friend, but they assume that the friendship lasts only as long as they are playing together. The quotes below were elicited as responses to the various moral dilemmas Selman used in his study:

Q   What kind of a person makes a good friend?

A   Boys play with boys, trucks play with trucks, dogs play with dogs.

Q   Why does that make them good friends?

A   Because they do the same things.

Children at this stage do not have very abstract understandings of concepts such as trust and intimacy, and they also have rather physical strategies for resolving conflict:

Q   If you and your friend are each trying to play with the same toy, how do you decide who gets it?

A   Punch her. Or just go play with something else.

Stage 1 of friendship development

At level 1 of perspective taking (early primary school) children understand that other people may think or feel differently from themselves, but they cannot visualize what other people think about *them*. At Stage 1 of friendship conceptions, children view a friend primarily as someone who gives them help, but they do not perceive the responsibility to reciprocate this help: 'You need a friend because you want to play some games and you have to get someone who will play the way you want him to'. Trust and intimacy are recognized more than in Stage 0, but still depend on how well the friend matches the child's own interests, or the extent to which the friend has good motives towards the child. In explanations of conflict and conflict resolution, the lack of reciprocity is also evident:

Q   What causes fights between friends?

A   If she calls you a name or something like that.

Q   How can you get to be friends again?

A   Make her take it back; make her say she was lying.

Friendships at Stage 1 then, are still rather transient, with children changing friends quite often.

Stage 2 of friendship development

By the second level of perspective taking (later primary school, middle childhood) children can understand another's view of themselves and are more aware of reciprocity. Friendship at Stage 2 means co-operation, each child taking account of the other's viewpoint. However, this is rather a 'fair-weather' type of reciprocity, since it is seen as necessary only in specific circumstances, and still does not underpin the whole friendship. Friendships at Stage 2 are seen as important and as valuable for themselves, not just in the service of the child's needs. Trust and intimacy are becoming salient, with a friend being someone who is told secrets and, importantly, will keep them. As a result, by Stage 2, friendships are rather longer lasting than before.

Stage 3 of friendship development

Pre-adolescents at the third level of perspective taking can stand not only outside themselves, but also outside their relationships and see them from the perspective of a third party. As a result, the focus is less on one or other of the friends, but more on the relationship itself. At Stage 3, friendships are defined by mutual support and understanding. Friendship is viewed as an intimate relationship that is maintained during minor conflicts. The intimacy can lead to greater concern with jealousy, and major conflicts are seen as ones which threaten the bond of trust established by this intimacy. 'A lot of times you will tell a friend some really private thing, something about your girlfriend or how you feel about somebody. If he goes out and asks that girl out, then you just can't trust him anymore, and you really can't be very good friends.'

Stage 4 of friendship development

The final level of perspective taking is typically only found in adolescence and adulthood. Individuals can recognize a general perspective on themselves and their actions. In Mead's terms, this is the 'generalized other'. At Stage 4 of friendship development, people recognize that others have complex and sometimes conflicting needs, each of which may be met by a different relationship. Friendships are seen as open to change and growth in the same way that people are. An important function of a close friend is to help provide the self with a sense of personal identity, and to attend to each other's deeper psychological needs. Trust is now viewed as a meeting of the twin needs of dependence and autonomy: 'trust is the ability to let go as well as to hang on'.

There is less possessiveness and jealousy than at Stage 3, since other relationships are recognized as necessary. In discussing the reasons for terminating a friendship, individuals for the first time will suggest that friendships might be 'grown out of'.

ACTIVITY 2

If you were able to carry out Activity 1, did your questions yield answers which would fit into these levels? Were there issues raised by the answers you received which are not covered by this model?

When you asked children about friendships in Activity 1, you may have received many answers which seem to straddle the levels, with statements that reflected thinking typical of at least two of them. This is often the case, and may indicate that development occurs only gradually, with later ideas about friendship not so much replacing earlier conceptions, but building on and reorganizing the earlier ways of thinking. Thus, children entering the third level, or even adults, will still talk of doing joint activities with a friend, much like the emphasis on playing together at the earlier levels, but now probably as only one of a more complex set of behaviours engaged in with friends.

The studies described so far, and many others which examine children's friendships, are based on asking children questions and expecting them to be able to put their views about this rather abstract notion of 'friendship' into words. Very few studies look at what children actually *do with* and *say to* their friends, and yet this would seem to be a very direct measure of what they understand about friendship. This approach would be particularly appropriate for children younger than those in the studies by Youniss and Selman. Young children's ability to express such ideas verbally is likely to be limited, and yet from their play it is evident that they live in a quite complex social world.

Some researchers have used the **observational method** to study children in the natural settings of their homes and nursery classes to uncover the complex rules governing friendship in young children (e.g. Corsaro, 1985; Denzin, 1977; Gottman and Parkhurst, 1980); an outline of the study by Corsaro is given in Box H. These studies of naturalistic behaviour have added to our understanding of children's friendships by stressing the importance of the social context in which children operate and the way concepts about friendships emerge to meet the demands of everyday interactions, rather than concentrating on asking each child for a reasoned account.

This approach is very much in keeping with the style of research advocated by symbolic interactionists such as Blumer (1969). This perspective sees the symbolic meanings people assign to their experience as crucial, and stresses the importance of examining both the emergence of meaning and the way meaning functions in the context of social interaction. Since meanings are seen as necessarily social—shaping and being shaped by interaction with others—then they are best examined in the context of ongoing interaction. While Youniss, and particularly Selman, examined concepts which were relevant to the symbolic interactionist perspective, they placed little stress on studying children in their natural social contexts. Instead, their emphasis was rather more on the development of the individual child's ability to take another person's perspective. In many ways, this emphasis on the individual is more closely allied to the theoretical position of Piaget. Whilst Piaget and Mead both stressed the importance of the ability to take the perspective of another person, Mead placed much greater emphasis on how this arises in social interaction, whereas Piaget saw it as one of a range of cognitive skills acquired by the individual child (see Chapter 3).

BOX H   Observing friendship in action

Corsaro observed children aged 3 to 5 years old at their nursery school over a period of a year. He used a number of techniques, including concealed observation from a specially constructed viewing area alongside the playrooms with a one-way mirror. He also used **participant observation** where he joined in with the children's activities and made notes inside the playrooms. Videotapes of the play sessions were analysed, as were interviews with the assistants at the nursery. Notes made during observations included the children's conversations, an accompanying description of the children's actions and any relevant background events during the conversations.

This is a typical example of such an observation:

The researcher (referred to as R and Bill), is observing two girls (referred to as B, aged three and Be, aged three years seven months) who are playing zoos, when L (another girl aged three years eight months) approaches:

B says to L	You can't play.
L to B	Yes, I can. I can have some animals too.
B to L	No, you can't. We don't like you today.
Be to L	You're not our friend.
L to B and Be	I can play here, too.
B to Be	No, her can't—her can't play, right Be?
Be to B	Right.
L to R	Can I have some of your animals, Bill (the researcher)?
R to L	You can have some of these.
B to R	She can't play, Bill, 'cause she's not our friend.
R to B	Why not? You guys played with her yesterday.
Be to R	Well, we hate her today.
L to all present	Well, I'll tell teacher (goes and fetches teaching assistant referred to as TA)
TA to B and Be	Girls, can L play with you?
B to TA	No! She's not our friend.
TA to B	Why can't you *all* be friends?
B to TA	No!
Be to B	Let's go outside, B.
B to Be	Okay

(Corsaro, 1985, pp. 124–5)

Corsaro (1985) collected some very rich data from the observational studies described in Box H, which led him to some interesting conclusions about young children's friendships. He noticed that the children he observed rarely engaged in solitary play. When they found themselves alone they would try to gain entry into ongoing activities with their playmates. However, these attempts to gain access were often resisted by the children already involved in activities, and this led to recurrent conflict. Corsaro suggested that children's concepts of friendship arise from this somewhat unstable social context, with claims of friendship used to try to gain access to a group and denials of friendship used to exclude intruders. Friendship was also discussed by the children during ongoing mutual activity, where it seemed to serve the purpose of strengthening the bond being formed between the children by the joint activity. Once again, Corsaro suggested that this strengthening is necessary because of the danger of disruption from other children.

Corsaro's research stresses the importance of the social context in determining the nature of the concepts children develop about friendship. The data support Youniss and Selman's findings with young children in indicating the prominence of a number of rather transient relationships based on mutual activity.

SAQ 3   Which of Selman's stages is illustrated by Corsaro's results?

Friendship, from Corsaro's perspective, becomes a concept actively constructed by the children in their dialogue with each other in order to establish and define their interactions. The children helped to shape their own experiences through their interactions with each other. They also attempted to gain control over their social worlds through their use of language. Corsaro's presentation of what goes on in interactions enriches the view of Selman and others, that friendship reflects an individual's developing ability to take the perspective of the other. Selman focused on the individual's ability in social perspective taking, while Corsaro stressed the role of language and interactions *within a social context*. Both, however, seek to establish the children's *own* perspective on their social world, which is very much the approach advocated by the symbolic interactionists. The child's perspective is often a very different one to that held by adults observing children.

So far in this chapter, we have discussed some of the developments in the concept of self and in social understanding from the earliest days of a child's life through to school. Although a number of theorists have implied that these processes of development are complete by adolescence, others, notably Erikson (1968) and Mead, have argued that we continue to mature, to alter our image of ourselves and learn more about how to interact with others as we grow older and experience a wider range of relationships. Throughout secondary socialization (see Section 3.2 above) in adulthood, people seek more information about their sense of self and about their roles in relationship to others, and they constantly adapt themselves to meet the challenge of new experiences and new beliefs.

Summary of Section 4

- In play, children experiment with alternative roles which allow them to perceive the world and themselves from different perspectives. It also allows them to prepare for new roles which they might adopt as they grow up.

- Symbolic play is particularly influential in encouraging children to develop representations of the social world.

- Selman suggests that concepts of friendship change with age and experience of interaction. At Stages 0 and 1, young children see friends as transitory playmates. At Stage 2, friends are viewed as people who give help and who are liked. At Stage 3, once the child becomes able to see things from another's perspective, mutual help and greater intimacy become important. Finally, at Stage 4, trust and the recognition of each other's needs underlie the older child's conception of friendship, which continues into adulthood.

- Corsaro's study of children's natural conversations with their friends suggests that they have a complex understanding of friendship and of the rules governing social behaviour, developed in their dialogue by the demands of the social context.

5 | Gaining information about the self

As Mead and Cooley stressed, to a great extent individuals derive information about themselves from other people (see Section 3.2 above). Each of us attends to the opinions, abilities and behaviour of various people in an attempt to find out about ourselves. We can learn how we are perceived by others (social feedback) and how we compare with others (social comparison). **Social feedback** is perhaps the earliest form of information we receive. As children, we are regularly told what other people think about our behaviour and about what we say, and this is a direct input into our self-concepts. Although other sources of self-information develop over time, we never lose our initial concern with the appraisals made of us by others. As we get older, this source of information, perhaps unfortunately, becomes more ambiguous and elusive. Once we are adults it is rare for others to tell us directly and honestly what they think of us. We have to become sensitive to subtle, often non-verbal cues indicating what another person thinks of us. We also become more sensitive to feedback from particular people who matter to us, and less bothered about what certain other groups may think. We concentrate on gaining information about what these particular people think of us and, as we shall explore below, about how we compare with those who matter to us.

5.1 Social feedback

In early, unsuccessful attempts to test the view that the adult self is a reflection of others' views, people were asked to describe themselves on a number of dimensions (such as sporty, honest, lazy, intelligent) and then a number of their acquaintances were asked to rate them using the same dimensions. The statistical estimate of the extent of agreement (the **correlation**) between the two sets of scores was calculated and found to be very high. For example, where people described themselves as easygoing, their friends tended to rate them as easygoing too. The conclusion was that these people had come to view themselves as easygoing as a result of the opinions held and expressed by these friends. But, put like this, you can probably see that things are just as likely to have happened the other way around.

As Gergen (1971) points out, high correlations between a person's view of him or herself and the view of other people are not adequate evidence to support the notion of a reflected self. Rather than a person's view being formed by the other people's opinions, it is always possible that the person has convinced others of a particular view of him or herself which they then express in their ratings. This type of correlation allows us to say that the two ratings are linked, but *not* to say which one has caused the other.

Much more convincing evidence for the reflected-self notion comes from studies such as Videbeck's (1960), where a person's self-concept is shown to be altered *directly* as a result of an evaluation made by another person; see Box I.

You should note the *deception* involved in Videbeck's study. Not only did he engage the students in the study without their knowledge, he also presented them with false information about their speech abilities, suggesting that an expert had rated them professionally. No doubt the students who received unfavourable feedback from the expert would have felt very bad about their abilities as a result. Although the experiment and the deception was explained to them afterwards, the effect on them may not have been entirely removed. In this and many other experiments in psychology, the researcher must be aware of such ethical problems and should attempt to eliminate or at least minimize any discomfort or unease which might be caused to the people involved in the study.

Videbeck's study suggests that other people's evaluations of us are important in determining our own views of ourselves. However, it would be unrealistic to attempt to generalize too much from his findings. Clearly, we are likely to take more notice of the evaluations made of us by some people rather than others; after all, the students in Videbeck's study thought that they were being judged by an expert. Would they have taken as much notice of an evaluation from a lay person? Also, we may be less likely to change our view of some aspects of ourselves than others. The students in Videbeck's study were attending a course to have their speech skills assessed and improved; they were expecting evaluation of their speech and, presumably, were willing to

BOX I   Self-concept and the reactions of others

Thirty students were enrolled in a speech class, and Videbeck used one of the sessions as an experiment (unbeknown to the students). The students were told that a man who came into the class was 'a visiting speech expert' who would listen to the students read a poem and then give each of them an independent appraisal of their speech abilities, in particular their voice control and communication of emotional tone. In fact the 'expert' was a **confederate** of Videbeck's, someone trained to act in the experiment in a particular way by the researcher. At random, the so-called expert gave half the class 'approving' evaluations and the other half 'disapproving' evaluations, *regardless* of the students' actual performances.

Both before and after the experimental session, the students were asked to evaluate their speech abilities on a series of nine-point scales, some of which were directly comparable to the abilities being assessed by the 'expert', while others were related abilities and others were unrelated (e.g.

their skills in social conversation). If the appraisal by the 'expert' had an effect on the students' self-concepts, their self-evaluations after the session should reflect this effect by being either more positive or more negative than before the session (depending on whether they received a positive or negative appraisal).

Videbeck found that students' self-evaluations of their speech abilities were indeed significantly affected by the 'expert's' appraisal, demonstrating the effects of other people's opinions on the self-concept. Students who had been given favourable feedback showed a general increase in their own evaluation of their abilities, an increase that was most marked for abilities like voice control, which were directly related to the 'expert' appraisal. Those who were given unfavourable feedback rated themselves as less able after the session, once again especially in the qualities most related to the 'expert's' appraisal.

accept it. As the results suggested, there was less change in their views of abilities not directly related to those that the expert had assessed. We may also ask whether someone would be as willing to accept an evaluation of central characteristics of the self-concept, such as his or her honesty?

To summarize, direct social feedback from other people can have a powerful influence on our self-concept. The strength of this influence, however, will vary depending on a number of factors such as the type of person giving the feedback, the attributes on which they comment, and how much they are in agreement with other people and with our own view of ourselves. Though the opinions of others are clearly important for the self-concept, a view which implies a simple and general acceptance of the evaluations made by others is clearly false. In the next section, we will consider another theory which has its roots in the symbolic interactionist tradition and which suggests that we do not internalize the views of others indiscriminately, but attend more to the views of particular others.

5.2 Social comparison theory

Festinger (1954) developed social comparison theory, concerning our sensitivity to other people's opinions. Whilst it is generally compatible with the interactionist perspectives of Mead, James and Cooley in its emphasis on the social origins of the self-concept, some of the detail and emphasis of the theory comes from a slightly different school. This other influence arises from the work of Kurt Lewin (who trained Festinger and who laid great stress on the experimental method) and Mustafa Sherif. These psychologists had stressed the socializing process of social interaction in groups rather more than its influence on the development of the self-concept. Sherif had conducted many important experiments on how group rules are established and enforced and emphasized the pressure to conform to a group (Sherif, 1936).

The basic tenet of **social comparison theory** is that we have a drive to validate our opinions and abilities (and thus, in a sense, ourselves), and that this drive enables us to operate effectively in our world. Festinger suggested that we prefer to use objective physical means for self-evaluation—such as timing how fast we can run—but for some abilities and opinions no such objective measures are available. For example, an opinion about the inevitability of war, or abilities as a father or as a composer, cannot be checked against an absolute physical standard. In such circumstances, where a physical standard is not available, social comparison theory suggests that we will look to *other people* for comparison. We may consult others directly, or through the media of books and magazines, which are full of advice about topics such as the 'right way' to bring up a child. As Festinger put it: 'An opinion, a belief, an attitude is "correct", "valid" and "proper" to the extent that it is anchored in a group of people with similar beliefs, opinions and attitudes' (Festinger *et al.*, 1950, p. 272). If neither physical nor social comparisons are available, Festinger proposed that the individual's self-evaluation would be unstable (that is, continuously altering) until a suitable comparison could be found.

Thus, we are more confident in our opinions and attitudes if they are shared by others. However, as we saw earlier, it is not just anyone who can influence our view of ourselves and, similarly, only some people can serve the social comparison function of helping us to evaluate our opinions. The other person (or persons) we compare ourselves with must be *similar* to us in relevant ways. Festinger suggests that we are motivated to seek and associate with people who are similar to us in order to allow us to make valid comparisons between their opinions and ours. It would not be very informative for a Socialist to look to a Conservative for comparison of their opinions about private education or expenditure on nuclear weapons, for example. Instead, we seek out generally similar others whose opinion we value.

But what happens when we find people who are generally similar to us disagreeing with some of our attitudes or opinions? One way of reducing any dissimilarity between ourselves and the other people is to change our own opinions and become more similar to the others. Another way is to try to persuade the others to change *their* opinions. Still another way would be to withdraw from that group as a comparison group and seek other, more similar people. All these ways of dealing with dissimilarity can be seen as leading to conformity with a group. Unity is re-established by either a change of attitude or the removal from the group of the 'deviant' person who disagrees with the group's views.

In the case of personal abilities, people also compare themselves with others who are similar. For example, we are more likely to assess our sports prowess by comparing ourselves with others in our team than with national stars, and the golf handicapping system is a formalized version of this. Unlike opinions, however, there is a scale of abilities such that we can become 'better'. As a result, we may choose to compare our abilities with others who are slightly better than ourselves to encourage us to improve, or with people slightly worse than us to make us *feel* we have improved.

The drive to make social comparisons results in a tendency to **conformity** within society; people generally prefer to be like other people. As was discussed in Section 2, the processes of becoming an individual and a member of a society are inextricably bound together, and in social comparison we have an example of this link. Whilst social comparison is an essentially individual process, with consequences for the self-concept (see below) it is also an important social regulator, since it binds people together in their influence on each other and results in similarity and conformity.

The effects of social comparison on the self-concept have been demonstrated in a number of experiments. Box J outlines a study conducted by Morse and Gergen (1970). Their experimental question was whether the mere presence of 'Mr Clean' or 'Mr Dirty' would affect the subjects' self-esteem ratings. If social comparison was operating, then waiting with 'Mr Clean' should cause the subjects to feel somewhat less positive about themselves in comparison with the immaculately turned out 'Mr Clean'. Waiting with 'Mr Dirty' should have the opposite effect and should increase the subjects' self-esteem. The results supported these predictions: the self-esteem of subjects who had waited with

---

BOX J   'Mr Clean' and 'Mr Dirty'

An advert was placed in a university newspaper for a part-time job in the research institute. When individual student applicants came for an interview for this job they were asked to fill in a number of forms, one of which was a measure of **self-esteem**, that is, how a person values various aspects of him or herself. Once the forms had been completed, the subject was asked to wait for a while before the interview, and was introduced to another applicant who was also waiting to be interviewed. This other person was, however, a confederate of the experimenter and not a real applicant.

For half the subjects, this other 'applicant' was smartly dressed, and carried a briefcase that contained sharpened pencils and philosophy and statistical books. The other subjects were asked to wait with a rather differently dressed person. He wore a dirty sweat-shirt and no socks, carried a battered novel and slouched around the waiting room. After some time waiting with one of these two 'applicants', the subjects were asked to fill in further forms, one of which was a second measure of self-esteem.

'Mr Dirty' increased, and the others who waited with 'Mr Clean' reported a lowering of their self-esteem. These changes were most marked for subjects who were found to have inconsistent, or poorly integrated self-concepts. Perhaps such people are more susceptible to changes in self-esteem because they have been evaluated in several different ways over time and remain less sure of their abilities and opinions. This is in line with Festinger's theory, since he believed that it is uncertainty that drives a person to seek social comparisons and act on the results.

Everyday life is replete with examples of the importance of social comparison. The proverbial idea of 'keeping up with the Joneses' captures part of what is implied by the concept. When the family next door purchases a new car some people may feel that their self-esteem is threatened unless they follow suit. Comparison with other relevant groups is an important element of wage negotiations, and unions are often as concerned with pay differentials as they are about the average wages of their members. These are not simply financial questions. One's feeling of self-worth and the contribution one is making to society are both bound up in the call for 'parity'.

The central notions of social comparison theory seem intuitively plausible and have some measure of empirical support. It is reasonable to assert that people want to have an accurate appraisal of their opinions and abilities and that in order to appraise these attributes they will have to compare themselves with others. There are criticisms of the theory, however. For example, the idea that only similar others can provide accurate appraisals can be questioned. It may be very informative on occasions to know about the abilities or opinions of people who are dissimilar to ourselves as well, such as those who lie at extreme positions on a scale of abilities (e.g. top and bottom marks in an exam) or who hold very discrepant opinions to our own. Indeed, if we only attended to people who agreed with us, we would never change. Despite these and other criticisms, Festinger's work has been important in social psychology for a number of reasons. The theory of social comparison has stimulated a great deal of research activity about how people evaluate themselves against others and what the social consequences of this comparison process are.

Summary of Section 5

- Social feedback, in the form of comments about us and our behaviour, is more direct and frequent for children. As adults we have to interpret more subtle messages about how others perceive us.

- The influence of social feedback will depend on a number of factors such as who is giving the feedback, what they are commenting on and how much their opinion is in agreement with our own.

- Social comparison involves comparing opinions, attitudes and abilities with relevant other people. Festinger suggested that we seek out similar others with whom to compare ourselves.

6 | Many selves?

Even when looking at a single feature of ourselves, the feedback we get from other people can be varied, even contradictory. The same person may be seen as considerate by some people and self-centred by others. If both points of view are accepted as valid, at least to some extent, then this inconsistency could lead to a potential threat to the person's integrated concept of him or herself. After all, we cannot be both fair *and* selfish. Or can we?

ACTIVITY 3

A common method for establishing people's views of themselves is the twenty statement test (TST) (Kuhn and McPartland, 1954). In this test, people are asked to give twenty statements in answer to the question, 'who am I?' You could do this now. Ask yourself the question, 'who am I?' and write down as many answers as you can up to twenty, starting each one with 'I am. . . .'.

You may like to carry this a little further by:

1 asking a couple of other people (perhaps of different ages) to give up to twenty answers to the 'who am I?' question; and/or

2 writing different (perhaps shorter) lists in answer to the 'who am I?' question, and thinking about different 'audiences' reading your answers (e.g. write one list as if a stranger was going to read it, another for a friend, or your boss, or a 'private' version just for yourself).

6.1 Roles

As we have seen, William James suggested that a person 'has as many social selves as there are individuals who recognize him and carry an image of him in their mind' (1892 (1961) p. 46; and see above Section 3.1). Many other writers, notably from the tradition of role theory in sociology, have also believed that an individual can hold a number of different self-perceptions without confusion or inconsistency. To understand how, we need to consider the notion of a **role**.

The word *role* derives from the Latin word *rotula*, or sheet of parchment wrapped around a wooden roller that contained the part that an actor recited on stage. In the theater, roles constrain actors' behavior, at least to some degree. Actors must say certain lines at certain times, engage in specific behaviors at specific moments, work with particular props, coordinate their actions with those of the other actors, and, in general, convey to the audience the character of the person they are playing. Within these constraints, of course, actors are free to display their own unique talents, fleshing out the character to give spontaneity and life to the author's words. They might ad-lib on occasion, throwing in or changing lines and dramatizing gestures to bring the character home and touch a responsive chord in the audience. Typically, the better the actor, the better his or her ability to improvise in a way that meets with the audience's approval. But the role still gives direction and purpose to the actor's behaviors, guiding them along a predetermined course.

(Schlenker, 1980, p. 66)

According to role theory, just as actors' behaviours are guided by their roles, people's normal social behaviour can be seen to be guided by the roles they occupy. A role can thus be seen as a set of expectations that the self perceives the 'generalized other' to hold for a pattern of behaviour in that situation. In our daily lives, we all occupy many different roles, for example, those of friend, student, mother, neighbour, customer, and grandchild. We behave in accordance with these many different roles, provided we know the rules for behaviour which make them up. Do not, however, think of this as slave-like obedience. We behave in accordance with our roles in the light of the overall requirements they specify. We do not stop being the people we are just because we fulfil the requirements of a role, just as actors can express their personal styles within the script for the role they are playing—they 'make the role their own'.

We can certainly view people as *making* roles for themselves, at least as much as we say they are *taking* their roles (Turner, 1962). This is where the influence of Mead's somewhat ambiguous concept of the 'I' comes into play. Being slightly distanced from social roles, the 'I' provides some degree of independence and individuality for the self, embellishing and individualizing the roles in order to prevent the self from being too externally constrained.

Look at Box K; when you did the TST in Activity 3, did your own responses tally with the findings presented there? There is, however, a note of caution to be added before we draw conclusions about how a person's self-concept is made up. In these types of test, people are usually answering the question, 'who am I?' for an experimenter, who is, most probably, someone they do not know. In a different context (for instance when friends ask them to describe themselves, or when they are thinking about themselves) the features they list may be rather different. What differences, if any, did you find in the lists you made for different 'audiences'? Also, there are differences between asking people to write down twenty short statements summing themselves up and asking them to talk at length in an unstructured interview, where the complexities of their views of themselves can be more fully explored. McCall and Simmons (1966) followed up the TST with such an interview, where people were asked questions such as, 'how important is it for you personally to be a . . .?'.

Each role carries with it certain expected rules for behaviour, which are generated by cultural values and beliefs, and which have often emerged because they perform a function in society. How do we become aware of these expected rules? How do we absorb our culture, learn to respond to the demands of the society in which we live and juggle with its conflicting demands? Obviously the media and our general education have a powerful influence. But to a large extent it is through communication and interaction with others, initially parents, that we learn roles and practise role behaviours.

The process of acquiring these roles and the cultural rules for behaviour is called socialization. The child gradually becomes an accepted member of a society when he or she understands and uses the rules and roles of that society. These are passed on to the child through interaction with experienced members of society. Indeed it is only possible to create and maintain the structure of a society, and to develop and transmit a culture *because we*

BOX K Describing the self

When asked to write twenty statements in answer to the question, 'who am I?' (the TST used in Activity 3, above) most people give more than half of their answers in role terms (e.g. male, married) and the rest in terms of personality traits or evaluations (e.g. sad, outgoing, good at sport). In one experiment using this test (Mulford and Salisbury, 1964), over one thousand adults were tested and their responses were analysed to discover the roles which people most frequently used to describe themselves. The four commonest types of description were in terms of:

	Role	Responses falling in this category
1	Family relationships (e.g. brother, mother)	70%
2	Occupation (e.g. nurse, clerk)	68%
3	Marital status (e.g. divorced, single)	34%
4	Religious identity (e.g. Christian, Hindu)	30%

Women used family categories more than men, who mentioned their occupation and sex more often. Age was mentioned most by the youngest (under-30s) and oldest (over-70s) in the sample.

humans have such specialized skills in social interaction. We have unique skills of communicating through spoken and written language and non-verbal systems of symbolic representation. As Mead and others stressed, it is only through symbolic interactions that we come to internalize our self-concepts, which include information about appropriate personal roles. Once again, we see the close links between the integrating and differentiating processes of social development which were raised in Section 2 and again in our discussion of social comparison. Whilst interaction and the acquisition of roles allow a child to become more of an individual, they also bind him or her more firmly into society.

On occasion, conflict can arise *between* the demands of two roles. This **inter-role conflict** arises when two or more of the roles which we occupy demand different behaviours from us. For example, a teacher may find his or her child in the school, or even in the class that he or she teaches, and have to balance the sometimes conflicting demands of the role of parent and that of teacher in dealing with the child in that context. Similarly, a plant foreman has to interact and deal with the conflicting demands of both workers and management within the same organization.

Another form of role conflict can arise when a person is aware of two or more sets of expectations with respect to the *same* role. This conflict *within* a role is called **intra-role conflict**. For example, there are several competing expectations for the role of a mother. To caricature the position, some people expect her to stay at home and give her time to the children; others suggest she should go out to work and engage a childminder or book the children into a nursery (if one is available). Each mother has to choose (more or less consciously and with varying degrees of conflict) between the various sets of expectations. Many coping strategies are developed to overcome conflict, such as establishing priorities, eliminating some sub-roles and rotating attention between roles (Hall, 1972).

The more of a person's life that is occupied with behaviours associated with a particular role, the more probable it is that the role and its behaviours will be internalized, that is, that they will become a crucial, and probably not conscious, part of the self and the personality. We have all heard of actors who talk of becoming the characters they play, particularly when the part requires considerable physical and mental effort. Roles provide anchors for self-definitions, and this can be seen particularly clearly when people are entering or leaving roles. This is perhaps best demonstrated in some of the work on ageing (e.g. Blau, 1973; Mutran and Burke, 1979). Such research suggests that, as family and job roles are lost, many older people fall into a 'role vacuum' and as a result suffer feelings of being 'useless'. These feelings are best overcome through establishing, or finding oneself in new roles, such as volunteer worker, Open University student or grandparent.

If people do not value the benefits of a particular role which they are in, or if they believe that they can't fulfil its requirements, problems can develop. When the self-concept contradicts the expectations of a role, behaviour in the role is likely to be poor, with such failures further reinforcing the belief that one cannot play that role. The person is not likely to internalize the role but instead may try to escape from its constraints, by leaving the job, for example. This emphasizes the interaction between the individual and the role, which was discussed earlier. Roles are not accepted as a package, but the 'I' actively 'negotiates' an appropriate way of coping with the external expectations for behaviour in a particular situation.

ACTIVITY 4

1   Choose two of the roles you listed for yourself in Activity 3 and write down a description of the rules for behaviour underlying each of them.

2   When you have done this, take each role in turn and try to set down how it is that you know these rules. Where did you learn the behaviour that is expected of you? Did (or does) any particular person or group hold these expectations of you?

3   Consider whether you experience any intra- or inter-role conflict in your life. Think of one example of each and write down how you (try to) resolve these conflicts.

6.2 Managing our 'masks'

As the previous section suggested, we all assume and have imposed on us a number of social roles which constitute expectations for how we should behave in various settings. Park suggested that:

In seeking to live up to the role . . . we find ourselves in a constant conflict with ourselves. Instead of acting simply and naturally, as a child, . . . we seek to conform to accepted models. . . . In our efforts to conform, we restrain our immediate and spontaneous impulses, and act, not as we are impelled to act, but rather as seems appropriate and proper to the occasion. Under these circumstances our manners, our polite speeches and gestures, our conventional and proper behavior, assume the character of a mask.

(1927, pp. 738–9)

Social interaction is viewed in this way by the dramaturgical theorists (e.g. Goffman, 1959) whose views are closely linked to the symbolic interactionist school described in Section 3. This is called **dramaturgical theory** because it draws attention to the theatre-like nature of social behaviour, emphasizing concepts such as roles, scripts and performance.

Goffman distinguishes three separate aspects of the self. The first two aspects—self as performer and self as audience to that performer—correspond to the 'I' and the 'me' of Mead's theory. The dramaturgical model adds a third aspect, of the self as the character performed. Dramaturgical theory says that, in taking the role of the other towards ourselves, we are bound to strive to create an appropriate impression and to act properly in our role. As a result, in studying the person, the dramaturgical theorists emphasize the importance of taking account of the character or mask he or she is seeking to sustain.

These masks, or, in McCall and Simmons' (1966) terminology, 'social identities' can be seen to include many of the roles and social positions people occupy, and which are often given as answers to the 'who am I?' question which you addressed in Activity 3. **Social identity** is the way a person is defined and regarded in social interaction. Just as situations must be defined by the partners in an interaction to determine what behaviour is appropriate, so people must *jointly* define their identities to clarify who they are and how they will act towards each other so as to co-ordinate their performance in the interaction. Any factor relevant to ourselves which might be noticed by other people has the potential to affect our relationships with them, and through these to affect our social identity. Such factors include the roles we occupy, our relative status, our appearance and our behaviour.

Social identities are what people attempt to monitor and control in front of others. The dramaturgical model of interaction suggests that people have an incentive to try to control their identities in interactions, because people's outcomes from an interaction are determined by how others define and regard them. Goffman (1959) and others (e.g. Schlenker, 1980) have catalogued a number of ways of attempting to present and control these identities. Such devices sometimes include attempts to influence the identities of the other person in the interaction. For instance, if one person wants to be seen as dominant, the other must be made to be (and feel) more submissive and less powerful. People can control the identities of others by actually influencing others' behaviour. This is the phenomenon of **altercasting**: the use of social influences to put another person into a particular identity. The person who wants to appear dominant will try many strategies to cause others to be submissive, such as bullying them, ridiculing them in front of others and ignoring their suggestions. If the altercasting is successful and the other person begins to behave submissively, then the desired, powerful identity is established for all others to see.

Subjective means can also be used to control the identities of others. For example, people who want to view themselves as very competent can achieve this by selective social comparisons. They will remember all the times that they performed more skilfully than others, and choose less skilful others to compare themselves with at every opportunity. These selective social comparisons allow people to conceptualize themselves in desired ways.

People do not have total control over their identities. So far, we have discussed the presentation of an identity as if it is a *consciously* planned and impeccably monitored operation. However, we are not always in control of the impressions others form of us; our attempts may be met with resistance if our partners do not want to accept either the identity we have tried to present or the identity we have tried to impose on them. Furthermore, we are not always consciously seeking to present any particular identity to others; in Mead's (1934) terms, we might be acting in the spontaneous 'I' mode.

6.3 A core self?

You may have been wondering, as you read about roles and masks in social interaction, whether this approach implies that people have many selves, each directed at a different audience, instead of having a *single self*, a unitary and coherent whole that is the core of their being. When we think about ourselves, we certainly do not feel as if we are constantly changing. Instead, we perceive a consistency over time, that we are in many ways the same person today as we were yesterday and will be tomorrow. This apparent paradox was raised earlier in the discussion about symbolic interactionism. In Section 3.1 the distinction between the 'I' and the 'me' was introduced. There, it was suggested that the 'me' part of the self-concept is more open to influence from the social context, and more likely to adapt to changing social demands, than the 'I'. Whilst the 'me' may internalize the various roles that the person adopts (or at least parts of these roles), the 'I' remains slightly apart, influenced but not dominated by the 'me', and providing a measure of independence from these role-expectations.

Our discussion of roles and masks raises the distinction between the public and private self, with the private self monitoring the success or failure of the public self's performance. A different approach in psychology, deriving from the humanistic tradition, suggests that this private self is in fact the authentic or core self and that this should become the focus of psychological enquiry. As will be discussed further in Chapter 9, humanistic psychologists see the search to uncover this authentic core self as the basic quest of all our lives.

The underlying 'personal style' which distinguishes one person's behaviour in the role of, for example, teacher, from another person in the same role is intuitively detectable but very difficult to analyse and research. Whilst distinctions between categories such as the 'I' and the 'me' have been made, too often the more individual category (the 'I' or 'authentic self') has been left somewhat unclear and under-researched.

Summary of Section 6

- People can appear to have several selves, behaving differently when in different social settings with different people.

- This chameleon-like quality of the self may be partly explained by the concept of role, where people conform to sets of expectations for behaviour appropriate to each particular social setting they find themselves in.

- We each occupy many roles, as is seen in answers to the twenty statements test.

- Conflict can arise between the demands of two or more of the roles we occupy simultaneously (inter-role conflict) or as a result of conflicting expectations within any one role (intra-role conflict).

- Dramaturgical theorists emphasize the theatre-like nature of social interaction. People are seen as actors who seek to manage the masks and identities which they adopt for the performances they give.

- We feel as if there is a true, or core, self as well as these various masks and roles. This might be labelled as the 'I', or as the authentic self (as the humanistic psychologists would call it). As yet, however, this remains somewhat intangible and difficult to research.

7 Reflection

Throughout this chapter we have presented a particular view of the interrelationship between the sense of self and a person's involvement in particular social interactions and in society at large. This has been based on the symbolic interactionist position, and some of the theories which have subsequently developed from it. To finish, we will look at this position rather more critically and evaluate its contribution to the study of the relationship between the self and the social world; we will also suggest some alternative ways of viewing this relationship.

A major problem with Mead's social psychology is that it was never systematically written up. The published material is in the form of collections of his various lectures and notes and as a result there are a number of inconsistencies, contradictions and obscurities. This makes it very difficult to evaluate his theory. Some concepts are, for example, rather poorly defined and vague. Thus, although Mead clearly specifies the nature of the socially defined 'me', the 'I' is much more loosely defined and is almost a catch-all category for all the 'not-me' aspects of the self, from biological urges to individual differences in life history. However, the theory is being continuously examined and reformulated by researchers working within Mead's framework.

Other issues, for example the role of emotion and irrationality in the development of the self and in social interactions, are almost completely ignored by Mead, as are the socially routine and repetitive aspects of social life. However, Mead's personal influence is evident here. He saw social interaction as a type of problem-solving, with people acting like scientists trying to work out how to behave and what meanings to attach to the behaviour of others. Thus, the rational and deliberate aspects of human social behaviour have received more attention than habits and emotions. The perspective will have to incorporate other concepts, such as those dealing with emotions and habits, if it is to generate wider theorizing in social psychology.

A further problem, arising in part out of the rather abstract and poorly-defined nature of many of the concepts, is that the theory does not seem to be easy to research. Mead described himself as a 'social behaviourist', meaning that he took as his starting point observable social behaviour. But he did not mean to look only at behaviour, and he emphasized the importance of establishing what people themselves make of their behaviour, that is, what it means to them as individuals. However, he gave very few guidelines about how his approach might be investigated and which methods would be appropriate. There has been a good deal of recent research which is nevertheless based on the symbolic interactionist position, notably Denzin's (1977) studies and his very readable accounts of children's interactions in their homes, and Corsaro's (1985) research in the nursery discussed in Section 4. Research from the symbolic interactionist perspective involves a particular, 'naturalistic' approach, which was initially advocated by Blumer, a close associate of Mead's. This involves:

the examination of particular instances of social life as they occur in their usual settings. They should be studied with some care and in some detail. The researcher should aim to see the world in the same way as those people he is studying. He should be prepared to live along with them throughout the course of their daily routines and to expose himself to those experiences which they typically encounter. He should aim for a sympathetic and sensitive understanding of their general outlook on the world.

(Cuff and Payne, 1984, p. 125)

Using such methods, the work of Denzin, Corsaro and others has gone some way to showing that symbolic interactionism is more than a purely speculative account of the self and social interaction, and the potential for further research is becoming clearer.

Further reading

BURNS, R. B. (1979) *The self concept: theory, measurement, development and behaviour*, London: Longman.
A very comprehensive, fairly complex account of many aspects of the self-concept, dealing with the theories presented in this chapter and many others. Also useful sections on methodology.

GOFFMAN, E. (1959) *The presentation of self in everyday life*, Harmondsworth: Penguin.
A classic, very readable account of the dramaturgical approach to social behaviour, drawing on examples from novels, newspapers and the author's own observations.

SLUCKIN, A. (1981) *Growing up in the playground*, London: Routledge and Kegan Paul.
The complex world of play, friendship and games in an easy-to-read account.

SMITH, P. K. (ed.) (1986) *Children's play: research developments and practical applications*, London: Gordon and Breach.
An accessible collection of articles on play.

References

BLAU, Z. (1973) *Old age in changing society*, New York: New Viewpoints.

BLUMER, H. (1969) *Symbolic interactionism: perspective and method*, Englewood Cliffs, NJ: Prentice-Hall.

BOWLBY, J. (1969) *Attachment and loss* (vols 1 and 2), New York: Basic Books.

BRAZELTON, T. B. (1976) 'Early parent–infant reciprocity', in V. C. Vaughan and T. B. Brazelton (eds) *The family: can it be saved?*, Chicago: Yearbook Medical Publishers.

BRAZELTON, T. B., KOSLOWSKI, B. and MAIN, M. (1974) 'The origin of reciprocity in the mother–infant interaction', in M. Lewis and L. Rosenblum (eds) *The effect of the infant on its caregiver*, New York: Wiley.

BRYSON, G. E. (1945) *Man and society: the Scottish inquiry of the eighteenth century*, Princeton, NJ: Princeton University Press.

COOLEY, C. H. (1902) *Human nature and the social order*, New York: Charles Scribner's Sons.

CORSARO, W. A. (1985) *Friendship and peer culture in the early years*, Norwood, NJ: Ablex Publishing.

CUFF, E. C. and PAYNE, G. C. F. (1984) *Perspectives in sociology*, 2nd edn, London: Unwin Hyman.

DAMON, W. (1983) *Social and personality development*, New York: W. W. Norton.

DARWIN, C. (1872) *The expression of the emotions in man and animals*, London: Philosophical Library.

DECASPER, A. J. and FIFER, W. P. (1980) 'Of human bonding: newborns prefer their mothers' voices', *Science*, no. 208, pp. 1174–76.

DENZIN, N. (1977) *Childhood socialization*, San Francisco: Jossey-Bass.

ERIKSON, E. (1968) *Identity: youth and crisis*, London: Faber.

FANTZ, R. L. (1961) 'The origin of form perception', *Scientific American*, vol. 204, pp. 66–72.

FESTINGER, L., BACK, K., SCHACHTER, S., KELLEY, H. and THIBAUT, D. (1950) *Theory and experiment in social communication*, Ann Arbor, Mich: Research Centre for Group Dynamics Institute for Social Research.

FESTINGER, L. (1954) 'A theory of social comparison processes', *Human Relations*, vol. 7, pp. 117–40.

FLAVELL, J. H., BOTKIN, P. T., FRY, C. L. WRIGHT, J. W. and JARVIS, P. E. (1968) *The development of role-taking and communication skills in children*, New York: Wiley.

GALLUP, G. (1977) 'Self-recognition in primates: a comparative approach to the bidirectional properties of consciousness', *American Psychologists*, vol. 32, pp. 329–38.

GARVEY, C. (1977) *Play*, Cambridge, Mass.: Harvard University Press.

GERGEN, K. (1971) *The concept of self*, New York: Holt, Reinhart and Winston.

GOFFMAN, E. (1959) *The presentation of self in everyday life*, Harmondsworth: Penguin.

GOTTMAN, J. and PARKHURST, J. (1980) 'A developmental theory of friendship and acquaintanceship processes', in W. A. Collins (ed.) *Minnesota symposia on child psychology*, vol. 13, Hillsdale NJ: Lawrence Erlbaum Associates.

HALL, D. (1972) 'A model of coping with role conflicts: the role behaviour of college educated women', *Administrative Science Quarterly*, vol. 17, pp. 471–86.

HARLOW, H. and HARLOW, M. K. (1962) 'Social deprivation in monkeys', *Scientific American*, vol. 207, pp. 136–44.

HERSHENSON, M. (1967) 'Development of the perception of form', *Psychological Bulletin*, vol. 67, pp. 326–36.

JAMES, W. (1890) *The principles of psychology*, New York: Henry Holt.

JAMES, W. (1892 (1961)) *Psychology: the briefer course* New York: Harper Torch Books.

KUHN, M. H. and McPARTLAND, T. S. (1954) 'An empirical investigation of self attitudes', *American Sociological Review*, vol. 19, pp. 68–76.

LEWIS, M. and BROOKS-GUNN, J. (1979) *Social cognition and the acquisition of self*, New York: Plenum Press.

MACCOBY, E. E. (1980) *Social development*, New York: Harcourt Brace Jovanovich.

MacLEAN, C. (1979) *The wolf children*, Harmondsworth: Penguin.

McCALL, G. J. and SIMMONS, J. L. (1966) *Identities and interactions*, New York: Free Press.

MAHLER, M. S. (1968) *On human symbiosis and the vicissitudes of individuation: infantile psychosis*, vol. 1, New York: International Universities Press.

MEAD, G. H. (1934) *Mind, self, and society*, Chicago: University of Chicago Press.

MORSE, S. and GERGEN, K. J. (1970) 'Social comparison, self-consistency and the concept of self', *Journal of Personality and Social Psychology*, vol. 16, pp. 148–56.

MOSS, H. A. (1967) 'Sex, age and state as determinants of mother–infant interaction', *Merrill–Palmer Quarterly of Behaviour and Development*, vol. 13, pp. 19–36.

MULFORD, H. and SALISBURY, W. (1964) 'Self-conceptions in a general population', *Sociological Quarterly*, vol. 5, pp. 35–46.

MUTRAN, E. and BURKE, P. J. (1979) 'Feeling "useless": a common component of young and old adults' identities', *Journal of Research on Aging*, vol. I, pp. 37–63.

OLSEN, D. R. (ed.) (1980) *The social foundation of language and thought*, New York: W. W. Norton.

PARK, R. E. (1927) 'Human nature and collective behaviour', *American Journal of Sociology*, vol. 32, pp. 733–41.

RICHARDS, M. P. M. (1971) 'Social interaction in the first weeks of human life', *Psychiat., Neurol., Neurochir.*, vol. 74, pp. 35–42.

SCHAFFER, H. R. (ed.) (1977) *Studies in mother–infant interaction*, New York: Academic Press.

SCHLENKER, B. (1980) *Impression management: the self-concept, social identity and interpersonal relations*, Monterey, CA: Brooks/Cole.

SELMAN, R. L. (1980) *The growth of interpersonal understandings*, New York: Academic Press.

SHERIFF, M. (1936) *The psychology of social norms*, New York: Harper.

SHOTTER, J. (1974) 'The development of personal powers', in M. P. M. Richards (ed.), *The integration of a child into a social world*, Cambridge: Cambridge University Press.

SMITH, A. (1759) *A theory of moral sentiments*, London.

STRYKER, S. and STATHAM, A. (1985) 'Symbolic interaction and role theory', in G. Lindzey and E. Aronson (eds.) *The handbook of social psychology*, vol. 1, 3rd edn, New York: Random House.

TURNER, R. (1962) 'Role-taking: process vs conformity?', in A. M. Rose (ed.) *Human behaviour and social processes*, Boston: Houghton Mifflin.

VIDEBECK, R. (1960) 'Self-conception and the reaction of others', *Sociometry*, vol. 23, pp. 351–9.

VYGOTSKY, L. (1933) 'Play and its role in the mental development of the child', *Soviet Psychology*, vol. 3, and in J. Bruner, A. Jolly and K. Sylva (eds) (1976) *Play: its role in development and evolution*, New York: Basic Books.

WINNICOTT, D. W. (1960) 'The theory of the parent–infant relationship', *International Journal of Psychoanalysis*, vol. 41, pp. 585–95.

WINNICOTT, D. W. (1964) *The child, the family and the outside world*, London: Pelican.

WOLFF, P. H. (1969) 'The natural history of crying and other vocalizations in early infancy', in B. M. Foss (ed.) *Determinants of infant behaviour*, vol. 4, London: Methuen.

YOUNISS, J. (1975) 'Another perspective on social cognition', in *Child Psychology*, vol. 9, Minneapolis: University of Minnesota Press.

Answers to SAQs

SAQ 1

(a) (i) approximately 38 per cent
(ii) approximately 2 per cent

(b) This implies that the children in the youngest age group (9 to 12 months) exhibited *some* self-directed behaviour when they touched themselves. Hardly any of the children touched the red mark, however. The red mark was put on their noses to test for self-recognition by eliciting from the children an explicitly self-directed piece of behaviour. Touching the mark on their noses would have indicated explicit self-recognition in Lewis and Brooks-Gunn's terms. Thus these younger children were deemed not to have a very well developed ability to recognize themselves since a low percentage of them touched this mark.

SAQ 2

	contingent movement	same physical appearance
(a) live video of themselves	✓	✓
(b) one week old video of themselves	✕	✓
(c) video of another child	✕	✕

SAQ 3

Corsaro's results support and illustrate Stage 0 of Selman's model of friendship development, where preschool children have a view of friendship as being based on mutual play. When they are not playing together, they do not class each other as friends.

chapter

3

THE DEVELOPMENT OF CHILDREN'S UNDERSTANDING

Paul Light and John Oates

Contents

1	**Introduction**	**80**
2	**The basis of Piaget's theory**	**82**
2.1	Object permanence	84
2.2	Representation	86
2.3	The sensori-motor stage	88
2.4	Processes in development	91
	Summary of Section 2	93
3	**The general theory**	**94**
3.1	The pre-operational child	96
3.2	Centration	98
3.3	Egocentrism	100
3.4	Conservation	101
	Summary of Section 3	106
4	**The development of social understanding**	**106**
	Summary of Section 4	113
5	**'Human sense': the social dimensions of understanding**	**114**
	Summary of Section 5	120
6	**Learning, teaching and development**	**121**
	Summary of Section 6	124
7	**Concluding comments**	**125**
	Further reading	126
	References	127
	Answers to SAQs	128

1 | Introduction

As you began to see in the previous chapter, the psychological development of children into adults is a complex process, involving not just the children themselves but also the social world in which they grow up. In this chapter, we are going to focus on the issue of development by looking at a central topic of developmental psychology, namely the development of mental or 'cognitive' abilities that are connected with acquiring, storing and using knowledge. Most early attempts at a scientific approach to the study of cognitive development took the form of case studies of single children, usually the children of the investigators. A landmark of this style of research is Charles Darwin's account of the development of his child William Erasmus (Doddy), from which Extract A below is taken.

EXTRACT A

During the first seven days various reflex actions, namely sneezing, hickuping, yawning, stretching, and of course sucking and screaming, were well performed by my infant. On the seventh day, I touched the naked sole of his foot with a bit of paper, and he jerked it away, curling at the same time his toes, like a much older child when tickled. The perfection of these reflex movements shows that the extreme imperfection of the voluntary ones is not due to the state of the muscles or of the coordinating centres, but to that of the seat of the will. At this time, though so early, it seemed clear to me that a warm soft hand applied to his face excited a wish to suck. This must be considered as a reflex or an instinctive action, for it is impossible to believe that experience and association with the touch of his mother's breast could so soon have come into play. During the first fortnight he often started on hearing any sudden sound, and blinked his eyes. The same fact was observed with some of my other infants within the first fortnight. Once, when he was 66 days old, I happened to sneeze, and he started violently, frowned, looked frightened, and cried rather badly: for an hour afterwards he was in a state which would be called nervous in an older person, for every slight noise made him start. A few days before this same date, he first started at an object suddenly seen; but for a long time afterwards sounds made him start and wink his eyes much more frequently than did sight; thus when 114 days old, I shook a paste-board box with comfits in it near his face and he started, whilst the same box when empty or any other object shaken as near or much nearer to his face produced no effect. We may infer from these several facts that the winking of the eyes, which manifestly serves to protect them, had not been acquired through experience. Although so sensitive to sound in a general way, he was not able even when 124 days old easily to recognise whence a sound proceeded, so as to direct his eyes to the source. . . .

. . . When four and a half months old, he repeatedly smiled at my image and his own in a mirror, and no doubt mistook them for real objects; but he showed sense in being evidently surprised at my voice coming from behind him. Like all infants he much enjoyed thus looking at himself, and in less than two months perfectly understood that it was an image; for if I made quite silently any odd grimace, he would suddenly turn round to look at me. He was, however, puzzled at the age of seven months, when being out of doors he saw me on the inside of a large plate-glass window, and seemed in doubt whether or not it was an image. . . .

When five months old, associated ideas arising independently of any instruction became fixed in his mind; thus as soon as his hat and cloak were put on, he was very cross if he was not immediately taken out of doors. When exactly seven months old, he made the great step of associating his nurse with her name, so that if I called it out he would look around for her. Another infant used to amuse himself by shaking his head laterally: we praised and imitated him, saying "Shake your head"; and when he was seven months old, he would sometimes do so on being told without any other guide. During the next four months the former infant associated many things and actions with words; thus when asked for a kiss he would protrude his lips and keep still,—would shake his head and say in a scolding voice "Ah" to the coal-box or a little spilt water, &c., which he had been taught to consider as dirty. I may add that when a few days under nine months old he associated his own name with his image in the looking-glass, and when called by name would turn towards the glass even when at some distance from it. When a few days over nine months, he learnt spontaneously that a hand or other object causing a shadow to fall on the wall in front of him was to be looked for behind. Whilst under a year old, it was sufficient to repeat two or three times at intervals any short sentence to fix firmly in his mind some associated idea. . . . The facility with which associated ideas due to instruction and others spontaneously arising were acquired, seemed to me by far the most strongly marked of all the distinctions between the mind of an infant and that of the cleverest full-grown dog that I have ever known. What a contrast does the mind of an infant present to that of the pike, described by Professor Möbius, who during three whole months dashed and stunned himself against a glass partition which separated him from some minnows; and when, after at last learning that he could not attack them with impunity, he was placed in the aquarium with these same minnows, then in a persistent and senseless manner he would not attack them!

(Darwin, 1877)

Darwin's efforts to treat his child's development as a scientific subject were not guided by any particular psychological theory, because none existed at the time and, as a result, his observations are rather piecemeal and unrelated. However, he was trying to tease out the influence of experience, learning, and instinctive behaviour, and to discern a developmental pattern. Most of the things he did with Doddy to test out his ideas would not be out of place in a piece of current research, for he realized that there are several intriguing areas where young children appear to think very differently from adults; for example, where Doddy is described as being unsure about the reality of objects seen in a mirror. Questions like this, as you will remember from the previous chapter, are still active topics of research.

Early accounts of development, like those of Darwin, were pioneering attempts to work out a scientific approach to studying a new subject, but it took many years of such studies before consistent methods of research began to emerge. Equally important were the clarification and definition of the issues and questions that might be asked about development. We must stress that, compared with many other natural sciences, and, indeed, with some other areas of psychology, developmental psychology is still to a large extent 'feeling its way'. It is a young science and still very much in a state of flux. In this chapter we shall be tracing just one of the historical threads of the subject, albeit a central one, by looking at how the development of mental abilities has been studied.

Studies of learning, and the development of knowledge were, for a long time, dominated by a belief that simple associations, like Doddy learning that putting on a hat and cloak was associated with going out, could account for mental development. Darwin saw a link here between humans and other living things: he seemed to believe that the main difference lies only in the speed of learning between different species. But few psychologists today would accept that the development of mind can be explained in such simple terms.

In this chapter, we start by introducing the developmental theory of Jean Piaget, which is generally acknowledged to have revolutionized the study of child development by offering a new, radically different perspective. We devote Sections 2 and 3 to an overview of some of the main features of Piaget's theory. For the most part, we will stick closely to Piaget's account, although we will make some general comments along the way. In the rest of the chapter we show how other researchers have taken up and tested some of Piaget's key ideas and, in so doing, have questioned some of the central assumptions of his theory.

However, although this will lead us to a reassessment of Piagetian theory, we will stress here that the theory has stimulated a vast number of research studies, only a few of which we can sample in this chapter. That so much research has been based on the sort of problems that Piaget first identified is really one of the best measures of the importance of his work to developmental psychology.

2 | The basis of Piaget's theory

For developmental psychology to achieve the status of a scientific discipline, there has to be broad agreement among researchers about its basic methods and observations, and about the nature of the central questions it is to address. Only then can knowledge be reliably accumulated. It is only quite recently that these requirements have begun to be met, and this is in large part due to the seminal work of the Swiss psychologist Jean Piaget (1896–1980).

Up to Piaget's time, the only 'grand theory' of the mental development of children was one derived from Darwin's evolutionary theory, and this is often summed up in the phrase 'ontogeny recapitulates phylogeny'. Put in simple terms, this means that the development of the individual (ontogeny) replays the development of the species (phylogeny). According to this view, put forward particularly by an American psychologist, G. Stanley Hall (Hall, 1907), the younger the child, the more primitive, in an evolutionary sense, are his or her mental abilities. So as the child grows older, his or her thinking will, at an early stage, be like that of a human ape-like ancestor, developing then into a stage like that of, say, a Neanderthal hominid, and only in later childhood will it resemble that of homo sapiens. Although now discredited, this view did at least suggest that children's mental abilities change in a systematic way with age. Hall's theory, being derived from Darwin's theory of evolution, was really an attempt to impose some sort of order, or structure, on something that had not really been studied as yet for its own sake. In other words, his theory did not start from the systematic observation of children as they developed. Piaget's theory, however, is based firmly on the observation of children's behaviour. He found that there are many problem-solving tasks in which children behave quite differently from adults and he believed that the way children's mental abilities develop towards those of adults could be described as passing through a regular series of stages.

Piaget's prolific writings had an extremely wide impact; they led many researchers into new territory and 'Piagetian' research became almost a discipline in itself. And it was not only psychologists who were influenced, for educationalists, particularly those concerned with younger children, were quick to use his ideas in developing new principles for curricula and teaching methods. 'Discovery learning', 'learning by doing' and 'learning through play', to instance some widely known examples, were developed and promulgated in the 1950s and 1960s with explicit reference to Piaget's work. It is still true to say that he is the single most important figure in developmental psychology today. But his findings, and his interpretations of them, are not accepted without question. Indeed, in recent years there have been quite fundamental reappraisals of some of the central tenets of Piaget's theory and the model of the developing child that it proposes.

Piaget started his career as a biologist, interested particularly in the processes by which organisms adapt to their environment during development. His interest in the development of children began in 1920 when he was invited to work in Alfred Binet's laboratory in Paris, helping to translate into French items originally developed by Cyril Burt in England for the very first 'intelligence test'. This test was destined to be used in French schools and later to form the basis of one of the most widely used intelligence tests, the Stanford–Binet. However, whereas an intelligence test focuses on items children get right, Piaget soon became interested in the underlying reasons for children sometimes giving *wrong* answers to the questions asked. These 'errors' seemed to him to be systematic rather than random, pointing towards some underlying consistencies in the children's developing mental abilities.

Piaget defined his task as the building up of a description and explanation of how intelligence develops in the individual child as a form of adaptation to the environment; a metamorphosis of his original biological interest into a novel psychological one. He coined the term **genetic epistemology** to sum this up. Epistemology is the study of knowledge, and was generally considered at the time to be primarily a philosophical pursuit. But Piaget's association of this with the word 'genetic' shifted his interest firmly into the field of developmental psychology, because by 'genetic' he meant growth and development rather than simply the action of genes. Although this focus on the growth of knowledge seems at first sight to restrict his interest to the intellectual domain, known as **cognition**, the implications of his ideas extended beyond cognitive development into many other areas, as we shall see later in this chapter.

2.1 Object permanence

Like Darwin, Piaget based many of his ideas on observations of his own children, Jacqueline, Lucienne and Laurent. It was such observations which led him to one of his central hypotheses about how infants' thought differs from that of older children and adults, a hypothesis that was quite startling in its implications for what the world is like for babies. Let us first look at one of these observations, of the infant Jacqueline's behaviour, as Piaget himself recorded it, reproduced here as Extract B.

EXTRACT B

Jacqueline tries to grasp a celluloid duck on top of her quilt. She almost catches it, shakes herself, and the duck slides down beside her. It falls very close to her hand but behind a fold in the sheet. Jacqueline's eyes have followed the movement, she has even followed it with her outstretched hand. But as soon as the duck has disappeared—nothing more! It does not occur to her to search behind the fold of the sheet, which would be very easy to do (she twists it mechanically without searching at all). But, curiously, she again begins to stir about as she did when trying to get the duck and again glances at the top of the quilt.

I then take the duck from its hiding-place and place it near her hand three times. All three times she tries to grasp it, but when she is about to touch it, I replace it very obviously under the sheet and she shakes it for a brief moment but it does not occur to her to raise the cloth.

Then I recommence the initial experiment. The duck is on the quilt. In trying to get it she again causes it to slide behind the fold in the sheet; after having looking at this fold for a moment (it is near her hand) she turns over and sucks her thumb.

I then offer her her doll which is crying. Jacqueline laughs, I hide it behind the fold in the sheet; she whimpers. I make the doll cry; no search. I offer it to her again and put a handkerchief around it; no reaction. I make the doll cry in the handkerchief; nothing.

(Piaget, 1955, pp. 36–7)

SAQ 1   (*SAQ answers are given at the end of the chapter*) Read through Extract B again. What do you think Piaget might have concluded from Jacqueline's apparent lack of interest in objects once they are out of sight? Have you seen anything similar in babies you know or have known?

BOX A   The Piagetian method

Piaget is often credited with having developed a new method for studying children's mental abilities, a method that is sometimes called 'clinical observation'. In contrast to, say, an intelligence test item which has a standard content and is given as far as possible in the same way to each subject, Piaget's approach was to follow up lines of interest with each child, exploring the reasons for the child's behaviour.

It is perhaps worth noting that the French language does not clearly differentiate between the concepts of 'experiment' and 'experience': what Piaget tends to call experiments are rather more loosely structured than that which we would recognize as an experiment, with its emphasis on standardization and control.

You can ask yourself how far Piaget's method, of which Extract B is a good example, is open to biasing the results. In that extract, for example, to what extent was the child's behaviour 'interpreted' by Piaget, as father and researcher? Is this really any different from Darwin's interpretations of Doddy's behaviour in Extract A? Keep this in mind particularly when you come to do a Piagetian task with a child yourself in Activity 1 in Section 3. These are points we shall return to later in this chapter.

From many observations, Piaget came to the belief that very young children are totally lacking in the concept of **object permanence**. As adults, we have a strong and pretty well unshakeable conviction that objects in the world have a continuing existence when they are not actually in our sight: we believe in a world 'out there' that is durable and stable. When we put something down we normally expect to find it again when we go back to the same place. And it is hard for us to imagine quite how the world would seem if we did not have this belief, because we cannot easily remember a time when we did not. But Piaget proposed that all of us go through a stage, very early in our lives, when we are completely without this belief. According to Piaget, the world is totally *impermanent* for the young infant, and exists only when actually being perceived in some way. If this is indeed true, then the baby is in a very real sense the 'centre of its world', and the disappearance and reappearance of objects is either 'magical' (if brought about by some agency other than the infant) or a direct result of the infant's actions.

This idea of 'centring'—that is, the sense of the baby feeling itself to be the centre and the moving force of its world—runs through much of Piaget's theory, particularly the ideas of **centration** and **egocentrism**. Centration basically refers to a tendency only to be able to deal mentally with a single aspect of a situation: in other words, to 'centre' on that aspect. In the case of very young children, this is a way of describing the apparently complete dominance of their own perceptions; for example, when an object disappears from their sight and they behave as if the object has ceased to exist altogether, they are 'centring' on their own perception. This particular sort of centring, where one's own viewpoint is dominant, was called 'egocentrism' by Piaget. By egocentrism, he meant centred on one's own perceptions or *actions* by a complete absence of conscious awareness of the separate existence of those of others, a quite different meaning from the everyday one of being selfish, which implies a conscious choice not to care about other people's feelings or needs. But, if at first the baby sees the world only as 'fleeting tableaux', how is the concept of an enduring, permanent world formed? According to Piaget, it is through the baby's own *actions*. Through the experiences of repeating actions and their effects, the baby comes to understand that actions have *consequences*. For example, in the earliest stages looking away from an object causes it to 'disappear' and looking back to the same location causes it to reappear. What is crucial to Piaget's view of what is happening in this rather commonplace occurrence is that the baby is storing something in the mind about both the act (looking away and back) and its effects (disappearance and reappearance). To introduce another of Piaget's terms, the baby is constructing a **representation**, a sort of model of the world, at this very early stage in terms of actions. We should note here that Piaget is implying that these representations, like the egocentric modes of thought referred to above, although mental, are also 'unconscious', in the sense that the baby is unaware of them.

As the baby becomes able to grasp objects, the potential for this sort of learning is greatly increased: things can be moved in and out of vision, and they can also be shaken. These are activities that the baby repeats again and again, taking obvious pleasure in the effects of such actions, and, according to Piaget, continuing to construct mental representations. Indeed, repetitive behaviour, doing things like dropping objects, putting one thing in another and so on, are a characteristic of early development. These repetitions all give the child a lot of information about the properties of objects in the world. It is also as if the child has some sort of motivation to repeat, over and over, things that he or she can do.

2.2 Representation

Before going into Piaget's ideas in any depth, it is worth briefly considering the concept we introduced at the end of Section 2.1, that of *representation*, which has to be dealt with by any theory of cognition, because 'knowing' is all about making internal what is external. Let us take an example of a cognitive act, the recognition of an object never seen before as a member of a known class, as when a child sees a particular dog that he or she has never seen before and correctly identifies it as a dog, rather than as some other animal such as a cat or a horse.

For this type of recognition to be possible, there has to be some sort of mental comparison between the novel object and something in memory of previous similiar experienced objects. Now, since this is not a comparison just of two objects in the world, which are both in view at the same time, there must be, in the child's mind, some sort of idea of what it is that makes an animal a dog and not some other sort of animal. And this idea is the 'representation'.

In fact, the way such ideas are represented in the mind and the way that representation develops are still lively research topics, but for the moment we will go on to an aspect of representation that Piaget considered to be important in development. This is the emergence of what he called **symbolic function**. The best example of what is meant by this can be seen in young children's play with objects, as we saw in the previous chapter. If a child, in play, uses something like a cardboard box to represent, say, a doll's cot, then this shows the sort of representation that Piaget called *symbolic*. The cardboard box is a *symbol* of a doll's cot, serving a function in play as a cot. The importance for Piaget of symbolic function, of one thing standing for another, lay primarily in the internalization, or mental representation, of such symbols.

Piaget himself did not give a great deal of attention to the emergence of language, but in language we see a prime example of symbolic representation. Words not only stand as symbols for objects, actions, feelings and so on, but can be put together in sentences in different ways to express or request almost anything. Piaget's main interest was in the representation of *actions*. It is not just the *existence* of objects that can be represented mentally, but also the child's *actions* on objects. The use of a previously carried-out action in a new situation shows that the action must have been mentally stored: that is, represented in some way.

BOX B   Definitions of key concepts in Piaget's theory

Object permanence
Piaget believed that very young babies are unable to realize that objects in the world have their own permanent, ongoing existence, and that for them objects are *impermanent*, existing only when being perceived in some way, in other words are 'out of sight, out of mind'.

Centration and egocentrism
According to Piaget, cognitive development is a progressive move away from thought that is *centred* on the child's own body. At first, everything is seen from the child's point of view and only from that, producing a profound *egocentrism*.

Representation
Cognitive development is concerned with *internalizing* knowledge about the world and actions on it. This internalized knowledge is *represented* in the mind in some way. Language is a form of representation, as are other types of *symbolic* representation such as the use of objects in play to *stand for* other objects. It is important to realize that these mental representations are not necessarily *conscious*: indeed, it is only later in development that an individual becomes consciously aware of them.

2.3 The sensori-motor stage

Piaget called the first two years of life the **sensori-motor stage** because this is the period in which the child's development is predominantly concerned with mastering the interactions of information from the *senses* and from *motor* actions in relation to the physical world. The child is learning how to achieve desired consequences such as getting an interesting object to the mouth to explore it further with the lips. In Piaget's words, the baby is learning how to use a means to achieve a desired end—that is, mastering 'means–ends relations'. But, according to Piaget, learning at this stage is entirely concerned with solving physical problems, and is not yet to do with more abstract mental problems. The sensori-motor stage is seen as establishing the foundations for all later developments, by the child's formation of representations of these motor sequences in a systematic, structured way. We are going to focus on this stage first, to look in detail at the *processes* that Piaget believed were involved in development, both during this stage and later.

Before we do so, however, it is worth noting that some children develop more slowly or faster than others, and even the development of an individual child may not always be maintained at a constant rate. Illness can slow down development and, when they have recovered, children often show a spurt of 'catch-up' growth, both mentally and physically. By way of analogy, it is as if an individual's development has a predetermined 'track', though this may not necessarily always be followed exactly.

Given, then, that a child's chronological age cannot be an exact measure of developmental age, it is clearly wrong to expect exactly the same developmental achievements to occur at the same age. So the ages given by Piaget for each stage or sub-stage are no more than indicative; individual children may pass through each or all stages earlier or later.

As shown in Table 3.1, the path towards these developmental achievements was seen by Piaget as marked by six sub-stages as follows:

1 Reflexes

During this period of about 6 weeks, the baby's activity is dominated by innate reflexive behaviours such as sucking, turning towards sounds and grasping objects placed in the palm of the hand. These **reflexes** are all behaviour patterns present in an organized form at birth, and this stage is primarily concerned with exercising and perfecting these.

2 Primary circular reactions

For the next 10 weeks or so, the baby begins to adapt the reflexes of the first sub-stage to the environment. Reflexes are no longer simply triggered as invariant patterns but show some adaptation to features of the world. **Circular reactions**, the repetition of simple behaviour patterns like waving the hands in front of the face, begin to appear as the child starts to explore the relation between actions and their effects. These are described as 'primary' since they are the first to appear, and as yet only involve the child's own body.

3 Secondary circular reactions

The child now begins to involve objects in circular reactions, and will repeat actions on these objects for their consequences. For example, a rattle will be shaken over and over again as the child explores the link between the shaking and the sound produced. As yet there is no sign of the child pursuing any mental goal, just repeating fortuitous events. This sub-stage lasts about 4 months, up to the age of 8 months.

4 Co-ordination of means–end relations

During this sub-stage, up to about the end of the first year, the child now develops the ability to act intentionally, to set out to achieve results by applying previously exercised behaviour patterns in particular circumstances. The child will now, for example, pick up a rattle in the cot in order to shake it, whereas in the previous stage the rattle would only be shaken if already in the hand. For Piaget, this period marked the beginnings of 'mental' intelligence, the first signs of abstract thought, freed from the here-and-now.

5 Tertiary circular reactions

Whereas in the sub-stage of secondary circular reactions (sub-stage 3) the child repeated actions for their effects, without any variation, actions are now varied, in order to explore the properties of objects. The child begins to experiment, and also to involve other people. The beginnings of using objects as tools also start now. This sub-stage takes up a further 6 months.

6 Invention of new means: mental combinations

Piaget describes this final sub-stage, up to the age of 2 years, as the one in which the child makes a fundamental progression, by beginning to move away from a total involvement with the here-and-now into the realm of

Table 3.1 The sensori-motor stage: the six sub-stages

Age	Sub-stage	Typical behaviours
0–6 weeks	1 Reflexes	Practice of innate reflexes such as sucking, grasping, looking
6–16 weeks	2 Primary circular reactions	Repetition of body movements for their consequences: e.g. putting hand to mouth and sucking it
4–8 months	3 Secondary circular reactions	Repetition of actions that have effects on the environment: e.g. kicking to shake cot and produce a sound
8–12 months	4 Co-ordination of means– ends relations	Child begins to combine actions to achieve results: e.g. pulling a cover away to get a rattle which is then shaken
12–18 months	5 Tertiary circular reactions	Experimentation begins as the child explores new ways of acting on the environment. Adults are drawn into activities
18–24 months	6 Mental combinations	Representation becomes apparent through emergence of language and symbolic play. Child becomes able to plan behaviour in simple ways

symbolic representation. The child is able to combine previously separate bits of behaviour to achieve goals, and to do so mentally. Symbolic play begins, as does the use of language and the ability to imitate the behaviour of others.

This brief summary of the successive achievements of the child as charted by Piaget gives an impression of the way he saw development as proceeding step by step, with each step building on what has gone before. Because of this, the stages and sub-stages of his theory have a necessarily invariant sequence. Although the precise timings for each sub-stage might vary, they have to be gone through in the same order by every child.

Extract C below, from Piaget's writing, gives his own brief overview of the central features of the sensori-motor stage. We will be discussing some of the terms he uses in Section 2.4.

EXTRACT C Sensori-motor stage

Before language develops, there is behavior that we can call intelligent. For example, when a baby of 12 months or more wants an object which is too far from him, but which rests on a carpet or blanket, and he pulls it to get to the object, this behaviour is an act of intelligence. The child uses an intermediary, a means to get to his goal. Also, getting to an object by means of pulling a string when the object is tied to the string, or when the child uses a stick to get the object, are acts of intelligence. They demonstrate in the sensori-motor period a certain number of stages, which go from simple reflexes, from the formation of the first habits, up to the coordination of means and goals.

Remarkable in this sensori-motor stage of intelligence is that there are already structures. Sensori-motor intelligence rests mainly on actions, on movements and perceptions without language, but these actions are coordinated in a relatively stable way. They are coordinated under what we may call schemata of action. These schemata can be generalized in actions and are applicable to new situations. For example, pulling a carpet to bring an object within reach constitutes a schema which can be generalized to other situations when another objects [sic] rests on a support. In other words, a schema supposes an incorporation of new situations into the previous schemata, a sort of continuous assimilation of new objects or new situations to the actions already schematized. For example, I presented to one of my children an object completely new to him – a box of cigarettes, which is not a usual toy for a baby. The child took the object, looked at it, put it in his mouth, shook it, then took it with one hand and hit it with the other hand, then rubbed it on the edge of the crib, then shook it again, and gave the impression of trying to see if there were noise. This behaviour is a way of exploring the object, of trying to understand it by assimilating it to schemata already known. The child behaves in this situation as he will later in Binet's famous vocabulary test, when he defines by usage, saying, for instance, that a spoon is for eating, and so on.

But in the presence of a new object, even without knowing how to talk, the child knows how to assimilate, to incorporate this new object into each of his already developed schemata which function as practical concepts. Here is a structuring of intelligence. Most important in this structuring is the base, the point of departure of all subsequent operational constructions. At the sensori-motor level, the child constructs the schema of the permanent object.

The knowledge of the permanent object starts at this point. The child is not convinced at the beginning that when an object disappears from view, he can find it again. One can verify by tests that object permanence is not yet developed at this stage. But there is there the beginning of a subsequent fundamental idea which starts being constructed at the sensori-motor level. This is also true of the construction of the ideas of space, of time, of causality. What is being done at the sensori-motor level concerning all the foregoing ideas will constitute the substructure of the subsequent, fully achieved ideas of permanent objects, of space, of time, of causality.

(Piaget, 1962)

2.4 Processes in development

So far, we have concentrated on describing the progression of development in the first two years as Piaget saw it and have said little about *how* he thought the changes came about. Before making this step we need to introduce another central concept of Piaget's. We have used the terms 'action' and 'behaviour pattern' to refer to simple pieces of behaviour such as shaking a rattle. As we saw in his description of the sensori-motor stage in Extract C, Piaget called these elements **schemata** (an alternative plural is **schemas**: this has the same meaning). He believed that the simple fact of possessing a schema created a motivation for its exercise, for its application to objects and situations, over and above the simple physical needs to apply them for ends such as feeding. We saw this in the very first sub-stage of the sensori-motor stage, where Piaget referred to the repetition of reflexes. Nowadays, psychologists generally prefer to use the term 'reflexes' for behaviours that are stereotyped (i.e. do not vary significantly) and are set off by specific inputs—for example, the infant closing the hand when the palm is pressed or turning the head towards a stroke on the side of the mouth. But the 'reflexes' that Piaget talked about were *pieces of behaviour*, or '*schemata*', that are able to change and adapt, after a period in which they are exercised over and over in a relatively fixed form.

At first, a schema such as sucking on an object placed in the baby's mouth does have a reflex or stereotyped quality about it, since it does not seem to be adapted at all to the properties of the object; the same action schema of sucking is evoked by a finger, a nipple or the corner of a cloth. Piaget described this sort of exercise of a schema as an **assimilation**, when the schema 'assimilates' different objects *without adaptation*. We see this sort of behaviour in the child at first applying sucking in a more or less indiscriminate way to any object that can be brought to the mouth, as a means of exploring that object. In this example, immediately recognizable to anyone who has watched young babies, we can also see the motivational element that

Piaget believed was an important process in development. It is as if sucking has a need to be exercised, at first just for itself, then on the baby's hands (a primary circular reaction) and later as a means to an end, the exploration of objects (a secondary circular reaction). Piaget saw this **intrinsic motivation** (as he called it) as a primary moving force in development, keeping the child actively applying schemas to new situations as they arise.

But gradually, the action schema of sucking becomes more adaptable, more responsive to differences in objects. This introduces the third central process in Piagetian theory of development, that of **accommodation**. This happens when schemas are *adapted* or modified to match the special characteristics of objects and situations. For example, the schema of reaching for and grasping objects is, initially, predominantly assimilative: it consists of a fairly crude 'swipe and grab' in the general direction of an attractive object. As the baby grows the schema becomes more refined and is adapted to the object's position and size: it begins to accommodate to the object. For example, a child with a new toy will try to play with it in a way that has never been tried

---

BOX C   Definitions of central processes in Piaget's theory

Schemas

A schema is an organized sequence of behaviour. Simple examples include sucking and grasping. More complex examples include opening a container to extract the contents, and putting on a pair of socks.

Assimilation

Piaget often talked of the 'aliment' (food) of the developing mind. Just as we eat food, break it down and make use of it, so we also take in information and fit it to knowledge we have already. This taking in, or 'assimilation', of experience does not imply any necessary change or development, but rather a fitting of what is 'out there' into existing mental representations. In other words, schemas can be applied in new situations without the need for adaptation: a baby may suck a novel object in exactly the same way as a familiar object, or a toddler may put on some new slipper-socks in the same way as ordinary socks, or a child may react to a new toy by trying out actions already practised with other toys. Piaget called this 'assimilative': the schema *assimilating* new objects into itself.

Intrinsic motivation

Piaget believed that the very existence of a schema in a child's repertoire of action *itself* created a motivation for its use: a motivation *intrinsic* in the schema.

Accommodation

This is in a sense the opposite of assimilation and occurs when mental structures actually change and grow. If a child reacts to the new toy by looking carefully at it and then trying a way of playing with it that has never been tried before, this is accommodative behaviour. Thus, schemas have to adapt to match the special characteristics of objects and situations. An example is when the child has to include rotating a lid (in order to open a container) in a schema that originally consisted of grasping and pulling at a lid. Accommodation implies two things: that children mentally create new forms of behaviour, and that these forms of behaviour match the characteristics of their objects—what Piaget called an 'adaptation'.

before. Whereas assimilative behaviour primarily serves the end of exercising schemas, accommodation reflects not only the growing adaptability of the schema, but also greater mental activity in the perception of the specifics of the situation to which the schema is adapted.

Piaget saw all behaviour as having assimilative and accommodative elements: assimilative to the extent that the application of a schema requires that it should already be present in the individual's repertoire, and accommodative to the extent that the schema adapts to the situation. The three processes—of intrinsic motivation, assimilation and accommodation—were three central elements in Piaget's explanation of how development progresses. We can see how this might account for the gradual, step-by-step development of behaviour by the gradual modification of schemas, each accommodation introducing new flexibility and adaptive possibilities for the next application.

This development can only occur, though, if the child is able mentally to store the results of these accommodations in some way, and Piaget saw this as happening through the process of *representation*. Throughout most of the sensori-motor stage, these representations were seen as having to do only with the child's own actions in the here-and now, but as we saw in Piaget's final sub-stage, this period ends with the child beginning to be able to act on these representations, to recombine then mentally.

Summary of Section 2

- Jean Piaget, a Swiss psychologist, was the first person to propose an overall theory of cognitive development, based on the way children of different ages behave.

- Piaget's theory is based on the idea that the mind of a young baby works in very different ways from the minds of adults, and that thinking passes through a series of distinct and consecutive stages *en route* to its adult form.

- Piaget believed that babies begin by having no understanding of the permanence of objects in the world.

- Piaget's theory states that a central aspect of development is a progressive move away from egocentric thought, where all perception of the world and its dynamics is initially *centred* on the child.

- Central to Piaget's theory is the development of mental *representations* of behaviour, and of the world and its objects.

- The first stage of development, according to Piaget, is one of *sensori-motor* development, in which babies are concerned with mastering the links between their behaviour and its effects in the world.

- Piaget saw the development of thought throughout childhood being brought about by the action of the three interlinked processes of *assimilation*, *intrinsic motivation* and *accommodation*.

3 | The general theory

We have introduced Piaget's developmental processes in the context of the first of his stages, the sensori-motor stage, to see the way they explain how behaviour can become more adaptive, in a step-by-step way. First, the ability develops to combine different schemas in order to achieve new ends. Second, the child represents schemas as if they were 'internal objects'. In other words, they become *representations* of actions. Piaget used a special term for schemas that achieve this status, he called them 'operations'. Finally, at the very end of the sensori-motor stage, the 2-year-old child becomes capable of combining representations into whole sets of actions to represent a whole system of possible behaviour rather than *individual actions*. He saw one of the goals of development in the first 2 years of life as being the achievement of a set of operations that are represented in this way, as a **structure**; that is, not just a random collection of unconnected actions, but as a co-ordinated set of possibilities for manipulating the world. And, reflecting this goal as one of 'acting on the world', he called it the achievement of **concrete operations**.

The development of this co-ordinated structure of operations was seen by Piaget as dominating the second of his four main stages of development, a stage to which he gave the name **pre-operational** because during this stage operations and their co-ordinations are still being developed. Let us first look at the whole structure of his theory's stages, before returning to the pre-operational stage in more detail.

Stage 1: Sensori-motor (from birth to about 2 years)

During this stage, the child's development is focused on the elaboration of action schemas, and the building up of a system of these schemas that is adaptable, primarily to objects in the environment. The stage concludes with the emergence of symbolic function: the ability to represent these schemas which begins to free the child from a total involvement in action.

Stage 2: Pre-operational (approximately from the age of 2 up to 6 years)

Being able to symbolize, to form mental representations, allows the child to move towards the development of a set of 'operations' that represent possibilities for acting on the world. During the pre-operational stage these are unco-ordinated, just as the early schemas of the sensori-motor stage were. The central task of the pre-operational stage is the building up of these operations. In this stage, the operations that are represented still remain tied to the level of action in the world.

Stage 3: Concrete operations (from about 6 to 12 years)

Throughout this stage the child is consolidating and co-ordinating the system of operations that emerged at the end of the previous stage, mastering the ability to act intelligently on the environment by planned behaviour, and reflecting on this application. At the end of this stage, when the system of mental operations is sufficiently developed and co-ordinated, it becomes possible to represent the operations themselves, much as schemas were represented earlier. This then frees the child from the concrete tie to action in the world and opens up the possibility of 'operating on operations', which marks the transition to stage 4.

Stage 4: Formal operations (from the age of 12 years onwards)

The ability to represent operations and to manipulate them independently of their concrete referents in the world allows the child to deal with abstract, hypothetical situations; pure logic becomes a possible tool of thought. The child begins to be able to think in a rational, scientific way, and to approach problems in a systematic, thought-out manner. The main achievement of this stage is the consolidation and co-ordination of the system of **formal operations**; that is, a purely abstract set of operations for manipulating the concrete operations of the previous stage.

Each stage is, according to Piaget, marked by characteristic modes of thought. The general progression through the stages is such that thought, and consequent action, become progressively less 'centred'. Through increasing abstraction of representation, 'mental operations' become less tied to concrete realities and egocentric perceptions.

BOX D   What is a stage of development?

Using the word 'stage' to describe a period of development may be just a recognition that children are capable of doing different things at different ages. This idea of stage allows one to describe these changes in terms of particular behaviours, ways of solving problems and so on, that appear to dominate in particular age ranges.

A rather stronger statement might be implied, however, such that there is some sort of abrupt change or discontinuity in development that establishes a boundary between one stage and the next. Indeed, if there is no such boundary implied, then it is rather dubious whether we would be justified in calling a particular period a 'stage' at all.

But using the word 'stage' also often carries with it a notion of sequence, that one stage must follow another stage in a set order. And this notion of sequence may also have 'strong' and 'weak' versions. The 'weak' version may simply assert that there is a

fixed sequence, whereas a 'strong' version may assert a causal relationship in which the completion of stage A is a necessary condition for the transition to stage B.

So you can see that the term 'stage' can have many different meanings. Often these are not explicit, and need teasing out.

Piaget's stages form a necessary sequence. No child is conceived of as missing out any of the stages, nor of passing through them out of sequence.

This has formed the basis of some criticism of his theory in that the stages may in a sense be self-defining as necessarily sequential, related more to the structure of knowledge in the domain concerned than to anything about the child. If the sorts of problems he set children were selected on the basis of such sequential knowledge structures, this may reinforce a strictly sequential theory of stages.

SAQ 2   In the light of what you have just read, what differences do you think there
are between the following two 'stage' statements?

(a) She is going through a babbling stage.

(b) She is going through a negative stage.

Do they imply different meanings of the word stage? What would be 'strong'
and 'weak' versions of these statements?

3.1 The pre-operational child

Piaget attached a great importance to the transition that is made at the end of
the sensori-motor stage, when the child begins on the road towards concrete
operations. During the pre-operational stage, although the child shows the
beginnings of reasoning at least in concrete situations, the various mental
operations that are being built up are not co-ordinated. Piaget used this
explanation to account for many intriguing phenomena, in the way children
appear to think, that characterize this stage. For, although children with the
new-found gift of language are able to carry out conversations with adults, to
engage with concrete problems and to offer explanations, in many situations
there still seems to be a very precarious grasp (or a bizarre lack of grasp) of the
properties of the physical world. It is this period that has been the focus of
most studies by other psychologists trying to confirm or revise Piaget's
theories of what the child is and is not capable of.

Piaget believed that it is only when the set of concrete operations has been
constructed that the child is fully able to distinguish between his or her own
egocentric viewpoint and the outside world. He offered in support many
observations of younger children's apparent **animism**—that is, their projection
of human feelings, behaviour and motives on to inanimate objects in the
world. The following collection of his observations is a good example (the
numbers in parentheses refer to ages in years and months):

Cli (3; 9) speaking to a motor in a garage: *'The motor's gone to bye-byes. It doesn't go
out because of the rain.'* . . .

Bad (3): *'The bells have woken up, haven't they?'*

Nel (2; 9) seeing a hollow chestnut tree: *'Didn't it cry when the hole was made?* To a
stone: *'Don't touch my garden! . . . My garden would cry.'* Nel, after throwing a stone
on to a sloping bank, watching the stone rolling down said: *'Look at the stone. It's
afraid of the grass.'*

Nel scratched herself against a wall. Looking at her hand: *'Who made that mark? . . . It
hurts where the wall hit me.'*

Dar (1; 8 to 2; 5) bringing his toy motor to the window: *'Motor see the snow.'* One
evening a picture (of some people he knew) fell to the ground. Dar stood up in bed,
crying and calling out: *'The mummies (the ladies) all on the ground, hurt!'* Dar was
watching the grey clouds. He was told that it was going to rain: *'Oh, look at the wind!
– Naughty wind, smack wind.*

Do you think that would hurt the wind?
Yes.' A few days later: 'Bad wind – No, not naughty – rain naughty. Wind good.
Why is the rain naughty?
Because Mummy pushes the pram and the pram all wet.' Dar couldn't go to sleep, so
the light was left on at his demand: 'Nice light.' . . . On a morning in winter when the
sun shone into the room: 'Oh, good! the sun's come to make the radiator warm.'

(Piaget, 1973, p. 241)

These examples, and anyone who regularly spends time with children aged
between two and four will be able to supply their own, suggest that the child
sees no irrationality in attributing intentions, feelings and consciousness to
inanimate objects. For Piaget, this was another instance of the pervasive
effects of the child's egocentrism, because it can be seen as the child
projecting his or her own feelings on to the world. A particularly revealing set
of observations was made by him of children's answers to questions about
how and why the sun and moon move, of which the following are good
examples:

Cam (6) said of the sun: 'It comes with us to look at us.
Why does it look at us?
It looks to see if we are good.' The moon comes out at night 'because there are people
who want to work.
Why does the moon move?
It's time to go and work. Then the moon comes.
Why does it move?
Because it's going to work with the men who work.
Do you believe that?
Yes.
That it works?
It looks to see if they work properly.'
Hub (6½): 'What does the sun do when you are out for a walk?
It moves.
How?
It goes with me.
Why?
To make it light, so that you can see clearly.
How does it go with you?
Because I look at it.
What makes it move when it goes with you?
The wind.
Does the wind know where you are going?
Yes. . . .'

(Piaget, 1973, p. 245)

Although it is clear that children at this stage are both aware of the possibility
of explaining events in the world and able to offer their own explanations,
their answers certainly seem to suggest that Piaget was right in believing that
this reasoning is still very much centred on the child's own self. The lack of
any system for reflecting on their own explanations seems sometimes to lead
them to charmingly circular reasoning:

Roc (6): 'Why is it cold in winter?
Because there is snow.

What is it that makes the cold?
The snow.

If there were no snow would it be cold?
No.

Is it the snow which makes the cold or the cold which makes the snow?
The cold makes the snow.

And where does the cold come from?
From the snow.'

(Piaget, 1973, p. 364)

3.2 Centration

Pre-operational children in Piaget's theory are basically egocentric, dominated by, or 'centred' on, their own perceptions because they are still very tied to the concrete world and their actions on it. Also, because the child lacks the ability to reflect on operations, his or her understanding of the world tends to focus on states, rather than on transformations, and the possibility of 'magical' causes of events seems unproblematic. Similarly, the child is unable to comprehend points of view different from his or her own, either in relation to other people's interests, feelings and so on, or even others' perceptions. A classic example of this particular difficulty is provided by children's responses to the 'three mountains' task described in Box E.

As used by Piaget, this task involves sitting the child beside a three-dimensional model of three mountains. A doll is put at the edge of the model, with a different view to that of the child, and the child's task is to show the experimenter what the doll's view is. Piaget used various ways of doing this so that the child would not have to describe it verbally. For example, the child has to arrange three cardboard mountains (like the model ones), or choose one of a set of drawings of the mountains model, drawn from different viewpoints, to indicate what view of the mountains the doll has.

Presented exactly in the form described in Box E, the problem is usually impossible for the child of up to about 8 years old to solve correctly. A common response is for children to indicate that the view they themselves have is also the one that the doll has. Piaget saw this as reflecting the inability of children to decentre from their own position: in other words, egocentrism. His explanation was that children in the pre-operational stage have not developed the ability to recognize that there are many different viewpoints on a scene like the three mountains, their own being just one of these, and that they also fail to recognize that the viewpoint changes as the viewing position changes. Although they may agree that this is so when their own position is changed, there is not the co-ordinated system of operations that would allow the child to predict the view from another point.

BOX E   The 'three mountains' task

'The mountains were made of *papier mâché* and were placed on a one metre square base. [Figure 3.1(a) shows the overall layout of the mountains and the viewing points A, B, C and D.] As seen from position A [the view shown in Figure 3.1(b)] the largest mountain was at the back of the display; it was grey with a snow-cap. A brown mountain was to the left, displaying a red cross on its summit. In the right-foreground was a green mountain surmounted by a small house. [The layout is shown in Figure 3.1(b).] There was a zigzag path down the side of the green mountain when viewed from position C and a rivulet descending the brown mountain when viewed from B. The only information given about exact sizes is that the heights of the mountains varied from 12 to 30 cm.

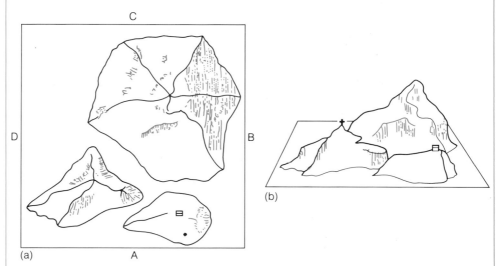

(a)   A

Figure 3.1 (a) Plan of the three mountains task; (b) view of the three mountains from position A
(Source: Cox, 1980)

The child was asked to represent the view of the mountains from his own position at A. Then a wooden doll (about two to three cm. high) was put at position C and the child was asked to represent the view that could be seen from there. This procedure was repeated for positions B and D. The child was then asked to move to position B (or C or D) and to represent the view from there; in addition he was asked to represent the view from A or other positions he had already occupied.

Piaget and Inhelder elicited three different modes of response. First, the child was asked to reproduce the doll's view by arranging three pieces of cardboard shaped like the mountains. Second, the child was asked to select the doll's view from a set of ten pictures (each measuring 20 by 28 cm.). In the third task, the child was asked to choose one picture and then decide which position the doll must occupy to have that particular view of the mountains.'

(Cox, 1980, pp. 63–4)

3.3 Egocentrism

If they are indeed unaware of the possibility of different viewpoints, and believe that their perceptions must be the same as everyone else's, then children in the pre-operational stage will be unable to alter their own viewpoint to take account of others. Piaget believed that this fundamental perceptual egocentrism created a barrier to true social interaction, and it is perhaps the main reason why he attached very little importance to any sort of social input to development. He had the firm belief that children of this age were unable to play *together*, and that children apparently playing together in groups were really just playing in parallel. His confirmation of this came partly from a series of observations of children at the Maisons des Petits de L'Institut Rousseau, where the following example of what he saw as egocentrism was recorded. Pie (presumably Pierre—Piaget abbreviates all names) was 6½ years old:

Pie (to Ez who is drawing a tram-car with carriages in tow): *But the trams that are hooked on behind don't have any flags.* (No answer.)

(Talking about his tram). *They don't have any carriages hooked on . . .* (He was addressing no one in particular. No one answers him.)

(To Béa), *'T'sa tram that hasn't got no carriages.* (No answer.)

(To Hei), *This tram hasn't got no carriages, Hei, look, it isn't red, d'you see . . .* (No answer.)

(Lev says out loud, '*A funny gentleman*' from a certain distance, and without addressing himself to Pie or to anyone else). Pie: *A funny gentleman!* (Goes on drawing his tram.)

I'm leaving the tram white.

(Ez who is drawing next to him says, 'I'm doing it yellow'), *No, you mustn't do it all yellow.*

I'm doing the stair-case, look (Béa answers, 'I can't come this afternoon. I've got a Eurhythmic class.')

What did you say? (Béa repeats the same sentence.)

What did you say? (Béa does not answer. She has forgotten what she said, and gives Ro a push.)

(To Béa). *Leave him alone.*

(Mlle B. asks Ez if he would like to come with her), *Come here Ez, it isn't finished. . . . Please teacher, Ez hasn't finished.*

(Without addressing himself to anyone,) *I'm doing some black stones. . . .*

(Id), *Pretty . . . these stones.*

(To Ez), *Better than you, eh?* (No answer. Ez had not heard the previous remark.)

(Piaget, 1959, pp. 6–7)

You may well feel that the children's behaviour in the above quotation is not *wholly* egocentric but that there are some examples of true interaction. And, of course, Piaget chose this extract specifically to support his viewpoint. The issue of whether play in children of this age range is primarily egocentric has been widely discussed as a theoretical and empirical question. For instance, in the previous chapter, children engaged in 'pretend' play are shown as reacting very much to each other, helping each other to play their roles. If you have an opportunity to do so, watch some children aged between 4 and 6 years old playing together. You will probably observe some tendency towards 'parallel but separate' play, but also some exchanges which seem much less egocentric. Certainly, though, children do appear to learn to involve themselves more in truly social play, in which they take account of their playmates' activity and speech, as they get older.

3.4 Conservation

Perhaps the best known and most widely researched of Piaget's standard tasks are those that he invented in order to study how children develop the ability to realize that there are things that do not change even when there are perceptual transformations; that is, to realize that just because something looks different from different angles does not necessarily mean the thing has itself changed. Just as in the 'three mountains' task the pre-operational child gives the impression of believing that his or her own perception of the model is the only one possible, so too in many other situations does own perception seem to be totally dominant, as if the pre-operational child has no understanding of a stable, independent 'world out there'.

The most widely researched task developed by Piaget tests what he called the ability of **conservation**. By this he meant that there is *conservation* of objects regardless of what they look like. For instance, the mountains remain the same regardless of viewpoint; similarly, a given amount of water remains the same whether it is in a tall glass or a short glass. In both cases, the reality of the object is conserved, despite a change in appearance. He proposed that pre-operational children do not appreciate that an amount of liquid stays the same regardless of the shape of the container that it is in. They would not, for instance, be able to understand that a litre of milk is still a litre of milk whether it is in a carton, a jug or a bowl. Someone who does appreciate this is said to have achieved *conservation of liquid*.

Piaget's classic conservation of liquid task was devised to give a standard way of assessing an individual's level of development in this area. It involves three basic steps:

1   First the child is shown two identical transparent beakers, A and B, each about two-thirds full of water, as shown in Figure 3.2(a). They are placed side-by-side in front of the child. The experimenter seeks the child's agreement that the quantities of water in each are the same, if necessary adding or taking away small amounts until the child is satisfied.

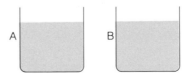

Figure 3.2(a) The initial display in the conservation of liquid task

2   As shown in Figure 3.2(b), the water from one beaker, A, is then all poured into another beaker, A2, which is either taller and narrower than the first one, or shorter and wider.

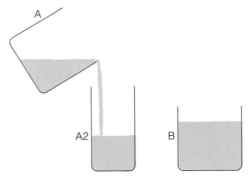

Figure 3.2(b) The transformation

3   This beaker is placed alongside beaker B as shown in Figure 3.2(c). The child is then asked whether there is now more water in the new beaker, A2, than in the other beaker, B, or less, or the same amount.

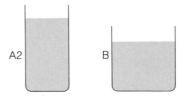

Figure 3.2(c) The transformed display

Typically, up to the age of about 6 or 7 years, the child will assert, when asked, that the amount of liquid has changed, and is now more (or less, depending on the arrangement and his or her perception of it). If the child is then asked why this is so, he or she will tend to say something like 'because it's taller', or 'because it's thinner'. The child's answers seem to indicate that his or her judgement of quantity is centred on the perceptual change brought about by the transformation.

Conservation, as Piaget defined it, is an ability that applies not only to amounts of liquid, but also to a whole range of other perceptual transformations. For example, another widely researched conservation is the conservation of mass. A child is shown two balls of a malleable material, such as plasticine or clay, and asked whether each ball has the same amount in it. Again, as for liquid, the amount is adjusted if necessary until the child is satisfied that both are equal.

In the next stage, one of the balls is rolled out into a sausage shape and placed alongside the other, untransformed, ball. Then, just as in the conservation of liquid task, the child is asked in the final stage whether there is more material in the sausage, or less, or the same amount. A 'non-conserver' will now say that the amounts are no longer the same, that the sausage now has more in it, and when asked why, is likely to say something like 'because you rolled it out'.

Piaget also studied children's behaviour in several other conservation tasks, including conservation of area, length and number.

SAQ 3   In Piaget's conservation of number task, the initial, untransformed display consists of two rows of counters—one black, one white—with an equal number of counters in each row. The two rows are placed side-by-side in front of the child as shown in Figure 3.3.

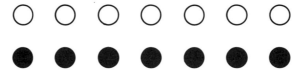

Figure 3.3 Two rows of counters in the conservation of numbers task

How could this display be transformed, and questions asked of the child, to find out whether the child is able to conserve number? What would 'conserving' and 'non-conserving' responses be?

ACTIVITY 1   Conservation

We suggest that you try out a conservation experiment yourself, with a child aged 5–6 years, to see how the child responds and to look critically at Piaget's interpretation of the results.

Conservation of mass (i.e. using two balls of plasticine or play dough) is probably the best one to use; if you wish you might also try one or more of the other conservations mentioned earlier.

Follow the three steps as described earlier in this section, that is:

First, form two balls of material and reach agreement with the child that the two are equal, that they have the same amount in each.

Second, roll one out into a 'sausage'.

Third, ask the child again, 'does this one have more plasticine (or dough) or does this one have more plasticine (or dough), or is there the same amount in each?' [Use exactly these words].

Now probe the child's answer to try and get a picture of why the child answered as he or she did. Ask why the response was given; ask about the effect of rolling out. Try rolling the sausage back into a ball and asking again.

Think about the form of words you used, and the effects of asking the pre-transformation and post-transformation question. What do you think the *child* means by his or her response? Could the task be done differently and get different results? Bear in mind the points raised in Box A in Section 2.1 when you do this task.

We will come back to the questions raised by this activity later in this chapter, and will try to use them to illustrate some of the ways in which developmental psychologists have attempted to reconceptualize the phenomena which Piaget first described for us.

For Piaget, the task of the pre-operational stage is to overcome a reliance on perception alone as being a direct and total picture of the world and to move towards a more abstract conception of perceptions as partial, needing to be supplemented by knowledge about the effects of transformations, breaking through the barrier of egocentrism. And this comes about, according to his theory, by the child representing a set of operations that can encompass transformations like the changes in perspective in the mountains task, or the rolling out of clay into a sausage, in a coherent system. This is achieved by the child representing the results of his or her own actions, and becoming able to reflect upon them as a result, in much the same way (but on a higher level of abstraction), as we saw in Sections 2.2 and 2.3, that representation frees the child from the constraints of the sensori-motor stage.

Extract D is Piaget's own summary of the key features of the pre-operational stage.

EXTRACT D   Pre-operational stage

. . . [The] symbolic function then brings great flexibility into the field of intelligence. Intelligence up to this point refers to the immediate space which surrounds the child and to the present perceptual situation; thanks to language, and to the symbolic functions, it becomes possible to invoke objects which are not present perceptually, to reconstruct the past, or to make projects, plans for the future, to think of objects not present but very distant in space – in short, to span spatio-temporal distances much greater than before.

But this new stage, the stage of representation of thought which is superimposed on the sensori-motor stage, is not a simple extension of what was referred to at the previous level. Before being able to prolong, one must in fact reconstruct, because behavior in words is a different thing from representing something in thought. When a child knows how to move around in his house or garden by following the different successive cues around him, it does not mean that he is capable of representing or reproducing the total configuration of his house or his garden. To be able to represent, to reproduce something, one must be capable of reconstructing this group of displacements, but at a new level, that of the representation of the thought.

I recently made an amusing test with Nel Szeminska. We took children of four to five years of age who went to school by themselves and came back home by themselves, and asked them if they could trace the way to school and back for us, not in design, which would be too difficult, but like a construction game, with concrete objects. We found that they were not capable of representation; there was a kind of motor-memory, but it was not yet a representation of a whole – the group of displacements had not yet been reconstructed on the plan of the representation of thought. In other words, the operations were not yet formed. These are representations which are internalized actions; but actions still centered on the body itself, on the activity itself. These representations do not allow the objective combinations, the decentrated combinations that the operations would. The actions are centered on the body. I used to call this egocentrism; but it is better thought of as lack of reversibility of action.

At this level, the most certain sign of the absence of operations which appear at the next stage is the absence of the knowledge of conservation. In fact, an operation refers to the transformation of reality. The transformation is not of the whole, however; something constant is always untransformed. If you pour a liquid from one glass to another there is transformation; the liquid changes form, but its liquid property stays constant. So at the preoperational level, it is significant from the point of view of the operations of intelligence that the child has not yet a knowledge of conservation. For example, in the case of liquid, when the child pours it from one bottle to the other, he thinks that the quantity of the liquid has changed. When the level of the liquid changes, the child thinks the quantity has changed – there is more or less in the second glass than in the first. And if you ask the child where the larger quantity came from, he does not answer this question. What is important for the child is that perceptually it is not the same thing any more. We find this absence of conservation in all object properties, in the length, surface, quantity, and weight of things.

This absence of conservation indicates essentially that at this stage the child reasons from the configuration. Confronted with a transformation, he does not reason from the transformation itself; he starts from the initial configuration, then sees the final configuration, compares the two but forgets the transformation, because he does not know how to reason about it. At this stage the child is still reasoning on the basis of what he sees because there is no conservation. He is able to master this problem only when the operations are formed and these operations, which we have already sensed at the sensori-motor level, are not formed until around seven to eight years of age. At that age the elementary problems of conservation are solved, because the child reasons on the basis of the transformation per se, and this requires a manipulation of the operation. The ability to pass from one stage to the other and be able to come back to the point of departure, to manipulate the reversible operations, which appears around seven to eight years of age, is limited when compared with the operations of the superior level only in the sense that they are concrete. That is to say, the child can manipulate the operations only when he manipulates the object concretely.

(Piaget, 1962)

In the next section of this chapter we turn to aspects of children's social development and social understanding in the preschool and early school years, and see how Piaget's theory has been extended to research in this field.

Summary of Section 3

- Piaget proposed that all children have to pass through a fixed sequence of four stages of cognitive development:

  1 The sensori-motor stage: 0–2 years (approximately)
  2 The pre-operational stage: 2–6 years (approximately)
  3 The concrete operational stage: 6–12 years (approximately)
  4 The formal operational stage: 12 years (approximately) onwards.

- Section 3 focused on Piaget's view of the characteristics of the child's thought in the *pre-operational* stage.

- According to Piaget, the pre-operational child is still locked into an *egocentric* view of the world, and this restricts his or her mental abilities in certain fundamental ways.

- Egocentrism means, amongst other things, that the child is *animistic*, projecting thoughts, intentions and feelings on to inanimate objects; for example, the sun shines *so that* people can see.

- Egocentrism also means that the pre-operational child is *unable* to comprehend points of view different from his or her own, the child is unable to recognize that a three-dimensional scene has several viewpoints apart from his or her own.

- Egocentrism also prevents the possibility of true interaction in play, which would involve taking account of other children's thoughts, feelings etc.

- The pre-operational 'non-conserving' child also lacks an understanding of underlying *constancies* in the world: for instance, when a piece of clay is rolled out, the child is unable to comprehend that its amount is conserved although its appearance is different.

4 | The development of social understanding

In Sections 4, 5 and 6 we shall be going beyond Piaget in a number of ways, but Piagetian theory will remain at the centre of the debate. All three sections share a common concern with the relationship between individual and social aspects of development. In Section 4 we shall be concerned with the way in which researchers have sought to extend Piaget's analysis to explain how the child comes to understand the social world, the world of *other people* and their feelings, meanings and intentions. In Section 5 we will see how other researchers have been working in the opposite direction: instead of using Piaget's account of intellectual development to explain the emergence of social understanding, they are seeking to demonstrate that the child's thinking and reasoning about the physical world depend on subtle processes of social interpretation. In Section 6 this emphasis on the social basis of 'learning to think' is extended into a wider consideration of the role of *teaching* in this process.

In our presentation of Piaget's ideas so far, we have concentrated mainly on the development of children's thinking and reasoning in relation to their physical environment—their ability to understand objects, amount, number and so on. Piaget was preoccupied with the foundations of children's mathematical, scientific and logical reasoning. When pressed on this, he expressed regret that he had not had time to give the development of children's understanding of their *social* world the attention it deserved. However, he argued that the fundamental course of development of understanding must be the same in respect of social understanding as it is for understanding of physical phenomena. In this section we will take a look at the development of children's social understanding in the light of Piaget's general theory, concentrating on research conducted with preschool and early school-age children.

We have seen that in Piaget's theory the pre-operational (predominantly the preschool) period is marked by an all-pervasive egocentrism—an inability on the part of the child to decentre from his or her own viewpoint. Piaget was mainly concerned with the consequences of this for the child's performance on individual cognitive tasks, but the concept of egocentrism also has obvious and important social dimensions. As we saw in relation to Selman's work in Chapter 2, many social situations demand that we make judgements about what another person is thinking, or feeling, or expecting. Such situations typically demand perspective-taking; that is, taking account of the other person's point of view on the situation.

To take a simple example, consider the familiar game of hiding a penny in one of two clenched fists so that your partner can try to guess which hand it is in. Partners may take turns at hiding the coin, or one may have a series of 'turns' before the other has a go.

ACTIVITY 2 A guessing game

If you have an opportunity to do so, try this game out with a preschool child. Hide the penny (or whatever) for the child on a number of occasions and note the pattern of his or her guessing. Then give the child some turns at hiding the coin for you.

Preschool children are usually enthusiastic about this type of game, but tend to make life all too easy for their opponent! When 'hiding' the coin, 3 and 4 year olds often neglect to close their fist, or to keep it closed, or they perhaps will bring out *one* fist only. If they manage to hold out two clenched fists they may gaze fixedly at the one containing the coin. In all these ways they seem to have difficulty in managing the situation so as to create genuine uncertainty for the other player.

Children a year or so older may do better, but even now if they have a series of turns at hiding the coin they will usually hide it in the same hand every time, or else alternate it regularly from left to right, making guessing very easy. Evidence from this and from other more complicated social guessing games (DeVries, 1970; Flavell, 1968) lends some support to the view that it is not until about the age which Piaget identified as the transition to concrete operational thinking, at 6 or 7 years, that children begin to make accurate judgements concerning other people's expectations. From this age, they show marked improvements in their ability to take account of what other people are thinking, and of what other people may think that *they* are thinking, and so on.

The ability to *lie* convincingly, and more generally to deceive others, depends upon having a clear grasp of what other people know and (more importantly) what they do *not* know. Preschoolers are typically very inept in this regard, and their attempts at lying and deceit are often engagingly naïve. Moreover, it seems that young children have difficulty understanding what it *means* to tell a lie. Piaget himself observed in an early study (Piaget, 1932) that children tend not to make the distinction between intentional and unintentional untruths. Any statement which does not correspond to the facts is a lie. A study carried out by Perner, Gruber and Wimmer (1985) in Austria, which provides supporting evidence, is described in Box F.

These findings are reminiscent of one of Piaget's best known observations, namely that young children judge moral culpability in terms of outcomes rather than intentions. Well-intentioned actions which result in major disasters (e.g breaking three cups while trying to help clear the table) are judged more blameworthy than disobedient actions with less dire

BOX F   Lies

Perner and colleagues worked with ten children at each of three age levels: 4½, 5½ and 6½. The children were tested individually, being presented at the outset with three dolls representing an older girl, a young girl and a young boy. The older girl doll is portrayed as possessing knowledge or information which she passes on to the young girl doll who in turn later passes it to the young boy doll. For example, in one scenario the young girl sees smoke rising above a wall, but cannot see its source. She asks the older girl (who is the other side of a wall, where she can see the source) where the smoke is coming from. The older girl tells the younger girl that it is (say) a bonfire, whereas the real child and the experimenter can see that it is coming from a chimney. The boy doll then comes along and asks the young girl doll where the smoke is coming from. She tells him it is from a bonfire.

As adults, we can see that in the first exchange the older girl told a lie (an intentional untruth) whereas in the second exchange the young girl was not lying, since she told what she believed to be the truth. Questioning by Perner and colleagues revealed that (apart from two of the youngest subjects) the children understood the stories and in particular understood that the young girl really did believe that the smoke came from a bonfire. Nevertheless, of the thirty children, twenty-nine consistently judged that the young girl had told a lie. The results strongly supported Piaget's early observation: children at these ages seem to judge whether something is a lie solely on the basis of its correspondence with the true situation, and not at all on the basis of the speaker's intentions.

consequences (e.g. breaking one cup while trying to reach some forbidden chocolates). Only from about the age of seven does the question of good and bad intent begin to figure in children's attribution of who was most at fault (Piaget, 1932).

The age of seven is, of course, significant in Piaget's theory since it is around this age that, in Piagetian terms, children reach the stage of concrete operational thought. In Piagetian terms, the parallel development of intellectual and social aspects of reasoning is reflected in the way that children, at this age, begin to develop moral systems or structures which enable them to make sense of behaviour within a social framework, rather than judging actions in isolation. Several more recent studies point to a similar conclusion. For example, Chandler (1977) studied how well young children can 'read' cues concerning other people's emotional experiences. Chandler had children interpret a story told in a comic-strip sequence of pictures in which (for example) a child sadly watches his father going away on an aeroplane, and later bursts into tears when he receives a present of a toy aeroplane. The postman who brings the present is perplexed, not being able to understand why the child is crying. Chandler was interested in the age at which children would begin to see both the reason for the child's reaction and the reason for the postman's perplexity. He found that it was not until 7 years of age that children began to succeed on tasks such as this. Younger children, even if they see why the child is crying, seem to lose sight of the fact that the postman would not share their knowledge of the relevant circumstances. Again, the issue of sorting out who has and who does not have certain pieces of information (and more generally of co-ordinating isolated events to form a whole co-ordinated system) is the central requirement for success.

However, when less complex techniques are used, young children do show some ability to judge the likely emotional experiences of others. For example, Box G describes a study by Light (1979) using a technique adapted from Borke (1971).

The 'faces' technique, of course, does not involve the same ability to differentiate who has what information as the Chandler technique. It really only demands that children recognize the emotional connotations of various situations. It is worth referring to your own experience at this point. Does such experience as you have with preschool children suggest that they are sensitive to, and have some understanding of, the emotional experience of others? While much anecdotal evidence does suggest that young children sometimes show this kind of 'empathy', there seems to be a lack of good research evidence in this area.

SAQ 4   What situations might lend themselves well to the assessment of empathy in preschoolers? Try to think of possible observational or experimental approaches to measuring young children's ability to judge and respond to other's emotions.

Verbal communication is another area where, according to Piaget, young children are limited by their egocentrism. Effective communication depends upon the speaker taking account of the listener's situation. As we saw in the

BOX G   Judging emotions

The procedure involved presenting the children (all within a week or so of their fourth birthday) with a blank-faced 2D cut-out doll together with a set of alternative 'faces' bearing different emotional expressions as shown in Figure 3.4. Boys had a set of 'boy' faces and girls a set of 'girl' faces, each including one happy, one sad, one frightened and one angry face. The doll figure was introduced as a child of the subject's own gender, and given a name (say 'Susan'). First the various faces were placed in turn on the doll and the child was asked, 'How's Susan feeling now?'. Almost all children were able to identify the emotional expressions as intended.

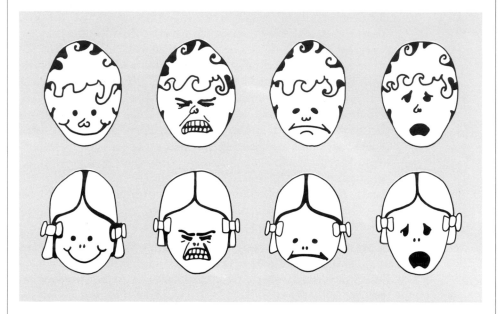

Figure 3.4 The set of facial expressions used in the study by Light (1979)
(Source: Light, 1979)

Then the child was told a series of ten stories about things which happened to 'Susan', and asked each time to 'pick a face' to 'show how she's feeling'. The stories included such events as dreaming about being chased by a tiger, having a ball snatched away while playing, having a pet rabbit die, and being invited to a birthday party.

Of the fifty-eight children tested, three used all four expressions appropriately throughout, and a further twenty-two used only one of them inappropriately. The 'happy' face was used accurately by the large majority of the children, while the other three were used with much lower but approximately equal levels of accuracy. Overall, although the children had evidently got some way to go before reaching adult levels of performance on this task, they showed considerable ability both to recognize emotional expressions and to recognize situations to which those expressions are appropriate.

previous section, Piaget saw the co-ordination of speaker's and listener's perspectives as distinctly lacking in the dialogue of preschoolers. Experimental work in this area has made extensive use of a research design introduced by Krauss and Glucksberg (1969) and described here in Box H.

Krauss and Glucksberg found that 5–6 year olds performed very poorly indeed on this kind of task, and did not improve with practice. They tended to produce very idiosyncratic descriptions (e.g. Mummy's hat) which might indeed have been accurate but were quite unhelpful to their partner. In other

BOX H   Assessing communication skills

A typical experiment might involve two children seated at opposite sides of a table, with an opaque screen between them. Each would have an identical set of cards. Krauss and Glucksberg (1969) used the shapes shown in Figure 3.5, though subsequent researchers have usually used less abstract shapes.

Figure 3.5 The set of cards used to assess communication skills
(Source: based on Krauss and Glucksberg, 1969)

A target card—for example, card 1 in Figure 3.5—is identified to one of the children (the speaker) by the experimenter. The speaker has the task of describing the card to his or her partner (the listener), so that the listener knows which card is being described and can correctly identify it from his or her own set. This procedure is then repeated, with the roles of speaker and listener being reversed. Thus, the task requires children to differentiate between the cards from the listener's point of view.

BOX I   Communication failure

The Robinsons' study followed the general procedure outlined above, except that the game was played between a single child and the experimenter. Line drawings of 'little men' were used—in one case the man has a hat, in another a flag, in another a flower, in another a flag and a flower (but no hat) and so on in various combinations. The Robinsons were interested in what happened when messages were misinterpreted and errors occurred. In some cases errors occurred because the child offered an ambiguous description (for example, saying 'he's got a flower' without saying whether he also had a flag). In other cases the experimenter deliberately made errors of the same kind. Whenever selection errors occurred the children were quizzed as to whose *fault* it was that things had gone wrong.

Sixty-four Australian infant school children between 5½ and 8 years of age were tested. Amongst the older children (7½–8 years), the blame was, with good reason, laid more often on the speaker than on the listener (though it has to be said that there was also a tendency to blame the experimenter rather than themselves, whoever was speaker!). Amongst the youngest children (5½–6 years), however, over 75 per cent of the children consistently blamed the *listener* for errors. It is not surprising then that the performance of children at this age does not seem to improve with practice: they do not appear to understand that inadequate *messages* can be responsible for failure of communication.

studies with more realistic pictures, the 5 and 6 year olds often gave very non-specific descriptions which could have applied to several different pictures—they knew which one they meant but there was no way their partner could have done. Box I describes a study by Robinson and Robinson (1976) in which children were asked whose *fault* it was when communication failed in this way.

These studies suggest that it is not until 7 or 8 years of age that children begin to be able to criticize their own verbal descriptions, or to see them from the point of view of the listener. However, there is no doubt that even preschool children can to *some* extent adjust their utterances to match their listener's requirements. For example, Maratsos (1973) taught children how to play a game and then asked them to tell a blindfolded as against a sighted listener how to play it. He found evidence that even children as young as 3 or 4 years made some adjustments to the way they described the game when talking to a blindfolded listener. Shatz and Gelman (1973) also found evidence that 4-year-old children tended to simplify their speech systematically when speaking to much younger children.

Here again, reflect on your own experience with young children. Can you think of situations in which they *do* adjust their communication in a way which reflects sensitivity to the listener? Equally, can you think of situations in which they conspicuously fail to do so? It is also worth thinking about times when we as adults fail to make suitable adjustments to those with whom we are trying to communicate. How often do we assume that people know things they in fact do not know, or that they are necessarily interested in the same things as we are? How often do we ignore what someone is trying to say if it does not fit with our preconceptions of that person or of a particular situation? Egocentrism in communication is clearly not an all-or-nothing phenomenon, overcome abruptly at a given age or stage. Rather, it would seem that the process of overcoming it is a gradual one, beginning early in life and continuing through adulthood, never really being completed. The same seems to be true of egocentrism more generally as we have seen throughout this section.

In this section we have taken a closer look at how children's ability to make *social* inferences develops. Piaget's claim was that children's social understanding develops in parallel with their understanding of the physical world. It follows from this that major changes might be expected to occur in the early school years, when egocentrism is overcome and operational thinking achieved. Studies we have mentioned lend support to this view, for example those concerned with: (1) young children's behaviour in guessing games; (2) their ability to judge lies and attribute fault in terms of *intentions*; and (3) their ability to recognize their listener's needs when framing verbal messages.

In all these cases, marked progress seems to be made at about the age of seven. On the other hand, other studies we have considered (e.g. judging emotions and some aspects of verbal communication) suggest that young children are far from totally egocentric. In the next section, we will examine work by researchers who reject Piaget's theory of parallel development and claim instead that children's intellectual development *depends* on their development of social understanding.

Summary of Section 4

- Piaget saw the development of social understanding as simply running in parallel with the development of mathematical or logical understanding.

- The preschooler, limited by egocentrism, is supposedly unable to make accurate judgements concerning other people's expectations. This is reflected in poor performance; for example, in social guessing games like 'hide the penny' where 'pre-operational' children tend to centre on individual features of a situation and ignore the whole pattern of relationships. So, in social situations we see evidence that children focus on isolated actions, and ignore their wider social meaning. We saw this in the case of attributing blame for misdeeds, or judging whether something is a lie.

- Preschoolers undoubtedly do have some ability to judge others' emotions, but in tasks which require them to disentangle the emotional perspectives of different characters (Chandler, 1977) they show little success before about the age of seven—that is, about the age which Piaget assigns to the experience of concrete operational thinking.

- Verbal communication abilities show a similar pattern, with some evidence of effective adaptation to the needs of the listener at an early age, but with evidence from experimental studies (e.g. Robinson and Robinson, 1976) that 5 and 6 year olds have little understanding of the basis of effective communication.

- Overall, it is clear that preschoolers are by no means *totally* egocentric, but their ability to reflect upon and make judgements about differing social perspectives is limited. Progress in overcoming the limitation seems to be gradual rather than abrupt.

5 | 'Human sense': the social dimensions of understanding

The work we reviewed in Section 4 reflects a process of generalization and extension of Piaget's theory in the social domain. But at the same time as this work has been going on, other researchers have been beginning to question the very distinction between social and intellectual development. Rather than seeing social and intellectual development as 'parallel' developments, which can be studied independently of one another, these researchers claim that the development of social understanding actually holds the key to children's intellectual development. According to this argument, the attempt to study cognitive development on its own has led Piaget and his followers systematically to underestimate children's abilities.

In 1978, Margaret Donaldson wrote a slim but significant book entitled *Children's minds*, based on her work with various colleagues and students at Edinburgh University. This exemplifies a completely new approach to 'adding a social dimension to Piaget', and involves an exploration of the social dimensions of the very tasks which Piaget invented to study individual intellectual development.

Broadly speaking, Donaldson's argument is that the preschool child is capable of much more subtle and sophisticated reasoning that Piaget allowed for, but that at this age reasoning is embedded in the familiar social situations of everyday life. The preschooler's apparent ineptitude on Piagetian tasks is seen as reflecting an inability to abstract (or, as Donaldson put it, to '**disembed**') reasoning from this familiar context. Seen from this standpoint, the developmental task of the early school years is not so much the creation of new forms of thought as the *freeing of existing forms of thought for use in new situations*. Donaldson argues that the experience of school itself has a significant role to play in this process.

These ideas are not entirely new. They were articulated in broad terms by the Soviet psychologist Lev Vygotsky in the 1930s, but Vygotsky's work was suppressed under Stalin and was not widely known in the West until the 1960s (Vygotsky, 1962). The American psychologist and educationalist Jerome Bruner developed some of the same arguments during the 1960s and early

1970s (e.g. Bruner, 1972). But it was not until the mid 1970s that any substantial body of research on these issues began to appear.

We will use two of Piaget's best known tasks, the 'three mountains' task and the conservation task, to illustrate our discussion. Both tasks were introduced in Section 3. The 'three mountains' task seemed to provide a striking illustration of the young child's apparent inability to recognize or take account of perspective differences. The results he obtained with this task led Piaget to say of the typical 4 or 5 year old that he 'appears to be rooted in his own viewpoint in the narrowest and most restrictive fashion so that he cannot imagine any perspective but his own' (Piaget and Inhelder, 1956, p. 242). By way of contrast, Box J reports a study by Hughes and Donaldson (Donaldson,

BOX J   Hiding from policemen

In this study, children between 3½ and 5 years of age were tested individually using an apparatus consisting of two 'walls' which intersected to form a cross. In the first stage the child was asked to judge whether a 'policeman' doll could see a 'boy' doll from various positions. Then the child was asked to 'hide the doll so the policeman can't see him', with the policeman at a given position. Then a second policeman was introduced, as illustrated in Figure 3.6, and the child was asked to hide the doll from both policemen. This required the child to consider and co-ordinate *two* points of view. Look at Figure 3.6 and work out where the doll should be placed (in this case the only effective hiding place is at C). This was repeated three times so that each time a different section was left as the only hiding place. The results were clear: 90 per cent of the responses given by the children were correct.

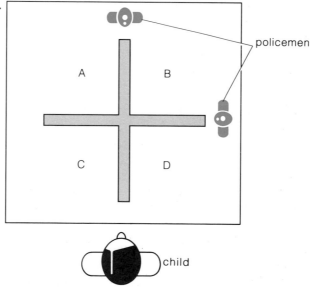

Figure 3.6 Plan of the experimental layout in the hiding game
(Source: Donaldson, 1978)

1978) in which children's ability to take account of perspectives other than their own was assessed in the context of a hiding game.

There are several differences between the 'hiding from policemen' task and the 'three mountains' task. The 'hiding from policemen' task requires that the child should work out only whether something will be visible from a given position, while the 'three mountains' task requires the child to work out exactly how a complex scene will *appear* from that position. But even so, Hughes' and Donaldson's results hardly seem consistent with Piaget's conclusion that the preschooler is 'rooted in his own viewpoint in the narrowest and most restrictive fashion'.

Donaldson's interpretation of the fundamental difference between these two tasks rests on the concept of **human sense**:

The point is that the *motives* and *intentions* of the characters are entirely comprehensible, even to a child of three. The task requires the child to act in ways which are in line with certain very basic human purposes and interactions (escape and pursuit)—it makes *human sense*. Thus it is not at all hard to convey to the child what he is supposed to do: he apprehends it instantly. It then turns out that neither is it hard for him to do it. In other words, in this context he shows none of the difficulty in 'decentring' which Piaget ascribes to him.

(Donaldson, 1978, p. 24)

The difficulty of the 'three mountains' task is seen, then, not so much in terms of the spatial complexity of the array (mountains were presumably familiar to Piaget and Inhelder's Swiss subjects!), but to the lack of *human sense* in the task. The task lacks any 'storyline' in terms of interpersonal motives or purposes. It is abstract in the sense of being arbitrary and cold-blooded. As Donaldson puts it, 'in the veins of three year olds, the blood still runs warm. . . .'.

ACTIVITY 3   Testing for egocentrism

If you have the opportunity to do so, try a few experiments with an even younger child—a 2 year old, say. Stick a different picture on to each side of a piece of card and show the child both sides. Then hold it up between you and ask which picture *the child* can see, and which picture *you* can see. Or stick a picture on to the bottom inside surface of a toy 'nesting cup' and ask the child, sitting at a little distance, to *show* you the picture. Does the child hold it up so you can see it, even though this means that he or she cannot? You may be able to think of other ways of testing the extent to which the child is aware that different people in different positions see different things.

Even as early as the first year or so of life we can see the beginning of such abilities. For example, babies of a year old can already point to things, and will look in the appropriate direction when things are pointed out to them. This ability seems to imply some recognition that what people see depends on which way they are looking. Indeed, there is evidence that from a very early age babies will follow the direction of someone else's gaze, so that if the mother looks round at something, the baby will often look there too. The argument is that right from the first year of life children are enmeshed in patterns of mutual social behaviour which involve the recognition of perspective differences. If egocentrism means behaving as if such differences do not exist, then young children are not egocentric. But if egocentrism is interpreted as referring to an inability to *think about* perspective differences explicitly and to make 'cold-blooded' abstract judgements about them, then young children may indeed be considered egocentric. In these respects their ability is indeed limited, and it is here that we see such marked changes in the early school years.

Before turning to the conservation task, we must give some attention to how this question of 'human sense' affects the way we, as well as young children, use language. Piaget tended to treat language as unproblematic. He took the view that when children use words, they meant exactly the same as adults, so one could use verbal questioning to get directly at the nature of the child's thought processes. We saw some examples of this in Section 3.

What this does not take into account is that word meanings often shift in subtle ways depending on the context in which they are used. Many words, such as 'bank', have a variety of quite distinct meanings, though we do not usually have difficulty deciding whether a finance house, or a sloping area, or a flying manoeuvre is meant. Sometimes the variations in meaning are quite subtle, however. Think about the word 'same', for example. If someone says to you 'that's the same man . . .', they are probably referring to a unique individual; whereas if someone says 'you and I have the same car', they are probably referring to a *type* of car rather than to one particular car. But if the two of you were allocated to the 'same' car at the Dodgems, it would probably once again mean the same *individual* car. The context of a word refers both to the sentence in which it is used (the linguistic context) and to the circumstances in which that sentence is uttered (the extralinguistic context). Both contain rich cues concerning the speaker's likely meaning, and Donaldson suggests that children, even more than adults, use this context to make a judgement about what is *meant*. The other side of the coin is that children are less likely to engage in any close analysis of the exact words *said*.

One of the examples which Donaldson uses concerns the word 'more', which, like the word 'same', occupies a key place in Piaget's conservation task (e.g. 'is there more juice in this glass, or more in that glass, or do they both have the same amount of juice?'). How do children understand the word 'more'? The study given in Box K, described by Donaldson (1978), was designed to find out.

It is not only in terms of the language used that the conservation test proves to be problematic. It has in fact become a favourite test-bed for investigators interested in the role of social processes in children's thinking and reasoning. One such study, by Light, Buckingham and Robbins (1979), is outlined in Box L.

It seems from this and similar studies that where the conservation task can be embedded in a context of socially intelligible activity, and especially where there is some reason for the transformation (the pouring from one beaker to another in this case) which the children can understand, then young children seem to grasp the essence of conservation. But in the standard Piagetian task they fail, perhaps precisely because they are *too* attentive to the social context. Why on earth should the experimenter start pouring things from one

BOX K   The meaning of 'more'

Donaldson and McGarrigle arranged a number of toy cars and garages on two shelves, one above the other, as shown in Figure 3.7. One shelf had five cars but six garages, so that one of the garages was empty. The other had four cars in four garages.

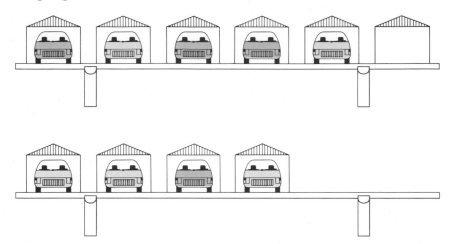

Figure 3.7 The 'cars and garages' display used in the study of the word 'more'

Preschool children were asked which shelf held more cars: in one condition, with the garages present as shown, and in another condition, with the garages absent. Without the garages *all* children gave the correct response, which seems to show that they know what 'more' means. But when the garages were present as shown, a substantial number (about a third) said the shelf holding only four cars had more. Why? Donaldson suggests that, when the garages are present, the children tend to read the situation in terms of the full set of cars which would be appropriate to the garages, so that the row of five cars in the six garages on the top shelf is seen as *lacking* a car. Thus, the child's interpretation of the whole term 'more' (so crucial to the conservation test) is affected by the way in which the situation is understood *as a whole*.

container to another for no apparent reason? Why should he or she ask the same question about which has more a second time if the child had answered it right the first time and nothing important had changed? Perhaps the child in this situation will not expect the adult to ask silly questions and will try to make sense of them in terms of what actually has changed, namely the *appearance* of the array (i.e. does it *look* different?). Thus, it may be children's very appreciation of these conversational conventions which leads them into error.

Think back to the conservation test you did as an activity in Section 3.4 (Activity 1). Did the child give you any hint as to how he or she understood the testing situation? Can you think of different ways in which you could have made the task more 'natural' and intelligible for the child: for example,

BOX L   A socially intelligible conservation task

In this study, eighty 6 year olds were tested in pairs. For half of them, the task was a standard Piagetian conservation task. Two identical beakers were filled to the same level with dried pasta 'shells'. When the children agreed that there was the same amount in each beaker, the contents of one were poured into a wider beaker. Now only 5 per cent of the children said that the quantities were the same; 95 per cent, in other words, appeared to be 'non-conservers'.

For the other half of the children the procedure was different. They were told at the outset that they were going to use the pasta shells in a competitive game. But after they had agreed that the two identical beakers contained the same amount, the experimenter 'noticed' that one of the beakers was dangerously chipped around

the rim. He looked around and found the alternative (larger) beaker and poured the contents in, asking the children before they started their game whether they had the same amount of shells each. This time 70 per cent of them judged that the quantities were equal; only 30 per cent appeared to be 'non-conservers'.

It may be that the 'game' element was important—that is, that when the children were thinking in terms of sharing out the pasta for a game their attention was focused on 'fair shares'. The chipped beaker gave a sensible, practical reason for transferring one lot of pasta to a different container. Under these conditions, far more children appeared to understand that the number of shells was unaffected by the perceptual change and were thus apparently 'conservers'.

by embedding the task within a game, or giving some reason for your own actions?

Donaldson (1978) and her colleagues argue that preschool children are neither as egocentric nor as lacking in logical skills as Piaget suggested. Some of Piaget's own tasks, including the 'three mountains' and conservation tasks, have been refashioned so that they make 'human sense', and have been shown to be very much easier as a result. We saw this first in relation to taking other people's perspectives (the 'policemen' task in Box J), then in relation to word meaning (the 'cars and garages' task in Box K), and finally in relation to conservation (the 'chipped beaker' experiment in Box L). These experiments strongly suggest that preschool children's reasoning seems to be 'embedded' in their understanding of social interchanges; development can be characterized as a process of 'disembedding' reasoning skills from the social contexts in which they evolve.

Outside of the testing situation, whether in the home or the school, the child's responsiveness to context will usually lead to a *correct* interpretation of adults' utterances. Indeed, it is probable that children often 'get the meaning' of what an adult is saying even when the adult uses words which the child doesn't really understand. This gives the child a way of making sense of the words themselves. Especially with words like 'number', which are not easy to *define*, this ability to make sense of the meaning in context may be an important mechanism for learning.

The processes of formal education may, as Donaldson (1978) claims, have an important part to play in this process. Through schooling, and perhaps particularly through learning to read and write, the child's attention is turned more and more towards the precise words used. This continues to be true for adults. Whereas in face-to-face conversation we attend to meaning-in-context, and often hardly notice the choice of words, when it comes to writing we do not have the same contextual support, and the words themselves have to convey a precise meaning. In this and other ways, school fosters an 'objective' attitude to language, in which statements or questions have a meaning in their own right, independently of the intentions or context from which they originate. To the extent that this view is correct, we can say that children from the age of 7 years onwards begin to succeed on Piagetian tasks not so much because they possess new logical competencies, but because they begin to appreciate the social rules of the testing situation, and to attend to the *language* that is used in that situation in a new 'objective' fashion.

The research we have considered in this section undermines the distinction implicitly drawn by Piaget between the domains of intellectual and social development. It is becoming clear that the kinds of task which Piaget set up to examine the *individual* child's cognitive competence actually create rather interesting and complicated *social* situations. Children's responses in such situations may be influenced to a very considerable extent by their reading of the adults' meanings and intentions. Recognizing this may help us not only to understand the nature of the psychological testing situation but also to recognize the inherently social nature of the processes through which the child's thinking develops. In Section 6 we shall explore some of the implications of this in relation to the processes of learning and teaching.

Summary of Section 5

- Donaldson (1978) argued that, contrary to Piaget's view, social and intellectual aspects of development are intimately connected, and that *all* the tasks which Piaget used had important social dimensions.

- Hughes and Donaldson (Donaldson, 1978) used a game involving hiding a boy from one or more policemen to illustrate their claim that young children do have an awareness of perspectives other than their own, and this produced good results even from preschool children, whereas Piaget's classic 'three mountains' task gave very poor results at this age.

- Donaldson interpreted the difference between the two tasks in terms of 'human sense'. For the preschooler, tasks have to make sense *socially*— that is, in terms of understandable motives and intentions etc.— otherwise the child cannot understand them at all.

- Part of the reason for this is that young children make inferences about what is *meant* rather than attending closely to the exact words *said*. Their interpretation of words is very dependent on context, as Donaldson and McGarrigle's 'cars and garages' study showed.

- Reconstruction of a standard Piagetian conservation task, so as to make it socially intelligible to the child, also results in very much improved performance, as the 'chipped beaker' study by Light *et al.* (1979) showed.

- Older children (of the age Piaget thought of in terms of 'operational' thinking) are seen by Donaldson (1978) as having achieved a degree of *independence* from the immediate context. Their thinking and reasoning is no longer 'embedded' in socially intelligible situations and they can function independently of these. Donaldson saw schooling (and especially learning to read and write) as important contributory factors in this development.

6 | Learning, teaching and development

Piaget once recounted at a conference the following anecdote concerning a child of 4 or 5 years old, sitting in his garden playing with stones:

Now to count these pebbles he put them in a row and he counted them one, two, three, up to ten. Then he . . . started to count them in the other direction . . . Once again he found ten. He found this marvellous . . . So he put them in a circle and counted them that way and found ten once again . . . He discovered that the sum was independent of the order.

(Piaget in Ripple and Rockastle, 1964, p. 12)

This example encapsulates two centrally important features of Piaget's theory. The first is that it is a *constructivist* theory, in that the child does not have knowledge innately, nor does he or she just receive it passively from others. Rather, knowledge is actively constructed by the child through active engagement with the world. The growth of knowledge involves a process of active adaptation to the world achieved through the twin processes of assimilation and accommodation. The child playing with the stones, in Piaget's example, is engaged in the process of building his own understanding of the world.

The second thing to note about this example is the way in which it underlines the *individualism* inherent in Piaget's approach. The emphasis, here as so often elsewhere, is on the child as a 'scientist', encountering the material world and engaging in a solitary quest for knowledge. Whether Piaget ever really intended to characterize the development of knowledge in quite such 'Robinson Crusoe-like' terms is questionable, but certainly one consequence of Piaget's influence has been that, until relatively recently, developmental psychology has had very little to say about the social dimensions of learning to think.

SAQ 5   In what sense or senses can Piaget's theory be described as 'individualistic'?

We saw in the last section how recent work by Donaldson and others on Piaget's own tasks has offered one way of opening up the social dimensions of the learning process. Another has been provided by the rediscovery of Vygotsky's early work (Vygotsky, 1962), which we also referred to briefly in the last section. Vygotsky's key idea was that the ability we have as adults to think and reason by ourselves and for ourselves is itself the outcome of a fundamentally social process. The baby, and later the child, are first and foremost social beings, able to engage with others but able to do rather little by themselves. As Vygotsky characterized it, the developmental process moves from an initial stage at which children are able to do things with others to a final stage at which they are able to do things by themselves. Consequently, Vygotsky saw the developing child's level of ability not so much in terms of what the child could do on his or her own, but rather in terms of what the child was capable of when given help. The child was envisaged as having a **zone of proximal** [or next] **development**: a spectrum of achievements which were beyond the child's unassisted grasp but which were attainable, given help and support from an adult. The teacher, to be effective, has to work sensitively within this zone.

This theoretical perspective has begun to prove very attractive to western developmental psychologists. Vygotsky himself died very young, and his own writings (e.g. Vygotsky, 1962) are fragmentary, offering little in the way of systematic evidence for his views. But his theory brings into the foreground an issue which developmentalists, under the influence of Piaget, have long neglected, namely the role of *teaching*. For Piaget, the young child's educational needs were conceived principally in terms of the provision of a rich and stimulating diet of experience, especially of the physical properties of objects. The teacher's role was seen principally in terms of diagnosing the child's readiness for new experiences and providing the appropriate environment in which those experiences could occur. This view emphasizes the constructive activity of the child but plays down the constructive role of the teacher. Vygotsky's stance differs in seeing the teaching–learning process as, above all, a *social* exchange in which shared meanings are built up through *joint* activity.

When we think of teaching we tend to think straight away in terms of what goes on in schools. But this kind of formal teaching is a fairly recent invention, while various other, typically less formal, modes of teaching must be as old as mankind. For present purposes, we mean to refer to those many situations in which somebody, often but not always an adult, works with the child with the more or less explicit aim of guiding the child's behaviour and developing the child's competence.

Bruner, for example, while working at Oxford in the 1970s, studied the kinds of early preverbal interactions of mothers and their babies discussed in Chapter 2. Bruner (1975) arranged for mothers to bring their infants to the laboratory at regular intervals over a 6-month period, the infants being 7 months old at the beginning of the study. None of the infants had any conventional speech at the beginning of the study, but all of them had at least single-word speech by the end of it. Mothers were videotaped feeding, bathing and playing with their infants. Bruner observed various regular patterns in the interaction of mother and infant, and sought to relate these to the development of language. For example, he describes the evolution of giving and taking of objects. Typically, at the outset, the focus is on the mother as agent. She dramatizes the act of handing the child a desired object by moving it slowly and by accompanying the movement with sounds of increasing pitch. Eventually the child begins to anticipate the arrival of the object, taking hold of it as it is passed. The child next becomes the agent in a reciprocal process of handing the object back to the mother. Through detailed case studies, Bruner traces the way the agents, actions and objects are gradually differentiated from one another in this process. He observes the way the mother's speech, marking parts of the sequence (for example, with a 'thank you'), becomes assimilated into the ritual game of exchange and eventually becomes part of the child's own repertoire. What Bruner is attempting to characterize here (and in the analysis of other similar exchanges, such as 'peekaboo') is not simply the learning of words, but rather the learning of 'conversational structures' which are basic to the structure of our language.

Over and above his specific interest in language, Bruner saw many of the child's most important intellectual achievements as being realized through this kind of spontaneous exchange in which the adult adopts an informal teaching role. The key concepts in his analysis are **contingency** and **scaffolding**. The adult's behaviour is 'contingent' to the extent that it depends upon, and follows immediately from, the child's previous response. The concept of scaffolding refers to the way that the adult can support or 'scaffold' the child's activity, supporting it in ways that allow the child to go beyond his or her present level of performance. The image is of scaffolding being used to assist the construction of a building; the scaffolding can then be removed once the building is erected. The child, like the building, will arrive at 'stand-alone competence' eventually, but only as a result of a good deal of constructive activity by others.

While Bruner was interested in the formats of spontaneously recurring interaction between parents and infants, Wood and Middleton (1975) at Nottingham University have adopted the same approach to the analysis of more structured exchanges. For instance, Box M describes a study in which adults were given the explicit task of teaching young children (3–5 year olds) how to assemble a kind of '3D jigsaw' made up of wooden blocks.

Teachers may provide 'scaffolding' for learners by highlighting important features of the task which might otherwise be forgotten. They may help children to analyse tasks and enable them to concentrate upon and master manageable aspects of it, one at a time. In these and other ways, whether the 'teaching' in question is formal or informal, adults shape, guide and foster young children's learning.

The world of school opens up a whole new domain for teaching and learning, with its own distinctive character. Here again, Vygotskyan ideas, long dormant, are shaping much current thinking—for example, about how the interchanges between teachers and children in the classroom shape the course of children's intellectual development (e.g. Edwards and Mercer, 1987). But it has to be admitted that the studies available to date are little more than beginnings: pointers to the possibility that the disciplines of developmental psychology and education may converge in years to come to offer a more integrated account of development and learning in the child.

BOX M Mothers as teachers

Wood and Middleton (1975) asked twelve mothers to teach their own 4-year-old children how to assemble the puzzle, so that the child would subsequently be able to do it on his or her own. The mothers had already been shown how to do the puzzle. The mother–child instruction session was videotaped and then the children had a go at completing the puzzle on their own.

The system of categories adopted reflects varying degrees of *control* which each instruction by the mother implicitly exerts over what happens next. In the list that follows, categories at the beginning of the list offer maximum scope for the child's initiative. Going down the list, instructions become progressively more controlling:

Level of control	Example
1 General verbal prompts	'Now you make something'
2 Specific verbal instructions	'Get four big blocks'
3 Indicates material	Points to block(s) needed
4 Prepares for assembly	Orients pairs so hole faces peg
5 Demonstrates	Assembles two pairs.

What Wood and Middleton found was that successful instruction was not associated with operating at one rather than at another of these levels of control, but with moving flexibly up and down this hierarchy according to how the child responded to the last instruction. An index of *contingency of instruction* was devised. High scores on this index were obtained by mothers who, when faced with a successful response to a previous instruction, shifted to a higher level, less controlling intervention, but when faced with a failure shifted immediately in the opposite direction. A mother's scores on this index proved to be the best predictor of the child's subsequent solo performance on the task. This kind of continuous monitoring of the child's current level of performance within the teaching–learning situation offers a good example of what Vygotsky meant by operating within the child's 'zone of proximal development'.

Summary of Section 6

- Piaget's theory is individualistic in emphasis, stressing the child's individual adaptation to the physical world and the resulting growth of logical and mathematical thinking. Little consideration is given to the processes of *social* transmission of knowledge from one generation to the next.

- Vygotsky, by contrast, saw the child as having a *zone of proximal development*: a spectrum of achievements attainable only with support from an adult. He was therefore interested in what the child could do *with help*, and with the ways in which adult–child interaction structured the development of children's thinking.

- Bruner's (1975) work with mother–infant pairs illustrates a Vygotskyan approach to early language learning. He analysed the spontaneous teaching strategies mothers adopt with their young infants, and sees this structured preverbal interaction as an important stepping-stone to language. The work of Wood and Middleton (1975) illustrates a similar approach, with mothers acting as teachers of their own preschool children.

- Such teaching seems to be successful to the extent that the adult can make his or her support delicately dependent upon the child's performance as it develops.

- Two concepts that studies both by Bruner (1975) and by Wood and Middleton (1975) use are: *scaffolding*, which describes the way in which the adult partner provides the necessary support for the successful completion of the child's action, and *contingency*, which describes the delicate dependence of the adult's action upon the immediately preceding action of the child.

- A Vygotskyan approach to such 'informal' teaching holds out the possibility of forging a better link between developmental psychology and the study of more formal teaching in the school context.

7 | Concluding comments

We could not hope to encapsulate all of developmental psychology within a single chapter and have not tried to do so. Aspects of emotional and social development are considered in the previous and subsequent chapters, and developmental issues will be touched upon here and there throughout this *Introduction to psychology*. In this chapter we have focused largely on the development of children's thinking, and have relied upon the work of Piaget to provide a framework for our discussion. This choice is not arbitrary, of course, since Piaget has provided the dominant theoretical framework for developmental psychology during its own formative years as a discipline.

Within our chosen domain, we have sketched Piaget's account of the beginnings of understanding in infancy, and of the process whereby this understanding is developed. We have given more detailed attention to his account of development during the preschool and early school years, which Piaget saw in terms of overcoming egocentrism and achieving 'operational' thinking. Two key tasks, the 'three mountains' task and the conservation task, were used to index these developments.

Piaget's theory is central to developmental psychology because Piaget 'set the agenda' for the discipline, and because more recent developments have often emerged in the form of critiques of, or reactions against, Piaget's position. We have seen that many particular aspects of Piaget's work have been questioned, and some of his claims clearly refuted. How much of the Piagetian edifice still stands? There is no real consensus on this as yet. Contemporary developmental psychologists would probably all agree that Piaget's main, lasting contributions have been his recognition that intellectual development involves qualitative changes in the ways children think, rather than simply gradual improvements in speed or accuracy, and his recognition that these qualitative changes come about through the child's own constructive activity. They would also agree that the immense volume of descriptive material which Piaget compiled concerning development from infancy to adolescence is one of the richest resources of the discipline.

On the other side of the account, Piaget's methods and techniques have sometimes generated misleading results, as we have seen both with the 'three mountains' task and with conservation. His claims for clear-cut *stages* in development are not widely accepted today, and well-publicized instances of, for example, 9-year-old children passing A-level Maths make any attempt to match ages and stages essentially unconvincing. Last but not least, Piaget's very *individualistic* emphasis has been rejected by many contemporary developmental psychologists. In Section 4 we saw some of the ways in which researchers have sought to extend Piaget's analysis to study the development of social understanding. In Section 5 we saw how other developmental psychologists, most notably Donaldson, have challenged Piaget 'on his home ground' by offering an analysis of individual cognitive testing as an essentially social process. And, finally, in Section 6 we highlighted the growing body of research which sees cognitive development largely in terms of *learning* (rather than 'natural' stage-by-stage *development*), and argues that to understand learning we are going to have to take the reciprocal process of *teaching* rather more seriously than we have done so far.

It is still only a relatively short time since Piaget's death. He has left behind him a thriving sub-discipline of developmental psychology, but one which still could be said to show more promise than achievement. It is odd, perhaps, that one of the last things to which western science should turn its attention is the development of thinking itself. Much more needs to be done before developmental psychology will be in any position to offer definitive answers, but the game is certainly afoot!

Further reading

More detailed treatment of the issues covered in this chapter, and of many other topics in developmental psychology, can be found in two other Open University courses in particular: *Personality, development and learning*, and *Cognitive development*. The following four associated Readers for these two courses contain a wide range of original research papers and discussion and review papers. They may be read independently of the courses themselves and should be available through bookshops and libraries.

BARNES, P., OATES, J., CHAPMAN, J., LEE, V. and CZERNIEWSKA, P. (eds) (1984) *Personality, development and learning*, London: Hodder and Stoughton/The Open University.

LOCK, A. and FISHER, E. (eds) (1984) *Language development*, London: Croom Helm/The Open University.

OATES, J. and SHELDON, S. (eds) (1987) *Cognitive development in infancy*, Hove: Lawrence Erlbaum/The Open University.

RICHARDSON, K. and SHELDON, S. (eds) (1987) *Cognitive development to adolescence*, Hove: Lawrence Erlbaum/The Open University.

We also recommend the following, which is a key publication in the field of research that has examined Piaget's theory:

DONALDSON, M. (1978) *Children's minds*, London: Fontana Books.

References

BORKE, H. (1971) 'Interpersonal perception of young children', *Developmental Psychology*, vol. 5, no. 2, pp. 263–9.

BRUNER, J. (1972) 'The nature and uses of immaturity', *American Psychologist*, vol. 27, no. 8, pp. 687–708.

BRUNER, J. (1975) 'The ontogenesis of speech acts', *Journal of Child Language*, vol. 2, pp. 1–19.

CHANDLER, M.J. (1977) 'Social cognition: a selective review of current research', in Overton, W. and McCarthy Gallagher, T. (eds) *Knowledge and development*, vol. 1, *Advances in research and theory*, New York and London: Plenum Press.

COX, M.V. (1980) 'Visual perspective-taking in children', in Cox, M.V. (ed.) *Are young children egocentric?* London: Batsford.

DARWIN, C. (1877) 'A biographical sketch of an infant', *Mind*, vol. 11, pp. 286–94, in Kessen, W. (1965) *The child*, New York: Wiley, pp. 118–29.

DEVRIES, R. (1970) 'The development of role-taking as reflected by the behavior of bright, average and retarded children in a social guessing game', *Child Development*, vol. 41, pp. 759–70.

DONALDSON, M. (1978) *Children's minds*, London: Fontana/Collins.

EDWARDS, D. and MERCER, N. (1987) *Common knowledge: the development of understanding in the classroom*, London: Methuen.

FLAVELL, J. (1968) *The development of role-taking and communication*, New York: Wiley.

HALL, G.S. (1907) *Aspects of child life and education*, New York: Appleton.

KRAUSS, R.M. and GLUCKSBERG, S. (1969) 'The development of communication: competence as a function of age', *Child Development*, vol. 40, pp. 255–66.

LIGHT, P.H. (1979) *The development of social sensitivity*, Cambridge, Cambridge University Press.

LIGHT, P.H., BUCKINGHAM, N. and ROBBINS, H. (1979) 'The conservation task as an interactional setting', *British Journal of Educational Psychology*, vol. 49, part 3, pp. 304–10.

MARATSOS, M. (1973) 'Nonegocentric communication in preschool children', *Child Development*, vol. 44, pp. 697–700.

PERNER, J., GRUBER, S. and WIMMER, H. (1985) 'Young children's conception of lying', *Cahiers de Psychologie Cognitive*, vol. 5, pp. 359–60.

PIAGET, J. (1932) *The moral judgement of the child*, translated by M. Gabain, London: Routledge and Kegan Paul.

PIAGET, J. (1955) *The child's construction of reality*, translated by M. Cook, London: Routledge and Kegan Paul. (First published in 1936.)

PIAGET, J. (1959) *The language and thought of the child*, translated by M. Gabain and R. Gabain, London: Routledge and Kegan Paul. (First published in 1923).

PIAGET, J. (1962) 'The stages of intellectual development of the child', *Bulletin of the Menninger Clinic*, vol. 26, pp. 120–8. Also reproduced in Munsinger, H. (ed.) (1975) *Readings in child development*, 2nd edn, New York: Holt, Rinehart and Winston, pp. 124–30.

PIAGET, J. (1973) *The child's conception of the world*, translated by J. Tomlinson and A. Tomlinson, London: Paladin.

PIAGET, J. and INHELDER, B. (1956) *The child's conception of space*, translated by F. J. Langdon and J. L. Lundzer, London: Routledge and Kegan Paul.

RIPPLE, R. and ROCKASTLE, V. (1964) *Piaget rediscovered*, Ithaca, NY: Cornell University.

ROBINSON, E. and ROBINSON, W. (1976) 'The young child's understanding of communication', *Developmental Psychology*, vol. 12, no. 4, pp. 328–33.

SHATZ, M. and GELMAN, R. (1973) 'The development of communication skills: modifications in the speech of young children as a function of listener', *Monographs of the Society for Research in Child Development*, vol. 38, no. 5.

VYGOTSKY, L.S. (1962) *Thought and language*, 2nd edn, Cambridge, MA: MIT Press. (First published in 1934.)

WOOD, D. and MIDDLETON, D. (1975) 'A study of assisted problem solving', *British Journal of Psychology*, vol. 66, no.2, pp. 181–91.

Answers to SAQs

SAQ 1

Basically, Piaget interpreted Jacqueline's behaviour as showing that her picture of the world was of objects that are basically *impermanent*. In other words, that once an object is not visible, it effectively has disappeared totally from existence. She seems unable to realize that an object is still there, even if not visible, and that it can be retrieved. Jacqueline was not unusual in this respect: it is common to see similar behaviour in other babies.

SAQ 2

(a) This statement is a fairly *strong* and clear use of the word stage to suggest that this baby is in a developmental period when a particular behaviour, in this case babbling, is dominant. It also probably suggests that this is a progression from the stage of uttering single sounds and that these are now *combined*. So in this sense, the previous stage may be seen as a *necessary* precursor, and babbling itself may be seen as a necessary precursor of the next stage. It is also implied that this stage is only gone through once: in other words, that there is some sort of underlying fixed sequence.

(b) This is a very different sort of statement: although it is talking about a dominant behaviour, negativity, it is unlikely that any of the further assumptions we drew out from the first statement are true here. Presumably children can 'go through a negative stage' any number of times: so there is not necessarily any underlying sequence, nor are there necessarily any implied precursor or successive stages. In terms of the discussion in Box D, this is a *weak* version.

SAQ 3

One of the rows of counters can be spread out, or placed closer together, so that the two rows are then of unequal length, but still each having the same number of counters, as shown in Figure 3.8.

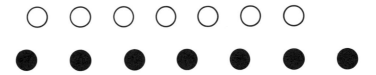

Figure 3.8 A transformed display in the conservation of numbers task

The child would then be asked whether one line of counters has more than the other, or the same, or less. When the child has answered, he or she would be asked to give reasons for his or her reply.

A 'conserving' response would be for the child to say that there is still the same number of counters in each row, and to explain this reply by saying 'none were added or taken away', or something similar.

A 'non-conserving' response would be for the child to say that there is no longer the same number of counters in each row and that one has more, or less, depending on the child's perception. The child will explain this change by saying 'because it's a longer (or shorter) row', or something similar.

SAQ 4

Direct observation of children in playgroups or similar situations would be one approach. In some ways this observation of naturally occurring instances seems the most valid approach, but we then have to rely to a large extent on chance to produce those occasions on which the children will show the kind of behaviour we are interested in.

Rich experimental situations could perhaps be produced by play-acting with children, encouraging them to play out roles and then judging how they and others involved would be feeling. This could build on young children's enthusiasm for pretend play, perhaps involving some favourite doll or soft toy.

As an alternative to the 'comic-strip' type of picture story used by Chandler (1977), one could perhaps use video sequences more akin to the cartoons which are such a familiar diet to young children these days. These would offer the possibility of a well-controlled, standard presentation but at the same time allow the children really to engage with the characters.

SAQ 5

Piaget's theory can be described as individualistic in at least two senses: (a) because he concentrated on describing the development of thinking and reasoning in the individual child, rather than on social aspects of development; and (b) because he treated these two domains as independent (parallel) aspects of development, thus implying that social processes play little or no part in the intellectual development of the individual.

4

PSYCHODYNAMICS: THE FREUDIAN APPROACH

Kerry Thomas

Contents

1	**An introduction to Freud's work**	**132**
2	**Basic assumptions of the psychodynamic approach**	**135**
2.1	Psychological determinism	135
2.2	The role of the unconscious	136
2.3	Goal-directed dynamics	137
2.4	Developmental approach	137
	Summary of Section 2	138
3	**Freud's model of the mind**	**138**
3.1	The topographical model: conscious, preconscious and unconscious	138
3.2	The psychical apparatus: id, ego and super-ego	139
3.3	The dynamics of personality: energy, conflict and anxiety	143
	Summary of Section 3	145
4	**Freud's developmental model: psychosexual stages**	**146**
4.1	Instincts and sexuality	146
4.2	Stages of psychosexual development	148
4.3	Childhood sexuality and personality development	149
4.4	The phallic stage and the Oedipus complex	152
	Summary of Section 4	157
5	**Psychoanalytic therapy**	**157**
5.1	Free association	160
5.2	Dream interpretation	163
5.3	The relationship between psychoanalyst and patient	166
	Summary of Section 5	170
6	**Evaluating psychodynamics**	**170**
6.1	The psychodynamic approach as science	171
6.2	Perhaps not traditional science, but scientific	173
6.3	Psychotherapy as a justification	175
	Summary of Section 6	178
	Personal acknowledgement	179
	Further reading	179
	References	181
	Answers to SAQs	183

1 | An introduction to Freud's work

Sigmund Freud is probably the most famous of all psychologists. His work
has had an important influence on the development of psychology and,
perhaps, an even more fundamental impact on western culture. Now, towards
the end of the twentieth century, few of us are aware on a daily basis of the
extent to which his ideas have been incorporated into the way ordinary
people think about motivation, personality and sexuality. His ideas, and
developments of them by other people, have influenced our conception of
morality, family life and childhood and thus perhaps the structure of our
society; and they have changed our attitudes to mental illness. Freudian
assumptions are now part of the fabric of literature and the arts. It is not the
function of this chapter to dissect these kinds of influences, but you should
remember that we no longer experience or live our lives in quite the same
way as people did before Freud, and that this is true whether you are a
psychologist or any other member of western humanity.

Freud's impact on the way we each live our everyday lives has been
dramatically summarized by Sherry Turkle, an American sociologist and
author of *Psychoanalytic politics* (1979). She has argued that Freud is
subversive. By this she means that his ideas have overturned the ways in
which we used to think of ourselves and our worlds, and that this new
approach potentially undermines our sense of security and order:

Freud is subversive and psychoanalysis delivers a subversive message in so far as it
calls into question what each of us . . . have as our commonsense understanding of
what it is like to spend a day in the world. That is to say, that we are centred actors,
we make our decisions, we're out there as kind of autonomous acting egos. That things
are as they seem, and that we can know reality. And most people, even in the 20th
century, post-Freud, have these sort of reassuring rules of realism as their way of
getting around their day. And Freud says, 'You can't do that. Wait a minute, that's not
true. Those three things are not true. You're not an autonomous actor, things are not as
they seem, and you really can never fully know the reality' . . . other philosophies,
other philosophers have delivered this message. And the difference it seems to me
about psychoanalysis is that it is a philosophy in everyday life. You have to confront it
when you confront the slip, when you confront your dream, when you confront these
very tangible pieces of the everyday that Freud casts into shadow and exhorts you to
use as windows onto this other reality.

(Turkle, 1987, p. 75)

This then is our starting point: the possibility that Freud's ideas about the
human mind can completely overturn our view of ourselves and of our worlds
by encouraging us to think about the *unthinkable*. By 'unthinkable' I mean
both those things that seem to be inaccessible and the things we find too
painful to think about. In one of his earliest books, *The psychopathology of
everyday life* (1901), Freud described many instances of how and when the
unthinkable (in both senses of the word) affects what healthy people do and
say in the course of ordinary life; some examples of these are given in Extracts
A to D. In colloquial English, these examples are called 'Freudian slips', but
Freud's translators gave them the invented Greek name **parapraxes**. Although
Freud has the reputation of being an extremely good writer, there has recently

been some controversy about certain aspects of the translation in the Standard Edition (SE) of his collected works (Strachey, 1953–66). It is undoubtedly difficult to convey in English the full meaning of some of his original German terms, so it is important to assess Freud's ideas carefully when reading his work (see Bettelheim, 1983).

EXTRACT A Mistakes

Here is an error of one of my patients: the fact that it was repeated in order to express a contrary meaning makes it particularly instructive. After protracted internal struggles this over-cautious young man brought himself to the point of proposing marriage to the girl who had long been in love with him, as he was with her. He escorted his *fiancée* home, said goodbye to her, and, in a mood of the greatest happiness, got on to a tram and asked the conductress for *two* tickets. About six months later he had got himself married but could not yet adjust himself to his conjugal bliss, he wondered whether he had done the right thing in marrying, missed his former relations with his friends, and had every sort of fault to find with his parents-in-law. One evening he fetched his young wife from her parents' house, got on to a tram with her and contented himself with asking for one ticket only.

(Freud, 1901, *The psychopathology of everyday life*, example added in 1919; SE 6, pp. 225–6)

EXTRACT B Slips of the tongue

Occasionally a slip of the tongue takes the place of a detailed characterization. A young woman who wore the breeches in her home told me that her sick husband had been to the doctor to ask what diet he ought to follow for his health. The doctor, however, had said that a special diet was not important. She added 'He can eat and drink what *I* want'.

(Freud, 1901, *The psychopathology of everyday life*, example added in 1910; SE 6, p. 70)

EXTRACT C Forgetting

I set store by high-quality blotting paper (*Löschpapier*) and I decided one day to buy a fresh supply that afternoon in the course of my walk to the Inner Town (the old, central part of Vienna). But I forgot for four days running, till I asked myself what reason I had for the omission. It was easy to find after I had recalled that though I normally *write* '*Löschpapier*' I usually *say* '*Fliesspapier*' (another word for 'blotting paper'). 'Fliess' is the name of a friend in Berlin who had on the days in question given me occasion for a worrying and anxious thought. I could not rid myself of this thought, but the defensive tendency . . . manifested itself by transferring itself, by means of the verbal similarity, to the indifferent intention [buying blotting paper] which on account of its indifference offered little resistance.

(Freud, 1901, *The psychopathology of everyday life*; SE 6, p. 159)

EXTRACT D Misplacing or losing things

A youngish man told me the following story: 'Some years ago there were misunderstandings between me and my wife. I found her too cold, and although I willingly recognized her excellent qualities we lived together without any tender feelings. One day, returning from a walk, she gave me a book which she had bought because she thought it would interest me. I thanked her for this mark of "attention", promised to read the book and put it on one side. After that I could never find it again. Months passed by, in which I occasionally remembered the lost book and made vain attempts to find it. About six months later my dear mother, who was not living with us, fell ill. My wife left home to nurse her mother-in-law. The patient's condition became serious and gave my wife an opportunity of showing the best side of herself. One evening I returned home full of enthusiasm and gratitude for what my wife had accomplished. I walked up to my desk, and without any definite intention but with a kind of somnambulistic certainty opened one of the drawers. On the very top I found the long-lost book I had mislaid.' With the extinction of the motive the mislaying of the object ceased as well.

(Freud, 1917a, *Introductory lectures on psycho-analysis*; SE 15, p. 55)

Freud used the examples of parapraxes, like those given in Extracts A to D, to illustrate how conflicts, wishes and trains of thought, of which one is not aware, can influence behaviour. The blotting-paper incident shows how, in trying to forget something painful, another topic which is the same phonetically is forgotten instead; and the lost book reveals unacceptable feelings of anger and being neglected. Freud made use of parapraxes to illustrate the workings of the mind in healthy and in neurotic people and they provide good examples of three of the basic assumptions of psychodynamics:

1   that nothing we do is accidental—psychological determinism;

2   that the unconscious has an important role in our behaviour; and

3   that the unconscious can produce effects in opposition to conscious will—goal-directed dynamics.

Before discussing these assumptions further, it will be helpful if we define some even more basic terms and ideas.

The term '**psychodynamics**' is used to denote the general approach which began with Freud, based on the idea that a large part of the human mind is unconscious and that the contents of the unconscious (the unthinkable) are the source of a great deal of our motivation. Wherever the word **dynamic** is used, it implies drive, force or motivation. Since Freud's time, psychodynamics has broadened into a more diverse collection of theories and clinical approaches, which nevertheless retain the basic idea of the dynamic unconscious. **Psychoanalysis** refers both to Freud's original attempt at providing a comprehensive theory of the mind, and also to the associated therapy. Thus the term encompasses both Freudian theory and Freudian therapy.

ACTIVITY 1

During the time you are working on this chapter note down any 'errors' and 'slips of the tongue and pen' that you (or your friends) make, and see if you can understand what might have been going on at a less conscious level.

All psychologists acknowledge the importance of processes that are not directly available to introspection and are thus, in some sense, 'not conscious'. You will find that people's 'errors' are sometimes studied in psychological experiments and in surveys of everyday mistakes as part of the scientific effort to understand psychological processes, without using the Freudian idea of a *dynamic* unconscious. The implication is that it may be possible to explain some, perhaps all, 'Freudian' errors in terms of quite different psychological models. For example, forgetting or losing objects may occur because of failures of attention or interference from other thoughts or activities.

2 | Basic assumptions of the psychodynamic approach

There are a number of fundamental tenets which are common to all the different schools of psychodynamics and which were the basis of Freud's original theory of psychoanalysis.

2.1 Psychological determinism

According to Freud's principle of **psychological determinism**, no aspect of human behaviour is accidental, although the 'no' in this phrase is probably too strong a word for most psychoanalysts today.

This does not mean that Freud denied the existence of events which are accidental, that is, events which are brought about by objects and forces outside the control of the individual who experiences them. If you are involved in a car accident, it may not be the direct result of your own behaviour but may be due to the other driver or the condition of the road. On the other hand, if you are frequently involved in motor accidents, then there might be a case for arguing that psychological factors are playing a part. Freud argues that most instances of so-called accidental behaviour have psychological determinants which can be identified.

When one thinks about determinism, it is common to think about one cause followed by one effect, as when a snooker cue hits a snooker ball and causes it to move across the table. Freud's conception of psychological determinism, however, does not state that each aspect of behaviour has a *single* cause. On the contrary, Freud believed in the principle of **overdetermination**, or multiple determination. According to this view, every psychic event is determined by the *simultaneous* action of several, different causes. For example, if I forget an appointment with a friend, this could be understood in terms of feelings (conscious and unconscious) about the friend, *and* about the holiday we were to plan at our meeting, *and* about the job I would have been neglecting if I had kept the appointment, and so on. Another example can be seen in dreams. These often seem to have a 'density' of meanings which can be unpacked and which represent the fusion of a number of different wishes and feelings with the content of one's ordinary waking life. Freud believed that it is possible to analyse not just the cause of a behaviour but the 'layers' of multiple causes and their multiple effects on that behaviour.

2.2 The role of the unconscious

This principle states that the unconscious mind plays a fundamental part in determining a person's behaviour.

Freud's most significant contribution to the study of human behaviour is his introduction of the crucial new concept of the **dynamic unconscious**. Freud did not discover the unconscious. In western culture and in modern times, this discovery is usually credited to the psychologist Adolf Meyer, in 1886. Also, other psychologists, notably William James and Johann Friedrich Herbart, had been emphasizing the role of the unconscious in mental life many years before Freud started his research, and it is likely that Freud studied these theories when he was a medical student. Freud's great contribution was to develop the idea that it is the unconscious, rather than that of which we are conscious and upon which we can exert our will, which is the fundamental source of all motivation.

Freud's psychological predecessors had thought of the unconscious as a passive 'storage cellar' for ideas and memories which are no longer important to the individual and thus drift out of conscious awareness. But Freud's view of the unconscious differed radically in that he believed the unconscious itself to be a dynamic force. This immediately raises the possibility of conflict between the contents of a rational conscious mind and the unknown contents and unpredictable effects of the unconscious with its unrecognized and largely uncontrollable sources of energy.

Conflict is the cornerstone of Freud's work, and more often than not, this is **unconscious conflict**. It is unrecognized for what it is and likely to be revealed indirectly as 'accidents', as disturbing emotional states, as destructiveness and all manner of unpleasant symptoms. It may also be revealed in dreams, which are often disguised representations of unconscious conflict. Unlike his predecessors, Freud believed that the material in the unconscious is mostly disturbing in nature and requires the expenditure of mental energy to prevent it from forcing its way into consciousness.

2.3 Goal-directed dynamics

This principle asserts that all behaviour is motivated *and* goal-directed. This proposition may seem obvious: how can any aspect of behaviour have no motivation or goal? But take the example of apathy. How can apathy be conceived of as goal-directed? For Freud, it is one of the ways in which a person defends certain aspects of the personality against disturbing thoughts or emotions by showing little interest in anything which might prove threatening.

One way or another, the idea that behaviour is goal-directed is common to most approaches within psychology. But this idea has been enhanced by Freud's psychoanalytic technique of looking for the goal underlying a person's behaviour; Freud looked for the function (or goal) that parapraxes, maladaptive behaviours and distressing symptoms serve in the context of the person's situation and personality. Although the idea of purposeful behaviour is not unique to the psychodynamic approach, the goal-directed nature of the unconscious and its role in determining behaviour is an original Freudian concept.

SAQ 1 (*SAQ answers are given at the end of the chapter*) Try to write out short (one sentence) definitions of the following terms:
  (a) psychodynamics
  (b) psychological determinism
  (c) overdetermination
  (d) dynamic unconscious
  (e) goal-directed dynamics

2.4 Developmental approach

Underlying Freud's approach is the idea that adult behaviour derives from the experience of the growing child. Freud placed great emphasis on the power of instinctual needs or drives such as hunger, thirst, and sex as the primary sources of motivation. But he did not believe that the development of a person is totally governed by instinctual and biological factors. He saw that the social environment, which places strict constraints on the gratification of instincts, crucially modifies and mediates the instincts and drives of the growing child. According to Freud, it is the conflict generated between instinct-based drives and the demands of society (ranging from the style of child rearing in the family right through to cultural norms and values) which is the basis of personality development *and* the origin of much mental illness. For this reason, it is essential to look at the developmental growth of an individual's personality in attempting to explain his or her present behaviour.

One of the most influential avenues of Freud's research focused on the question of how the personality of an individual develops, and so the psychodynamic approach places great significance on the resolution of conflicts which initially arise during the first five years of life. Since Freud, many psychologists of different kinds have also stressed the importance of the first five years of life (for example, Piaget whose work was described in Chapter 3), but the psychodynamic movement was the first psychological discipline to give such an emphasis to the early period of life.

Summary of Section 2

The basic tenets of psychodynamic theories are:

- *Psychological determinism*: no behaviour is accidental.

- *The crucial importance of the unconscious*: a large part of the mind is not directly accessible to consciousness, and the unconscious is the source of motivation.

- *Goal-directed motivation*: all behaviour is motivated and goal-directed. Much of our behaviour is directed towards goals of which we are not conscious. These goals may be in opposition to our conscious intentions.

- *Developmental approach*: in psychodynamics, the first five years of life are seen as the source of experiences and conflicts which are crucial to the development of personality.

3 | Freud's model of the mind

Freud developed a general theory of human nature and psychology based on his clinical work with individual patients and his observation of everyday behaviour. His model of the mind is a complex system of interrelated concepts and theories which need to be mapped on to one another to provide a view of the causes which determine human behaviour.

3.1 The topographical model: conscious, preconscious and unconscious

According to Freud, the **psyche** (the mind) has three different qualities or levels: the conscious, preconscious and unconscious. He describes these levels in his **topographical model** of the mind.

What did Freud mean when he spoke about the unconscious, preconscious and conscious levels of the psyche? In *An outline of psycho-analysis* (1940), he starts from the *fact* of consciousness. No one can deny that we are *aware of* some parts of our mental life; this is the **conscious** level. Introspection makes it clear that a perception, thought, or memory may be conscious at one moment and 'gone' the next. Freud argues that these gaps in our conscious awareness make it necessary to have a concept such as the unconscious. But *within* the unconscious he makes three important distinctions. Some processes and contents of the unconscious can become conscious easily—we can recall some memories without hesitation, and we can develop *trains of thought* starting from a single conscious thought. According to Freud, this material is in the **preconscious**. The contents of the preconscious are 'not conscious' but they can easily become so. Second, in the **unconscious** proper there is material which can 'through our efforts, be made conscious, and in the process we may have a feeling that we are often overcoming very strong resistances' (Freud, 1940, p. 160). And, third, there is a great deal else in the unconscious which can probably never become available to consciousness.

Freud's view of the unconscious was essentially *negative*. He believed that the contents of the unconscious are neither conscious nor easily available to consciousness for good reason—they have been repressed well out of reach of our awareness because they are painful or in some sense dangerous. In Freud's model of the mind the unconscious is dynamic. It contains memories, perceptions, fantasies, impulses and conflicts which must be 'pushed back' or repressed in order to make life in the real world less conflictful, less threatening and less painful. For the most part, this defensive strategy is a healthy process of adaptation to the environment and social pressure, and it is relatively uncostly to the individual. But Freud believed that for some people the process of developing defence mechanisms leads to neurotic disorders which can be relieved by bringing repressed painful memories and conflicts back into consciousness during psychoanalysis.

3.2 The psychical apparatus: id, ego and super-ego

In addition to the levels of the topographical model, Freud elaborated his model of the mind as a psychological apparatus consisting of three structures: the id, ego and super-ego. He believed that human behaviour is determined through the *interaction* of these three parts, which can therefore also be thought of as the structural components of personality. Freud's own diagram of his model of the mind was rather 'brain-shaped', but it is important to remember that the levels of the mind and the id, ego and super-ego do *not* correspond to any anatomical structures within the brain. Rather, they are abstract concepts which derive their meaning from within the psychoanalytic explanation of behaviour; see Figure 4.1.

The **id** is the instinctual force of behaviour, driving all behaviour in the direction of immediate gratification of the individual's biological needs, the instinctual drives of hunger, thirst, sex, and so on.

The **ego** maintains the individual as a whole, whilst at the same time adapting to external reality. It learns to compromise between the outside world, the id instincts and the demands of the super-ego. The functions of the ego are always directed towards *external reality* and so include most of the functions

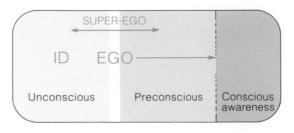

Figure 4.1 Diagram of the relations between id, ego and super-ego and levels of consciousness
(Source: adapted from Freud, 1933)

discussed later in this book—memory, perception, learning, motor skills and action.

The **super-ego** represents the internalization of demands normally generated outside the individual by his or her culture or society (as opposed to the id which is made up of demands generated within individuals). These demands are initially communicated to the child through the dictates and parenting styles of the family, and they give rise to the **ego ideal** (the child's concept of the behaviour of which his parents' will approve) and the **conscience** (the child's conception of the behaviour his parents will condemn as morally bad). It is as if the parents were *inside* the child's head waiting to challenge and judge his or her behaviour whenever id impulses arise which do not conform to the norms of society. Freud's theory thus places great emphasis on the influence of parental attitudes in the formation of the child's personality.

As Figure 4.1 shows, Freud elaborated his ideas of the id, ego and super-ego *in relation to* the levels of the mind he had already formulated. While the overall function of the ego is to enable the individual to adapt and, where necessary, repress instinctual drives so as to be able to live comfortably in the external and socially constraining world, its activities are not necessarily conscious, or even preconscious. Freud discovered, through the process of psychoanalysis, that patients are by no means always conscious of the tactics (the defence mechanisms) the ego employs to ward off forbidden impulses and anxiety-producing thoughts. The psychoanalyst may observe changes in the patient's behaviour or in the flow of what he or she is saying, but the patient may be completely unaware of why this is happening. Freud concluded that some of the functions of the ego must be unconscious. He also found that some of the demands of the super-ego operate at an unconscious level. So, as Figure 4.1 shows, the ego and super-ego span all three levels of consciousness. The id, in contrast, is entirely unconscious. Some of Freud's own descriptions of the qualities and functions of the three structures and their levels of consciousness are given in Extracts E to G.

EXTRACT E The id

It is the dark, inaccessible part of our personality; what little we know of it we have learnt from our study of the dream-work and of the construction of neurotic symptoms, and most of that is of a negative character and can be described only as a contrast to the ego. We approach the id with analogies: we call it a chaos, a cauldron full of seething excitations. . . . It is filled with energy reaching it from the instincts, but it has no organization, produces no collective will, but only a striving to bring about the satisfaction of instinctual needs subject to the observance of the pleasure principle. The logical laws of thought do not apply in the id, and this is true above all of the law of contradiction. Contrary impulses exist side by side, without cancelling each other out . . . there is no recognition of the passage of time, and—a thing that is most remarkable and awaits consideration in philosophical thought—no alteration in its mental processes is produced by the passage of time. Wishful impulses which have never passed beyond the id, but impressions, too, which have been sunk into the id by repression, are virtually immortal; after the passage of decades they behave as though they had just occurred.

(Freud, 1933, *New introductory lectures on psycho-analysis*; SE 22, pp. 73–4)

It contains everything that is inherited, that is present at birth, that is laid down in the constitution—above all, therefore, the instincts, which originate from the somatic [relating to the body] organization and which find a first psychical expression here (in the id) in forms unknown to us.

(Freud, 1940, *An outline of psycho-analysis*; SE 23, p. 145)

EXTRACT F The ego

[T]he ego seeks to bring the influence of the external world to bear upon the id and its tendencies, and endeavours to substitute the reality principle for the pleasure principle which reigns unrestrictedly in the id. For the ego, perception plays the part which in the id falls to instinct. The ego represents what may be called reason and common sense, in contrast to the id, which contains the passions. All this falls into line with popular distinctions which we are all familiar with; at the same time, however, it is only to be regarded as holding good on the average or 'ideally' . . .

Thus in relation to the id it is like a man on horseback, who has to hold in check the superior strength of the horse; with this difference, that the rider tries to do so with his own strength while the ego uses borrowed forces. The analogy may be carried a little further. Often a rider, if he is not to be parted from his horse, is obliged to guide it where it wants to go; so in the same way the ego is in the habit of transforming the id's will into action as if it were its own.

(Freud, 1923, *The ego and the id*; SE 19, p. 25)

[The ego] has the task of self-preservation. As regards *external* events it performs that task by becoming aware of stimuli, by storing up experiences about them (in the memory), by avoiding excessively strong stimuli (through flight), by dealing with moderate stimuli (through adaptation) and finally by learning to bring about expedient changes in the external world to its own advantage (through activity). As regards *internal* events, in relation to the id, it performs that task by gaining control over the demands of the instincts, by deciding whether they are to be allowed satisfaction, by postponing that satisfaction to times and circumstances favourable in the external world or by suppressing their excitations entirely. It is guided in its activity by consideration of the tensions produced by stimuli. The raising of these tensions is in general felt as *unpleasure* and their lowering as *pleasure*. . . . An increase in unpleasure that is expected and foreseen is met by a *signal of anxiety*; the occasion of such an increase, whether it threatens from without or within, is known as a *danger*. From time to time the ego gives up its connection with the external world and withdraws into the state of sleep, in which it makes far-reaching changes in its organization.

(Freud, 1940, *An outline of psycho-analysis*; SE 23, pp. 145–6)

EXTRACT G   The super-ego

The long period of childhood, during which the growing human being lives in dependence on his parents, leaves behind it as a precipitate the formation in his ego of a special agency in which this parental influence is prolonged. It has received the name of *super-ego*. In so far as this super-ego is differentiated from the ego or is opposed to it, it constitutes a third power which the ego must take into account. . . .

The details of the relation between the ego and the super-ego become completely intelligible when they are traced back to the child's attitude to its parents. This parental influence of course includes in its operation not only the personalities of the actual parents but also the family, racial and national traditions handed on through them, as well as the demands of the immediate social *milieu* which they represent. In the same way, the super-ego, in the course of an individual's development, receives contributions from later successors and substitutes of his parents, such as teachers and models in public life of admired social ideals. It will be observed that, for all their fundamental difference, the id and the super-ego have one thing in common: they both represent the influences of the past—the id the influence of heredity, the super-ego the influence, essentially, of what is taken over from other people—whereas the ego is principally determined by the individual's own experience, that is by accidental and contemporary events.

(Freud, 1940, *An outline of psycho-analysis*; SE 23, pp. 146–7)

SAQ 2   Using words rather than a diagram, explain briefly how the levels of the topographical model (unconscious, preconscious, conscious) map on to the structures, id, ego and super-ego.

3.3 The dynamics of personality: energy, conflict and anxiety

Freud believed that the dynamics of personality are based on conflict. The id, ego and super-ego interact with external circumstances in such a way as to be in continual conflict, and this conflict has to be resolved by the ego. This is true at any particular moment—in a snapshot view of the personality—*and* it is true over time—in a developmental view of how a person learns to resolve the conflict from infancy onwards. People's moment-to-moment behaviour and their long-term personalities (in the sense of consistent patterns of behaviour over time) depend on having an ego strong enough to resolve past and present conflicts and on the particular mechanisms that the ego habitually uses to achieve the resolution.

In Freud's theory, all conflict is initially fuelled by instinctual needs originating in the id, illustrated in Extract F by the metaphor of the rider (the ego) using the energy of his horse. Freud called this instinct-based energy the **libido**. Using a further metaphor, which he called the **economic view**, he likened the distribution and movement of the libido in the psyche to the investment and movement of capital in an economic system. Thus, libido associated with conflicting impulses or ideas could, in the service of resolving a conflict, be withdrawn, moved (displaced) and reinvested in other behaviours or ideas. Freud believed that no description of the psychic state is complete until it is assessed in the semi-quantitative terms of the economic view.

In most branches of psychology, questions about motivation—what it is that fuels human action—are problematic and are often ignored. Attempts to describe motivation, whether in psychology or in everyday language, tend to entice one into materialist metaphors about physical systems (mechanical, electrical and hydraulic), or in this case the monetary system. For example, Freud's psychodynamics are often thought of in terms of a **hydraulic model**: pressure building up in one part of the mind and having to be pushed back and controlled by 'dams' which might fail and lead to catastrophic flooding. His own vocabulary was a mixture of physical metaphors and an attempt to talk about psychic energy and its movements around the psyche in terms of economics, value, investment and capital. Freud's translators compounded these difficulties by inventing a Greek-based terminology to replace the original German. It makes sense to us to think of ideas and memories as being *charged with* or *invested with* energy. But the translators invented the verb 'to cathect' instead. If you read Freud, you will need to understand the use of this term. For example, when you are hungry, your id generates a demand for food (i.e. it cathects the need for food) and your ego may respond by cathecting first images of food and then plans for getting food. Thus, images and ideas about food are invested with libido. **Cathexis** is the quantity of energy attached to an idea—rather like a quantity of electric charge. It can be moved from one idea to another, perhaps as a diversionary tactic. If there is no food available, in order to reduce unpleasant feelings of hunger, your ego might withdraw libido from food images (a process of decathexis) and, in its place, cathect the idea of going out jogging. This would be a displacement of libido which would defend the ego by warding off tension.

Freud's theory is called an **instinct theory** because instinctual needs in the id are the fundamental source of psychic energy, that is libido. And his version of psychodynamics is an **ego psychology** because the health and well-being of the individual depends on the strength of the ego and its ability to harness instinctual energy to subdue or to compromise with the demands of the id, the super-ego and external reality.

The id is always governed by the **pleasure principle** and makes demands on the ego for the satisfaction of its instinctual needs. The term 'pleasure principle' is shorthand for a tendency on the part of the id to keep instinctual tension at an optimal level by avoiding pain and seeking pleasure. The ego has somehow to modify these demands within the restrictions imposed on it by the super-ego. At the same time, the ego has to consider the id's demands in terms of the possibilities presented by external reality, thereby functioning in accordance with the **reality principle**. According to the classical Freudian view, the ego gradually gains strength in infancy and childhood, and so the reality principle is achieved slowly in the course of development. In contrast, the pleasure principle is innate and leads to the gratification of instinctual demands through wish-fulfilling fantasies, *with no recourse to reality*.

One of the results of conflict between the ego, id and super-ego and external reality is the experience of **anxiety**. This experience is centred within the ego and it is the ego's job to reduce or remove the anxiety by one means or another, thus making life more bearable. Sometimes anxiety is a signal of an **external danger**. The ego deals with this **objective anxiety** by avoidance or some other realistic action in the outside world. But psychodynamics makes it plain that by no means all danger resides in the outside world. Much anxiety is a signal (which we experience consciously) of **internal danger** which more often than not remains unconscious. This internal danger resides in childhood memories of painful events (**trauma**), fantasies associated with id impulses and frustrations, and the fear of a punishing super-ego. When these memories and fantasies are awakened by thinking or remembering, or when they are echoed (perhaps unconsciously) by evocative events in later life, what is experienced is the threat of repetition of the original (now unconscious) traumatic moment or the original (now unconscious) conflict.

Internal danger, like external danger, is signalled by anxiety which can sometimes be overwhelming. Since the danger is internal, it cannot be avoided by 'fight or flight' or any realistic action in the outside world. It can only be warded off, that is, prevented from reaching consciousness or removed from consciousness by one or more of the ego **defence mechanisms**. In Freud's terminology, **neurotic anxiety** is associated with danger originating in instinctual impulses, and **moral anxiety** with the condemnations of the super-ego. The ego defence mechanism that has been most central to psychodynamic theory is **repression**. This prevents the substance of the internal danger from reaching consciousness—all anxiety-arousing memories of earlier dangers are shut out of awareness and kept locked away in the unconscious. And, by warding off the danger, anxiety is reduced or removed.

Ego defences are usually unconscious. They are not necessarily unhealthy; indeed they are an important process within a normally functioning personality. Although they may prove inadequate in the long term, these defences provide the ego with a means of short-term control over inner conflicts and anxiety. If defence mechanisms are unconscious, how is it possible to know what they are? In psychodynamics, they can be known through the process of psychoanalysis. Psychoanalysis is, in part, directed at understanding a person's defence mechanisms and reaching a point at which the patient can 'see' and accept the analyst's interpretation of the defence and 'own' the painful or disturbing 'material' that is being warded off.

Freud's psychodynamic theory is primarily concerned with the conflicts, defences and symptoms which originate in the id impulses of *infantile and childhood sexuality*. This raises the question of the relation between psychic energy in general—the libido—and sexuality. In the next section we discuss this together with Freud's view of how children develop through a series of psychosexual stages.

Summary of Section 3

- According to Freud's topographical model the psyche has three different qualities or levels: conscious, preconscious, and unconscious. The contents of the preconscious are not conscious but can easily become so. In the unconscious, there is material which is not conscious but which can, with difficulty, become so. There is also material which is unlikely ever to reach consciousness.

- Freud described the mind as made up of three non-anatomical structures: the id, ego and super-ego. The id contains instincts which are the innate driving forces of behaviour. The super-ego is constructed from the internalized demands made upon a person by culture and society and initially communicated to the child by the words and deeds of parents. It is the source of the child's 'conscience'. The ego maintains the person as a whole in the midst of conflict between id instincts, the dictates of the super-ego and the pressures of external reality.

- Freud's theory is an instinct theory. The instinctual needs of the id are the source of psychic energy called 'libido'.

- Freud's version of psychodynamics is an 'ego psychology' because at its centre is the idea that the health and well-being of the person depends upon the ability of the ego to resolve psychic conflicts generated by interactions between the id, super-ego and reality.

- Freud believed that psychic conflict and the way it is resolved is a crucial part of personality.

- Anxiety is often a conscious signal of unconscious, internal danger which cannot be averted by 'fight or flight'. Instead, ego defence mechanisms such as repression protect the person from this anxiety. These defence mechanisms are usually unconscious.

- According to Freud, most internal danger originates in powerful instinctual impulses, and the conflict between these id impulses and super-ego prohibitions.

4 | Freud's developmental model: psychosexual stages

Freud's entire work is built on the idea that adult behaviour, healthy and unhealthy alike, is driven by instinctual impulses and desires that originate in the id in childhood—for the most part wishes with a sexual content which were prohibited by society and thereafter remain concealed by defence mechanisms. Within the metaphor of the economic view we might say that these childhood wishes, which are always 'alert' in the unconscious, provide the psychic capital which is invested in the ventures of adult life.

A simplistic reading of these ideas would lead us to a common caricature of Freud's work: that it is all about sex and that sex underlies everything we do. As with most caricatures, there is some truth in this. Freud believed that it is the sexual instinct, in a broad sense, that is the source of psychic energy, the libido. He believed that sexual impulses arising in the id are present from the earliest weeks of life and that infants and young children are sexual beings. The centrality of sexuality in life, and the idea that childhood sexuality is a normal feature of development, provoked outrage and disbelief among professionals and the public at large. But Freud was determined not to compromise on these points, nor on his use of the word 'sexual'. He believed that he was confronting his readers' defences about sexuality. However, behind the caricature, in Freud's extensive writing, there is a powerful developmental theory. This theory of psychosexual development is unique in psychology because it attempts to link three areas of development: the unfolding of physical growth, the gradual organization of the instinctual sexual drive *and* the child's increasing attempts to understand and to represent, internally, the *meaning* of his or her behaviour *as a result of* interactions with parents, siblings and peers.

> ACTIVITY 2
>
> As you read the rest of this section, you may find it helpful to make a chronological chart which will allow you to compare Freud's version of child development with the ideas of Mead and his followers (Chapter 2) and Piaget (Chapter 3). List the theorists down the left-hand side of a page and then go back to Chapters 2 and 3 and find the most appropriate time intervals (months at first, perhaps, and then years) to write across the top of the page. Finally, fill in the stages or phases or developmental goals that each theorist discusses under the appropriate age.

4.1 Instincts and sexuality

It is a mistake to think, as many people do, that Freud believed the sex instinct (i.e. the drive to reproduce) is the *only* one humans have. However, it is the instinct on which Freud focused most of his attention and he believed it to be central to human nature. He began his theoretical work with the idea of two basic groups of antagonistic instincts: those concerned with reproduction (sexual instincts) and those concerned with self-preservation (ego instincts). He thought that the conflict between these two instincts was the source of neurosis. Later, however, he came to believe in a more general **life instinct**, which he called **Eros**, made up of sexual, life-preserving and creative drives whose energy source is the libido. In addition to the life instinct, and as a result of his earlier work on the relation between natural mourning processes in bereavement and depressive illness (1917b), Freud came to the conclusion that people also have a fundamental **death instinct (Thanatos)**. The death instinct is an urge to give up the life-struggle and return to quiescence; it includes a death wish and the drive to self-destructive acts. The idea of a death instinct and its relation to aggression has remained controversial and is beyond the scope of this chapter.

As an instinct theory, Freud's work is based on biological concepts. He described all instincts as originating in the physical body (i.e. not in the mind), as having a source of energy, and as having a goal—that is, a piece of consummatory behaviour which reduces tension and/or gives pleasure. When such goals are not achieved, the organism experiences frustration leading to tension or pain, which eventually mobilizes psychological defence mechanisms. Freud believed that, in addition to a bodily source, energy and a goal, instincts require an 'object'—that is, another individual or an environmental agency which helps the person (the subject) to achieve the goal. Thus, for an infant, hunger arises in the body, is energized by the libido, the goal is sucking the nipple and receiving nourishment, and the object is the nursing mother (or the breast itself). For post-pubertal sexuality, the source is genital, the energy is libidinal, the aim is orgasm and the giving and receiving of semen, and the object is the loved-one. By including the need for an object (another person) in his concept of an instinct, Freud opens the door to the influence and impact of the social environment on the human biological organism. This aspect of Freud's work is called **object relations**.

It is important to realize that, in psychodynamics, the use of the term 'object' nearly always refers to another *person* (not a *thing*) with whom the individual is in a significant relationship. Mental representations of objects (people) which have attained significance for a child are called **internal objects** (internal representations of people). The processes by which an infant creates a complex inner world of internal objects, highly charged with emotions, is central to psychodynamic theories.

Freud developed a view of the major instincts as made up of component instincts, that is, innate fragments of behaviour which are combined and organized *during a child's development* to give shape to the full instinct. But it was only for the sexual instinct that he worked out the details of this developmental course. He first wrote about the 'component instincts of the sexual drive' in *Three essays on the theory of sexuality* (1905) at a time when he was already postulating that disturbances of sexuality underlie some forms of mental illness. The evidence came from many of his patients in the course of psychoanalysis. Freud learned that they enjoyed sexual excitements and gratifications that were not directly related to the 'mechanisms' of reproduction. For this reason, he called these activities 'perversions', a word we probably would not want to use today. The important point is: why should such 'perversions'—or, indeed, why should ordinary sexual foreplay which is not directly related to insemination—be exciting and gratifying? Freud concluded: 'This gives us a hint that perhaps the sexual instinct itself is no simple thing, but put together from components which have come apart again in the perversions' (Freud, 1905, p. 162). Freud's theory of psychosexual development was the result of trying to understand how the components of the sexual instinct arise piecemeal in childhood and then become combined in adult sexuality.

4.2 Stages of psychosexual development

According to Freud's theory of psychosexual development, the components of the sexual instinct, each having as its source a part of the body which is capable of giving pleasurable sensations (called **erotogenic zones**), emerge in a *predetermined developmental sequence*. This progression starts with the mouth, then moves to the organs of elimination (the urethra and more importantly the anus), and then to the genitals. Freud specified that before puberty the genital erotogenic zone is essentially phallic, that is, either the penis or the clitoris. This is because he believed that these organs are equivalents, and that females do not experience their vaginas as a source of pleasurable sensations until puberty. At each stage, children focus on the sensations of the relevant bodily zone. These sensations may be satisfying or frustrating and they gain particular psychological significance *in relation* to the people in the child's world who satisfy or frustrate them. The order of these stages is fixed but they can overlap, and as centres of interest and potential gratification they can be returned to in later periods of life.

The **oral stage** is thought to be roughly from birth to 1 year. Here the source of pleasurable sensations is the mouth: the mucous membrane of the lips, the tongue, sucking, and, later, the pleasure of biting. The **anal stage** lasts from 1 to 3 years approximately. This stage centres on the pleasurable sensations experienced in the mucous membranes of the rectum and anus and the feeling of the faecal mass inside the body and as it is released. By this time the child's muscular growth and sphincter control has reached the point where he or she can take pleasure in 'holding' or 'letting go' faeces. The **phallic stage**, from 3 to about 5, centres on the penis in boys and the clitoris in girls and culminates in the emotional crisis called the Oedipus complex (see Section 4.4). There then follows a period of quiescence called the **latency period**. After this, puberty begins and the components of the sexual instinct come together in adult genital sexuality, the **genital stage**. Figure 4.2 shows these stages, together with the development of the ego and super-ego.

To understand the full implications of Freud's theory of development, we need to go beyond this description of psychosexual stages. We need to ask four questions:

* In what sense are the sensations at each stage *sexual*?
* Does the infant or child experience the sensations in isolation or as part of relating to other people?
* What might the pleasures and frustrations experienced at a particular stage *mean* to a child?

- What effect might gratifications or frustrations at each stage have on the child's developing personality?

The importance of Freud's theory of psychosexual stages is that it provides a single framework within which we can ask a wide range of questions which span physical, emotional, cognitive, social, sexual and personality development.

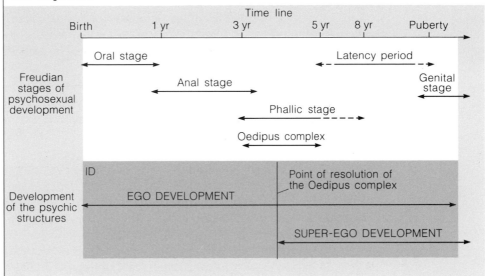

Figure 4.2 Developmental aspects of Freudian theory

4.3 Childhood sexuality and personality development

In what sense are the psychosexual stages sexual?

It has been found that in early childhood there are signs of bodily activity to which only an ancient prejudice could deny the name of sexual and which are linked to psychical phenomena that we come across later in adult erotic life—such as fixation to particular objects, jealousy, and so on. It is further found, however, that these phenomena which emerge in early childhood form part of an ordered course of development, that they pass through a regular process of increase, reaching a climax towards the end of the fifth year, after which there follows a lull. During this lull progress is at a standstill and much is unlearnt and there is much recession. After the end of this period of latency, as it is called, sexual life advances once more with puberty; we might say that it has a second efflorescence. And here we come upon the fact that the onset of sexual life is *diphasic*, that it occurs in two waves—something that is unknown except in man . . .

The first organ to emerge as an erotogenic zone and to make libidinous demands on the mind is, from the time of birth onwards, the mouth. To begin with, all psychical activity is concentrated on providing satisfaction for the needs of that zone. Primarily, of course, this satisfaction serves the purpose of self-preservation by means of nourishment; but physiology should not be confused with psychology. The baby's obstinate persistence in sucking gives evidence at an early stage of the need for satisfaction which, though it originates from and is instigated by the taking of nourishment, nevertheless strives to obtain pleasure independently of nourishment and for that reason may and should be termed *sexual*.

(Freud, 1940, *An outline of psycho-analysis*; SE 23, pp. 153–4)

If you have children or have the opportunity to observe infants and small children, you might like to consider whether Freud's statements about children's sexuality fit with your observations. You may even be able to remember some of your own childhood feelings and sensations, and your 'theories' about sexuality and reproduction. Many of you will have seen a baby nursing at the breast; how would you describe its expression? What kind of pleasure does it remind you of? Of course we cannot claim to *know*, but often it looks like some very intense, almost orgasmic experience. It is not unusual for a toddler to recreate this expression of bliss if given the opportunity to suck a feeding bottle belonging to its infant sibling. And the tantrums and jealousies that can follow a small child's glimpse of its mother breast-feeding a new baby are often far more intense than those we, as 'rational' adults, might expect to be associated with mere nourishment. It is observations like these, together with evidence from psychoanalysis, that convinced Freud, and many others after him, of the existence of childhood sexuality. But we need to clarify two issues.

First, again in Freud's own words: 'It is necessary to distinguish sharply between the concepts of "sexual" and "genital". The former is the wider concept and includes many activities that have nothing to do with the genitals' (1940, p. 152). When Freud uses the word 'sexual' he is referring to sensations, pleasures, satisfactions, excitements, and intense emotions that are *not necessarily* to do with genital sexuality. But this qualification should not be an excuse to downgrade the impact of the word. The sensual, tension-releasing and emotive states that Freud and many other psychodynamic theorists have in mind when they use the word 'sexual' have the same kind of intensity, potential for comforting and for reducing tension, and the same kind of significance in the life of infants and children as the psychological states associated with genital sexuality have for adults.

Freud's theory goes beyond the *biological survival function* of self-contained, autoerotic pleasure associated with the removal of hunger, or the release of discomfort through the elimination of urine or faeces. Instead, Freud is concerned with the *psychology* of how infants and children experience and deal with the pleasures and frustrations of each psychosexual stage *in relation to the people that take care of them*.

Therefore, when Freud uses the word 'sexual', it carries many connotations, often simultaneously: it is an amalgam of biological functions, intense erotic sensation, sensual pleasure, the nature and control of intimate relationships, and the experience and communication of emotion.

What is the role of other people in children's experience at each psychosexual stage?

Newborn infants are thought to have little or no conception of other people as separate beings. If anything, they begin by experiencing other people as extensions of themselves (see Chapter 2, Section 2). But soon they behave as though they are aware that other people are in some sense separate and are involved in providing, or not providing, satisfactions and comfort. Psychoanalysts, in contrast to the developmental psychologists whose work is described in Chapter 2, believe that some sense of self or ego (albeit fragile and fragmentary) begins to emerge at or very near the beginning of life. Many psychoanalysts since Freud (e.g. Mahler and Winnicott who were mentioned in Chapter 2, and Melanie Klein) have been concerned with *object relations*; that is to say, they have centred their work on the developing relation between the infant ego and significant other people, initially the mother. Freud, with his instinct-based theory, was not *so* concerned with object relations, but he did stress that the quality and pattern of gratification or frustration, tolerance or punishment that infants and children meet in the social environment *in response to the impulses and fantasies that are characteristic of each psychosexual stage*, will determine the child's personality and moral development and be the major influence in his or her socialization. It is clear that Freud believed that a child's experience of and with other people in the first five years of life has a crucial and permanent effect on development.

What might the pleasures and frustrations experienced at a particular stage mean to a child?

The importance of other people as the source of the *meanings* of these early experiences of sexuality can be illustrated with the following example. Consider what a 2-year-old boy (or girl) might experience when refusing to use the potty. In *choosing* to keep for himself the pleasurable, autoerotic bodily sensation of retaining his faeces he is, at the same time, controlling his own pleasure and experiencing autonomy. In addition, the erotic pleasure and experience of choice and autonomy is amplified and given further significance by virtue of the *social meaning* of this behaviour. When he refuses to deposit his faeces in the potty, he deprives his mother of what *she* wants; he withholds from her what might be thought of as his 'gift' to her. Thus, with this one act, he is experiencing, and in some important sense combining, pleasurable bodily sensations and what is probably his first opportunity to exercise power and withhold love from his mother, with all the implications that this may have for expressing his feelings toward her.

What might be the effect on personality of gratification or frustration at each stage?

Freud attributed personality traits in normal adults to an interaction between inherited patterns of the sexual instinct, with its progression through the erotogenic zones (in which there are individual differences in overall strength and variations), and the constraints of the social environment. He believed that unresolved conflicts at each stage in infancy and childhood can lead to anxiety and the mobilization of ego defences, and, if the conflicts are excessive, to neurotic illness. Conflict can arise at a psychosexual stage *either* because of too much frustration *or* because of too much gratification. Both situations make it difficult for the infant or child to move on to the next stage. In Freud's theory of development, it is **fixation** at a particular stage (or some degree of fixation) that accounts for patterns of personality traits in adults. Difficulties encountered during a psychosexual stage, or in moving out of one stage to the next, can also cause an adult to return to that stage—to regress— later in life, as a defence against current problems. This process of **regression** is another ego defence mechanism.

An infant weaned too early (or too late) would tend, as an adult, to seek out oral gratification of one kind or another. This might be just overeating or smoking. Or it could be more pronounced, perhaps showing itself in some exaggerated form of sexual behaviour or, it has been suggested, in alcoholism or drug abuse. Since the oral stage includes not only a sucking phase, but biting too, a typical oral character type might be optimistic, generous and talkative, or aggressive, verbally and physically. Adult personality traits associated with each phase can, confusingly, appear in directly opposing forms. For example, fixation at the oral stage can lead to excessive passivity and dependence—as experienced by a baby who is totally provided for. Or, as a defensive reaction against longed-for dependency, oral fixation may lead to the opposite, that is, to exaggeratedly independent traits. This is an example of another defence mechanism called **reaction formation** in which the person unconsciously produces the opposite feelings and behaviours to those that might arouse anxiety.

People who have a degree of fixation at the anal stage typically show some combination of three character traits: they are orderly (included here is conscientiousness and concern about cleanliness), parsimonious (sometimes to the point of avarice), and obstinate (sometimes to the point of rage and revengefulness). These traits are seen as products of the child's experience of toilet training. We have already seen that a 2-year-old, as a result of the physical development of musculature and sphincter control, is able to make choices that have an important social impact. He is now in a position to exercise some control *vis-à-vis* his caretakers, and to express his emotions through his behaviour. He can be 'good' and express love by giving his parents the 'gift' they want, and he can be 'clean' and please his parents. Or he can express anger and punish them by making a mess, or he can express anger by control—by refusing to give them what they want. Thus he connects the pleasurable sensation of 'letting go' or 'holding on' with an act that potentially has several social meanings. So, through acting in his social world in relation to his instinctual impulses and needs, and learning to deal with the responses he receives, the child's personality develops. This illustrates Freud's basic position on personality: it is the result of conflict between inherited patterns of instincts, revealed in needs and behaviour, and the environment.

4.4 The phallic stage and the Oedipus complex

According to Freud, the phallic stage is of particular importance for the growth of a healthy personality. Unresolved conflicts at this stage can result in boys growing up to be mother-fixated and girls growing up to be father-fixated—each, in adult life, searching for a sexual partner that resembles the parent. Difficulties at the phallic stage can also lead to more general problems of gender identity and to a weak moral sense.

In the phallic stage, all children are thought to go through a crucial developmental crisis which leads to the consolidation of appropriate gender identity and gender roles and the formation of the super-ego. This crisis is called the **Oedipus complex**. (In girls it has been called the Electra complex, but the term is rarely used.) At around the age of four, erotic sensations originating in the penis or clitoris become associated with sexual fantasies, conscious and unconscious. These fantasies are about the parents' sexuality, about how reproduction works and where babies come from, and about the child's need to love and possess the parent of the opposite sex. The emotions that are stirred up include intense envy and jealousy. The child envies the same-sex parent's qualities and powers and wants them for him or herself in order to become the love object of the opposite-sex parent. At the same time, the child is jealous of the attention and love given to the same-sex parent and wants to dispossess and get rid of this same-sex parent and take his or her place. Thus, for example, a boy will be envious of his father's attributes, powers and sexuality and jealous of his father's possession of his mother. The boy wishes to be like his father and even to *be* his father and thus take his place. This is the source of identification with the same-sex parent and the origin of the process of learning appropriate gender roles.

Up to this point, during the oral and anal stages, boys and girls have had similar experiences. But in the phallic stage, the development of boys and girls diverges. Exactly how this happens is still controversial. Both boys and girls tend to be closer to their mothers in their earliest years. For boys this emotion is eroticized in the phallic stage leading to feelings of rivalry with the father, and fantasies of displacing him. This is the parallel with the legendary Oedipus, son of a king and queen in ancient Greece. As an infant, Oedipus was abandoned on a mountain-side to die, in order to avoid a prophecy that he would grow up to kill his father and marry his mother. But he was rescued by shepherds and brought to the court of a king in another country. In early manhood, he returned to his own land where, almost immediately, he killed a man (his father) in a quarrel and then married an older woman (his mother), the queen. In Freud's theory this tragedy is re-enacted in each generation in fantasy. Freud believed that the Oedipus complex is true for all cultures and all historical periods. However, the universality of the Oedipus complex, its exact form and its centrality in development are now controversial. (Freud's discovery is described in Extract H.)

EXTRACT H Freud's discovery of the universality of the Oedipus complex

Freud struggled with the idea of the Oedipus complex for some time before it came to him clearly, almost exactly one year after the death of his own father in 1896. He expressed his realization of its universality in a letter to his friend Fliess:

A single idea of general value dawned on me. I have found, in my case too, [the phenomenon of] being in love with my mother and jealous of my father and I now consider it a universal event in early childhood. If this is so, we can understand the gripping power of *Oedipus Rex*, in spite of all the objections that reason raises against the presupposition of fate; the Greek legend seizes upon a compulsion which everyone recognizes because he senses its existence within himself. Every one in the audience was once a budding Oedipus in fantasy, and each recoils in horror from the dream fulfilment here transplanted into reality . . .

Fleetingly the thought passed through my head that the same thing might be at the bottom of Hamlet as well. I am not thinking of Shakespeare's conscious intention, but believe, rather, that a real event stimulated the poet to his representation, in that his unconscious understood the unconscious of his hero. How does Hamlet the hysteric justify his words, 'Thus conscience does make cowards of us all'? How does he explain his irresolution in avenging his father by the murder of his uncle . . .? How better than through the torment he suffers from the obscure memory that he himself had contemplated the same deed against his father out of passion for his mother . . .? His conscience is his unconscious sense of guilt.

(Freud, in a letter to Fliess, dated 15 October 1897; Masson, 1985a, pp. 272–3)

During the Oedipus complex, a boy's feelings for his mother and rivalry with his father lead him to fantasize (consciously and unconsciously) that he can get rid of his father and take his place. But fantasizing the death of his father evokes extreme anxiety and he fears some dreadful retaliation. Freud believed that at around the age of four, a boy's anxiety would focus on castration as an appropriate punishment for the crime of desiring his mother. He thought that, at this age, boys realize for the first time that girls do not have such a prized possession—that is, a penis—and they think that girls must have been castrated already. In order to defend himself against **castration anxiety**, the boy 'becomes his father'. In doing this, he uses two defence mechanisms: **identification** and **introjection**. He identifies with the aggressor (in fantasy his retaliating father) and in so doing he introjects (takes in) his father's attitudes and moral values. Identification and introjection are the source of the boy's super-ego and also enable him to develop an appropriate gender identity. Freud called this process the resolution of Oedipal conflict. Once the Oedipal conflict is resolved the boy puts aside his sexual libido for the duration of the latency period.

Freud had a great deal more trouble with his theory about how *girls* deal with these conflicts, and eventually he concluded that the process for girls was more difficult. At the beginning of the phallic stage, girls, like boys, have their mothers as their primary love object. In the course of their development, girls not only have to switch to having a man as love object but, according to Freud, they also have to change their main genital zone from the clitoris to the vagina. Freud thought that at about 4 years old, girls discover that they lack something that boys have and 'from that time forward fall a victim to envy for the penis. . . . A little girl . . . makes her judgement and her decision in a flash. She has seen it and knows that she is without it and wants to have it' (1925, p. 252). This concept of **penis envy** has received much criticism. Girls are thought at first to deny this envy and then to fantasize a hidden penis and to develop a sense of inferiority which may later lead to a character trait of envy and jealousy. The hurt to a girl's self-love and esteem caused by lack of a penis—a lack for which she blames her mother—brings about a giving up of clitoral sexuality for the development of femininity. Because she blames her mother she now turns to her father as love object, with the hope of getting from him a child to replace her anatomical deficiency. Freud also believed that, with such a circuitous pathway as this, girls do not fully resolve their Oedipal conflict and that the result is a less well developed super-ego and moral sense. Not surprisingly, this interpretation has led to a strong feminist critique of Freudian theory as male-centred and phallus-centred.

There is now evidence, from observational studies and from psychoanalysis, that girls experience their vaginas as erotogenic from an early age. In addition, it is increasingly clear that *both* sexes have an early awareness of the vagina and have fantasies which reflect the value and psychological importance of the vagina and female procreativeness as well as the phallus (i.e. penis–clitoris). Many psychodynamic theorists now question the phallus-centred concept of penis envy and believe that each sex may envy the attributes, potential creativity and power of the other. The *fact* that in our society, and in many others, female attributes and female creativity are less visible and often depreciated while male qualities are more visible, more valued, and thus more enviable, may be a product of male-dominated cultures rather than a biological inevitability.

Freud's difficulty in accounting for female development proved to be an important turning-point for psychodynamics since it focused more attention on the **pre-Oedipal stage**. In *Female sexuality* (1931) Freud wrote: 'A female's first object, too, must be her mother: the primary conditions for a choice of object are, of course, the same for all children' (p. 228). Freud concluded

that the *duration* of this attachment had also been greatly underestimated. In several cases it lasted until well into the fourth year—in one case into the fifth year—so that it covered by far the longer part of the period of early sexual efflorescence. Indeed, we had to reckon with the possibility that a number of women remain arrested in their original attachment to their mother and never achieve a true change-over towards men. This being so, the pre-Oedipus phase in women gains an importance which we would not have attributed to it hitherto.

(Freud, 1931, pp. 225–6)

In this paper, Freud expressed his surprise at finding that, for girls at least, *the pre-Oedipal years are of vital importance.* Up to this point his work had centred on the Oedipus complex at age four or five as being by far the most important psychosexual hurdle for children. Now he suggested that:

Since this [pre-Oedipus] phase allows room for all the fixations and repressions from which we trace the origin of the neuroses, it would seem as though we must retract the universality of the thesis that the Oedipus complex is the nucleus of the neuroses. But if anyone feels reluctant about making this correction, there is no need for him to do so . . . we can extend the content of the Oedipus complex to include all the child's relations to both parents.

(ibid.)

Freud's attempt to understand female sexuality is one of the most controversial aspects of his work. But, ironically, it was his own dissatisfaction with this part of his theory that led to the most influential developments of psychodynamics. Freud's rethinking of his position on female sexuality, as we have seen, suggests a refocusing of attention away from Oedipal conflict at age four or five, and towards the importance of children's fantasies about their parents' sexuality, their own sexuality and object relations *from the very beginning of life.* This is the province of object relations theories such as those of Klein, Winnicott, Fairbairn and many others who have worked largely since Freud's time, from about the 1930s to the present. Much psychodynamic theory and practice today, especially in

Britain, is an amalgam of Freud's work (or sometimes Jung's theories) with those of Klein or other object relations theorists. Some further reading on these important figures is listed at the end of the chapter.

Like the resolution of conflict at earlier psychosexual stages, resolution of the triangular relationships of Oedipal conflict and its impact on personality development depends upon an interaction between each child's particular, innate patterns of instincts and the social environment that he or she experiences. This social environment is a reflection of society's norms and values, the prescribed structures of family life *and* the personalities and attitudes of particular parents, and the ways they deal with their children's needs, impulses, fantasies and anxieties.

The end of the Oedipus complex marks the start of the *latency stage*, during which children are believed to turn aside from their sexuality and attend to other aspects of development. More demands are made on the child's behaviour through schooling and interactions with other social groups outside the family. Many skills, practical, social and intellectual, have to be learned (see the discussion of Piaget's work in Chapter 3). The super-ego, established in the Oedipus complex of the phallic stage, continues to develop during latency and the genital stage through the individual's contact with society and culture. At puberty, the child enters the *genital stage* when the component sexual instincts become organized into adult genital sexuality.

SAQ 3   So far in this chapter, five ego defence mechanisms have been mentioned which are used to reduce anxiety. See if you can remember what they are.

To end this section we will briefly summarize the relationship between the psychosexual stages and the id, ego and super-ego (see Figure 4.2). The unconcious id with its libido is the source of instinctual sexual impulses which, as physical development proceeds, find gratification in different areas of the body during the oral, anal, phallic and genital stages. The experience of these impulses, and the fantasies, frustrations and pain they cause in accommodating to reality, largely represented by caretakers, lead to anxieties. The developing ego unconsciously tries to deal with these by employing appropriate and inappropriate defence mechanisms. Central to Freud's theory is the defensive response to the Oedipus complex during the phallic stage which, through identification and introjection, results in the internalization of parental attitudes to form the super-ego, the source of the child's conscience and moral sense. The interactions between id, ego, super-ego and external reality, together with the use of defence mechanisms, determine personality. But this interaction depends on the innate strength of instinctual impulses and innate tendencies to employ particular defences. It also depends on the details of the environment the infant encounters, and in particular how he or she is treated by the family. Thus, according to Freud, whether personality development is normal or abnormal in a particular child depends on the innate qualities of his or her instincts, how he or she is brought up, and the appropriateness of defence mechanisms at each psychosexual stage.

Summary of Section 4

- A developmental approach is central to Freud's work.

- Freud believed that a child's experiences of other people in the first five years of life have a crucial and permanent effect on development.

- The theory of psychosexual development states that the components of the sexual instinct emerge in a predetermined sequence of stages which parallel physical development. They are (a) the oral stage, (b) the anal stage, (c) the phallic stage, (d) the latency period and (e) the genital stage.

- Freud believed that the Oedipus complex, which occurs during the phallic stage, is the most important developmental hurdle. It is the stage at which children experience sexual feelings toward the parent of the opposite sex and anxiety-provoking envy and jealousy towards parents of the same sex. Resolution of Oedipal conflict leads to gender identity and the formation of the super-ego, the source of the child's moral sense. Freud believed that failure to move through this stage results in the most severe neuroses.

- Achievement of gender identity follows a different course for boys and girls, but Freud acknowledged that his description of girls' development is problematic.

- Personality development is seen as the outcome of the experience of psychological conflict and conflict resolution during each psychosexual stage *in relation* to the child's caretakers. It is determined by an interaction between innate instinctual factors and the child's social environment.

- Freud believed that disturbances of infantile sexuality caused by parental repression, punishment or over-gratification (or, sometimes, actual seduction, see below) results in fixation at the various stages, leading to neuroses.

5 | Psychoanalytic therapy

It must be stressed that Freud's model of the mind was derived from his clinical experience and observation. Throughout his life's work there was a two-way exchange between theory and therapy. His first ideas were developed to explain the behaviour of patients suffering from **hysteria**, a mental illness much more rare today than in Freud's times, in which physical symptoms, such as partial paralysis or blindness, have no physical explanation. These early ideas from clinical work formed the basis for new therapeutic techniques. These led Freud to expand the range of neuroses he investigated and this, in turn, led to the development of more sophisticated theory. And so the cycle continued. The techniques he used during psychoanalysis can thus be considered as research tools. They revealed unconscious processes and provided the material from which Freud formulated hypotheses, which he then tested by applying them to the cases of other patients. Because Freudian theory and therapy are so interwoven it is important to understand both facets of his work in order to appreciate either one.

The overall goal of psychoanalytic therapy is to bring about a fundamental change in patients' personalities so that they are released from their neurotic disorders. **Neurosis** is a form of mental disorder which is not a physical disease of the nervous system, that is to say, it has no known organic origin. Neurotic disorders of the personality are usually distinguished from the more serious psychoses in which patients periodically lose touch with reality.

Freud believed that neurosis is caused by the repression of disturbing, anxiety-producing feelings associated with psychological conflicts in early childhood. Sometimes neuroses follow from *real*, damaging events in early life, such as an illness which disrupts feeding in the first weeks of life, an early loss of a loved parent, or some degree of sexual abuse. When a child has suffered serious physical and/or emotional damage (a trauma), the original external danger is represented internally and becomes a potential internal danger, signalled by anxiety when memories are roused or conflicts of a similar kind are encountered in later life. But internal dangers and severe anxiety can also be the product of fantasies without actual damaging events. In these cases, it is the child's fantasies associated with the id impulses of each psychosexual stage and the conflict between these fantasies and a punitive super-ego (the internal representation of a punishing parent) that is the internal danger (usually unconscious) and the source of anxiety. Freud assumed that the patient's ego was too weak to cope with such conflicts, whether based on real or fantasized events, and defended itself by repressing them into the unconscious. However, psychological conflicts do not go away. Often they find expression as neurotic symptoms like anxiety states, phobias and obsessions, such as compulsive hand-washing, some forms of depression, and many psychosomatic disorders where physical symptoms are thought to be of psychological origin.

At first, Freud believed that sexual seduction was the cause of hysteria. His evidence was the material about seduction that his patients, mostly female, described in the course of psychoanalysis. Later, in 1897, he changed his mind on this, largely because he could not believe that sexual abuse of children and young adults could be as widespread as this evidence suggested. He concluded that much (but not necessarily all) of what he heard from his patients was fantasy, and that sexual fantasies, in particular of seduction by an adult loved one, are universal and not found only in those presenting as patients. The importance of fantasy of all kinds, as a driving force underlying behaviour and as a crucial source of conflict and anxiety, became central to psychoanalytic theory from this point on.

Recently, many analysts and others have judged Freud harshly on this account. The most extreme critiques of his 'change of mind' have come from feminists and from those who work with abused children. Some people have claimed that Freud's revision of his original seduction theory was the result of his own ego defences protecting him from the horror of accepting that sexual abuse of children is not such a rare occurrence. One theorist has even suggested that Freud's revision of his seduction theory was a cover-up (Masson, 1985b). Perhaps the majority of psychoanalysts today take a middle course on this painful question, to a large extent *believing* what children say and what adults report later, but also acknowledging the crucial role of fantasy in mental life (see Miller, 1985 and 1987).

Freudian psychoanalysis aims to bring infantile conflicts from the unconscious into consciousness and then to help the patient deal with these at a conscious level. Thus, classical Freudian psychoanalytic therapy can be considered to comprise three stages:

1   Identification of defence mechanisms, especially repression, that keep the conflict (and sometimes the memory of a trauma) in the unconscious.

2   Release of this material to consciousness.

3   Redirection of the emotional energy (libido) associated with the defence mechanism, thereby allowing the patient's ego to recognize the conflict and deal with it (emotionally, cognitively and/or behaviourally) in relation to current reality. In this way the patient's ego becomes stronger and better able to deal with conflicts, both those originating in the past and those occurring in current life.

Freud developed various techniques for getting around the controlling forces of the defence mechanisms and thus releasing unconscious material. He began by using **hypnosis**, and visited Charcot in Paris in 1885 to study hypnotic techniques in the treatment of patients with hysteria. Charcot and others found that a suggestion to walk or to see, made while the patient was hypnotized, often removed the patient's symptom, but the original symptom of paralysis or blindness would sometimes be replaced by another. When Freud began his private medical practice as a neurologist in Vienna, he used hypnosis to attempt cathartic cures of psychosomatic conditions. Instead of using hypnotic suggestion to remove symptoms directly, Freud used hypnosis to release memories and the patients appeared to 're-live' the associated emotions. The combination of hypnotically induced 'confession' and release seemed to have a healing effect.

At first Freud, and his friend and colleague Breuer, believed that this **catharsis**—the 'cleansing' effect of the released emotion—was the source of the cure. However, a young patient of Breuer's, referred to in the case reports as Anna 'O', changed this view. She had a hysterical paralysis and other physical symptoms including an unexplained cough. An improvement in her symptoms came, not after hypnotic 'release', but after she remembered the original occasion of her cough whilst under hypnosis. She remembered that, whilst nursing her dying father, she had heard music coming from a neighbouring house. Her desire to go to the dance rather than nurse her father caused her such painful guilt that this memory was repressed, only to produce the cough whenever she heard dance music. Thus it was Breuer and Anna 'O', rather than Freud, who could be said to have effected the first 'talking cure'.

Freud found that hypnosis was an unreliable way of releasing memories and replaced it by the method of free association. Initially, free association was more or less forced on him by a patient who was determined to talk about anything and everything that came into her head. The development of the technique was a crucial step in the history of psychoanalysis and it is now the major method for reaching unconscious material. The other major techniques are dream interpretation and analysis of Freudian slips (parapraxes) such as forgetting and misplacing and other behavioural manifestations of psychological conflict like those illustrated in Section 1. Parapraxes sometimes need very little interpretation, but in other cases the details and context of the error or slip can be unravelled, almost as with dreams, to reveal important areas of unconscious conflict and pain. Finally, the relationship itself, between psychoanalyst and patient, is used to uncover unconscious processes which underlie habitual patterns of relating to important others throughout the patient's life.

5.1 Free association

Free association requires patients to say whatever comes into their minds, regardless of how personal, painful, fleeting or inconsequential it may seem to be. Freud did not view free association as producing random utterances but maintained that, like all mental events, the thought processes governing it are *determined* by unconscious forces. Essentially, the analyst is asking the patient to bypass the conscious editing which normally occurs during speech production. Free association provides the basic material for psychoanalysis. Everything that the patient says during a psychoanalytic session is material for the analysis. The patient may talk about events and feelings in his or her life outside the session or in the session itself (the 'here and now'), including feelings and fantasies about the analyst. Memories may come to light, sometimes from distant childhood. Very often the patient will experience strong emotions—rage, weeping perhaps, and physiological changes such as cramps, blushing, sexual arousal or even nausea—as a result of what he or she talks about, or the disturbing memories that come to light, and as a reaction to interpretations from the analyst. Often the flow of associations will dry up, or there will be silences, or odd changes of topic. All of these are signs of **resistance**, conscious or unconscious, and are treated by the analyst as crucial evidence about the patient's conflicts.

ACTIVITY 3 (Optional)

Try the following free association exercise with the help of a tape recorder. Don't take this exercise too seriously; its aim is to help you appreciate how much conceptual editing you normally do when you speak. In a typical analysis the patient lies on a couch with the analyst sitting slightly behind, out of the patient's line of vision. This minimizes the more conventional aspects of a two-person interaction. Place your tape recorder out of sight and try to forget about it.

Sit or lie comfortably. You could close your eyes. Now say *whatever* comes into your head. Try not to censor anything, and try not to be constrained by a need to 'make sense' because, in this context, 'making sense' can be a kind of logical censorship and may be a defence. For instance, you don't have to complete your sentences. If a new thought or image occurs to you whilst you are still talking, then break off and follow the new train of thought. You might have to practise a few times before you become unselfconscious.

If you find that you can do this, you might like to search the tape for topics or themes that you return to several times, or for juxtapositions of ideas that at first look unrelated but, on reflection, are associated with the same feeling. An exercise like this, that you do for yourself, is unlikely to tell you anything of consequence about your unconscious processes, but it should give you some evidence that *meaningful* processes do operate below the level of your awareness.

It is a widely-held misconception that most of psychoanalysis is concerned with recreating accurate memories of significant *events* that have happened in childhood. Usually this is a small, although valuable, part of the outcome of free association. In general, what is more important is the recovery of childhood fantasies, feelings and misperceptions. These are very often brought to light in a roundabout way, woven together with memories of relatively unimportant happenings; Freud called them **screen memories**. Freud believed that a screen memory persists, often with great clarity and often recurring frequently in free association, *because it has a hidden content* which can be revealed by interpretation rather as if it were a dream. Screen memories are remembered because they symbolize, with particular aptness, some important aspect (rather than specific event) of the childhood situation. Extract I gives an example of a screen memory from Freud's own self-analysis. This description first appeared in *The psychopathology of everyday life* in 1901, but further interpretation led to an important footnote being added in 1924, revealing yet another layer of unconscious process and providing a vivid illustration of the principle of overdetermination.

EXTRACT I A childhood memory

I should like now to give a single example of the way in which a childhood memory, which previously appeared to have no meaning, can acquire one as a result of being worked over by analysis. When I began in my forty-third year to direct my interest to what was left of my memory of my own childhood there came to my mind a scene which had for a long while back (from the remotest past, as it seemed to me) come into consciousness from time to time, and which I had good evidence for assigning to a date before the end of my third year. I saw myself standing in front of a cupboard ('*Kasten*') demanding something and screaming, while my half-brother, my senior by twenty years, held it open. Then suddenly my mother, looking beautiful and slim, walked into the room, as if she had come in from the street. These were the words in which I described the scene, of which I had a plastic picture, but I did not know what more I could make of it. Whether my brother wanted to open or shut the cupboard—in my first translation of the picture I called it a 'wardrobe' ('*Schrank*')—why I was crying, and what the arrival of my mother had to do with it—all this was obscure to me. The explanation I was tempted to give myself was that what was in question was a memory of being teased by my elder brother and of my mother putting a stop to it. Such misunderstandings of a childhood scene which is preserved in the memory are by no means rare: a situation is recalled, but it is not clear what its central point is, and one does not know on which of its elements the psychical accent is to be placed. Analytic effort led me to take a quite unexpected view of the picture. I had missed my mother, and had come to suspect that she was shut up in this wardrobe or cupboard; and it was for that reason that I was demanding that my brother should open the cupboard. When he did what I asked and I had made certain that my mother was not in the cupboard, I began to scream. This is the moment that my memory has held fast; and it was followed at once by the appearance of my mother, which allayed my anxiety or longing. But how did the child get the idea of looking for his absent mother in the cupboard? Dreams which I had at the same time (as the analysis of this memory) contained obscure allusions to a nurse of whom I had other recollections, such as, for example, that she used to insist on my dutifully handing over to her the small coins I received as presents—a detail which can itself claim to have the value of a screen memory for later experiences. I accordingly resolved that this time I would make the problem of interpretation easier for myself and would ask my mother, who was by then grown old, about the nurse. I learned a variety of details, among them that this clever but dishonest person had carried out considerable thefts in the house during my mother's confinement and had been taken to court on a charge preferred by my half-brother. This information threw a flood of light on the childhood scene and so enabled me to understand it. The sudden disappearance of the nurse had not been a matter of indifference to me: the reason why I had turned in particular to this brother, and had asked him where she was, was probably because I had noticed that he played a part in her disappearance; and he had answered in the elusive and punning fashion that was characteristic of him: 'She's "boxed up" ("*eingekastelt*")'. At the time, I understood this answer in a child's way [i.e. literally], but I stopped asking any more questions as there was nothing more to learn. When my mother left me a short while later, I suspected that my naughty brother had done the same thing to her that he had done to the nurse and I forced him to open the cupboard ('*Kasten*') for me. I now understand, too, why in the translation of this visual childhood scene my mother's slimness was emphasized: it must have struck me as having just been restored to her. I am two and a half years older than the sister who was born at that time, and when I was three years old my half-brother and I ceased living in the same place.

(*Footnote added 1924*)   Anyone who is interested in the mental life of these years of childhood will find it easy to guess the deeper determinant of the demand made on the big brother. The child of not yet three had understood that the little sister who had recently arrived had grown inside his mother. He was very far from approving of this addition to the family, and was full of mistrust and anxiety that his mother's inside might conceal still more children. The wardrobe or cupboard was a symbol for him of his mother's inside. So he insisted on looking into this cupboard, and turned for this to his big brother, who (as is clear from other material) had taken his father's place as the child's rival. Besides the well-founded suspicion that his brother had had the lost nurse 'boxed up', there was a further suspicion against him—namely that he had in some way introduced the recently born baby into his mother's inside. The affect of disappointment when the cupboard was found to be empty derived, therefore, from the superficial motivation for the child's demand. As regards the *deeper* trend of thought, the affect was in the wrong place. On the other hand his great satisfaction over his mother's slimness on her return can only be fully understood in the light of this deeper layer.

(Freud, 1901, *The psychopathology of everyday life*; SE 6, pp. 49–52)

SAQ 4   (a) In Extract I, what was the screen memory?

       (b) Outline the unconscious fantasy which Freud interpreted from the main part of the extract.

       (c) In 1924, many years later, Freud interpreted another, deeper layer of unconscious fantasy symbolized by this same screen memory. Try to outline what this was.

5.2 Dream interpretation

Although free association, and the various kinds of material it supplies, is the primary technique for gaining access to the unconscious in adults, dreams are also important. Analysts vary in the emphasis they put on the use of dreams, but, in the history of psychoanalysis, dreams were known as 'the royal road' to the unconscious. They have provided much evidence that unconscious processes and their interpretation are relevant to normal people as well as to those with a mental disorder.

It is common for patients to bring their dreams to psychoanalytic sessions; some keep detailed notes of what they dream each night. A dream has both **manifest content**—the story and images and **latent content**—the hidden dream thought originating in the unconscious. The manifest content reaches consciousness when one wakes up and remembers the dream, but the dream thoughts—the unconscious processes—are still hidden and can only be reached by unravelling the dream-work. **Dream-work** is the work done by the ego during sleep to convert the desires of the unconscious id into a 'story' that is acceptable to the defensive ego: 'The study of the dream-work teaches us by an excellent example the way in which unconscious material from the id . . . forces its way into the ego, becomes preconscious and, as a result of the ego's opposition, undergoes the changes which we know as *dream-distortion*.' (Freud, 1940, p. 165).

Interpreting dreams is seen in psychodynamics as a way to reveal the *processes* of the unconscious. It was through the study of dreams that Freud reached the distinction between primary process thinking and secondary process thinking. **Primary process thinking** is characteristic of unconscious mental activity and can be seen in dreams when several ideas and images become fused or condensed and symbolize other ideas, and when space and time are ignored. Primary process thinking is under the influence of the pleasure principle; it reduces tensions by 'hallucinations' which are essentially wish fulfilments. **Secondary process thinking** is what we call logical, grammatical and realistic conscious thought. Day-dreaming and creative fantasy are a mixture of the two, and can therefore sometimes provide access to unconscious material.

Freud's basic thesis about dreams is that they are wish fulfilments which are created in the preconscious *in order to protect sleep*. Thus, wishes that originate in the unacceptable desires of the id and/or in the residues of waking life are elaborated by dream-work to the point at which they are acceptable to the ego. For example, a hungry person might dream that he or she is eating a good meal (an example of straightforward wish fulfilment); someone who has fallen in love with his friend's wife might dream of an affair with a completely different woman who happens to have the same name. In this example the wish is fulfilled, but its disturbing content is disguised. However, all of us have experienced frightening dreams that actually wake us up. How does Freud account for these? He thought of dreams as compromises:

It must not be forgotten that dreams are invariably the product of a conflict, that they are a kind of compromise-structure. Something that is a satisfaction for the unconscious id may for that very reason be a cause of anxiety for the ego. . . . Anxiety dreams are mostly those whose content has undergone the least distortion. . . . A dream is invariably an *attempt* to get rid of a disturbance of sleep by means of a wish fulfilment, so that the dream is a guardian of sleep. The attempt may succeed more or less completely; it may also fail, and in that case the sleeper wakes up, apparently woken precisely by the dream. So, too, there are occasions when that excellent fellow the night-watchman, whose business it is to guard the little township's sleep, has no alternative but to sound the alarm and waken the sleeping townspeople.

(Freud, 1940, pp. 170–1)

ACTIVITY 4

You may like to try to keep a record of your own dreams and perhaps discuss them with friends or fellow students. Could they represent some kind of wish fulfilment? You will need to keep a pencil and paper near your bed to write down what you can remember of your dreams as soon as you wake. Alternatively, make some notes when you wake and then write out the dreams later. You will find that details are lost from memory very quickly. You will also probably find that when you start to write down what, at first, seems like a fairly simple, short dream, it turns out to be much longer and more complicated as you write. This is an example of condensation.

When a dream is to be interpreted, the usual technique is to ask the patient to free associate around the content of the dream, perhaps concentrating on words or images that patient or analyst think are particularly significant. Very recent events and earlier memories may be worked into the dream by this method. By revealing the latent content the analyst can help to bring repressed material into the patient's consciousness. Dreams are usually interpreted in the context of other material the patient has brought to the analyst on previous occasions, and often interpretation relates not to single dreams but to *sequences* of dreams. The manifest content of dreams (the story) is meaningful *within the life of the particular patient* rather than in a universal sense. Interpreting a dream is a much more personal and complex matter than using a 'dream-book' to look up the meaning of the dream as one might use a dictionary. Nevertheless, Freud did believe that the process of dream-work—the creation of an acceptable story—follows a set of universal rules, rather like the grammar of a language. These are discussed at length in his book *The interpretation of dreams* (1900). Extract J is an example of both the 'grammar' of dreams and the need to know something of the context of the dream. Without knowledge of the religious background of the man who had this dream it is not possible to arrive at the interpretation that Freud made.

EXTRACT J   A short dream interpretation

This dream consisted only of two short pictures: *His uncle was smoking a cigarette although it was a Saturday.—A woman was caressing and fondling him* (the dreamer) *as though he were her child.*

In regard to the first picture the dreamer (a Jew) remarked that his uncle was a pious man who never had done and never could do anything sinful like that [smoke on the sabbath]. In regard to the woman in the second picture nothing occurred to him [in his associations] except his mother. These two pictures or thoughts must obviously be seen in connection with each other. But how? Since he expressly disputed the reality of his uncle's action, it is plausible to insert an 'if': 'If my uncle, that pious man, were to smoke a cigarette on a Saturday, then I might let myself, too, be cuddled by my mother.' This clearly means that cuddling with his mother was something impermissible, like smoking on a Saturday to a pious Jew.

(Freud, 1917a, *Introductory lectures on psycho-analysis*; SE 15, p. 186) (italics in original)

Freud believed that, whilst dreams must be interpreted within the context of the dreamer's own life, they also make use of symbols that are universal for all humanity. In dreams, these symbols serve to disguise the latent content of the dream and protect the dreamer from the underlying anxiety. According to Freud, most dreams protect the sleeper from instinctual needs and most of these are sexual; thus, in his theory of dreams, most of the symbols 'stand for' or disguise aspects of sexual life. (Not all psychodynamic theorists agree with Freud's theory of dreams or with the details of his dream symbolism; see, in particular, Jung, 1935.) Examples of **dream symbolism** from Freud's work, are given in Extract K.

EXTRACT K   Freudian dream symbols

The range of things which are given symbolic representation in dreams is not wide: the human body as a whole, parents, children, brothers and sisters, birth, death, nakedness. . . . The one typical—that is regular—representation of the human figure as a whole is a *house*. . . . One's parents appear in dreams as the . . . King and Queen or other honoured personages; so here dreams are displaying much filial piety. They treat children and brothers and sisters less tenderly: these are symbolized as *small animals* or *vermin*. Birth is almost invariably represented by something which has a connection with *water*: one either falls into the water or climbs out of it, one rescues someone from the water or is rescued by someone—that is to say, the relation is one of mother to child. . . .

It is a striking fact that, compared with this scanty enumeration, there is another field in which the objects and topics are represented with an extraordinarily rich symbolism. This field is that of sexual life—the genitals, sexual processes, sexual intercourse. The very great majority of symbols in dreams are sexual symbols. . . .

[T]he male organ finds symbolic substitutes . . . in things that resemble it in shape . . . such as *sticks, umbrellas, posts, trees* and so on; further, in objects which share with the thing they represent the characteristic of penetrating into the body and injuring—thus sharp *weapons* of every kind, *knives, daggers, spears, sabres,* but also *fire-arms.* . . . In the anxiety dreams of girls, being followed by a man with a knife or fire-arm plays a large part. . . .

[Dreams] can treat the sexual organ as the essence of the dreamer's whole person and make him himself *fly.* Do not take it to heart if dreams of flying, so familiar and often so delightful, have to be interpreted as dreams of general sexual excitement. . . .

The female genitals are symbolically represented by all such objects as share their characteristics of enclosing a hollow space which can take something into itself: by *pits, cavities* and *hollows,* for instance, by *vessels* and *bottles,* by *receptacles, boxes, trunks, cases, chests, pockets* and so on. *Ships* too fall into this category. Some symbols have more connection with the uterus than with the female genitals: thus, *cupboards, stoves* and, more especially, *rooms.* . . .

[W]e may enquire how we in fact come to know the meaning of these dream-symbols, upon which the dreamer himself gives us insufficient information or none at all.

My reply is that we learn it from very different sources—from fairy tales and myths, from buffoonery and jokes, from folklore (that is, from knowledge about popular manners and customs, sayings and songs) and from poetic and colloquial linguistic usage. In all these directions we come upon the same symbolism . . ..

(Freud, 1917a, *Introductory lectures on psycho-analysis;* SE 15, pp. 153–9)

5.3 The relationship between psychoanalyst and patient

The basic aim of psychoanalytic therapy is to bring about a fundamental change in the patient's personality. The analyst forms an alliance with the patient's ego in order to help control or to mitigate the id impulses and/or the unreasonable super-ego demands which underlie the unresolved conflict. Before therapy, the patient's ego defends itself by various defence mechanisms, such as repressing the conflict into the unconscious. After therapy, the patient's ego should be stronger and capable of handling the opposing demands of the id, super-ego and external reality. This transformation in the functioning of the ego is brought about in three stages. First, defence mechanisms are identified; second, the repressed conflict is brought into consciousness by employing the techniques outlined in the previous section; and, third, the patient is helped to cope with the conflict in a more realistic way. These phases are repeated many times for each conflict that is dealt with.

This continually repeated process of bringing material into consciousness and then, with the help of interpretation and the support of the analyst–patient relationship, attempting to link it with current reality and allow the negative emotions to be *expressed* rather than *repressed*, is called **working through**. A patient in analysis tries to take in the *full* implications of new information gained through interpretations, but this integration process can take a very long time. Working through is a combination of learning how to live with a new emotional reality and mourning the loss of illusions that were part of the ego's defence. Because of the patient's defences and limited capacity to accept and connect the different levels of meaning in an interpretation, understanding comes piecemeal and slowly. It rarely *feels* like a dramatic insight. Indeed the *conscious* progress of acceptance, learning and change may be imperceptible to the patient for long periods.

The slowness of making unconscious material conscious and the difficulty of accepting interpretations is, to a large degree, the result of the patient's resistance. Resistance may be shown in the form of unwillingness or inability to co-operate with the analyst. For example, a patient may: turn up late for appointments, or forget them altogether; stop having dreams or fail to remember them; be unwilling or unable to continue during free association; try to change the topic, argue about the interpretation, find it impossible to understand what the analyst is saying or even leave the session altogether. Extract L gives Freud's description of these processes.

EXTRACT L   Resistance and working through

[W]e should not forget that the conscious filling-in of the gaps in his perceptions—the construction we are presenting him with—does not mean as yet that we have made the unconscious material in question conscious to him. All that is true so far is that the material is present in him in two records, once in the conscious reconstruction he has been given, and besides this in its original unconscious state. Our continued efforts usually succeed eventually in making this unconscious material conscious to him himself, as a result of which the two records are brought to coincide. The amount of effort we have to use, by which we estimate the resistance against the material becoming conscious, varies in magnitude in individual cases. For instance, what comes about in an analytic treatment as a result of our efforts can also occur spontaneously: material which is ordinarily unconscious can transform itself into preconscious material and then becomes conscious—a thing that happens to a large extent in psychotic states. From this we infer that the maintenance of certain internal resistances is a *sine qua non* of normality. A relaxation of resistances such as this, with a consequent pushing forward of unconscious material, takes place regularly in the state of sleep, and thus brings about a necessary precondition for the construction of dreams.
(Freud, 1940, *An outline of psycho-analysis*; SE 23, pp. 160–1)

Resistance is an active force which influences the course of analysis. Although it slows the progress of the therapy, it is an important source of information for the analyst about the nature of the repressed conflict. As we have seen, the stuff of psychoanalysis is not necessarily long-lost memories. Much of what patients provide is a jumble of memories and feelings from yesterday, long ago, recently and today; it can include material about what is happening in the outside world, and *right now in the analytic session*. Of course, much of this material is about relating to other people, including the analyst. In all this material, and sometimes *especially* in the ways of relating to the analyst, there is evidence of defence mechanisms at work—grist for the psychoanalytic mill.

It is important to realize that psychoanalysis as a therapy has developed considerably. By the end of Freud's life, he and other analysts were already aware of processes occurring during psychoanalysis that were not adequately dealt with by the techniques Freud had originally developed. Initially, he had believed that, as long as traumatic memories of events and fantasies in childhood were identified and brought to the consciousness, the 'release' this afforded would be the cure. Gradually, Freud and others have realized the importance of *working through* the material released from the unconscious. Another major development has been the use of the relationship between analyst and patient as a tool in the therapy.

In the early days of psychodynamic theory, the patient in analysis was thought of as a 'historical child'. Psychoanalysis was seen as a reconstruction of the past and an emotional replay, but 'getting it right this time'. However, quite soon Freud realized from his own and from other analysts' experiences of the intensity of patients' feelings about their analysts, that the route to 'getting it right this time' is, in some sense, a re-living of emotional relationships *through the relationship with the analyst*. The process that occurs between patient and analyst is known as **transference**. This choice of word reflects the original idea that patients transfer feelings that historically belonged to some other relationship on to the current relationship with the analyst. For example, since Freud and his contemporaries tended to focus on conflicts arising in the Oedipal stage, they interpreted their patients' intense emotional transference in terms of Oedipal relations of passionate love, envy, jealousy and rivalry with parents.

Over the years it has become increasingly clear to practising analysts that the *process* of transference—that is, its occurrence followed by interpretation and the working through of what is happening—is one of the most important tools they have. It has become so central to theory and practice that many, though not all, analysts believe that making interpretations about transference is what distinguishes psychoanalysis from other forms of psychotherapy. When attention is focused on the transference and what is happening in the here and now, the historical reconstruction of childhood events and the search for the childhood origins of conflicts may take second place.

The feelings associated with transference can be very intense, irrespective of the sexes of patient and analyst. They can take many forms—a childlike dependence on the analyst, a passionate erotic attachment, overestimation of her qualities, jealousy about all those connected with her, envy of her family, and so on—all of which are instances of **positive transference**. Within the course of analysis, the feelings often become hostile—a **negative transference**. A well-known and much caricatured feature of psychoanalysis is that the analyst takes a lot of trouble to remain unknown as a person, saying very little, and nothing about herself. One of the reasons for this is that, in the absence of real information about the analyst as a person, there is plenty of opportunity for transference fantasies to develop. The psychological distance also ensures that an ordinary, reciprocal relationship does not develop.

Just as transference is one of the areas of development of Freudian theory, so too is **counter-transference**, the feelings the analyst has about the patient. In Freud's time, counter-transference feelings, such as irritation, dislike, sexual attraction and so on, were considered to be a failing on the part of the analyst. These feelings were to be controlled absolutely. They were never to be acted upon, or shown, or discussed between analyst and patient, and apart from this strict self-control on the part of the analyst they were to be ignored. Now, counter-transference is considered an unavoidable outcome of the analytic process, irrespective of how well prepared the analyst is by analytic training and its years of required personal analysis. The same behavioural rules of self-control still apply, but most modern analysts are trained to *observe* their own counter-transference feelings and to *use* these to increase their understanding of the patient's transference and defences.

In addition to the transference relationship, the analyst is also available to the patient in a more general, supportive role which is sometimes called the **therapeutic alliance**. As unconscious conflicts and impulses are brought to consciousness, it is important that the patient deals with them in the 'safe' context of the therapeutic session rather than in the outside world, and without **acting out** the impulses, either in the session or in real life. The analyst and the framework of the fixed and regular therapeutic hour provides a 'container' which 'holds' the patient, enabling him to feel sufficiently secure to continue to explore and experience painful emotions. It also gives a reliable, fixed point in the day or week when he knows he can express himself, verbally, without restriction; this helps him to control impulses and avoid acting out his difficulties in the outside world. Within that safe 'container', the patient and analyst can work through the insights and interpretations at the patient's own pace.

From a practical standpoint, psychoanalysis has the disadvantage that it involves a great deal of expense in terms of time, money and energy. An analysis usually lasts for several years and sometimes much longer, and commonly requires four or five sessions each week. For these reasons, many psychotherapists who base their work on psychodynamic principles carry out what is called **psychoanalytic psychotherapy**. This is a shortened form of therapy in which the patient attends sessions once or twice a week for perhaps a year or two. Sometimes there is a contract between patient and therapist as to how long they will work together and what they will try to achieve. In this kind of therapy, transference is often, though not invariably, less important and the therapist tends to play a more active role in guiding the work into areas of conflict which are thought to be significant to the patient's symptoms and goals for the therapy. There are other circumstances where an analyst might decide to limit the extent and intensity of analysis on the grounds that patients with some types of mental disorder may be at risk of a more serious mental illness if their defences are reduced and certain kinds of unconscious material are released into consciousness.

SAQ 5   List the ways of gaining access to unconscious material that have been mentioned so far in this chapter.

Summary of Section 5

- The techniques that Freud used during psychoanalysis can be considered as research tools with which to study unconscious processes.

- Freudian psychoanalysis aims to bring infantile desires and conflicts from the unconscious into consciousness, and then to help the patient deal with these at a conscious level in the context of current reality. The therapeutic alliance between analyst and patient provides support whilst the patient's ego gains in strength.

- The main techniques in use today for gaining access to unconscious material are: free association; dream analysis; analysis of resistances, of slips and errors; and of transference and counter-transference. Some analysts make use of creative fantasy including art.

- Freud believed that dreams are wish fulfilments which protect sleep. The painful and disturbing wishes, which are the latent content of the dream can be elaborated or translated into symbols in the manifest content which the waking ego can accept.

- The material of psychoanalysis is not necessarily an accurate reconstruction of real childhood events. Fantasies, misperceptions and screen memories are equally important, and the stuff of current, everyday life—including the relationship with the analyst—is crucial.

6 | Evaluating psychodynamics

There are several possible criteria for an assessment of Freud and of psychodynamics more generally. As academic, scientific psychologists we might be most concerned about whether or not the theories are 'true'; that is to say, do they represent the workings of the human mind *as they really are*? However, if you are a medical practitioner or a therapist or a person who is distressed by mental illness, you might be more concerned about whether or not psychoanalysis can provide a cure. A philosopher of science might be most concerned about how it is possible ever to *know* about the unconscious, when, by definition, it is something of which we are unaware, and about the sort of evidence that we should be willing to accept in support of psychodynamic processes. And whether you are a philosopher or a person in the street, you may well want to question the assumptions about human nature that underlie psychodynamics. Many people are worried by Freud's emphasis on sexuality. And many people, especially women and feminists, are concerned and angry about his view of female sexuality and the implied inferiority of women. However, since Freud's death there have been many developments in psychodynamic theory and some of the common critiques of his theory have already been addressed by other psychodynamic theorists.

6.1 The psychodynamic approach as science

Freud himself had no doubt that what he was doing was science. He was a trained scientist in a sense we would accept today, and he believed that he was working as a scientist towards theories which describe the truth about the workings of the human mind, the causes of human behaviour and mental illness. Furthermore, his work has been presented to the public and to professionals as science and as medical science for the last hundred years or so. But, ironically, it is from the point of view of traditional science that his ideas have provoked most criticism. A scientific psychologist would start with the question: Is psychodynamics a scientific model of the workings of the human mind that can be supported by empirical evidence?

According to most versions of how science works in its efforts toward truth, theories on their own are not sufficient. First, theories have to be supported by the evidence of our senses. Such **empirical evidence** can take many forms, such as measurements, detailed observations of events that happen, counting the frequency with which events happen, classifications of the range of events that occur and so on. But there has to be a high level of agreement among the scientists concerned about what is being measured or counted or observed, and about what conclusions can be drawn. In other words, there must be a high degree of **objectivity**. Second, empirical evidence has to *fit* with the theory. Starting with the theory and the concepts it uses, a scientist makes a prediction about what will happen under certain specified conditions. If the prediction is incorrect then the theory which generated it may have to be modified or even dropped altogether. But, if the prediction is upheld, this is taken as evidence that the theory is worth keeping and working with, for the time being at least, until it generates a crucial prediction which cannot be supported empirically, or until a better (i.e. more powerful or more simple) theory comes along. The crucial question for us here is whether psychodynamics conforms to this kind of scientific standard.

There have been many attempts to test predictions based on Freud's ideas and a notable collection and discussion of these can be found in *Fact and fantasy in Freudian theory* (Kline, 1972). Kline concludes on the basis of these studies that there *is* support for some Freudian ideas. But he also states that it would be a mistake to assume from this that other aspects of Freud's work, unsupported by the evidence or as yet untested, irrespective of how difficult they may be to test, can be accepted too.

One of the studies discussed by Kline is Hall's test of aspects of Freud's theory of the Oedipus complex, using analysis of dream material (Hall, 1963). Almost 3000 dreams were collected from nearly 2000 people. Overall, the samples were evenly split by sex, and the age range of participants was from 2 to 80. Hall concluded from Freud's theory of the Oedipus complex that, for both sexes, the early representation of the father in dreams is as a stranger, but that, because of the Oedipal conflict, dreams of male strangers and aggressive male strangers will be more common for males than for females. Hall's specific predictions were that:

1   in all dreams there would be more male than female strangers;

2   the dreams of males would contain more male strangers than the dreams of females;

3   in all dreams there would be more encounters with aggresive males than with aggressive females;

4   these encounters with aggressive males would be more frequent in the dreams of males than females; and

5   when asked to free associate about the male strangers in their dreams the participants would give more associations about fathers and about authority figures than about anything else.

Hall found that the first four of these predictions were upheld and the fifth was marginal.

However, many researchers, notably Eysenck, are convinced that, even when there seems to be empirical support for a Freudian idea, there are always other, simpler explanations which are just as valid. For example, in *The experimental study of Freudian theories* (1973), Eysenck and Wilson, in the course of a critique of Kline's conclusions about the empirical support for Freudian theories, outline another explanation for Hall's findings. Eysenck and Wilson draw on Eysenck's own theory of dreams (Eysenck, 1957):

This theory asserts that the mind in sleep . . . continues to be concerned with the problems of everyday life; the dream being a more primitive form of mental activity than waking thought, this dream activity expresses itself in pictorial and symbolic form. The function of symbolism is not to avoid the censor; it serves an adjectival function, i.e. it makes more precise the meaning of certain concepts. You may dream of your mother as a cow, or as a queen; this signifies her nutritive or disciplinary functions. . . . The predictions from such a theory lead to much the same deductions as do those by Hall from Freudian theory. We normally have more aggressive encounters with male strangers, particularly when we are males ourselves, simply because more males are aggressive, and more so towards other males. Both males and females tend to encounter more male strangers in the course of their work.

(Eysenck and Wilson, 1973, p. 123)

Eysenck and Wilson go on to suggest what seems to be a rather dubious alternative explanation for the pattern of dreams: that male strangers are not met in the home, where women spend most time, but they are met at work, where men spend their days (note that 500 of the sample were under the age of 18). However, it is plain that Eysenck and Wilson are right to question whether one needs Freud's Oedipus complex to account for these dreams.

It is frequently the case that, even where a prediction based on Freudian theory is supported by empirical evidence, another explanation, from everyday cultural expectations or from another kind of psychological theory, can also account for the findings. But this may be in part because the methods available to test Freudian ideas require us to dissect his wide-ranging and coherent ideas into small segments, and to trivialize his propositions. It is not easy to think of how the traditional scientific approach can assess predictions that, for instance, deal with the emotional intensity of love, envy and Oedipal rivalry that Freud attributes to a small boy or deal with the holistic nature of the Oedipus complex.

The traditional scientific approach has difficulty with theories such as Freud's which do not lend themselves to the formulation of unambiguous predictions. The subtlety of Freud's ideas matches the complexity of human behaviour. It is in the nature of psychodynamic theory that effects can have several different causes simultaneously, and also that causes can lead to several different effects. For instance, one might predict that an ego-defensive manoeuvre will be made, but not which one. Freud's theory of psychosexual stages suggests that fixation at a given stage will lead to certain patterns of behaviour, but which ones? Sometimes the possible outcomes of a prediction are diametrically opposed. For example, according to Freud, anal fixation leads to retentiveness (shown behaviourally as avarice) *and* expulsiveness (shown as excessive generosity). Fixation at the oral stage can lead to excessive dependence on oral gratification *or*, by reaction formation, to overt behaviour which displays exactly the opposite trait, exaggerated independence. The principle of overdetermination does not lend itself to experiments aimed at objectively elucidating cause and effect.

Despite Kline's efforts, many people believe that psychodynamic theories *by their very nature* cannot be properly subjected to this kind of scientific test. For the most part, it is not possible to set up predictions which can be definitively tested. Some psychologists believe that, for this reason, Freudian theories have no validity and therefore no place in psychology (see Eysenck 1972 and 1985), but other psychologists believe that there are other ways of being scientific.

6.2 Perhaps not traditional science, but scientific

Most psychoanalysts claim that *experimental* validity is an inappropriate yardstick for evaluating psychodynamic theories. They believe that the theories are verified in practice, in the patient–analyst interactions. This is well illustrated in a postcard sent by Freud to Rosenzweig, a psychologist who had been attempting an experimental demonstration of repression. Freud wrote:

I have examined your experimental studies for the verification of psychoanalytic assertions with interest. I cannot put much value on these confirmations because the wealth of reliable observations on which these assertions rest make them independent of experimental verification. Still, it (experimental verification) can do no harm.

(Quoted in MacKinnon and Dukes, 1962, p. 703)

There is plenty of evidence that Freud and those who came after him *worked scientifically* with regard to rigorous data collection, the generation of theoretical ideas followed up with further observations, tests of the effects on patients of their interpretations, and adjustments of the theoretical ideas where necessary. Over the years, large numbers of detailed case reports have been written and a growing community of psychoanalytically-orientated practitioners discuss and compare their findings (although there is the considerable problem of disguising data so as to protect the confidentiality of the patient). So, in so far as science is the systematic formulation of concepts and theories based on detailed and repeated observation, then the major part of psychodynamic theory is *scientific*. But, even if we accept a less traditional view of what science comprises, there are still some important problems to consider.

Is it possible to be objective about psychoanalytic evidence? Most of the material on which psychodynamic theories have been based, and with which they are tested during therapy, takes the form of utterances made by patients to analysts. The meaning of these utterances is conferred by the context of that particular patient's life and therapy, and usually only the analyst hears them. It is extremely difficult, if not impossible, for observers to have access to, to understand, to categorize and to agree about what is happening—all the steps that are necessary to achieve objectivity.

Related to the question of objectivity is the problem of replication. How can psychoanalytic findings be replicated? Can it ever be possible to get identical results on different occasions? Although there have been some tests based outside the consulting room using behavioural observation, surveys, dreams and so on, the vast majority of the evidence for psychoanalysis comes from case material collected during psychoanalytic sessions, in the context of the continuing story and the continuing relationship between a particular patient and analyst. Another independent 'observer' can never be introduced to take the analyst's place with the patient and try to repeat the findings; if this were ever attempted the whole situation would immediately change.

Another difficulty is that of looking for evidence of general rules about human nature and human behaviour by studying only those people who have presented themselves to the consulting room because they are ill or unhappy. There are two possible responses to this criticism. First, it is not uncommon in science to study a system that has gone awry in order to clarify one's understanding of how it works; and, second, by no means everyone who undertakes psychoanalytic therapy is 'ill'. Psychoanalysts work in a variety of settings, clinical and otherwise, and post-Freudians, especially those who work in the tradition of Jung, analyse people who are searching for understanding and meaning in their lives rather than a cure for an illness.

Finally, there is the well-known criticism that Freud based his theories on the minds and habits of late nineteenth century, Viennese, middle-class neurotics. Certainly Freud's patients were a limited sample, and in no sense representative of humankind. More recently, the range of people who have been studied through participation in analysis has greatly increased. Both Anna Freud and Melanie Klein and her followers have studied infants; Jung attempted anthropological studies, although these have also been severely criticized; and feminist psychoanalysts have listened to women patients in a less male-centred theoretical framework. Some therapists work regularly with psychotic patients, and, in general, the cultural and ethical milieu today is rather different from that in which Freud lived. Nevertheless, the universality of some of Freud's work is questionable. Freud's comments to Fliess about the universality of the Oedipus complex draw on history and literature (Extract H), but we can quibble about a theory that depends on a mother–father–child triad as an inevitable pattern of living. There have been, and still are, many social groupings in which recognition of kinship and living arrangements are rather different. On the other hand, this does not rule out the possibility of the universal existence of rivalry, jealousy and envy, especially in relation to sexuality; some such evidence can even be observed in animals, especially primate groups. Some support for the universality of Freud's ideas might be inferred from the kind of influence they have had in the West over the last century. Virtually everyone refers to Freudian slips, assumes unconscious motivations and is captivated by dream analysis. Something in Freudian thought resonates in all of us, which is perhaps a sign that his theories and those of his followers do appeal to general human characteristics.

6.3 Psychotherapy as a justification

We have seen that there are many standpoints from which to evaluate a theory. However critical we may be of its scientific status and its ultimate truth, psychodynamics *may* be justified because the understanding it provides enables therapists to make people feel better. So, *does* psychotherapy based on psychodynamics cure mental illness? Inevitably, it depends on what kind of mental illness: some severe mental disorders are clearly the province of psychiatry and are not amenable to a 'talking cure'. But even for the kinds of neurotic illness that Freud believed he could alleviate, there is no simple answer.

The therapeutic effectiveness of psychoanalysis has never been 'proven'. Several writers have attempted to review the evidence for cures, but this is a very difficult task. It is difficult to define what constitutes a cure. It is also common for studies of the effectiveness of psychoanalysis and psychotherapy to fail to distinguish between the various types of mental illness that are being treated. It has been said that the question 'does psychotherapy cure?' is as meaningless as 'does medicine cure? (Gleitman, 1986). Another serious problem is how to classify the therapy that a patient has received. Rachman and Wilson (1980) devote a chapter to the effectiveness of psychoanalysis, concluding that 'there is still no acceptable evidence to support the view that psychoanalysis is an effective treatment' (p. 76); but it is never clear how they define psychoanalysis. This is common: most of the assessments of therapeutic success refer to psychotherapies of various kinds, often mixed together in the same study. These may be psychodynamic, but not specifically Freudian in that they may be based on other 'schools' such as those of Jung or Klein. Or they may be 'talking cures' which do not depend on the idea of the dynamic unconscious, for example, Roger's 'client-centred' therapy and other *humanistic* approaches which will be described in Chapter 9.

One of the biggest difficulties in assessing the outcome of any psychotherapy is the fact that many people who suffer from the less severe forms of mental illness get better *without having any treatment.* Eysenck (1952 and 1966) surveyed about twenty articles which reported the outcome of psychotherapy with neurotic patients. He concluded that about sixty per cent of those treated, improved. But he also claimed that the rate of **spontaneous remission**—that is, people who would have got better without any treatment—would have been seventy per cent. On the basis of more recent evidence, it seems that the percentage of people with neurotic illness who improve without treatment is closer to forty per cent (Bergin, 1971). There are other reviews still more encouraging for psychotherapy (Luborsky *et al.*, 1975; Smith and Glass, 1977; Landman and Dawes, 1982). Smith and Glass assessed a series of reviews of psychotherapeutic effectiveness, covering about 400 studies in all, and they concluded that psychodynamic psychotherapy is effective, but no more so than other kinds of psychotherapy.

One of the questions always asked when a patient feels better is: how do we know which part of the therapeutic process caused the improvement? Perhaps psychotherapeutic success has nothing to do with psychodynamic theories. For instance, Truax (1963), who studied eclectic psychotherapy and Rogerian client-centred psychotherapy as well as psychodynamics, found that when the psychotherapist was empathetic and had positive regard for the patient, the patient showed more improvement (see also Truax and Carkhuff, 1967). Fiedler (1950) has shown that the extent of the therapist's experience is a greater determinant of the therapeutic outcome than the school of psychodynamics. Lomas (1987) has questioned the value of *psychoanalytic interpretation* as an instrument in the cure, arguing that the process of psychoanalysis, together with the experience of transference, is curative, but the meaningfulness of the interpretation is not part of this effect.

Finally, in so far as psychoanalysis and other forms of psychodynamic psychotherapy do have a therapeutic effect, there is some evidence that it is only suitable for certain kinds of people, primarily those who are well-educated and articulate. It has been found that people accepted for treatment have tended to be young, *attractive, verbal, intelligent* and *successful* (the YAVIS effect). The emphasis which the process of psychoanalysis places upon verbal communication suggests that patients need to be of a certain intellectual level and, in practice, they have usually been middle class. Working-class patients with the same symptoms tend to be referred to a behaviour therapist, a clinical psychologist or to psychoanalytically-orientated group therapy. This is, in part, a reflection of the YAVIS effect put into action by referring agencies and by some psychoanalysts themselves, but is also a result of the availability of psychodynamic psychotherapy. In the United Kingdom, it is difficult to find such treatment on an individual as opposed to a group basis in the National Health Service (NHS). Outside the NHS, treatment can be costly, especially if more than one session per week is considered. But, as more people undergo training as psychoanalysts and psychodynamic psychotherapists, treatment is increasingly available and within the financial reach of a wider range of potential patients. This easing of access, together with the extension of psychodynamic work with children, with those who are mentally and physically handicapped, and with some psychotic patients who have serious communication difficulties, is beginning to suggest that psychodynamic treatment can help a wide range of people.

It is clear that psychodynamics does not offer the 'whole truth' about the workings of the mind. Freud recognized this, although he did hope at the beginning of his working life that scientific development of his ideas would eventually provide such a picture, right down to the biology of the brain. Today, when metaphor is an acceptable way of extending formal understanding (e.g. computer analogies for the workings of the mind), it has become usual to say that psychodynamic theory has the quality of a particularly vivid metaphor. But there is a danger that this is pejorative and minimizes its contribution, allowing scientific psychologists to keep their academic distance. The basic tenets of psychodynamics are no more metaphorical than theories about thinking and memory. And there is a sense in which the so-called metaphor of sexuality in Freud's work may be closer to reality as we experience it than some of the more conventional scientific metaphors and models of psychological life that you will meet in later chapters of this book. And there is a further problem: *if* Freud's ideas are correct then they will, inevitably, challenge our own psychological defence mechanisms, thus making us resistant to his approach and perhaps influencing our attitudes to the evidence he, and others, have presented.

When we assess what psychodynamics has to offer, it is important to remember that psychodynamics did not end with Freud. His work set the agenda for a great deal more. Many important contributions to psychology have been made by other analytic theorists, during Freud's lifetime and since. Some of this work is an extension of Freud's ideas—see, for example, the work of Erickson on developmental stages throughout life; some is a reaction against Freud—see, for example, the work of Jung who did not believe in the centrality of the sexual instinct and who thought of the unconscious in a much more positive way, as the source of all our potential and creativity. Some common criticisms of Freud have, in fact, already been ameliorated or even overturned by more recent work—see, for example, the ideas of the psychoanalyst Karen Horney who reinterpreted penis envy as a cultural phenomenon in a male-dominated society; and Fromm who believed that social forces are more important in psychodynamics than innate instincts. A constant exchange of views and theoretical adjustments in the light of evidence and new ideas is now commonplace in the psychodynamic world.

Psychoanalysis has made an important, perhaps unique, contribution to psychology in the area of emotional development and the creation by each individual of his or her emotionally charged representation of the world. This is even more the case today as a result of two psychodynamic approaches that have become particularly influential in Britain: those of Melanie Klein and the object relations school (which includes Winnicott who is mentioned in Chapter 2). Whereas at the centre of Freud's theory there is a conflict between instincts and society, for Klein and for the object relations theorists the main concern is how the infant and small child learns to relate to and to represent internally the important people in his or her social environment. The way an infant responds to and interacts with these figures, both in reality and fantasy, affects the developing self, emotional states, mental health and relations with other people and with the world at large *throughout life*. Both of these post-Freudian developments have pushed the focus of interest back to the earliest weeks and months of life; no longer is the 4-year-old's Oedipus complex at the centre of the stage. Pre-Oedipal conflicts, beginning almost at birth, set the scene for psychological development. This contribution of psychodynamics seems to be converging, to some degree, with other approaches in developmental psychology. Although Klein, Winnicott and Piaget were interested in very different aspects of child development, what each of them says is largely compatible and in some instances unexpectedly similar.

Psychodynamics provides a starting point for understanding human behaviour *in its entirety*. What the various psychodynamic schools offer are attempts to understand the unity and complexity of human behaviour, something which more conventional psychological approaches find difficult. However, in the last twenty years or so, psychology in general has been more willing to accept what we, in this chapter, have called the basic tenets of psychodynamics. The importance of *development* for understanding the mind has been widely acknowledged. But you will also find, as you continue to study psychology, that many approaches outside psychodynamics acknowledge and take account of processes that occur beyond awareness. For example, those who study memory or perception or learning, are able to design experiments which throw light on what is happening at the non-conscious level. Currently in psychology, much attention is given to the influence of *meaning* on what organisms do. For example, the emotional content of words can affect what a person learns; the meaningfulness of a story makes it much easier to remember than isolated words; and an individual's prior expectation can dramatically affect what is perceived. These examples implicitly acknowledge the role of some motivational force which is not necessarily available to conscious awareness. But, unlike psychodynamics, other approaches to psychology pay little or no attention to the possibility of conflict between 'rational will' and non-conscious processes.

Finally, any evaluation of Freud must take account of the enormous impact his ideas have had on the cultural life of the West in the twentieth century. Although this topic is well beyond our scope here, you may find it useful to speculate on why his ideas have been so influential, and why they have grasped the imagination of so many people, despite being at odds with many of our culturally accepted (and religious) beliefs about ourselves. Even those who are opponents of Freud's work are very involved and excited by their attempts at disproof or disparagement. Freud himself would say (as he did about the Oedipus complex) that this degree of involvement with the ideas is because, for all of us, they are distant echoes of personally experienced 'truths'.

Summary of Section 6

- Psychoanalysis as a theory does not stand up well to the criteria of traditional scientific methods. There are problems with: experimental method; objectivity; replication; formulation of unambiguous predictions; and *empirical* evidence.

- There have been attempts to test hypotheses derived from Freudian ideas outside the consulting room, but the findings are controversial.

- There is now a community of psychoanalysts who work scientifically in the sense of testing their ideas in clinical practice and reporting their findings. But problems remain. The essential privacy of the method; the sample of people studied; protection of patient's identities when reporting findings.

- Freud's original psychoanalytic theories have been especially criticized on the grounds of: the narrow sample; claims that the processes are universal and culture-free; his views on women and female sexuality.

- There have been many attempts to evaluate the effectiveness of psychodynamic therapy. The findings are unclear because of difficulties with: categorizing the presenting illness; defining a 'cure'; spontaneous remission rates; variations of treatment across psychodynamic 'schools'; and, when a cure occurs, difficulty in specifying *what* it is that has had the therapeutic effect.

- Since Freud, some of the problematic areas in his work have been reworked or changed by other theorists. In Britain especially, psychodynamic theory is moving away from the centrality of instincts (with its focus on sexuality) toward object relations more generally. This move focuses attention on psychological development, particularly in the early mother–infant relationship.

Personal acknowledgement

I would like to thank Jon Slack whose work in an earlier Open University psychology course provided a starting point for this chapter.

Further reading

Original works by Freud
FREUD, S. (1900) *The interpretation of dreams*, Pelican Freud Library, vol. 4 (SE 4 and 5).

FREUD, S, (1901) *The psychopathology of everyday life*, Pelican Freud Library, vol. 5 (SE 6).
Both of these original works are fascinating and not difficult to follow.

Dictionary
RYCROFT, C. (1972) *A critical dictionary of psychoanalysis*, Harmondsworth UK, Penguin Book.
Rycroft's slim dictionary of psychoanalytic terms is an indispensable handbook for any reader who is new to psychoanalytic literature. It includes some terms that belong to psychodynamic traditions other than Freud.

Background on Freud
STRACHEY, J. 'Sigmund Freud: a sketch of his life and ideas; and chronological table.'
This very useful and short outline and table is reprinted at the beginning of every volume of the Pelican Freud Library.

GAY, P. (1988) *Freud: A life for our time*, London: Dent & Sons.
This is a biography of Freud which includes a great deal of detail about his work. It is written by a historian with a psychoanalytic training.

Sociological approach
BOCOCK, R. (1976) *Freud and modern society*, London: Van Nostrand Rieinhold.
In this book Freud's work is presented from a sociological point of view.

Critique
GELLNER, E. (1985) *The psychoanalytic movement*, London, Paladin Books.
This is a learned and somewhat angry critique, from a philosophical point of view.

EYSENCK, H. J. (1985) *Decline and fall of the Freudian empire*, Harmondsworth: Viking.
This is almost a caricature of a critique. It is so angry as to be amusing and is well splattered with exclamation marks.

Other psychodynamic approaches
STORR, A. (1973) *Jung*, London: Fontana Modern Masters.

STORR, A. (1983) *Jung: selected writings*, London: Fontana.
Jung's original writing and his ideas are difficult. The first of these two books is an excellent short introduction; the second is a collection of extracts from original works by Jung, with editorial comments which bind the extracts into a coherent, short version of Jung's ideas.

SEGAL, H. (1972) *Introduction to the work of Melanie Klein*, London: The Hogarth Press and the Institute of Psychoanalysis.
There are no easy introductions to Klein; this is the easiest and best.

PHILLIPS, A. (1988) *Winnicott*, London: Fontana Modern Masters.
This is an introduction to the work of Winnicott, an influential British analyst who has contributed new ideas to theory and practice.

WINNICOTT, D. W. (1986) *Home is where we start from*. Harmondsworth: Penguin.
This is a posthumous collection of essays.

From the point of view of the consumer
CARDINAL, M. (1983) *The words to say it*, London: Picador.
A moving novel based on the author's experience of classical Freudian psychoanalysis.

HERMAN, N. (1985) *My Kleinian home*, London: Quartet Books.
Nini Herman eventually became a therapist; on her way to this goal she encountered three therapies: Freudian, Jungian and Kleinian.

DINNAGE, R. (1988) *One to one: the experience of psychotherapy* Harmondsworth: Viking.
A collection of 20 'cases' where the patients tell their own stories (good and bad) about their treatment.

References

BERGIN, A. E. (1971) 'The evaluation of therapeutic outcomes', in A. E. Bergin and S. L. Garfield (eds) *Handbook of psychotherapy and behaviour change*, New York: John Wiley.

BETTELHEIM, B. (1983) *Freud and man's soul*, London: The Hogarth Press.

EYSENCK, H. J. (1952) 'The effects of psychotherapy: an evaluation', *Journal of Consulting Psychology*, vol. 16, pp. 319–24.

EYSENCK, H. J. (1957) *Sense and nonsense in psychology*, Harmondsworth: Penguin.

EYSENCK, H. J. (1966) *The effects of psychotherapy*, New York: International Science Press.

EYSENCK, H. J. (1972) 'The experimental study of Freudian concepts', *Bulletin of the British Psychological Society*, vol. 25, pp. 261–7.

EYSENCK, H. J. (1985) *Decline and fall of the Freudian empire*, Harmondsworth: Viking.

EYSENCK, H. J. and WILSON, G. D. (1973) *The experimental study of Freudian theories*, London: Methuen.

FIEDLER, F. E. (1950) 'A comparison of therapeutic relations in psychoanalytic, non-directive and Adlerian therapy', *Journal of Consulting Psychology*, vol. 14, pp. 436–55.

FREUD, S. (1900) 'The interpretation of dreams', in J. Strachey (ed.) (1953) *Standard Edition*, vols. 4–5.

FREUD, S. (1901) 'The psychopathology of everyday life', in J. Strachey (ed.) (1960) *Standard Edition*, vol. 6.

FREUD, S. (1905) 'Three essays on the theory of sexuality', in J. Strachey (ed.) (1953), *Standard Edition*, vol. 7, pp. 123–245.

FREUD, S. (1917a) 'Introductory lectures on psycho-analysis', in J. Strachey (ed.) (1963) *Standard Edition*, vols. 15–16.

FREUD, S. (1917b) 'Mourning and melancholia', in J. Strachey (ed.) (1957) *Standard Edition*, vol. 14, pp. 237–58.

FREUD, S. (1923) 'The ego and the id', in J. Strachey (ed.) (1961) *Standard Edition*, vol. 19, pp. 1–66.

FREUD, S. (1925) 'Some psychical consequences of the anatomical distinction between the sexes', in J. Strachey (ed.) (1961) *Standard Edition*, vol. 19, pp. 241–58.

FREUD, S. (1931) 'Female sexuality', in J. Strachey (ed.) (1961) *Standard Edition*, vol. 21.

FREUD, S. (1933) 'New introductory lectures on psycho-analysis', in J. Strachey (ed.) (1964) *Standard Edition*, vol. 22.

FREUD, S. (1940) 'An outline of psycho-analysis', in J. Strachey (ed.) (1964) *Standard Edition*, vol. 23.

GLEITMAN, H. (1986) *Psychology*, 2nd edition, New York and London: W. W. Norton.

HALL, C. S. (1963) 'Strangers in dreams: an experimental confirmation of the Oedipus complex', *Journal of Personality*, vol. 31, no. 3, pp. 336–45.

JUNG, C. G. (1935) *The Tavistock lectures*, London: Routledge.

KLINE, P. (1972) *Fact and fantasy in Freudian theory*, London: Methuen.

LANDMAN, J. T. L. and DAWES, R. M. (1982) 'Psychotheraputic outcome: Smith and Glass' conclusions stand up under scrutiny', *American Psychologist*, vol. 37, pp. 504–16.

LOMAS, P. (1987) *The limits of interpretation*, Harmondsworth: Penguin.

LUBORSKY, L., SINGER, B. and LUBORSKY, L. (1975) 'Comparative studies of psychotherapies: is it true that everyone has won and all must have prizes?', *Archives of General Psychology*, vol. 32, pp. 995–1008.

MacKINNON, D. W. and DUKES, W. F. (1962) 'Repression', in Postman, L. (ed.) *Psychology in the making*, New York: Alfred A. Knopf, pp. 662–744.

MASSON, J. M. (ed.) (1985a) *The complete letters of Sigmund Freud to Wilhelm Fliess 1987–1904*, Cambridge, Mass: Harvard University Press.

MASSON, J. M. (1985b) *The assault on truth*, Harmondsworth: Penguin.

MILLER, A. (1985) *Thou shalt not be aware*, London: Pluto Press.

MILLER, A. (1987) *The drama of being a child*, London, Virago Press.

RACHMAN, S. J. and WILSON, G. T. (1980) *The effects of psychological therapy*, 2nd edition (vol. 24 of *International Series in Experimental Psychology*, general editor H. J. Eysenck), Oxford: Pergamon Press.

SMITH, M. L. and GLASS, C. V. (1977) 'Meta-analysis of psychotherapy outcome studies', *American Psychologist*, vol. 32, pp. 752–60.

STRACHEY, J. (ed.) (1953–66) *The standard edition of the complete psychological works of Sigmund Freud*, vols. 1–24, London: The Hogarth Press and the Institute of Psychoanalysis.

TRUAX, C. (1963) 'Effective ingredients in psychotherapy', *Journal of Counselling Psychology*, vol. 10, pp. 256–63.

TRUAX, C. and CARKHUFF, R. (1967) *Towards effective counselling and psychotherapy*, Chicago: Aldine Press.

TURKLE, S. (1979) *Psychoanalytic politics*, London: Barnett Books (in association with André Deutsch).

TURKLE, S. (with IGNATIEFF, M., RIEFF, P. and HARTMAN, G.) (1987) 'Psychoanalysis: nothing sacred', in Bourne, B., Eichler, U. and Herman, D. *Voices: psychoanalysis*, Nottingham: Spokesman (in association with The Hobo Press).

Answers to SAQs

SAQ 1

(a) *Psychodynamics* is the basic idea that a large part of the mind is unconscious and that the unconscious is the source of a great deal of our motivation. Psychodynamics is also the name given to an approach to psychology based on this premise. It includes Freud's work (psychoanalysis) *and* that of other theorists, some of whom have remained within the classical Freudian tradition and some of whom have extended and challenged his ideas.

(b) *Psychological determinism*, in psychodynamic theory, is the idea that, not only is no behaviour accidental, but all behaviour is the outcome of an underlying causal pattern of motivation, most of which originates in the unconscious.

(c) *Overdetermination*: behaviour is usually the outcome of 'layers' of multiple causes which have their effects simultaneously, rather than the outcome of single cause and effect pairs or chains of such pairs.

(d) *Dynamic unconscious*: the unconscious mind is the source of motivation and exerts a crucial influence on what we do. It is the dynamic unconscious (rather than consciousness, upon which we can to some degree exert will) that is the fundamental source of mental energy and direction.

(e) *Goal-directed dynamics*: all behaviour is directed towards goals, many of which are unconscious and may be in opposition to conscious will. This includes apparently maladaptive behaviour and 'errors' (parapraxes) which also have some function for the individual (e.g neurotic symptoms function to protect the ego from anxiety).

SAQ 2

The id is totally unconscious. The ego and the super-ego are both partly unconscious and partly preconscious; those parts of the ego and super-ego that are preconscious are potentially available to consciousness.

SAQ 3

Repression, regression, reaction formation, identification and introjection. You could also include therapeutic resistance, mentioned later in the chapter.

SAQ 4

(a) The screen memory is Freud's image of himself standing in front of the cupboard demanding something and screaming, while his older half-brother holds the cupboard door open. Freud then sees his mother come in from outside; she looks slim and beautiful.

(b) Analysis of the screen memory, together with some questions asked directly of his mother, revealed important feelings, events and fantasies which were, up to this point, still unconscious, that is, not consciously part of the memory. Freud discovered that a familiar family nurse had disappeared at around the time he places this memory. He concluded that the underlying fantasy was that the nurse had been shut up in the cupboard by his half-brother *and* that he had been afraid that his mother, who had also 'disappeared' temporarily to give birth to his sister, had also been shut up in the cupboard. He was happy to see her restored to him—slim again.

(c) The footnote to this screen memory reveals a yet deeper layer of unconscious fantasy: that the cupboard was symbolic of his mother's body and he, as a 2-year-old who had recently gained a baby sister, was demanding to see and to know whether there were any more unwanted siblings still hidden and waiting to be born. Freud's much older half-brother stood in place of his father as a rival for his mother's affection. The footnote added in 1924 illustrates that different levels of interpretation yield different, simultaneous causes for the significance and persistence of the memory—an example of the principle of overdetermination.

SAQ 5

Hypnosis; free association; dream analysis; analysis of parapraxes; interpretation of creative fantasies, art and day-dreams; analysis of resistance in therapy; and analysis of transference and counter-transference.

Overview of Part II

It is important to realize that Mead, Piaget and Freud all studied child development because they thought it provided the key to understanding the psychology of the adult. If each offers a partial view, this is because they were trying to understand different aspects of the adult's psychological world. Mead was mainly concerned with the development of identity, Piaget was more concerned with the development of reasoning powers, and Freud's interest lay in development in the emotional sphere. The three perspectives are not complementary to each other in the sense that a full picture of development will emerge if we put them all together. Neither are they wholly contradictory. All three theories were seeking some sort of universal description of development, but the methods used to do this have been many and varied. You have come across the use of simple observation, clinical interviewing, psychoanalysis and more or less rigorously designed experiments. Each of the three approaches we have looked at has tended to prefer one or two of these methods, valuing certain kinds of evidence over others. To some extent, this makes it difficult to test the benefits of one perspective against another.

Ages and stages

You have seen that all three perspectives share a concern with trying to draw up some sort of general, objective 'chart' of the course of development in all children, and that they were attracted by the idea that development can usefully be seen as a sequence of consecutive stages. However, none of these theories assumes that these stages occur at absolutely precise ages. Piaget was particularly concerned that his theory of the development of mental operations should not be used as an indication that a child who cannot perform the water conservation task should be considered backward. All the theorists assume that, when a child acquires some new knowledge or social skill, a previous stage must have been passed in order to progress to the next stage. This notion of an ordered sequence of stages is strongest in Piaget's theory. In his terms it would be inconceivable that a child could understand how to count objects before grasping a more primitive concept like object permanence (see Chapter 3, Section 2.1).

Piaget and Freud both saw development as basically an individualistic process, something that goes on primarily *within* each child. A broader view of development sees it as embedded in the social world in which children live. The apparent stage-like quality of development may have more to do with how the growing competencies in the child interact with social conditions. To take a Piagetian example from Chapter 3, Section 3.1, an 'animistic stage' may really be a reflection of the way parents talk to young children about the 'feelings' of inanimate favourite toy animals. It is interesting, too, to note the apparently different levels of development implied by Piaget's 'egocentric' conversation described in Chapter 3, Section 3.3, and the 'sharing of roles' conversation with much the same aged children, in Chapter 2, Section 4.1. The reason for this difference may be a cultural one between the modern American children and the Swiss children recorded in the 1930s. Or it may be something to do with the different expectations of the researchers investigating different aspects of child development. Finally, to turn to a Freudian example, it has been claimed that in cultures with different weaning and child-rearing practices, children do not inevitably display the psychosexual stages exactly as described by Freud.

The role of experience in development

Although it may seem obvious that experience of some kind is necessary for children to develop, the exact role of experience is treated rather differently in each of the three theories. For Mead and his followers, social experience was central. Without constant interactions with other people, without being able to communicate symbolic meanings, the child cannot internalize its own concept of self. The 'me' is constructed by children coming to see themselves as reflections of other people's impressions. This might be taken to imply that everyone's self-concept is simply an amalgam of society's needs and roles, yet people often react quite differently in what appear to be the same circumstances. Indeed, Mead recognized this diversity and proposed the concept of the 'I' to cover the more individual spontaneous and creative aspects of the self. However, the 'I' remains rather less well explained than the 'me', and with less clear origins.

Experience plays an important role in Piaget's theory, as can be seen from the baby's reactions to objects in the sensori-motor stage (see Chapter 3, Section 2.3). The ability to *assimilate* experiences—that is, to understand them in the light of previous knowledge—and the ability to *accommodate* new experiences by creating new ways of understanding, are the chief mechanisms for learning, as described in Chapter 3, Section 2.4. Nevertheless, Piaget has always tended to play down the importance of teaching, language and other social experiences in the emergence of mental operations such as understanding numbers and volume conservation. It may well be true that a child has to be intellectually 'ready' to acquire knowledge. But children also need the ability to make sense of what an adult wants from them and to make socially appropriate responses, as demonstrated by the experiments described in Chapter 3, Section 5. In other words, the unfolding of mental operations is not just a function of the individual child's development.

Early experience is considered all-important in Freudian theory. But much more crucial than *actual* experiences is the continuing effect on social behaviour of fantasies, conscious and, more importantly, unconscious, which are stimulated by these experiences. These unconscious fantasies may influence later behaviour, as seen in Freudian slips (see Chapter 4, Sections 1 and 5.1). Memories of early events will be distorted as the result of defence mechanisms, which repress undesirable conflicts, and often project unacceptable feelings on to our interpretations of other people.

Despite this picture of individuals driven by their inner desires and frustrated instinctual drives, external reality is an essential ingredient in Freud's theory of development. It is because the ego has to deal with 'reality' that frustrations and anxieties arise. Relations with the mother, and later the father, are crucial for how the psychosexual stages, especially the Oedipus complex, are resolved. The personalities and neuroses of adults are a direct result of experiences undergone in early childhood, even though these may only operate at an unconscious level.

Running through all the chapters in Part II is an unresolved tension, one that is coming more and more to dominate debate in developmental psychology. It is a tension between the *social* and the *individual* aspects of development. Psychology in general, and developmental psychology in particular, tries to explain the behaviour, the thoughts and the feelings of the individual person. But, increasingly, we are coming to see much adult behaviour, and the development of children, as operating in a social framework. You will see, in later chapters, just how intricate this relationship may be, and how it must lead us to question the existence of an individual personality separate from the surrounding social world.

PART III
THE FOUNDATIONS OF BEHAVIOUR

Introduction to Part III

Does the emphasis on the importance of social experience in the chapters in Part II ignore other equally important determinants of human behaviour? One crucial factor is the fundamental biological characteristics shared by humans and other animals. Freud himself laid great stress on biological factors, believing that people with 'weak' nervous systems were less likely to be able to cope with the anxiety caused by stress and so were more likely to develop a neurosis in later life.

Chapter 5 outlines the physiological activity of the nervous system, in particular how information is processed by the brain. It also discusses the issue of how evolution and genetics have contributed to the wide range of behaviour in animal species, including humans. The kinds of questions raised have important implications for our views of the nature of psychological processes. How does the brain work and what are the effects of physiological processes on behaviour? In what sense are we biological beings like all other animals, determined by the processes of evolution and the way our bodies function?

While accepting the crucial role of inherited biological factors in behaviour, it is impossible to ignore the vast amount of learning that goes on throughout life. Without the ability to learn from experience, the survival of animals will be at risk. So Chapter 6 goes on to discuss how learning occurs. The focus in this chapter is on the basic mechanisms involved in acquiring new information and learning new skills. Most of the research reported is concerned with rats and pigeons learning relatively simple responses. The basic idea is that animals learn to adapt their behaviour in response to changed circumstances. Some psychologists argue that exactly the same principles can be used to explain the way humans learn to avoid painful objects, to speak a new language and to communicate with other people.

The discussion of biology and learning in animals raises two important issues. The first is just how much can be learnt about human behaviour from studying the behaviour of animals. The second is the yet trickier question of whether it is ethical to carry out experiments on animals in laboratories, albeit care is taken to avoid unnecessary pain. We are just raising these questions here but you will find that they are considered further in the overview of Part III.

chapter

5

BIOLOGICAL PERSPECTIVES

Frederick Toates

Contents

1 **Introduction: biology and its relevance to psychology** **192**
Summary of Section 1   195

2 **The physiology of the cell**   **195**
2.1 Nerve cells (neurons)   196
2.2 Synapses and chemical transmitters   201
Summary of Section 2   206

3 **Genetics and evolution**   **207**
3.1 The cell and the gene   207
3.2 Evolution   209
3.3 The selfish gene   214
Summary of Section 3   218

4 **Motivation**   **218**
4.1 The principle of homeostasis   219
4.2 Homeostasis and motivation   220
4.3 The motivation of drinking   220
4.4 The motivation of feeding   222
4.5 Anorexia nervosa   227
Summary of Section 4   229

5 **Depression**   **229**
5.1 The biochemistry of depression   230
5.2 Types of depression, and explanations   233
5.3 Inheritance and depression   235
5.4 Animal models of depression   240
5.5 Evolution and fitness   240
5.6 Types of explanation and their implications   241
Summary of Section 5   243

6 **Concluding comments**   **243**
Personal acknowledgements   245
Further reading   245
References   246
Answers to SAQs   248

1 | Introduction: biology and its relevance to psychology

This chapter is primarily about the biological bases of psychology. However, its implications are broader than that, and concern the nature of different types of explanation in psychology. Basically, we shall ask the question, 'what have the biological sciences got to offer psychology?'. In trying to answer this, we shall base much of our discussion around two behavioural phenomena: feeding and depression. These have been selected as case studies to illustrate the relevance of biology to psychology. This relevance concerns both normal behaviour, such as understanding the day-to-day eating and drinking activities of an animal, and abnormal behaviour: that is, when such systems go wrong. Some of the general explanatory principles that will be discussed in these case studies could be adapted and applied to other phenomena in psychology.

First, in order to bring out some of the issues involved in using biology as an explanatory tool in psychology, we shall look at an example of the way in which the lay public sometimes tacitly employs biological concepts and metaphors. Read the following (imaginary) conversation and try to formulate as clearly as you can a list of the issues that it raises concerning the relationship between biology and psychology.

Bill 'I loved biology in school—how the eye works, so I can see things. How I can hear your voice. I often wonder about the brain. They say it's all done there. But how do I know when my belly is empty and I need to eat? How do I feel it? Do you ever wonder about these things? Trouble is, I think too much about these things.'

Jean 'Yes, but you spend far too long worrying about these things and you never get anywhere with it all. Now take Harry. He's ill again with depression and that's simply because he thinks too much about things. He really doesn't have a lot to be depressed about. He should try bringing up three children on his own.'

Bill 'That's tough. Funny thing, depression. I've read that depression and that sort of thing run in families. It's something biological, you know. Something is wrong with poor old Harry's brain. He's a bit—er—funny, you know. His nerves just break down once in a while, like the bits of an old car.'

Jean 'I don't believe it. First, it's all in the genes. Now it's his nerves. Depression is all in the mind. In any case, if it runs in families, how can we explain that Harry's brother is as normal as you or me?'

Bill 'I have no idea. In any case, I guess, I'm lucky. I know I worry too much, but I sleep well, and have a good appetite. I adore food. Only problem is that I'm a bit overweight. Yet my little niece is as thin as a rake, and she thinks she's fat.'

Jean 'You do overeat a bit, and that's because your body must need those few extra calories. I don't know about your niece. Weird isn't it? She can't need so much food as others. A doctor might help in her case. But I'm telling you, Harry just needs to pull himself together. Chuck all those silly pills in the bin.'

Bill 'It's a marvellous thing, your brain, you know. Scientists work for years studying rats' brains, trying to understand them. But they still can't tell us why poor old Harry's off sick.'

Jean 'Of course they can't explain it by looking at rats. Harry's a human not a rat. He's not stupid or dim. He can reason; he has a mind and can pull himself together. A rat can't reason—it's just a biological thing. Harry needs to learn to snap out of it.'

Bill 'I still think that's a bit harsh. After all, he can't help it, but I admit he does feel sorry for himself most of the time.'

You probably came up with a variety of different issues that are raised by this conversation, and which relate to assumptions in biology. My list is as follows:

1   That a study of the normally functioning body can give useful insight into psychological phenomena, such as seeing, hearing and feeling hunger.

2   That depression might 'run in families'. If so, by what means could it be transmitted from one generation to the next? Would we expect each family member to exhibit the trait? Is 'running in families' synonymous with an effect being 'biological'?

3   That looking at how the brain works might be a useful approach to explaining mental illness.

4   That there could be something abnormal about the brain when a person is in a state of depression. Could such an abnormality be the cause of the abnormal mental state of depression?

5   That, in contrast with assumption 4 above, it is possible for a mental state of suffering to be 'all in the mind', having no basis in a corresponding brain state; that is, it would be 'disembodied'. This distinguishes it from a physical illness.

6   That nerves can break down, by analogy with bits of a car wearing out.

7   That, in understanding a phenomenon such as depression, whose best-known aspect is in the realm of human feelings, it might be useful to observe the behaviour of another species, in this case the rat.

8   That the quantity of food eaten reflects the body's need for calories.

9   That a class of behavioural abnormality, undereating or overeating, can be explained by events in the body.

As the chapter proceeds, we shall return to consideration of Jean, Bill and Harry and the issues raised by this discussion. We shall use a knowledge of biology to illuminate Jean and Bill's argument, and to see where it needs challenging or refinement.

To go first to basics, what is biology and what has its study to offer psychology? Biology is defined as the study of life. Looking at the Greek roots of the word, *bios* is the word for 'life' and *logos* is the word for 'study'. Biology concerns itself with the whole range of living organisms—that is, animals, plants, bacteria and viruses—and their interdependence. We are concerned here only with animals, including those of the human variety.

There are three main aspects of investigation which we might place under the heading of a 'biological perspective' on psychology. First, there is the comparative method; that is, the study and comparison of different species of animal. When psychologists look at species other than humans, it is generally with a long-term goal of understanding human behaviour. As a matter of standardization and historical tradition, rats and pigeons are their favourite species, particularly when looking for general principles of learning that might apply across species. Observations on primates such as the chimpanzee and rhesus monkey have provided useful insights into human social behaviour. (Another comparative discipline, ethology, involves the study of the behaviour of a wider range of different species—for example, geese, finches and newts—for their own intrinsic interest value. The intellectual roots of ethology are as a branch of zoology, though there is now considerable overlap with psychology.)

In animal studies within psychology, most usually, simple **animal models** are proposed and their explanatory value put to the test, including their applicability to humans. The term 'model' refers to something (e.g. the rat), which is, of course, rather different from the ultimate target of interest (the human). In this case, 'model' carries the meaning that (a) the rat is assumed to have certain behavioural and structural *features* in common with the human, and (b) for various reasons the rat can be used as the basis for explanation. These reasons have to do with, amongst other things, the rat being simpler and experimentation easier. Certain aspects of complex human behaviour can sometimes be better understood in this way.

Contrary to what is sometimes said, the comparative approach does not involve making the naïve assumption that people behave just like rats (except when the approach is misused). Rather, we suppose that, by studying rats and pigeons, and by employing due caution, we might gain some understanding of human behaviour. We can also investigate what kinds of problems different species have been required to confront in order to survive and flourish in their natural habitat, and compare this study with the behaviour and environment of our own species.

The second major aspect of investigation, in which biological knowledge can contribute to psychological insight, concerns the structures that make up the body, how they function and how certain naturally produced chemicals (termed 'biochemicals') and hormones influence them. Understanding of the components of the human nervous system has been aided by investigation of the relatively simple nervous systems of sea-slugs and squids. The study of the working of the structures of the body is known as physiology. We can ask how prescribed drugs affect behaviour by their interaction with the nervous system. For example, we might like to know exactly how, and where, 'poor old Harry's' antidepressant drugs act upon his brain.

Finally, there is the investigation of inheritance. This concerns the study of what an animal inherits from its parents, and the mechanisms of this inheritance. This study is termed genetics. In the present chapter, we are concerned with the role of inheritance in nervous system structures that play a part in behaviour. Investigators wish to know whether, for example, a tendency to depression is inherited from one generation to another.

In the discussion in the rest of the chapter, we use each aspect of the biological approach—the comparative, the physiological and the genetic—to help illuminate human behaviour. Use of the comparative approach will be implicit in much of what we discuss. We shall need to discuss the physiological and genetic approaches explicitly and in some detail, and I introduce these in Sections 2 and 3, respectively.

Summary of Section 1

- There are three main areas of investigation that come under the general heading of a 'biological perspective on psychology'.

- The comparative approach looks for similarities and differences between different species. Models based on animal behaviour are proposed as an aid to our understanding of human behaviour. For example, we might ask whether anything resembling depression is to be found in species other than humans.

- By looking at the components and structures of the body, and how they work (i.e physiology), we can gain an understanding of the biological foundations of behaviour. For example, we might like to know how dieting agents exert their effects on the nervous system.

- The science of genetics concerns itself with inheritance. By studying genetics we can discover how nervous system structures that determine behaviour can be inherited from one generation to the next.

2 | The physiology of the cell

Consider a few of the behavioural psychologist's favourite subjects—the rat, pigeon and human—as a sample of different animal species. The body of each animal is made up of a number of different **organs**. An organ may be defined as a distinct structure within the body serving a particular function. For example, the heart is an organ whose function is to circulate the blood, and the kidney is an organ which serves to eliminate waste substances from the blood. The brain is an organ concerned with processing information.

Within a given organ, the material that forms its structure is termed 'tissue' (for example, muscle tissue and brain tissue). When we compare different animal species, we see an enormous diversity in their forms and behaviours. However, the composition of tissue from one animal is very similar to that from another: bone tissue from a bird, for example, is much like human bone tissue. Differences in function and appearance are achieved largely by differences in shape and how such tissues are put together.

It surprises most people to know just how much of an animal's body is made up simply of water. Something between 60 per cent and 70 per cent of the body weight of a rat, dog or human is water. This water is distributed in various places, some is in the blood, comprising its fluid part, the **plasma**. However, a much larger part of the body water is in the tissues; their solid components can be considered to be suspended in fluid.

When we reduce body tissue to its component parts, its basic building block is the **cell**. Tissue is composed of many small cells, and these are the natural units of study for the biologist. For example, the human brain is made up of something like 10 000 000 000 nerve cells.

According to where it is located—for example, kidney cell or heart cell—each type of cell is specialized to perform a particular function: red blood cells, for instance, are specialized to carry oxygen towards the various organs of the body. Because of their smooth surface, these cells are transported around the body with ease in their fluid medium, the plasma, as Figure 5.1 shows. Most of the other cells of the body are found at a fixed location, rather than being transported around. For example, a type of cell in the eye is specialized to detect light, and such cells enable us to see.

All cells are surrounded by a cell wall, called a **membrane**, which to some extent keeps the constituents of the fluid environment within the cell apart from the fluid environment that bathes the cell. Figure 5.1 shows some cells, their surrounding membranes and the fluid environment that bathes them (called 'interstitial' because it fills up the space between the cells). The interstitial fluid serves as a medium of communication between the cells and the blood.

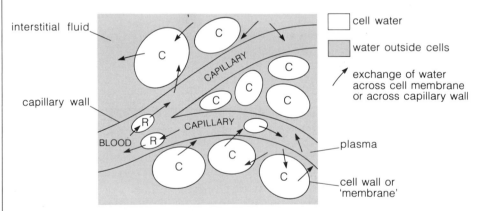

Figure 5.1 Some of the general cells of the body (C), showing the cell wall or membrane that surrounds them, and the fluid medium (the interstitial fluid) that occupies the spaces between them. Also shown are some red blood cells (R) in a capillary (Source: Mook, 1987, Figure 3.4)

2.1 Nerve cells (neurons)

We shall be concerned mainly with a particular type of cell, the **nerve cell** or, as it is more often called, the **neuron**. The total collection of all such neurons in a body constitutes the **nervous system**. Figure 5.2 shows a major part of the human nervous system, the **central nervous system** (CNS). This consists of the brain and the spinal cord, which are made up of millions of neurons. Other neurons, of which only four are shown, carry information to and fro

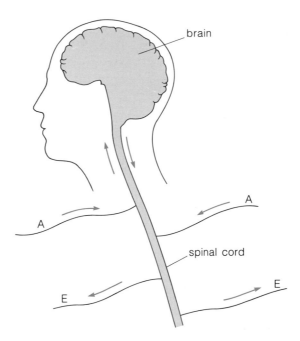

Figure 5.2 The central nervous system (CNS). This consists of the brain and the spinal cord. Also sketched are four of the numerous peripheral neurons, forming part of the peripheral nervous system. Two of those shown are afferent (A), carrying information from the periphery of the body to the CNS. Two others are efferent (E) carrying information from the CNS to the periphery

between the central nervous system and the various regions of the body (e.g. the foot). Such neurons are termed 'peripheral'.

Neurons come in various shapes and sizes, from very small to a metre or more in length. By probing a neuron with a piece of apparatus we can detect a small electrical voltage in the cell; the individual cell is like a small battery. When this electrical voltage remains constant, the cell is said to be 'resting', but when the voltage changes up and down, we describe the cell as being *active*. Many nerve cells have the property of very rapidly changing their electrical state. The cell suddenly changes its voltage and then just as suddenly returns to its original condition. Changes of this kind are termed **action potentials** (see Figure 5.3).

The more frequently a cell changes its voltage in this way, or in other words 'fires', the more active it is said to be. Changes in electrical voltage constitute the signalling system (or 'language') of the nervous system.

Neurons—that is, nerve cells—are defined as a distinct class of cell by virtue of the particular function that they serve, that of handling *information*. That is to say, given that changes in electrical activity are the language of the nervous system, transmitting changes in electrical state from one region to another can be described as a transfer of information. An alternative vehicle for the transfer of information in the body is provided by **hormones**. These are chemicals that are secreted into the blood at one location and exert an effect at a more distant location.

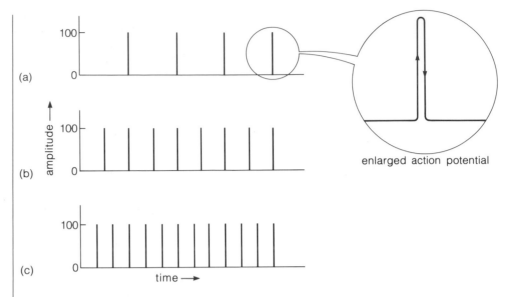

Figure 5.3 A recording of the activity of a neuron over a period of time, shown somewhat simplified. 0 represents the resting state of the neuron, 100 represents the extent of the action potential. (a) Over the period of observation, the neuron changes its electrical state four times: that is, it exhibits four action potentials; (b) the neuron now is more active, showing a higher frequency of action potential generation; and (c) the neuron is more active still. One action potential (circled) is shown enlarged with the time-scale slowed down. Note that the action potential is characterized by a sudden change from the resting state and a return to the resting state

For some neurons, 'handling information' means serving the function of communication over considerable distances in the body. To visualize this function, try a simple exercise: move the thumb of your left hand. The decision to move your thumb was made in your brain. The information was then transmitted to the muscles controlling your thumb, where the command was executed. By their firing, neurons carried this information from your brain to the muscles controlling your thumb. Figure 5.4 shows, in a rough sketch, the pathway involved. Over the first part of the journey, the information travels along neuron 1, within the CNS. Within the spinal cord the information is transferred to neuron 2, a neuron which then proceeds to leave the spinal cord, carrying information to the muscle controlling the thumb. A pathway consisting of neurons, over which information travels, is termed a **neural pathway**.

Over a long distance, information can be transmitted by a number of neurons acting in sequence. Activity in one cell influences that of its neighbour at the junction between the cells. In the case shown in Figure 5.4, neuron 1 carries the information some of the way and then neuron 2 takes over.

SAQ 1   (*SAQ answers are given at the end of the chapter*) What is meant by saying that neuron 1 in Figure 5.4 is active and that activity in neuron 1 instigates activity in neuron 2?

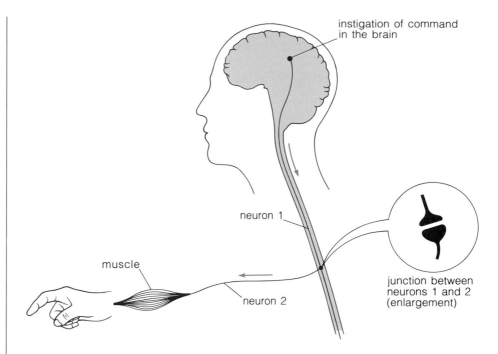

instigation of command in the brain

neuron 1

junction between neurons 1 and 2 (enlargement)

muscle

neuron 2

Figure 5.4 Pathway involved in moving the thumb

Neurons are one of the means by which action is executed. They are also the means by which events arising in the environment are signalled to the central nervous system. Neurons within the central nervous system *process* this information. By the term 'environment' is usually meant the world external to the body. However, in physiology and biological psychology, the word is sometimes also used to refer to the tissues of the body, the 'internal environment' of the body.

Suppose that you tread on a nail. This damage to the tissue of the body soon comes into your conscious awareness. A neuron, whose tip is located in your foot at the site invaded by the nail, is stimulated by the damage and becomes active. The activity is transmitted along the length of this neuron to the spinal cord, and from there to the brain. Figure 5.5 illustrates this. A section of the spinal cord and a neuron, one of a class known as **nociceptors**, are shown. The nociceptor is a neuron that is sensitive to tissue damage at the vicinity of its tip. At the spinal cord, there is a junction between the nociceptor and another neuron. In a relay fashion, this second neuron will transmit the message to the brain. Amongst other things, a transfer of information might be fed to the muscles of the vocal apparatus, which would then be activated, and you would let out a scream.

SAQ 2   In Figure 5.5, are the nociceptor, and the neuron with which it connects, within the central nervous system?

Take another example to illustrate the transfer of information by neurons, as illustrated in Figure 5.6.

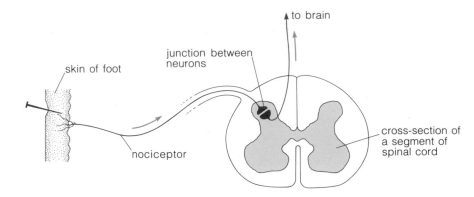

Figure 5.5 A specialized neuron termed a 'nociceptor' that detects tissue damage and conveys this information to the spinal cord. The tip of the nociceptor is at the skin, where it is sensitive to damage in its immediate vicinity. This information is conveyed in the form of action potentials to the spinal cord. At the spinal cord, the nociceptor forms a junction with another neuron that conveys the signal on tissue damage up to the brain

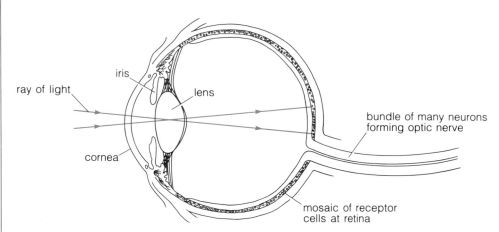

Figure 5.6 The eye and the optic nerve which carries information to the brain. Light passes through the cornea and the lens to hit the retina. Here it influences the electrical activity of some of the mosaic of small light-sensitive neurons ('receptors') that are distributed over the retina. These neurons communicate with others that carry the information in the optic nerve to the brain

Light is absorbed by specialized **light receptors** situated at the retina, the light-sensitive surface at the back of the eye. The electrical state of these receptors is changed by light absorption. In other words, they convert light energy into an electrical signal. These receptors influence other cells at the retina, and the signal is, by such stages, transmitted to the brain.

Suppose that your body is deficient in energy or water, as a consequence of a period of deprivation of one or the other. In the case of water deprivation, the quantity of water held in the cells (including neurons), in the spaces between the cells and in the blood (see Figure 5.1) will fall. A specialized neuron, which is sensitive to the quantity of water contained within it, changes its activity level, and this causes you to be motivated to seek water. At a conscious level, humans report the sensation of thirst. In the case of food deprivation, a neuron would signal deficiency of energy, which would motivate the search for food and would form part of the system associated with conscious feelings of hunger.

Neurons that convey information *to* the central nervous system (for example, the nociceptor shown in Figure 5.5) are termed **afferent neurons**. They convey information either to the spinal cord, as in Figure 5.5, or directly to the brain, as in the case of the neurons forming the optic nerve (Figure 5.6).

Neurons that convey information *from* the central nervous system are termed **efferent neurons**, and a type of efferent neuron is the **motor neuron**. A motor neuron carries a message from the spinal cord to a muscle: an example of a motor neuron is neuron 2 in Figure 5.4. As another example, a motor neuron transmits a signal to the muscle of a foot, so as to pull the foot off a nail.

The majority of neurons in the body are neither afferent (i.e. stimulated directly by events in the environment) nor efferent (i.e. carrying signals to muscles), but are located in the central nervous system, between afferent and efferent neurons. Neurons of this class—for example, neuron 1 in Figure 5.4—are known as **interneurons**. They are the neurons which, amongst other things, play a role in processing incoming information and generating strategies of action in response to it.

2.2 Synapses and chemical transmitters

We now need to consider in more detail the junction between neurons, as shown, for example, in Figures 5.4 and 5.5. The junction between neurons is known as a **synapse**, and an example of one is shown enlarged in Figure 5.7.

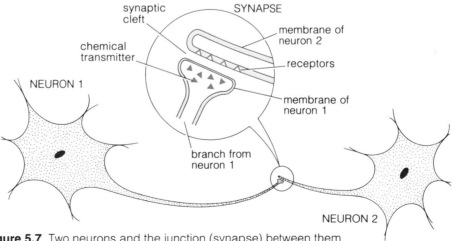

Figure 5.7 Two neurons and the junction (synapse) between them

It is at the synapse that activity (i.e. electrical changes) in one neuron is able to influence the activity of another. In this chapter, our discussion of synapses covers only the most important kind in the human nervous system, the **chemical synapse**. This class of synapse consists of part of the membrane (i.e. cell wall) of each of the two neurons and of the gap between them. By focusing upon events in the two cells that come together at a chemical synapse (henceforth termed simply 'the synapse'), let us see how one neuron is able to influence its neighbour.

At the chemical synapse, a neuron, when active or 'excited', causes a **chemical transmitter** to be released from its ending. In Figure 5.7, neuron 1 is one of this kind. Its terminal is shown enlarged. Observe the chemical transmitter stored at the terminal. Suppose neuron 1 is active. It is causing the chemical to be released from its terminal into the cleft between the cells, known as the **synaptic cleft**, through the thinned area of membrane. The chemical transmitter moves across the membrane into the cleft and attaches itself to the membrane of neuron 2 on the other side of the cleft. One consequence of this transmission of chemical across the synapse can be that neuron 2 then becomes electrically active. In this way, information is transmitted from one neuron to another.

SAQ 3   In the case shown in Figure 5.7, suppose neuron 1 shows a burst of activity. Briefly summarize a sequence of possible events in neurons 1 and 2.

The chemical transmitter substance that is released from one neuron and influences an immediately adjacent neuron is also termed a **neurotransmitter**, or sometimes a **chemical messenger**. There are various different chemical substances employed as neurotransmitters in the nervous system. (Later, in Section 5, we shall discuss neurotransmitters in our study of depression, since there is evidence that depression is associated with abnormalities in some of these chemicals.)

We said that the neurotransmitter attached itself to neuron 2, and thereby was able to make active (or 'excite') this cell. It is now necessary to look closer at this process. In Figure 5.7, consider the part of neuron 2 that is immediately adjacent to neuron 1 in the synapse (within the part of the diagram that has been enlarged and shown encircled). This is the region of neuron 2 that forms part of the synapse; it is the point of synaptic contact between neurons 1 and 2. The surface, or membrane, of neuron 2 at this point contains what are known as **receptors**. When the molecules (chemical particles) of transmitter substance released by neuron 1 collide with the membrane of neuron 2, the receptors catch them and form an association. The analogy of a key and a lock is usually used to illustrate this; the transmitter is analogous to the key and the receptor to the lock. If the key fits into the lock, the door opens. Opening the door is analogous to exciting neuron 2. For information to be transmitted across a synapse, the configuration of the molecules of the transmitter substance must fit the receptors.

The nervous system employs a number of different transmitters. Figure 5.8 shows two adjacent synapses employing two different ones. Neuron 1 is currently firing and releases neurotransmitter A, which fits the receptors of neuron 2. Suppose that a membrane (of neuron 4) at one of the two synapses contains receptors for neurotransmitter B. When active, neuron 3 releases transmitter B, and so neurons 3 and 4 form part of a neural pathway. At the moment captured in Figure 5.8, neuron 3 is inactive. However, some of transmitter A, released as a result of activity in neuron 1, drifts into the synaptic cleft between neurons 3 and 4. Using our analogy, neurotransmitter A is the wrong key for this particular lock, and so would not form an association with the receptors for B at neuron 4. In other words, neuron 4 cannot be influenced by the presence of transmitter A. Thus, neuron 1 can be active, exciting neuron 2, and spilling some transmitter A in the direction of neuron 4, but neuron 4 remains uninfluenced. Only when neuron 3 is active and transmitter B is released into the synaptic cleft would neuron 4 be influenced. By employing chemically distinct transmitters, the nervous system is able to eliminate interference ('cross-talk') between synapses and thereby between pathways.

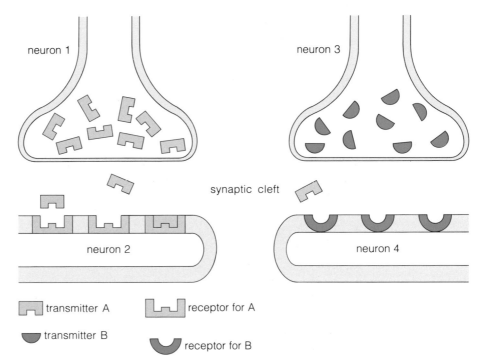

Figure 5.8 Two adjacent synapses employing different transmitters

Transmitter substance is constructed, or to use the correct expression, *synthesized*, within a neuron and is stored at its terminal. As you have seen, when the neuron is active the substance is released from the terminal. A neuron is characterized by the transmitter that it synthesizes, stores and releases. For example, one transmitter is **serotonin**, and a neuron that synthesizes, stores and releases it is termed **serotonergic**. Examination of the brain reveals that different regions sometimes tend to employ different transmitters. For example, one can speak of neurons in a region as constituting the 'cholinergic system', meaning a pathway of neurons all employing the transmitter acetylcholine.

SAQ 4   Of what would a serotonergic synapse consist?

SAQ 5   Look at Figure 5.9. At synapse 1, which neuron influences which?

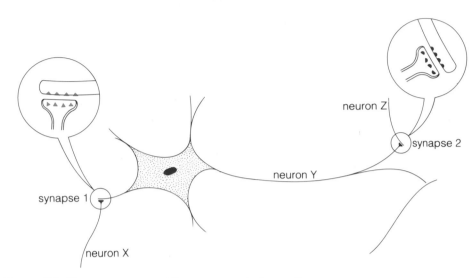

Figure 5.9 Three neurons and the synapses between them

Note that, in Figure 5.9, at synapse 1, neuron Y is unable to influence the activity of neuron X. This is because, at this synapse, X releases transmitter and Y only has receptors for this transmitter. However, at synapse 2, neuron Y is able to influence neuron Z. This is because at synapse 2 the transmitter is released from Y and the receptors are at Z. Therefore, neuron Y is both a receiver of input (from X) and a giver of output (to Z). In fact, this is the way in which most neurons (i.e. the interneurons) function.

Apart from cutting down on cross-talk, there are other reasons why the nervous system uses a number of different transmitter substances. A function that can be served by employing more than one neurotransmitter is illustrated in Figure 5.10.

So far, we have spoken about one neuron *exciting* another at a synapse. Suppose that synapse 1 in Figure 5.10 is of this kind. Activity in neuron A increases the activity level of neuron C to above C's background (i.e unstimulated) level. However, some neurotransmitters exert quite the opposite effect to this; that is, they suppress electrical activity. Suppose synapse 2 is of this kind; that is, it is an **inhibitory synapse**. When neuron B is active, there is a *suppression* of activity in neuron C.

The graphs at the bottom of Figure 5.10 illustrate this. When neither neuron A nor neuron B is active, there is a low 'background' level of activity in neuron C (graph i). When neuron A is active, neuron C is activated (graph ii). Conversely, when neuron B is active, neuron C is inhibited to a level that is below its resting level (graph iii). When both neurons A and B are simultaneously active, their effects tend to cancel out (graph iv). Whether a synapse is excitatory or inhibitory depends upon properties of the transmitter substance and receptors.

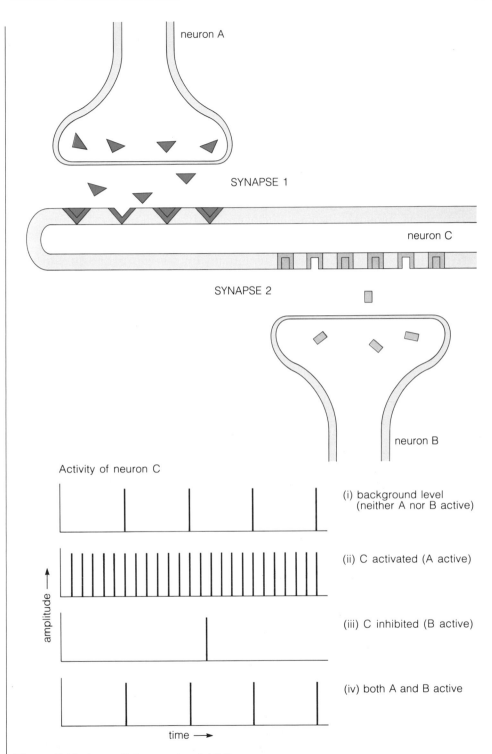

Figure 5.10 An excitatory and an inhibitory synapse

The three neurons A, B and C show how the nervous system can *process* information as well as just conveying it from one place to another in the body. For instance, a high level of activity in neuron C conveys the information that 'there is high activity in neuron A, but relatively little activity in neuron B'. To understand the function served by the process of inhibition, consider again Figure 5.5. If we tread on a thorn, the nociceptor is activated and a message is passed to the brain. We might scream and step off the object. However, on very rare occasions, the brain might need to inhibit such a reaction. For instance, if we are running for our lives and the only escape is through a field of thorns, it could be advantageous for the message labelled 'to brain' in Figure 5.5 to be inhibited. There is indeed evidence for such inhibitory inputs in the region of the synapse shown.

It should not be difficult now to appreciate the importance to psychology of studying neurons. The information that reaches our central nervous system, concerning events both in the outside world and in the internal environment of the body, does so in the language of electrical changes in neurons. To perceive the external world by visual, auditory, touch or smell channels, it is necessary first that neurons are excited by events in the world. Information processing, which is discussed elsewhere, has, as its physical basis, the neural structures of the central nervous system. Our action upon the world, our behaviour, is mediated via muscles that derive their activation from the central nervous system.

Summary of Section 2

- The body is composed of cells. One particular class of cell, the nerve cell or neuron, is distinguished by the function it serves, that of communication of information.

- The total collection of all the neurons of the body constitutes the nervous system. Of this collection, those located in the brain and spinal cord constitute the central nervous system. Others, which are outside these areas, are termed 'peripheral'.

- The communication function of a neuron occurs by changes (e.g. by action potentials) in its electrical voltage.

- Information is carried *to* the central nervous system by afferent neurons and is carried *from* the central nervous system by efferent neurons. Information processing within the central nervous system is carried out by interneurons.

- One neuron influences a neighbouring neuron at a synapse. At a chemical synapse, transmitter is released from one neuron, migrates across the synaptic cleft, and is taken up by receptors on the membrane of the second. As a result of this take-up, the electrical activity of the second neuron is changed. The change can be an increase in activity (excitation) of the second neuron to a level above its background rate, or a decrease (inhibition) to below this level.

- A neuron is characterized by the transmitter that it synthesizes, stores and releases at its terminal, at the synapse. For example, a serotonergic neuron releases serotonin. A synapse is similarly characterized by its transmitter substance. For example, at the serotonergic synapse, serotonin is released from one neuron and serotonin receptors are present at the second neuron.

3 | Genetics and evolution

The discussion so far has emphasized the structure and function of the nervous system. Now is the time to stop and take stock of how we come to *possess* our nervous systems. This section looks at some of the factors that determine the form of the nervous system. To achieve this we need to go back to basics, from the special case of the neuron (the nerve cell) to the general properties of all cells. We shall then return to the specifics of the neuron in the context of development and evolution.

3.1 The cell and the gene

If you examine a cell (not just a neuron, but almost any cell) under a high-powered microscope, it is possible to detect characteristic structures: the membrane surrounding the cell and structures within it (see Figure 5.11). These structures are termed organelles (the word means 'little organs'). A and B in Figure 5.11 are organelles. One particular organelle within the cell, labelled C, is especially important. It is termed the **nucleus**.

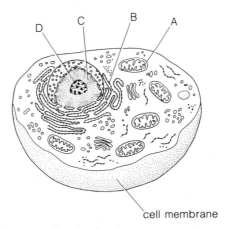

cell membrane

Figure 5.11 Diagram of a generalized cell, shown cut away to reveal its constituents. A, B, C and D are explained in the text

The nucleus of every cell in the human body (other than sperm or egg cells) contains forty-six thread-shaped structures called **chromosomes**; one such is pinpointed in Figure 5.11 and labelled D. These chromosomes are composed, in part, of a complex chemical called **deoxyribonucleic acid** (or DNA for short). The DNA on each thread carries what we could term 'units of information' called **genes**.

What do we mean by the definition of genes as 'units of information'? From the time of conception onwards, the genes act together with environmental factors to influence every aspect of bodily structure and function, such as skin colour, hair colour, height, intelligence and temperament. Some people refer to genes as 'blueprints', by analogy with the design that a draughtsman produces for an engineering product. You might say, for instance, that the genes are the blueprint for your particular hair colour. However, although this analogy might be viable for some characteristics, it can be deceptive, since it seems to imply a fixed plan that is inevitably realized in the course of time. It might encourage us to disregard the importance of the environmental factors. Such characteristics as weight, intelligence or temperament, depend upon a complex interaction between genes and environment. To see genes as 'units of information' (rather than blueprints) that contribute to the outcome is likely to be less misleading.

We now need to consider two important properties of living systems: **replication** and **reproduction**. Consider the growth of a human baby from a fertilized egg; that is, from a single cell. This process of growth is possible because the cells from which the baby is formed repeatedly divide. Consider the initial cell dividing into two cells. Each of these two cells divides to give four cells. These then divide to give eight. So from one cell, we get four, eight, sixteen, thirty-two cells and so on. Each time that a cell divides into two, the DNA in its nucleus is copied. The new cell, although specialized to perform a particular function (e.g. communication, as in the case of a neuron), contains an exact replica of the DNA in the original cell. This replication of cells is a process that occurs within the one organism (see Figure 5.12).

Note that in replication each chromosome pair is copied exactly. We need to ask where that first cell with its full complement of genes came from in the first place. Reproduction (see also Figure 5.12) concerns the production of a *new* organism from the cells of its parents. The egg or sperm cell contains only one half of each chromosome pair. At fertilization, the two halves come together, one from the male sperm and the other from the female egg. Unlike replication, in the process of reproduction what is formed is a cell that is not an *exact* replica of either of the parent cells.

Every human being, including of course yourself, derives from the *fusion* of two cells into a single cell. An egg cell from the mother fuses with a sperm cell from the father. As a result, the gene-carrying chromosomes of the egg (coming from the mother) are paired with the corresponding gene-carrying chromosomes of the sperm (coming from the father). Thereby the newly formed cell has a *novel* set of chromosomes. After extensive cellular replication, and a long period of development and interaction with the environment, accompanied unfortunately by some wear and tear, the final product is the *you* of today.

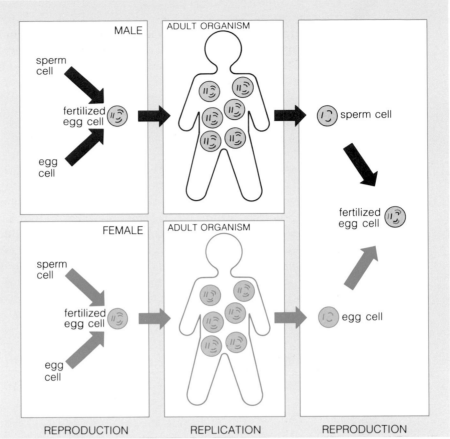

Key: ⫽ gene pair 1;   ⌐ gene pair 2;   ⌣ gene pair 3;

Figure 5.12 Processes of replication of cells within the individual male and female, and reproduction of a new animal. (For simplicity, only six—three pairs—of the forty-six paired chromosomes are shown within each cell)

Suppose one asks, 'by what process does an animal come to acquire genes of a particular kind?'. As you have just seen, one answer might be that the animal got its genes because its parents 'gave' them to it, by the process of combining component chromosomes. However, another way of approaching this question is to consider events over a very long time-scale, over many thousands of generations, and to ask why some genes have survived and others have fallen by the wayside. This is the process of evolution, to which we now turn.

3.2 Evolution

Up until the nineteenth century, the dominant view or, as some might say, 'dogma', on how to explain the diversity of different types of animal in existence in the world was in terms of God's creation. A divine purpose was revealed in this work, and humans formed a pivotal role in this plan. We were created as beings fundamentally different from animals in the important respect that we were endowed with an immortal soul, free will and moral insight.

Today, the dominant explanatory mechanism to account for the diversity of animal forms is **Darwin's theory of evolution by natural selection**. Before I describe this, it is worth mentioning briefly that there is still controversy over the extent to which Darwin's theory is compatible with, or directly antagonistic to, the Biblical account. Opinions vary from atheists holding that Darwin made God redundant, to the belief that evolution is the mechanism of God's creation. Another view, associated with Sir Fred Hoyle amongst others, is that evolution in Darwin's terms is only part of the story and that there is a purposive intelligence at work in the universe (Hoyle, 1983). So now let us see what Darwin's theory is about.

We will make our starting point the estimate that life in its simplest form first appeared on earth about 4000 million years ago. Turning abruptly to today, there are now over one million different species of organism in existence. Imagine watching a film that speeded up these 4000 million years into just a few hours. Starting the film at the origin of life, you would see the development of an enormous divergence of different species, from the simple to the more complex. The complex forms of animal, such as ourselves, would appear only in the last second or so of the film. Over the length of the film, we would see that some species have prospered and increased in numbers over the earth, and then declined. A very large number have become extinct. How do we begin to explain the changes in form of animals and the change in their numbers? Darwin developed his theory to explain this. The starting point of Darwin's theory is that the physical characteristics of an organism are important for its individual survival and for its success in reproducing itself.

SAQ 6   What characteristics of a rat, a kestrel, a peacock and a fish might be important in these regards?

Within a given species, individual animals vary in the individual characteristics that are relevant to their survival and reproduction. For example, some rats have stronger legs than others, and some kestrels have better eyes than others. Some male peacocks will have brighter, or bigger, and thereby more attractive, tails than others. The stronger the rat's legs, the faster it can run. The faster it can run, the longer it is likely to live, and, in general, the more offspring it will leave to posterity.

The environment is such as to allow only *some* of the offspring of an organism to flourish. Some will die, for example, of starvation or be caught by a predator before reaching sexual maturity. Suppose that a feature that gives an animal an advantage is passed to its offspring by a mechanism of inheritance. For example, consider a rat possessing genes that contain information for producing particularly strong legs. Such a rat will endow at least some of its offspring with similar genes, coding for strong legs. Because of their greater speed, rats of this kind will prosper at the expense of slower rats. They will expand in numbers. In other words, the population of rats will change or *evolve*.

By this stage, you might wonder why the legs simply do not go on forever getting stronger and stronger, and thus why a 'lightning-fast' super-rat does not evolve. The answer is that, apart from advantages, 'super legs' would bring disadvantages. For example, the rat would get heavier, which would necessitate higher energy input and more food being found. Being bigger, the number of bolt-holes available to the rat in an emergency would diminish. Evolution would be expected to find a compromise, in effect trading off advantages and disadvantages.

The term 'natural selection' refers to traits, such as strong legs, being perpetuated according to their survival value in a particular environment. In the language of evolution theory, we might say that a successful organism is one that is well *adapted* to its environment and so survives to donate its adaptive genes to its offspring.

SAQ 7   The camel's excellent temperature control system enables it to survive in arid desert conditions. Give some further examples of organisms that could be described as well *adapted* to their environment.

Clearly, in order to reproduce, an organism must survive to the age at which it is sexually mature. After that, the longer it stays alive at an age at which it is able to reproduce, the greater are its chances of endowing posterity with offspring. In biology, the term **fitness** (not to be confused with athletic prowess!) refers to the ability of an organism to survive and produce offspring that can themselves survive and produce offspring. It is possible to identify two factors which contribute to fitness: **fecundity** and **viability**.

An animal's fecundity is defined as the number of fertilized eggs to which a sexually reproducing organism contributes. Viability is an individual fertilized egg's chances of surviving long enough to reproduce. For example, fish produce very large numbers of eggs but few survive. Viability is low. Primates have a low fecundity (few fertilized eggs) but high viability for a given egg.

Let us now return to an assumption that we made earlier in the development of the present argument: that characteristics are inherited from one generation to another. For example, we assumed that a rat with stronger than average legs will tend to endow its offspring with stronger than average legs. How would such inheritance work?

You might have reasoned that it is all very well for us to assume that rats with relatively strong legs endow their offspring with strong legs, but how does a rat with stronger than average legs arise in the first place? One, now-discredited, view is as follows. A particular rat is born with average legs but exercises them more than normal, and thereby strengthens them (possibly a rat equivalent of a jogging fanatic!). By virtue of its prudent physical investment, such a rat's offspring have stronger than average legs. At one time it was seriously suggested that, if such characteristics are *acquired* in the lifetime of an individual, they can be transmitted to its offspring. For this to happen, the change in the leg muscles of the energetic rat would need to be able to change the coding of its genes, since it is only by passing on genes that inherited characteristics can be given to a new organism (see Figure 5.12). We know of no route whereby changes in the coding in a gene could occur as a result of changes having taken place in a muscle. It would be hard to find a serious scientist these days who believes in the optimistic idea that acquired characteristics can be transmitted genetically. The optimism is evident in the assumption that such desirable characteristics as acquired wisdom or muscular prowess would be inherited. However, one might, more pessimistically, ask whether having a limb amputated would influence the genetic information responsible for forming the next generation's limbs. To go to absurd lengths, it might be asked whether dying one's hair blond would lead to blond-haired children. These days, the favoured theory to explain the mechanism of inheritance is as follows.

Recall that the combination of chromosomes at fertilization yields a novel set of chromosomes. Suppose two components (A and B) are needed for strong legs; neither on its own is enough. The father's genes might provide A and the mother's provide B. The unique combination has an advantage over the genes of either parent. Another process also occurs. Occasionally in the process of inheritance a **mutation** appears, by chance, in a gene carried by one parent. As a result of this, an offspring deviates in some respect from what might be expected on the basis of that parent's genes. Such an offspring is termed a **mutant**. The mutation might or might not prove viable. Suppose the mutant form is able to reproduce. Then the mutation can be copied in the mutant's offspring which subsequently follow. In other words, a mutation can be inherited.

It is *as if*, in the environment, the mutation is tested by the process of natural selection. If it has greater fitness than a comparable non-mutant, then animals of the mutant type will increase in frequency. Mutations that are adaptive will prosper, whereas maladaptive mutations will decline in frequency. In practice, most mutants tend to be less fit than the parent form, but a small number are fitter. This *is* evolution by natural selection: that is, in effect, testing out different solutions to the question of what is the fittest form for each species. For example, at the time of the industrial revolution in Lancashire, it became adaptive for certain moths to have a darker colouring. This made it more difficult for predators to spot them against soot-darkened trees, and darker moths increased in frequency.

So far, we have talked about the inheritance of physical characteristics, such as the strength of a leg or the colour of a tail. However, you might feel that we have spent rather long on basic biology for what should be an introduction to psychology. The reason that we have laboured the point is that, on first encounter, evolution is easier to understand in the context of the inheritance of such physical characteristics as strength of legs. However, it is also very relevant to understanding the inheritance of characteristics of the nervous system that underlie the performance of particular behaviours.

Genes were described earlier as 'units of information' that play a role in determining the structure of the developing organism. All the cells of an organism, their form and their interconnections, are determined by gene–environment interaction. Recall from Section 2 that the nervous system contains particular types of cell, called neurons, and their interconnections through synapses. The nervous system is the physical base for the processes that organize behavioural strategies. For example, memory is stored in the nervous system, probably coded in the form of connections between neurons. By means of the nervous system, genes exert their role in behaviour. Some examples make this clear.

The decision by an animal whether to attack or flee from a rival is organized by the nervous system. A factor that plays a role in determining the tendency to attack is the level of the hormone testosterone in the body. The relationship between this level and the attack tendency is not a simple one, and the reader is cautioned against extending the example to humans. However, let us consider that, for males of a particular species, the red deer, the tendency to attack increases over a certain range as the level of testosterone in the blood increases. This occurs because testosterone sensitizes particular neurons that play a key role in the decision to attack. Being in a sensitized state these neurons are relatively easy to trigger by the presence of a rival animal.

Suppose that a mutant male now appears which, by virtue of its genetic endowment, has a secretion rate of testosterone somewhat elevated above normal. As a consequence, this animal has a higher than normal tendency to attack. This could prove adaptive. The male might manage to secure a large number of females for itself, driving away all potential competitor males and producing a relatively large number of offspring. As a result, the mutant gene controlling testosterone secretion would increase in frequency in the future population. However, by contrast, the mutant character trait of high aggressiveness could prove to be maladaptive.

Could you suggest a way in which such a mutation could be maladaptive?

The animal might pick an inordinately large number of fights with other animals. Some of these it might win, but sooner or later it might lose. Even if it 'wins', it might sustain injuries that could later prove damaging. A wound might turn septic. The animal might invest so much time and energy in seeing off potential rivals that it ignores other needs.

This example can serve to introduce two fundamentally different kinds of explanation in animal behaviour, the **causal** and the **functional**. A causal explanation is in response to a question of the kind, 'how do we explain the behaviour of an animal in terms of events happening at the given point in time?'. These events concern the stimuli impinging upon it, the current state of its nervous system and the mechanisms in the brain. Suppose we ask, 'why do male red deer show heightened aggression in the mating season?'. The causal explanation would be in terms of the properties of the nervous system, its sensitization by testosterone, and the instigation of aggression by the presence of a rival male. A functional explanation is in terms of the animal's evolutionary history. It is in response to the question, 'how has such behaviour benefited the fitness of the animal's ancestors and how will it benefit the offspring?'. A functional explanation for heightened aggression in red deer during the mating season is that such fighting increases the animal's fitness, since this is a time when females are sexually receptive.

For another example of these two types of explanation, consider the body-weight of a guinea-fowl hen during incubation of her eggs (Hogan, 1980).

Food is placed only 50 centimetres from the nest, and yet she fails to eat and allows a major fall in body-weight. A causal explanation would be that a neural signal exerts *inhibition* on the feeding system. This signal arises from activity within the system controlling incubation. In terms of a functional explanation, the weight loss could hardly be to the benefit of her own body. She normally regulates body-weight closely. The fall in weight itself is a possible *cost*. However, persisting with incubation is to the *benefit* of the eggs, and, by this means, to the mother's overall fitness; that is, her ability to pass on genes to future generations. The more often she leaves the eggs, the greater are the chances that they will chill or be eaten by a predator. A perhaps still more convincing example of a cost being incurred in the interests of the young, is the feigning of injury done by some birds in order to lure a predator towards an 'easy target' and away from the nest.

Functional explanations of behaviour are a rich source of misunderstandings. Do the red deer or the bird have foresight over what is the best course of action to maximize fitness? Our earlier discussants, Bill and Jean, would doubtless invoke 'it's all just instinct' and 'it's for the good of the species'. It is instinct, in the sense that animals do not have to learn these strategies by trial and error or imitation. They do indeed enable the species to survive. Unfortunately, although what Bill and Jean might have to say on this matter could have some descriptive value, its usefulness in explanation would not be great.

A currently favoured approach to explanation, which can be illustrated by the hen, is as follows: (1) the mother's behaviour in such a situation, in apportioning time between feeding or incubation, is *partly* determined by genes, as realized in her nervous system; (2) by adopting the behaviour shown, she maximizes the chances that her genes will be passed on; and (3) genes therefore can be said to exert a *self-perpetuating* influence. In other words, the information units of the gene will favour behaviour (e.g. large investment of time in incubation) that most effectively leads to the genes' own perpetuation.

How far can we go in explaining behaviour in these terms? So far, the explanations given in the chapter have been fairly uncontroversial. However, examination of the full implications that some theorists attach to the self-perpetuating role of genes sometimes generates passionate debate, as the next section describes.

3.3 The selfish gene

Animals are said to act in such a way as to maximize their fitness. The following example will show how this notion has come to be at the core of contemporary biology and why, in recent years, it has entered popular discussion in such places as the BBC2 television programme *Horizon* and *The Guardian*. The ideas expressed here are controversial and I cannot do justice to their wide implications. I can, however, introduce you to the debate that now occupies a number of prominent thinkers in philosophy, and in the biological and social sciences.

Newcomers to the area often accept the logic of gene perpetuation, but do so with the help of a fallacy. The fallacy is to consider the gene to have a conscious and almost clairvoyant power over the best course of action for the animal to take in order to serve the gene's own perpetuation. The fallacy represents an attempt to answer the question, 'how does the gene, and thereby the animal, *know* what is best?'. This is not the right sort of question to ask. Rather, we need to assume that those genes that provide information that maximizes their own chance of perpetuation are the ones that are around today. These are the genes to have been 'naturally selected'. The others have 'fallen by the wayside'.

A number of theorists argue that, metaphorically speaking, it is *as if* genes are selfish: genes that provide information that best suits their own perpetuation will be perpetuated. Some have argued that one of the more significant contributions to evolutionary biology was the book entitled *The selfish gene* by Richard Dawkins, published in 1976, which developed this argument.

In spite of the concepts *survival of the fittest* and *nature red in tooth and claw*, the notion is deeply embedded in our view of life that animals *act for the good of the species*. Do they? The question is a complex one and contains a booby-trap for the unwary. Unfortunately, attractive as it sounds, there is little evidence that what is for the good of the species can exert an influence on the evolutionary process. A gene coding for pure altruism to other members of one's own species would not prosper in a competitive and hostile world. By the logic of the selfish-gene argument, genes will contribute information in nervous system structures that will bias animals to act in such a way as to perpetuate their own genes, and, in so doing, the species as a whole often *incidentally* benefits.

You might feel that the mother hen's investment in incubation could not be called selfish, but another example will perhaps lend more credence to the appropriateness of the expression. Figure 5.13 concerns the behaviour of wild Olive baboons in Tanzania (Packer, 1977). In (a) male A is copulating with a female with whom he has formed a bond. Male B is standing by. In (b) along comes male C. Male B solicits the help of male C, by rapidly and repeatedly pointing his head alternately at C and A. By this gesture, male C is persuaded to join B in threatening A. Male A leaves the female and is engaged in combat with C. In (c) in the meantime, Male B quickly mates with the female.

So far, this might appear to make little sense in terms of the argument about selfish genes. Obviously it is a way of perpetuating B's genes, but what is in it for C? If anything, there would appear to be considerable *cost* rather than *benefit* to C; he might get injured, and all in the cause of assisting B? According to Dr C. Packer (1977), who made these observations, the benefit to C is as follows. In enlisting the help of C, animal B forms a pact (or *coalition*) with C. On a subsequent occasion, B will serve as the decoy, allowing C to mate. Later, C will again serve as decoy. So after all, each male is pursuing a strategy that selfishly perpetuates his own genes. Although we can make sense of this behaviour in functional terms, it raises profound questions of a casual kind. These questions concern the complexities of the intelligence involved in animals B and C forming a pact that will be 'honoured' on future occasions.

Figure 5.13 Coalitions in male Olive baboons

The action of the incubating fowl clearly has the result of benefiting the survival of the species as a whole. However, this is an incidental spin-off. By the selfish-gene argument, it can only be *explained* in terms of a strategy for perpetuating the bird's own individual genes. If species survival were a factor in the explanation of behaviour, then the action of the Olive baboon presents profound problems. To help the species prosper, one imagines that male A should be left undisturbed. Engaging him in combat runs some risk for all the baboons concerned. For example, a leopard might use the opportunity to sneak up on them. However, the behaviour helps perpetuate B's and C's genes.

It is clear, then, that the 'selfish-gene' debate raises some profound questions and these often serve to generate more heat than light. It undoubtedly gives insight into some aspects of behaviour. However, its opponents argue that examples can be found in nature that do not yield to explanation in terms of gene perpetuation. They note that both (1) the interactions between gene and environment in determining nervous system structure, and (2) the interactions between nervous system and environment in determining behaviour are extremely complex, especially in humans. They argue that this complexity often precludes any simple mapping between genes and behaviour.

One question that this discussion might have raised in your mind is, 'have we got beyond all this in human society?'. Is genuine altruism, with no increase in fitness to the altruist, a myth in animals? Is altruism, with no ulterior motive, a myth in human society? The 'selfish-gene approach' has been characterized by some opponents as being male dominated and imbued with a sexist and reactionary bias. Examples such as baboon mating are in danger of being used as prescriptions for human social behaviour. To the opponents, the richness of human and animal behaviour cannot be reduced to the actions of a series of gene-perpetuation machines. To them, there is something profoundly sordid about even asking the question as to whether one can see any relevance of all this to human societies. However, Richard Dawkins has always strongly cautioned against any simple extrapolation from his ideas to complex human social behaviour.

Whatever the extent to which we can gain insight into human behaviour by looking at animals, the examples chosen should give you a feel for an *aspect* of the process of evolution. Over millions of years, various solutions have been 'tested'. A criterion for good 'design', with regard to both physical and behavioural characteristics, is the fitness of the animal. There might be an optimal solution to be found by natural selection. For example, a tendency to neither excessive timidity nor bullying might represent a good design. A moderate level of attack readiness could be the best. The optimal solution at one point in time might not be so at another. Evolution should be regarded as an 'on-going' process that is, in effect, testing the appropriateness of different designs. Some mutations will prove adaptive and will prosper; others will be maladaptive and become selected out. A large number of mutations might confer no advantage or disadvantage on the holder. Another possibility to consider is that the adaptive or maladaptive significance of some mutations might become apparent only after many generations.

When you consider the fact that information on the structure of the brain, the connections between neurons, the type of neurotransmitter that the cell synthesizes etc., is carried genetically, then the importance of genetics and evolution for the study of behaviour becomes apparent. We showed their relevance to behaviour, considering specifically the examples of feeding, incubation, sex and fighting. In Section 4, we consider again the range of possible activities with which, at any point in time, an animal might need to be engaged in order to stay alive and reproduce, and we shall look more closely at the causal mechanisms that underlie those various activities.

Summary of Section 3

- A sperm cell from the male and an egg from the female fuse to give a new cell. This cell inherits genes from both parents.

- This cell replicates in the course of development to give the millions of cells of the body.

- The genes are 'units of information' that interact with environmental factors to determine the form of the developing organism. As with other parts of the body, the structure of the nervous system is determined in this way.

- In the process of inheriting genes, mutations sometimes occur. These mutations can be adaptive (i.e. give increased fitness) or maladaptive (or neither) relative to the non-mutant gene.

- Evolution occurs by (a) the formation of novel combinations of genes and (b) adaptive mutations increasing in frequency in a population. Maladaptive mutations decrease in frequency. Over time, populations can change in both their physical and behavioural characteristics.

- There is a tendency for those genes that provide information that favours their own perpetuation, to prosper. Some use the term 'selfish gene' in this context, meaning that the behaviour of an animal is to be understood in terms of maximizing the chances of perpetuating its own genes. The area is one of much passionate debate, and extrapolation to human social behaviour is fraught with hazards.

4 | Motivation

There are many activities that an animal in the wild needs to perform in order to survive and pass on its genes. Some of the more obvious activities would be eating; drinking; mating; control of body temperature by hibernating, migrating or nest building; fleeing from predators or attacking rivals; and exploring the environment. These activities all contribute to an animal's fitness. In the last section we considered some decisions, whether to fight, feed or incubate eggs. The role of neurons and their sensitization by testosterone in making the attack decision was discussed. Both external factors (e.g. an intruder) and internal factors (e.g. nervous system pathways sensitized by testosterone) contribute to the attack tendency. The term **motivation** refers to the tendency for an animal to engage in a particular activity, and incorporates both internal and external contributions to this tendency. For instance, an animal that is *moved* to pursue food and ingest it is said to be acting under the influence of feeding motivation.

Depriving an animal of food for a period of time is a powerful way of increasing its hunger motivation by changing its internal state. We sometimes describe the internal contribution to motivation by the term **drive** (Toates, 1986). A rat deprived of water for 24 hours would be said to have a higher thirst drive than one deprived for 12 hours. One can study levels of drive by placing an animal in an apparatus in which the animal works to obtain food or water by pressing a lever (in the case of the rat) or pecking a key (for the pigeon). This apparatus is termed a **Skinner box** and is fully described in the next chapter. Use of this apparatus shows that an animal deprived of food for 24 hours would probably press a bar to earn food more energetically than one deprived for 12 hours.

Some activities, such as drinking, eating and temperature control, serve the interests of the animal's own bodily integrity. Lack of water will lead to dehydration and damage to the body tissues. Lack of food and the consequent energy depletion in the body will likewise compromise its physical integrity. If body temperature goes beyond certain limits, this is hazardous to survival. Fleeing from danger also serves the integrity of the body, though of course by different means to the activities of feeding and drinking. Exploration of the environment by an animal such as a rat would serve its fitness by establishing where food, water and potential bolt-holes are located. In contrast to the other activities, mating does not usually help the animal's individual survival chances. Rather, its contribution to fitness is *directly* through reproduction.

For a complete picture of motivation, we would need to look at a range of activities—for example, feeding, sex and aggression—and try to understand the biological bases of these systems in the animal's nervous system. We shall, however, concentrate upon a particular class of system (described by the term 'homeostasis') that is concerned with the integrity of the body. It is relatively easy to illuminate the biological bases of this class of system, and show its relevance to behaviour.

4.1 The principle of homeostasis

The important physiological parameters of the body, such as water content and temperature, do not normally depart far from their *optimal* values. What do we mean by this? The optimal value is that at which the body functions best. Consider the following example. For human body temperature to rise more than a tiny amount above 37°C is indicative of something being wrong. Normally, if such a deviation from optimum occurs, corrective action is automatically taken to restore conditions to optimum. This property of the body, to maintain its important parameters at an optimal level for the current goal (e.g. watching television or swimming), and to take corrective action when they depart from this, is known as **homeostasis**.

Can you think of some instances in which the body would take automatic action in response to a deviation in a physiological parameter?

An elevation in temperature above normal causes sweating, which reduces temperature back to normal. A fall in temperature causes shivering, which generates heat by muscular activity thereby causing the temperature to rise back up to normal. Swelling of body fluids to above their normal levels by drinking an excess of water causes an increase in urine flow until the excess has been eliminated and body fluids return to normal.

4.2 Homeostasis and motivation

So, how does the principle of homeostasis relate to motivation? The constancy of the internal parameters of the body depends not only upon intrinsic physiological processes, but also upon the animal's behaviour in the external environment. For example, whereas an excess of water is normally lost by urination, a deficiency of water motivates the behavioural mechanism of drinking. Rats and other animals search out a place to drink when they are deficient in water. The supply of energy to the body involves feeding motivation. Temperature can be controlled by intrinsic mechanisms—for example, the shivering and sweating mentioned above—but there are also behavioural means of control. For example, we put on, or take off, clothes, we build houses or we emigrate to Florida. Section 4.3 explains how physiological indicators of water deficiency become transferred into motivation and action.

4.3 The motivation of drinking

Figure 5.1 showed some of the cells of the body, which might have been, for example, skin cells or cells in the lungs or heart. Note the supply of blood to these cells, and the fluid environment within which the cells exist. Recall that something between 60 per cent and 70 per cent of the weight of the human, dog, bird or rat is water. Water is lost from the body by a variety of different means, according to the species. In the service of temperature regulation, humans lose water by sweating. Rats spread saliva over their bodies. To eliminate unwanted substances, urine is formed and excreted. This water is lost first from the blood, but, as the water content of the blood falls, water migrates from the cells and the spaces between them into the blood. Normally, after a certain loss of water from the body, thirst is aroused. The animal is *motivated* to seek water and drink until the deficit is repaired. If water is unavailable, the motivation level increases as the deviation from the optimal level of water gets larger. A homeostatic system that takes corrective action in response to a deficit, so as to correct the deficit, is an example of a **negative feedback system** (Toates, 1980).

How does the system detect the deviation from optimal fluid state? It is believed that there are two types of receptor that monitor different aspects of the internal fluid environment and instigate a motivation signal when their particular local environment is in deficit (Fitzsimons, 1987; Rolls and Rolls, 1982). One detector is sensitive to the volume of a blood vessel, and drinking motivation is instigated when blood volume falls. Another detector consists of a cell, or, more precisely, a specialized neuron in the brain. When the neuron shrinks, this signals to the neural mechanisms that instigate the search for water. In effect, this cell serves as an indicator or 'sample' of the state of all of the cells of the body; its state of shrinkage serves as a sample of general cellular shrinkage due to dehydration. For a familiar analogy, consider that a thermostat on a wall is sensitive only to the temperature of its immediate environment, but none the less the temperature of the whole house can still be satisfactorily regulated with such a detector.

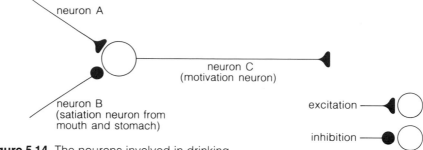

Figure 5.14 The neurons involved in drinking

Figure 5.14 shows a simplified representation of part of the system relating body water and the motivation to drink (Toates, 1980, 1986). Neuron A is a 'sample cell' which is sensitive to its own fluid environment. When its water content falls, the cell becomes active. Neuron A makes an excitatory synapse upon neuron C, the 'motivation neuron'. When neuron C's activity level exceeds a threshold, the rat initiates a search for water and ingests it. Neuron B is a 'satiation neuron', which fires in response to the presence of water in the stomach and the passage of water through the mouth. Neuron B makes an *inhibitory* synapse upon C. The importance of the satiation neuron is as a mechanism to switch drinking off at the appropriate time.

Figure 5.15 shows the responses of some of the neurons involved in the drinking system. Our observations commence at time 0. Note the activity level in neuron A arising from loss of water. Initially, there is no activity in neuron B. As a result of the excitation from neuron A, neuron C is active. The rat is motivated to search for water. At time t_1 the rat commences drinking. Over the course of the drink, which lasts from time t_1 to t_2, the activity of neuron A declines very slightly.

Looking at Figure 5.15, why does the activity in neuron A decline?

The activity in neuron A declines because a little of the water taken into the stomach is already being absorbed into the blood, and thereby into the cells, restoring their fluid volume. Note the rise in activity of neuron B ('the satiation neuron') over the course of the drink. Water passing through the mouth and into the stomach causes activity in this neuron.

How do you account for the fall in activity of neuron C over the period t_1 to t_2 in Figure 5.15?

The activity in neuron C depends upon the *net effect* of the excitation it receives from neuron A and the inhibition it receives from neuron B (i.e. the

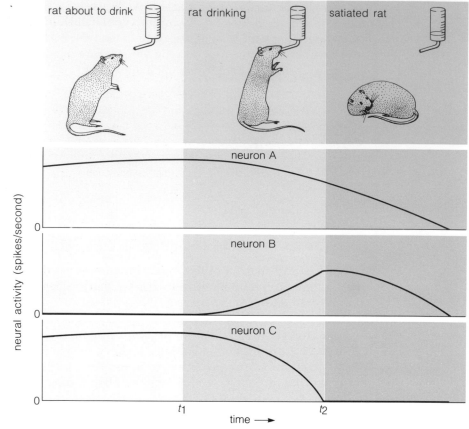

Figure 5.15 Responses of drinking system

difference between excitation and inhibition). As the activity of A declines and that of B increases, so the activity of C declines. At time t_2 the effects of A and B are equal and opposite, and so the activity of C is brought to zero. The rat switches off drinking and enjoys the bliss of satiety.

SAQ 8   In terms of the overall efficiency of the rat, what function does the inhibitory neuron (B) in Figure 5.15 serve?

Having gained some insight into the biological foundations of a motivational system, we can now turn to a more complex system, feeding. This is a motivation less well understood than drinking, and the role of social factors in its determination is more evident.

4.4 The motivation of feeding

Can you think of some of the factors that might influence a human's decision to feed? There are basically two kinds of factors: those internal (or 'intrinsic') to the human, such as the level of energy (e.g. glucose), and those external (or 'extrinsic'), such as the quality and availability of food in the refrigerator. However, there also exist more complex individual and social factors, which we consider later in this section.

An intrinsic factor that plays a part in hunger motivation and the decision to feed is to do with the need for *energy* in the cells of the body. It is therefore useful to return briefly to consideration of the cell. In Section 2, we described the structure of the cell, its nucleus and membrane. We also discussed a particular type of cell, the neuron. In the case of this type of cell, we mentioned synthesis of transmitter substance and the existence of a small electrical voltage in the cell. Changes in this voltage are the signal that the nervous system employs for communication. In other words, the cell is like a small process plant. Chemicals are being synthesized and released. An electrical voltage is being generated. Like any other process plant, the activity requires energy. This energy is in the form of substances such as glucose that are derived from the foods we eat. The blood carries glucose to the cells, glucose is transported across the cell membrane, and into the cell, where it is used as an energy source. Other substances such as fats, vitamins and amino acids are also needed in our diet, but for our purposes we shall concentrate on energy.

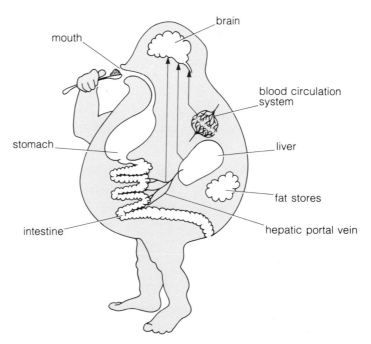

Figure 5.16 Some of the sites in the body that have been proposed for the detector of body-energy state

In order to maintain a supply of energy to the cells, the body requires a mechanism for recognizing its energy state and generating a motivational signal that represents this state. The signal detecting internal energy state would act together with information on, amongst other things, the availability of foods to generate the command to ingest or avoid food. Where, in the body, is the mechanism for detecting energy state? A number of proposals have been made, as Figure 5.16 indicates. Ingested food passes through the mouth and into the stomach, and then into the intestine. It is absorbed across the wall of the intestine into the hepatic portal vein (a large blood vessel) and then passes to the liver. From the liver, nutrients are distributed by the blood to the various tissues of the body. A detector of energy state might be located in the hepatic portal vein, in the liver or somewhere in the blood circulation system. At the moment, the most likely candidate would seem to be a detector of energy availability in the liver (Toates, 1986). When energy level falls, motivation to eat tends to be aroused, and when it is elevated we tend to experience satiety. Figure 5.17 shows how this might be achieved. Suppose for some reason feeding tendency arises unless it is inhibited. The top part of the figure illustrates a condition of energy abundance. The detector cell is taking up substantial quantities of glucose from the blood and is generating action potentials. Activity in this cell might then inhibit feeding tendency. The lower part of Figure 5.17 indicates a deficiency of energy take-up by the cell. This could be because blood glucose level is low. The cell is inactive and so no inhibition is exerted upon feeding tendency. Being uninhibited, feeding motivation would lead to ingestion. Such a detector of internal energy state is part of the story, but it is only part.

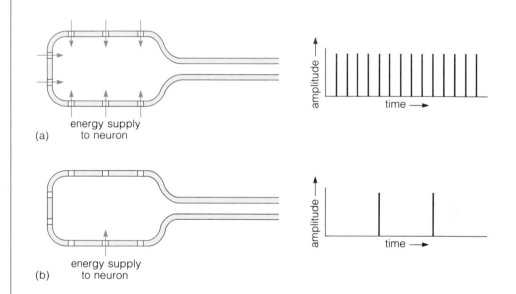

Figure 5.17 The sensitivity of a neuron to energy supply. (a) When energy supply is high, the frequency of action potentials generated is high, as shown in the graph; (b) when energy supply is low, the frequency of action potentials generated is low

Let's now consider some factors *external* to the animal that might play a role in motivation. A rat might neglect its standard diet, but avidly ingest chocolate biscuits. (A similar behaviour is occasionally seen in humans!) We would say that the chocolate biscuits have a relatively high **palatability** or **incentive** value to the rat. To investigate the role of novelty in arousing ingestion, we need to compare an animal's intake when there is a choice of food with its intake when only a single diet is available throughout. Box A describes such an investigation.

BOX A Investigating the role of novelty

The result shown in Figure 5.18 illustrates the power of variety of diet to arouse ingestion (LeMagnen, 1967). The columns show the amount of food in grams eaten by rats in a 2-hour feeding session. In phase I of the experiment, on four successive days, rats are fed for 2 hours with one of four different foods, A, B, C and then D. Each food is basically the same, but made to taste slightly different by the addition of an arbitrary flavour tag, such as lemon juice or almond. Note that, from observations in phase I, there is not much difference in the amount eaten between the four diets; they are equally attractive. Now consider phase II of the experiment. On the first day (test day 1), rats are given 30 minutes of access to diet D, followed by 30 minutes of access to diet B, 30 minutes with diet A and then 30 minutes with diet C. If novelty arouses ingestion, it would be expected that rats would eat more on those days when variety was provided. Compare their total intake over the 2-hour session on the first test day (15 grams) with test day 2 when they were given 2 hours access to diet C only (total intake 6 grams). As successive days show, it is clear that variety is a powerful stimulus to ingestion.

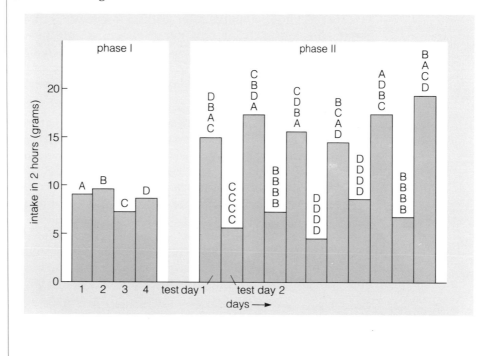

SAQ 9 In the experiment described in Box A, the researchers changed the food dish every 30 minutes even on those days when the identical diet (e.g. CCCC) was given throughout the 2-hour session. Why?

Although the distinction between internal (or drive) and external (or incentive) factors is useful for some purposes, a sharply defined dichotomy can also be misleading. To illustrate this, consider a situation experienced by the American psychologist Martin Seligman. Seligman had what was to become a famous meal in a restaurant which included as its most notable and exotic ingredient *sauce Bearnaise*. Some hours later, Seligman was taken ill with a gastrointestinal disorder.

How do you think Seligman felt towards *sauce Bernaise* subsequently?

The thought of it was repulsive, and he would have been unlikely to be attracted to such a flavour for sometime afterwards.

Seligman had formed an association between the taste and the subsequent ill-effects, a phenomenon that you will study in greater detail in the next chapter. Seligman's claim to fame was that he actually recognized the phenomenon for its psychological interest and implications. You might have experienced a similar phenomenon. I certainly have: I couldn't face the thought of the Greek dish *hummus* for 10 years after having eaten it a few hours before being taken ill. The illness had nothing to do with the meal. I knew that fact intellectually, after visiting my doctor, but my nervous system none the less formed an association between the taste and illness. My intellect could not overcome the basic feeling of nausea. A rat in a similar situation, given *sauce Bernaise* or *hummus*, would shun the diet in the future. A bird eating a poisonous butterfly and becoming sick would tend to shun similar-looking butterflies in the future.

The relevance of this phenomenon to our discussion is that, in the presence of a particular food that has negative associations, the motivation to ingest is low. The animal might have a need to ingest, in that a period of deprivation might have been imposed. The food might be of an intrinsically acceptable kind, in that the animal would readily have ingested it prior to the experience. So, motivational states depend not only upon the animal's internal physiological state and the intrinsic quality of the food, but also upon any internalized *associations* that the animal has formed with the substance (Epstein, 1982; Toates, 1986). This association need not be a negative one. Diets that are followed by beneficial consequences, such as recovery from illness, are favourably labelled by the rat (Rozin and Kalat, 1971; Booth, 1987).

This has been a brief survey of the three principal factors that we need to consider in discussing the motivation to ingest food: (1) energy state of the body; (2) palatability and novelty of food; and (3) internalized learned associations. Learned associations can be very complex, as in the case of persuasion by the advertising industry. Feeding is related in part to energy needs in terms of the flow of energy into the cell. However, particularly in humans, feeding is a complex behaviour with various connotations. It is a social behaviour serving a social communication function. Starvation can be used as an instrument of political protest as in hunger strikes. Identifiable biological factors, as seen in rat models, will give us useful insight, but this needs to be viewed in terms of the social matrix within which the animal exists. A powerful illustration of this point is provided by the condition termed 'anorexia nervosa', which we look at in Section 4.5.

4.5 Anorexia nervosa

The condition termed **anorexia nervosa** has been characterized as '. . . the relentless pursuit of thinness through self-starvation, even unto death' (Bruch, 1974). It is a puzzling phenomenon.

Just to give us an initial orientation with which to approach this, recall two phenomena discussed earlier. In Section 4.4, I described instances in which ingestion of food depends not only upon its intrinsic quality and the subject's internal energy state, but also upon the associations or *connotations* of the food for the individual. Recall also the experiment discussed in Section 3.2 regarding incubation in the guinea-fowl, in which the hen allowed her body-weight to fall. The result of this experiment was described in terms of maximizing fitness.

What is the important message of these results as far as the control of feeding and regulation of body-weight are concerned?

These results show that, to understand what is happening to the feeding- and weight-regulating systems, it is sometimes necessary to consider them in a broader behavioural context. Behaviour is the outcome of an *interaction* of factors. In the example of the hen, feeding, or its absence, could be understood fully only by considering the other activities. The dominant activity was incubation and this was able to exert inhibition upon the feeding system. These examples give just an initial lead in the attempt to make sense of anorexia nervosa in that they suggest, for understanding the anorexic, the need to consider (a) the associations or connotations of food and (b) the feeding system in the context of other systems and activities.

According to definitions given by The American Psychiatric Association, for a patient to be classified as suffering from anorexia nervosa, it is necessary to rule out any form of identifiable 'organic pathology' as the fundamental cause. The expression 'organic pathology' means abnormality somewhere in the body tissues; for example, a failure of the cells of the body to take up glucose from the blood, a breakdown in the neurons that detect energy level, or a failure of the cells in the brain to synthesize a transmitter substance. Therefore, anorexia nervosa represents a failure to eat, for which no identifiable cause can be found within the tissues of the body. The definition does not preclude the possibility that, in the future, some underlying organic pathology might be identified in a causal role, though that would seem to be the most unlikely explanation. Anorexia nervosa afflicts predominantly young women; only about 5 per cent of sufferers are male.

The word 'anorexia' means loss of appetite, but, in the present context, is something of a misnomer. Although the patient will often *appear* to have no appetite, it can be misleading to focus attention upon this (Palmer, 1980). She (or he) is by no means always lacking in appetite; some subjects report strong hunger and have binges. Rather, the patient could more accurately be described as being phobic about a normal weight or obsessed with slimness. Feeding and starving are secondary to this consideration. The behaviour serves the *purpose* of slimness. The phobic attitude towards weight sets this condition apart from other eating disorders, such as loss of appetite secondary to depression or a phobic fear of contamination by objects including food (for example, the germ phobia of the aircraft maker and film producer, Howard Hughes).

In anorexia nervosa, food intake is often followed by self-induced vomiting or compulsive exercise rituals designed to burn off surplus calories. A significant number of anorexics appear to have a distorted perception of their body size, seeing themselves as being larger than they really are.

There have been numerous attempts to explain the condition, in terms of, amongst other things, a desperate plea for attention, pathological dynamics within the family, a protest strike against the demands of awakening sexuality, or a response to oppressive societal pressures for slimness directed primarily towards women. (The latter is well described by the feminist writer Susie Orbach, in her book *Hunger strike*.) Of course, these are not mutually exclusive explanations.

The ramifications of the difficulty are expressed well by Dr R.L. Palmer in his book *Anorexia nervosa*:

There can be few more difficult experiences for a parent than to see their child wasting away while refusing the offers of food which seem such a tantalizingly simple solution to the problem. It is often suggested that the young people who fall ill with anorexia nervosa come from families with more than their fair share of interpersonal and other problems. If this is indeed true then the anguish of the parents may well be the greater for it.

(Palmer, 1980)

Indeed, in some circles family therapy is the favoured course of action for this disorder.

Although there is no identifiable physiological *cause* to be found in the tissues of the body, once weight starts to fall there are profound disturbances in physiology. Amongst other things, menstruation stops. Once the condition is initiated, it then becomes extremely difficult to tease apart cause and effect in so far as the psychological condition of not eating and the associated organic pathology are concerned.

Although the understanding of this condition is still very incomplete, for our purposes it serves well to illustrate the point that feeding is to be explained only *partly* in terms of events in the tissues of the body. It is also necessary to consider social interactions and the subject's own interpretation of her (or his) situation. Feeding or starving can serve a variety of ends concerned with self-image, social aspirations and role in life. A human's behaviour is so often at odds with what we might at first predict from simple rat-based explanatory models, such as homeostasis and fitness maximizing. Section 5 looks at depression, another example of where human behaviour 'goes wrong'.

Summary of Section 4

- Some motivations contribute to preservation of the integrity of the individual animal's body; for example, the motivation to escape from danger. A class of such motivations—for instance, feeding, drinking and temperature control—contribute to this end as part of the mechanism of homeostasis.

- In homeostatic systems, a deviation from the optimal level in a physiological parameter causes motivation appropriate to restoration of the optimum, an example of a negative feedback system. For instance, a deficit of water arouses the motivation to ingest water. Ingested water restores normality.

- Some motivations do not contribute to bodily integrity, but are concerned more directly with reproduction. Sexual motivation is obviously an example of this.

- The body contains specialized neurons that detect fluid and energy states. Their signals contribute towards the decisions as to whether to seek food and water and ingest. Activity in 'satiation neurons' inhibits motivation.

- Two basic kinds of factors influence the motivation to ingest a given food: the internal (e.g. the energy level of the body), and the external (e.g. the palatability of food). However, there are also more complex individual and social factors such as the learned associations that the animal has formed with the food.

- The condition anorexia nervosa is a particular example of a pathological condition of self-imposed starvation for which there is no identifiable organic cause, emphasizing the importance of such influencing factors as self-image and family dynamics.

5 | Depression

This section looks at depression as a case study to illustrate the relevance of neurotransmitters, neurons, genetics and the comparative approach to understanding a complex human phenomenon. It illustrates the relationship between the approaches but also highlights the pitfalls that await the unwary in attempting to apply biology to phenomena in psychology.

Depression should not be thought of as a single or 'unitary' phenomenon; there exist different classes of depression (Willner, 1985). For example, in one type of depressive disorder, phases of depression alternate with phases of mania characterized by unrealistic optimism, high levels of energy and heightened activity. Space precludes discussion of this disorder here. We shall be concerned only with the class of depressive disorder not showing mania.

Probably everyone has some idea of what depression is like. Although they might have escaped it themselves, many know of a relative or friend who has been treated for this condition. They will have seen their behaviour and heard of their mental anguish.

Depressed people are likely to report being down in spirit, feeling powerless to influence events, are low in energy, and have feelings of apathy and/or pessimism: that is, they feel hopeless and helpless. They are unmotivated to engage in their usual activities. If they do engage in them, they derive little or no pleasure from them. They have difficulty in concentration and might report having a low self-image and feelings of guilt. Thoughts often turn towards suicide and death. Signs of depression include waking early, eating rather little (though, for some people, overeating), little or no positive interest in sex and withdrawal from social contact and activities (Sutherland, 1976; Willner, 1985).

Depressed patients tend to show an increased sensitivity to negative events, such as criticism for example. Their sensitivity towards positive elements, such as favourable feedback on their performance, tends to be decreased. Controlled experiments have shown that, for depressives, recall of events, such as incidents in a story, tends to be biased towards negative events (Breslow, Kocis and Belkin, 1981). A leading theorist and pioneer in developing techniques for treating depression, Aaron Beck, has summarized these aspects of depression as a **negative cognitive set** which is revealed as a bias in behaviour, thinking, fantasy and dreams.

Try to list some of the external and some of the internal factors that you think might be important in the causation of depression.

You have probably listed such external factors as the loss of something valuable to the person, as in divorce, bereavement and unemployment, and such internal factors as the physiological changes occurring during an attack of influenza, or following the birth of a child, or accompanying the female menstrual cycle or menopause.

5.1 The biochemistry of depression

Currently, much research on depression is focused on the neurotransmitters dopamine, noradrenaline and serotonin, amongst others. Whether one of these is particularly important, or whether their interaction is more crucial, is a question still open to debate. However, researchers are converging on the opinion that in some way an abnormality at certain *key synapses* within the central nervous system has a crucial role to play in depression. Figure 5.19 shows some possible abnormalities at a key site in a person's nervous system. In principle, one or more of these might play a role in depression. The abnormality could exert a bias in the nervous system towards those behaviours and feelings that we term depression.

Some of the evidence on the role of factors in the central nervous system that play a primary role in depression comes from looking at patients who

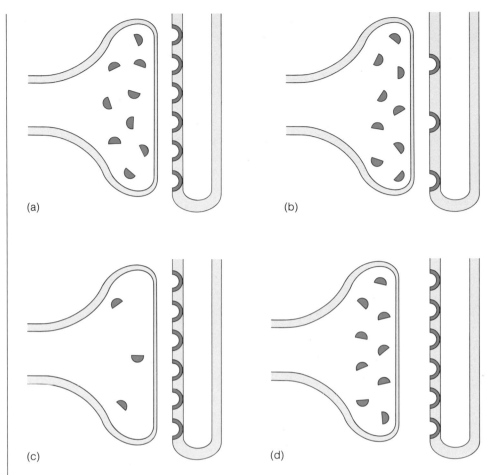

Figure 5.19 Possible abnormalities at a key site in a person's nervous system: (a) shows a normal synapse and (b), (c) and (d) show forms of abnormality. The synapse shown in (b) has an abnormally low number of receptors on the post-synaptic membrane. This would mean that even for a normal release of transmitter, the effect on the post-synaptic neuron would be lower than normal. (c) represents the case of an abnormally low level of synthesis and storage of transmitter. An action potential in this neuron would cause relatively little chemical to be released into the cleft. (d) represents an abnormally wide synaptic cleft. Transmitter would tend to leak out before reaching the receptors on the post-synaptic membrane

experience depression as a side-effect of other disorders or of the treatment of these disorders with chemicals. One of the most influential findings appeared in the 1950s, and biochemical theories of depression date from this time. Patients suffering from hypertension were given the drug reserpine to lower blood pressure. One of the side-effects of this treatment in a significant percentage of patients was depression (Fries, 1954). Reserpine causes a depletion of the brain's neurotransmitter, noradrenaline, and this suggested that depression might at least sometimes be associated with abnormally low levels of activity in synapses employing noradrenaline.

Further evidence has been provided by the effects of another drug, called iproniazid, which increases the noradrenaline level in the brain (reviewed by

Willner, 1985). This drug has an antidepressant effect which indicates that it might counteract the low levels of noradrenergic activity at crucial synapses.

Whatever the broader implications, one might think that the results of reserpine administration clearly show the influence of an internal factor in depression, and in a sense they do. However, when we look closely at the results, we see it is more accurate to consider the interaction of several factors. Those patients reporting depression induced by reserpine were those who, earlier in their lives, had experienced depression. Reserpine did not tend to cause depression in patients not having had an earlier experience of depression. This result has caused some, for instance Paul Willner (1985), to argue that reserpine *biases* or sensitizes a part of the nervous system towards depression. External environmental events and memories of earlier depression then act in combination with the sensitized part of the nervous system to generate the experience of depression.

You should be able to suspect already that a question of the kind, 'is depression biological or social?' can sometimes, if not always, be fundamentally misleading.

Another valuable source of evidence on depression comes from looking at patients suffering from Parkinson's disease. This disease is associated with a deficiency of the neurotransmitter dopamine, caused by a degeneration of dopamine-containing neurons. Patients suffering from Parkinson's disease also tend to suffer from depression, thus suggesting the possibility that dopamine deficiency plays a role in depression.

Why do we need to be careful in our interpretation of such a result?

Dopamine deficiency might have a direct effect upon both depression and Parkinson's disease. However, we need also to consider the possibility that the depression is a consequence of the *psychological* impact of Parkinson's disease upon the victim, rather than something sharing the same biochemical basis. In fact, though, there is a high incidence of depression even in the early stages of the disease, when the symptoms of Parkinsonism are only mild. Attempts have been made to compare Parkinsonian patients and, as a control condition, non-Parkinsonian patients who have a similar physical disability. This might show whether the impact of disability alone can account for depression. The non-Parkinsonian patients show a much lower incidence of depression (Robins, 1976), suggesting a primary role for dopamine deficiency in Parkinsonian patients.

Another piece of evidence to implicate a role for dopamine in depression is that drugs which have a similar effect to dopamine on the central nervous system often produce an improvement in the depressed patient's condition. There is also evidence that electroconvulsive therapy (ECT), which can be effective in cases of severe depression, boosts the dopamine system (discussed by Willner, 1985). This treatment consists of passing a brief electric current through the patient's brain.

5.2 Types of depression, and explanations

As an initial classification, it is useful to distinguish between factors internal and external to the subject, in discussing the causes and treatment of depression. However, rather as we saw for feeding, such a classification needs careful qualification. As we look more deeply into the subject, a neat dichotomy between two such sets of factors can sometimes be inherently misleading.

Depression is often classified as **endogenous**, in which the cause is said to be internal (e.g. a chemical transmitter imbalance) or **exogenous**, in which we describe the cause as external (e.g. loss of a marital partner). The term 'reactive' is sometimes used in a similar, if not identical sense, to 'exogenous'. Again, the external–internal distinction is a valid one up to a point, and has proved to be useful in some therapeutic interventions. However, if this is taken to be an exclusive categorization, it can be misleading. That is to say, it is wrong to ignore endogenous factors in exogenous depression and vice versa.

A person suffering from an endogenous depression will not experience misery in a psychological vacuum divorced from events in the external environment. Rather, the external environment will interact with a nervous system that is biased towards a depressive reaction by internal events. Events in the external environment that might otherwise represent reasonable challenges would be seen as the cause for hopeless despair. For a given abnormal internal condition, one could imagine the two extreme conditions of external factors being such as to accentuate (e.g. threat of unemployment, divorce) or minimize (e.g. finding a supporting partner) the chances of a full-blown depression reaction.

Now imagine external factors, such as a divorce, which are seen as the prime causes of exogenous depression. The effect of such external events will depend upon the sensitivity of the nervous system to a depression reaction (e.g. the levels of certain neurotransmitters).

Figure 5.20 represents a useful way of viewing the complex interaction between internal and external factors as determinants of depression. Events in the external environment impinge upon the sense organs and are detected and perceived by the subject. The subject places an interpretation upon these events (Oatley and Bolton, 1985). Changes at certain central key synapses will bias the interpretation towards the negative, which will in turn change the state of the key synapses. This will lead the subject to construe the world as even more negative. Anticipating failure, the subject will be unmotivated to pursue normal goals. The consequences will shift the system still further in the direction of depression. Like the motivational systems described earlier, this process exhibits feedback (Toates, 1980). However, it is characterized as **positive feedback**, since a deviation from normal at a central synapse can become self-reinforcing and self-amplifying. By contrast, for a negative feedback system, deviations are self-eliminating. Action returns the system to normal.

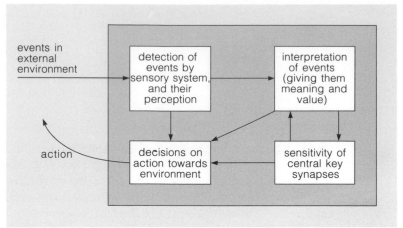

Figure 5.20 A way of conceptualizing depression

SAQ 10   Looking back to Section 4.3, give an example of a negative feedback operation in motivation that stands in contrast to the positive feedback operation just described.

Clearly then, fundamental errors can be made in attributing weightings of importance to internal factors (e.g. synaptic changes) or external factors. Both sets of factors are obviously crucial and are inextricably *interactive*.

We now consider another good example of an occasion when a neat internal–external dichotomy can be misleading. To do so, it is first necessary to discuss stress. Some researchers find it useful to divide the factors that play a role in depression between immediate causes and long-term sensitizors. This is not a clear-cut distinction; there exists a grey area of overlap, but it is a useful first approximation. A well-known long-term sensitizor is *stress* (Anisman and Zacharko, 1982). Examples of this include years of marital disharmony and the threat of unemployment. Some authors prefer the expression *strain* to refer to the long-term predisposing factor. A study by George Brown and Tirril Harris, in inner London, identified the strain experienced by unemployed women bringing up three or more young children on their own (Brown and Harris, 1978). This study identified the absence of social support as being a significant factor; a confiding relationship was an 'antidote' to depression.

In the case of stress caused by environmental events, we can identify the physical basis as a biochemical change in a region of the brain known as the *locus coeruleus*. This has been investigated by examining the brains of animals that had been exposed to stress. Techniques are available for identifying the quantities of different neurotransmitters at specific brain sites. A lengthy period of exposure to stress results in changed activity levels of certain neurotransmitters. Specifically, there is an increased activity in neurons containing acetylcholine relative to the activity of those containing noradrenaline and dopamine. So, is stress an external or internal factor? It is the outcome of complex external–internal interactions, associated with identifiable changes in the brain.

SAQ 11 Recall Bill's statement at the beginning of this chapter, regarding Harry's disorder: 'His nerves just break down once in a while, like the bits of an old car'. Does this fit our understanding of the basis of depression in the nervous system?

5.3 Inheritance and depression

Can you recall Bill's statement: 'I've read that depression and that sort of thing run in families'? Jean retorted: '. . . if it runs in families, how can we explain that Harry's brother is as normal as you or me?'.

Having been introduced to genetics in Section 3.1, you are now in a better position to consider this discussion. Bill is right: depression does indeed, to some extent, run in families. That is to say, the children of people suffering from depression tend to suffer from depression more than do the children of non-depressive parents (McGuffin and Katz, 1986).

In principle, is there a possible explanation for this that makes no appeal to genetics?

One might argue against the role of genetics by claiming that being brought up by a depressed parent is almost bound to be a depressing experience for the growing child. In addition, a depressed style of interacting with the world could be imitated. So, if we find a tendency for transmission of depression from one generation to another, we would need also to consider the environmental factor before rushing in with a genetic explanation. Let us be sure now that we know exactly what we mean by a 'genetic factor' in depression. Let's hope that we can be rather more sophisticated in our discussion than were Jean and Bill in theirs.

Recall that, in Section 3.1, we saw that genes are units of information that act in complex interaction with environmental influences to determine the structure and behaviour of an animal. Possibly, by the process of inheritance, some genetic units of information could bias certain individuals towards depression. If, however, we simply look at families, it is impossible to tease apart the influence of genetics and environment: these two factors are inevitably *confounded*. Most probably both factors play a role.

A possible way of approaching this question is to compare identical and non-identical (known as fraternal) twins brought up by their natural parents. Biologically, these types of twin are very interesting. Identical twins are genetically identical, being derived from a single fertilized egg which has divided into two. Fraternal twins derive from two different fertilized eggs, and have, on average, only 50 per cent of the genes in common. Suppose we look at a number of identical and fraternal twins, and administer to each a questionnaire that is designed to measure their depression. The questions would be of the kind, 'how often have you contemplated suicide?' and 'does life have a purpose for you?'. Let us say that 10 is a maximum score of depression and 0 is no sign of depression.

Look at Figure 5.21.

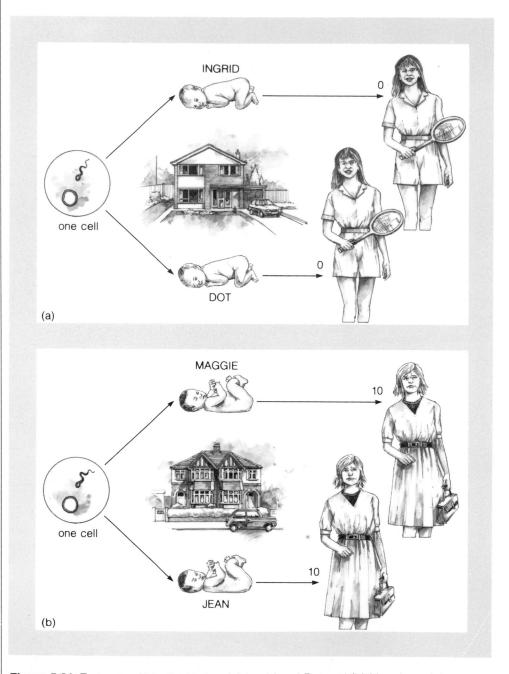

Figure 5.21 Two sets of identical twins: (a) Ingrid and Dot and (b) Maggie and Jean. Identical twins derive from a single fertilized egg, and so are genetically identical. The numbers refer to the depression scores of the individuals

Ingrid and Dot are a pair of identical twins, coming from a single cell. Neither is depressed. Each has a score of 0 on a depression index. Maggie and Jean are another pair of identical twins. They are both very depressed. Each has a score of 10. From looking at a number of such pairs, we could get a measure of the extent to which the two halves of the pair are alike in their score. This is a special type of correlation known as **concordance**. This sample of two pairs would give the maximum possible concordance. Of course, in reality the science of behaviour is never as neat as that! The point is simply that one can get a measure of concordance. Now look at Figure 5.22 which shows two pairs of fraternal twins: that is, twins coming from separate cells. Again, we could work out the concordance for a large number of such pairs.

Which type of twins, identical or fraternal, would you expect to have the higher concordance if there is a significant genetic contribution to depression?

Since identical twins are more alike genetically, one would expect higher concordance for identical than for fraternal twins.

In practice, when such studies have been carried out, it has indeed been found that the concordance in depression scores is higher for identical than for fraternal twins. How do we explain this? Note that within each of the pairs of twins, the environment is assumed to be constant, so presumably we could attribute the greater concordance of identical twins to their greater genetic similarity.

Look carefully at the four pairs of twins in Figures 5.21 and 5.22. Can you see that there is another possible interpretation for the closer concordance in depression of identical rather than of fraternal twins?

The figures suggest that identical twins dress alike and seem to have similar interests (e.g. both Ingrid and Dot appear to like tennis), which is not true for our fraternal twins. Based upon anecdotal evidence, this might seem a reasonable assumption. Someone might even argue that the similarity in dress of Ingrid and Dot is the result of genetics. On the other hand, it could also be argued that identical twins are *treated* more similarly than are fraternal twins. Possibly, the environment channels identical twins into pursuit of very similar activities. Of course, our diagrams exaggerate reality, but the point is that we must be very cautious in simply stating that the environment is as similar within fraternal as within identical twins. Some authors claim that the common assumption, suggested in our figures, of a closer similarity of treatment of identical as compared with fraternal twins is simply not true in practice (Eysenck, 1977). Given the higher concordance in depression scores for identical as compared with fraternal twins, this would strengthen the argument for a genetic contribution to depression. The point is that trying to tease apart the roles of genes and environment is like walking over an intellectual mine-field. Mercifully, you are not expected for the moment to negotiate your way through, but merely to recognize the existence of the mines. We return to this topic in Chapter 7.

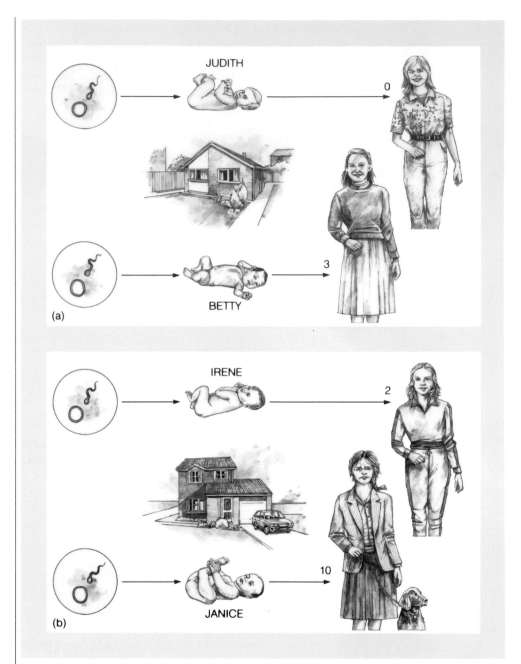

Figure 5.22 Two sets of fraternal (i.e. non-identical twins): (a) Judith and Betty and (b) Irene and Janice. Fraternal twins derive from two different fertilized eggs, and, though similar genetically, are not genetically identical. The numbers refer to the depression scores of the individuals

Another possible approach to this question, which addresses the issue of the confounding effect of similar environments, is to look at twins who have been brought up in different environments; for example, by different foster-parents. Again, a genetic contribution towards depression might be expected to reveal itself in a larger concordance in depression scores for identical rather than for fraternal twins. Indeed, this has been found. However, one also has to avoid mines here. First, the sample of subjects is not typical. Twins who have been adopted will be likely to have come originally from deprived families. This raises the question of the generality of any findings in this area. Second, even if the twins were looked after by foster-parents from almost immediately after birth, there is still an environmental factor present in what could be a crucial early stage of life. This might well have been stressful. Even before birth, the twins would have been exposed to any influences in the blood of the mother, such as an elevation in stress hormones which might bias towards later depression. If there exists any chance for confounding influences to exert a role, someone will probably sooner or later draw attention to them.

Having pointed out the mines, we can now make some more positive and intellectually satisfying statements. Let us return to the discussion between Bill and Jean, and to Jean's argument that '. . . if it runs in families, how can we explain that Harry's brother is as normal as you or me?'.

We are now in a position to sharpen the logic of this debate. First, we need to be clear as to whether Bill had considered the environmental factor. If he had, and was referring specifically to genetic transmission, then our answer would be that only 'units of information' can be transmitted genetically. This information interacts with the environment to give a behavioural outcome. Suppose Harry's brother is not his identical twin. Their genes will therefore not be identical. Perhaps the genetic contribution towards depression is less in the case of Harry's brother. However, it might be greater, and yet Harry's brother might be fortunate enough to live in a very stress-free environment. He might have a harmonious family life and a secure job, scoring low on the strength of environmental stress factors. In other words, there is nothing fixed and immutable in the realization of such a genetic transmission of information. The good mental health of Harry's brother is not necessarily an argument against a genetic factor. By analogy, the much-quoted favourite great-uncle who smoked eighty cigarettes a day and yet still managed to live to be ninety-five, is not a convincing argument against a causal role of smoking in lung cancer.

SAQ 12   Can you recall from Section 3.1 why, in the context of the present subject-matter, we were reluctant to employ the expression 'blueprint' for the information content of the genes?

We are also in a good position now to see what is probably a fundamental misunderstanding in Jean's statement 'First, it's all in the genes. Now it's his nerves'. The genes and the nervous system are not two mutually exclusive sites at which a problem could be identified. Genetic differences between two individuals can give rise to a difference in their nervous systems. So, a genetic contribution towards depression would most likely be mediated via the neurons of the central nervous system. The various abnormalities shown in Figure 5.19 could be inherited genetically.

5.4 Animal models of depression

We noted in Section 1 that one possible way of trying to gain understanding of a complex human phenomenon is to take a comparative look at animal models that approximate to the human condition. The question as to whether animals experience subjective states of mental anguish is unanswerable, though from logical extrapolation and ethical considerations it would seem safest to assume that such advanced species as monkeys, rats and cats do. What we can investigate is whether there are *behavioural* manifestations of depression in animals, a topic that is discussed further in the next chapter.

Recall that one of the behavioural signs of depression in humans is disengagement from incentives; such natural incentives as food and sex lose much of their appeal. There is a reluctance to engage in normally pleasurable behaviours. Behaviour analogous to this can be observed in animals when the activity of the dopaminergic pathways (i.e. pathways composed of neurons that employ dopamine as their transmitter) is reduced (Wise, 1982). In an experiment, a rat whose neurons are deficient in dopamine, bar-presses in a Skinner box less energetically for natural rewards, such as food.

Another possible animal model of depression that is somewhat more natural consists of the reaction of an infant monkey to separation from its parents (McKinney, 1984). Such an animal goes through a phase of protest followed by a period of silent withdrawal from activities, sitting hunched in a corner. The latter might in some ways be analogous to human depression.

5.5 Evolution and fitness

At this stage, it is interesting to view depression in terms of the concepts of evolution and fitness. We argued that evolution is an arbiter of fitness, that animals exhibiting even a marginal advantage are likely to be selected at the expense of others. The phenomenon of depression might appear to make little sense in these terms. After all, in humans, depression is sometimes linked with suicide and impotence, factors that we hardly associate with the maximizing of fitness. So is depression maladaptive? If it is, we might ask how it has evolved. Alternatively, we might ask the surprising questions, 'could there be an evolutionary advantage for an animal to adopt the depression strategy of withdrawal and disengagement at certain times?' and 'could this help to explain human depression?'. It is possible to envisage that it might be to an animal's advantage to behave with a strategy of withdrawal from activity when active coping with external circumstances proves impossible. For example, suppose an abandoned baby monkey adopts a protest strategy of shrieking for a while. It finds that this fails to do any good in the sense of bringing help. The best thing to do then might well be to disengage from the world, conserve energy, stay quiet, and avoid predators and the intolerable stress of repeated failure. We might call this a *depression strategy* for coping. The baby monkey might solicit help this way.

At this point we need to sound some loud notes of caution; there are several fundamental misunderstandings that can so easily arise.

Misunderstanding 1: 'That whatever exists, in the form of a physical characteristic or a propensity to behave in a certain way, must have arisen by a process of evolutionary competition in the struggle for fitness maximization'. The reasonable assumption that characteristics that increase fitness will prosper, does not lead logically to the conclusion that *all* human traits have emerged from the historical struggle for fitness competition. For example, it would be misleading to argue that red blood cells are red because this colour conferred an advantage on the first animal that possessed it.

Misunderstanding 2: 'That if we observe behaviour in an animal and can see where it might confer an advantage, then analogous behaviour in humans also confers a similar advantage'. The animal model can sometimes give us a useful hint or pointer to the evolutionary basis of something, but uncritical extrapolation is to be avoided. A trait arising in the process of evolution might no longer confer any advantage on humans. We are no longer simply at the mercy of evolutionary competition, but have created cultures and institutions like the National Health Service and the Family Planning Association which play a role in determining who shall survive and reproduce and who shall not.

From a plausible suggestion on the evolutionary origin of depression, it does *not* follow that the behaviour of depressed people is necessarily to their benefit. The misunderstandings listed above should caution you in using evolutionary arguments. The magnitude of the human reaction of depression is often out of all proportion to its possible benefits, so that it is an enormous burden both for the sufferer and for his or her relatives. We should perhaps view long-term depression as an aberration of a potentially adaptive behavioural strategy. Similarly, gross overeating is doubtless maladaptive. However, it represents an aberration of an adaptive mechanism, that of the arousal of feeding motivation by available and palatable food. It could be argued that, were it not for the human trait of charity, depressed and other disadvantaged people would be unlikely to survive.

5.6 Types of explanation and their implications

In his comprehensive review published in 1985 and entitled *Depression— a psychobiological synthesis*, Paul Willner of the City of London Polytechnic poses a question of fundamental importance: 'What is the relationship between biochemical events in the brain and the experiences that people have when they are depressed?'. One aspect of any possible answer arising from Willner's analysis is clear: the biochemical level of discourse does not provide a better language that we should strive to speak at all times. That would constitute unwarranted **reductionism**. Reductionism is the process of trying to explain events at one level simply in terms of a more basic level. In this case, it would mean reducing the explanation of psychology to physiology or biochemistry. Mental events do not simply *reduce to* a more scientific account at the biochemical level.

Willner proposes that to bridge the conceptual gap between neurochemistry and subjective experience, we need to identify four levels of explanation:

biochemical, physiological, cognitive and experiential. In these terms, 'cognitive' refers to the processing of information: the way in which the brain handles information. This is the domain of mainstream experimental psychology. The term 'experiential' refers to our subjective experience, the content of our consciousness.

We need to consider not only the four levels, but also the relationships between adjacent levels. Consider first the relationship between biochemical and neurophysiological levels. Boosting the production of dopamine or injecting substances that mimic dopamine increases the level of activity at synapses in certain of the brain's neural pathways. These changes in neural pathways will change the way that the brain processes information. Greater sensitivity in certain dopaminergic pathways could bias decision making towards going forward, engaging in contact with the world, rather than retreating and disengaging.

Going in stages from the biochemical to the experiential, at each level new properties appear or **emerge**. These properties depend upon what happens at the lower level but cannot simply be reduced to it. By analogy, complex social phenomena depend, of course, upon individuals, but the phenomena cannot be explained purely in terms of the properties of individuals. Rather, a new domain of discourse, social psychology, with its own principles and explanatory terms, opens up as we move to a new level.

Willner poses the question: 'Is depression a biochemical abnormality or an agonizing subjective experience?'. I am sure that by now you would agree with Willner that a reasonable answer is that depression is bound to be both. Which aspect or 'level' we emphasize depends upon the purpose of our description. To discuss personal anguish with another human being would be the most appropriate level of discourse under some conditions. However, in the search for an antidepressant, it might be more appropriate to focus attention upon the biochemical level.

As Willner points out, undue emphasis upon depression as a biochemical disorder can lead to a parallel emphasis upon biochemical *solutions* to the problem in the form of drug prescriptions. As part of, say, a social or political argument on mental health, emphasis upon drugs and ECT might be felt to have sinister implications. It might detract from reasonable changes that could be made in the social environment of depressed people. On the other hand, it would be thoroughly misleading to deny a biological base to mental phenomena. As for other phenomena such as feeding/hunger or fear, the biological and the subjective should not be seen as rival accounts, but rather as complementary accounts of a complex phenomenon.

Summary of Section 5

- The behavioural and experiential phenomena termed depression arise from a complex *interaction* between events internal and external to the depressed person.

- Sometimes we need to focus upon *either* the external *or* the internal contribution, but we should always be aware of the inevitable role of both sets of factors.

- There appears to be a genetic contribution to depression, though its investigation is fraught with pitfalls. The genetic contribution would, in all probability, be mediated via synapses between certain neurons in the central nervous system.

- It is possible to propose animal models of depression that can give insight into features of the phenomenon.

- It is useful to consider four levels of discourse in a full account of depression: biochemical, physiological, cognitive and experiential. An intellectual challenge arises in attempting to relate these levels. No level is superior as an explanation.

6 | Concluding comments

This brief tour of the brain and behavioural sciences should have given you a greater appreciation of the discussions in psychology that appeal to a biological level of explanation. You should now be aware of some of the more obvious pitfalls that await the unwary traveller in this area.

In the course of the discussion of motivation and depression, we identified relevant external events, such as food and stressors. We also identified internal events, such as fluid and energy levels in the body and changes in neurotransmitter levels at key synapses. An area of crucial importance is the *interface* between these two sets of factors as well as their complex associations. Thus, feeding motivation depends in part upon the memories evoked by foods. Similarly, depression depends upon the interpretation of external events and the bias exerted on this process by certain key synapses.

Perhaps the most important message is the need to avoid superficially attractive and simple dichotomies, implied by questions such as, 'is depression *mainly* biological *or* social?' and 'is aggression *either* social *or* biological?'. Consider the question, 'is feeding mainly biologically determined?'. As we have seen, feeding is influenced by factors in the tissues of the body, such as energy levels, and also by the quality and availability of food. In addition, it is influenced by a variety of other factors, such as social dominance in a colony of rats and desired body shape in humans. The challenge lies in seeking an explanation of the modes by which these various factors *interact*.

In this chapter, I have deliberately not attempted to dichotomize the animal into biological and non-biological parts. There is a biological *level* or perspective in looking at behavioural systems, using the particular body of knowledge held by the biological sciences. However, that does not mean that living systems are in part biological and in part non-biological. At the end of the day, there is one whole integrated animal. There are areas in which biology has been able to contribute much and other areas in which insight from biology has either been less impressive or seems less appropriate to the problem. For example, biology has not made much contribution to understanding complex human reasoning. We are not yet in a position to attempt mapping between human mental skills and their physical base in the neurons of the brain. However, that in no way denies that reasoning involves neurons in the brain as its physical base.

The discussions raised in this chapter are of profound importance to our society; they are much more than simply intellectual debating points. The prescription of massive doses of antidepressants and tranquillizers each year for mental anguish often involves tacit or explicit assumptions about what is going on at a biological level. For example, we might assume that the most useful focus for intervention against mental pain is the central nervous system. Alternatively, we might feel that there is something fundamentally wrong or sinister in treating the nervous system with chemicals, when the problem could be more humanely tackled by changes in society. However, we might, as a compromise position, acknowledge that, while the problem would be most usefully solved at a social level, we sometimes need to turn, as individuals, to chemical cures as the only means at our very limited disposal. These are not issues for which we can give you correct answers, but we can at least teach you the basic biology and psychology that is relevant to the debate.

It would not be an exaggeration to say that the issues raised in this chapter are amongst some of the most fundamental to confront human beings, having implications not only in politics but also in philosophy and religion. To end this chapter, let us briefly return to Jean's comments, reported at the start of the chapter: 'Depression is all in the mind' and 'A rat can't reason—it's just a biological thing'. We need to ask whether a condition of mental anguish, or mental joy for that matter, can be 'all in the mind'. Such an assumption involves the belief, either explicitly or tacitly, in a basic dichotomy, or duality, between mind events and brain events. On this view, some things have a physical embodiment—for example, they are represented by the activity of nerve cells—whereas other things have an existence independent of nerve cells. Such a duality is one that would receive little support amongst neuroscientists these days. The consensus view, in so far as it exists, is that mental phenomena are associated with corresponding brain phenomena. The nature of the correspondence is one about which there is much discussion, but all you need to note is the belief that mental events are in some sense embodied in brain events.

Discussion of whether a rat can reason would really take us out of our depth, but, given the title of the chapter, we must not evade the issue as to whether 'it's just a biological thing'. On one level, it is indeed just biological. Look at its brain under a microscope and all you will see are neurons and connections between them. On very high powered magnification, you will see the components of neurons; that is, the membranes, nuclei and transmitter substances. This is all very much within the domain of the biological sciences. On the other hand, if you were to look at my brain under a microscope, you would not find anything more psychologically revealing. The point is that on one level, we, humans and rats, are just biological. However, on another level humans are conscious beings with private feelings. To deny the latter is to fly in the face of common sense. The challenge comes in trying to relate our private conscious states to our biological states. Such a challenge has attracted some of the best minds (and, presumably, their brains) in the history of civilization, but I am sure you will accept that to attempt to resolve its inherent dilemmas goes beyond our brief here!

Personal acknowledgements

I am most grateful to Alastair Ewing and David Robinson of the Biology Department, The Open University, and to Heather McLannahan of Region 13 of The Open University for their valuable comments on an initial draft of the chapter.

Further reading

1 About the nervous system and behaviour:

Two books which provide good, 'user-friendly' and richly illustrated guides to the whole subject are:
BLOOM, F.E. and LAZERSON, A. (1988) *Brain, mind and behaviour*, New York: W.H. Freeman; and
KALAT, J.W. (1988) *Biological psychology*, Belmont, CA: Wadsworth.

A simplified introduction to how the neuron works and to general principles of neural systems can be found in:
TOATES, F. (1986) *Biological foundations of behaviour*, Milton Keynes: The Open University Press.

2 On genetics and behaviour:

A good general introduction to the whole area of biological psychology, with a section on genetics and behaviour, is:
KALAT, J.W. (1988) *Biological psychology*, Belmont, CA: Wadsworth;
and an introduction set in the context of general biology is contained in:
OPEN UNIVERSITY COURSE S102 *A science foundation course*, Units 20 and 21, Milton Keynes: The Open University Press.

3 On evolution:

For an easy-to-read introduction to evolution theory, you could try:
RIDLEY, M. (1985) *The problems of evolution*, Oxford: Oxford University Press.

For an account of Darwin's theory of evolution, as it relates to issues in psychology, you might refer to:
BOAKES, R.A. (1984) *From Darwin to behaviourism*, Cambridge: Cambridge University Press.

An easy-to-read introduction to evolution set in the context of the other biological sciences is to be found in:
OPEN UNIVERSITY COURSE S102 *A science foundation course*, Units 19 and 21, Milton Keynes: The Open University Press.

The following is a much discussed book, and one that is easy to read. It has been written by one of the best-known names in the area, and gives an account of his belief that genes tend to carry information coding for selfishness:
DAWKINS, R. (1976) *The selfish gene*, Oxford: Oxford University Press.

4 *On motivation:*

A well-written introduction to the subject, relating it to health issues and every-day life, is:
LOGUE, A.W. (1986) *The psychology of eating and drinking*, New York: W.H. Freeman.

PALMER, R.L. (1980) *Anorexia nervosa*, Harmondsworth: Penguin, is a cheap, easy-to-read paperback describing this unusual phenomenon; and
TOATES, F. (1986) *Motivational systems*, Cambridge: Cambridge University Press, is an account of various motivational systems (e.g. feeding, drinking, sex), showing the similarities and differences between them.

5 *On depression:*

The following is a detailed academic review of depression with a large number of references. It describes Willner's view of depression, which is summarized in the present chapter:
WILLNER, P. (1985) *Depression—a psychobiological synthesis*, New York: John Wiley.

For a personal account of the experience of depression and therapy, written by a well-known experimental psychologist, see:
SUTHERLAND, S. (1976) *Breakdown*, London: Weidenfeld and Nicolson.

6 *Refer to the following for the broad issues raised by the biological perspective:*

This book introduces the ideas of levels of explanation and discusses reductionism and some of its broader implications:
TOATES, F. (1986) *Biological foundations of behaviour*, Milton Keynes: The Open University Press.

References

ANISMAN, H. and ZACHARKO, R.M. (1982) 'Depression: the predisposing influence of stress', *The Behavioural and Brain Sciences*, vol. 5, pp. 89–137.

BOOTH, D.A. (1987) 'How to measure learned control of food or water intake', in Toates, F. and Rowland, N. (eds) *Feeding and drinking*, Amsterdam: Elsevier, pp. 111–49.

BRESLOW, R., KOCIS, J. and BELKIN, B. (1981) 'Contributions of the depressive perspective to memory function in depression', *American Journal of Psychiatry*, vol. 138, pp. 227–30.

BROWN, G. and HARRIS, T. (1978) *Social origins of depression*, London: Tavistock.

BRUCH, H. (1974) *Eating disorders: obesity, anorexia nervosa and the person within*, London: Open Books.

DAWKINS, R. (1976) *The selfish gene*, Oxford: Oxford University Press.

EPSTEIN, A.N. (1982) 'Instinct and motivation as explanations for complex behaviour', in Pfaff, D.W. (ed.) *The physiological mechanisms of motivation*, New York: Springer, pp. 25–58.

EYSENCK, H.J. (1977) *You and neurosis*, London: Temple Smith.

FITZSIMONS, J.T. (1987) 'Some methods for investigating thirst and sodium appetite', in Toates, F. and Rowland, N. (eds) *Feeding and drinking*, Amsterdam: Elsevier, pp. 393–425.

FRIES, E.D. (1954) 'Mental depression in hypertensive patients treated for long periods with large doses of reserpine', *New England Journal of Medicine*, vol. 251, pp. 1006–8.

HOGAN, J.A. (1980) 'Homeostasis and behaviour', in Toates, F.M. and Halliday, T. (eds) *Analysis of motivational processes*, London: Academic Press, pp. 3–21.

HOYLE, F. (1983) *The intelligent universe*, London: Michael Joseph.

LEMAGNEN, J. (1967) 'Habits and food intake', in Code, C.F. (ed.) *Handbook of physiology (section 6) alimentary canal vol. 1*, Washington, DC: American Physiology Society, pp. 11–30.

McGUFFIN, P. and KATZ, R. (1986) 'Nature, nurture and affective disorder', in Deakin, J.F.W. (ed.) *The biology of depression*, London: Gaskell, pp. 26–52.

McKINNEY, W.T. (1984) 'Animal models of depression: an overview', *Psychiatric Developments*, vol. 2, pp. 77–96.

MOOK, D.G. (1987) *Motivation—the organization of action*, New York: W.W. Norton.

OATLEY, K. and BOLTON, W. (1985) 'A social–cognitive theory of depression in reaction to life events', *Psychological Review*, vol. 92, pp. 372–88.

ORBACH, S. (1987) *Hunger strike*, London: Faber.

PACKER, C. (1977) 'Reciprocal altruism', in *Papio anubis, Nature*, vol. 265, pp. 441–3.

PALMER, R.L. (1980) *Anorexia nervosa*, Harmondsworth, Penguin.

ROBINS, A.H. (1976) 'Depression in patients with Parkinsonism', *British Journal of Psychiatry*, vol. 128, pp. 141–5.

ROLLS, B.T. and ROLLS, E.T. (1982) *Thirst*, Cambridge: Cambridge University Press.

ROZIN, P. and KALAT, J.W. (1971) 'Specific hungers and poison avoidance as adaptive specializations of learning', *Psychological Review*, vol. 78, pp. 459–86.

SUTHERLAND, S. (1976) *Breakdown*, London: Weidenfeld and Nicolson.

TOATES, F. (1980) *Animal behaviour—a systems approach*, Chichester: Wiley.

TOATES, F. (1986) *Motivational systems*, Cambridge: Cambridge University Press.

WILLNER, P. (1985) *Depression—a psychobiological synthesis*, New York: John Wiley.

WISE, R.A. (1982) 'Neuroleptics and operant behaviour: the anhedonia hypothesis', *The Behavioural and Brain Sciences*, vol. 5, pp. 39–87.

Answers to SAQs

SAQ 1

We mean that the electrical voltage of neuron 1 is changing up and down; it is firing. By its firing, neuron 1 instigates corresponding changes in neuron 2.

SAQ 2

For most of its length the nociceptor is outside the CNS, and thereby is part of the peripheral nervous system. However, it enters the spinal cord, and so part of it is within the CNS. The neuron with which it forms a connection is wholly within the CNS.

SAQ 3

A sequence of possible events would be: (1) neuron 1 is active; (2) neuron 1 releases chemical transmitter from its terminal; (3) the chemical transmitter migrates across the synaptic cleft; (4) the chemical transmitter attaches itself to neuron 2; and (5) in response to the attachment of chemical transmitter, neuron 2 becomes active (i.e. exhibits action potentials).

SAQ 4

A serotonergic synapse would consist of a junction between two neurons, one of which synthesizes, stores and then releases serotonin into the synaptic cleft. At the membrane of the second neuron there are receptors for serotonin. Consequently, activity of the first neuron causes release of serotonin, a substance which fits the 'lock' at the second neuron.

SAQ 5

Neuron X influences neuron Y by releasing transmitter at synapse 1, and Y contains receptors for this transmitter.

SAQ 6

There are probably very many different answers that you will have arrived at, but some possible examples are as follows. The strength of the rat's legs determines its ability to run fast, and hence its chances of escaping a predator. The physical characteristics of a kestrel's eye determine how good its vision is, and how successful it is at catching voles. The tail feathers of a male peacock influence its attractiveness to the female and hence its chances of successful reproduction. The speed of reaction of a fish to a disturbance determines whether it will form a heron's meal.

SAQ 7

You will doubtless have arrived at a rich variety of different reasons. The zebra's stripes offer good camouflage. The owl's excellent nocturnal vision serves its ability to find prey.

SAQ 8

The inhibitory neuron serves to switch drinking off when the rat has drunk an amount of water commensurate with its need for water. Water takes time to be absorbed into the cells. Without the influence of the inhibitory link, which is activated by water passing through the mouth and into the stomach, the rat would drink very much more than needed. This would waste time. Also, the excess would later need to be excreted in the urine after being warmed to body temperature: a waste of heat.

SAQ 9

The hypothesis under test was whether variety in the diet increased ingestion. Suppose, in the condition of receiving diet C throughout, the rat had been left undisturbed for the 2 hours. It could be argued that the increased ingestion seen in the variety-diet condition (e.g. DBAC) relative to the same-diet condition was due to the fact that in the former the rats were disturbed every 30 minutes by the changing of dishes. Possibly the stress of the experimenter's intrusion arouses feeding. In any experiment, the *control* condition (same food throughout), must be identical to the *experimental* condition (variety of foods), in every respect except for that of the variable (in this case, variety versus constancy of diet) under investigation.

SAQ 10

A fall in the level of body fluids causes action to be taken in interaction with the environment so as to correct the deviation from optimum. The rat drinks water, or, for example, works to obtain water in a Skinner box.

SAQ 11

This might serve as a convenient metaphor for what happens in a mental disorder such as depression, but on closer examination we would wish to refine it. Nerves do not literally snap, like the car's piston which has been subjected to years of metal fatigue. Rather, the physical embodiment of mental disorder, the 'breakdown', appears to be an excess or deficiency of key neurotransmitters or their receptors, at certain sites. (However, in some diseases of the nervous system, nerves do degenerate physically.)

SAQ 12

We were reluctant to employ the expression 'blueprint' because it has connotations of a fixed plan that will inevitably be realized by development and thus might encourage us to disregard the importance of the environmental factors.

chapter **6** # BEHAVIOURISM AND ITS CONSEQUENCES

Frederick Toates and Ingrid Slack

Contents

1	**Introduction**	**251**
1.1	The beginnings of behaviourism	252
	Summary of Section 1	254
2	**Classical conditioning**	**255**
2.1	Pavlov's classical conditioning experiment	255
2.2	Interpretations and developments of Pavlov's experiment	259
	Summary of Section 2	262
3	**Instrumental conditioning**	**263**
3.1	Edward Thorndike: the law of effect	263
3.2	The instrumental contingency and stimulus–response psychology	266
	Summary of Section 3	267
4	**Burrhus F. Skinner: operant conditioning**	**268**
4.1	Invention of the Skinner box	269
4.2	Shaping	270
4.3	Operant conditioning and reinforcement	270
4.4	Skinner's dissent from stimulus–response psychology	272
4.5	The discriminative stimulus	274
4.6	The impact of Skinner's approach	276
	Summary of Section 4	278
5	**Starting the cognitive shift**	**279**
5.1	Edward Tolman: purposive behaviour	280
5.2	The cognitive approach	281
	Summary of Section 5	284
6	**Classical and operant conditioning reinterpreted**	**284**
6.1	Classical conditioning and flexible behaviour	285
6.2	Expectancy and prediction	287
6.3	The Skinner box: learning an association between a response and its outcome	294
	Summary of Section 6	296
7	**The biological challenge**	**296**
7.1	The misbehaviour of organisms	298
7.2	The Garcia effect	300
	Summary of Section 7	303
8	**Summary, overview and applications**	**303**
	Personal acknowledgements	307
	Further reading	307
	References	308
	Answers to SAQs	310

1 | Introduction

Like Chapter 4, this chapter will look at one of the great movements, or, as they are known, 'schools', of psychology: namely, behaviourism. The psychologists who contributed to the behaviourist school laid particular emphasis upon the way in which learning occurs. So, before we go on to describe the movement, we need to ask: 'What is meant by the term "learning"?'.

We are all familiar with a variety of examples of learning, such as learning to speak French, learning to play hockey and learning that a particular café is closed on Sundays. At a certain level of understanding, we seem almost intuitively to know what we mean by the word 'learning'. However, it is not easy to define *exactly* what is meant by the term. One point does seem clear: that learning arises from our *experience* of the world. At one time we do not know something or we lack some skill; after appropriate experience we do know something or do exhibit the skill.

One of the tasks of any theory of learning is to attempt to define the characteristics that are common to all examples of learning. If successful, we would then see each example as being a specific case of a general theory. At first glance, one might think that some kinds of learning involve acquiring information in the form of knowledge (e.g. learning history) that might not be revealed directly in behaviour, whereas other kinds of learning (e.g. how to swim) are revealed almost wholly in skilled behaviour. A large part of this chapter is concerned with describing the behaviourist attempt at constructing a 'grand theory' that would explain all cases of learning. The chapter will outline the background to this attempt, what its aspirations were and the extent to which it succeeded. The limitations and failures of the behaviourist endeavour will also be discussed.

In order to describe this attempt at building a theory of learning, we raise here, right at the start of the chapter, two fundamental sets of questions that will be central to the discussion throughout. Don't worry if these questions seem difficult at this stage. You are not expected to have ready answers to them. They are introduced at the beginning simply to give you an orientation towards the issues that will be raised. The first set of questions is of the kind: 'What is learning?', 'What exactly do we learn?', 'How does behaviour change as a result of experience?'. The second set of questions looks at the broader context in which explanations of learning appear, and consists of such issues as: 'What is the science of psychology about?', 'Is psychology a science having a status comparable to that of physics and biology?', 'What can it hope to achieve?', 'What are the kinds of data that are appropriate to the science of psychology?', 'Should psychologists go about their research in a similar way to biologists and physicists?'.

There is considerable overlap between these two sets of questions. The answer to a question of the kind, 'what is learning?', will inevitably reflect our broader view of what psychology is all about. Since most experiments in this area used either rats or pigeons, our discussion of these two sets of questions will revive from the start a further question that was raised in the last chapter: 'To what extent can we extrapolate from animals to humans?'.

For a large section of the academic community in psychology, the first half of this century saw a revolutionary change both (1) in the way the subject of psychology was perceived and (2) specifically in the way the phenomenon of learning was explained. Understanding of this change can best be gained by first discussing briefly the kind of psychology to which it stood most strongly in opposition.

1.1 The beginnings of behaviourism

What is the appropriate subject matter for a science of psychology? One answer to this was given by Wilhelm Wundt, professor of philosophy at the University of Leipzig between 1875 and 1920. To Wundt, psychology was the science of *consciousness*. People who acted as 'observers' in Wundt's laboratory were asked to reflect inwards on the contents of their consciousness; that is, to *introspect* about sensations and feelings, and to report these as accurately as they could. Such a method is termed **introspection**. Clearly, a science built upon such an endeavour, relying upon a report from the subject, would be a very different science from, say, biology, which is based upon direct observation of living organisms without any possibility of their participation in the process of reporting their inner states.

Partly as a revolt against introspection, a very different view of what a science of psychology should be about was proposed by the American, John B. Watson (1876–1958). To Watson a science of psychology should be based exclusively upon *public* data; that is to say, data derived from the direct observations made by one or more persons. This is in distinction to the essentially *private* origin of the data generated by introspection, origins that are not open to direct checking by other people. In Watson's view, the data used in science should be observable by a community of scientists; no one person should have any kind of privileged access to them. It must be possible to check the data. By being open to inspection, the experiment from which the data are derived is available for exact replication by others. By this criterion, the contents of a person's consciousness are ruled out as valid data, since they are not open to direct inspection by others. They are available only as second-hand data, relying on the verbal accounts of the person describing his or her own sensations. The introspectionist school was dedicated to checking and comparing data between many subjects. However, the data (e.g. spoken reports of conscious states) had inescapably private origins.

Data open to public examination consist of (1) such things as the amount of light falling on the subject's eye or the amount of sound reaching his or her ears, and (2) the subject's behaviour (e.g. movement of limbs and muscles, sweat secreted onto the skin, saliva secreted into the mouth). Something observable that influences the subject's sense organs, such as the light entering the eyes, the heat falling on the skin or the sound reaching the ears, is known as a **stimulus** (plural, 'stimuli'). What the subject does immediately after the arrival of a stimulus, such as to blink the eyes, withdraw the hand from a hot object or run from a bear, is known as the **response**. To Watson, a science of psychology consists in the study of the relationship between these two sets of observable data: what is done to the subject and what the subject does, in other words, stimuli and responses.

Explanations of the relationship between stimuli and responses should be made in terms of measurable events within the nervous system, such as the activity of particular sets of neurons. Mental events—the *unobservable* contents of consciousness—had no place in Watson's science and were accordingly thrown out. To Watson they provided nothing more than speculation and games with words, and were within the domain of philosophy rather than psychology. Like Freud, Watson saw the role of a science of psychology as that of providing an account of behaviour, and one that would neatly map onto an understanding of how the brain works. However, Watson considered neither conscious nor unconscious aspects of a mind to have a valid role to play in achieving the goal of explaining behaviour.

You might wish to object at this stage on the grounds that, for you, a rich and personally unique inner mental world exists and concerns such things as wishes, plans and fears. You might argue that this mental world can often be divorced from any particular piece of behaviour. Watson, in his attempt to banish mental states from psychology, argued that even thinking can be anchored firmly to behaviour. In his argument, thinking is really only feedback from the muscles involved in lip and throat movements that are too small to be easily observed. In other words, thought is really nothing more than inner speech, a form of behaviour ('talking to oneself').

Watson observed the success of other sciences such as biology, physics and chemistry, and noted that they were based upon observable data. Furthermore, the essence of their success was reliable and reproducible *measurement*. A physicist had equipment for the precise measurement of, for example, the intensity of a light or the speed of sound. Watson wanted to model psychology on these other sciences, and to do so he had to emphasize the importance of unambiguous observation and measurement of behaviour. In this approach, the unobservable and unmeasurable terms 'consciousness' and 'mental states' had no role to play. The school of psychology associated with Watson is termed **behaviourism** since it saw the study of behaviour as being the *only* appropriate subject matter for a science of psychology.

The various stimuli that impinge upon the sense organs can be reliably measured: for example, the intensity of a ringing bell. The responses that these stimuli elicit from the animal, such as the blink of an eye or the twitch of a muscle, can also be accurately measured. So a science of behaviour would consist of documenting and explaining the relationship between stimuli and responses.

Learning is a topic central to building a science of psychology, irrespective of one's view of the kind of science that psychology should follow. So what was Watson's view of learning, given his general assumptions of what psychology should be about? As you might have guessed, to Watson the criterion by which learning was judged to have taken place (the 'index of learning') was a *change* in behaviour. For example, if a new stimulus at first evokes no response, but after repeated presentation it does evoke a response, this would be evidence of learning. For instance, a child might be asked in school, 'what is the French for thank you?'. At first the child might utter something incomprehensible. After being corrected over several days, the child comes to respond with the word 'merci'. It is this *change* in the behaviour of speaking that is seen as the **index of learning**.

Fortunately for Watson, some years before his behaviourist manifesto, some experiments had been performed in Russia that provided just the material he needed for a behaviourist interpretation of learning. Their impact in the West was not fully appreciated until Watson launched his behaviourist crusade. Section 2 will consider these experiments in some detail before returning to their implications for Watson's behaviourism.

Summary of Section 1

- There are some fundamentally different approaches to the study of psychology. What a school of psychology considers to be the appropriate way to study a phenomenon such as learning depends upon its broader approach to psychology as a whole.

- One approach to psychology, influential at the turn of the century, was that of introspection, asking people to describe the contents of their own consciousness.

- In contrast to introspection, John Watson proposed that psychology should concern itself with observable and therefore public data. Such data consisted of (1) events in the environment (stimuli) and (2) behaviour (responses). Watson proclaimed the behaviourist revolution.

- Watson attempted to model psychology along the lines of such sciences as physics and biology, by emphasizing the need for precise measurement. Stimuli that impinge upon an animal, and the animal's responses, were to be measured.

- According to Watson, events within the animal (human and otherwise) should be described in purely biological terms. Mental events should be avoided as they are unobservable and therefore their study is unscientific.

- In Watson's view, learning consists of a change in behaviour, measured in terms of a change in the response to a stimulus.

2 | Classical conditioning

One of the best known figures in the history of psychology is the Russian researcher Ivan Petrovich Pavlov (1849–1936), though in fact he did not consider himself to be a psychologist. Pavlov was trained as a physiologist and initially investigated the process of digestion, for which he was awarded the Nobel prize for medicine.

2.1 Pavlov's classical conditioning experiment

Pavlov was interested in the factors that cause a dog to secrete saliva from glands in the mouth and gastric juices from glands in the stomach. The normal stimulus to elicit secretion of saliva is the presence of food in the mouth. Using rigorously controlled experimental conditions, Pavlov was able to make accurate measurements of the amount of salivation elicited by this stimulus. In this way, he was able to describe the properties of the **salivation reflex**. A reflex is a fixed, automatic response (e.g. salivation) to a particular stimulus (e.g. food in the mouth). Pavlov's goal was accurate measurement of the relationship between the stimulus (food in the mouth) and the response (salivation).

If Pavlov's research had been confined to the study of such reflexes, then his scientific achievement, though notable, would have remained firmly within the bounds of physiology. However, Pavlov occasionally ran into what was at first an unwelcome complication to reaching his goal. He noticed that often the dog would start to salivate *before* the food was placed in its mouth. The sight of the experimenter bringing the food was sometimes sufficient to elicit salivation. Pavlov termed secretions evoked by such stimuli **psychic secretions**. This was in distinction to the secretion evoked by the stimulus of food in the mouth, and referred to the more remote and less tangible nature of the stimulus; for example, the dog sensing the arrival of Pavlov bringing food.

Fortunately for psychology, Pavlov changed his attitude towards such psychic secretions. Rather than seeing them as a contaminating influence upon the science of physiology, he came to regard them as phenomena worthy of study in their own right. He went on to devise formal experiments to measure the properties of psychic secretions in dogs, a series of experiments that now have a place in the popular imagination and every-day vocabulary.

Pavlov raised the question as to what kind of stimulus could serve to elicit psychic secretions. He had already observed that the sight of food and the experimenter bringing it could serve in this capacity. What other kinds of stimuli were able to elicit salivation? What was the nature of their relationship to food? Pavlov's experimental procedure is outlined in Box A. Pavlov introduced new terminology to describe the stimuli and responses in his experiment. Food in the mouth was termed the **unconditional stimulus**, abbreviated as either **UCS** or **US**. The logic underlying the use of this term is that food is able *unconditionally* to elicit salivation; it does not rely upon a prior pairing with another stimulus. The salivation caused by the food is

BOX A   Pavlov's experiment

Figure 6.1 shows Pavlov's dog held in a harness. The experiment required that the dog's capacity for movement was minimal. For rigorous scientific experimentation, Pavlov also needed to have tight control over the stimuli to which the dog was exposed. The dog had not been exposed before to the stimulus of the sound of a bell and Pavlov observed that the ringing of a bell did not elicit salivation. He called the bell a **neutral stimulus**, abbreviated as **NS**. He then rang the bell and immediately afterwards presented food. He repeated this pairing of bell and food a number of times. The response of salivation was reliably evoked on each presentation of bell and food. Pavlov then tested the bell in the *absence* of the food to see what happened. The bell *on its own* now elicited the secretion of a certain amount of saliva. The bell, previously a neutral stimulus, now had acquired the capacity to elicit salivation, by virtue of its repeated pairing with the presentation of food.

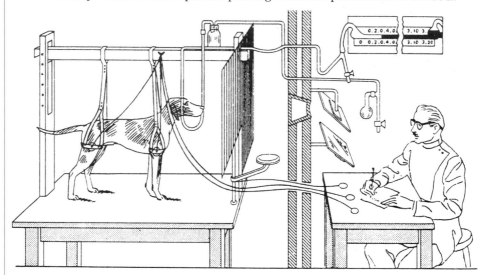

Figure 6.1 Pavlov's experimental set-up. The dog is held in a harness while it is stimulated with food and the bell. The flow of saliva is measured (Source: Geldard, 1963)

termed the **unconditional response** (abbreviated as **UCR** or **UR**). The reflex relating the stimulus of food in the mouth to the response of salivation was termed the **unconditional reflex**.

Following its pairing with food, the bell, hitherto a neutral stimulus, became a **conditional stimulus** (**CS**). The term 'conditioned' is sometimes used instead of conditional. The origin of the term 'conditional' is that the power of the bell is *conditional upon* its pairing with food; it has no unconditional power to elicit salivation. Following the pairing of bell and food, the salivation caused by the bell acting on its own was termed the **conditional response** (**CR**). The reflex relating the bell to salivation was termed the **conditional reflex**.

The procedure demonstrated by Pavlov, whereby a neutral stimulus (e.g. a bell) becomes a conditional stimulus by virtue of its pairing with an unconditional stimulus (e.g. food), was termed **conditioning**. Pavlov's technique was the first conditioning experiment to gain recognition. Subsequently, to distinguish this from other forms of conditioning, whose significance became apparent somewhat later, Pavlov's technique and result became known as **classical conditioning**. An alternative expression is **Pavlovian conditioning**. The sequence of classical conditioning is shown in Figure 6.2.

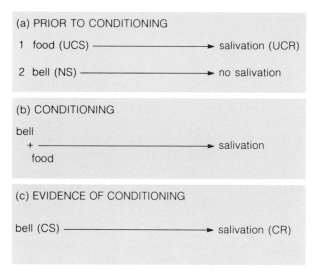

Figure 6.2 Summary of Pavlov's experiment. (a) Prior to conditioning, the stimuli are tested: (1) the unconditional reflex: food (UCS) elicits salivation (UCR) and (2) the bell (NS) does not elicit salivation; (b) the conditioning procedure of presentation of the bell and, immediately following, food; and (c) testing for conditioning: the bell (CS) has now acquired the power to elicit salivation (CR)

SAQ 1   (*SAQ answers are given at the end of the chapter*) Suppose that a follower of Pavlov had observed that a human subject jerked his foot in response to an electric shock to the sole. Flashing a blue light caused no movement in the foot. After a few pairings of blue light followed by shock, the light acting on its own elicited a jerk of the foot. In this example, what is (a) the unconditional stimulus; (b) the unconditional response; (c) the neutral stimulus; (d) the conditional stimulus; and (e) the conditional response?

But what has Pavlov's experiment on salivation to do with *learning*? Before conditioning, the dog had been shown to respond to the food in its mouth. This did not involve learning. Rather, it revealed an unconditional reflex, genetically determined and common to all dogs. Originally, the dog did not respond to the bell by salivating. Following conditioning, the dog responded to the bell with salivation. Its behaviour towards the previously neutral stimulus of the bell had *changed* as a result of experience. In behaviourist terms, this would be the *index of learning*, indicating that the dog had 'learned' to salivate to the bell. What serves as the conditional stimulus depends upon the events in the life of a particular dog. In the case studied by Pavlov, it was exposure to a bell paired with food.

Pavlov's experiment, with a dog held in a harness, would seem far removed from the natural environment of a dog. However, when we consider the life of an animal in the wild, it is clear that the capacity to learn through classical conditioning has adaptive value (see Chapter 5, section 3.2). For example, suppose an animal samples a new food with a distinctive visual appearance. On first encounter, the sight of the food does not itself elicit salivation. However, by repeated pairing of the sight of the food and food in the mouth, salivation and secretion of digestive juices come to be triggered by the *sight* of food. The food would thereby arrive in a stomach that is already prepared physiologically to accept it. This facilitates the process of digestion.

Subsequent researchers have found the timing of bell and food in relation to one another to be an important factor. The bell normally needs to be sounded about 0.5–1 second before the presentation of food to obtain the best effect. If the bell is sounded after the presentation of food, conditioning is impossible. If it is presented more than a few seconds before food, the conditioning effect is weak. This principle of timing—whereby for classical conditioning to occur the CS needs to come at the same time as, or just before, the UCS—is known as the principle of **temporal contiguity**. In the laboratory this timing is determined by the experimenter.

In a situation such as that studied by Pavlov, the sequence of events to which an animal is exposed is known, in psychology jargon, as the **contingency**. Whether the animal learns anything on exposure to the contingency is a further consideration; the contingency is simply how things are arranged. The origin of the meaning of this term is that the experiment is arranged in such a way that the occurrence of one event is *contingent upon* the occurrence of another. A **classical contingency** consists of two *stimuli* occurring in a fixed time order. In Pavlov's experiment, the contingency is between the two stimuli of bell and food, as shown in Figure 6.2(b). The full significance of the term contingency will become apparent later in the chapter.

SAQ 2   If a sudden puff of air is applied to the human eye, a blink of the eye is invariably observed. This reaction does not have to be learned. It is a reflex that serves to defend the eye against damage. How might you attempt to classically condition this reaction? In your answer, identify the meaning of the following terms:
(a) unconditional response (UCR);
(b) conditional response (CR);
(c) unconditional stimulus (UCS);
(d) conditional stimulus (CS);
(e) neutral stimulus (NS);
(f) temporal contiguity.

SAQ 3   What is the contingency in the leg-jerk experiment described in SAQ 1?

Following the establishment of salivation to the sound of a bell, Pavlov investigated the effect of repeatedly sounding the bell *without* presenting food. After a number of such presentations, the amount of salivation evoked by the bell declined, and finally (after twenty or so trials) the bell lost its capacity to produce salivation. Pavlov described the procedure of applying the CS in the absence of the UCS as **extinction**, the result being described as the animal's response to the bell alone becoming 'extinguished'.

SAQ 4   In the experiment described in SAQ 2, (a) how would you extinguish the conditional response? and (b) how would you know when extinction is complete?

2.2 Interpretations and developments of Pavlov's experiment

Pavlov's demonstration of classical conditioning is easy to repeat and literally thousands of similar experiments have been performed since his day. There can be no doubt as to the validity of his findings. However, controversy enters the picture when we try to *explain* the result. A major theme of this chapter will be the different kinds of explanations for the learning taking place in Pavlov's experiment. For the moment, we will consider the interpretation placed on the result by Watson and the American behaviourists.

Classical conditioning, as described in Pavlov's terms, fitted exactly to Watson's ideas about what a science of psychology needed. Watson, as president of the American Psychological Association, was in a powerful position to promote awareness of Pavlov's experiment, and to advance the behaviourist view that associations between observable stimuli and responses should be the basic units on which a science of psychology is built. This would be particularly true of the scientific study of learning. Pavlov's experiment concerned precisely measurable stimuli and responses. There was no need to postulate that the dog had conscious or mental states mediating the linkage between a bell and food. To Watson, this encapsulated what *learning* was all about: a *change* in behaviour as a result of experience. Some forms of learning might be complex, but, by patient observation and analysis, Watson believed they could be reduced to the simple units of conditioned responses. Watson proceeded to test the generality of Pavlov's procedure, with the help of a healthy infant, little Albert, who was destined for a place in the history of psychology.

Watson observed that Albert showed little or no fear reaction towards a white rat. Watson then tried banging loudly a piece of metal just behind Albert's head. This evoked Albert's withdrawal from the location of the noise. Watson then produced the loud noise at the same time as presenting the white rat. After such pairing of rat and loud noise, Watson observed Albert's reaction to presentation of the white rat on its own. The rat now elicited a reaction of withdrawal.

SAQ 5   In relation to little Albert, how would you define the terms (a) NS, (b) CS, (c) UCS, (d) CR, (e) UCR, (f) unconditional reflex and (g) conditional reflex?

Watson and his followers interpreted the learning that occurs on exposure to a classical contingency (pairing of a neutral stimulus with an unconditional stimulus) as being the result of a strengthening of an association between a stimulus and a response. For example, in Pavlov's experiment, repeated experience strengthens the association between the stimulus of the bell and the response of salivation. From experiments of the kind carried out on Pavlov's dogs and little Albert, grew what is termed **stimulus–response psychology** (often abbreviated as **S–R psychology**). This term conveys the ideas (1) that what is learned consists of a relationship between a stimulus and a response, and (2) a science of psychology consists of investigating such associations. As you can see, the name of the S–R movement derives from the nature of the association that was thought to be formed (i.e. between a stimulus and a response), rather than from the contingency employed in forming the association (i.e. between two stimuli).

SAQ 6   In the terms of S–R psychology, in the case of little Albert, what is the association being strengthened?

The behaviourists rejected mental events as candidates for forming the linkage between the stimuli and the responses in such experiments. They argued that the linkage could only be explained, if at all, in the language of physiology. In its specific details, Watson's explanatory theory changed several times, but Figure 6.3 shows the essence of his approach. It concerns how he believed the associations between stimuli and responses were formed in the brain. There are some strong connections in the brain; for example, between the stimulus of food in the mouth and the response of salivation. There are assumed also to be numerous weak and normally ineffective links in the brain—for example, pathway X in Figure 6.3—which provide the base for conditioning.

The model of classical conditioning shown in Figure 6.3 contains some speculation. For instance, Watson had no concrete evidence to support the existence of a network of weak links such as X. Rather, the model was based on the general understanding of how the brain functions that prevailed at the time. The model predicts that the CS will produce a CR that is like the UCR. The size of the CR depends upon the strength with which the link X is made. Typically, if the UCR is twenty drops of saliva, the CR might be fifteen.

SAQ 7   Suppose a neutral stimulus has become a conditional stimulus by pairing with an unconditional stimulus. What is the procedure called when the CS is subsequently presented a number of times without the UCS? In Pavlov's salivary conditioning experiment, what is the effect of this procedure?

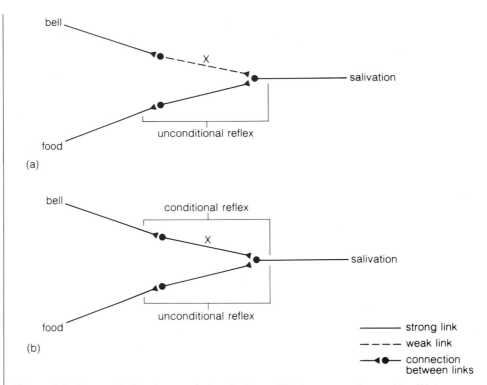

Figure 6.3 A speculative theory of classical conditioning, as envisaged by Watson.
(a) Prior to conditioning. Food in the mouth causes saliva secretion. Sounding the bell
does not elicit salivation, since link X is not sufficiently strong; (b) following pairing of the
bell and food. The fact that the pathways from bell and food have been excited together
on a number of occasions results in a strengthening of the link X between them. Now the
bell, even in the absence of excitation by food, is able to elicit some salivation

SAQ 8   In Watson's model, based upon brain processes and shown in Figure 6.3, what
         might you suppose would be the brain process corresponding to extinction of
         the conditioned salivation reflex?

Subsequent work on rats has shown that the conditioning that occurs on
exposure to a classical contingency can be a very robust phenomenon.
Suppose a rat is exposed to a few pairings of a tone (neutral stimulus) and
shock (unconditional stimulus). The tone is then tested in the absence of the
shock. This constitutes imposing extinction conditions. Sometimes a hundred
or more presentations of the tone alone need to be given before signs of fear
are eliminated.

An S–R theory of the kind proposed by Watson is often termed *mechanical* or
mechanistic. This is by analogy with such mechanical gadgets as cigarette
dispensing machines, and emphasizes the simple, stereotyped way in which
the output (the salivation or cigarette packet) is tied to the input (bell or
money). Whether one believes that S–R theory does justice to explaining the
behavioural phenomena is a question we shall leave for the moment.

The *classical contingency* that we have considered in this section is that between two stimuli: (1) the NS, which becomes a CS, and (2) the UCS. The examples were (a) bell and food in Pavlov's experiment and (b) rat and loud noise for little Albert. In each case, a neutral stimulus acquires some potency to elicit a response as a result of its pairing with a stimulus that unconditionally provokes a response. Section 3 looks at a different contingency and describes its relevance. Experiments using this other type of contingency were being explored in depth in America at around the same time that Pavlov and Watson were advancing the cause of classical conditioning. The results obtained from the two contingencies contributed to the general case for a behaviourist interpretation of psychological phenomena.

Summary of Section 2

- Pavlov devised an experimental procedure whereby a neutral stimulus becomes a conditional stimulus by virtue of its pairing with an unconditional stimulus. This procedure became known as classical, or Pavlovian, conditioning.

- Pavlov presented a neutral stimulus (e.g. a bell) just before a stimulus (e.g. food) that unconditionally evoked a response (e.g. salivation). This arrangement of stimuli is an example of a classical contingency. The stimulus of the bell was shown to acquire some of the response-evoking power of the food.

- In Pavlov's experiment, the food is the unconditional stimulus (UCS). The salivation elicited by the food is the unconditional response (UCR). After conditioning, the bell (previously a neutral stimulus) becomes the conditional stimulus (CS). The salivation elicited by the bell is the conditional response (CR).

- The association between an unconditional stimulus and an unconditional response is termed an unconditional reflex.

- The association between a conditional stimulus and a conditional response is termed a conditional reflex.

- Pavlov found that if the CS is presented in the absence of the UCS a number of times, the CS generally loses some or all of its capacity to evoke the conditional response. The procedure of presenting the CS without the UCS is known as extinction. When the CR fails to appear to the CS, the response has been extinguished.

- Watson welcomed the classical conditioning experiment as showing the basic unit of learning in terms of a stimulus–response association. The basis of the S–R association was described in terms of a theory based upon possible connections in the brain.

3 | Instrumental conditioning

The last section considered classical conditioning and the stimulus–response model of learning. Classical conditioning refers to a contingency in which two stimuli (NS and UCS) are paired. In the typical laboratory study of classical conditioning, the stimuli are entirely under the control of the experimenter. For instance, the dog is presented with food and a bell; its own behaviour plays no role in their presentation. This section looks at a type of conditioning in which the contingency is fundamentally different to this. The nature of the contingency is best illustrated by considering one of the first experimenters to have worked with this approach.

3.1 Edward Thorndike: the law of effect

One of the pioneers of American psychology was Edward L. Thorndike (1874–1949), famous for his puzzle box with which he studied learning by cats, as described in Box B.

BOX B   The puzzle box

A hungry cat was put into a box and food was placed outside the box, as shown in Figure 6.4.

In order to get out of the box, it was necessary for the cat to manipulate a latch that held the door in place. In other words, a *contingency* was arranged between the animal's behaviour and a consequence, escape. Escape was contingent upon a *response*. At first, when placed in the box, the cat would act somewhat frenetically, struggling and meowing. After a while, apparently by accident, the cat would perform the necessary manipulation and thereby earn its freedom and access to the food. The cat would then be returned to the box for the next trial. Thorndike recorded the length of time elapsing between placing the cat in the box and the cat opening the door, and this was used as the index of learning. Over a series of such trials, the length of time before the cat escaped decreased, although this trend was accompanied by a certain amount of variability. The assumption was that the shorter the time to escape, the stronger was the learning. A **learning curve** can be drawn to illustrate the gradual reduction in escape times, as shown in Figure 6.5.

How did Thorndike explain the result of the puzzle-box experiment? He considered a number of possible explanations that might be offered. Did the cat show sudden insight into the problem? Thorndike dismissed this as an explanation on the grounds that, if insight were involved, the form of the learning curve would be expected to display a sudden fall in the escape time, as the animal twigged how to solve the puzzle. This hypothetical situation is represented in Figure 6.6.

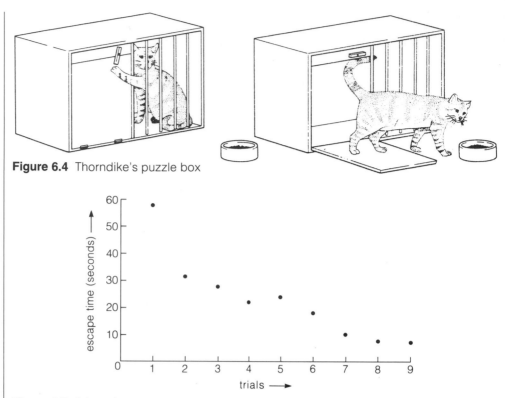

Figure 6.4 Thorndike's puzzle box

Figure 6.5 A learning curve obtained from the puzzle box for an individual cat

In Thorndike's experiments, the escape time decreased gradually over a number of trials, thus supporting the idea of gradual learning rather than sudden insight. Thorndike arrived at the conclusion that learning involves the gradual formation of an association between the *stimulus situation* of the puzzle box and the particular *response* that was instrumental in escape, a stimulus–response (S–R) association. The strength of this association increases gradually over the trials, as reflected in the gradual decrease in escape times. Note that, in this theory, an association is not formed between thoughts or ideas, but between the stimulus (the box) and a response (muscles involved in pulling the latch). Thorndike's argument is as significant for what it implicitly denies as for what it asserts. Contrary to a commonsense view, it denies that an animal comes to associate a response with its outcome. According to Thorndike's view, an animal cannot learn to anticipate the consequences of its actions; the consequences merely (one might say, 'blindly') strengthen stimulus–response associations.

Having argued that learning consists of the formation of new stimulus–response associations, Thorndike turned his attention to the mechanisms underlying learning. What is it that determines that certain combinations of stimulus and response shall be associated, and not others? Thorndike at first observed apparently random behaviour on the cat's part. What was it about the puzzle box that later determined that the stimulus situation (e.g. front wall of the box) would be associated with a particular response (e.g. manipulating latch)? According to Thorndike, learning occurs only if a response has some

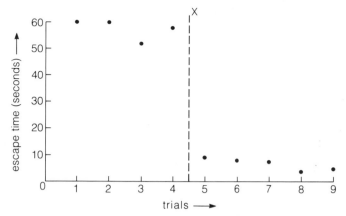

Figure 6.6 The learning curve that might be expected if the cat solved the problem by insight. There would be a sudden fall at some point (point X), in this case shown after the fourth trial, after the solution was obtained

effect, as represented in Figure 6.7. The term 'response' means activity by a set of muscles, in this case the muscles controlling the paw movements that were successful in opening the latch. Of the many responses that occur in this situation, only those that lead to favourable consequences, such as escape, will be learned.

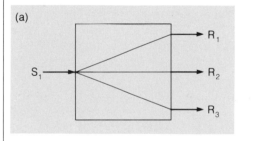
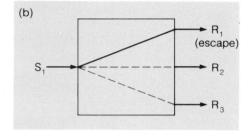

Figure 6.7 A model of learning, as proposed by Thorndike. (a) At the start, the stimulus situation (S_1) of the box could make contact with any one of a number of different responses (R_1, R_2, R_3 . . . etc.); (b) of this range of responses, it is only the connection of S_1 with R_1 that is strengthened, because R_1 is the response that leads to escape and to food

In Thorndike's experiment, the effect is escape and gaining food. Other responses (e.g. scratching the floor with the left back leg), which might potentially have formed an association with the stimulus situation, did not do so because they had no significant effect. If the effect is one such as the gaining of food, then an association will be formed between the stimulus situation and the particular response that led to food. Thorndike proposed the **law of effect**, which states that responses having favourable consequences will be learned. In Thorndike's own words:

Of several responses made to the same situation, those which are accompanied or closely followed by satisfaction to the animal will, other things being equal, be more firmly connected with the situation, so that, when it recurs, they will be more likely to recur; those which are accompanied or closely followed by discomfort to the animal will, other things being equal, have their connections with that situation weakened, so that, when it recurs, they will be less likely to occur.

(Thorndike, 1911, p. 244)

SAQ 9   With reference to Figure 6.7, suppose that, by some bizarre twist of fate, instead of escape and food, the consequence of response R_1 was an electric shock to the paw. What would be the predicted effect on future behaviour?

The process of strengthening the association between a particular stimulus and response would later be termed **reinforcement**, because it 'reinforces' the association. The notion of reinforcement strengthening an S–R association was to become a central feature in both the development of behaviourism and later arguments against the school. The agent responsible for reinforcement, in this case food (and escape), would be termed the **reinforcer**.

In a way very similar to Pavlov and Watson, Thorndike speculated about the events in the nervous system that would mediate between stimulus and response, being convinced that any explanations should be sought at the biological level. In particular, he considered a strengthening of connections between neurons as a possible basis of learning.

If you suppose that the notions of satisfaction and discomfort do not entirely fit a science of behaviour based upon purely observable data and avoiding mentalism, you would be quite right. However, Thorndike was aware that he might be criticized for this, and attempted to define a satisfying state, strictly in behavioural terms, as '. . . one which the animal does nothing to avoid, often doing things which maintain or renew it' (Thorndike, 1911, p. 245). However, some theorists (e.g. Watson) were later to challenge Thorndike over the question of whether he had really eliminated mental events from his explanation.

3.2 The instrumental contingency and stimulus–response psychology

In Thorndike's experiment, learning was defined in terms of forming associations between stimuli and responses, in a rather similar way to the account given earlier for classical conditioning. However, the technique used to produce the learned association was fundamentally different. In classical conditioning, two stimuli (e.g. food and a bell) are presented to the animal. The animal's own behaviour is not a factor in this sequence of events. By contrast, in Thorndike's experiment, the animal's own behaviour is *instrumental* in the sequence of events; that is, manipulation by the paw causes the door to open and escape to be possible. For this reason, the type of conditioning studied by Thorndike is termed **instrumental conditioning**, in contrast to classical conditioning.

Another way of expressing this difference is in terms of the *contingency* in operation. In a classical conditioning experiment, the contingency is arranged between two stimuli; for example, a bell and food. Behaviour does not play a role in the contingency. For instance, suppose, on one occasion, Pavlov's dog failed to salivate. It would still get the food. An **instrumental contingency** is arranged between a *response* and a reinforcer. For example, Thorndike's cat only received the food *if* it manipulated the latch. Obtaining food was *contingent upon* the animal's response.

SAQ 10   In the following situations in which conditioning of a pet is described, state whether an instrumental or classical contingency is involved in the relationship between (i) and (ii):

(a) (i) when a dog pulls on a rope, (ii) its master appears and takes it for a walk;

(b) (i) when a cat pushes against a panel, (ii) a nearby cat-flap opens and the cat can enter the house;

(c) every time a cat owner goes to open a tin of cat food and (i) to give it to the cat, (ii) she first reaches to a high shelf for a can-opener. In time the cat starts to show signs of excitement whenever the owner reaches up to the top shelf.

Thorndike argued that a simple principle of learning, that of forming S–R associations, could explain much, if not all, of what animals and humans learn. He believed that complex behaviour called intelligent or creative could really be reduced to learning a number of simple S–R associations. For example, according to Thorndike, the cats were not showing insight in escaping from the puzzle box. In arguing the case for seeking common principles of learning applicable between different species, Thorndike was an important influence in the development of comparative psychology. In the spirit of Darwin (Chapter 5, Section 3.2), Thorndike tried to break down the fundamental dichotomy between animals, seen to be endowed simply with blind instincts, and humans, having a creative and intelligent capacity. Watson emphasized the importance of classical conditioning and Thorndike pioneered instrumental conditioning. To both Watson and Thorndike, animal and human behaviour and learning could be explained largely in terms of S–R connections.

The instrumental contingency pioneered by Thorndike was soon to occupy the attention of a number of distinguished researchers.

Summary of Section 3

- Thorndike's puzzle box was the apparatus for the first scientific study of instrumental conditioning, a type of conditioning fundamentally different from classical conditioning. In this apparatus, escape and food were contingent upon a manipulatory response by a cat.

- An instrumental contingency is one in which an animal's behaviour is instrumental in determining some outcome. There is a contingency between a response and a reinforcer.

- The gradual decrease in escape time was used as an index of learning.

- Thorndike proposed the law of effect: as a result of the consequences of a response, an association between the stimulus situation and the response is strengthened, a process later termed reinforcement.

- The agent responsible for this reinforcement was termed the reinforcer (e.g. food).

- In Thorndike's view, an animal cannot learn to anticipate the consequences of its actions; an association is not formed between thoughts or ideas.

4 | Burrhus F. Skinner: operant conditioning

One of psychology's most famous names, Burrhus Frederick Skinner (born 1904), followed in the tradition of Thorndike. When Skinner started his research in the 1930s, the favourite technique for studying instrumental conditioning was the maze, as illustrated in Figure 6.8.

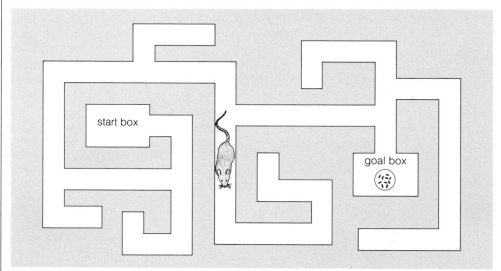

Figure 6.8 Maze used in instrumental conditioning

A rat was released from the start box and, if it found its way to the goal box, it obtained a morsel of food. In other words, the animal's behaviour in running the maze was instrumental in obtaining reinforcement. After each trial, the rat needed to be removed from the goal box and returned to the start box, and the next trial was initiated. The rat's speed in reaching the goal box and the number of errors made on the way were noted. A rat might take twenty or more trials to learn the maze. A learning curve could then be constructed to show how the speed with which the rat ran the maze increased over trials, and this speed used as an index of learning.

4.1 Invention of the Skinner box

Skinner sought a way of investigating instrumental behaviour that was more economical with time—economical for both the rat and Skinner. This simple consideration led to the invention of the now-famous **Skinner box** (named this by other researchers). Figure 6.9 illustrates the Skinner box.

Figure 6.9 Skinner box for rats, showing also chart recording of lever-pressing. On the chart, each vertical line represents a single press on the lever

The apparatus consists of a box containing a lever (sometimes termed 'bar') and a tray. If the lever is lowered, a pellet of food is automatically dropped into the tray. An automatic recorder consisting of chart paper and a pen is linked electrically to the Skinner box. The paper moves across the pen at a constant speed. When the lever in the Skinner box is pressed, the pen makes a mark on the chart paper. A succession of lever-presses is shown, thus indicating the number of times the rat presses the lever within a given period of time.

By the use of this piece of apparatus, an instrumental contingency can be arranged between lever-pressing by a rat and the arrival of the reinforcer, food. Every time the rat presses the lever, a pellet of food is delivered into the food tray. As Figure 6.10 shows, an adaptation of the same basic apparatus allows the response of key-pecking by a pigeon to be reinforced with food. When the pigeon pecks the key, a morsel of food is delivered.

Figure 6.10 Skinner box for pigeons

Skinner and his followers were able to leave these automated pieces of apparatus to run themselves. On returning, the psychologist could inspect the chart and see the record of lever-pressing activity of the animal. Any number of rats or pigeons could be run simultaneously, each in its own Skinner box. Factors such as the size or quality of pellet or the hours of food deprivation could be varied and their effect on the rate of lever-pressing observed.

Following training, the effect of omitting food could be observed, a procedure termed *extinction*. When no pellets are delivered for a lever-press, the rat is said to be 'placed on extinction conditions'. On extinction conditions, following a period of often frenetic activity, the rat will slow up and then cease responding. The response of lever-pressing is said to have extinguished.

SAQ 11   (a) (i) What led to extinction in Pavlov's experiment? (ii) What contingency was removed?

(b) (i) What led to extinction in the Skinner box? (ii) What contingency was removed?

4.2 Shaping

Labour saving as the invention of the Skinner box was, the psychologist was still not entirely redundant in Skinner's laboratory, because one part of the procedure was labour intensive. In principle, one could simply leave a novice rat in the Skinner box and in time, as part of its exploration and manipulation of the environment, it would doubtless happen to press the lever. However, it might take a very long time before the rat would press hard enough to earn a pellet. It would take still longer before the rat would be pressing regularly. To shorten this phase of acquisition, Skinner used a procedure termed **shaping** to modify the behaviour of his rats, as follows.

Given that the experimenter's goal is to obtain a rat that presses the lever, Skinner reinforced **successive approximations** to this goal. First, the experimenter would deliver the rat a pellet just for going near to the lever. Once the rat had been conditioned to go near the lever, the criterion for obtaining reinforcement would be made slightly more demanding so that the rat would need to touch the lever to earn a pellet. When the rat was touching the lever frequently, the criterion for obtaining reinforcement was that the rat should lower the lever slightly. The next step was full lowering of the lever, at which point the apparatus delivered a pellet automatically. The use of the word 'shaping' to describe this procedure was chosen deliberately. By analogy with a potter shaping an unformed lump of clay by successive approximations to form a vase, so Skinner gradually shaped the behaviour of a naïve rat into that of a trained rat.

4.3 Operant conditioning and reinforcement

The type of conditioning studied by Skinner clearly involved an *instrumental* contingency in that the rat's behaviour was instrumental in the sequence of events. It is, however, usually described as **operant conditioning**. The meaning of this expression is that the subject operates upon the environment to cause an effect; it performs **operants**. The words 'instrumental' and 'operant' would seem then to be virtually synonymous, and indeed some psychologists treat them in this way. However, other psychologists use the term operant to mean the particular type of instrumental conditioning that is exemplified by an animal's behaviour in the Skinner box. In the maze, the experimenter initiates each trial. By contrast, the crucial feature of the Skinner box is that the rat is *self-pacing*. The rat in a Skinner box is, in a sense, master of the situation when it comes to the instigation and timing of each operant.

In Skinner's apparatus, food would be described as **positive reinforcement**. The tendency to lever-press increases by virtue of the contingency between lever-pressing and food. The adjective 'positive' is used to denote that reinforcement occurs by the *gain* of something: for example, food. Suppose the rat is subjected to a loud noise that it can *terminate* by lever-pressing. The loud noise would be termed **negative reinforcement**. The adjective 'negative' refers to something that is reinforcing by virtue of its termination. Both positive and negative reinforcement lead to an *increase* in the frequency of performing a given behaviour, that being reinforced. Finally, suppose the presentation of electric shock were contingent upon some behaviour: moving to one particular part of a cage, for instance. The tendency to perform this behaviour would be expected to *decrease*. The rat would learn to stay away from the area associated with shock. Used in this way, electric shock would be termed **punishment**. At this point, it is vital to stress that Skinner's whole emphasis has been strongly placed upon positive reinforcement.

SAQ 12   A psychology student wishes to see whether the procedures of the Skinner box can be generalized to reforming the behaviour of her husband. The husband pays little attention to his wife and the wife wishes to increase the amount of attention paid to her. The husband dislikes the music of Max Bygraves but loves Michael Jackson. Sometimes when the husband comes home, Max Bygraves is being played on the cassette player. The wife switches it off when the husband pays her attention. Sometimes when the husband pays the wife attention, she switches on Michael Jackson. When he hides behind the newspaper she switches on Max Bygraves. Try to identify where the wife is employing the three contingencies: (a) punishment; (b) negative reinforcement, and (c) positive reinforcement.

Skinner was able to use his apparatus to study some of the properties of operant conditioning. A brief account of just one of these will give you a feel for his research. Skinner was particularly interested in what he termed **schedules of reinforcement**. As we have described the Skinner box so far, the schedule has been one of **continuous reinforcement**; that is, each lever press is reinforced with a pellet of food. Skinner compared behaviour reinforced in this way with what happens when the schedule is arranged as one of **partial reinforcement**. Under this condition, reinforcement is not given for every lever-press. For example, the apparatus can be programmed so that only every tenth lever-press earns a pellet of food. Suppose that a rat or pigeon is exposed to a partial-reinforcement schedule and then placed on extinction conditions; that is, food is omitted entirely. The animal will persist with lever-pressing for longer than one exposed to a continuous reinforcement schedule.

Skinner and his followers (known as 'Skinnerians') see the rat in a Skinner box as a suitable model for explaining even complex human social behaviour. Just as the food pellet reinforces the hungry rat's bar-pressing, so, for example, could a smile be described as a social reinforcer for the response of saying good morning. The frequency of saying 'good morning' is assumed to be increased by such positive reinforcement. To Skinnerians, behaviour is shaped and maintained by its *consequences*.

SAQ 13   (a) A follower of Skinner is called into a school to advise on the behaviour of little Johnny. The Skinnerian notices that when little Johnny is quiet— drawing, writing or looking out of the window—the teacher pays no attention to him. Johnny throws a rubber at another child. The teacher pays attention to Johnny, by scolding him. Five minutes elapse and Johnny throws a pencil. How might the Skinnerian describe this situation? In your answer, identify: (i) the different behaviours exhibited; (ii) the reinforcer; and (iii) which behaviour was being reinforced.

(b) What might the Skinnerian recommend to change Johnny's behaviour?

The example of Johnny's behaviour illustrates the point that what might be maintaining a behaviour is unintentional reinforcement, even where punishment was intended.

Skinner's practical work was enormously influential, suggesting the general principle that behaviour can be shaped by application of the instrumental contingency. Apart from experiments, Skinner was also concerned with the S–R theory of behaviour and relating his data to this. However, he was soon to lose faith in this theory, as the next section will describe.

4.4 Skinner's dissent from stimulus–response psychology

To understand why Skinner ran into trouble reconciling his experimental data with stimulus–response theory, it is useful first to reconsider classical conditioning. In this type of conditioning, the stimuli assumed to form part of S–R associations are clearly defined events that occur at a particular point in time. For example, the onset and termination of the sound of a bell or the flash of a light (two commonly used neutral stimuli) can be rigorously controlled and measured, as can the presentation of the unconditional stimulus (e.g. food).

By contrast, in instrumental conditioning the stimulus component of the proposed S–R association is vague. Thorndike described the interior of the puzzle box as the 'stimulus situation'. It is not clear how to improve upon the expression 'stimulus situation'. In a similar vein, some people refer to the stimulus of the lever in the Skinner box. However, suppose one wished to account for the timing of a trained rat's behaviour. The rat is put into a Skinner box and at first it explores the food tray. Then it sniffs the floor. Then, at perhaps 53 seconds after being put in the box, the rat presses the lever. Why 53 seconds and not 51 seconds? We cannot easily appeal to the 'stimulus of the lever', since this stimulus has been present throughout. We are led into theoretical speculation of the kind that the stimulus must have been slightly different or was able to capture the rat's attention at precisely 53 seconds. The behaviourists entertained such ideas, but the problem with theorizing of this kind was that it represented precisely the kind of unsupported speculation that behaviourism was designed to combat. One ends up virtually introspecting for the rat, to try to capture its thoughts!

Up until 1935, Skinner was still speculating that, in the Skinner box, the stimulus of the lever must be eliciting the response of pressing; this S–R association was being reinforced. However, he was not very enthusiastic about the inclusion of such an ill-defined stimulus in an account of behaviour that in all other respects was based firmly upon observables. The response (lever pressing) and the reinforcer (delivery of the food pellet) could be measured precisely. By 1938, in a radical move by Skinner, the notion of a stimulus eliciting a response had been eliminated from his account of operant conditioning. In doing this, Skinner divided the population of responses that an animal can show into two classes: elicited and emitted.

Elicited responses were those that could reliably be associated with an eliciting stimulus, such as the innate response of salivation to food or to the conditional stimulus of a bell. To Skinner, elicited responses were typically secretions of glands and were the business of researchers into classical conditioning. **Emitted responses** were responses such as touching a lever in a Skinner box, often involving the whole animal, for which *there was no obvious stimulus applied immediately before the response occurred*. Animals were simply said to emit freely such 'arbitrary' responses from time to time. If they are reinforced, their frequency increases. The question of *why* animals emit such behaviour was not one that Skinner was willing to pursue. He felt that, in attempting to do so, the psychologist would inevitably get bogged down. Progress could be made by simply taking as given (1) the animal's tendency to emit responses and (2) reinforcement. Hence, at a stroke, Skinner believed he had cleansed the science of psychology of all theoretical speculation.

Note the difference between Figures 6.11 and 6.7. In both cases, a response is reinforced by its effect. But in Figure 6.11, unlike the earlier model, there is no longer a defined stimulus that becomes associated with the response. In Skinner's model of behaviour, all that can be observed is (1) behaviour, (2) the instrumental contingency of reinforcement that shapes and maintains that behaviour and (3) the environment within which the contingency is applied. To Skinner, this was enough, and in his laboratory he could exert perfect control over (2) and (3). Such control in turn brought behaviour under control.

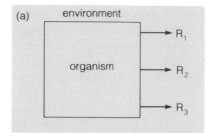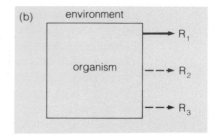

Figure 6.11 Skinner's view of behaviour. (a) An animal freely emits a number of different and somewhat arbitrary responses; (b) one of these (R_1) is reinforced, and hence the frequency of emitting this response increases. The frequency of other responses might correspondingly decline

4.5 The discriminative stimulus

Skinner recognized that, in every-day life, the availability of reinforcement is often signalled by changes in the environment. For example, in his terms, an 'out-of-order' sign on a cigarette machine announces that reinforcement will not follow the response of inserting money, and people withhold inserting money. Could rats and pigeons learn whether to respond, according to a signal as to the availability of reinforcement? If so, we would then say that they are able to show **discrimination**.

The way such an ability to discriminate is tested is as follows. Suppose a rat is trained to press a lever in a Skinner box, and after several days it is reliably pressing and obtaining its daily food in a one-hour session. Reinforcement availability is then restricted and this is signalled by the light in the Skinner box. During the one-hour session, the lights are switched on for 2 minutes and then off for 2 minutes throughout the session. Over a 2-minute period with the lights on, food is delivered in response to a lever-press. Food is then made unavailable for the next 2 minutes when the lights are off, and in turn is available again for 2 minutes with the lights on, and so on throughout the hour. The effect of introducing this schedule on the rat's lever-pressing is shown in Figure 6.12, which compares when the reinforcement conditions are first changed, a little later and then considerably later. Note that at first the rat increases its frequency of lever-pressing during the 'food-not-available' 2 minutes (as shown in part a).

SAQ 14   Consider for a moment a 2-minute period of 'food not available', in isolation. This period corresponds to imposing which of the conditions that we have already discussed?

After some experience, the rat is pressing equally in the two time periods (part b). Somewhat later, the rat is not pressing at all in the 'food-not-available' period and concentrating all of its efforts into the 'food-available' period (part c). In this way, Skinner was able to bring the behaviour of the rat under the control of a particular stimulus present in the environment, light and dark. The rat's behaviour was showing *discrimination* between light and dark.

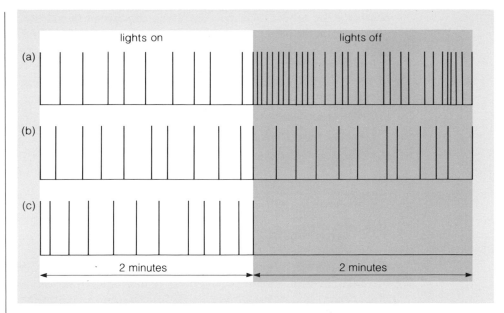

Figure 6.12 A rat is placed under the terms of 'lights on, reinforcement available' and 'lights off, reinforcement unavailable'. (a) Lever-presses observed immediately after these terms are imposed; (b) lever-presses observed 1 hour later; (c) lever-presses observed 2 days later

Skinner quite reasonably termed such a stimulus a **discriminative stimulus**. Unfortunately, therein lies a major source of the confusion endemic to many accounts of Skinner (see Catania, 1984; Carpenter, 1974, for a discussion of this confusion): the discriminative stimulus is not the same as the stimulus in stimulus–response psychology. In S–R psychology, the stimulus is said to *elicit* a response. The response follows the stimulus. By contrast, in Skinner's formulation, as the example of light–dark discrimination showed, behaviour is only brought under the control of the discriminative stimulus *after* the behaviour has been emitted. Skinner defines the discriminative stimulus purely in terms of observables. He makes no theoretical commitment to how this discriminative stimulus exerts its influence, beyond denying that it is an elicitor of the response. It is merely a feature of the environment that is manipulable by the experimenter and is observed to exert some control over lever-pressing.

Since the 1930s, Skinnerian psychology has studiously avoided all theoretical speculation involving unobservables.

SAQ 15 Imagine that the following events take place in a psychology laboratory. The laboratory is rapidly running out of the special food pellets that fit into Skinner boxes. The students are instructed to be as economical as possible with them but still to produce as much lever-pressing behaviour as possible. Karen and Wayne investigate the following. First, the rat's behaviour is shaped and it is soon lever-pressing reliably for a pellet for each response. The students then programme the equipment so that the rat needs to press 10 times to earn each pellet. After two sessions on this schedule, they return the conditions to one pellet for each lever press. They then alternate sounding a buzzer for 5-minute periods with 5-minute periods of silence. They only reinforce the rat for lever-presses when the buzzer is sounded. After several sessions the rat is pressing only when the buzzer is sounded. The rat is then returned to the conditions of each lever-press being reinforced with food. Finally, the food is omitted altogether and the number of lever-presses observed. With respect to this example, explain the meaning of the expressions:

(a) continuous reinforcement;

(b) partial reinforcement;

(c) discriminative stimulus;

(d) extinction.

4.6 The impact of Skinner's approach

Skinner and his followers applied their ideas in a number of fields. For instance, in education emphasis was placed upon treating each pupil as an *individual* learner, making learning interesting, and reinforcing correct responses rather than punishing bad behaviour. Teaching machines were developed in which the individual is given feedback (positive reinforcement) for correct responses. In guidance and therapy, for, say, marital disharmony, Skinnerians argued that abnormal behaviour could be maintained by hidden positive reinforcers (e.g. attention or sympathy). This shifted emphasis from blaming a person for misbehaviour towards dispassionate analysis of the possible sources of underlying reinforcement.

His *Notebooks* bear witness to how, in day-to-day experiences, Skinner applies the principles of positive reinforcement to understanding behaviour. For example, he observed:

When we were on the train from London to Exeter, two young girls, perhaps four and two, came into our compartment with their parents. For half an hour they were beautifully behaved. Then the younger tried to get a comic book away from her sister. They fought and the younger girl cried. The parents separated them and immediately got out a bag of sweets. 'To keep them quiet?'. Possibly, but in any case to reinforce fighting and crying.

(Skinner, 1980, p. 66)

Skinner has found the principles of positive reinforcement invaluable in understanding his life and organizing events within it. The principle also appears in some surprising contexts. For example, his autobiography, *Particulars of my life*, describes the following memory of childhood in Susquehanna, Pennsylvania:

I learned the technique of masturbation quite by accident, when I was perhaps eleven. Up to that point sexual play had consisted of undirected handling of genitalia. One day another boy and I had gone out of town on our bicycles and walked up a creek, beside which we were later to build a shack. We were sitting in the sun engaged in rather idle sex play when I made several rhythmic strokes which had a highly reinforcing effect. I immediately repeated them with even more reinforcing results.

(Skinner, 1976)

To Skinner, psychology is not only a science, but a social movement and
Skinner has often been compared to a missionary. To him, psychology should
be used primarily as a tool to solve the social ills of the world. To Skinner, the
task of a science of psychology it not to speculate about events in the mind or
even in the brain, but rather to be a tool in building a Utopian society based
upon positive reinforcement. Such problems as crime and urban decay are
seen by Skinner as being the consequence of society not accepting a culture
that is based upon a technology of positive reinforcement. In Skinner's eyes,
the way to change the behaviour of criminals is not to punish them, or to
psychoanalyse them, or to try to change their attitudes or personalities, but
simply to shape desirable behaviours by the use of positive reinforcement.
Acceptance of such a technology of behaviour change involves abandoning
some of our most cherished ideals, such as the notion that man is a free agent.
One of Skinner's most famous books, *Beyond freedom and dignity* (Skinner,
1971), describes the urgent need for such a programme of social change.

A poll of Americans conducted in 1975 found Skinner to be the most famous
living scientist (Guttman, 1977; Herrnstein, 1977). Indeed, by this poll, he was
in the top forty of the most significant people ever to have lived (Jesus Christ
being first). However, as you will doubtless have imagined, his ideas have also
provoked much criticism and cynicism. Some have argued against the
simplification inherent in the assumption that rats pressing levers for food
provide an adequate model for solving the complex ills of human society.
Some see the Skinnerian model as sinister, and ask who in society decides
which desirable behaviour to reinforce and with what reinforcer? His political
philosophy of building a Utopian society based upon positive reinforcement
earns the contempt of both sections from the right, who see it as an attack
upon the cherished ideals of freedom and responsibility, and sections from
the left (e.g. Rose and Rose, 1976), to whom it is an anathema to locate the ills
of society at the level of individual reinforcement contingencies rather than
economic power.

In that he was concerned with observable behaviour and made no appeal to
mental events in the explanation of behaviour, Skinner should be seen to be
firmly in the 'hard-nosed' behaviourist tradition of Watson. However, his
rejection of the value of pursuing the S–R theory of learning is a significant
departure from this trend. Discussion of Skinner concludes the account of the
mainstream or 'hard-nosed' behaviourists. Section 5 considers a theorist who
shared, if nothing else, Skinner's scepticism towards the S–R theory of
learning. However, this theorist, Tolman, was a psychologist whose influence
was to be in a quite different direction to that of Skinner.

Summary of Section 4

- By the invention of the Skinner box, Skinner pioneered a particular kind of instrumental contingency: that between a response of lever-pressing and reinforcement. Conditioning as a result of this contingency is known as operant conditioning.

- In operant conditioning, the subject operates upon the environment to cause an effect; it performs operants.

- Gain of such things as food increases the frequency of the response on which its presentation is contingent. Food is a positive reinforcer.

- Removal of an aversive condition, such as a loud noise or electric shock, increases the frequency of the response on which the removal is contingent. In this context, loud noise or shock is a negative reinforcer.

- Application of an aversive condition, such as electric shock or loud noise, decreases the frequency of the response on which its presentation is contingent. In this context, electric shock or a loud noise is a punisher.

- A contingency involving the reinforcement of each lever-press is termed continuous reinforcement. Reinforcing only some lever-presses (e.g. every tenth) is known as partial reinforcement.

- Omitting the reinforcement from an operant contingency is a procedure known as extinction. When the animal ceases to respond, the response is described as extinguished.

- Skinner identified two classes of response: elicited and emitted.

- Elicited responses are those associated with an eliciting stimulus.

- Skinner does not seek to identify a stimulus associated with emitted behaviour. However, behaviour can later be brought under the control of a discriminative stimulus, by reinforcing responses in the presence of the stimulus but not in its absence.

- Skinner sees the task of a science of behaviour as being to account for behaviour in terms of the reinforcement of freely emitted operants, both in the laboratory and in society.

5 | Starting the cognitive shift

Rather like the original behaviourist movement, the voices of dissent raised against behaviourism and the stimulus–response theory of learning have some of the features of a revolution in science. Such revolutions occur when an established body of theory is shown to be inadequate and a 'better theory' is available. By a 'better theory', we mean one that explains a wider set of data, and can account for results that the old theory found difficult to explain. However, scientific revolutions do not generally throw out all of the old theory. Features of it remain intact. Experiments inspired by the old theory can often be reinterpreted in terms of the new theory. Like revolutions in government, there is often a long history of dissent marked by local uprisings. When the revolution takes place, evidence against the established position can sometimes be found from long ago. Before we describe the nature of the non-Skinnerian strand of the dissent against the S–R theory of learning, it is useful to reiterate the essence of S–R psychology, in order to establish exactly what was, and what was not, in dispute.

Pavlov had demonstrated that, by pairing a neutral stimulus with an unconditional stimulus, the neutral stimulus became a conditional stimulus that acquired some of the properties of the unconditional stimulus. In the hands of Watson and others, the theory that was employed to explain this effect was in terms of strengthening an association between a stimulus and a response. As a biological explanation of the process underlying conditioning, excitation from the neutral stimulus was somehow supposed to feed into the pathway in the brain that links the unconditional stimulus to the unconditional response. By so doing, the neutral stimulus acquired some of the response-evoking strength of the unconditional stimulus. In instrumental conditioning, Thorndike, Skinner and others had demonstrated the ability of reinforcement to change the behaviour of an animal. As a result of the *effect* of a particular behaviour on the environment in generating reinforcement, that behaviour would emerge as dominant from an unformed repertoire of different behaviours. In the theoretical speculations of Thorndike (though not Skinner), the effect served to cement the linkage between the stimulus situation and the response that proved instrumental in obtaining reinforcement. Thus, both classical and instrumental conditioning were explained in terms of forming new S–R associations.

What is not in doubt is the validity of the experiments under discussion. For example, it is easy to classically condition a rat or to demonstrate the shaping of a rat in a Skinner box by the use of reinforcement. These experiments have been repeated by generations of psychologists with the same results. Controversy concerns only the validity and usefulness of applying an S–R theory to these results. The dissenters fall into two main camps: (1) those within the 'hard-nosed' behaviourist camp who wish to keep a distance from speculative theorizing (i.e. Skinner, described in Section 4), and (2) those outside the camp who prefer theories other than the S–R (e.g. Tolman, described next). An additional source of dissent, described in Section 7, arises from those looking at differences in learning capacity between different species of animal.

5.1 Edward Tolman: purposive behaviour

Edward C. Tolman (1886–1959) was one of the most famous dissenters against the S–R theory of psychology. Tolman had one foot firmly in the behaviourist camp in so far as he felt that the answers to the interesting questions of psychology were to be found by looking at rats running in mazes. The early 'hard-nosed' behaviourists, such as Watson, had urged psychology to exorcize the ghost of mentalism in favour of the model of S–R connections. In keeping with Watson, Tolman did not want a return to a psychology based upon mental events and consciousness. However, Tolman did not share Watson's faith that a science of behaviour could be based upon the general explanatory power of the S–R model.

By observing the behaviour of rats negotiating mazes, Tolman concluded that such behaviour appears to be governed by a *purpose*. Rather than being a stereotyped *response to* stimuli, behaviour is directed *towards* a goal. The rat successfully learning a maze is not simply associating particular stimuli (e.g. corners in the maze) with particular limb responses, as S–R theory would suggest. Doubtless, Tolman was partly led to his conclusions, in a rather non-behaviourist fashion, by his own intuitions about mental processes and his own behaviour. Tolman did not wish to imply that the animal has any *conscious* strategy for getting to the goal. Somewhat cautiously, he argued that the rat acted *as if* it had a purpose. To convey this sense he used the term **purposive** to describe the behaviour. In terms that fit closely to the notion of behaviour being 'purposive', Tolman argued that the rat acts as if it has an **expectancy** of what will be obtained at the goal (the term 'expectancy' is often used synonymously with 'expectation'). By denying that the rat is simply responding to stimuli, Tolman reasoned that such behaviour could not be *reduced* to a series of S–R associations.

The most important feature of animal behaviour that led Tolman to the notion of 'purposive behaviour' is its *flexibility*. He acknowledged that there might exist reactions to some stimuli that appear to be stereotyped responses and can be characterized as 'reflexive'. However, he argued that, on closer scrutiny, the S–R model could not give a convincing explanation for the richer aspects of animal behaviour, such as the rat negotiating a maze. The rat adapts its leg movements according to the circumstances; it does not repeat the same stereotyped sequence of motor responses each time. What was common from one trial to the next was not the sequence of motor responses performed by the rat's muscles, but rather the goal that the rat attained. To Tolman, it was pointless to look at individual leg movements and to base a theory of learning upon these. Rather, he argued that one needs to understand how learning enables the rat to *adapt* its behaviour to reach the goal. Tolman and his followers backed up their claim with some very clever experiments that have now become classics of psychology.

Macfarlane (1930), a student of Tolman's, trained rats to negotiate their way through a maze that was flooded to a depth of several inches with water. The reward in the goal box was food on dry land. Not surprisingly, the rats opted to swim through the maze. Macfarlane then drained the water from the maze and placed the rats in the start box. The rats were able to run through the maze without making an error. Considering the leg movements, the rat's responses were, of course, different between the wet and dry mazes. The stimuli in the maze were also different: wetness and dryness of the maze floor, for example. Clearly, what the rats had learned was something about the maze *divorced from the actual limb responses involved in negotiating the maze.* We have drawn particular attention to the last statement since it is the crux of the distinction between Tolman's approach and an S–R approach.

According to Tolman, the rat learns something about the experimental situation, of the kind: 'food is over there near the window' and 'the path to the left leads to the path that leads to the food'. It learns about relationships between things: for example, between food and window. In other words, rather than learning a stereotyped association between a stimulus and a response, Tolman argued that animals learn a relationship between *stimuli.*

5.2 The cognitive approach

The model of learning proposed by Tolman is characterized by the term **cognitive**, which refers to the storage of a particular kind of *information* in the brain. This information is about the world outside but it does not specify the muscles involved in negotiating the animal's way in the world. In the cognitive account, the rat learns *facts* (or **cognitions**) not responses. The stimulus of the window carries information to the rat concerning the window's association with food. In Tolman's terms, while negotiating a maze, rats form a **cognitive map** of the maze. This is an internal representation of the maze stored in the brain. Subsequent behaviour is then based upon (1) cognitions about the layout of the maze and where food is located with reference to the cognitive map, and (2) the prevailing circumstances: to swim or to run through the maze, for instance.

To speak of cognitions in animals does not suppose that their cognitive capacity is exactly like that of a human. Whether animals consciously reason on the basis of their cognitions is a matter of speculation. We don't know. We do know that humans can use language to express the knowledge in their brains, and therefore a cautious distinction between animal and human cognition would seem to be in order.

To an S–R behaviourist, learning consists of associations between stimuli and responses. To a cognitivist, such as Tolman, it consists in the assimilation of information that is not tied directly to behaviour. Stimulus–response theory represents an attempt to explain directly the *performance* of the rat. The input is stimuli and the output is behaviour. The theory tries to account for *all* of the path that lies between input and output, in terms of S–R associations, some learned and some innate. By contrast, a cognitive theory of learning attempts to account for a smaller part of the relationship between input and output. It does not try to prescribe exactly *how* learning of cognitions will be utilized in behaviour. In addition to incorporating learning, a model of behaviour expressed in cognitive terms would need to take into account the animal's goal and its capacity for flexibility of behaviour in the face of varying environmental conditions.

A good example of a rat's formation of a cognitive map and how this can be utilized in giving flexibility to behaviour was provided by an experiment carried out by Tolman, Ritchie and Kalish (1946), described in Box C.

BOX C   The experiment of Tolman *et al.*

In an experiment performed by Tolman *et al.* (1946), rats were required to learn one of two things in order to get to food. The maze used in this experiment is shown in Figure 6.13. Each rat was released alternately from positions S_1 and S_2. For half the rats (group 1), food was always obtained by turning right. That is to say, on running from S_1, food was obtained at F_1, and on running from S_2 it was found at F_2. These rats were required to learn a particular *response*—that is, to turn right—in order to get food. Stimulus–response theory would suggest that this should be a relatively easy task for the rat. For the other half (group 2), food was always available in a given *place* (for example, at F_2), irrespective of the location from which they started running. To earn food, rats in group 2 always needed to go to the same place. To do so, each rat in group 2 was required to make different responses, turning left on running from S_1 and right on running from S_2.

Rats required to learn to go to a given *place* (group 2) were much more successful at solving their problem than were those required to make a given *response* (group 1). Within eight trials, all of the eight rats given the place-learning task had solved the problem. None of the rats required to learn a specific response was able to learn as fast as this.

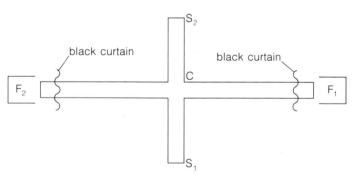

Figure 6.13 Experiment performed by Tolman *et al.* (1946)

The experiment of Tolman *et al.* was conducted in a rich environment with many cues outside the maze. In such an environment, rats are easily able to learn about places and their relationship to food (group 2). This supports Tolman's contention that rats learn information about the environment in the form of a cognitive map. Response learning is not impossible (group 1), but, in such an apparatus, it is relatively difficult for rats to utilize response-based information. Of course, in the natural habitat, food might normally remain in one place for periods of time and so the rat's facility for place learning can be seen to have adaptive value.

Tolman and his students were able to marshall other evidence to support their argument that an animal's behaviour involves an *expectancy* of what is in the goal box. Tinklepaugh (1928) trained monkeys on a task that involved earning a piece of banana or lettuce on an instrumental contingency. During the course of this experiment, Tinklepaugh played a trick on the monkey. The monkey observed the experimenter placing a piece of banana under an inaccessible container. Then, out of sight of the monkey, the banana would be replaced by a relatively unattractive, but normally acceptable, item of food for a monkey, a piece of lettuce. The monkey would then be given access to the container. Its reaction could only be described as one of frustration. It would not eat the lettuce, but would carefully inspect the container. On occasion, it would shriek at the experimenter, suggesting that an expectancy about the quality of the food had not been fulfilled.

If an animal is motivated to pursue a goal and has an expectancy of the quality of the goal, what is responsible for constructing the animal's cognition concerning the goal? What is the procedure by which animals learn about goals? To theorists in the tradition of S–R psychology, something concerned with *ingestion* of food, or the consquences of ingestion, was assumed to reinforce an S–R connection. Tolman rejected the S–R model, but what about the notion of reinforcement with which it is associated? How do we explain that Thorndike's cats escaped the puzzle box faster on successive trials (see Figure 6.5), unless something is being strengthened over time? Similarly, rats running in mazes became faster over successive trials.

In Tolman's terms, what is being strengthened in the maze is as follows. As the rat gains in experience, cues that lead to the goal-box, such as particular arms in the maze, become better *predictors* of the way to food. The expectancies that food is in the goal-box and that a particular route leads there, are *strengthened* over these trials. There is no better way to confirm a rat's expectancy that food is in the goal-box, and to teach it how to negotiate the maze, than to make it hungry and reward it with food in the goal-box. Tolman did not doubt the effectiveness of the *procedure* of reinforcement; he merely denied that the *process* by which it works is one of strengthening S–R associations. Rather, he saw reinforcement as acting to strengthen cognitions concerning the expectancy of food in a certain location.

Tolman's ideas were somewhat masked by the dominant Skinnerian and other 'hard-nosed' behaviourist positions in the period between about 1950 and 1970. However, from the late 1960s to the present day there has been a strong shift in favour of the cognitive approach. Section 6 considers how the ideas of Tolman lead on naturally to a cognitive interpretation of both classical conditioning and the behaviour of the rat working for food in a Skinner box.

Summary of Section 5

- Edward Tolman was one of the most famous dissenters against the S–R theory of learning.

- Tolman argued that behaviour is purposive, that animals assimilate knowledge about their environment and can show flexibility in reaching goals.

- According to Tolman, an animal acts as if it has an expectancy as to the outcome of its behaviour, e.g. food will be found in the goal-box of a maze.

- Information on, for example, the layout of a maze and the location of food therein is represented internally and held in the brain in the form of a cognitive map of the maze.

- Purposive behaviour depends upon what the animal has learned, its expectancy of what is at the goal and the prevailing circumstances.

6 | Classical and operant conditioning reinterpreted

One of the fundamental differences between stimulus–response theory and Tolman's cognitive theory was that the latter allowed for the flexibility of behaviour. A variety of different strategies and movements, involving various muscles, could be recruited according to prevailing circumstances. By contrast, the S–R theory of instrumental learning would only permit a fixed response to appear in any given situation.

Tolman suggested that a similar flexibility might also apply to classical conditioning. Perhaps what is learned is not a new stimulus–response association but a relationship between two stimuli; for example, between the bell and food. If, in the maze, the rat learns to expect food over by the window, then in Pavlov's experiment the dog might have learned to *expect* food on hearing the bell. Subsequent theorists were able to marshall a number of bits of evidence to show that what is learned in a classical conditioning experiment is indeed an *expectancy* of the unconditional stimulus, triggered by presentation of the conditional stimulus. Sections 6.1 and 6.2 consider this evidence. First, we look again at what is learned in classical conditioning and see whether there can be flexibility in the expression of such learning in behaviour.

6.1 Classical conditioning and flexible behaviour

To test whether an expectancy rather than a fixed S–R association is formed during classical conditioning, experiments need to allow flexibility in the expression of learning to be revealed. Pavlov's experiment did not allow the dog much scope for varying behaviour. It was held in a harness (see Figure 6.1) and the index of learning was simply the quantity of saliva secreted. It is difficult to imagine how flexibility could be manifested in such an experiment, and so it cannot be used to discriminate between S–R and cognitive models. Both models predict that a dog held in a harness will salivate in response to the bell. Subsequent experiments have clearly shown that an animal is able to reveal flexibility in the expression of classical conditioning, when given the opportunity to do so.

Consider an experiment in which a mild electric shock (unconditional stimulus) is applied to the floor on which a rat is standing. The rat's unconditional response to the shock is to flee, if escape is possible. In a confined space, the rat jumps or flinches. Then, on one or two occasions, a tone (neutral stimulus) is paired with the electric shock. Following such pairing of tone and shock, what is the rat's response to presentation of the tone alone? If escape is possible, the rat will probably flee. If it is not possible, the response to the tone is often one of freezing (immobility) (Gray, 1988; Bolles, 1970).

This experiment shows that, following a given pairing of conditional and unconditional stimuli, the conditional response (e.g. freezing) can be very different in form to the unconditional response (e.g. fleeing, jumping or flinching). What the rat learns then is not to perform a particular *response* to the conditional stimulus. It does not simply transfer the unconditional response to control by the conditional stimulus. Rather, it appears to learn an *expectation* of shock. In response to the conditional stimulus, it acts in a way that is appropriate to the occurrence of shock in the near future. Such behaviour exhibits *flexibility* in that it is adjusted to the circumstances. If the environment permits it, the animal might be able to avoid the shock altogether by fleeing.

It is possible to see the advantage of this flexibility in terms of survival in the natural habitat. Fleeing or jumping in response to, say, the pain of tissue damage caused by a fox's claws, as it makes an abortive attempt at capture (analogous to electric shock in a laboratory experiment), would make sense. However, freezing might be an adaptive strategy in response to a cue signalling that a predator is in the vicinity (analogous to the tone), in a situation where escape is impossible. By remaining motionless, the rat might' avoid detection by the predator. Note that a model of classical conditioning as represented in Figure 6.3, in which the CS simply connects with the pathway linking UCS to UCR, could not account for such flexibility. All that this model could possibly predict, as a result of conditioning, is a CR that is similar in form to the UCR.

Interestingly, some 300 years before Pavlov, an 'experiment' (if we could call it that) was reported that involved a classical contingency, but allowed flexibility in the expression of learning. The experiment, described in 1615 by the Spanish playwright Lope de Vega, remained hidden from the world of psychology until apparently it was told to the American learning theorist O. Hobart Mowrer (Mowrer, 1960). The significance of the experiment becomes very apparent in the light of a reconsideration of classical conditioning.

The experimenter was a monk, who as a punishment for his sins was made to eat his food from the floor of the monastery. To compound the unfortunate soul's misery, the monastery cats were allowed free access to compete for the food with the monk. All the monk's attempts to get rid of the cats were either ineffective or so obvious as to draw the attention of his seniors, until one day he discovered classical conditioning.

I put them all in a sack, and on a pitch black night took them out under an arch. First I would cough and then immediately whale[1] the daylights out of the cats. They whined and shrieked like an infernal pipe organ. I would pause for awhile and repeat the operation—first a cough, and then a thrashing. I finally noticed that even without beating them, the beasts moaned and yelped like the very devil whenever I coughed. I then let them loose. Thereafter, whenever I had to eat off the floor, I would cast a look around. If an animal approached my food, all I had to do was to cough, and how that cat did scat!

(Mowrer, 1960, p. 24)

A cognitive interpretation of this experiment is as follows (Toates, 1986). Following the line of Tolman, the pairing of cough and trauma creates an expectation. The cough revives a memory of the trauma, and the cat then takes action appropriate to the expectation of trauma. Precisely what form this action takes will depend crucially upon the context in which the cat finds itself when the cough is sounded. For example, in the sack it might crouch, in the kitchen it might flee, and cornered in a room, attack would be a possibility. The degrees of freedom open to the subject were greater than in Pavlov's experiment, and thereby the exact nature of what is learnt is somewhat better revealed.

Consideration of a large number of results showing flexibility in the expression of classical conditioning led the Canadian psychologist Dalbir Bindra (1922–1980) to propose, in the spirit of Tolman, the general model that Pavlovian conditioning consists of forming expectancies (Bindra, 1974, 1978). By convention, this is represented as CS → UCS, which summarizes the assumption that presenting a conditional stimulus creates an expectancy that the unconditional stimulus will occur. On its own, this statement does not tell us what the rat will *do* when the CS is presented. Its behaviour depends not only upon the expectation but also upon such factors as the possibilities that the environment offers and what is the most appropriate thing to do in the circumstances. For example, in Bindra's terms, in the Pavlovian experiment, presenting the bell creates an expectancy for food. In response to the bell, the animal acts *as if* food is being given. The Spanish cats learned a cough–trauma expectancy and their behaviour depended upon their environmental context. In other words, on exposure to a classical contingency, what is learned is an accurate reflection of the contingency. Animals learn an

---

[1]Whale: a word meaning to beat or to flog.

association between two stimuli, rather than an association between a stimulus and a response.

This section has described the details of how the expectancy acquired by classical conditioning is *utilized* in purposive behaviour. The description of classical conditioning in terms of creating an expectancy followed logically from the work of Tolman. In parallel with this, other researchers have been concerned with looking more closely at the details of the process by which the expectancy is formed in the first place and this is the topic of Section 6.2.

6.2 Expectancy and prediction

So far we have spoken of such unconditional stimuli as shocks, food, the impact of the claws of a fox and the caning by a monk, these all being things that are of some immediate importance to the survival chances of an animal. They are all stimuli to which the animal reliably *responds*. We have seen that the animal is able to form expectancies of such events based upon the occurrence of conditional stimuli (e.g. a cough associated with a beating).

Can the animal only show expectancies of immediately *important* events, those to which it normally responds? Suppose two neutral stimuli—for example, a bell and a light—are paired on a number of occasions, the bell coming just before the light. Will the rat come to expect the light when the bell is sounded? The measurement of any such expectancy poses difficulties but a number of rather ingenious experiments have shown that animals do indeed have the capacity to form such expectancies (Dickinson, 1980). One of these experiments is described in Box D.

As shown in Box D, an animal can therefore form expectancies between two neutral stimuli that have been presented together. However, expectancies are more readily formed between neutral stimuli and such things as shock and food. The outcome of experiments of this kind, showing that animals can come to expect even neutral stimuli, has led a number of researchers to rephrase expectancy theory slightly. In the newer and broader terms, it is said that animals form expectancies of one *event* following another *event* (Dickinson, 1980; Mackintosh, 1983). In such terms, prediction of a biologically important event (an unconditional stimulus) such as shock or food is seen as just a special case of the general theory. The theory states that, if one event (E_1) occurs just before another event (E_2), the animal can form an expectancy of E_2. This is represented as $E_1 \rightarrow E_2$: given the occurrence of event E_1, the animal can come to expect event E_2 to occur.

This is an appropriate point to take stock of how far we have now come with developing the cognitive approach to classical conditioning. At no stage have we doubted the validity of Pavlov's experiment. We have merely changed the interpretation of it. We now see this experiment as a special example of a general principle: that when two events are paired, the occurrence of one event (E_1) can lead the animal to expect the subsequent event (E_2). We have also seen that what the animal *does* in response to E_1 (and thereby the expectancy of E_2) depends upon the context in which the animal finds itself.

BOX D   Testing for an expectancy

In phase 1 of the experiment, neither a tone nor a light are seen to evoke any obvious behaviour on the part of the rat, apart from an increased tendency to investigate the apparatus (Figure 6.14). In phase 2, the tone is paired with light. In phase 3, the light is paired with shock on a number of occasions. In phase 4, the rat's reaction to each of the stimuli is tested. The light now comes to evoke fear (e.g. a reaction of freezing). Therefore it is known that in phase 3 the rat learned to expect the shock on presentation of the light. The question is whether, in phase 2, the rat learned an expectancy between the tone and the light, even though this was not revealed in behaviour. Would the rat expect the light on hearing the tone? In phase 4 of the experiment, when the tone was presented on its own, the rat showed signs of fear to the tone (e.g. freezing).

Note that the tone was never paired with shock. The logic of the argument is that presenting the tone creates an expectation of the light which in turn creates an expectation of the shock. The rat therefore exhibits fear to the tone. In such an experiment, careful controls also need to be run to make sure that it is specifically the *pairing* of light and tone that is responsible for the result. If a control group is run in which the rat is exposed to tone and light at random times in phase 2, then the tone does not come to evoke fear in phase 4.

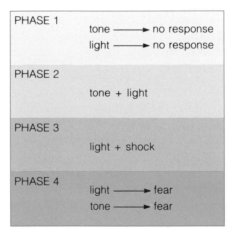

Figure 6.14 Experimental procedure for demonstrating the formation of an expectancy between two neutral stimuli

Sometimes it might react to E_1 in much the same way as it does to E_2: for example, the salivation that is evoked by the tone (E_1) in Pavlov's experiment is much like the salivation evoked by the food (E_2). In other cases, the response to E_1 is very different to the response to E_2. For example, the response of freezing to a tone (E_1) is rather different to the response of fleeing or flinching made to the shock (E_2) with which it has been paired.

SAQ 16   In cognitive terms, based upon prediction of events (i.e. using the expressions
          E_1 and E_2), what is learned in Pavlov's salivary conditioning experiment?

The capacity of an animal to form $E_1 \rightarrow E_2$ expectancies gives it an enormous
adaptive advantage in the world. Expressed in other words, the ability means
that it is able to form *predictions* of what is about to happen in the world. It
can then take action appropriate to this prediction: for example, to flee, to
salivate or to freeze. The rat's ability to form predictions is similar in some
basic ways to the much more sophisticated capacity for prediction that
humans have developed, though we must be cautious not to go too far with
such comparisons. Weather forecasting is a good example. By making a
forecast, one cannot of course change the weather—the environment remains
the same. What changes is the person's *relation to* the environment, staying
indoors or running to shelter on hearing the forecast of a hurricane. Similarly,
in the laboratory, by learning that a tone predicts shock, represented as
(tone)→(shock), a rat cannot stop the shock. However, it can take appropriate
action, fleeing or freezing.

Suppose a rat is exposed to a couple of pairings of tone and (2 seconds later)
shock in a laboratory cage. It rapidly learns that, by leaping onto a platform
when the tone occurs, it can avoid the shock. The shock is then disconnected
by the experimenter. However, for a hundred or more trials, the rat still leaps
on hearing the tone. Why, you might be asking, doesn't the rat's behaviour
extinguish? The rat seems to be acting on the cognition (tone)→(shock) and
yet the shock does not occur. Even if it did still occur, the rat would not be
around to feel it. By comparison, the conditional salivation response of
Pavlov's dog to a tone would soon have ceased if food did not follow the tone.
There are two things to be said in answer to this issue. First, in cognitive
terms the rat has probably learned that the tone predicts shock *at a particular
place*. By its action on hearing the tone, the rat is no longer in that place to
revise its cognition (tone)→(shock) to one of (tone)→(no shock). Second, such
behaviour can be seen to have adaptive value. Suppose, in the wild, as a
result of an encounter, the rat has learned a cognition (distinct sound)→(pain
of a fox's claws). It might be best for the rat to take action for the rest of its life
in response to such a distinctive sound. It would not make sense for the rat to
require a 'booster dose' of the claws once in a while in order to maintain the
cognition (tone)→(claws) intact.

We have now come a long way from viewing the animal in terms of simple
mechanical analogies of coins in slot machines. This analogy and the model
shown in Figure 6.3 are now seen to be wholly inadequate in explaining what
is learnt on exposure to the classical contingency. However, to reject an
earlier attempt at an explanation of the process underlying conditioning is
clearly not enough; in the new terms, we need to provide an explanation of
the process underlying the formation of a prediction. What is it about the
occurrence of a traumatic event that means the animal can so quickly and
efficiently form an association between an E_1 (e.g. tone) and the traumatic
event (E_2)? To answer this, it is now necessary to look in more detail at the
description of the rat being able to form a prediction of what will happen in
the future, a prediction that is triggered by the presentation of E_1.

We guess that, by now, you are probably convinced that the capacities (1) to form predictions of the immediate future and (2) to be able to respond flexibly to those predictions, can confer a crucial advantage on an animal. A rat forewarned is a rat forearmed! However, it would seem reasonable to suppose that the rat has not the luxury of an unlimited brain capacity to devote exclusively to forming predictions. Its brain must engage in a variety of other activities and so the rat must allocate priorities. Seen in this light, forming some predictions might be expected to take priority over forming others. In considering issues of this kind, the explanation of what *function* something serves (see also Chapter 5, Section 3.2) can sometimes be very helpful in understanding how it works.

As a thought exercise, consider designing an efficient rat. What sort of events would it be most important for a rat to be able to predict?

From the perspective of designing an efficient rat you might imagine that it is particularly important for it to form predictions of biologically significant events, such as the arrival of a predator or food. Priority should be given to this and indeed such predictions are very readily formed. Another consideration is that it would be particularly useful for the rat to form predictions of *unexpected* events. On first encounter, this factor might seem more subtle than the consideration of biological significance, or, alternatively, it might be so obvious as to have been taken for granted. However, its consideration turns out to hold the key to understanding how expectations are formed.

Suppose, as a result of exposure to a few paired presentations of tone and shock, a rat has learned that a tone (E_1) predicts shock (E_2); it expects shock when it hears the tone. Now suppose that, following this learning, a light (let's call it E_1'') is presented at the same time as the tone on a number of occasions, just before the shock. Would it be to the rat's advantage to form a predictive association between the light (E_1'') and the shock (E_2)? If the rat were to have unlimited brain capacity, it might be useful. On the other hand, the shock was not unexpected. It was predicted by the tone. The rat would not have been caught unawares by the shock. Therefore, it might be adaptive for a nervous system of limited capacity not to form an *additional* expectancy, this one with the light. So much for armchair speculation about designing an efficient rat, but what does a real rat do in this situation? Is it the case that to form a predictive association with an event, a subsequent event needs to be unexpected? A now-classic series of experiments inspired by Leon Kamin (1969) provides the answer. Box E describes one representative example.

The experiment described in Box E shows that a predictive association is not formed between an event E_1'' (tone for group 1) and a following event E_2 (shock for group 1), if E_2 is already predicted by another event E_1 (light for group 1).

How do we explain the process underlying this somewhat paradoxical result? To do so, for the moment, you will need to think about things in a slightly different way to that which is appropriate to understanding earlier parts of the chapter. Rather than starting by thinking about an event E_1 and then

BOX E   How to present the (un)expected to a rat

GROUP 1	GROUP 2
PHASE 1 light + shock	——
PHASE 2 light + tone + shock	light + tone + shock
PHASE 3 light ——→ fear tone ——→ no fear	light ——→ fear tone ——→ fear

Figure 6.15 Arrangement of light, tone and shock

In phase 1 of the experiment, a group of rats (group 1) was exposed to a pairing of a light (E_1) followed by a shock (E_2) for eight trials. Group 2 experienced nothing during this phase (see Figure 6.15). For group 1, in phase 1, by classical conditioning, the light should acquire the capacity to elicit fear. After experiencing these eight trials, the shock would be *expected* on presentation of the light. For both groups, in phase 2, a compound stimulus consisting of the light *plus a tone* was paired with the shock over eight trials. Would the tone acquire any capacity to elicit fear? For those in group 1, would the rat's prior experience with the light (in phase 1) affect the capacity of the tone to become a conditional stimulus for fear?

In phase 3, the tone and the light were then each tested to see whether they evoked any fear. Rats in group 1 showed no fear of the tone. They showed fear of the light. For rats in group 2, unlike those in group 1, both the tone and the light acquired a strong fear-evoking capacity (e.g. freezing).

considering a following event E_2, you now need to start the explanation by considering E_2. Suppose that the system works in the following way. The occurrence of an *unexpected* event like the first shock (E_2) for rats in group 2 (phase 2) is the trigger that initiates a search for a cue (E_1) that might serve to predict the event. The rat scans its memory of recently arrived information, asking, in effect, 'what has just happened in the world that might have caused event E_2?'. On finding such an event (E_1), an expectancy, $E_1 \rightarrow E_2$, is formed. Rats in group 2 find two such events, light and tone, and a predictive association is formed with both. However, if on the basis of an established E_1 (the light for rats in group 1), the event E_2 is expected (the shock for rats in group 1 during phase 2), then no such scan is made. Therefore, if after an event E_1 has formed a predictive relationship with E_2, *two* events, E_1 and E_1'', are presented together, and just before E_2, then no predictive association is formed with event E_1''.

SAQ 17   Describe the first shock experienced by rats in each group in phase 2 of the experiment, using the expressions 'predicted', 'expected', 'unexpected', E_1 and E_2.

Note that a model of the kind shown in Figure 6.3 could not account for this result. In the traditional language of classical conditioning, simply pairing a neutral stimulus (e.g. the tone for group 1) with an unconditional stimulus (e.g. shock) is not *sufficient* to produce conditioning to the neutral stimulus. Subsequent experiments showed that Kamin's result (Kamin, 1969) was not due to the tone failing to be processed by rats in group 1, by being blocked out by the light: the tone was processed but did not enter into a predictive association with the shock.

So the animal is now seen to be looking for predictors, events that will enable it to take action to predict other events such as shock or food. On finding a predictor, it no longer searches for further predictors, since such a search is initiated only by unexpected events. Now consider again what would constitute a system of prediction for an efficient rat. It needs to establish predictors for significant events and it needs to be able to take action in a flexible way when the predictor appears. Given that it has a limited capacity to handle information, it cannot afford to set up new predictors for events that are already well predicted. There is one final consideration: the efficient rat would need to find a *reliable* predictor (E_1) for a significant event. A variation on a simple and familiar example can make vividly clear what is meant by 'reliability of a predictor'.

Suppose a village appoints a lookout to alert the inhabitants to when a wolf appears and threatens the sheep. Clearly, someone who cries 'wolf' too often when there is no wolf would not constitute a wholly reliable lookout. However, he might be tolerated. It might be considered much more serious if he repeatedly *fails* to spot a wolf when one really is present. The lookout might plead that he has reliably spotted a number of wolves even though he has missed several. Surely to employ him is better than having no lookout at all. The villagers might argue that they have limited resources. If they dismiss him, they might then be able to employ a really reliable lookout. With the help of this analogy, you should be better placed to appreciate a crucial experiment reported by Rescorla (1968). Rescorla wondered whether a tone that is paired with a shock on only *some* occasions would be utilized by the animal as a predictor of shock. If it were to be utilized it would fail to give warning of a number of shocks. Rescorla's experiment is described in Box F.

So how are we to interpret the difference between the two conditions shown in Figure 6.16, such that group 1 did, and group 2 did not, develop fear to the tone? A moment's glance at Figure 6.16 shows that, for group 1, shock never occurs in the absence of the tone. However, for group 2, shock is as likely to occur in the absence of the tone as in its presence. Suppose the rat's nervous system functions in the way suggested in the discussion of Kamin's experiment. The occurrence of an unexpected event such as shock or food (E_2) is the trigger for a scan of sensory information arriving just before the event. Rescorla's experiment shows that if an E_1 (e.g. sound) occurs *each* time a significant event (E_2) happens, an $E_1 \rightarrow E_2$ expectancy will be formed. However, if an E_1 occurs on only *some* of the occasions on which an E_2 occurs, then an expectation is less likely to be formed between them.

BOX F Rescorla's experiment

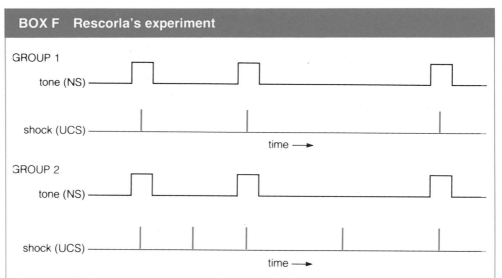

Figure 6.16 Experiment reported by Rescorla (1968)

Rescorla compared the conditions of tone (E_1) and shock (E_2) administered to two groups of rats (groups 1 and 2), a sample of which is shown in Figure 6.16. For each group of rats, there is an equal number of presentations of tone. The shocks given to group 1, in temporal contiguity with the tone, are also given to group 2 at exactly the same point in time. However, the rats in group 2 receive additional shocks in between those paired with the tone. What is the effect of these additional shocks on the process of forming an expectancy between tone and shock? If a simple pairing of a neutral stimulus with an unconditional stimulus were all that is involved in conditioning, we would expect to obtain as much conditioning of fear to the tone for rats in group 1 as in group 2. There are an equal number of tone–shock pairings for the two groups.

In fact, rats in group 2 failed to develop any conditional fear to the tone. In the terms of classical conditioning, as with Kamin's experiment (Kamin, 1969), pairing of a neutral stimulus with an unconditional stimulus is therefore not *sufficient* to transform a neutral stimulus into a conditional stimulus. Those in group 1 did develop fear to the tone.

Seen in terms of the function served, for rats in group 2 the tone is not a *reliable* signal for shock in spite of a number of tone–shock pairings. It failed to give warning of shock on a number of occasions. By contrast, for group 1 the tone has a highly reliable predictive value, each occurrence of shock being heralded by the tone. For group 1, the tone carries the vital information that 'in the presence of the tone, shock is more likely to happen than in the absence of the tone'. The conclusion arrived at by modern learning theorists is that the occurrence of events that impinge upon the nervous system is the trigger for the animal to search for predictive cues. The nervous system of rats in Rescorla's group 1 would rapidly find the tone to be a reliable predictor of shock. For rats in group 2 it would not be; the nervous system processes would remain open for finding a reliable predictor.

The argument is that the animal's nervous system is programmed so that predictive relationships are established between events. As Dickinson (1980) expresses it, the animal is organized so as to learn the **causal texture** of its environment. Out of the mass of events that impinge upon an animal's sense organs, processes in the central nervous system seem able to select what is the most reliable predictor of a significant event.

So both in Tolman's mazes and in classical conditioning, a cognitive model in terms of learning the predictive relationship between events seems to fit the data very well. In the maze, the rat normally learns something of the kind 'food is over there by the window'. In a classical conditioning experiment, depending upon the context of the events, the rat learns that one event predicts a subsequent event. So far in the cognitive shift section, we have not looked at applying cognitive ideas to the operant contingency and the Skinner box. Can we apply a cognitive interpretation to what the animal learns in this situation? An attempt to do this was presented in what has now become a highly influential paper published in 1972 by Robert Bolles of the University of Washington, Seattle (Bolles, 1972).

6.3 The Skinner box: learning an association between a response and its outcome

In the typical operant contingency, the arrival of food is contingent upon the response of lever-pressing. Bolles (1972) argued that what an animal learns in the operant contingency is not a relationship between a stimulus and a particular response, but rather an *expectation* that a response will produce a given outcome. Thus, the Skinner box is to be seen as an instrument for teaching the rat an expectation, 'lever-press yields food'. In such terms, shaping is the phase during which the rat is learning the association between its behaviour and an outcome. One could develop the argument by saying that each reinforced lever-press serves to confirm the rat's expectation (lever press)→(food).

In what way is Bolles' account of instrumental conditioning different from that of Thorndike and Skinner? The theory is fundamentally different to Thorndike's account, in which the animal is assumed to form no association between a response and its outcome. Rather, Thorndike saw reinforcement as blindly strengthening a stimulus–response association. Bolles' approach should also be seen as distinct from that of Skinner, who makes no commitment to a theory attempting to explain the process underlying learning in the Skinner box and meticulously avoids all reference to unobservable events. Thus, cognitions (e.g. the outcome to be expected from making a response) form no part of Skinner's account.

SAQ 18   In Section 5.2, an experiment by Tinklepaugh that involved a monkey receiving a piece of banana or lettuce was described. In what way does the result of this experiment support Bolles' account?

There are a number of pieces of evidence to favour Bolles' model. Rats show signs of stress if the expectation towards which they are working is not confirmed. For example, if a rat that has formed the expectation (lever press)→(food) is then placed on extinction, it will immediately show hormonal changes characteristic of stress (Gray, 1988; Levine, 1985). Incidentally, it pays to keep your fingers well away from the front end of the rat at this stage! Extinction provides a further piece of evidence in favour of the cognitive model. Section 4.3 described a partial reinforcement schedule; that is, a schedule in which only some lever-presses are reinforced.

Can you recall from Section 4 the effect of a partial reinforcement schedule as far as extinction is concerned?

A rat trained on a partial reinforcement schedule takes much longer to extinguish than one trained on a continuous reinforcement schedule. When, back in the behaviourist era, this result first appeared, it was described as a paradox. In terms of reinforcing stimulus–response associations, surely continuous reinforcement should lead to a stronger association than partial reinforcement. Surely the continuously reinforced rat would persist for longer after imposition of extinction conditions.

However, if one applies Bolles' model, one can begin to make sense of the phenomenon. In order to extinguish the habit of lever-pressing, the rat needs to revise its cognition (lever-press)→(food) to a new cognition (lever-press)→(no food). The transition to extinction conditions from continous reinforcement is obviously an abrupt one. The change is from *each* lever-press yielding food to *no* lever-press doing so. By contrast, for partial reinforcement, the rat has already been exposed during training to a number of occurrences of lever-press followed by no food. For example, to obtain one pellet it might have needed to press ten times. Therefore, following partial reinforcement, the application of extinction conditions is not so obviously different to the training conditions. The clearer the difference between extinction conditions and the prior reinforcement conditions, then the easier it would be for the animal to revise its cognition. It is therefore logical to expect that formation of the cognition (bar-press)→(no food) will take longer following partial reinforcement.

Bolles acknowledges his debt to the work of Tolman and sees his own theory as following in this tradition. Whereas Tolman worked mainly with mazes, Bolles has worked primarily with Skinner boxes, but the conclusions are entirely compatible. In Bolles' own words: '. . . when my animals learn they are acquiring temporally organized information . . . In effect, Tolman's animals were always "getting to" some expected outcome whereas mine were typically "waiting for" some outcome'.

According to Bolles, the expectancy (e.g. a pellet following a lever-press) is embodied somewhere in the rat's central nervous system. It is exploited in behaviour when (1) the rat is in the presence of the lever and (2) the outcome is motivationally relevant to the rat. For instance, a period of food deprivation makes food a desired outcome. As with Tolman, Bolles' theory does not enable us to predict exactly when a rat will use its cognition in producing behaviour. When the motivation of the rat makes food desirable, the cognition (response)→(food) will be utilized in the gaining of food by lever-pressing. Interestingly, the instrumental contingency is one arranged between behaviour (e.g. lever-pressing) and an outcome (e.g. food) and in the Skinner box what the animal actually learns appears to correspond to this contingency.

In the next section, we consider some further evidence in favour of Bolles' model and this will be in the context of the differences in learning ability between different animals, characterized as a 'biological approach to learning'.

Summary of Section 6

- A cognitive interpretation of classical conditioning is that the animal constructs an expectancy that presentation of a conditional stimulus will be followed by presentation of an unconditional stimulus, as represented by (conditional stimulus)→(unconditional stimulus).

- When a conditional stimulus is presented an animal can respond flexibly (e.g. to flee or freeze), depending upon prevailing circumstances.

- In broad terms and to emphasize a cognitive interpretation, we now speak of one event (E_1) serving as a predictor of another (E_2), represented as $E_1 \rightarrow E_2$; that is, if E_1 occurs then the animal can come to expect E_2 to occur also.

- An unexpected event (E_2) is the cue for the nervous system to scan for a reliable predictor E_1 of the event E_2.

- The most reliable predictor (E_1) is one that predicts each occurrence of an event E_2. The animal gives priority to finding a reliable predictor; it is organized so as to learn the causal texture of its environment.

- A cognitive interpretation of operant conditioning in the Skinner box is that what the animal learns is an expectancy that a response will produce a given outcome, as represented by (response)→(outcome).

7 | The biological challenge

In several important respects the behaviourism of Pavlov, Watson, Thorndike and Skinner owed a great deal to the influence of the biological sciences. First, the work of Darwin on the theory of evolution (see Chapter 5, Section 3.2) had emphasized a continuity between species in the animal kingdom. This made it seem viable to attempt to derive theories of learning that applied across all species, including humans. For example, Pavlov felt that general laws of learning could be derived simply by looking at the salivation reflex in dogs. In a similar vein, Skinner was fond of holding up to an audience a record of operant responding and challenging them to state whether it was rat, pigeon or monkey that was being studied. Darwin's theory had also underlined the importance of the adaptive value of behaviour. The early behaviourists were able to point out the adaptive value of classical conditioning in terms of preparing the animal for the arrival of the unconditional stimulus. Of course, they did not describe this capacity in the richer cognitive terms of classical conditioning giving the capacity of prediction. None the less, just the capacity for taking reflexive advance action of, say, salivation in response to a tone could clearly be seen to confer an important advantage. Instrumental conditioning was also clearly of adaptive value since it enables the animal to gain biologically important things such as food and water. Also, at the turn of the century, the growing awareness of brain mechanisms and the function of neurons gave a scientific language in which to couch descriptions of processes between incoming sensory information and the resulting behaviour.

However, zoology is concerned as much with *differences* between animals as with their common properties and problems in survival. In time, the behaviourists were accused of not paying sufficient attention to the differences between different species in their learning capacity. Also, considering a given animal, they were felt to have underestimated the richness and differences of learning capacity according to the task presented. The notion of a typical or representative animal—for example, the rat or pigeon—lost much of its earlier appeal. Bolles (1979) argued: 'What is this strange concept of a "representative" animal? Whom does the pigeon represent? Does it stand for you or me, the rat, the flatworm, or even other birds?'. Herrnstein (1977) was equally sceptical about the generality of a simple law of learning that disregarded species differences: 'And until someone makes a stalking, pouncing predator out of a cow or moose and extinguishes those responses in a cat, scepticism seems tenable'.

In other words, depending upon the species, there are important constraints on what an animal can learn. One animal might readily learn to perform a certain response whereas another would find the task quite impossible. An animal might already be 'equipped' to perform certain responses; a cat's stalking, for example. Before describing these constraints, it is necessary to review certain key principles of learning that emerged from the behaviourist era. Pavlov had shown that in classical conditioning the timing of the presentation of the neutral stimulus and the unconditional stimulus was crucial; that is, the principle of temporal continguity. Ideally, the bell should be sounded no more than a few seconds before the food was presented. If it were sounded after the food was given, then the bell acquired no capacity to elicit salivation. This result, of course, makes good sense when viewed in terms of the predictive role of the bell in signalling a biologically important event. If the bell were sounded much more than a few seconds before the food was presented, then again conditioning was very difficult to achieve. The two things that were to be associated needed to occur closely in time. In a similar way, in operant conditioning, it was found that reinforcement needed to follow the response rather closely in order to change the frequency of the response. If food were delayed by just a second or so following the response, then conditioning was difficult or impossible.

The neutral stimulus used in classical conditioning was thought to be *arbitrary*. If a tone could come to elicit salivation so could a light or any other stimulus. Similarly, in operant conditioning, if food could reinforce lever-pressing so as to increase its frequency, it could equally well reinforce a rat standing on the back legs, so that this arbitrary behaviour would increase in frequency. However, in time, experiments were to show (1) that the principle of temporal contiguity is of limited validity; (2) that the cues that can become conditional stimuli are not arbitrary but constrained; and (3) which response could be successfully reinforced with which reinforcer is also highly constrained. These constraints can be seen as reflecting differences in the biological capacities of the animals under study.

A number of now classic experiments showed that (1) animals were often incapable of learning apparently simple tasks that they 'should' readily have learned and, conversely, (2) they were sometimes capable of feats of learning that defied established belief. Both kinds of result led to the same conclusion: that by genetics and early learning, animals of a particular species come to learning situations already biased towards learning some things and against learning others.

7.1 The misbehaviour of organisms

Breland and Breland (1961) published a paper entitled 'The misbehaviour of organisms', the title being a parody of Skinner's famous book *The behaviour of organisms*. Breland and Breland had set up a small business training animals along Skinnerian lines for the entertainment industry. In many cases it proved relatively easy to shape the behaviour of their subjects, including reindeer, cockatoos, porpoises and whales. However, a number of 'recalcitrant' animals were encountered. Their experiences with a raccoon exemplify the kind of difficulty:

Raccoons condition readily, have good appetites, and this one was quite tame and an eager subject. We anticipated no trouble. Conditioning him to pick up the first coin was simple. We started out by reinforcing him for picking up a single coin. Then the metal container was introduced, with the requirement that he drop the coin into the container. Here we ran into the first bit of difficulty: he seemed to have a great deal of trouble letting go of the coin. He would rub it up against the inside of the container, pull it back out, and clutch it firmly for several seconds. However, he would finally turn it loose and receive his food reinforcement. Then the final contingency: we put him on a ratio of 2, requiring that he pick up both coins and put them in the container.

Now the raccoon really had problems (and so did we). Not only could he not let go of the coins, but he spent seconds, even minutes, rubbing them together (in a most miserly fashion), and dipping them into the container. He carried on this behaviour to such an extent that the practical application we had in mind—a display featuring a raccoon putting money in a piggy bank—simply was not feasible. The rubbing behaviour became worse and worse as time went on, in spite of nonreinforcement.

(Breland and Breland, 1961)

The failure that Breland and Breland described as '. . . one of the most annoying and baffling for a good behaviorist' concerned pigs who were required to deposit coins in a piggy bank. For the first weeks and even months, things went very well; like all pigs, these subjects had ravenous appetites, were easy to work with and to condition. But then, pig by pig, with monotonous regularity, things went wrong:

> He might run over eagerly for each dollar, but on the way back, instead of carrying the dollar and depositing it simply and cleanly, he would repeatedly drop it, root it, drop it again, root it along the way, pick it up, toss it up in the air, drop it, root it some more, and so on.

(Breland and Breland, 1961)

Breland and Breland describe these results as 'a clear and utter failure of conditioning theory', for which their background in behaviourism had not prepared them. Animals should not 'drift away' from behaviours that have been reinforced, towards behaviours that have not been reinforced, such as rooting. In each case of misbehaviour, Breland and Breland noted that the animal drifted into food-getting behaviour typical of the species in question. In rubbing the coins, the raccoon was demonstrating 'washing behaviour', which would normally, for example, remove the inedible outer layer of a crayfish. The pig shows its species-typical rooting, normally in the service of gaining food. Breland and Breland coined the expression **instinctive drift** to describe the shift towards such species-typical behaviour. In each case, the animal was dealing with an object that had acquired a food-related significance. In each such case, it acted towards it in a species-typical way that would be appropriate to real food.

Robert Bolles used 'misbehaviour' in support of his cognitive model of learning.

According to Bolles, what is learned in a Skinner box?

The animal is said to learn a (response)→(outcome) cognition. Bolles argued that, depending upon the species, an animal will sometimes come to a new learning situation already possessing a particular kind of (response)→(outcome) cognition. The expectancy might be innate or learned through prior experience in the animal's normal environment, or most likely a combination of the two. This might interfere with the (response)→(outcome) cognition that the animal is required to learn in the new situation. The success at shaping an animal will depend upon the degree to which the cognitions required of the animal are compatible with those that it brings to the situation. For the pigs, their (rooting at food-related cues)→(gain of food) expectancies interfered with learning the relationship between placing the money in a certain location and gaining food. The racoon, it would seem, brought to the situation an expectancy of the kind (rubbing food-related objects)→(food).

The instrumental contingency of reinforcement can therefore be seen to have practical limitations. In some cases, animals cannot learn even though an instrumental contingency is in effect (Breland and Breland's raccoons and pigs). In such cases, the contingency as arranged by the experimenter (e.g. food is contingent upon depositing a coin in a box) is not reflected in the animal's learning and behaviour. Only certain behaviours in certain species can be shaped by certain reinforcers. A similarly profound challenge to the generality of the principles of learning was posed by Garcia and Koelling (1966).

7.2 The Garcia effect

Garcia and Koelling (1966) raised two fundamental and, it turned out, related questions: (1) for events to be associated, do they always need to occur closely together in time? and (2) can any neutral stimulus become a conditional stimulus? Restating these questions in the cognitive terms developed in Section 6.2, we would ask: (1) how far apart can two events E_1 and E_2 be and still allow an $E_1 \rightarrow E_2$ predictive association to be formed? and (2) can *any* event (E_1) be utilized as a predictor of another event E_2?

Typically, such things as (a) bells and food presentation or (b) lights and electric shock had been associated, and the principle of temporal contiguity shown to hold. However, could it be that this principle is valid for only certain classes of events? Garcia and Koelling tested several stimuli to see whether an association could be formed with illness experienced a long time after the stimuli were presented. These researchers made the astonishing claim that, in an experiment on rats, they had been able to form an association between two events that were separated not by a second or two, but by several hours. The experiment was conducted as described in Box G.

Garcia and Koelling's result challenged not one, but several cherished beliefs. Not only was the association formed over a vast interval of time, but it was formed in a single trial. Traditionally, learning had been viewed as something requiring a number of trials. Also, a particular kind of association was formed. The stimulus that was associated with nausea was not arbitrary. The association was specifically one between *taste* and nausea. In other words, in cognitive terms, rats readily form (taste)→(nausea) predictive associations over long intervals. Testing the rat in the presence of the ringing bell and flashing light shows that they form with difficulty, or not at all, (sound)→(nausea) or (visual stimulus)→(nausea) associations.

This result is usually placed under a 'biological challenge' heading since it shows that, rather than learning *any* association, a rat sometimes learns just what would be most appropriate for a rat in the wild to learn. Normally, a rat identifies food by taste rather than by sight or sound. Also, the unfortunate consequences, such as gastric illness, of ingesting a poisonous food, would be experienced, not immediately, but some time after ingestion. It is not difficult to appreciate the *adaptive* value (Chapter 5, Section 3.2) of readily forming an association specifically with taste and being able to form an association between events separated over long intervals of time. This learning phenomenon is now generally termed the **Garcia effect**, in honour of its discoverer.

The Garcia effect is seen as an example of the nervous system having a bias towards forming certain associations. The rat is said to be **prepared** to form an association between taste and ill-effects, but **contraprepared** to associate, say,

BOX G Garcia and Koelling's experiment

Rats were exposed to a novel taste—for example, a solution of saccharin—which they drank. Tasting this solution could be regarded as an event E_1. Contact between the rat's tongue and the drinking spout was the automatic trigger to activate a bell and flashing light. These served as two other events. An hour or so later, or even up to 12 hours later in some cases, the rats were given an injection that made them feel ill (nausea reaction). After this single experience, would the rats be able to associate the illness with one or more of the events, the taste, the light or the sound? In other words, would they be able to treat one or more of these events (E_1) as predictors of nausea (E_2)?

To test for the formation of a conditional association between the taste of saccharin and illness, on a subsequent occasion rats were presented with the same saccharin solution, but with the bell and light not operating. They declined to ingest it. The implication was that the rats had formed an association between the taste of saccharin and ill-effects experienced some hours after ingestion. On another occasion, they showed no reluctance to ingest *plain* water even though drinking it activated the ringing bell and flashing light. Thus, the rats had not formed an association between a sound or a light and illness. Figure 6.17 summarizes the experiment carried out by Garcia and Koelling.

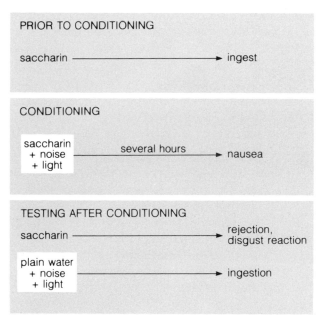

Figure 6.17 Summary of Garcia and Koelling's experiment. Prior to conditioning, the saccharin solution was acceptable. The rats' tongue movements in ingesting it caused a bell to ring and a light to flash: In the conditioning phase, rats experienced nausea some time after ingesting the saccharin solution. They were then tested under one of two conditions: (a) with a saccharin solution, which they declined, or (b) with plain water, where the tongue movements caused the bell to ring and the light to flash. They ingested the plain water

sound and subsequent ill-effects (Seligman, 1970). In the terms developed in Section 6.2, the nervous system scans for a cue (E_1) predictive of nausea (E_2), and is biased towards using *taste* as the predictive cue (E_1).

SAQ 19   Consider the two following situations, in the terms of a cognitive approach:

(a) a rat is exposed to tone closely followed by a shock;

(b) a rat is exposed to a novel food followed 3 hours later by illness.

In each case, consider what is learned by exposure to the situation and (i) define E_1 and E_2; (ii) describe the relationship between E_1 and E_2; and (iii) describe how the rat's subsequent behaviour is changed as a result of exposure to the situation.

The Garcia effect is most readily shown when the taste is a novel one. It is difficult or even impossible to condition an aversion to familiar plain water. This makes good sense both in terms of mechanism and function. A rat will have had a lifetime's experience of (plain water)→(benign consequences), which would need to be unlearned. By contrast, a substance with a novel taste would have no learned associations and would stand as a likely candidate for predicting a consequence such as nausea; that is, to become an E_1. Considering the natural environment of an animal, it is more likely that a novel rather than familiar food would be the cause of any experience of nausea. Similarly, many people who report conditioned aversions do so in the context of illness experienced after ingesting exotic, rather than familiar, foods.

SAQ 20   Can you recall a similar effect to that obtained in Garcia and Koelling's experiment that was experienced by the psychologist Martin Seligman and described in Chapter 5?

The Garcia effect is one factor amongst others that can explain why it is so difficult to kill wild rats by poisoning. They have a refined capacity to sample a very small amount of a novel food and wait for the consequences. Birds, which commonly identify foods by their visual appearance—the colour of berries, for example—are able to form (visual cue)→(nausea) associations over long intervals. Gustavson (1977) studied the effectiveness of poisoning wolves with sheep meat, in an attempt to deter them from killing sheep. It was found that, after such poisoning, they would sometimes act submissively when confronted with a sheep.

The biological approach served to confirm the cognitive model in terms of the animal forming predictive associations. Both the biological and cognitive approaches are generally seen as serious challenges to several of the early behaviourist assumptions.

Summary of Section 7

● The biological approach is characterized by looking at differences in learning capacity between different species, and asking how these capacities relate to the natural environment of the species.

● Animals sometimes bring species-specific (response)→(outcome) expectancies to a learning situation. When the animal is exposed to a contingency that requires it to learn something at odds with its existing (response)→(outcome) expectancy, it might fail to learn; that is, it might 'misbehave'.

● Under some conditions animals can learn $E_1 \rightarrow E_2$ predictive associations even though E_1 and E_2 might be hours apart. With a given E_2 (e.g. illness/ nausea), some E_1s (e.g. taste) will form an association more easily than will others (e.g. sound). This is known as the Garcia effect.

8 | Summary, overview and applications

This chapter started by describing the aims of a revolution. Watson was in revolt against the prevailing schools of psychology: introspection and psychoanalysis, for example. A psychology based upon mental events and consciousness would be replaced by a rigorously scientific psychology dealing only with observable data, throwing out all unobservables in the process. Explanations would be couched in terms of measurable stimuli and responses, linked by stimulus–response associations, thus originating stimulus–response psychology. These S–R associations would be open to analysis in terms of the known physiology of the brain. In spite of some fundamental differences with Watson's position, Skinner was later to give enormous momentum to the behaviourist movement and applied it to such areas as education policy and mental health care. Learning of skills such as French and golf would be described in the same simple terms that apply to rats running mazes.

So how does the movement look now? Looking back to this era, some students greet their introduction to behaviourism with incredulity. How could the behaviourists have believed, they ask, that animals are simply collections of S–R associations? Such students tend to see the cognitive shift as a process analogous to reinventing the wheel. They argue: 'If they didn't know already, anyone would have guessed that animals could do cognitive tricks!'. A similar incredulity is sometimes expressed by zoologists familiar with the richness and diversity of animals. For example, contemporary zoologists sometimes argue that, of course, rats can show taste–nausea learning over long intervals, since, from basic evolutionary considerations, one would expect them to have evolved such a facility. Of course, temporal contiguity would not apply.

As you will already have gathered from reading the previous chapters, the mind and consciousness are now firmly back, having a respectable place in the science of psychology. A simple but comprehensive and mechanistic S–R model of learning applicable to all species, including humans, and situations, couched strictly in terms of observables, failed to explain the richness of learning and behaviour. We now need to recognize a variety of different ways in which knowledge of the world is acquired, in both rats and humans, such as learning cognitive maps. So has the behaviourist revolution failed? By his rigid insistence on modelling psychology upon the other sciences, did Watson serve only to set the subject back? It might be argued that cognitive psychology and the study of consciousness would have advanced at a much greater pace were it not for behaviourism. Some might even go so far as to argue that Watsonian behaviourism was, in effect, a curse upon psychology, but we would caution against this view. An overview of the different strands and developments of behaviourism will show why we feel this.

First, the behaviourists produced some ingenious experiments that have had a profound impact on psychology. The outlook of behaviourism forced psychologists to be rigorous in their methodology and language, to cut out much vague theorizing. It is one thing to suppose with the benefit of hindsight that animals must have evolved the capacity for constructing cognitive maps or exhibiting taste–nausea associations over long intervals. It is quite another to demonstrate these phenomena under rigorously controlled conditions.

Acknowledgement of Pavlov's pioneering studies owed much to their popularization by American behaviourism. Though the theoretical intepretation of the classical and instrumental conditioning experiments has changed, their validity and importance in numerous areas is beyond dispute. For example, Pavlovian conditioning is of central importance in understanding why some apparently reformed drug addicts suddenly relapse. By exposure to environments that in the past were associated with drug taking, some of the physiological and mental changes that characterize drug craving are recreated (Stewart, de Wit and Eikelboom, 1984; Siegel, Krank and Hinson, 1987). Classical conditioning has proved invaluable in understanding such phenomena.

It is true that few, if any, now have faith in the stimulus–response theory of behaviour. However, the two principal challengers to the theory, Tolman and Skinner, have each in their very different ways spawned massively productive schools of psychology.

Tolman's disenchantment with S–R psychology led him to pursue a cognitive approach. In this respect, Tolman seems nearer the commonsense view of animal and human behaviour. In particular, a nation of pet-lovers, such as the British, would have some difficulty regarding their cherished ones, whether four- or two-legged, as merely a series of S–R connections. There has always been an abundance of stories concerning the demonstration of insight and creative leaps by animals, both within the discipline of psychology and outside. Tolman's was an attempt to *explain* the learning processes that play a role in purposive and flexible behaviour. In so doing, terms such as purpose, goal, cognition and cognitive map were used. These have a distinct mentalistic flavour about them and in a sense Tolman had only one foot in the behaviourist camp. Perhaps Tolman's experiments carried so much conviction because he used the same bits of apparatus as were used by the 'hard-nosed' behaviourists and at the same time challenged S–R theory in its own terms; for example, to argue which arm a rat would be expected to take in a maze.

In contrast to Tolman, Skinner has shunned all reference to cognitive terms in accounting for the *causes* of behaviour. Rather, he has stuck rigidly to the doctrine of basing a science of psychology upon observables, in this case behaviour and the contingencies of reinforcement that shape and maintain behaviour. In Skinner's terms, conscious feelings and cognitions *depend upon* such reinforcement. Cognitions are not something to be employed in the explanation of behaviour. Thus, Skinnerians and cognitive psychologists have really pursued two quite different goals. To some extent, an individual might subscribe to the ambitions of both schools, acknowledging both the cognitive nature of the learning *process* and the importance of the reinforcement *procedure* (Bindra, 1978; Toates, 1984).

The behaviourist revolution in essence was based upon two forms of contingency, the classical and instrumental. As we have seen, in neither case does it appear that animals learn an S–R association when exposed to these contingencies. Rather, they learn an expectancy; for example, a (stimulus)→(stimulus) expectancy in classical conditioning (summarized as $E_1 \rightarrow E_2$). In the Skinner box they appear to learn a (response)→(outcome) expectancy. In each case what is learned is a reflection of the contingency as arranged by the experimenter. The process of learning during exposure to these two contingencies is firmly within the cognitive domain. These two expectancies seem to have a very wide application in diverse species and learning contexts. However, the details need careful qualification. Exactly which expectancies can be formed and over what time periods will depend upon the species and the events being associated. Breland and Breland's 'misbehaving' animals failed to exhibit learning that was a reflection of the contingency arranged by the trainer.

In cognitive terms, the expectancy learned when exposed to a classical contingency gives animals the capacity of *prediction* over their environment. This clearly has adaptive value. The animal can take action and thereby be prepared for, say, food arriving in the stomach or the arrival of a predator from the undergrowth. The expectancy learned in the instrumental contingency gives the animal *prediction*, and in addition it gives the animal *control*. The animal can actually change the course of events by its action: obtain food or escape from a hot environment, for instance.

The notions of prediction and control are crucial in a number of areas. For example, animals exposed to a situation in which they can do nothing to control the onset of painful stimulation seem to suffer great stress and form a cognition of the kind (response)→(no effect). When the environment is changed so that they are able to exert control, it sometimes proves impossible for them to revise the cognition (response)→(no effect) to one of (response)→(effect). They remain passive and show signs similar to humans experiencing depression (Chapter 5, Section 5). Seligman (1974) termed this *learned helplessness*, and some approaches to treating human depression are characterized by trying to structure the patient's cognitions so as to undermine the notion of helplessness. Attempts are made to teach them cognitions of the kind (action)→(effect on the environment). In a similar vein, it is now recognized that the welfare of farm animals depends in part upon creating an environment in which the animal can experience some prediction and control (Wiepkema, 1987; Toates, 1987). For example, rats sometimes prefer to work for food in a Skinner box rather than eat free food (Osborne, 1977; Gardner and Gardner, 1988). By analogy, it might be a contribution towards good animal husbandry to allow domestic animals to perform operant tasks for some of the necessities of life, such as food and heat.

In Sections 6.2 and 7.2, the notion of the animal being programmed to search for the *most reliable predictor* emerged. In Rescorla's experiment (Figure 6.16b), it was shown that the tone acquired no power to predict shock in spite of the fact that it occasionally came just before the shock. The tone was not a reliable predictor, since the shock was just as likely to occur in its absence as in its presence. Where it is a good predictor, as in Figure 6.16a, then it acquires predictive capacity. In the wild, one can imagine that, out of the variety of possible events that are present and which might be used as predictors, the animal's nervous system has the task of selecting the best one. A similar task was faced by the rat experiencing nausea. If taste, auditory and visual cues are simultaneously present during ingestion, the rat is biased in favour of forming an association with the taste cue. The adaptive value of this is that taste is most likely to characterize food for the rat. Incidentally, in the Seligman experience described in Chapter 5, Section 4.4 and in SAQ 20 of the present chapter, he specifically formed an association between *taste* and nausea. As far as is known, he developed no aversion to the waiter or the wallpaper in the restaurant, in spite of their simultaneous presence during the tasting experience.

We would like to leave the chapter by considering the broader implications of behaviourism. Skinner's approach rests upon a single simple assumption that freely emitted behaviour can be reinforced and will thereby increase in frequency. We saw in Section 7.1 that there are some serious constraints on the universality of this principle, as illustrated, for example, by misbehaving raccoons. However, Skinner can still point to an immense success at shaping behaviour in a wide variety of species. To what extent the technology involved in shaping the behaviour of the rat in a Skinner box is a suitable model for solving the problems of the world is not something open to proof. Rather, it remains more an act of faith as to whether society can get the garbage cleaned from the streets and criminals reformed by the optimum use of positive reinforcement. Given the differences of opinion on the subject, it is not something about which we can present a consensus view. We hope that it will provide a fruitful source of speculation for you.

Personal acknowledgements

We are most grateful to Derek Blackman (University of Wales, Cardiff), Robert Boakes (University of Sussex), Robert Bolles (University of Washington), Nick Mackintosh (University of Cambridge) and Madeline Watson (Longfield CE Middle School) for their helpful comments on earlier drafts of this chapter.

Further reading

The historical background to behaviourism relating it to developments in nineteenth-century biology can be found in:
BOAKES, R.A. (1984) *From Darwin to behaviourism*, Cambridge: Cambridge University Press.

For a biography of John Watson and an account of the early days of behaviourism you could try:
COHEN, D. (1979) *J.B. Watson: the founder of behaviourism*, London: Routledge and Kegan Paul.

A good and entertaining account of behaviourism and its consequences, written in terms of the main personalities involved, is:
BOLLES, R.C. (1979) *Learning theory*, New York: Holt, Rinehart and Winston.

In the context of a broad critique of Freudian theory, H.J. Eysenck's excellent book is also in part an account of the relevance of classical conditioning to clinical psychology. It should be interesting to contrast Eysenck's account of neurosis with that presented in Chapter 4.
EYSENCK, H.J. (1986) *Decline and fall of the Freudian empire*, Harmondsworth: Penguin.

For a well-written introduction to the issues involved in the so-called 'Beyond freedom and dignity' debate (Skinner's view of behaviour and society) you might look at:
CARPENTER, F. (1974) *The Skinner primer: beyond freedom and dignity*, New York: The Free Press.

A comprehensive and detailed discussion of Skinner's psychology, involving contributions from a large number of psychologists, for and against Skinner can be found in:
CATANIA, C. and HARNAD, S. (eds) (1988) *The selection of behaviour*, Cambridge: Cambridge University Press.

And for an excellent account of Skinner's view of what is wrong with society and how to put it right refer to:
SKINNER, B.F. (1971) *Beyond freedom and dignity*, Harmondsworth: Penguin.

For a well-balanced critique of behaviourism, showing its relation to zoology and economics you could try:
SCHWARTZ, B. (1986) *The battle for human nature*, New York: W.W. Norton.

For two well-written books on learning, as viewed from a cognitive perspective, see:
DICKINSON, A. (1980) *Contemporary animal learning theory*, Cambridge: Cambridge University Press; and

MACKINTOSH, N.J. (1983) *Conditioning and associative learning*, Oxford: Clarendon Press.

A review of learning from a cognitive perspective, pointing out the common misunderstandings of the nature of classical conditioning, can be found in:
RESCORLA, R.A. (1988) 'Pavlovian conditioning—it's not what you think it is', *American Psychologist*, vol. 43, pp. 151–60.

For an account of the relationship between learning theory and motivation theory, developing some of Tolman's ideas, you might refer to:
MOOK, D.G. (1987) *Motivation—the organization of action*, New York: W.W. Norton; and
TOATES, F. (1986) *Motivational systems*, Cambridge: Cambridge University Press.

Introductory discussions of the biological perspective on learning can be found in:
BOLLES, R.C. (1979) *Learning theory*, New York: Holt, Rinehart and Winston; and
DOMJAN, M. and BURKHARD, B. (1986) *The principles of learning and behaviour*, Pacific Grove: Brooks/Cole.

For a detailed examination of the issues in the biological perspective, together with contributions from a number of prominent theorists in the area, see:
GARDNER, R.A. and GARDNER, B.T. (1988) 'Feedforward versus feedbackwards: an ethological alternative to the law of effect', *The Behavioural and Brain Sciences*, vol. 11, pp. 429–93.

References

BINDRA, D. (1974) 'A motivational view of learning, performance and behaviour modification', *Psychological Review*, vol. 81, pp. 199–213.

BINDRA, D. (1978) 'How adaptive behaviour is produced: a perceptual–motivational alternative to response–reinforcement', *The Behavioural and Brain Sciences*, vol. 1, pp. 41–91.

BOLLES, R.C. (1970) 'Species-specific defense reactions and avoidance learning', *Psychological Review*, vol. 77, pp. 32–48.

BOLLES, R.C. (1972) 'Reinforcement, expectancy and learning', *Psychological Review*, vol. 79, pp. 394–409.

BOLLES, R.C. (1979) *Learning theory*, New York: Holt, Rinehart and Winston.

BRELAND, K. and BRELAND, M. (1961) 'The misbehaviour of organisms', *American Psychologist*, vol. 16, pp. 681–4.

CARPENTER, F. (1974) *The Skinner primer: beyond freedom and dignity*, New York: The Free Press.

CATANIA, A.C. (1984) 'The operant behaviourism of B.F. Skinner', *The Behavioural and Brain Sciences*, vol. 7, pp. 473–5.

DICKINSON, A. (1980) *Contemporary animal learning theory*, Cambridge: Cambridge University Press.

GARCIA, J. and KOELLING, R.A. (1966) 'Relation of cue to consequence in avoidance learning', *Psychonomic Science*, vol. 4, pp. 123–4.

GARDNER, R.A. and GARDNER, B.T. (1988) 'Feedforward versus feedbackwards: an ethological alternative to the law of effect', *The Behavioural and Brain Sciences*, vol. 11, pp. 429–93.

GELDARD, F.A. (1963) *Fundamentals of psychology*, New York: John Wiley.

GRAY, J.A. (1988) *The psychology of fear and stress*, Cambridge: Cambridge University Press.

GUSTAVSON, C.R. (1977) 'Comparative and field aspects of learned food aversions', in Barker, L.M., Best, M.R. and Domjan, M. (eds) *Learning mechanisms in food selection*, Waco: Baylor University Press, pp. 23–45.

GUTTMAN, N. (1977) 'On Skinner and Hull—a reminiscence and projection', *American Psychologist*, vol. 32, pp. 321–8.

HERRNSTEIN, R.J. (1977) 'The evolution of behaviourism', *American Psychologist*, vol. 32, pp. 593–603.

KAMIN, L.J. (1969) 'Predictability, surprise, attention and conditioning', in Campbell, B.A. and Church, R.M. (eds) *Punishment and aversive behaviour*, New York: Appleton-Century-Crofts, pp. 279–96.

LEVINE, S. (1985) 'A definition of stress?', in Moberg, G.P. (ed.) *Animal stress*, Bethesda: American Physiological Society, pp. 51–69.

MACFARLANE, D.A. (1930) 'The role of kinesthesis in maze learning', *University of California Publications in Psychology*, vol. 4, pp. 277–305.

MACKINTOSH, N.J. (1983) *Conditioning and associative learning*, Oxford: Clarendon Press.

MOWRER, O.H. (1960) *Learning theory and behaviour*, New York: Wiley.

OSBORNE, S.R. (1977) 'The free food (contrafreeloading) phenomenon: a review and analysis', *Animal Learning and Behaviour*, vol. 5, pp. 221–35.

RESCORLA, R.A. (1968) 'Probability of shock in the presence and absence of CS in fear conditioning', *Journal of Comparative and Physiological Psychology*, vol. 66, pp. 1–5.

ROSE, H. and ROSE, S. (1976) *The political economy of science*, London: The Macmillan Press.

SELIGMAN, M.E.P. (1970) 'On the generality of the laws of learning', *Psychological Review*, vol. 77, pp. 406–18.

SELIGMAN, M.E.P. (1974) 'Depression and learned helplessness', in Friedman, R.J. and Katz, M.M. (eds) *The psychology of depression: contemporary theory and research*, Washington: V.H. Winston, pp. 83–125.

SIEGEL, S., KRANK, M.D. and HINSON, R.E. (1987) 'Anticipation of pharmacological and nonpharmacological events: classical conditioning and addictive behaviour', *Journal of Drug Issues*, vol. 17, pp. 83–110.

SKINNER, B.F. (1971) *Beyond freedom and dignity*, Harmondsworth: Penguin.

SKINNER, B.F. (1976) *Particulars of my life*, London: Jonathan Cape.

SKINNER, B.F. (1980) *Notebooks*, Englewood Cliffs: Prentice-Hall.

STEWART, J., DE WIT, H. and EIKELBOOM, R. (1984) 'Role of unconditioned and conditioned drug effects in the self-administration of opiates and stimulants', *Psychological Review*, vol. 91, pp. 251–68.

THORNDIKE, E.L. (1911) *Animal intelligence*, New York: Macmillan.

TINKLEPAUGH, O.L. (1928) 'An experimental study of representative factors in monkeys', *Journal of Comparative Psychology*, vol. 8, pp. 197–236.

TOATES, F. (1984) 'Models yes; homunculus, no—a commentary on the paper by Professor B.F. Skinner', *The Behavioural and Brain Sciences*, vol. 7, pp. 650–1. Reprinted in Catania, C. and Harnad, S. (eds.) (1988) *The selection of behaviour*, Cambridge: Cambridge University Press.

TOATES, F. (1986) *Motivational systems*, Cambridge: Cambridge University Press.

TOATES, F. (1987) 'The relevance of models of motivation and learning to animal welfare', in Wiepkema, P.R. and van Adrichem, P.W.M. (eds) *Biology of stress in farm animals: an integrative approach*, Dordrecht: Martinus Nijhoff, pp. 153–86.

TOLMAN, E.C., RITCHIE, B.F. and KALISH, D. (1946) 'Studies in spatial learning: II. Place learning versus response learning', *Journal of Experimental Psychology*, vol. 36, pp. 221–9.

WIEPKEMA, P.R. (1987) 'Behavioural aspects of stress', in Wiepkema, P.R. and van Adrichem, P.W.M. (eds) *Biology of stress in farm animals: an integrative approach*, Dordrecht: Martinus Nijhoff, pp. 113–33.

Answers to SAQs

SAQ 1

(a) The unconditional stimulus is the electric shock; (b) the unconditional response is the jerk caused by the shock; (c) the neutral stimulus is the blue light prior to its pairing with shock; (d) the conditional stimulus is the blue light after its pairing with shock; and (e) the conditional response is the jerk elicited by the blue light.

SAQ 2

A stimulus not having the capacity to elicit eye-blink, such as a tone, would be identified. Such a stimulus is termed the neutral stimulus (NS). On a number of occasions the neutral stimulus would be presented just before application of the puff of air. After a number of such pairings, the capacity of the tone to elicit eye-blink in the absence of the puff of air would be tested. The puff is the unconditional stimulus (UCS) and the eye-blink in response to it is termed the unconditional response (UCR). The neutral stimulus, the tone, becomes the conditional stimulus (CS) following pairing with the puff. The eye-blink caused by the tone acting on its own is termed the conditional response (CR). Temporal contiguity refers to the timing such that the neutral stimulus is presented immediately before the puff.

SAQ 3

The contingency is that between two stimuli, the blue light and the shock.

SAQ 4

(a) The tone would be presented a number of times without the puff of air.
(b) Extinction would be complete when the subject's eye no longer blinked in response to the tone. The conditional response (CR) of blinking to the tone (CS) would have been extinguished.

SAQ 5

(a) NS is the neutral stimulus, the rat prior to conditioning; (b) the CS, the conditional stimulus, is the rat after conditioning; (c) the UCS, the unconditional stimulus, is the loud sound; (d) the CR, the conditional response, is the fear reaction of withdrawal evoked by the rat following pairing with the noise; (e) the UCR, the unconditional response, is the withdrawal reaction evoked by the sound; (f) the unconditional reflex is the reflex that relates the stimulus of the loud noise to the response of withdrawal; and (g) the conditional reflex is the reflex that relates the conditional stimulus of the rat to the response of withdrawal.

SAQ 6

The association between the white rat and the reaction of withdrawal is being strengthened.

SAQ 7

The procedure is termed extinction. The effect is to reduce the amount of saliva secreted in response to the CS, a phenomenon also termed extinction.

SAQ 8

If learning consists of a strengthening of the linkage X, as Watson's model implies, then logically, extinction would consist of a weakening of this linkage. The result would be to return the system to the condition shown in Figure 6.3(a). (Another possibility is that extinction corresponds to an *inhibitory* link—Chapter 5, Section 2.2—appearing in parallel with X and opposing the excitatory influence.)

SAQ 9

The probability that the animal would perform response R_1 would decrease.

SAQ 10

(a) Instrumental, because pulling the rope is instrumental in alerting the master; (b) instrumental, because pushing against the panel is instrumental in opening the flap; (c) classical, because the capacity of the cat owner's reaching behaviour to evoke excitement in the cat depends upon the pairing of this behaviour with food presentation.

SAQ 11

(a) (i) Omitting presentation of food; (ii) the contingency between bell and food.
(b) (i) Omitting presentation of food; (ii) the contingency between lever-pressing and food.

SAQ 12

(a) Playing Max Bygraves; (b) switching Max Bygraves off; and (c) playing Michael Jackson. Note that the very same thing, the music of Max Bygraves, can serve as either punishment or negative reinforcement. It is the *contingency* that defines the role the stimulus serves. Of course, for many people, the music of Max Bygraves serves as a positive reinforcement. Individual differences are important.

SAQ 13

(a) (i) On the one hand, drawing, writing and looking out of the window and, on the other, throwing things around; (ii) the reinforcer is the teacher's attention; and (iii) the disruptive behaviour of Johnny is being reinforced by the teacher's attention.

(b) As a solution, the teacher might try omitting to show attention when Johnny is disruptive, in the hope that his behaviour will extinguish. In addition, Johnny's good behaviour should be reinforced. For example, whenever Johnny sits drawing, the teacher might smile approvingly at him.

SAQ 14

The condition is that of extinction.

SAQ 15

(a) Continuous reinforcement refers to when each lever-press is reinforced with a pellet of food; (b) partial reinforcement refers to when only some lever-presses are reinforced, e.g. every second or every hundredth. In this example, it is the phase in which every tenth lever-press is reinforced; (c) discriminative stimulus refers to the buzzer. The rat can discriminate this and behaviour can be brought under the buzzer's control; (d) extinction is when no pellets are given for lever-pressing.

SAQ 16

A predictive relationship is established between the bell (E_1) and the food (E_2) such that the bell predicts the appearance of food, represented as $E_1 \rightarrow E_2$.

SAQ 17

For rats in group 1, the first shock experienced in phase 2 (E_2) would be expected on the basis of the light (E_1). It would be predicted by the light. For rats in group 2, the first shock in phase 2 would be unexpected. It would not have been predicted by any event.

SAQ 18

Tinklepaugh's monkey showed signs of expecting a banana as a result of lifting the lid and displayed frustration on finding the expectation not confirmed.

SAQ 19

(a) (i) E_1 is the tone and E_2 is the shock; (ii) the tone (E_1) predicts the shock (E_2), represented as $E_1 \rightarrow E_2$; and (iii) the tone which was previously a neutral stimulus is now the cue that elicits a response such as fleeing, if escape is possible, or freezing, if escape is not possible.

(b) (i) E_1 is the food and E_2 is the illness; (ii) the taste (E_1) predicts the illness (E_2), represented as $E_1 \rightarrow E_2$; and (iii) as a result of exposure to this situation the rat now avoids the food.

SAQ 20

Seligman developed a conditioned aversion to *sauce Bernaise* as a result of illness following some hours after ingesting a meal characterized by this flavour. Of course, in this case the predictive association was formed with the wrong event!

Overview of Part III

In Chapter 5 reference is made to evolutionary and other biological explanations of animal behaviour. This includes behaviour which might appear 'altruistic' in the interests of preserving the species. A rather different way of considering this kind of behaviour is in terms of the 'selfish gene'. Analysis of the hens' and baboons' behaviour described in Chapter 5, Sections 3.2 and 3.3, is cited as evidence in support of arguments which are still the subject of much debate. Throughout Chapters 5 and 6 the interaction between internally generated biological activity and responses to external events is a constant theme.

Chapter 6 concentrates on the effects of experience in changing animals' behaviour. Particularly impressive are experiments showing that rats are capable of learning quite complex cognitive representations of relationships between events in the environment, enabling them to produce responses that will achieve optimal consequences. However, you may have wondered at times, when reading about the ability of pigeons to discriminate between light and dark, and rats learning the location of goal boxes, whether even the most sophisticated cognitions of animals can match those of quite a small child performing one of Piaget's water conservation tasks. The question of whether one should *extrapolate* from animals to humans is a very important one arising from both Chapters 5 and 6, and merits further discussion here.

Extrapolations of animal behaviour to humans

Since Darwin, most people have accepted the process of evolution, including the implication that we ourselves are animals which have developed from primitive organisms. Evolution supports the view that there are likely to be *continuities* between the biological systems of similar species. On the basis of this, scientists study the nervous systems of mammals, such as cats and rats, in order to draw conclusions about neural activity in the human nervous system. Similarly, studies of physiological abnormalities in the secretion of substances like noradrenaline and serotonin, associated with learned helplessness in rats, have been used to explain mood changes typical of human depression.

There has been much more debate about the value of extrapolations based on work in the behaviourist tradition. As described in Chapter 6, Section 1, some typical ways of studying learning prior to the emergence of behaviourism included armchair philosophical speculations about the existence of knowledge and introspective self-analysis. (It was not until later that Piaget and other psychologists began to make careful observations of children's behaviour.) In this historical setting, Pavlov's objective measurements of a dog's saliva in a tube as an index of learning seemed to represent an enormous step forward. Surely, as Watson thought, it must be possible to measure all learning in terms of changes in observable behaviour. Skinner's innovation of automating the study of behaviour in rats and pigeons in the Skinner box offered even greater opportunities of measuring learning as responses to changing contingencies of reinforcement.

Up till this point, as explained in Sections 2, 3 and 4 of Chapter 6, behaviourists viewed learning as *direct* stimulus–response links. However, Tolman's exploration of the purposive and flexible nature of rats' behaviour, examined in Section 5, initiated the idea that there may be *mental* events going on inside the animal's brain. A cognitive map of the environment, the knowledge that food is near the window, implies a mental representation, a *cognition* which may guide behaviour. This is very different from the notion of direct links between stimuli and responses, the basis of S–R psychology. The 'cognitive shift', described in Chapter 6, Sections 5 and 6, represents an elaboration of Tolman's ideas, demonstrating that rats can have cognitions about events which are likely to lead to other more or less satisfying events, and even that animals search for something which can act as a predictor to explain a novel event.

Can the same principles of conditioning explain human learning? Looking at the classical conditioning and operant conditioning experiments, it is easy to think of comparable examples of when human conditioning occurs. Albert came to fear the white rat. A child or adult quickly learns not to touch a hot electric plate, even on a new 'ceramic' electric hob. Often we give other people, or even ourselves, little rewards, such as a chocolate biscuit, to encourage desired behaviour like writing an essay.

There are many examples, like these, which may be used to support the notion that human behaviour can be manipulated by altering the contingencies of reinforcement. But the million dollar question is how to explain the complex learning which enables people to write an essay in the first place: the ability to speak, read and write a language, and to acquire knowledge about the topic of the essay; the acquisition of the difficult skills of marshalling points in a logical order; and selecting grammatical sentences to express what you want to say. Even this list does not exhaust all the necessary factors, including the motivation to excel. It has always proved difficult to provide explanations based on animal studies for the gradual learning of mental skills, many of which are resistant to ordinary teaching.

The difficulties of extrapolating from one species to another are especially great when the species are very different from each other. Humans are most similar to the higher primates in terms of physiology and behaviour, and are very different from the rats and pigeons used in the experiments described in Chapter 6. Different animals may have very different characteristics (such as sense organs and manipulative skills), cognitive abilities (ability to learn), and ecological factors (typical habitat and experiences). These and other biological constraints (see Chapter 6, Section 7) may be enough to make extrapolation impossible. A good example of this is demonstrated by the mirror reflection studies in Chapter 2, Section 2.2. During their second year, children are able to recognize reflections of themselves in a mirror. Chimpanzees, after some experience, were also able to learn to recognize their own 'red noses', whereas marmosets never learned this skill. Interestingly, marmosets could probably be conditioned by a food reinforcement to touch their noses only in the presence of the discriminative stimulus of a mirror. But would this behaviour, making it look 'as if' they recognized themselves, actually prove that they had this ability?

The whole issue of extrapolation—how much we can or should extrapolate from animal studies—is not at all easy to resolve. It would appear at first sight that the more cognitive rats are shown to be, the more they behave in a 'human' way. But we have to query whether representations of simple associations between the whereabouts of a goal box with food, or a light as a predictor of shock, fully correspond to the complexities of people's 'cognitive maps' of their physical and social environments.

One of the other main differences between animals and humans is the ability of humans to use language. (Indeed, one of the attractions of animal studies for the early behaviourists was that rats could *not* be asked any questions about internal mental events.) People are constantly talking to each other, and perhaps the greater part of human learning is communicated to us by other people through language. Learning is measured by written answers to examination questions, as well as by the ability to act in new ways, all of which are observable indicators of new learning. The crucial role of language as a unique reflection of human cognition will be discussed further in Chapter 13.

Ethical considerations

These were first raised in Chapter 1, Section 4.3. The code of the British Psychological Society reflects the much greater concern in recent years about letting subjects know what is involved in a psychological study and subsequently debriefing them in such a way that they are not left emotionally perplexed or upset by their experiences.

There are equally strict regulations, laid down by the Experimental Psychology Society, governing the use of animal subjects in laboratory experiments. These include provision of basic needs such as warmth, feeding, and clean, safe accommodation. There have been significant shifts in opinion and practice about the limits governing the use of animals in research. Certainly many of the conditioning experiments carried out up until even a decade ago would never be considered acceptable these days. There is, also, much more emphasis on letting animals show what they are capable of, often in more naturalistic settings, as in the biological experiments described in Chapter 6, Section 7.

The possible infliction of distress on animals is carefully considered in relation to the aims of the research and the benefits which are likely to be gained from new knowledge. Although these benefits are not always of immediate practical application, medical advances have often arisen from what may have looked like 'pure' scientific research. Some examples of the applications of psychological theories to human problems will be described in Part VII.

There will inevitably be differences in opinion about the practice of using animals in experiments, the aim of which is to add to psychological knowledge about the biological and learning capabilities of different species. The answer to the earlier question concerning how much we can learn about humans from animal studies is also relevant. If it is impossible to extrapolate the results from biological and physiological research on animals, this clearly weakens the case for carrying out animal studies. But conflicting views will still remain. We hope that, whatever your individual views on this question, you will appreciate that a book about psychological approaches, which left out the important strand of research into animal biology and behaviour, would present a one-sided account of psychological theory and research.

PART IV
INDIVIDUAL DIVERSITY

Introduction to Part IV

The three chapters in Part IV appear to represent a shift in emphasis from the chapters in Part III. In the first place, the focus is exclusively on the capabilities of the human species as opposed to other animals. The second point is that psychologists who study intelligence and personality are interested in accounting for the way in which individuals differ from each other. Of course, the theories described in Part II are also concerned with the development of individuals. Piaget described the growth of intelligence, Mead the development of social experience and Freud the origin of personality types. Similarly, the accounts of genetics and learning in Part III suggest basic mechanisms for producing the variety of behaviour found in animals. Considering all this, you may wonder why we need to include special chapters in Part IV dealing with individual differences in intelligence, personality and experience. However, as you will see, research in these areas comes from a tradition in which individual diversity is the key topic.

Chapter 7 outlines some of the ways in which psychologists have attempted to develop IQ tests as objective measures of intelligence. Within the psychometrics tradition, intelligence tests are used as a standard against which individuals' intelligence can be measured. Sections 3 and 4 of Chapter 7 move on to the fascinating question of what underlies the range of people's IQ scores. Is it due to heredity, or to different social and cultural experiences, or to a mixture of the two? Are there any genuine differences in intelligence between people of different ethnic origins? Finally, are there different kinds of intelligence: creative or practical as well as intellectual? These issues are discussed in the chapter and the evidence carefully examined.

Chapter 8 also focuses on differences between individuals but this time in terms of personality. Personality has in some ways proved a more difficult concept to pin down than intelligence, perhaps because there are so many facets to personality. Different people may have conflicting views of another person's personality or character traits, depending on how well they know them. Even more confusingly, people's personalities may appear to vary from day to day because they do not always behave consistently in every situation. None the less, some psychologists have attempted to devise psychometric personality tests and questionnaires to decide whether people have a particular personality trait or exhibit a particular personality type, such as being introverted or extraverted. Other psychologists accept the uniqueness of each individual's personality and try to explore the way each person typically experiences the world.

It is the nature of personal experience which is taken up in Chapter 9. The emphasis is on the diversity of people's experiences, and their potential for personal growth. The humanistic perspective offers alternatives to theories which see individual experience as being largely constrained by general principles of human learning and development, and by the physical and social environments.

The three chapters in Part IV together stimulate discussion of some of the most difficult issues in psychology. Questions about the extent to which intelligence and personality are fixed or are liable to change, the role of internal biological factors and of culture, the extent to which we are consciously in control of our experience, will be examined further in the overview of Part IV.

chapter 7 ASPECTS OF INTELLIGENCE

Andrew M. Colman

Contents

1	**Introduction: individual differences and the basics of intelligence testing**	**323**
1.1	What is intelligence?	324
1.2	Correlation	325
1.3	Galton and Binet	326
1.4	The concept of the intelligence quotient	328
1.5	The normal distribution	329
1.6	Conversion to IQ scores	331
1.7	Advantages of the statistical approach	332
	Summary of Section 1	332
2	**Modern psychometric approaches to intelligence**	**333**
2.1	Wechsler scales	333
2.2	British Ability Scales	336
2.3	Raven's Progressive Matrices and the Mill Hill Vocabulary scale	337
2.4	General intelligence and specific factors	338
2.5	How accurate are IQ tests?	341
2.6	Does intelligence decline in later life?	342
	Summary of Section 2	344
3	**The nature–nurture controversy**	**344**
3.1	Heritability of IQ	345
3.2	Separated identical twins	347
3.3	Family studies	350
3.4	Adoption studies	351
3.5	Conclusions	353
	Summary of Section 3	354
4	**Race and intelligence**	**354**
4.1	Racial admixture studies	356
4.2	Racial crossing studies	357
4.3	Test bias	358
4.4	Environmental influences on IQ	360
	Summary of Section 4	361
5	**Cognitive styles**	**361**
5.1	Field dependence–independence	361
5.2	Convergence–divergence	363
5.3	Concluding comments	365
	Summary of Section 5	366
	Further reading	366
	References	367
	Answers to SAQs	371

1 | Introduction: individual differences and the basics of intelligence testing

People differ from one another, not only physically but also psychologically. Some people are self-assertive while others are submissive, some are persevering while others are fickle, some are outgoing while others are shy, some are trusting while others are suspicious, and so on. Allport and Odbert (1936) carried out a dictionary search and found 4500 distinct adjectives in the English language denoting psychological differences between people. Each of these adjectives relates to a personality **trait**, a more or less consistent pattern of behaviour that a person possessing the trait would be likely to display in certain circumstances. When we describe someone as shy, for example, we implicitly assume that he or she would probably show signs of embarrassment when meeting strangers.

The study of **individual differences** in psychology arises from the fact that different people do behave differently, in ways that are to some degree consistent and predictable, not only when meeting strangers, but also in many other circumstances. The ancient Greeks were the first to notice these differences and to attempt to explain them. Their doctrine of the four **temperaments**, which was widely accepted for many centuries, sought to explain individual differences in terms of the mixture of four fluids or humours in people's bodies. Optimistic or sanguine people were thought to have in their bodies a predominance of blood (*sanguis*), depressive or melancholic people an excess of black bile (*melaina chole*), short-tempered or choleric people an excess of yellow bile (*chole*), and apathetic or phlegmatic people a predominance of phlegm (*phlegma*). Although the physiological basis of the doctrine of the four temperaments was undermined by biological research during the Renaissance, the classification has survived in a modified form in some modern personality theories. This is discussed in greater detail in Chapter 8.

The first systematic study of individual differences using modern research methods was Francis Galton's study of intelligence in England in 1884. Since then psychologists have devoted particular attention to individual differences in intelligence and thinking. These differences have been more thoroughly investigated than any others in psychology, partly because of their uniquely important effects on people's educational prospects and prospects in life generally, and partly because of their controversial social implications.

In this chapter, some of the fundamental ideas and research findings related to individual differences in intelligence and thinking will be discussed. This will provide you with an introduction to one of the most important classes of individual differences in psychology.

ACTIVITY 1

Think of someone who seems to you to be very intelligent. List the person's qualities that led you to this judgement. Did you choose someone who is academically clever? How would you define intelligence? Are there other kinds of intelligence?

1.1 What is intelligence?

Intelligence can be defined informally as intellectual ability. A person who solves a difficult crossword puzzle quickly or gives the right answer to a tricky mathematical problem or gets a high score on an IQ (intelligence quotient) test is showing intelligent behaviour, and it is reasonable to infer that such a person is intelligent. Someone who does badly at the same tasks is not showing intelligent behaviour and *may* have a low intelligence, but the inference is uncertain in this case because other explanations are possible. Poor performance, even on an IQ test, might be due to tiredness, lack of interest or motivation, test anxiety, or many other causes apart from low intelligence.

Until fairly recently, psychologists who devised IQ tests tended to base their definitions of intelligence on their own preconceptions about intellectual ability and the types of behaviour associated with it. By the early 1920s there were almost as many different definitions of intelligence in the psychological literature as there were psychologists writing about intelligence. Some of the early expert definitions are shown in Box A.

In 1981, the American psychologist Robert J. Sternberg and his colleagues asked a large group of experts to rate many different kinds of behaviour according to how characteristic of intelligence they considered each one to be (Sternberg *et al.*, 1981). A statistical technique called factor analysis, which will be explained in Section 2.4, was used to search for common themes.

BOX A   Early definitions of intelligence

A famous symposium on 'Intelligence and its measurement' was published in the *Journal of Educational Psychology* in 1921. Fourteen experts gave their own informal definitions of intelligence, some of which may be paraphrased as follows:

1   The ability to carry out abstract thinking (L.M. Terman).
2   The ability to give responses that are true or factual (E.L. Thorndike).
3   The capacity to inhibit instincts, coupled with analytical ability and perseverance (L.L. Thurstone).
4   The ability to acquire abilities (H. Woodrow).
5   The ability to learn or to profit by experience (W.F. Dearborn).
6   The ability to adjust oneself to relatively new situations in life (R. Pinter).
7   The ability to adjust oneself to the environment (S.S. Colvin).
8   The capacity for knowledge and knowledge possessed (V.A.C. Henmon).

After 1921, many other informal definitions appeared in the psychological literature (see Miles, 1957, for an interesting summary and discussion).

Three factors which emerged from the analysis were: **verbal intelligence**, **problem solving** and **practical intelligence**. Sternberg interpreted these as the major **components of intelligence**, at least according to expert opinion.

Sternberg and his colleagues also showed that experts and non-experts have remarkably similar conceptions of intelligence. When ordinary people were asked to rate the same kinds of behaviour as the experts, there was almost complete agreement about how characteristic each one is of intelligence. In technical terms, the correlation between the two sets of ratings was 0.96, which is very high. The technique of correlation is often used in the study of intelligence and in other branches of psychology, so it is worth pausing briefly to explain it.

1.2 Correlation

The technique of **correlation** is simply a method of assessing whether, and to what extent, one measure varies together with another. Two measures that are related to each other are co-related (hence correlated), and the statistical technique for determining how strongly they are correlated is called correlation. As a child grows, for example, his or her arms and legs get longer, and this simultaneous change in the same direction is called **positive correlation**. Two unrelated measures that vary independently of each other are said to be uncorrelated. The length of a child's arms and the amount of rain that falls in Singapore, for example, are uncorrelated. If high scores on one measure tend to go with low scores on the other, such as the age of a preschool child and the number of grammatical errors he or she makes, then there is a negative correlation between the two measures.

The usual **index of correlation** ranges from zero (0.00), for uncorrelated measures, up to +1.00 for a perfect positive correlation and down to −1.00 for a perfect negative correlation. The further a correlation is from zero, the more closely the two measures are related to each other, either positively or negatively.

The high positive correlation of 0.96 that Sternberg and his colleagues found shows that the experts and non-experts tended to rate the various kinds of behaviour very similarly, and this suggests that their conceptions of intelligence were very similar. There were two slight differences. First, only the experts considered motivation to be an important ingredient of intelligence; second, the non-experts attached more importance than the experts to social aspects of intelligence, such as the ability to make witty remarks and to understand jokes.

SAQ 1   (SAQ answers are given at the end of the chapter) Try to estimate, on the basis of common sense, whether the correlation between each of the following pairs of measures is highly or moderately positive, close to zero, or negative:

(a) height and weight among adults;

(b) height and age among children;

(c) alcohol intoxication and manual dexterity.

1.3 Galton and Binet

Francis Galton, a cousin of the biologist Charles Darwin, constructed the world's first intelligence test in England more than a century ago. He also carried out the first empirical studies designed to determine the extent to which differences in intelligence are (1) hereditary or (2) due to the different environments in which people grow up. In the firm belief that hereditary factors are overwhelmingly important, he founded the *eugenics movement* which aimed to improve the hereditary stock of the human population by selective breeding; that is, by encouraging intelligent people to have more children than less intelligent people. He was also the first psychologist to suggest that racial groups differ in innate intelligence.

Galton's intelligence test was based on his theory about the mental processes involved in thinking, reasoning and problem solving. He believed that mental ability depends on the capacity to perceive subtle differences, so that, as he put it, 'the more perceptive the senses are of difference, the larger is the field upon which our judgement and intelligence can act' (Galton, 1883). Galton therefore assumed that measures of **sensory discrimination**, the ability to detect small differences through the sense organs, should be good tests of intelligence.

In 1884, at the International Health Exhibition in the South Kensington Museum, Galton set up a stall where visitors could have their mental abilities tested for 3 pence, and more than 9000 men and women took up his offer. This was the first and one of the largest studies of intelligence ever undertaken. It was also unusual, to say the least, that the subjects paid the researcher for their participation rather than the other way round. Galton's tests measured **reaction times** (the speed with which people can react to signals), visual and auditory discriminations (the smallest differences in the lengths of lines and the pitches of musical notes that they can detect), touch sensitivity (the minimum distance between a pair of pinpricks that they can feel as separate rather than as a single pinprick), and various other sensory and motor functions (e.g. the maximum number of taps they can make with a stylus in a minute).

It soon became clear that Galton's theoretical approach to the measurement of intelligence was misconceived. In particular, the American psychologist Clark Wissler reported in 1901 that the various sensory and motor tests did not correlate with one another when he tried them out on college students (Wissler, 1901). People who scored very highly on one test did not necessarily score highly on the others and vice versa. Galton's assumption that all the tests measured the *same* general intellectual ability could not, therefore, be right. Worse still, Wissler reported that *none* of the tests correlated with students' examination marks. On the other hand, marks in different subjects, such as mathematics and English, did correlate with one another, which was in line with the commonsense assumption that intelligence plays a part in academic achievement in all subjects. Wissler concluded that the sensory and motor tests were not good measures of intelligence, and Galton's sensory–motor approach to the measurement of intelligence was abandoned in favour of direct tests of reasoning ability.

The first useful intelligence test was developed by Alfred Binet and Theodore Simon in France in 1905. Binet had been asked by the Minister of Public Instruction to find a means of detecting mentally subnormal children and classifying them as '*débiles*' or 'morons' (mildly subnormal), 'imbeciles' (severely subnormal), or 'idiots' (profoundly subnormal), with a view to putting them in special classes or schools in which teaching could be geared to their abilities. Intelligence tests are still used for that purpose, although the terms used to denote mental handicap are now less offensive.

Binet worked out a commonsense, pragmatic way of measuring intelligence, in sharp contrast to Galton's earlier theoretical approach. Binet's was a commonsense approach in that it assumed that the best way to measure a child's intelligence is to test the child's ability to follow instructions, to exercise judgement and to solve a wide variety of problems generally associated with intelligence. The final version of the Binet–Simon scale contained fifty-four items arranged in order of difficulty, from following the movement of a lighted match with the eyes, through naming parts of the body and counting backwards from twenty, to working out what time a clock face would show if the hour and minute hands swapped places.

SAQ 2   Without looking at your watch, try to work out what time a clock face would show if the hour and minute hand swapped places at 1.55.

Binet's method was pragmatic in that items were selected for the scale according to how well they correlated with an independent criterion known to be associated with intelligence. The problem, of course, was to find a suitable independent criterion for intelligence. You might think that it is impossible to find such a criterion, because if one existed there would be no point in constructing intelligence tests, but you would be wrong. Binet was the first to realize that *age* is an ideal criterion. It is an indisputable fact that as children grow older their ability to solve problems generally increases.

Binet and Simon administered the items of their intelligence test to representative groups of children of various ages (standardization samples). They found that on many items the older children performed better than the younger children. This was good evidence that these items were indeed measuring intelligence. On this basis they were able to establish **test norms**. The idea behind test norms is to provide standards of 'normal' or average ability against which other children's scores can be compared.

Binet and Simon established norms for each age group by recording the average number of items that children at each age level could pass. This enabled them to introduce the concept of **mental age**. If, for example, a 10-year-old child could pass only those items that 6-year-olds in the standardization sample could pass, then it was reasonable to infer that the child was functioning at a mental age of 6 and was therefore retarded by about 4 years. Binet defined 'morons' ('*débiles*') as people whose mental age had not increased beyond the norm for 11-year-olds, 'imbeciles' as those who had developed only up to a mental age of 5 years, and 'idiots' as those whose mental development stopped short at a mental age of 2 years.

Binet was fiercely critical of other psychologists, such as Galton, who considered intelligence to be a fixed and hereditary quantity. 'We must protest and react against this brutal pessimism', he wrote in 1909. 'With practice, enthusiasm, and especially method, one can succeed in increasing one's attention, memory, and judgement, and becoming literally more intelligent than one was before' (Binet, 1909). He even went to the lengths of developing a programme of intellectual exercises to improve mental fitness in the way that physical exercises improve bodily fitness. These 'mental orthopaedics', as he called them, were designed to raise the intelligence of mentally retarded children.

SAQ 3   (a) What evidence is there that Galton's tests were not good measures of intelligence?
(b) What evidence is there that Binet's tests do measure intelligence?
(c) How do Galton's and Binet's tests differ in content?

1.4 The concept of the intelligence quotient

The rest of Section 1 describes the techniques used for calculating IQ scores. If you find these difficult, read on and come back after finishing the chapter.

The idea of mental age led to the invention of the intelligence quotient, which is what the letters IQ stand for. In 1912 the German psychologist William Stern pointed out the obvious fact that a person's mental age tells us nothing about his or her intelligence unless we also know the person's actual (chronological) age (Stern, 1912). Imagine three 10-year-old children called Anne, Beatrice and Charles. Anne has a mental age of 7 years and is therefore obviously below average intelligence for her chronological age of 10. Beatrice has a mental age of 10 and is therefore of average intelligence. Charles has a mental age of 12 and so is above average intelligence. Stern hit upon the ingenious idea of dividing mental age by chronological age and regarding this quotient, which he called the **intelligence quotient**, as an index of intelligence.

In symbols, Stern's quotient is the fraction MA/CA; that is mental age (MA) divided by chronological age (CA). The American psychologist Lewis Terman later introduced the abbreviation **IQ** for intelligence quotient and suggested multiplying Stern's fraction by 100 to convert it to a percentage (Terman 1916). The revised concept of the IQ therefore is defined as:

$$IQ = \frac{MA}{CA} \times 100.$$

According to this formula, Anne, with a mental age of 7 and a chronological age of 10, has an IQ of 7 divided by 10, multiplied by 100, which works out as 70. This means that her mental age is 70 per cent of her chronological age. Beatrice, whose mental and chronological ages are both 10, has an IQ of 10 divided by 10, multiplied by 100, which comes to 100, which is average for her age. Charles, whose mental age is 12 and whose chronological age is 10, has an IQ of 12 divided by 10, multiplied by 100, which comes to 120, so his mental age is 20 per cent higher than his chronological age. The most important point to notice is that an IQ of 100 is average by definition, so IQs below 100 are below average and IQs above 100 are above average.

SAQ 4 (a) Elizabeth, Andrew and William are all 5 years old. On an IQ test Elizabeth passes only those items that an average 4 year old in the standardization sample passed, Andrew passes only those that an average 5 year old passed, and William passes only those that an average 6 year old passed. Use the formula *IQ = mental age (MA) divided by chronological age (CA), multiplied by 100* to work out Elizabeth's, Andrew's and William's IQ scores.

(b) Mark is 20 years old and Philip is 40 years old. They both pass only those items that an average 20 year old in the standardization sample passed. Using the formula, calculate their IQs. Does the answer seem fair to Philip when you think about it?

Although IQ is defined in most elementary psychology textbooks according to the mental age/chronological age formula shown above, it is seldom calculated that way today. The main reason for this is that the definition leads to absurdities when it is applied to adults. Beyond the age of about 17 or 18, people do not show any increase in intellectual ability, as measured by IQ tests. Mental age tends to stabilize, although in later life it may even decline (a point we will come to in Section 2.6). Average 40 year olds perform on IQ tests at about the same level as average 20 year olds. Yet, according to the old MA/CA formula, a 40 year old person performing at the level of a 20 year old has an IQ of 20 divided by 40, multiplied by 100, which comes out as an IQ of only 50. This would imply that the 40 year old is severely retarded or, in the new terminology of educational psychology, suffers from 'severe learning difficulties'. To put it another way, the standard textbook definition of IQ is weighted unacceptably against age and is actually nonsensical when applied to middle-aged and elderly people.

1.5 The normal distribution

In 1939, David Wechsler introduced a purely statistical definition of IQ that avoids the problems of the old mental age/chronological age formula (Wechsler, 1939). His definition is used by virtually all contemporary psychologists who construct IQ tests. The basic idea is straightforward. An intelligence test is given to large samples of people from each age group in the population. Each person is given a test score according to how many items he or she answered correctly; the numbers of people with each possible test score are then counted. Figure 7.1 shows a typical pattern of test scores. For simplicity's sake, the data in Figure 7.1 are taken from a small sample of twenty people given a test containing just ten items. In practice, much larger samples are needed, and the tests usually include more items.

Listed along the horizontal axis (line) of Figure 7.1 are test scores: 0 items correct, 1 item correct, and so on. Each square in the diagram represents a person who achieved the test score shown directly below it. The number of

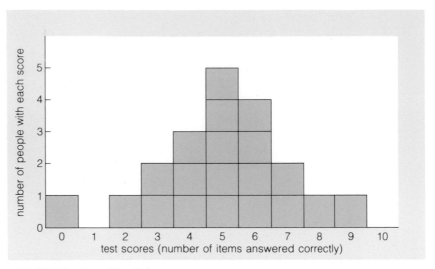

Figure 7.1 Distribution of intelligence test scores (out of 10) for a sample of twenty people

squares above each test score represents the number of people who achieved that test score: two people scored 3, for example, and three people scored 4 on the test. Figure 7.1 represents the **distribution** of test scores in the sample. You will notice that there are more people with scores near the middle (test scores of 5 or 6) than there are with very low or very high test scores.

SAQ 5   In Figure 7.1:

(a) How many people achieved test scores of 5 or 6?

(b) How many people scored more than 7?

(c) How many people scored less than 3?

(d) What is the mean (average) test score of the sample? (*Hint*: add up the total scores in each column and divide the sum of these total scores by the number of people, i.e. twenty.)

When an intelligence test is given to a very large sample of people, it is found in practice (and there is a mathematical theorem that shows why it happens) that the distribution of scores closely resembles the bell-shaped **normal distribution** shown in Figure 7.2; the 'height' of the 'bell' represents the number of people with each test score. Here again, most of the test scores are close to the mean (average) (represented by the 'bulge' in the centre of the 'bell'). The further away a test score is from the mean, the fewer the people who achieve that test score.

The normal distribution is symmetrical: 50 per cent of test scores fall below and 50 per cent above the mean. Figure 7.2 also shows the percentage of test scores that fall within certain evenly spaced distances from the mean of the normal distribution. These distances are expressed in terms of a measure of variability called the **standard deviation** (abbreviated **SD**). Standard deviation

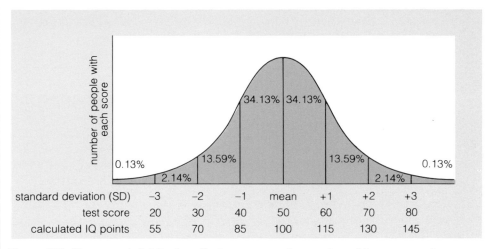

Figure 7.2 The normal distribution. Test scores are the number of items correctly answered out of 100. IQ scores are calculated from these (see text)

is a measure of the extent to which scores deviate from the average score. Scores that are one standard deviation from the mean are closer to the average than scores that are 2 standard deviations from the mean. Notice that 34.13 per cent of test scores fall within one standard deviation above the mean, and the same percentage of test scores fall within one standard deviation below the mean.

SAQ 6 In Figure 7.2:

(a) What percentage of people have test scores between 20 and 30?

(b) What percentage of people have test scores between 70 and 80?

(c) What percentage of people have test scores between 20 and 40?

1.6 Conversion to IQ scores

By convention, the mean of a normal distribution of IQ scores is set at 100. As shown in Figure 7.2, the mean test score of 50 is accordingly converted to a mean IQ of 100 points. Every other test score can be converted to IQ points according to how many standard deviations above or below the mean it falls. Again by convention, each standard deviation is assigned a value of 15 IQ points. A test score of 40 (see Figure 7.2) is one standard deviation below the mean test score of 50, shown by an SD of −1. To convert it to an IQ, we simply take the mean IQ of 100 and subtract 15 (one standard deviation) from it, giving a calculated IQ of 85 points. Similarly, a test score of 60 is one standard deviation above (+1) the mean test score of 50, so the equivalent IQ is 100 plus 15, which is 115 points. One last example: a test score of 20 is 3 standard deviations below (−3) the mean test score. The equivalent IQ is therefore 100 minus 45, which is 55 points.

SAQ 7   In Figure 7.2, what is the equivalent standard deviation and calculated IQ of the following test scores: (a) 80; (b) 30; and (c) 70?

1.7 Advantages of the statistical approach

The distributions in Figures 7.1 and 7.2 each represent the test scores of a particular age sample. If they were scores of 8 year olds, for example, then the test score of any particular 8 year old could be converted to an IQ by the statistical method based on standard deviations outlined in Section 1.6.

There are two main reasons why this method of calculating IQ scores is preferable to the old formula of mental age divided by chronological age, multiplied by 100. First, it eliminates the absurdities that arise when the old MA/CA method is applied to adults. You will remember that 40 year olds who achieve the same test score as average 20 year olds end up with IQs of only 50 when the old MA/CA formula is used, although their performance is, in reality, average for their age. The statistical method involves comparing a person's test score with the average for people in the *same* age group. This means that since the average scores of these age groups are the same, the test scores of both 20 year olds and 40 year olds will then be compared against the same mean.

The second advantage of the statistical approach is that an IQ score calculated in this way indicates a person's intelligence relative to his or her peers in a way that is easy to understand. A person with an IQ of 130, for example, is in the top 2½ per cent for that age group, as is clear from Figure 7.2.

Summary of Section 1

- Intelligence can be defined informally as intellectual ability, although this can cover many different types of thinking, including verbal intelligence, problem solving and practical intelligence, which were interpreted by Sternberg as components of intelligence.

- The technique of correlation is used to measure the degree to which abilities are related to each other.

- Two measures that relate to each other are correlated; two unrelated measures that vary independently of each other are uncorrelated.

- The intelligence quotient (IQ) was originally defined by a formula, devised by Stern, comparing mental age and chronological age.

- These days, IQ is measured by comparing people's performance on intelligence tests with norms for their own age groups, a purely statistical definition of IQ introduced by Wechsler in 1939.

2 | Modern psychometric approaches to intelligence

Psychometrics (from the Greek *psyche*, meaning 'mind', and *metron*, meaning 'measure') focuses on the *measurement* of intelligence. Psychometric comparisons between people with different IQ scores have dominated the study of intelligence ever since the turn of the century. Research into the nature of intelligence and the psychological processes involved in thinking were rather neglected until comparatively recently, and some of the developments in this area will be discussed in Section 5.

In 1916, Lewis Terman of Stanford University translated and adapted the Binet–Simon scale for use in the United States, and the **Stanford–Binet scale**, as it became known, was the prototype of nearly all subsequent IQ tests. As we saw in Section 1.3, in constructing tests for children, Binet had used the independent criterion of age as a basis for choosing suitable test items. This was a reasonable thing to do because older children are obviously better than younger children at following instructions, exercising judgement and solving problems. However age cannot be used as an independent criterion of intelligence in constructing tests for adults as we saw in Section 1.4, and the problem was one of how to select test items which would stretch the abilities of adults and thus reflect their true level of intelligence.

Psychologists solved this problem simply by extending or extrapolating the tests. Terman, for example, included a vocabulary subtest in his Stanford–Binet scale and used the method of extrapolation to make it applicable to adults. When testing children, he found that 6-year-olds could generally define common words like *orange*, older children could define less common words like *lecture*, and only teenagers could define uncommon words like *philanthropy*. He therefore extended or extrapolated this scale so that it could be used with adults by including very uncommon words like *sudorific* (which means sweat-producing). A similar method of extrapolation can be used with other types of test items. The commonsense assumption is that intelligent adults should be able to cope with more difficult items than less intelligent adults.

The Stanford–Binet scale is still used by researchers and educational psychologists. The most recent version of it, published in 1985, is unusual among IQ tests in so far as it is explicitly designed to minimize sexual and ethnic bias in its questions. There are many other intelligence tests available today, and the ones most often used are the Wechsler scales, the British Ability Scales, Raven's Progressive Matrices and the Mill Hill Vocabulary scale, which are described below in Sections 2.1, 2.2, and 2.3, respectively.

2.1 Wechsler scales

The Wechsler scales are based on an adult IQ test originally developed by the American psychologist David Wechsler in 1939. There are now three different Wechsler scales for use with different age groups: the **Wechsler Adult**

Intelligence Scale (revised) or WAIS-R, the Wechsler Intelligence Scale for Children (revised) or WISC-R, and the Wechsler Preschool and Primary Scale of Intelligence or WPPSI. Each of these scales has to be administered individually by a trained tester and each yields three separate scores: verbal IQ, performance IQ and full scale IQ. Some simulated items of the type used in the verbal and performance subtests of the Wechsler Intelligence Scale for Children (revised) are shown in Box B.

The items that make up the Wechsler scales are remarkably diverse and many of them—for example, the questions about the writer of *Tom Sawyer* and the meaning of 'flexible' in Box B—seem to be measures of knowledge or memory rather than of thinking ability. Wechsler's view was that knowledge reflects intelligence because intelligence is needed to acquire knowledge. It is certainly possible to criticize some of the items. Perhaps the most questionable items are in the Comprehension subtest which often asks for judgements based on general knowledge. Even so, each of the Wechsler subtests has been shown to be positively correlated with each of the others. This means that people who get high scores on one subtest tend to get high scores on the others, and vice versa. The correlations between various subtests of the Wechsler Adult Intelligence Scale (revised) are shown in Table 7.1.

Table 7.1 is called a **correlation matrix**. It shows the correlations between people's scores on each subtest and each other subtest. The names of the subtests are listed down the side and in the same order across the top. The first column, for example, contains the correlations between scores on the Information subtest and scores on each of the other subtests. There is a dash rather than a correlation at the top of the first column, in the row labelled Information, because the correlations in the matrix are between scores on *different* subtests. The second row, labelled Digit Span, shows a correlation of 0.46 between the Digit Span and the Information subtests. The third row, labelled Vocabulary, shows a correlation between scores on the Vocabulary

Table 7.1 Average correlations between WAIS-R subtests

Subtest	Information	Digit Span	Vocabulary	Arithmetic	Comprehension	Similarities	Picture Completion	Picture Arrangement	Block Design	Object Assembly	Digit Symbol
Information	—										
Digit Span	.46	—									
Vocabulary	.81	.52	—								
Arithmetic	.61	.56	.63	—							
Comprehension	.68	.45	.74	.57	—						
Similarities	.66	.45	.72	.56	.68	—					
Picture Completion	.52	.37	.55	.48	.52	.54	—				
Picture Arrangement	.50	.37	.51	.46	.48	.50	.51	—			
Block Design	.50	.43	.52	.56	.48	.51	.54	.47	—		
Object Assembly	.39	.33	.41	.42	.40	.43	.52	.40	.63	—	
Digit Symbol	.44	.42	.47	.45	.44	.46	.42	.39	.47	.38	—

(Source: data adapted from Wechsler, 1981, p. 46)

BOX B   Simulated items of the type used in the verbal and performance subtests of the Wechsler Intelligence Scale for Children (Revised)

(*Answers in brackets*)

Verbal subtests

Information
How many wings does a bird have? (Two)
What is steam made of? (Vaporized water)
Who wrote *Tom Sawyer*? (Mark Twain)

Vocabulary
What is a desk? (A writing table)
What does 'flexible' mean? (Easily bent)

Arithmetic
Sam had three pieces of candy and Joe gave him four more. How many pieces of candy did Sam have altogether? (Seven)
Three women divided eighteen golf balls equally among themselves. How many golf balls did each person receive? (Six)
If two buttons cost 15p, what will be the cost of a dozen buttons? (90p)

Comprehension
What should you do if you see someone forget his book when he leaves a restaurant? (Run after him with it)
What is the advantage of keeping money in a bank? (Security)
Why is copper often used in electrical wires? (It is a good conductor)

Similarities
In what way are a lion and a tiger alike? (They are both animals)
In what way are a saw and a hammer alike? (They are both tools)
In what way are an hour and a week alike? (They are both periods of time)

Performance subtests

Picture completion
The subject points out the missing elements in several line drawings; for example, a wheel missing from a pram.

Picture arrangement
The subject arranges a number of pictures into a sequence so that they tell a meaningful story.

Block design
The subject arranges painted wooden blocks to copy designs formed by the examiner.

Object assembly
The subject fits a number of shapes like jigsaw pieces together to make recognizable objects.

(Adapted from The Psychological Corporation, 1974)

and the Information subtests of 0.81 and a correlation between the Vocabulary and Digit Span subtests of 0.52. There are no correlations in the top right of the matrix because they would merely repeat what is in the bottom left. The correlation between Information and Digit Span is missing from the first row, for example, because it is the same as the correlation between Digit Span and Information shown in the second row.

If there were no relation between the Block Design subtest (a non-verbal test of abstract problem solving) and the Information subtest (a verbal test of knowledge), to pick two of the most dissimilar subtests, then the correlation between these two would be zero. In fact, Table 7.1 shows that it is 0.50, which is higher than the correlation of 0.47 that exists between the heights and weights of adult men in Britain (Knight, 1984, p. 29). Most of the correlations between the Wechsler subtests are above 0.50, and this is surprising and inexplicable to anyone who doubts the existence of general intelligence, suggesting as it does that there is a global mental ability underlying performance on all the subtests, as we shall see in Section 2.4.

SAQ 8   In Table 7.1, what are the correlations between the following subtests:
(a) Vocabulary and Information?
(b) Vocabulary and Comprehension?
(c) Comprehension and Information?
(d) Object Assembly and Block Design?

2.2 British Ability Scales

The British Ability Scales (BAS), first published in 1979, are a set of twenty-three tests designed to measure an even wider diversity of mental abilities than are the Wechsler scales. The BAS yields visual IQ, verbal IQ and general IQ scores. It can be used with children and adolescents up to 17 or 18 years of age. Its subtests can be classified according to the following six mental processes: speed of information processing, reasoning, spatial imagery, perceptual matching, short-term memory, and retrieval and application of knowledge. Speed of information processing, which is supposed to underlie performance on all other subtests, is the most unusual component of the BAS. Its presence reflects the influence of modern information-processing approaches to intelligence, to which you will be introduced in the chapters in Part V.

The various subtests of the BAS, like those of the Wechsler scales, each correlate significantly with each of the others, and general IQ scores derived from the BAS correlate quite highly with independent measures of scholastic and academic attainment (Elliott, 1983, chapters 9 and 10). Correlations between general IQ and school tests of mathematical attainment range from 0.62 to 0.81 for children of different ages. Correlations between general IQ and tests of reading attainment range from 0.67 to 0.72. Lastly, correlations between the British Ability Scales' general IQ and 'O' level (now GCSE) grades in various subjects range from 0.24 (English literature) to 0.63

(mathematics). These correlations suggest once again that different measures of intellectual performance tend to be related and that there is a general intellectual ability underlying IQ test scores.

2.3 Raven's Progressive Matrices and the Mill Hill Vocabulary scale

Raven's Progressive Matrices, first published in 1938 and revised several times since then, is a *non-verbal* test designed to measure abstract reasoning ability through the use of meaningless geometric diagrams. SAQ 9 asks you about one of the easiest items from the test.

SAQ 9   In Figure 7.3, which of the numbered diagrams at the bottom would complete the arrangement at the top?

The Raven's Progressive Matrices test is designed to cover a very wide range of mental ability and to be usable with subjects irrespective of age, sex, nationality, or education. Scores on Raven's Progressive Matrices correlate

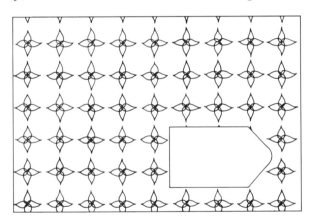

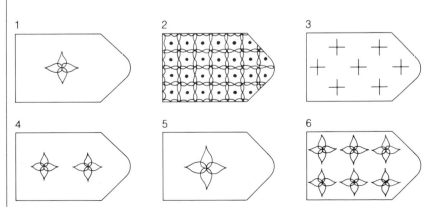

Figure 7.3 An easy item from Raven's Progressive Matrices
(Source: Raven *et al.*, 1983, item A5)

highly with those on other intelligence tests. Correlations with the Wechsler scales, for example, range from 0.54 to 0.88, and correlations with measures of educational attainment, such as school grades and examination results, are generally between 0.20 and 0.60. Many psychologists believe that Raven's Progressive Matrices provide the purest available measure of general intelligence, uncontaminated by cultural and educational influences. But research to be discussed in Section 4 casts doubt on that belief.

The Mill Hill Vocabulary scale, published in its original form in 1944 as a verbal companion to Raven's Progressive Matrices, consists of a list of eighty-eight words divided into two sets of forty-four. The subject's task is to explain the meanings of the words or (in an alternative form of presentation) to select the correct synonym for each word from a list of six alternatives provided. Most children with a mental age of 5 years can explain the meanings of the first few words (*cap, loaf, unhappy*), and between the ages of 5 and 16, children of average intelligence can usually define about three additional words per year. The most difficult words in the list, which only a small minority of adults can define, include *recondite, exiguous* and *minatory*. The correlation between scores on the Mill Hill Vocabulary scale and Raven's Progressive Matrices is 0.75, which is remarkably high considering that they are two utterly different ways of measuring intelligence.

There are many other intelligence tests in common use. The most popular are paper-and-pencil, multiple-choice **group tests** that can be administered to large numbers of subjects at the same time. The types of test items most often featured in these tests, apart from those already described, are analogies, odd-one-out items, and number sequences. Examples of each type are given in SAQ 10.

SAQ 10   Can you solve the following (difficult) intelligence test items? They are similar to ones found in paper-and-pencil group IQ tests.

(a) *Analogies*
C is to X as F is to:
(i) M   (ii) U   (iii) L   (iv) V   (v) H.

(b) *Odd-one-out*
Which of the following is the odd one out?
(i) goal   (ii) line   (iii) sore   (iv) hurt   (v) wand.

(c) *Number sequences*
What is the missing number in the following sequence?
0, 2, 8, 18, . . .

2.4 General intelligence and specific factors

Scores on different IQ tests correlate highly with one another, partly because a new test is not considered valid *unless* it correlates with existing tests. To that extent, validating a new IQ test is rather like hoisting oneself with one's own bootstraps. But that is not the whole story. The most impressive finding to emerge from decades of research into intelligence is the way in which different types of tests and subtests correlate with one another no matter how different they are in content. People who score highly on one test generally score highly on others, and people who score badly on one tend to score badly on the rest. It is difficult, in fact, to devise *any* set of intellectual problems that are not more easily solved by people with high IQs than by those with low IQs. People who do not believe that IQ tests measure intelligence are hard put to explain this well-established fact or to point to anything that *does* indicate intelligence in commonsense terms but does not correlate with IQ scores.

Most contemporary psychologists interpret the fact that different IQ tests and subtests correlate with one another, although not perfectly, as evidence that they must all be measuring a single common factor, which the British psychologist Charles Spearman (1927) called *g* (for **general intelligence**). This implies that people are either intelligent, average, or unintelligent across the board, depending on their levels of general intelligence.

A rival interpretation championed by the American psychologist Louis Leon Thurstone (1938) focused on the other side of the coin—the fact that the correlations between IQ subtests are not perfect and that certain groups of test items usually correlate more highly with one another than with items in other groups of tests. Thurstone believed that these clusters of correlated items indicate the existence of seven independent **primary mental abilities**. He labelled these Number, Word Fluency, Verbal Meaning, Memory, Reasoning, Spatial Perception and Perceptual Speed. His assumption was that intelligence is made up of *independent* abilities, so that a person may score highly on some groups of test items and poorly on others. A person with good Word Fluency, for example, would be expected to score well on all the items which test that particular ability, but the same person may or may not score highly on items which test the Perceptual Speed ability.

The statistical technique of **factor analysis** has been used in an attempt to settle the argument about general intelligence versus specific abilities. The details of factor analysis are complicated, but the underlying idea is easy to grasp. Factor analysis begins with a correlation matrix such as the one shown in Table 7.1. A mathematical technique is then used to scan the matrix for clusters of high correlations, indicating groups of tests or subtests that are all attributable to a common underlying factor. The purpose of factor analysis is to reduce the matrix of correlations to the smallest possible number of factors that can account for all the correlations in the matrix. This process is analogous to that of reducing all the colours of the rainbow to the three primary colours—red, green and blue—of which they are all composed. If all the tests or subtests measure the same general intellectual ability, then only *one* main factor ought to come out of the analysis. This would be evidence in favour of Spearman's concept of general intelligence (*g*). If, on the other hand, the various tests or subtests measure several independent abilities, then several factors should emerge from the analysis.

When factor analysis is applied in an effort to decide objectively whether intelligence is a single general ability or a set of independent specific factors, the results are ambiguous to say the least. It is not difficult to see why this is so. If Spearman was right, and all tests and subtests measure *g* with varying degrees of accuracy, then there should always be very high correlations between all intelligence subtests, especially between those subtests which are the best measures of intelligence.

If, on the other hand, Thurstone was right and different groups of items measure relatively independent primary mental abilities, there should be clusters of high correlations between subtests measuring the same factor, and correlations close to zero between subtests measuring different factors. One might, for example, find high correlations between subtests involving visual ability, and high correlations between subtests involving verbal ability, but zero correlations between visual and verbal subtests.

In practice, the correlation matrix which shows correlations between IQ subtests usually turns out like the correlations between the WAIS-R subtests shown in Table 7.1. It is difficult to decide whether the pattern confirms Spearman's theory of a general factor g or Thurstone's theory of independent primary mental abilities. As you can see from the answers to SAQ 8, Vocabulary, Information and Comprehension seem to form a cluster of high correlations (all over 0.68), as do Object Assembly and Block Design (0.63). But the correlations between subtests belonging to different clusters are nowhere near zero as Thurstone's theory demands; the lowest correlation in the whole table is 0.33. Factor analysis cannot produce clear-cut results with messy data like these. When applied to the Wechsler scales, it usually generates three factors, labelled Verbal Comprehension, Perceptual Organization and Memory (Wechsler, 1981, p. 50). But these factors are not independent because correlations between subtests belonging to different groups are substantial, as we have seen.

The evidence that has accumulated since the 1930s, when Thurstone's views were most influential in the United States (though not so much in Britain), strongly supports the theory of general intelligence. Without accepting that theory in some form it is hard to explain the significant correlations that exist between all intelligence tests and subtests, no matter how diverse. But Thurstone was right in thinking that different people with the same IQ can have very different intellectual strengths and weaknesses.

Modern IQ tests are often designed so that separate scores can be calculated for different aspects of intelligence. The Wechsler scales, as we have seen, measure verbal IQ, performance IQ and full scale IQ. The British Ability Scales measure verbal IQ, visual IQ and general IQ. People with identical general IQ scores can, and often do, have quite different patterns of ability, which may tell us more about them than do their global IQ scores (the average of all their subtest scores). For example, some people are excellent at verbal thinking but rather weak at visual thinking. It is a mistake, however, to believe that the different mental abilities are completely independent. The notion of an overall general intelligence, represented by global IQ, and the rival notion of specific abilities, represented by various factors such as verbal or visual ability, undoubtedly both contain a portion of the truth.

2.5 How accurate are IQ tests?

The accuracy of an IQ test, or of any measuring instrument for that matter, consists of two main ingredients: reliability and validity. The **reliability** of a test is the consistency and stability with which it measures. If a tape measure is a reliable measure of length, then it should show **consistency** in results if we measure objects with different parts of the tape. It should also show **stability** in the sense that it should give the same results if we measure the same objects with it on two separate occasions. If the tape measure is not consistent and stable, perhaps because it tends to stretch, then it is not a reliable measure. The same idea applies to psychological tests such as IQ tests. If an IQ test reliably measures general intellectual ability, then scores on some test items should correlate highly with scores on the other items. People's scores on the test on two separate occasions should also correlate highly.

There are three main techniques for establishing the reliability of tests. The first establishes **split-half reliability**, which shows the test's consistency. Researchers give the test to a large group of people and record the score that each person gets on the odd-numbered test items and the even-numbered items. The researchers then work out the correlation between these two sets of scores, each of which represents half of the items. If all the test items measure the same general ability, then people who do well on the odd-numbered items should tend to do well on the even-numbered items, so the correlation should be high. If the correlation is low, with many people scoring very differently on the two halves of the test, then the test is not reliable.

The second technique determines the **parallel-form reliability** of a test. Some tests, such as the Stanford–Binet scale and the Mill Hill Vocabulary scale, come in two equivalent forms each containing similar kinds of items. In these cases, the parallel-form reliability of the test can be assessed by giving both forms of the test to a large group of people and working out the correlation between their scores on the two forms. Once again, the correlation will be high if the test is reliable.

The third technique establishes **test–retest reliability**, which is an index of the test's stability. Researchers give the test to a large group of people on two separate occasions and work out the correlation between the two sets of scores. If the test is reliable, then people who score highly on the first occasion should score highly on the second, and those who score badly on the first occasion should score badly on the second. In other words, the correlation between the two sets of scores should be high; if it is not, then the test is not reliable. Good IQ tests have very high reliabilities. The split-half and test–retest reliabilities of the Wechsler Adult Intelligence Scale and the British Ability Scales (general IQ) are both 0.95.

The second ingredient of a test's accuracy is its **validity**. A test is said to be valid if it measures what it purports to measure. There are many ways of assessing a test's validity, of which the most important are various types of criterion validation. In the case of IQ tests, **criterion validation** involves giving the test to children of different ages or different levels of educational attainment. If an IQ test is a valid measure of intelligence, it ought to correlate significantly, although not perfectly, with measures of educational attainment. It follows that children who do well at school should *tend* to score higher on IQ tests than those who do badly at school. This expectation has been confirmed by numerous careful research studies (Jensen, 1980; Mackintosh and Mascie-Taylor, 1985). Correlations between IQ scores on the one hand and marks in 'O' level (now GCSE) examinations, or scores on school tests of reading attainment or mathematics on the other, are typically found to lie between 0.40 and 0.70. If IQ were a *perfect* predictor of educational attainment as measured by such tests, then the correlations would be 1.00; if IQ were quite unrelated to educational attainment, then the correlations would be zero. The fact that the correlations lie somewhere between these two extremes suggests that IQ tests are valid measures of intelligence, and also that intelligence contributes substantially to scholastic performance, but that the two are not identical.

Another method of validating an IQ test is by correlating scores from it with scores from other IQ tests of known validity. This method, called **congruent validation**, ensures that the new test measures whatever the other tests measure. A new IQ test would be considered suspect if it gave scores that did not correlate highly with those from established IQ tests.

It is important to understand that a test can be reliable but not valid. A test that purports to measure intelligence, for example, may in fact simply be measuring reading ability. Such a test could be very reliable, in the sense that it gives consistent and stable scores, but it would not be a valid intelligence test because it would be measuring reading ability rather than intelligence. On the other hand, a test that is known to be valid must be reliable, because it cannot measure accurately what it is supposed to measure unless it is consistent and stable.

2.6 Does intelligence decline in later life?

It is worth commenting briefly on the long-term stability of intelligence. Young children's intellectual ability increases as they grow older, but this increase levels off when people reach the age of about 17 or 18 years. IQ scores indicate intellectual ability relative to the average for people of the same age. The question naturally arises as to whether people's IQs then remain stable over long periods of time. IQ tests are not reliable for very young children, under about 5 years of age, so it is hardly surprising that IQs at that age do not correlate very highly with IQs in later life, even though the correlations are well above zero. From about the age of 7 years, IQ scores tend to stabilize: people's IQs at the age of 7 correlate about 0.70 with their own IQs at the age of 17.

Does intelligence decline in middle age? There is a great deal of evidence that average intelligence, at least as measured by the 'pure' reasoning tests and subtests, is highest among 18–30 year olds and significantly lower in older groups. On Raven's Progressive Matrices, for example, average 20 year olds solve about 45 of the 60 matrices correctly, average 40 year olds solve about 37, and average 60 year olds solve only about 28 (Raven, Court and Raven,

1983). A similar progressive decline with age has been reported on the performance scales of the WAIS-R (Wechsler, 1981) and on other non-verbal tests and subtests (Bates and Schaie, 1976). These data used to be accepted stoically as evidence that intelligence declines quite precipitously after about 30 years of age. It is now known that the findings arise from something quite different and less alarming.

Most of the findings showing a decline in intelligence with age have been based on studies in which groups of people of different ages were compared. These are called **cross-sectional studies** because they focus on a cross-section of the population—comprising, that is, *different* age groups—at a particular time. Recent research (e.g. Schaie, 1983) has used **longitudinal studies** in which researchers tested and retested the *same* group of people at different times rather than different age groups at the same time. In other words, they followed the IQ test performance of one group of people as they got progressively older. (People of the same age who are tested repeatedly in a longitudinal study are called an **age cohort**.) In the longitudinal studies, a decline in intelligence was found only after the age of about 60.

Why, then, do 50-year-old people score lower in cross-sectional studies than 30 year olds? The reason seems to be that younger generations are more intelligent than their elders, or at least better than their elders at solving 'pure' reasoning problems in IQ tests. When a person born in 1930, for example, is tested and retested later in life, there is little decline in IQ. But that person's IQ is likely to be slightly lower than that of someone born 20 years later. A comparison with height is instructive. Young adults are taller, on average, than members of their parents' generation, because people today tend to grow taller. The reason why 50 year olds are generally shorter than 30 year olds is not that they have begun to shrink with age but that they belong to a shorter age cohort, and there is a similar cohort effect with intelligence.

The evidence is quite unambiguous. Like physical stature, average levels of intelligence, at least as measured by non-verbal tests like Raven's Progressive Matrices, have been rising steadily over the past half century or so, not only in Britain, but also in Belgium, Canada, France, New Zealand, the Netherlands, Norway, the United States and probably Japan (Flynn, 1987; Lynn and Hampson, 1986). This must be the reason, or at least a substantial part of the reason, why older cohorts do less well in the tests. Even the decline after the age of 60, which shows up not only in cross-sectional but also in longitudinal studies, may have nothing to do with age as such. It may be due to the tendency for intelligence to decline, probably as a side-effect of illness, in people who are close to death. Age cohorts over 60 are bound to include a minority who are suffering from various kinds of illnesses, and the decline in average intelligence after the age of 60 may be due entirely to the decline in intelligence in that minority group.

Summary of Section 2

- Modern intelligence tests include the Wechsler scales, the British Ability Scales, Raven's Progressive Matrices and the Mill Hill Vocabulary scale.

- A correlation matrix shows the correlations between scores on several tests or subtests.

- Factor analysis is a statistical technique for analysing clusters of correlations to identify underlying factors.

- Spearman's theory of general intelligence assumes a single *g* (general intelligence), reflected by high correlations between all tests and subtests. Thurstone's theory emphasizes several clusters of correlations associated with primary mental abilities.

- The *reliability* of a test depends on its being a consistent and stable measure, as demonstrated by split-half, parallel-form and test–retest correlations.

- The *validity* of a test is the extent to which it measures what it purports to measure. Criterion validation involves correlating IQ scores with measures of educational attainment and with other IQ tests. Congruent validation ensures that the new test measures whatever the other tests measure.

- While cross-sectional studies indicated a steep decline in IQ for older age groups, longitudinal studies indicate that intelligence does not decline as much as was formerly believed.

3 | The nature–nurture controversy

For over a century a controversy has raged in psychology over the relative contributions of heredity (**nature**) and environment (**nurture**) to intelligence. Lewis Terman and other early American psychometricians believed intelligence to be a fixed and innate mental capacity. Many of them were members of eugenic societies which campaigned in favour of sterilization laws to prevent people with very low IQs from having children, and against immigration from southern, central and eastern Europe. A number of sterilization laws were passed in the United States, beginning with the Act for the Prevention of Idiocy in Pennsylvania in 1905. In the state of Virginia alone, where a similar law was passed, over 7000 people with low IQs were compulsorily sterilized between 1924 and 1972. In 1912 a psychologist called Henry Goddard administered IQ tests to immigrants at the receiving station in New York harbour and reported, incredibly, that most of the Italians, eastern

Europeans and Jews were 'feebleminded' (Goddard, 1913). The infamous Immigration Restriction Act of 1924 limited the number of Jewish refugees from Nazi Germany who were able to escape to the United States, as a result of which hundreds of thousands perished in concentration camps after being refused entry into the United States. The writings of Terman, Goddard and other American psychometricians, while not a direct cause of these deplorable measures, lent intellectual credibility to them (Fancher, 1985; Gould, 1981; Colman, 1987).

In Britain, Cyril Burt, later to be knighted for his services to educational psychology, advised the Consultative Committee on Secondary Education in 1938 that intelligence is a fixed and hereditary factor which can be measured reliably by the time a child is 11 years old. His advice was incorporated into the Education Act of 1944 which introduced the 'eleven-plus' examination based largely on IQ tests. Children who failed the eleven-plus were denied entry to grammar schools which prepared pupils for higher education and were sent instead to academically inferior secondary modern schools, where they remained even if their intellectual or scholastic ability improved dramatically in later years.

Is it true that a person's intelligence is a fixed and hereditary characteristic, as eye colour is, or is it a variable characteristic traceable to environmental influences? Stated in that way, the question is misleading for two main reasons. First, there is no necessary connection between the fixedness of a characteristic on the one hand and its genetic or environmental origins on the other, as the question implies. An example to illustrate this is an illness called phenylketonuria. This is a purely hereditary disease caused by a single recessive gene and associated with severe mental retardation. Nevertheless, the effects of this hereditary disease can be prevented by a single environmental change: by eliminating phenylalanine, which is present in food proteins, from the patient's diet. This shows that a hereditary characteristic need not be fixed and unmodifiable. It is also the case that a fixed, unmodifiable characteristic need not necessarily be hereditary. This applies, for example, to mental retardation resulting from oxygen deprivation at the time of birth.

Second, it is meaningless to pose the heredity-versus-environment question about intelligence as an either/or issue. In order to have any human intelligence a person needs a brain, and it is impossible to have a brain without inheriting the necessary genes *and* acquiring the food, oxygen, parental care and other environmental requirements for its growth.

3.1 Heritability of IQ

The question about which psychologists argue is slightly more complicated: to what extent are *differences* in IQ *between people* genetically determined? In technical terms, the question is, 'what is the heritability of IQ?' The **heritability** of a characteristic in a specified population is the *proportion* of the variability of that characteristic that is attributable to genetic differences between individuals. The heritability of IQ is therefore that proportion of the variability—that is, the differences between individual IQ scores—that is attributable to genetic differences between people in the population.

Two hypothetical limiting cases will help to fix the concept of heritability and clarify the point at issue. Imagine first a perfectly egalitarian utopia in which no one is advantaged or disadvantaged relative to anyone else with regard to any environmental factors that might affect IQ. In that society any IQ differences observed between people, and therefore also the variability of IQ, would necessarily be due *entirely* to genetic factors (nature), so the heritability of IQ would be 100 per cent. Now imagine a science-fiction dystopia (the opposite of utopia) populated entirely by clones who share identical genes. In that case, since there are no genetic differences between people, any observed variance in IQ would necessarily be due entirely to environmental factors (nurture) and so the heritability of IQ would be zero.

If education influences IQ, and it is hard to believe that it does not, then any increase in equality of educational opportunity is likely to lead to the paradoxical result that hereditary factors become increasingly important in producing differences between people. Because heritability is defined as the *proportion* of the IQ differences due to the heredity, then if differences due to environmental factors play a smaller role, it follows that the remaining proportion due to hereditary factors automatically becomes relatively larger. In fact, there is empirical evidence to show that this has happened. A study of Norwegian twins born in the 1930s, 1940s and 1950s confirms that, as equality of educational opportunity increased in that country, the estimated heritability of intelligence increased correspondingly (Heath *et al.*, 1985).

How can the heritability of IQ be estimated? The problem would be easily solved if researchers could hold either environmental or hereditary factors constant as in the hypothetical utopia and dystopia discussed above. Experimental biologists routinely perform similar experiments on plants to determine the heritability of various characteristics, but it is manifestly impossible to settle the IQ question by such methods. Psychologists are limited to *indirect* methods of estimating the heritability of IQ, and the results are highly controversial.

Researchers have used three main methods for estimating the heritability of IQ: studies of separated identical twins, family studies and adoption studies. Galton pioneered two of these methods in a primitive way and reported his results in a book entitled *Hereditary genius: an inquiry into its laws and consequences* (Galton, 1869). His family study consisted of an examination of the family trees of 415 highly distinguished people in various walks of life. He found that their blood relatives were also eminent much more often than would be expected by chance, and, furthermore, that their close relatives were more often eminent than their more distant relatives. For example, 48 per cent of their sons, 7 per cent of their grandsons, and only 1 per cent of their great-grandsons were eminent. Genius thus seemed to run in families rather like red hair, which was already known to be hereditary, and Galton concluded that differences in mental ability are also largely hereditary.

SAQ 11   Galton found that intelligence seemed to run in families, and he inferred from this that differences in intelligence are mainly due to heredity. Can you think of any other explanation for his finding?

Galton's adoption study capitalized on the common practice of nepotism in the Roman Catholic Church, whereby popes used to adopt young boys from ordinary backgrounds and raise them in their homes as 'nephews'. Galton argued that these boys had similar environmental advantages to those enjoyed by the natural sons of other eminent men but none of the genetic advantages: 'the social helps are the same but the hereditary gifts are wanting' (Galton, 1869). His investigation showed that the popes' 'nephews' seldom attained eminence in later life, although almost half the natural sons of other eminent men did so. He interpreted these findings as further evidence that intelligence is largely hereditary.

Galton's family and adoption studies were quaint and interesting but hardly convincing. Sections 3.2, 3.3 and 3.4 are devoted to a review of the evidence that has accumulated since then. For over a century psychologists have tried to resolve the nature–nurture question in relation to IQ, using both refinements of Galton's methods and studies of separated identical twins. However, all this research effort has produced no very definite conclusions.

3.2 Separated identical twins

As explained in Chapter 5, section 5.3, **identical twins** are formed when a single ovum, fertilized by a single sperm, splits in two and grows into two separate individuals. The twins have identical genes, which means that they are the same sex and very similar in all hereditary characteristics. Non-identical twins develop from two separate ova fertilized by two separate sperms at about the same time; they may be the same or opposite sex and share about half their genes in common, just like ordinary siblings (brothers and sisters). Both identical and non-identical twins are normally brought up together and share a common environment.

Identical twins are very occasionally separated soon after birth and raised in different homes. The importance of these rare cases is that these twins share only their genes, not their environments, in common. Any similarity in their IQs beyond what is to be expected by chance would seem, on the face of it, to be attributable to their genetic identity. Some psychologists regard studies of separated identical twins as the most convincing data available concerning the heritability of IQ, but the results are, in reality, curiously inconclusive. Only four such studies have so far been published, partly because suitable cases are extremely hard to find. The results, in descending order of the sizes of the studies, and of the correlations reported, are summarized in Table 7.2.

By far the largest and most influential of the published studies, and the one reporting the highest correlation, was carried out by Sir Cyril Burt of University College London between the 1940s and 1960s. It is also the only one purporting to show that the home environments of the twins were quite

Table 7.2 Studies of the correlation between the IQs of separated identical twins

Study	Number of twin pairs	Correlation
Burt (1955, 1958, 1966)	53	0.86
Shields (1962)	37	0.77
Newman, Freeman and Holzinger (1937)	19	0.67
Juel-Nielsen (1965)	12	0.62

different. If separated identical twins are raised in similar home environments, then the correlation between their IQs is hard to interpret because it might be due to environmental similarities rather than to the genetic similarities. Burt reported that the correlation between the twins' home environments, which he rated on a scale from 'higher professional' to 'unskilled', was close to zero, which suggests that the massive 0.86 correlation between their IQ's must be due to genetic differences alone, implying that the heritability of IQ is 86 per cent.

In 1974, the American psychologist Leon Kamin drew attention to certain anomalies in Burt's data which seemed to strain the laws of probability (see Box C), and in 1979, Leslie Hearnshaw's official biography of Burt proved beyond doubt that the data were faked. Burt simply fabricated IQ scores to prove his hereditarian point, and he even went to the lengths of publishing papers in psychological journals with fictitious co-authors.

The second largest study (Shields, 1962) reported a correlation of 0.77 between the IQs of thirty-seven pairs of separated identical twins in England. This study, unlike Burt's, can be criticized on the grounds that the twins' environments were quite similar (Kamin, 1974). In more than half the pairs, the 'separated' twins were raised in different branches of the same family; often one member of the pair stayed with the mother while the other was raised by a grandmother or aunt. If these pairs are removed from the sample, the correlation in the remaining thirteen pairs drops to 0.51. But in several of these cases the twins' environments were still similar because both twins attended the same school, played together, and so on. Shields' data therefore overestimate the heritability of IQ to an unknown degree because the correlation between the twins' IQ scores might be due chiefly to their similar environments.

The next largest study (Newman et al., 1937) reported a correlation of 0.67 between the IQs of nineteen pairs of separated identical twins in the United States. This study contains three serious flaws. First, there is abundant evidence that the twins' environments were similar, as in the Shields study (Kamin, 1974). Second, the researchers used a flawed method of recruiting subjects for their study. To avoid accidentally including non-identical twins in their sample, they excluded all pairs who said in reply to a preliminary questionnaire that they were at all dissimilar in appearance or behaviour. This biased the sample from the outset in favour of twins who were extremely similar, because twins who were noticeably dissimilar were not included.

BOX C Kamin's unmasking of Burt's fraud

Three years after Burt's death, Kamin (1974) pointed out several 'numerical impossibilities' in Burt's data. Kamin's most devastating discovery was the existence of inexplicable identical correlations in the data. Burt claimed to have tested his twins on both individual and (presumably less reliable) group IQ tests. He initially reported data from twenty-one pairs of separated identical twins. By 1958 he claimed to have tested over thirty pairs, and by 1966 his sample had purportedly grown to fifty-three pairs. He reported the correlations as shown in Table 7.3.

Table 7.3 Inexplicable identical correlations in Burt's data

Date	Number of twin pairs	Correlation	
		Group test	Individual test
1955	21	0.771	0.843
1958	30+	0.771	0.843
1966	53	0.771	0.863

The fact that the correlations, with one exception which may be a typing error, remain identical to three decimal places with different sample sizes, strains the laws of probability and the credulity of the reader. Kamin concluded that 'the numbers left behind by Professor Burt are simply not worthy of our current scientific attention' (Kamin, 1974).

This is a serious methodological error in a study in which it is precisely the degree of similarity that is at issue. The third flaw is the confounding of IQ with age. The researchers measured the twins' IQs with the original 1916 Stanford–Binet scale, which is notorious for its faulty standardization for different age groups. A properly standardized IQ test should yield average scores of 100 for all age groups because an IQ of 100 is average *by definition*. However, the 1916 Stanford–Binet scale yields higher average scores for younger than for older age groups (see the discussions in Sections 1.4 to 1.6). The correlation between the twins' IQs in the study by Newman *et al.*, may therefore be due, at least in part, to their identical ages rather than their identical genes.

The last and smallest study (Juel-Nielsen, 1965), carried out in Denmark on twelve pairs of separated identical twins, reported a correlation of 0.62. Juel-Nielsen measured the twins' IQs with a Danish translation of the Wechsler Adult Intelligence Scale (WAIS) which had not been standardized on a Danish sample, and this resulted in IQ being confounded with age as in the study by Newman *et al.* (Kamin, 1974). A second flaw was that, in many cases, the twins' environments were similar, as in the Shields study.

3.3 Family studies

A child inherits half its genes from each of its parents and therefore shares half its genes with each of them. It follows from this that non-identical twins and ordinary siblings share about 50 per cent of their genes in common, a grandparent shares about 25 per cent of genes with each grandchild, and so on. In family studies these different degrees of genetic relatedness are compared with IQ correlations between the corresponding relation pairs. The underlying assumption is that, if the heritability of IQ is high, then the IQ correlations between different categories of relatives should decrease in an orderly fashion as the degree of genetic relatedness decreases.

The most influential family study (Erlenmeyer-Kimling and Jarvik, 1963) reported a remarkably orderly pattern of correlations between numerous different categories of relatives. Some of the data, as summarized in tabular form by Jensen and Eysenck, are shown in Table 7.4.

Table 7.4 Correlations between IQ scores of different categories of relatives

Relationship category	Average IQ correlation
Identical twins raised together	0.87
Identical twins raised apart	0.75
Siblings raised together	0.55
Siblings raised apart	0.47
Parent–child	0.50
Non-identical twins (opposite sex)	0.49
Second cousins	0.16
Unrelated	−0.01

(Source: summarized by Jensen, 1969, p. 49, and Eysenck, 1971, p. 62, from Erlenmeyer-Kimling and Jarvik, 1963)

Most of the correlations correspond uncannily closely to the proportions of genes that each of the categories of relatives share in common. It is now known that the data, which were obtained from fifty-two separate research reports, are indeed too good to be true (Kamin, 1974; Paul, 1985; Colman, 1987). One example will suffice to show how unreliable the data are. Look at the correlation of 0.47 for siblings raised apart. It is based on three published investigations, one by Burt and a mythical co-author of his whom he called Howard, which reported correlations of 0.46, 0.34 and 0.23. The average of these three numbers is not 0.47, as shown in Table 7.4, but 0.34, which is way below the theoretical figure of 0.50 that corresponds to the proportion of genes siblings share in common. There are numerous similar errors and distortions, all in the direction of making the data appear to support the simple genetic theory. To make matters worse, the data include many correlations fabricated by Burt to support that theory.

Erlenmeyer-Kimling and Jarvik's data were discredited in the mid 1970s, but they continue to be cited in textbooks as evidence for the heritability of IQ. Of the nineteen textbooks of genetics published between 1978 and 1984 that devoted more than half a paragraph to the heritability of IQ, twelve cited the data as evidence, and in many of these books it was the *only* evidence cited (Paul, 1985). One of the books included a dramatic insert on 'Scientific fraud: the case against Sir Cyril Burt', but also stated that 'the measured heritability of IQ is relatively high' and gave the Erlenmeyer-Kimling and Jarvik data, which incorporate Burt's fraudulent figures, as evidence for this conclusion (Tamarin, 1982, pp. 291–2).

More reliable family studies have been done in recent years. To translate the findings into numerical estimates of heritability, mathematical models have to be used, and these models include a large number of assumptions which some critics consider unacceptable. They all assume, for example, that identical and non-identical twins raised together experience the same environmental background, and that living with a very intelligent or a very unintelligent sibling has no direct effect on a child's IQ. The evidence from the best family studies suggests that the heritability of IQ probably lies somewhere in the range of 30–60 per cent (Henderson, 1982), but many psychologists consider the evidence to be unconvincing.

3.4 Adoption studies

Children who are adopted early in life share none of their genes with their adoptive parents but about 50 per cent with their natural mothers who relinquished them soon after they were born. It is reasonable to assume that, if IQ differences are due mainly to environmental factors, then the IQs of adopted children should correlate more highly with those of their adoptive parents than with those of their natural mothers with whom they have never lived. If IQ is highly heritable, on the other hand, then roughly the reverse should be found. The IQs of adopted children should correlate moderately highly with those of their natural mothers, who donated 'nature' in the form of half their genes, and not at all with the IQs of their adoptive parents, who provided 'nurture'.

Two classic adoption studies (Burks, 1928; Leahy, 1935) reported correlations of only 0.13 and 0.18, respectively, between the IQs of adopted children and those of their adoptive parents. These correlations are virtually zero and are certainly much lower than those found between the IQs of children raised by their natural parents and the IQs of those parents, which suggests that genes are important. But the results are hard to interpret because the IQs of the adoptive parents in both studies were mostly high and closely bunched together (Kamin, 1974, chapter 5; Eysenck and Kamin, 1981, chapter 15). Why is this a problem? The answer is that it may have artificially depressed the correlations. The point is that, if the adoptive parents are all very intelligent, then there is no scope for correlations throughout the range from low to high IQs. To understand this statistical point, consider personal income and diet as measured by calorie intake. There is undoubtedly a high correlation between these two things in the world's population as a whole. But it would probably all but disappear if only well-off people in Britain were included in the sample, because well-off people are, for the most part, equally well fed. The same thing may have happened in the Burks and Leahy studies. The adoptive parents were nearly all highly intelligent.

Skodak and Skeels (1949) were the first to examine both the IQs of adopted children and those of their *natural* mothers. They found the correlation to be 0.44 in sixty-three children adopted before the age of 6 months. For decades this finding was considered the most powerful of all the evidence showing the heritability of IQ to be high, because there seemed to be no possible environmental explanation for such a substantial correlation between the IQs of children and the IQs of their mothers from whom they were separated in early infancy.

Perhaps surprisingly, there *is* an environmental explanation, and it is called **selective placement**. Children are not delivered to their adoptive homes by storks. They are usually sent there by adoption agencies who used, before the Second World War, to place most children in well-off homes. Since the war, as adoption has become more popular, the agencies have generally tried to place each child with adoptive parents whose intellectual and educational level roughly matches those of their natural mothers. In the Skodak and Skeels study, children of natural mothers with high IQs had often been placed with college-educated adoptive parents in wealthy homes which probably provided good environments for the development of their IQs, while children of low-IQ natural mothers had generally been placed with less well educated adoptive parents in poorer homes (Kamin, 1974, chapter 5). What follows from this is that the correlation between the children's IQs and those of their natural mothers may have been due to selective placement in environments related to their natural mothers' IQs rather than to hereditary factors.

More recent adoption studies have avoided some of the pitfalls of earlier research by focusing on parents who have raised both adopted and natural children in their homes. All the children are brought up in the same environment by the same parents, so any significant difference between the parent–child IQ correlations for the adopted children and the natural children in these households would seem to be attributable to the sole difference that only the *natural* children share genes in common with their parents.

The results of two large American studies using this improved research design are shown in Table 7.5.

Table 7.5 Correlations between IQs of adoptive mothers and IQs of their natural and adopted children

	Mother–Child correlation	
	Natural children	Adopted children
Scarr and Weinberg (1977)	0.34	0.29
Horn, Loehlin and Willerman (1979)	0.20	0.22

In Scarr and Weinberg's (1977) Minnesota study, the parents and their natural children were white and the adopted children were mostly black or of mixed race. The mother–child IQ correlation was slightly higher for the natural children, but the difference was not statistically significant (which means that it could easily have been due to chance). In Horn *et al.*'s (1979) Texas Adoption Project, as it is called, there was a slight difference, which was also non-significant, in the opposite direction. Both sets of results suggest that the heritability of IQ is low because of the similar mother–child correlations regardless of whether or not the genes were the same.

Further evidence pointing to this conclusion comes from families in both studies with more than one adopted child and a natural child or more than one natural child and an adopted child. The correlations in these families between pairs of natural children (with half their genes in common), pairs of adopted children (genetically unrelated) and natural–adopted pairs (genetically unrelated) were all very similar. None of the correlations differed significantly from the others, although the first of these should surely have been higher than the others if the heritability of IQ is high.

In both studies correlations were also reported between the adopted children's IQs and those of their *natural* mothers. In the Minnesota study the correlation between the IQs of the adopted children and the estimated IQs of the mothers who relinquished them was 0.32. But this is probably attributable to selective placement because the correlation was later shown to be almost the same (0.33) when the IQs of children unrelated to the mothers but living in the same adoptive homes were substituted in the calculation (Kamin, 1974, chapter 5). In other words, the natural mothers' IQs correlated just as highly with the IQs of the other children in the adoptive homes as with the IQs of their own children. This is surprising and can be explained only by selective placement. In the Texas study the correlation was 0.31 between the IQs of adopted children and those of their natural mothers, and it was 0.19 when children sharing the same environment but none of the mothers' genes were substituted in the calculation. In this case, selective placement explains most of the original correlation, though not all of it.

3.5 Conclusions

Most people, including psychologists, seem to hold strong views about the heritability of intelligence. The research evidence has signally failed to settle the question once and for all or to provide a half-way convincing estimate of the relative contributions of heredity (nature) and environment (nurture) to individual differences in IQ scores. Studies of separated identical twins, family studies and adoption studies are all fraught with different but seemingly insuperable problems.

Any estimate of heritability is at best only a very rough approximation, and it applies only to a single population at a single point in time. The amount of environmental variation differs from one society to the next, and it even changes over time within the same society. A consequence of this is that the heritability of IQ is itself a variable quantity that can never be pinned down and carved in stone as a universal and eternal verity. Precise estimates give a false air of scientific exactitude because they are not based on properly controlled experimental studies. Controlled experiments on heritability are impossible to perform on human subjects for practical and ethical reasons. The research that has been done is non-experimental and inadequately controlled, and it is foolhardy to overinterpret its findings. The data come from studies that are always imperfect, often seriously flawed and occasionally downright fraudulent.

Depending on which studies you consider best, which you are willing to ignore, and which simplifying assumptions you are willing to accept, you can arrive at an estimate of the heritability of IQ anywhere from zero to about 70 per cent. There is another, probably wiser, option, and that is simply to suspend judgement on this issue. It is certainly not necessary to hold a view about the heritability of IQ because, whether it is high or low or zero, the degree to which we can influence people's IQs by suitable environmental means is an entirely separate (and much more important) question. Whatever the heritability of IQ, improvements in education, housing, social environments, and nurture in general can only be of benefit to society as a whole and all the individuals within it.

Summary of Section 3

- Attempts to measure the proportion of the differences in IQ attributable to heredity have used studies of separated identical twins, family studies and adoption studies.

- The apparently high correlations that have been recorded between the IQ scores of separated identical twins are not necessarily due to the twins' identical genes. One alternative explanation is the fact that, although separated, the twins are often raised in similar environments. There are cases also, where figures may have been doctored in a fraudulent manner.

- The reported correlations due to kinship in families are ambiguous, because genetic and environmental influences are difficult to separate.

- Correlations between the IQs of adopted children and those of their natural mothers may be due to selective placement of the children in home environments similar to those of their natural parents.

- In all these studies it is very difficult to sort out the degree to which differences in intelligence are due to heredity (nature) as opposed to environmental factors (nurture).

4 | Race and intelligence

An acrimonious debate about race and intelligence began when Arthur Jensen of the University of California, Berkeley, published a paper entitled 'How much can we boost IQ and scholastic achievement?' (Jensen, 1969). Hans Eysenck of the University of London summarized Jensen's ideas in a book entitled *Race, intelligence and education* (Eysenck, 1971). The point at issue in this debate is the interpretation of the evidence showing that black Americans score about 15 points *lower*, on average, on IQ tests than do white

Americans (Shuey, 1966; Scarr, 1981). Also, people of West Indian descent in Britain score between 5 and 13 points lower, on average, on IQ tests than do members of the indigenous white population (Mackintosh and Mascie-Taylor, 1985; Mackintosh, 1986). Jensen and Eysenck both argued that the differences are due mainly to genetic differences between the black and white races, and their writings generated angry emotional reactions. Literally hundreds of criticisms were published, and there were calls for Jensen's dismissal from the American Psychological Association. Students began disrupting his classes, and his university had to hire a bodyguard to protect him. Reactions to Eysenck in England were only slightly less extreme.

Before examining the evidence on this question, it is worth mentioning two theoretical points that are relevant to it. The first is that modern techniques of genetic analysis have shown only about 7 per cent of human genetic differences of all kinds to be attributable to racial differences (Rose et al., 1984, pp. 119–27). This suggests that race, like beauty, is only skin deep and that race differences in intelligence are therefore unlikely to be due to genetic factors. The second theoretical point is that some 70 per cent of Afro-Americans and Afro-Caribbeans have at least one white ancestor, and 15 per cent have more white ancestors than black; the ancestry of black Americans and West Indians is, on average, 20 per cent white (Reed, 1969). These facts also make it unlikely that there are any very marked inborn psychological differences between the black and white populations. The question is empirical, though, and there is evidence that bears more directly on it.

Jensen and Eysenck argued that race differences in IQ are mainly due to genetic factors, and they based this conclusion largely on evidence which they believed showed that the heritability of IQ is high. They reasoned that, if IQ differences in the general population are due mainly to heredity, then IQ differences between the black and white groups within the population must also be due mainly to heredity. The argument is now known to be invalid, as the biologist Richard Lewontin demonstrated with the following famous analogy (Rose et al., 1984, p. 18). Two handfuls of seed are taken from the same sack and planted in separate plots, which differ from each other only in that the second plot is deficient in nutrients. The plants in the first plot grow tall and those in the second are stunted. This is illustrated in Figure 7.4.

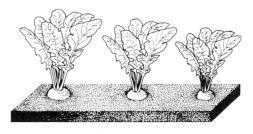
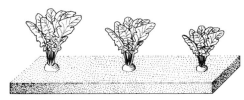

plot A   rich in nutrients   plot B   deficient in nutrients

Figure 7.4 Lewontin's analogy. Within each plot, genetic differences make some plants grow taller than others. Because of environmental differences (nutrients), however, the plants in plot A grow taller than the plants in plot B

ACTIVITY 2

Examine Figure 7.4 carefully. Then think about Lewontin's analogy and try to anticipate where it is leading.
(a) Will the difference *between* the plants in the two plots be due to genetic factors, environmental factors, or both?
(b) There will also be differences between individual plants *within* each plot. Will these *within*-group differences be due to genetic factors, environmental factors, or both?
(c) What can you conclude from the answers to (a) and (b) about race differences in intelligence?

The average difference *between* the two groups of plants will be due entirely to environmental factors (nutrients), because the seeds come from the same sack and are therefore genetically the same, on average. On the other hand, differences between plants *within* each plot will be due entirely to genetic factors because the environment is identical for all seeds in the same plot. In other words, heritability is 100 per cent within each group, but the average difference between the two groups is due entirely to environmental factors. Lewontin's analogy shows that, even if the heritability of IQ is very high, the differences between racial groups may be entirely attributable to environmental factors.

The argument based on heritability is fallacious, as shown above. However, we should examine the empirical evidence for the genetic or environmental origins of the black–white IQ gap. This comes from racial admixture and crossing studies, to which we can now turn.

4.1 Racial admixture studies

Racial admixture studies capitalize on the fact, mentioned earlier, that black people have varying amounts of white ancestry. If the black–white IQ gap is mainly due to genetic factors, then obviously black people with a great deal of white ancestry, and therefore many 'white' genes, should have higher average IQs than those with no white ancestry. It is difficult to estimate a person's proportion of white ancestry accurately, so the results of racial admixture studies are not absolutely conclusive.

One of the earliest and best studies (Witty and Jenkins, 1936) focused on ninety-one black children with the highest IQs of all the many thousands in the Chicago public school system. When the researchers classified these high-IQ black children according to proportion of white ancestry by examining their family trees, they found no evidence that they had more white ancestry than did a comparison group of ordinary black Americans. The results showed, for example, that 14.3 per cent of the high-IQ children had predominantly white ancestry, compared to 14.8 per cent of the comparison group. If genetic factors are at the root of the black–white IQ gap, then there should have been substantially more children with predominantly white ancestry in the high-IQ group. In fact, the distribution of white ancestry was remarkably similar in both groups of children, and the brightest child in the sample, a girl with an astonishing IQ of 200, was one of the ones who had no known white ancestry at all.

Sandra Scarr and her colleagues carried out the most carefully controlled racial admixture study yet reported (Scarr *et al.*, 1977). They used biochemical methods based on blood samples to estimate racial ancestry in a sample of Minnesota schoolchildren and found no relationship between racial ancestry and IQ scores on any of the four separate tests that they used. These findings confirm those of Witty and Jenkins (1936). They suggest strongly that the IQ difference between black and white Americans does not stem from genetic causes.

4.2 Racial crossing studies

Racial crossing studies focus on black, white and mixed-race children who happen to be raised in similar environmental circumstances. If genetic factors are mainly responsible for the IQ difference between the races, then the white children should have higher average IQs than the mixed-race children, and the mixed-race children should have higher average IQs than the black children. If environmental factors are all-important, on the other hand, then black, mixed-race, and white children raised in similar circumstances should have similar average IQs.

The problem, of course, is to find children from the different race groups raised in truly similar environmental circumstances. The most obvious objection to this line of research is that it is difficult or impossible to raise black, white and mixed-race children in comparable environments because racism is itself an important environmental factor to which only the black and mixed-race children are likely to be exposed. If they score lower than the white children on IQ tests, critics of the research can always argue that the supposedly equal environments actually favoured the white children. Interestingly, this objection turns out to be beside the point because, when they are raised in similar circumstances, the black and mixed-race children do not, in fact, score lower than the white children. In all three racial crossing studies that have been published, children from the different racial groups were found to have remarkably similar average IQs. The results of these studies are shown in Table 7.6.

Table 7.6 Average IQ scores of black, mixed-race and white children raised in similar environments

| Study | Average IQ | | |
	Black	Mixed-race	White
Eyferth (1961)	—	96	97
Tizard *et al.* (1972)	107	106	103
	98	99	99
	106	110	101
Scarr and Weinberg (1976)	97	109	111

Note: The children in the Tizard *et al.* study were given three separate IQ tests.

The children in Eyferth's (1961) study were *Besatzungskinder* (occupation children), the illegitimate offspring of sexual liaisons between American occupation troops and German women after the Second World War. Some of their American fathers were black and some were white. All the children were raised by their white mothers in post-war Germany where anti-black prejudice was, and is, comparatively rare. The mixed-race children, who inherited half their genes from their black fathers, and the white children, whose genetic make-up was entirely white, differed by only a single point in average IQ.

Barbara Tizard and her colleagues (Tizard *et al.*, 1972) gave young children living in 'residential nurseries' in England three separate IQ tests. It is clear from Table 7.6 that the black and mixed-race children scored consistently *higher*, on average, than the white children, though the differences were very small and non-significant.

The third racial crossing study, carried out by Sandra Scarr and Richard Weinberg in the United States (Scarr and Weinberg, 1976), was the Minnesota inter-racial adoption study already discussed in a different context in Section 3.4. The black, mixed-race and white children in the study were all living in white adoptive homes. Scarr and Weinberg pointed out that the black children were not really raised in the same environmental circumstances as the others. They were adopted later in life and had less well educated adoptive parents than the mixed-race and white children. The mixed-race and white children were found to have very similar average IQs, but the black children scored 12 to 14 points lower, on average, than the other groups (see Table 7.6). Only the mixed-race and white children were raised in truly comparable environmental circumstances, according to the researchers, and the similar average IQs of these two groups suggest that environmental rather than genetic factors account for IQ differences between the races.

4.3 Test bias

Many people, especially non-psychologists, believe that it is hardly surprising that black people get lower average scores on IQ tests than white people. The reason they usually give is that the tests are probably biased. Let us examine this popular explanation a little more closely.

It is certainly true that most conventional IQ tests were constructed by white, middle-class, male psychologists, standardized on white samples, and validated by correlating their scores with tests of scholastic attainment in white schools. (The Wechsler scales, the British Ability Scales, and the newest version of the Stanford–Binet scale are exceptions: at least their standardization samples contained members of ethnic minorities.) But these facts, in themselves, do not prove that the tests are biased. The claim that IQ tests are biased, if it means anything intelligible, implies that they underestimate the true intelligence of black people.

It is not clear what this claim amounts to in the absence of any measure of true intelligence apart from IQ tests themselves. It might mean that IQ tests underestimate the ability of black people to excel at school examinations and other activities usually assumed to require intelligence. There is a great deal of evidence to show that IQ tests are not biased against black people in that sense. IQ tests predict scholastic attainment just as well for black as for white children in the United States (Jensen, 1980). In Britain also, two studies based on large, random samples of schoolchildren showed that IQ scores correlate highly with school tests of mathematics and reading ability among both West Indian and white 11-year-old children. If anything, the West Indian children do slightly *worse* on the school tests than their IQ scores suggest they should do (Mackintosh and Mascie-Taylor, 1985; Mackintosh 1986).

It could be argued that IQ tests are biased against black people in a different sense. Perhaps they fail to take account of various forms of educational and general environmental deprivation that cause black people to do badly in IQ tests *and also* in school examinations and all other activities requiring intelligence. This is a misleading argument. It is equivalent to saying that unemployment statistics are racially biased because they show that black people in Britain are twice as likely to be unemployed (or in the case of Pakistanis and Bangladeshis three times as likely) as white people.

Of course educational and general environmental deprivation adversely affect the development of intelligence. Poverty, overcrowding, poor housing and amenities, and similar environmental factors are all associated with relatively poor performance on IQ tests (Mascie-Taylor, 1984) and a disproportionate number of black people certainly grow up in educationally and environmentally deprived circumstances. It is these inequalities rather than any bias in the tests themselves which are responsible for this poor performance.

To avoid accusations of test bias, psychologists have constructed a number of **culture-fair tests** which depend to a minimum degree on information and language. Although no test is completely **culture-free**, some are clearly more cultural-fair than others. Raven's Progressive Matrices, which was decribed in Section 2.3, is the best known and most respected of the culture-fair tests. Perhaps surprisingly, the evidence shows that black people in the United States and Britain often perform worse on culture-fair tests than on culturally loaded tests such as the Mill Hill Vocabulary scale. Jensen interpreted this as further evidence that the black–white IQ gap is due mainly to genetic factors. He argued that, if the IQ gap is due to genetic influences, it should show up more markedly on culture-fair tests (Jensen, 1969, p. 81).

Three studies carried out independently in Britain cast doubt on this interpretation, and on the whole notion of culture-fairness. They all showed that Asian children who had recently immigrated into Britain scored badly on Raven's Progressive Matrices and on other supposedly culture-fair tests, but that those who had lived in Britain for several years scored as well as white children (Ashby, Morrison and Butcher, 1970; Sharma, 1971; Mackintosh and Mascie-Taylor, 1985). In all three studies, the Asian children's average IQ scores rose by 15 to 20 points after they had lived in Britain for 5 years, although their actual intelligence could hardly have changed so dramatically in such a short time. These findings decisively dispel the myth that Raven's Progressive Matrices and similar tests are even remotely culture-fair. They suggest, on the contrary, that people from certain cultural backgrounds are at a disadvantage on these tests until they learn new ways of approaching IQ tests.

4.4 Environmental influences on IQ

The National Child Development and Child Health and Education studies in Britain (Mackintosh and Mascie-Taylor, 1985; Mackintosh, 1986) investigated environmental factors such as father's occupation, family size, family income, and neighbourhood quality that might influence children's IQs. The researchers tried to match each West Indian child with a white child in similar environmental circumstances in order to see whether the IQ gap persisted when the environmental factors were equalized in this way. Some of the West Indian children were so deprived that the researchers could find no suitable white counterparts for them among more than 10,000 children randomly selected from the whole population for each study, but among the successfully matched pairs the IQ gap was indeed greatly reduced. In the National Child Development Study, an 11-point average difference between West Indian and white IQ scores decreased to a 5-point difference, and in the Child Health and Education study, a 9-point gap decreased to 3 points. Similar results have been reported in the United States and elsewhere. Blau (1981), for example, compared 500 white and 500 black American children and found that by statistically eliminating environmental factors, such as socio-economic status and family structure, the IQ gap was reduced from about 15 to 3 IQ points.

Do findings like these prove that black–white IQ differences are due to environmental rather than genetic factors? Unfortunately they do not, and to believe that they do is to commit the so-called *sociologist's fallacy* (Mackenzie, 1984). The reason is that the artificial suppression of environmental differences can obscure real genetic differences. To see this clearly, consider one environmental factor, socio-economic status, a little more closely. It is possible, *at least in principle*, that high intelligence helps people to get good jobs and salaries and may therefore partly determine socio-economic status. If this is so, then researchers who compare black–white pairs of similar socio-economic status, or equalize this environmental factor statistically, are bound to find smaller IQ differences between the races. Intelligent people, both black and white, would still end up in the higher-status jobs and less intelligent people, both black and white, would end up in lower-status jobs, so people of similar socio-economic status would tend to have similar IQs.

Black people in the United States and Britain undoubtedly score lower, on average, than white people on conventional IQ tests. It is worth noting that members of some ethnic minorities, such as Jews and Orientals (Chinese and Japanese), in the United States score higher, on average, than the general white population, and the same is probably true in Britain. Psychologists do not fully understand the reasons for any of these racial differences, although they seem to be due chiefly to environmental differences between the groups. The suggestion by Jensen, Eysenck and others that the differences are largely due to genetic factors seems hardly credible in the light of the evidence that has accumulated since the early 1970s, from racial admixture and racial crossing studies in particular.

Summary of Section 4

- Jensen and Eysenck have argued that average differences in IQ scores between members of different racial groups are due to genetic differences between the races.

- Findings from racial admixture and racial crossing studies show that black, white and mixed-race children brought up in similar environments have similar IQ scores.

- There is no evidence that IQ tests are biased against black people in Britain or the United States.

- Some of the environmental factors that cause black people to score lower on IQ tests than white people have been identified, but they are not fully understood.

5 | Cognitive styles

We have concentrated so far on differences in overall intelligence as measured by IQ tests. However, people differ from one another, not only in their overall levels of intellectual ability but also in the *way* they think. Different people tend to display distinctive styles in the way in which they think, remember, perceive and generally process information, and these are known as **cognitive styles**. These styles affect people's functioning in virtually all areas of their lives. Psychologists have discovered numerous cognitive styles which appear to be quite distinct from general intelligence. Research in this area deals with the *manner* in which people think rather than their *ability* to think. The various cognitive styles that have been identified relate to different *modes* of mental functioning rather than to different *levels* of mental ability.

Cognitive styles develop slowly and cannot easily be modified by experience or training (Messick, 1976; Morrison, 1988). They seem to be deeply rooted in personality structures, and some of them may even be biologically based (Witkin, 1976). Research into cognitive styles has its roots in cognitive psychology and personality theory. Most of the techniques used to investigate them are therefore based on the methods of experimental and clinical psychology, in contrast to the psychometric methods used in the study of intelligence. In Sections 5.1 and 5.2, two of the most important cognitive styles will be discussed: field dependence–independence and convergence–divergence.

5.1 Field dependence–independence

Field dependence–independence is a cognitive style discovered accidentally by the American psychologist Herman Witkin in 1949, which has been extensively studied since then (Witkin, 1949, 1976; Witkin *et al.*, 1972, 1974;

Hampson, 1982, chapter 2). In simple terms, people are **field dependent** if their thoughts and perceptions are strongly influenced by external factors (the 'field'), and they are **field independent** if their thoughts and perceptions depend mainly on internal cues. Many people are neither field dependent nor field independent but fall somewhere between these two extremes.

The most popular tests for measuring field dependence–independence are the rod and frame test, the rotating room test and the embedded figures test. The **rod and frame test** is conducted in a completely darkened room. The subject's task is to adjust a luminous rod to the vertical position within a tilted rectangular frame. All the subject can see is the rod surrounded by the tilted frame. Field-dependent people are strongly influenced by the tilted frame and tend to align the rod with it. Field-independent people, on the other hand, ignore the frame and concentrate instead on internal gravitational cues in judging when the rod is in the upright position.

In the **rotating room test** the subject sits on a pivoted chair in a tilted room and tries to adjust the chair to the upright. This test also produces marked individual differences. Astonishingly, some field-dependent people think that they are sitting upright when the chair is, in reality, tilted as much as 30 degrees from the vertical.

The **embedded figures test** appears superficially to be quite different from the other two tests, but it also measures field dependence–independence. In this test the subject tries to locate simple geometric figures embedded in a series of complex diagrams.

SAQ 12   Figure 7.5 presents a difficult item from the embedded figures test (Witkin *et al.*, 1971). The simple figure on the right is embedded in the complex diagram on the left. Can you see it and trace it out? It took Witkin's student subjects an average of 2 minutes 24 seconds to solve this puzzle correctly.

 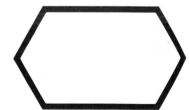

Figure 7.5 A difficult item from the embedded figures test
(Source: Witkin, 1950)

Field-dependent people are distracted by the overall complexity of the diagrams and have difficulty finding the embedded figures. Most field-independent people find the figures popping out of the diagrams without effort on their part.

In these three tests, the field-independent cognitive style is associated with superior peformance. Scores on all these tests correlate with one another: people who align the rod with the tilted frame also tend to align their bodies with the tilted room and have difficulty finding the embedded figures.

After decades of research into field-dependent and field-independent children and adults, it is clear that these cognitive style differences are associated with numerous other characteristics. Because they rely on their own internal cues, field-independent people are analytical and logical. They tend to gravitate towards occupations such as engineering, science teaching and experimental psychology, and they are often regarded by others as ambitious, inconsiderate and opportunistic. Field-dependent people, on the other hand, pay more attention to the environment and therefore excel at interpersonal relations. They are generally considered to be popular, friendly, warm and sensitive; they tend to prefer occupations such as social work, elementary school teaching and clinical psychology. Achievement in a particular occupation also relates to these cognitive style differences. In one study, for example, highly successful psychiatric nursing students were found to be much more field dependent than equally successful surgical nursing students, who tended to be field independent (Quinlan and Blatt, 1973).

Some researchers, notably the Canadian psychologist Philip Vernon (1972), have argued that field independence is merely an aspect of intelligence. Research has shown that field-independent people generally achieve higher, and field-dependent people lower, IQ scores on performance subtests of IQ tests such as the Wechsler scales. In other words, field independence and scores on these subtests are correlated. What is more, between the ages of about 5 and 17 years, people generally become increasingly field independent. This strengthens Vernon's claim that field independence is merely an aspect of intelligence, because intelligence also increases with age up to about 17 years.

Nevertheless, there are good reasons for believing that field independence is not equivalent to general intelligence. Girls and women, for instance, are generally found to be more field dependent than boys and men, although there is no evidence of any difference in general intelligence between the sexes. It is, in fact, field *dependence* which is associated with superior functioning in various kinds of situations involving social interaction. Field-dependent people have been found, for example, to be better than field-independent people at interpreting information from the social environment. They are better at attending to, decoding and remembering facial expressions and verbal messages concerned with social relations and attitudes (Witkin, 1976; Hampson, 1982). The evidence suggests that field-dependent people may be more socially intelligent than field-independent people, and that IQ tests fail to measure this kind of intelligence.

5.2 Convergence–divergence

Convergent thinking is a cognitive style characterized by a tendency to focus on a single best solution to a problem. Convergent thinkers are at their best when dealing with problems that have unique solutions. At the opposite extreme is the **divergent thinking** style, characterized by the fluent production of a variety of novel ideas relevant to the problem in hand. Divergent thinkers prefer, and perform better at, open-ended problems which do not have unique solutions. These cognitive styles, first identified and named by the American psychologist J.P. Guilford in the 1950s, have been investigated by Getzels and Jackson (1962), Wallach and Kogan (1965), Hudson (1966, 1968) and many others.

Convergent thinking is measured by conventional IQ test items which have unique correct answers (though you may think that the answer to SAQ 10, which involved the anagrams of boys' and girls' names, required a heap of 'divergent' imagination). Tests of divergent thinking tap more creative types of thinking. A typical item from a test to measure divergent thinking is the following: 'How many uses can you think of for a brick?' In his study of English schoolboys, Hudson (1966) found that many boys could think of only three or four answers in about 3 minutes, but most of those whom he identified as divergent thinkers gave ten or more answers. One of Hudson's divergent thinkers, for example, gave the following set of answers: 'To break windows for robbery, to determine the depth of wells, to use as ammunition, as pendulum, to practise carving, wall building, to demonstrate Archimedes' Principle, as part of abstract sculpture, cosh, ballast, weight for dropping things in river, etc., as a hammer, keep door open, footwiper, use as rubble for path filling, chock, weight on scale, to prop up wobbly table, paperweight, as firehearth, to block up rabbit hole'. Some other items from tests of divergent thinking are given in Box D.

BOX D   Some tests of divergent thinking

1   How many words can you think of ending in '-tion'?
2   How many words can you think of that mean roughly the same as 'hard'?
3   How many objects can you think of that are round and edible?
4   Suppose that people no longer needed or wanted to sleep. How many consequences of this can you think of?

(Adapted from Guilford, 1959)

Several interesting differences between convergent and divergent thinkers have been discovered. Hudson (1966, 1968) found that, even while they are still at school, convergers usually specialize in physical sciences, mathematics, or classics, hold conventional attitudes and opinions, pursue technical or mechanical interests in their spare time, and tend to be emotionally inhibited. Divergers, on the other hand, usually specialize in the arts or biology, hold unconventional attitudes and opinions, have spare-time interests involving interaction with other people, and tend to be emotionally uninhibited.

Some psychologists believe that divergent thinking is equivalent to creativity. It is certainly true that conventional IQ tests measure only convergent thinking and that, beyond an IQ of about 140, intelligence plays a negligible role in explaining the original contributions of creative people in various fields. It may also be true, though this is more controversial, that divergent thinking is a necessary component of creative ability. But scores on divergent thinking tests correlate only modestly with independent criteria of creative ability, such as critical acclaim among professional artists. There is more to creativity than divergent thinking. Personality characteristics such as a willingness to take risks, self-confidence, perseverance and curiosity no doubt play a part in creative achievement.

If divergent thinking is an essential prerequisite of exceptional intellectual performance, it is ironic that candidates for higher education are selected largely on the basis of their ability to do well in school examinations which, for the most part, tap only convergent thinking. It is worth remembering that many creative geniuses, including scientists like Albert Einstein, had undistinguished school records.

5.3 Concluding comments

Psychologists have identified numerous cognitive styles apart from the ones discussed in this section. Field dependence–independence has been investigated more thoroughly than any other cognitive style, but research into convergence–divergence has also contributed significantly to our understanding of individual differences, especially individual differences in thinking.

The psychometric approach to the study of intelligence, discussed in earlier sections, concentrates on individual differences in global intellectual ability as measured by IQ tests. The object of research into cognitive styles, on the other hand, is to describe and understand individual differences in people's manner of thinking rather than in their ability to think. Research into cognitive styles highlights the fact that there are important cognitive differences between people, apart from overall differences in intelligence.

Some recent critics have argued that field independence in particular, and cognitive styles in general, are simply specialized mental abilities (Morrison, 1988). The implication is that cognitive styles are really aspects of intelligence. It is certainly true that field-independent people are better than field-dependent people at ignoring external distractions when judging whether luminous rods or their own bodies are upright and when locating a simple figure embedded in a complex diagram. Field-independent people therefore perform better on these tests than field-dependent people. But there are situations requiring social skills and creative thinking in which the field-independent cognitive style could be a handicap rather than an advantage (Witkin, 1976; Hampson, 1982).

Although tests of cognitive styles inevitably appear to favour one particular cognitive style rather than its opposite, researchers have sometimes managed to devise alternative tests of the same cognitive styles in which the advantage is reversed. Whether or not this could be done with all cognitive styles is an open question.

Most of this chapter has focused on the psychometric approach, which assumes that IQ tests measure all important aspects of intelligence. IQ tests certainly seem to tap intellectual skills such as logical thinking and the ability to acquire information and to use it effectively. But there are arguments to suggest that a broader approach to intelligence might be useful. A recent theorist, Sternberg (1984), has emphasized the importance of analysing the underlying processes and skills that are required to do specific tasks. In his view, intelligence includes the ability to transfer skills to novel tasks and to execute mental operations rapidly, smoothly and effortlessly. Analysed in this way, the concept of intelligence is broadly applicable to performance on practical problems in everyday life as well as formal intelligence tests. In general, research into individuals' intelligence and cognitive styles has drawn attention to the *variety* of intellectual abilities and ways of thinking.

Summary of Section 5

- Cognitive styles refer to differences in people's manner of thinking rather than their overall level of intellectual ability.

- Field independence is characterized by the ability to make judgements based on internal cues. Field dependence involves more reliance on external factors.

- Convergent thinkers are best at logical thinking and solving problems with unique solutions. Divergers tend to produce a wide variety of novel ideas, and tend thus to perform better at problems which do not have unique solutions.

- Cognitive styles have advantages and disadvantages. People who score highly on field independence and convergence tend to do well on IQ tests. Divergers tend to be more intuitive and creative and, if they are also field dependent, are more likely to display social intelligence.

Further reading

The following two books contain excellent accounts of the history of intelligence testing. The second also explains the basic statistical ideas very clearly. They are both very well written:

FANCHER, R.E. (1985) *The intelligence men: makers of the IQ controversy*, New York, W.W. Norton.

GOULD, S.J. (1981) *The mismeasure of man*, New York: W.W. Norton.

For an orthodox account of psychometric approaches to intelligence, with masses of factual information clearly presented, you might refer to:

JENSEN, A.R. (1981) *Straight talk about mental tests*, London: Methuen.

A summary of the arguments and evidence on both sides of the nature–nurture debate is presented in the following book. The authors are leading figures in the debate representing opposite points of view:

EYSENCK, H.J. and KAMIN, L.J. (1981) *Intelligence: the battle for the mind*, London: Macmillan.

The main controversies surrounding intelligence and a few other issues in psychology are dealt with in:

COLMAN, A.M. (1987) *Facts, fallacies and frauds in psychology*, London: Hutchinson/Unwin Hyman.

The best general introductions to the study of cognitive styles are found in the following two books. The first contains contributions from leading researchers into cognitive styles. The second is an introductory textbook:

MESSICK, S. and Associates (1976) *Individuality in learning: implications of cognitive styles and creativity for human development*, San Francisco: Jossey-Bass.

GOLDSTEIN, K.M. and BLACKMAN, S. (1978) *Cognitive style: five approaches and relevant research*, New York: Wiley.

References

ALLPORT, G.W. and ODBERT, H.S. (1936) 'Trait-names: a psycho-lexical study', *Psychological Monographs*, vol. 47, whole no. 211.

ASHBY, B., MORRISON, A. and BUTCHER, H.J. (1970) 'The abilities and attainment of immigrant children', *Research in Education*, vol. 4, pp. 73–80.

BATES, P.B. and SCHAIE, K.W. (1976) 'On the plasticity of intelligence in adulthood and old age', *American Psychologist*, vol. 31, pp. 720–5.

BINET, A. (1909) *Les idées modernes sur les enfants*, Paris: Flammarion.

BLAU, Z.S. (1981) *Black children/white children: competence, socialization, and social structure*, New York: Free Press.

BURKS, B.S. (1928) 'The relative influence of nature and nurture upon mental development: a comparative study of foster parent–foster child resemblance and true parent–true child resemblance', *Yearbook of the National Society for the Study of Education* (Part 1), vol. 27, pp. 219–316.

BURT, C. (1955) 'The evidence for the concept of intelligence', *British Journal of Educational Psychology*, vol. 25, pp. 158–77.

BURT, C. (1958) 'The inheritance of mental ability', *American Psychologist*, vol. 13, pp. 1–15.

BURT, C. (1966) 'The genetic determination of intelligence: a study of monozygotic twins reared together and apart', *British Journal of Psychology*, vol. 57, pp. 137–53.

COLMAN, A.M. (1987) *Facts, fallacies and frauds in psychology*, London: Hutchinson/Unwin Hyman.

ELLIOTT, C.D. (1983) *British Ability Scales, manual 2: technical handbook*, Windsor: NFER-Nelson.

ERLENMEYER-KIMLING, L. and JARVIK, L.F. (1963) 'Genetics and intelligence: a review', *Science*, vol. 142, pp. 1477–9.

EYFERTH, K. (1961) 'Leistungen verschiedener Gruppen von Besatzungskinder in Hamburg: Wechsler Intelligenztest für Kinder (HAWIK)', *Archiv für gesamte Psychologie*, vol. 113, pp. 223–41.

EYSENCK, H.J. (1971) *Race, intelligence and education*, London: Temple Smith.

EYSENCK, H.J. and KAMIN, L.J. (1981) *Intelligence: the battle for the mind*, London: Macmillan.

FANCHER, R.E. (1985) *The intelligence men: makers of the IQ controversy*, New York: W.W. Norton.

FLYNN, J.R. (1987) 'Massive IQ gains in 14 nations: what IQ tests really measure', *Psychological Bulletin*, vol. 101, pp. 171–91.

GALTON, F. (1869) *Hereditary genius: an inquiry into its laws and consequences*, 2nd edn (reprinted 1978), London: Julian Friedmann.

GALTON, F. (1883) *Inquiries into the human faculty and its development*, London: Macmillan.

GETZELS, J.W. and JACKSON, P.W. (1962) *Creativity and intelligence: explorations with gifted children*, New York: Wiley.

GODDARD, H.H. (1913) 'The Binet tests in relation to immigration', *The Journal of Psycho-Asthenics*, vol. 18, pp. 105–7.

GOULD, S.J. (1981) *The mismeasure of man*, New York: W.W. Norton.

GUILFORD, J.P. (1959) 'Three faces of intellect', *American Psychologist*, vol. 14, pp. 469–79.

HAMPSON, S.E. (1982) *The construction of personality: an introduction*, London: Routledge and Kegan Paul.

HEARNSHAW, L.S. (1979) *Cyril Burt: psychologist*, London: Hodder and Stoughton.

HEATH, A., BERG, K., EAVES, L., SOLAAS, M., COREY, L., SUNDET, J., MAGUS, P. and NANCE, W. (1985) 'Education policy and the heritability of educational attainment', *Nature*, vol. 314, pp. 734–6.

HENDERSON, N. (1982) 'Human behavior genetics', *Annual Review of Psychology*, vol. 33, pp. 403–40.

HORN, J.M., LOEHLIN, J.C. and WILLERMAN, L. (1979) 'Intellectual resemblance among adoptive and biological relatives: the Texas Adoption Project', *Behavior Genetics*, vol. 9, pp. 177–207.

HUDSON, L. (1966) *Contrary imaginations: a psychological study of the English schoolboy*, London: Methuen.

HUDSON, L. (1968) *Frames of mind: ability, perception and self-perception in the arts and sciences*, London: Methuen.

JENSEN, A.R. (1969) 'How much can we boost IQ and scholastic achievement?', *Harvard Educational Review*, vol. 39, pp. 1–123.

JENSEN, A.R. (1980) *Bias in mental testing*, London: Methuen.

JUEL-NIELSEN, N. (1965) 'Individual and environment: a psychiatric–psychological investigation of monozygotic twins reared apart', *Acta Psychiatrica et Neurologica Scandinavica*, Monograph Supplement 183.

KAMIN, L.J. (1974) *The science and politics of I.Q.*, Harmondsworth: Penguin.

KNIGHT, I. (1984) *The heights and weights of adults in Great Britain*, London: Her Majesty's Stationery Office.

LEAHY, A.M. (1935) 'Nature–nurture and intelligence', *Genetic Psychology Monographs*, vol. 17, pp. 235–308.

LYNN, R. and HAMPSON, S. (1986) 'The rise of national intelligence: evidence from Britain, Japan, and the USA', *Personality and Individual Differences*, vol. 7, pp. 23–32.

MACKENZIE, B. (1984) 'Explaining race differences in IQ: the logic, the methodology, and the evidence', *American Psychologist*, vol. 39, pp. 1214–33.

MACKINTOSH, N.J. (1986) 'The biology of intelligence?', *British Journal of Psychology*, vol. 77, pp. 1–18.

MACKINTOSH, N.J. and MASCIE-TAYLOR, C.G.N. (1985) 'The IQ question', in *Report of Committee of Inquiry into Education of Children from Ethnic Minority Groups*, London: Her Majesty's Stationery Office, pp. 126–63.

MASCIE-TAYLOR, C.G.N. (1984) 'Biosocial correlates of IQ', in Chester, R. (ed.) *Proceedings of the Twelfth Annual Symposium of the Eugenics Society, London, 1983*, Driffield: Nafferton Books, pp. 99–127.

MESSICK, S. (1976) 'Personality consistencies in cognition and creativity', in Messick S. and Associates, *Individuality in learning: implications of cognitive styles and creativity for human development*, San Francisco: Jossey-Bass, pp. 4–33.

MILES, T.R. (1957) 'On defining intelligence', *British Journal of Educational Psychology*, vol. 27, pp. 153–65.

MORRISON, D.L. (1988) 'Predicting diagnosis performance with measures of cognitive style', *Current Psychology: Research and Reviews*, vol. 7, pp. 136–56.

NEWMAN, H.H., FREEMAN, F.N. and HOLZINGER, K.J. (1937) *Twins: a study of heredity and environment*, Chicago: University of Chicago Press.

PAUL, D.B. (1985) 'Textbook treatments of the genetics of intelligence', *Quarterly Review of Biology*, vol. 60, pp. 317–26.

QUINLAN, D.M. and BLATT, S.J. (1973) 'Field articulation and peformance under stress: differential prediction in surgical and psychiatric nursing training', *Journal of Consulting and Clinical Psychology*, vol. 39, p. 517.

RAVEN, J.C. COURT, J.H. and RAVEN, J. (1983) *Manual for Raven's Progressive Matrices and Vocabulary Scales. Section 3: standard progressive matrices*, London: H.K. Lewis.

REED, T.E. (1969) 'Caucasian genes in American Negroes', *Science*, vol. 165, pp. 762–8.

ROSE, S., KAMIN, L.J. and LEWONTIN, R.C. (1984) *Not in our genes: biology, ideology, and human nature*, Harmondsworth: Penguin.

SCARR, S. (1981) *Race, social class, and individual differences in IQ*, Hillsdale, NJ: Lawrence Erlbaum Associates.

SCARR, S., PAKSTIS, A.J., KATZ, S.H. and BARKER, W.B. (1977) 'Absence of a relationship between degree of white ancestry and intellectual skills within a black population', *Human Genetics*, vol. 39, pp. 69–86.

SCARR, S. and WEINBERG, R.A. (1976) 'IQ test performance of black children adopted by white families', *American Psychologist*, vol. 31, pp. 726–39.

SCARR, S. and WEINBERG, R.A. (1977) 'Intellectual similarities within families of both adopted and biological children', *Intelligence*, vol. 1, pp. 170–91.

SCHAIE, K.W. (1983) *Longitudinal studies of adult psychological development*, New York: Guilford.

SHARMA, R. (1971) Unpublished PhD thesis, cited in Mackintosh and Mascie-Taylor (1985).

SHIELDS, J. (1962) *Monozygotic twins brought up apart and brought up together*, Oxford: Oxford University Press.

SHUEY, A.M. (1966) *The testing of negro intelligence*, 2nd edn, New York: Social Sciences Press.

SKODAK, M. and SKEELS, H.M. (1949) 'A final follow-up study of one hundred adopted children', *Journal of Genetic Psychology*, vol. 75, pp. 85–125.

SPEARMAN, C. (1927) *The abilities of man*, London: Macmillan.

STERN, W. (1912) *Psychologische Methoden der Intelligenzprüfung*, Leipzig: Barth.

STERNBERG, R.J. (1984) in Anderson, J.R. and Kosslyn, S.M. (eds) *Tutorials in learning and memory*, San Francisco, CA: W.H. Freeman.

STERNBERG, R.J., CONWAY, B.E. and BERNSTEIN, M. (1981) 'People's conceptions of intelligence', *Journal of Personality and Social Psychology*, vol. 41, pp. 37–55.

TAMARIN, R.H. (1982) *Principles of genetics*, Boston, MA: Willard Grant Press.

TERMAN, L.M. (1916) *The measurement of intelligence*, Boston, MA: Houghton Mifflin.

THE PSYCHOLOGICAL CORPORATION (1974) *Wechsler Intelligence Scale for Children—revised*, Cleveland, OH: The Psychological Corporation.

THURSTONE, L.L. (1938) *Primary mental abilities*, Chicago: University of Chicago Press.

TIZARD, B., COOPERMAN, O., JOSEPH, A. and TIZARD, J. (1972) 'Environmental effects on language development: a study of young children in long-stay residential nurseries', *Child Development*, vol. 43, pp. 337–58.

VERNON, P.E. (1972) 'The distinctiveness of field dependence', *Journal of Personality*, vol. 40, pp. 366–91.

WALLACH, M.A. and KOGAN, N. (1965) *Models of thinking in young children*, New York: Holt, Rinehart and Winston.

WECHSLER, D. (1939) *The measurement of adult intelligence*, Baltimore, MD: Williams and Wilkins.

WECHSLER, D. (1981) *WAIS-R manual: Wechsler Adult Intelligence Scale—revised*, Cleveland, OH: The Psychological Corporation.

WISSLER, C. (1901) 'The correlation of mental and physical tests', *Psychological Review*, Monograph Supplement 3, no. 6.

WITKIN, H.A. (1949) 'The nature and importance of individual differences in perception', *Journal of Personality*, vol. 18, pp. 145–60.

WITKIN, H.A. (1950) 'Individual differences in ease of perception of embedded figures', *Journal of Personality*, vol. 19, pp. 1–15.

WITKIN, H.A. (1976) 'Cognitive style in academic performance and teacher–student relations', in Messick, S. and Associates, *Individuality in learning: implications of cognitive styles and creativity for human development*, San Francisco: Jossey-Bass, pp. 38–72.

WITKIN, H.A., DYK, R.B., FATERSON, H.F., GOODENOUGH, D.R. and KARP, S.A. (1974) *Psychological differentiation: studies of development*, Hillsdale, NJ: Lawrence Erlbaum Associates.

WITKIN, H.A., LEWIS, H.B., HERTZMAN, M., MACHOVER, K., MEISSNER, P.B. and WAPNER, S. (1972) *Personality through perception: an experimental and clinical study*, Westwood, CT: Greenwood Press.

WITKIN, H.A., OLTMAN, P.K., RASKIN, E. and KARP, S.A. (1971) *A manual for the ebedded figures test*, Palo Alto, CA: Consulting Psychologists Press.

WITTY, P.A. and JENKINS, M.D. (1936) 'Intra-race testing of Negro intelligence', *Journal of Psychology*, vol. 1, pp. 179–92.

Answers to SAQs

SAQ 1

(a) Moderately positive;

(b) highly positive;

(c) negative.

SAQ 2

About 10 minutes past 11.

SAQ 3

(a) They do not correlate with one another or with students' examination marks.

(b) Older children perform better on his tests than do younger children.

(c) Galton's tests measure sensory and motor functions; Binet's tests measure the ability to deal with problems intelligently.

SAQ 4

(a) Elizabeth: $\frac{4}{5} \times 100 = 80$; Andrew: $\frac{5}{5} \times 100 = 100$; William: $\frac{6}{5} \times 100 = 120$.

(b) Mark: $\frac{20}{20} \times 100 = 100$; Philip: $\frac{20}{40} \times 100 = 50$. This is absurd because there is no reason to believe that Philip's intelligence is below average. We would not think an adult of 40 mentally retarded just because he obtained the same score on an IQ test as a 20 year old.

SAQ 5

(a) 9;

(b) 2, i.e. scores of 8 and 9;

(c) 2;

(d) $0 + 2 + (2 \times 3) + (3 \times 4) + (5 \times 5) + (4 \times 6) + (2 \times 7) + 8 + 9 = 100, \div 20 = 5$.

SAQ 6

(a) 2.14%;

(b) 2.14%;

(c) $2.14\% + 13.59\% = 15.73\%$.

SAQ 7

(a) $80 = 3$ standard deviations above ($+3$ SD) the mean, i.e. $3 \times 15 = 45$ IQ points above 100; $100 + 45 = 145$ IQ points.

(b) $30 = -2$ SD $= 2 \times 15 = 30$ points below 100; $100 - 30 = 70$ IQ points.

(c) $70 = +2$ SD $= 2 \times 15 = 30$ points above 100; $100 + 30 = 130$ IQ points.

SAQ 8

(a) 0.81;

(b) 0.74 (you will have had to look down the Vocabulary column to find the correlation with Comprehension. The blank half of the matrix is a mirror image of the other half);

(c) 0.68;

(d) 0.63.

SAQ 9

Diagram number 6.

SAQ 10

(a) (ii) (there are two letters before C and after X in the alphabet, and there are five letters before F and after U).

(b) (ii) (the anagrams Olga, Rose, Ruth and Dawn are female names; Neil is a male name). We congratulate you if you got this one right!

(c) The missing number is 32 (the differences between adjacent numbers are 2, 6, 10, 14—that is, every other even number).

SAQ 11

Galton's critics pointed out that people with eminent relatives may be successful because of superior *nurture*, in the form of wealth, education and personal connections, rather than superior *nature*, in the form of hereditary factors.

SAQ 12

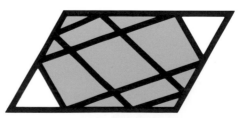

Figure 7.6 A difficult item from the embedded figures test with the embedded figure picked out
(Source: Witkin, 1950)

8

DIMENSIONS OF PERSONALITY

Kerry Thomas

Contents

1	**Personality and common sense**	**374**
1.1	Dispositions and consistency	375
1.2	Personality development and change	376
1.3	Unique individuals versus patterns of similarity	377
	Summary of Section 1	378
2	**Allport's trait theory**	**378**
2.1	Personality traits as the source of consistency	379
2.2	Whole people—a living synthesis	381
2.3	Focus on the present and on conciousness	381
	Summary of Section 2	383
3	**Eysenck's type theory of personality**	**383**
3.1	What is a personality type?	383
3.2	Eysenck's personality types	386
3.3	Eysenck's psychometric approach to personality types	388
3.4	The biological basis of Eysenck's typology	391
3.5	Experimental evidence for Eysenck's theory of personality types	393
3.6	The elaboration of Eysenck's types in the social world	394
	Summary of Section 3	396
4	**Kelly's personal construct theory**	**397**
4.1	People as 'scientists'	397
4.2	Personal constructs	397
4.3	The repertory grid	398
4.4	Properties of constructs and construct systems	401
4.5	What does Kelly mean by personality change?	403
	Summary of Section 4	406
5	**Different ways of understanding personality**	**406**
5.1	Testability: idiographic and nomothetic	407
5.2	Personality and motivation	409
5.3	Experience and consciousness	410
5.4	Consistency in behaviour	410
	Summary of Section 5	412
	Further reading	412
	References	413
	Answers to SAQs	414

1 | Personality and common sense

The idea of personality is a most intriguing concept for many of us, in western culture at least. We have a long literary tradition which in one way or another is concerned with describing, analysing and understanding what people are like, and how their personalities affect their lives. Everyday language is full of adjectives and phrases which refer to personality characteristics and to the assumptions we make about what personality is. We will start with some commonsense assumptions and use them to illustrate what psychologists' theories attempt to formalize.

In everyday life we talk about famous 'personalities' of stage and screen; we are all familiar with 'strong' personalities and 'weak' ones. We read about politicians with 'real' personalities, those who can charismatically 'project' their personalities. We know people 'without personality' and some with personality problems. And we may have read about those with multiple personalities. We believe that our children go through stages of personality development; we encourage personality growth and are ambivalent about the possibility of personality change. We readily classify people about whom we know very little using a descriptive, often pejorative, shorthand of personality called a **stereotype**. Examples of stereotypes are: 'redheads have quick tempers', or 'Scotsmen are mean with money'. We confidently make intuitive predictions about the behaviour and intentions of our friends and colleagues using 'commonsense' personality theories. We often do this by describing people in terms of personality characteristics called personality traits. Employers' references are good examples of this:

Ms Smith is a resourceful manager. She is without question honest and dependable, tactful and courteous in dealing with staff at all levels, and forthright in making her views known on issues of substance. She is justifiably ambitious, but perhaps too liable to act without consulting other interested parties . . .

The theories about others that we carry around with us are called **implicit personality theories** (or naïve personality theories). The activities which follow will remind you how much we all use these implicit theories of personality in everyday life.

ACTIVITY 1

Write out a description of the personality of one person you know well, and also of one or two people you know only slightly. Limit yourself to two or three minutes on each description.

In Activity 1, it is likely that you described your friends and acquaintances in terms of **personality traits** such as 'warm', 'friendly', 'trustworthy', 'not-very-academic', 'sporty', and perhaps as personality types like 'introverted, intellectual type' or 'beefy, sports type'. The odds are that you described the person you know well in terms of several trait labels, which confer on him or her quite a degree of individuality. For those that you know less well, it is more likely that you put them into broader categories that represent personality types, or even stereotypes. This may reflect the fact that you have less information about them and are going beyond any information you do have. It may also reflect a useful process of arriving at a simple, overall description that has some worthwhile predictive value. Even if you only know enough about a person to stereotype him as an unsociable, introverted type, this type label might mean that you don't waste time inviting him to join a noisy group to go to a football match.

ACTIVITY 2

The list of personality characteristics below is a combination of trait labels from descriptions of two real people. See if you can sort them out to form two characteristic trait profiles each consisting of five trait labels. In other words, which five are likely to go together? Does this leave five that also go together?

(a) impervious; (b) independent; (c) confident; (d) introvert; (e) witty; (f) secretive; (g) outgoing; (h) selfish; (i) arrogant; (j) alert.

You were probably able at least to start grouping these traits into personality types without knowing whose personality was being described. This demonstrates that in everyday life we do use trait and type theories; we are aware that not all combinations of traits are equally likely. (The original descriptions were: (a), (d), (f), (h), (i) and (b), (c), (e), (g), (j).) According to our implicit personality theories we do not expect that someone we think of as being jolly, outgoing and intelligent will also be cold. Nor do we expect someone who is shy, quiet and studious to be aggressive.

The clustering of personality characteristics in implicit personality theory extends beyond behavioural characteristics. 'Opinionated' or 'dogmatic' are personality trait words, but the actual *content* of people's systems of beliefs and feelings about the world (i.e. their attitudes) also seem to be part of our implicit theories about other people. We have stereotyped expectations about attitudes and beliefs that go together. Who expects a 'hanger and flogger' to be pro-abortion or a member of the Campaign for Nuclear Disarmament, or to be a person who is always open to new ideas?

What are the assumptions about personality that the person in the street uses and that psychologists might try to understand, explain and perhaps improve upon?

1.1 Dispositions and consistency

First, it is clear from most of our ordinary language that we think of personality as something that belongs to each of us. It is something that each of us has somewhere inside, just as we have stomachs, lungs and livers. It is this feature that enables all of us to use 'personality', or personality type, or personality traits (such as friendly, sociable, honest) to explain *why* someone is *consistent* in his or her behaviour across many different situations and over quite long periods of time. The idea that our personalities *dispose* us to act in certain, consistent ways seems to be fundamental to almost all theories of personality. This leads to the notion of **disposition** in both commonsense theories and in formal theories put forward by psychologists. Without this underlying idea of consistency, the idea of personality seems to vanish, leaving people's behaviour unpredictable and perhaps no more than a reaction to the situations they find themselves in.

Some formal theories attempt to identify the basic cause of personality; in other words, what it is that gives rise to consistency in a person's behaviour. Perhaps it is biological and innately determined by our genetic make-up. Alternatively it might be something learned as part of social development which then provides a particular way of viewing the world. As we saw in Chapter 4, Freud accounts for consistencies in behaviour with the notion of an inner organization of id, ego and super-ego which mediate the conflict between biology (inherited patterns of instincts) and society (the child's social environment). For Freud, this results in the development of broad classes of personality types (oral, anal etc.). Other theorists use the concept of the personality trait to account for the underlying consistency in personality.

However, there is an approach to personality theory which questions whether personality *is* something that resides in each of us. Some psychologists believe that our behaviour is largely influenced by the situations in which we find ourselves and that what we believe to be consistent behaviour is the result of social norms and roles. Some would add to this the possibility that we make conscious attempts to *appear* consistent. We shall return to this in Section 5.

1.2 Personality development and change

Ordinary language shows that we think of personality as something that is both relatively unchangeable *and* open to some development. Most of us can tell stories about people who seem to have had the same temperament 'from the day they were born'. There is now considerable evidence that some characteristics, such as emotionality, activity, sociability and energy level, appear early and are especially consistent and difficult to alter (Buss and Plomin, 1984). But it is also commonplace to hear of people who have changed their personalities dramatically, seemingly through their own efforts or perhaps by undergoing therapy.

Just as commonsense views of personality vary, psychologists' theories also differ about whether personality is present from birth and is basically inherited, or whether it develops gradually throughout childhood, and perhaps beyond. They also consider how personality might develop, and when it crystallizes. Some personality theories make the issue of change central, others pay little or no attention to it.

The term 'personality', in ordinary usage, often carries value judgements and implications about the health and mental stability of the individual. Formal personality theories differ in the emphasis they put on clinical aspects. Some, as we saw in the work of Freud in Chapter 4, are based on people who have some degree of mental disorder. Other theorists believe that the study of personality should begin with *normal* individuals. Yet other theories, some of which you will meet in the next chapter (Chapter 9) on humanistic psychology, go beyond normality and concentrate on the enrichment of personality, and the pursuit of well-being and happiness.

1.3 Unique individuals versus patterns of similarity

In everyday life we tend to use the word 'personality' in two distinct ways. We use the notion of personality to emphasize the integration, consistency, and uniqueness of a whole individual. However, we also use the idea of personality to emphasize dimensions of similarity and difference between people. In this latter case, the focus is on *aspects* of people's behaviour, rather than on the uniqueness of a whole individual. We do this when we categorize people into broad types or when we compare people according to certain traits; for example, some people are very optimistic, some are slightly optimistic, and some are pessimistic. However, a statement like this leaves a great deal about the whole personality of each person unsaid.

Psychologists' theories also can be divided into two basic approaches. It is possible to focus on exploring the behaviour, experiences, feelings and lives of *whole individuals* in depth. This is called the **idiographic approach**. Because this approach is concerned with the personality of individuals, it is considered neither desirable nor possible to make generalizations about how people's personalities differ.

On the other hand, people can be *systematically* ranked or ordered on the basis of personality traits such as optimistic–pessimistic, or emotional–stable. If the extent to which people possess these traits can be *measured*, then there is the possibility of carrying out complex comparisons of individual differences. This is the realm of **psychometrics** (mental measurements). As we saw in Chapter 7, psychometrics has led to the development of intelligence tests. Personality can also be studied in this way, using tests and questionnaires to measure aspects of personality. Psychologists use psychometric methods to describe and predict the behaviour of people *in general* in order to arrive at general laws of behaviour. This is called the **nomothetic approach** to personality. Psychologists' nomothetic theories of personality have to be stated clearly enough to be evaluated in terms of tests and evidence.

This rest of this chapter describes three theories that have been chosen to illustrate different aspects of personality theory and different ways of going about the study of personality. The first theory, that of Gordon Allport (1897–1967), is an idiographic theory, in which the consistency of each individual's behaviour is explained by the concept of the personality trait. The second theory, that of Hans Jürgen Eysenck (born 1916) is a nomothetic theory which uses psychometric methods to order people on dimensions of personality, notably extraversion–introversion. Eysenck's theory concentrates on the similarities and differences between people, and the basic source of consistency in behaviour is the personality type. The third theory is that of George Kelly (1905–66). This is essentially an idiographic approach to the way in which unique individuals view and make sense of their worlds. You will see, though, that it is not always easy to categorize theories as wholly idiographic or nomothetic.

Summary of Section 1

- Everyone has commonsense theories of personality. These are called implicit personality theories. They tend to describe people in terms of personality traits, personality types and stereotypes.

- Personality, both in commonsense and in formal psychological theories, usually depends on the notion of consistency of behaviour, over time and in similar situations.

- Psychological theories of personality are concerned with such issues as whether personality is inherited; or whether it develops gradually during childhood; and whether it can be changed in later life. Some theories approach personality from the perspective of abnormal psychology and some are more concerned with the normal person.

- The idiographic approach to personality studies unique individuals in depth, often drawing directly on people's inner experiences.

- The nomothetic approach to personality aims for general rules about personality through the systematic study of similarities and differences between people. It often uses psychometric methods; that is, measurement of personality characteristics.

2 | Allport's trait theory

Allport published *Personality: a psychological interpretation* in the USA in 1937. It was one of the first theories of personality outside the clinical and psychodynamic Freudian traditions, and it was a reaction against the stress on the past, on unconscious motivation and abnormal personality. Allport also stepped outside the nomothetic assumptions of the behaviourist and experimental approaches to psychology current at the time. He stated that the experience of unique, normal, human adults should be at the centre of the study of personality. Personality theories should *not* be built on observations and speculations about children, neurotics or animals: 'Some theories . . . are based largely upon the behaviour of sick and anxious people or upon the antics of captive and desperate rats. Fewer theories have derived from the study of healthy human beings, those who strive not so much to preserve life as to make it worth living' (Allport, 1955, p. 21).

In his book, Allport reviewed about fifty definitions of personality and arrived at his own version (updated in 1961): 'Personality is the dynamic organization within the individual of those psychophysical systems that determine his characteristic behaviour and thought' (Allport, 1937 and 1961, p. 28). The building blocks of his theory are personality traits. Later in his work on personality, Allport listed what he believed to be the requirements of a good theory of personality (1960). Several of these are used here to present an outline of his work.

2.1 Personality traits as the source of consistency

Allport believed that the first requirement of a good theory of personality is that personality should be thought of as *contained within the person*. By this he meant that personality should not be explained in terms of social roles or the influence of environmental situations. His own theory is built around the concept of **personality traits** which he saw as the source of consistency in human behaviour. Personality traits are also responsible for differences between people in how they respond to the same situation: 'The same fire that melts the butter hardens the egg' (Allport, 1937, p. 102).

According to Allport, the structure of personality is made up of inner, personal dispositions which determine behaviour, called **traits**. He believed that traits exist as actual entities: 'A trait . . . is independent of the observer, it is really there. . . . There are . . . mental structures in each personality that account for the consistency of behaviour' (Allport, 1937, p. 289).

How do traits determine behaviour? Allport defined a trait as a mental structure which could 'render many stimuli functionally equivalent and initiate and guide equivalent forms of adaptive and expressive behaviour' (ibid, p. 295). This can be seen in Figure 8.1 which shows how having the trait of friendliness disposes a person to see a range of situations (stimuli) as ones in which 'sociable' responses are likely to be relevant and appropriate. Depending on the precise situation, the trait will result in similar but not identical responses. The adjectives that describe the behaviours (e.g. outgoing, helpful, warm, attentive), are all characteristic of an underlying, unifying trait, identified as friendliness (or sociability).

Figure 8.1 The trait of friendliness unifying several situations (stimuli) and responses

Because Allport placed great value on the commonsense view of personality, he started his search for personality traits with the English language. He and his assistant searched through a dictionary and found nearly 18 000 adjectives which describe people's personality characteristics (Allport and Odbert, 1936). Each adjective like 'cheerful', 'fastidious', 'lazy', 'mean' and 'honest' describes an *aspect* of an individual's personality but does not attempt to sum up the *whole* of it. He referred to these adjectives as **trait labels**.

Since there are potentially so many traits, how many make up an individual's personality? Allport believed that there are relatively few basic traits that interact with each other to produce the enormous variation we actually see in people's behaviour. He assumed that people's personalities are influenced by their most important personality traits. The most important and most general traits are called **cardinal traits**; these are all-pervasive, determining principles. For example, some people's lives seem to be built around competitiveness and success, and here the cardinal trait might be achievement. In others, lifelong selflessness and devotion to others and to duty might be a cardinal trait—Florence Nightingale is the example often quoted. However, few people have lives like this, organized around a single, clear, outstanding cardinal trait. Allport suggested that personalities of this kind are relatively rare.

At a less general level are **central traits**. These are the basic dispositions that characterize an individual. Allport suggested that there are rather fewer of these than one might expect, perhaps between five and ten. For example, if a person could be described as energetic, busy, friendly, reliable and competent, these would be his central traits. **Secondary dispositions** are less general, less consistent and not so easy to observe. They are more like specific idiosyncrasies, such as the range of a person's preferences. They are closer to, but not quite as specific as, habits or attitudes.

How is it possible to discover a person's traits? Allport believed that traits could be observed indirectly through the *frequency* with which a person displays a particular kind of behaviour, the *range of situations* in which broadly the same kind of behaviour occurs, and the *intensity* of the preferred mode of responding. He also recommended the use of interviewing people, asking them directly about themselves and their plans and intentions. And he also suggested using documents, letters and diaries as a source of evidence.

Allport carried out a famous idiographic study of a woman called Jenny on the basis of her many letters to a friend, written over a period of eleven years. He asked thirty-six trained 'judges' to rate the letters for evidence of specific central personality traits. The work started with 198 trait names, but eventually Allport thought that Jenny's personality was described accurately in terms of just eight central traits: quarrelsome/suspicious, self-centred, independent, dramatic, artistic, aggressive, cynical, and sentimental. The research was published as *Letters from Jenny* (Allport, 1965) and it is a very good example of the idiographic approach. Allport was concerned with describing the whole personality of a single individual.

According to Allport, traits are not fully present at birth but develop as the result of learning in a complex environment. Nevertheless, he thought that physique (body type), temperament (innate emotional disposition) and intelligence are the inherited raw materials from which the individual's traits develop in interaction with the environment.

This description of the role of traits in Allport's theory of personality provides a sketch of what he considers to be the basic source of consistent behaviour. However, to appreciate his work it is necessary to put the trait concept into the context of his whole theory. The main value of his theory is its comprehensive account of what he sees as the psychological functioning of the *whole person*.

2.2 Whole people—a living synthesis

Allport's second requirement for a personality theory was an emphasis on the *whole* personality of individuals. As mentioned earlier, he began working in the 1930s when the *scientific* study of psychology, particularly in the form of behaviourism, was becoming a crusade (see Chapter 6). The move to a scientific approach, in all fields of psychology led to the study of aspects of people's behaviour (e.g. how they learn responses) rather than whole functioning individuals. This approach is based on the argument that human beings are so complex that psychologists have to focus on particular psychological processes, like learning, IQ or memory, and this is the only way of arriving at general laws to explain behaviour. Allport believed strongly that the psychological study of personality should not lose sight of the whole, unique person in the service of pursuing scientific generalizations. He considered that any attempt to understand personality by measuring isolated aspects of personality on rating scales was mistaken unless these measures could be recombined to give a sense of the whole person—a living synthesis.

Allport believed that his use of the concept of trait permitted a living synthesis. Although the study of traits focuses on individual *aspects* of people, traits can be recombined to give a sense of the *whole* person. Allport's personality theory aims to provide a detailed description of individuals rather than comparisons between limited aspects of their personalities. The theory does not set out to make predictions about what people in general will do. It is essentially idiographic.

2.3 Focus on the present and on consciousness

Allport's third and fourth requirements of a good personality theory were that it should explain behaviour in terms of the present motives and intentions of the individual rather than in terms of the past; and that conscious intentions, directed by the 'self', should be at the centre of the theory. Although personality may be the result of an interaction between genetic dispositions and social learning, it is the *here and now* that is important for understanding the personality of the whole individual. It is the current mixture of personality traits that determines behaviour.

Again this is at odds with the dominant traditions that preceded Allport. Probably the most important contribution to personality up until the 1930s came from the psychodynamic approach, particularly the work of Freud. There is a revealing anecdote about an interview Allport had, in his early twenties, with Freud in Vienna (see Extract A). This encounter could have been the reason that Allport became strongly anti-psychodynamic.

EXTRACT A Allport's encounter with Freud

[Freud] did not speak to me but sat in expectant silence for me to state my mission. I was not prepared for silence and had to think fast to find a suitable conversational gambit. I told him of an episode on the tramcar on my way to his office. A small boy about four years of age had displayed a conspicuous dirt phobia. He kept saying to his mother, 'I don't want to sit there . . . don't let that dirty man sit beside me.' To him everything was schmutzig [filthy]. His mother was a well-starched Housefrau, so dominant and purposive looking that I thought the cause and effect apparent.

When I had finished my story Freud fixed his kindly therapeutic eyes on me and said, 'And that little boy was you?' Flabbergasted and feeling a bit guilty, I contrived to change the subject. While Freud's misunderstanding of my motivation was amusing, it also started a deep train of thought. I realized that he was accustomed to neurotic defenses and that my manifest motivation (a sort of rude curiosity and youthful ambition) escaped him. For therapeutic progress he would have to cut through my defenses, but it so happened that therapeutic progress was not here an issue.

(Allport, 1968, pp. 383–4)

In contrast to Freud's emphasis on unconscious determinants, Allport's theory of personality focuses on *conscious* motivation. Motivation and feelings as experienced in the present, rather than as energy from the past, are responsible for behaviour. Allport believed that the psychodynamic theorists had 'a kind of contempt for the "psychic surface" of life. The individual's conscious report is rejected as untrustworthy, and the contemporary thrust of his motives is disregarded in favour of a backward tracing of his conduct to earlier formative stages' (Allport, 1960, p. 96). 'When we set out to study a person's motives, we are seeking to find out what that person is trying to do in this life—including, of course, what he is trying to avoid and what he is trying to be. I see no reason why we should not start our investigation by asking him to tell us the answers as he sees them' (Allport, 1960, p. 101). This quotation illustrates how Allport stressed the determinant role of conscious thought and planning, and the belief he had in the reliability of people's statements about their motivations.

Because of his emphasis on the here and now, Allport believed that personality is always *growing*, becoming something different. He believed that the driving force of behaviour should be in the present, avoiding the possibility of stagnation in outdated childhood motives. Thus 'a student who first undertakes a field of study in college because it is required, because it pleases his parents, or because it comes at a convenient hour may end finding himself absorbed in the topic, perhaps for life. The original motives may be entirely lost. What was a means to an end becomes an end in itself' (Allport, 1961, p. 235). As people develop, their motivations become stabilized and **functionally autonomous**. This is an important concept in Allport's theory. It means that, in the adult, earlier sources of motivation come to have a current meaning in that goals are chosen in terms of their congruity with a person's self-image, self-identity, and desire for growth.

In Allport's terminology the self is called the **proprium**. His theory describes how the proprium develops during childhood. This focus on the self (proprium) is similar to that of Mead (see Chapter 2, Section 3). However, Allport was particularly concerned with how people *consciously experience* their lives. This is yet another example of how Allport's work was different from the psychology of his time. He believed that personality, whilst always organized, is also always changing and adapting in the course of learning and psychological growth. Some of these ideas were taken up by later psychologists working within the humanistic tradition (see Chapter 9).

Summary of Section 2

- Personality traits are the building blocks of Allport's theory. They are mental structures that give rise to consistency in behaviour. Cardinal traits and central traits are particularly important in accounting for an individual's personality.

- Allport's trait theory centres on the whole personality of healthy individuals. It is an example of the idiographic approach.

- He believed that the study of personality should focus on individuals' present motives and conscious experiences rather than the unconscious motivational effects of the past, as in Freud's work.

- According to Allport, personality is always growing and has the potential of becoming something different.

3 | Eysenck's type theory of personality

Just as we all use a naïve personality theory based on individual personality traits, we also seem to find categorizing people into broader types almost irresistible. Indeed it may be that there is some benefit in this for simplifying the social world. From ancient times in both East and West there have been systems for typing people on the basis of their astrological birth signs. These have a strong element of predestination—people become the types they were born to be. The ideas that personality is inherited and is based on biological structures have remained in type theories in various modified ways.

The work of the British psychologist, H.J. Eysenck, is a modern type theory notable for the breadth of its scope. It is based on the idea that types of personality are distinguished by fundamental differences in their nervous systems, differences which are probably inherited. Eysenck attempts to understand the causes of behaviour, ranging from specific habits to value systems and political ideology. And the neurophysiological basis of the theory provides it with a unique capacity for testing the hypotheses it generates using experimental methods.

3.1 What is a personality type?

In the West, personality types first appeared in Greek culture, perhaps originating with Hippocrates in the fourth century BC. The idea was developed later, in the second century AD, by Galen. Galen's typology linked four personality types with the relative dominance of one of four body fluids—blood, phlegm, yellow bile and black bile. A **sanguine** person was thought of as particularly energetic, a **phlegmatic** person as sluggish, apathetic and relatively unreactive, a **choleric** person was characterized as irritable, and a **melancholic** person was depressive. These four types are descriptions of what we would call **temperaments**, that is stable general features of personality that may well have their origins in biology, and are present, to some degree, at birth or very soon after (Buss and Plomin, 1984).

Many of the early theories of personality types, whether based on folk wisdom or early empirical studies, made use of the idea that personality is related to some quality of the nervous system and/or physical build. Thus Kretschmer (1925) discovered a systematic correlation between people's physical build and the propensity to develop certain psychiatric disorders. Sheldon (1940) worked out a threefold typology of temperament related to physique. Here we find the short, fat, jolly person and the tall, thin thinker, with the muscular, energetic, assertive athlete somewhere in between. These are undoubtedly stereotypes, but Sheldon carried out extensive measurements of physique and ratings of temperament and life preferences to arrive at this scheme.

Type theories start from the position that it is the personality type to which an individual belongs which is of primary importance. It is from these basic types that secondary characteristics (traits and more specific behaviours) follow, more or less inevitably. Type theories stress the importance in the causation of personality of a small number of processes, stages or structures internal to the individual. But this does not necessarily mean that we have to put people into a very small number of pigeon-holes representing 'pure' types.

As Kretschmer wrote, 'the concept of type is the most fundamental concept of all biology. Nature . . . does not work with sharp contrasts and precise definitions . . . fluid transitions are the rule [but] groupings arise which we encounter again and again; when we study them objectively, we realize that we are dealing here with the focal-points of frequently occurring groups of characteristics, concentrations of correlated traits' (Kretchmer, 1948). Thus the idea of a typology still permits plenty of room for individual variation. The extremes are the pure types, but there is also a range of other possible clusters of characteristics under the broad umbrella of a type. For example, a few individuals may seem to be excessively withdrawn or extravagantly outgoing, but most people fall somewhere in between these two extremes.

Thus to understand what is implied by a typology we need to consider, not only the descriptions of 'pure' types, but also the **personality dimensions** on which people vary. For example, returning to Sheldon's stereotypical 'short, fat, jolly person' versus his 'tall, lean, thinker', we can see that these types are examples of individuals who can be placed at the extremes of certain physical and psychological dimensions.

SAQ 1   (*SAQ answers are given at the end of the chapter*) What are the dimensions (or principles) that Sheldon uses to distinguish between these two 'types'?

Eysenck's type theory is based on three personality dimensions: extraversion–introversion, neuroticism–stability, and psychoticism. (This third dimension, psychoticism, is less well researched than the others and will not be discussed in this chapter.) Just as with Sheldon's stereotypes, Eysenck's 'pure' types are the people who are extremely extraverted or introverted. In other words, they are placed at either extreme of the **extraversion–introversion dimension**. Similarly, some individuals are extremely neurotic or stable, with the majority of people having intermediate positions on the **neuroticism–stability dimension**.

Eysenck used the two main personality dimensions of extraversion–introversion and neuroticism–stability together to chart four 'pure' personality types. In Figure 8.2, the two personality dimensions form a cross, with neuroticism–stability as the vertical axis and extraversion–introversion as the horizontal axis. Depending on their scores on these two dimensions, each individual can be placed in relation to the dimensions. At the extremes are people with very high or very low scores. Those who score very highly on both neuroticism and extraversion fall into the personality type of neurotic extravert. Because they score highly on *both* dimensions they are placed between the two dimensions. Other extremes are neurotic introverts, stable extraverts and stable introverts. As shown in Figure 8.2, most average people fall somewhere in the middle, without extreme scores on either dimension.

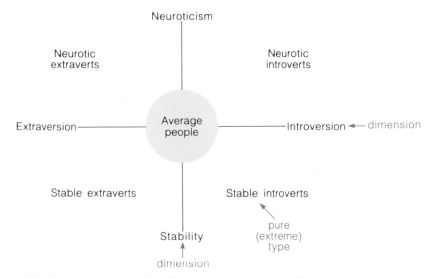

Figure 8.2 Eysenck's personality dimensions and personality types

SAQ 2   Which of the four extreme personality types would have high scores on both introversion and neuroticism?

3.2 Eysenck's personality types

According to Eysenck, it is a person's type that brings about consistencies in behaviour and thereby gives rise to his or her personality. The type to which a person belongs is the result of that person's position on the extraversion–introversion and neuroticism–stability dimensions. Eysenck suggests that the structure of personality consists of a **hierarchy** of levels (see the example for introversion in Figure 8.3). A person's type determines his or her personality traits, these traits determine habitual responses, and these habits, in turn, determine specific responses.

The trait clusters that Eysenck associates with extraversion and with neuroticism are shown in Figures 8.4 and 8.5. Note that neuroticism, as Eysenck uses the term, is not the same as neurotic as used by Freud. In Freud's work neurotic is a clinical or subclinical state resulting from unresolved conflicts between the impulses of the id, usually sexual, and the constraints of the super-ego and reality. For Eysenck, neuroticism is a personality dimension based on the relative stability or instability of the nervous system.

Where have Eysenck's ideas about personality types come from? What is the evidence for the clusters of traits associated with types like introvert, extravert and neurotic?

First, Eysenck's theory is built upon a long, historical tradition of typing personality in terms of different kinds of nervous system. One of the first experimental psychologists, Wundt, suggested that Galen's fourfold typology—sanguine, phlegmatic, choleric and melancholic—could be thought of as the interaction of two dimensions, each representing a different aspect of *nervous system activity*. He suggested that the nervous system could vary in reactiveness: quick versus slow and strong versus weak.

Eysenck's neuroticism–stability dimension and his extraversion–introversion dimension are similar, respectively, to the slow/quick and strong/weak

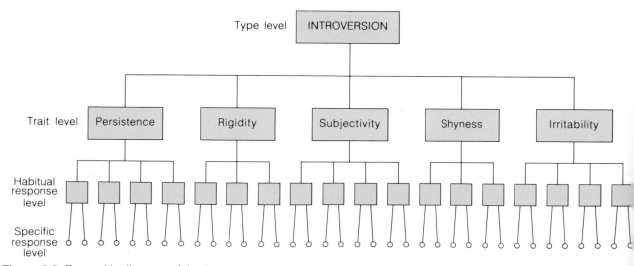

Figure 8.3 Eysenck's diagram of the hierarchical organization of personality

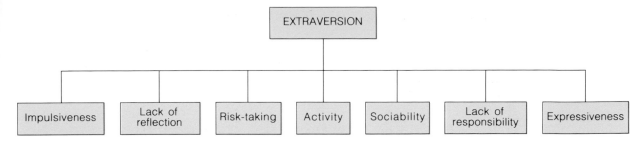

Figure 8.4 Personality traits associated with extraversion

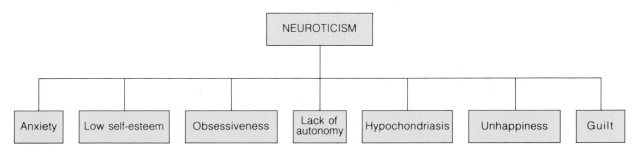

Figure 8.5 Personality traits associated with neuroticism

dimensions of earlier theorists. As we shall see below, Eysenck's particular contribution is that he has found a basis for these dimensions in modern scientific knowledge about the neurophysiology of the nervous system.

Second, Eysenck draws on the work of the psychiatrist and psychodynamic theorist Jung. Jung's typology was based on his own detailed clinical observations. He differentiated people into types on the basis of the way they deal with the outside world. Jung suggested a twofold division of people into introverts and extraverts. (Within each of these categories he also divided people into those whose best developed 'psychological function' is either thinking, feeling, sensing or intuiting.) The extravert 'goes out to meet stimulation'. 'The earliest sign of extraversion in a child is his quick adapatation to the environment, and the extraordinary attention he gives to objects and especially to the effect he has on them' (Jung, 1923, para. 896). The introvert, in contrast, characteristically steps back from new situations, taking an extra moment or two to ponder; he or she almost never unequivocally welcomes newness, but after initial hesitation tends to take in the stimulation in terms of his or her own subjectivity. 'Very early there appears a tendency to assert himself over familiar objects, and attempts are made to master them . . . when he asks questions it is not from curiosity or from a desire to create a sensation, but because he wants names, meanings, explanations to give him subjective protection against the object' (ibid., para. 897). Jung saw both these stances as habitual ways of relating to the world, each of which has its own advantages and disadvantages. However, Jung emphasized that, although types exist, the vast majority of people are not 'pure' types and that people vary on continuous dimensions.

Third, over many years, Eysenck and his co-workers have collected empirical evidence of differences between people in their everyday behaviour and feelings. Eysenck has developed questionnaires in which people can give self-reports of their behaviour, preferences and thoughts. The data collected from these questionnaires provide the basis for Eysenck's psychometric approach to personality.

3.3 Eysenck's psychometric approach to personality types

Psychometrics is the science of measuring psychological variables. The work described in Chapter 7 is an excellent example of psychometric techniques and their use in formulating theories about intelligence. Eysenck's personality theory depends vitally on the use of psychometric measurement, derived from questionnaire responses, to establish what he believes are the universal structures of personality. This is the basis of his nomothetic approach. Activity 3 gives some of the questionnaire items taken from *Know your own personality* (Eysenck and Wilson, 1975).

ACTIVITY 3

Try these examples of questionnaire items which assess extraversion–introversion. Don't spend too long thinking about them but give the answer 'yes' (Y), 'no' (N), or 'don't know' or 'sometimes' (?) to each item. The instructions normally advise you to try to avoid putting a '?' except when you really cannot decide.

It is not possible in an activity like this to obtain an accurate measure, so you will not be able to compare yourself with others or with norms on the basis of these few questions. What you will be able to see, however, is the kind of question that Eysenck uses and the difficulties of trying to respond to them.

1 Are you inclined to be slow and deliberate in your actions?

2 Are you generally very enthusiastic about starting a new project or undertaking?

3 Are you inclined to rush from one activity to the next without pausing for rest?

4 Generally, do you prefer reading to meeting people?

5 Are you fairly talkative when with a group of people?

6 Do you enjoy spending long periods of time by yourself?

7 When the odds are against you, do you still usually think it worth taking a chance?

8 When you are catching a train, do you often arrive at the last minute?

9 Are you rather cautious in novel situations?

10 Do you like planning things well ahead of time?

11 Do you often change your interests?

12 Do you often buy things on impulse?

13 If you are watching a slapstick film or farcical play do you laugh louder than most of the people around you?

14 Are you able to maintain outer calm in the face of an emergency?

15 Do you subscribe to the philosophy of 'Eat drink and be merry for tomorrow we die'?

16 Do you like to have time to be alone with your thoughts?

17 Do you seldom stop to analyse your own thoughts and feelings?

18 Do you frequently become so involved with a question or problem that you have to keep thinking about it until you arrive at a satisfactory solution?

19 Are you inclined to be over conscientious?

20 Are you normally on time for appointments?

21 Are you inclined to live each day as it comes along?

To get an approximate indication of whether you are on the extravert or introvert side of the scale, you can score your responses using the guide at the end of the chapter.

Questions like those in Activity 3 require only a simple response of 'yes', 'no', or 'don't know'. It is also possible to use the same kinds of questions to form **personality rating scales** which give respondents more opportunity to make finer discriminations in their self reports on behaviour or feelings. For instance, the first question in Activity 3 could become transferred into an **item** in a rating scale as follows:

Are you inclined to be slow and deliberate in your actions?

always   often   sometimes   rarely   never.

This is an example of a five-point scale with the requirement to circle *one* of the five possible ratings. The answers would be scored from 5 (always) to zero (never.) In a personality rating scale, the responses to all the items would be scored and these scores summed over the entire questionnaire to arrive at an overall score on a personality dimension.

Eysenck and many others have shown that people differ systematically in the scores they achieve. A few people have scores which place them at the extremes of the extraversion and neuroticism dimensions, but most have scores which place them towards the centre of the distribution of scores, as in the bell-shaped normal distribution described in Chapter 7, Section 1.5. There the distribution showed that there are more people with average intelligence than with either very high or very low IQ scores. Similarly, most personality scores would be bunched in the middle of the bell, with fewer at each extreme.

How does Eysenck conclude from psychometric evidence that the *structure* of personality can be formulated in terms of a limited number of personality dimensions which underlie the responses people make to questionnaire items? In order to understand this, it is necessary to make a clear distinction between people's responses to each item and the patterns of scores they get over the whole questionnaire.

Each questionnaire item has some **face validity**. That is, from ordinary experience, a question like 'Are you fairly talkative when with a group of people?' can be assumed to reflect an aspect of sociable behaviour. But when many items of this sort are presented to many people it is also possible to show *statistically*, using the method of **correlation**, that people who say 'yes' to this particular item also tend to say 'yes' to other, similar items. These similar items—the items which tap fairly specific behavioural tendencies related to social behaviour—can be shown, empirically, to 'go together'; that is, to correlate. These correlations are used to identify clusters of items which represent *traits*, like sociability or impulsiveness.

Eysenck's theory states that traits are derived from types (as shown in Figures 8.4 and 8.5). To demonstrate the existence of a type, it is necessary to look for patterns among the traits. This is done using the statistical technique called **factor analysis**, which was described in Chapter 7, Section 2.4. Using factor analysis it is possible to show, statistically, that people who get high scores on the trait of sociability also tend to get high scores on the trait of impulsivity, the trait of risk-taking and all the others shown in Figure 8.4 for extraversion. Similarly, people who get low scores on one trait will tend to get low scores on the other traits, and those with medium scores tend to have medium scores for all the traits.

What this means is that the traits themselves can be shown to form clusters of correlations. It is these clusters that provide evidence for the existence of types. The scores that people get for whole clusters of traits give an index of their types. The cluster of extraversion traits shown in Figure 8.4 is quite different from the cluster of neuroticism traits shown in Figure 8.5. The empirical finding that these clusters of traits *exist* is important evidence for the structure of personality that Eysenck has suggested, although, as we shall see below, this is not the only evidence.

Just as we have considered patterns in scores at the level of specific items clustering into traits, and traits clustering into types, it is also possible to look at relationships between people's scores at the type level. Using factor analysis, it is possible to find out, for instance, whether people who get high scores on the extraversion–introversion dimension (i.e. are highly extravert) will always get similarly high scores on neuroticism. In other words, if you know someone's score on extraversion, does it enable you to predict his or her score on neuroticism?

A central tenet of Eysenck's theory is that the underlying biological cause of extraversion is quite unrelated to the biological cause of neuroticism. He therefore hypothesized that knowing a person's score on the extraversion dimension would tell you nothing at all about that person's position on the neuroticism dimension. This is shown in Figure 8.2 where the vertical axis (neuroticism) and the horizontal axis (extraversion) cross at right angles. It is possible for someone to be either a neurotic extravert or a neurotic introvert, which indicates that the scores on the two dimensions are unrelated. This hypothesis has been repeatedly tested over many years using different versions of Eysenck's personality rating scales and different populations of respondents. It is generally concluded that the evidence supports his idea that the extraversion–introversion is unrelated to the neuroticism—stability dimension.

In the course of his research, Eysenck and his co-workers have refined several versions of personality questionnaires to measure the personality dimensions in his theory. These are in continuous use today, notably the MPI (the Maudsley Personality Inventory) and the EPI (the Eysenck Personality Inventory). Using these questionnaires, a vast amount of research has been conducted on a wide range of individual differences in psychology, the basic dimensions of which correlate with people's scores on the extraversion and neuroticism scales, in other words, with their personality type.

3.4 The biological basis of Eysenck's typology

Thus far we have considered the psychometric evidence for the structure of personality. Eysenck's theory also states how the two main dimensions are represented biologically, and this opens up the theory to a different kind of testing. By making claims about the differences between the personality types in terms of their neurophysiological make up, it is possible to devise laboratory experiments to test specific hypotheses about the four personality types that can be derived from Figure 8.2: stable extraverts, stable introverts, neurotic extraverts and neurotic introverts. In the main, the evidence has supported Eysenck's theory. Before considering how these experimental tests are carried out, what is the relationship that Eysenck suggests exists between biological differences and behaviour?

Eysenck believes that a person's position on the personality dimension extraversion–introversion is caused by the level of arousal in the brain, and that their position on the neuroticism–stability dimension is caused by the stability or lack of stability (i.e. the *lability*) of the autonomic nervous system. The **autonomic nervous system** is that part of the nervous system that controls involuntary activities such as breathing, digestion and heart rate.

What do we mean by **arousal level**? Most people know what it is like to drink strong coffee and feel very wakeful and stimulated in a general sense. Similarly, if one is chronically tired or pleasantly bored, there is a sense of lack of stimulation. The first of these states is one of high arousal and the second is low arousal. Levels of arousal are controlled by a particular structure in the lower part of the brain, called the **ascending reticular activating system** (ARAS). The ARAS is thought to operate like an amplifying system. Stimulation (nerve excitation) is constantly reaching the brain from nerve cells all over the body. These nerve impulses are channelled through the ARAS which can either dampen down the level, reducing arousal in the higher centres of the brain, or amplify the stimulation, increasing the arousal level. According to Eysenck, the observed differences in the behaviour of extraverts and introverts is caused by genetic differences in the ARAS.

Eysenck has proposed that there are genetically determined individual differences in the ARAS which affect the usual levels of arousal that we experience. Through their behaviour, people tend to adjust these levels to a comfortable optimum. He suggests that introverts are chronically overaroused from birth. From this it follows that introverts behave in a way that attempts to *reduce* their arousal level. In contrast, extraverts are chronically underaroused and so tend to behave in a way that *increases* their arousal level. In other words, introverts try to correct their chronic overarousal by avoiding extra stimulation from the outside world. Extraverts try to correct their chronic underarousal by looking for stimulation and new experiences in their everyday behaviour.

The idea that it is introverts who are overaroused and extraverts who are underaroused may appear paradoxical. It is as if introverts have some internal 'volume control button' which is constantly turned up too high, whereas for extraverts this same control is turned too low. Their everyday behaviour has to compensate for this, either by avoiding extra stimulation, resulting in typical introverted behaviour, or by dashing about looking for more stimulation like a typical extravert. (Of course, most people, with average scores on the extraversion–introversion dimension, must have a medium degree of arousal.)

According to this strong claim, extraversion/introversion is an inherited condition. It follows that a person's development, in whatever kind of social and physical environment, will lead inevitably to a range of behaviours, both specific (at the level of habits and specific responses) and more general (at the trait and type level), which will serve to adjust the balance of arousal, the whole acting as a biological homeostatic mechanism (see Chapter 5).

Eysenck is indeed a proponent of the importance of genetic factors in behaviour. He has used twin studies (see Chapter 7, Section 3.2) to support his theory about the genetic basis for both personality and intelligence dimensions. For instance, he claims that Shields' twin study (1962) showed more similarity in extraversion scores for identical twins compared with fraternal twins. The problems of establishing the heritability of individual differences have been clearly illustrated in Chapter 7. Despite this, Eysenck's own position is that 'we might be justified in saying that some three-quarters of individual differences in personality, insofar as these are related to E[xtraversion] and N[euroticism], are genetically determined' (Eysenck, 1970, p. 454).

Eysenck's theory about the biological basis of the neuroticism–stability dimension is less well worked out than the extraversion–introversion dimension. He believes that neuroticism is concerned with the **lability** of the autonomic nervous system, and is essentially an index of the emotionality of the individual. Those people who are low on the neuroticism dimension are emotionally stable and somewhat insensitive in general, using the terms in an everyday sense. People who are high on the dimension are, in contrast, emotionally labile. They tend to over-react emotionally and are more sensitive to pain and other emotional stimulation. Again the theory assumes that emotionality is an inherited characteristic and claims support from twin studies. There is a substantial amount of evidence that emotionality, along with some other aspects of temperament, can be observed very early in life and persist into adulthood (Buss and Plomin, 1984).

3.5 Experimental evidence for Eysenck's theory of personality types

How does arousal level affect behaviour? In answering this question, Eysenck drew upon psychological research which relates states of the nervous system to the learning and performance of tasks. For instance, Pavlov suggested that the ease with which classical conditioning occurs depends on the type of the nervous system in question. Pavlov suggested that a 'weak', easily aroused nervous system is relatively easy to condition. Eysenck saw a parallel between a weak nervous system and the chronic overarousal associated with introversion, implying that introverts should be relatively easy to condition. Pavlov had also identified what he called a 'strong' or underaroused nervous system which would be resistant to conditioning. Eysenck claimed that, since it is extraverts who have a low level of arousal, they would be less easy to condition than introverts. From this follows a whole string of predictions, many of which have been tested (see Box A). Eysenck also made predictions based on the low arousal of extraverts and the high arousal of introverts about

---

BOX A   Two experimental tests of Eysenck's theory

1 Conditioning and extraversion–introversion

Differences in the ease with which conditioning occurs in introverts and extraverts are not consistent, but under some conditions they can be demonstrated. Eysenck and his associates have focused upon the speed and strength with which subjects form classically conditioned associations (Chapter 6, Section 2). An example is the association between a puff of air as the unconditional stimulus (UCS) and a tone (neutral stimulus). Eysenck and Levey (1972) found that under some circumstances introverts form an eye-blink association more quickly than extraverts. These circumstances consisted of (a) presenting the UCS on only some occasions and (b) using a weak puff of air. When the conditioning is made difficult, introverts do condition more easily that extraverts, as predicted by Eysenck's theory.

2 Boredom and performance

In a bizarre but classic experiment in 1963, Spielman used two groups of subjects, already identified as being extravert or introvert on the basis of their questionnaire responses, to perform a boring mechanical task. They were simply to tap on a metal plate, using a metal stylus. The apparatus was constructed so that an accurate record could be kept of the length of time the stylus was actually touching the plate. As you might expect, the subjects became gradually more fatigued, and the time the stylus was not in contact with the plate increased. Measurement of the time the stylus was not in contact with the plate gave an index of performance, called 'involuntary rest pauses' (IRPs). From the trials, Spielman found that extraverts produced up to fifteen times more IRPs as compared with introverts. The finding had been predicted from the notion that, since extraverts have less arousal and more quickly build up a reaction against the activity ('inhibition') than introverts, they get bored and behave, in effect, like fatigued people. In contrast, the introverts have enough 'natural' internal arousal to keep them going. These differences are likely to be particularly visible in a long, boring manual task in the laboratory.

how they would react to performing tedious tasks in the laboratory. Because they have a low level of arousal (compared with introverts) extraverts will become bored more easily and will persevere less. Depressant drugs, including alcohol, which reduce the arousal level, will make normally overaroused introverts behave more like extraverts. Stimulant drugs, including caffeine, should decrease the performance of introverts by making their arousal levels even higher, but, by raising the normal low arousal level of extraverts, reduce their need for stimulation-seeking behaviour.

Finally, there is another important point to be made about Eysenck's theory and its relation to biological variables. We have seen that there is psychometric evidence for his theory of personality and that this rests largely on the measurement and analysis of self-report questionnaires about behaviour, feelings, preferences, beliefs etc. We have also seen that there is evidence for the biological substrate of Eysenck's personality differences. This being the case, it is possible that **performance measures** could be used to assess personality. For example, if extraverts and introverts differ substantially on a whole range of simple manual tasks, it may be possible to devise valid and reliable tests that depend on *measurement of actual behaviours in a test situation*, as opposed to self-report ratings. This further objectification of personality measurement has long been the dream of many personality theorists. But, while it would seem feasible in the case of Eysenck's approach, in practice this has not been developed. The reasons for this are the complexity and inconvenience of setting up performance measures as compared with the simple, cheap and demonstrably reliable questionnaires, like the one in Activity 3.

3.6 The elaboration of Eysenck's types in the social world

Eysenck believes that his three basic dimensions of personality are the relatively simple starting points for personality, and that personality becomes more diverse and idiosyncratic in terms of actual behaviour as individuals experience the interaction of their basic type with the realities of everyday life. Initial biological differences, such as level of arousal, *cause* individuals to learn from and behave in the environment in different ways. Although (according to Eysenck) the basics of personality are present at birth, differential experience of environments produces the different behaviour that we observe in the different personality types.

Nevertheless, his theory does suggest that there are heavy constraints on the kind of personality that an individual can develop. Perhaps more than any other theorist, Eysenck stresses the inevitability of certain paths of development for each personality type, particularly for those people at the extremes of the personality dimensions. This is particularly clear in his suggestion that socialization processes act in a quite different way in extraverts and introverts, leading to substantial differences in *social behaviour*. This is one of the most controversial aspects of Eysenck's work. He has hypothesized that, because extreme extraverts condition less easily during their lifetimes and especially during childhood, they are less amenable to the ordinary socialization processes and, as a result, are more likely than introverts to become deviants and sociopaths. The other side of this coin is that introverts, since they are more easily conditioned, are more likely to be oversocialized, conscientious, anxious and guilt-ridden.

Eysenck has also made a link between people's political ideologies and their underlying personality types. It has long been established, using questionnaires, that people in general have political beliefs and attitudes that can be ranged on a single axis corresponding to a **radical–conservative dimension** (political left versus political right). As with Eysenck's personality dimensions, there is likely to be a normal distribution of people along the radical–conservative dimension, with most clustering in the middle but with some people being at either extreme. Eysenck has contributed the idea that there is a second dimension, independent of the first, which corresponds to general social attitudes to a range of topics. He has called this second dimension of social attitudes the **tough-mindedness–tender-mindedness dimension (T dimension)**. By introducing this T dimension it is possible to understand certain similarities between the two political extremes. Eysenck has argued that right-wing extremists (Fascists) and left-wing extremists (Communists) are 'similar' in their extreme tough-mindedness (Eysenck, 1954). He worked on political attitudes some time ago, and Figure 8.6 shows, in a very dated form, the kinds of attitudes that were held by people whose radical–conservatism and T scores placed them on the two dimensions.

Eysenck concluded that the radical–conservative (right wing–left wing) dimension represents true social attitudes acquired during one's lifetime by experience in the social and political world. In contrast, the T dimension is a result of 'a projection on to the field of social attitudes of certain fundamental personality traits. . . . [A] person's social attitude (Radical, Conservative, or

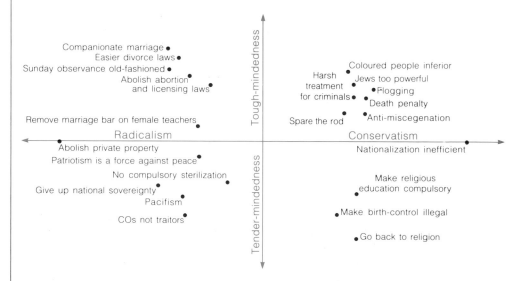

Figure 8.6 Distribution of attitudes in relation to tough-mindedness and radicalism. (Please note that this scale was devised in 1954 when opinions and statute laws were very different from now)

intermediate) would seek expression in terms of the fundamental personality variables so closely related to the T [dimension]' (Eysenck, 1954). In his book *The psychology of politics* (1954), Eysenck suggested a relationship between extraversion and tough-mindedness, and introversion and tender-mindedness. However, by 1978, he claimed that this was a small effect and that tough-mindedness is really a projection of his third personality dimension, psychoticism (Eysenck and Wilson, 1978). An evaluation of this evidence is beyond us here, but it is fair to say that the evidence is not entirely convincing.

There is some appeal in a theory which can unite so many different levels of psychological variation and account for them with a simple biological model. However, if this simplicity makes the theory more easily accepted without due caution (particularly since typing of people also seems to be intuitively appealing), then there are dangers in a model that links social conformity and deviance and political affiliations to inherited personality characteristics. Nevertheless, taking the theory as a whole, together with the mass of empirical evidence that has accumulated over many years, there is no question that Eysenck's contribution is unique. It is a comprehensive theory which forces comparisons with other theories which have narrower and less testable views of personality.

Summary of Section 3

- Type theories state that consistency in behaviour is the result of a person's type. 'Pure' types are defined as the relatively few individuals who occupy extreme positions on personality dimensions.

- In Eysenck's theory there are three personality dimensions: extraversion–introversion, neuroticism–stability, and psychoticism.

- Eysenck's theory is nomothetic and relies heavily on psychometric measurement using personality questionnaires. Factor analysis of scores has revealed the dimensions which Eysenck believes constitute the underlying structure of personality.

- Eysenck has related his personality dimensions to neurophysiology. This makes it possible to test the theory experimentally. Extraversion–introversion is thought to be related to chronic arousal levels in the brain, and neuroticism–stability to lability of the autonomic nervous system.

- Eysenck's personality theory has also been extended into the controversial area of social conformity and deviance, and political ideology.

4 | Kelly's personal construct theory

Kelly's approach to understanding personality is very different from that of any other personality theory. For Kelly, and those who work in his tradition, the essence of the endeavour is to understand each individual in her or his own terms. Like Allport's, it is an idiographic theory. For Kelly, personality is not quantifiable and it is not possible to generalize across individuals. Physiology and genetic inheritance are irrelevant, and the only motivational basis is that the person is alive and trying to make sense of the world in order to survive and prosper. It can be considered a *personality theory* because it deals with the typical ways in which each person experiences the world and this results in some consistency in behaviour.

4.1 People as 'scientists'

All personality theories make assumptions about human nature, and in some cases these are so arresting or counter-intuitive as to be major features of the theory. Freud's work is of this kind, with its view of people as being driven by unconscious instinctual drives which, when unacceptable to the socialized individual, have to be warded off by defence mechanisms. Kelly's view of what it is like to be a person is very different from that of Freud but, like Freud, his underlying assumptions about human nature are basic to the whole theory.

Kelly's view of being a person can be summed up in the idea that people act as **scientists**. Scientists proceed by formulating theories and hypotheses about what the world is like and then testing them out. In this way scientists achieve **models** of the world. Kelly believed that we all behave with respect to our worlds as if we are scientists. The aim is to build up a model of the world which will allow us to predict events; in this way we can gain mastery over the environment. The essence of Kelly's approach is that the ideas, thoughts and theories we have about reality arise out of our experience in the world. The unique model we form of the world relatively quickly becomes an idiosyncratic framework which we use to interpret further experiences. In Kelly's theory of personality the underlying *consistency* in a person's behaviour is a direct outcome of the way each unique individual builds a unique model of what the world is like. According to Kelly, each person's behaviour follows directly from this model of the world, that is, from the way the person interprets experiences and events.

The specific hypotheses we have (at a given time) about the world are called personal constructs. And the framework which acts as a model of the world is called a **construct system**.

4.2 Personal constructs

The **personal constructs** in Kelly's theory are formulated as pairs of opposing concepts which we apply to the world of objects and people around us. For example, you may tend to see people as being either *kind or cruel*, either *frightening or gentle*, either *extravert or introvert*. These are known as **bipolar constructs** because they are expressed in terms of two opposite poles.

You may wonder whether Kelly's extravert–introvert bipolar construct is the same as Eysenck's extraversion–introversion dimension. It is essential to grasp a crucial distinction here. Eysenck's dimensions are used as *objective* personality scales on which everyone can be scored. In complete contrast, Kelly's bipolar constructs are the basis for each individual's way of viewing the world. If a person is shown to have a bipolar construct defined by the poles of introversion and extraversion, this simply means that the person tends to use this construct to judge other people. Eysenck's dimensions are objective nomothetic scales for measuring personality; Kelly's constructs represent an idiographic approach to discovering each individual's idiosyncratic model of the world.

Since personal contructs are the building blocks of Kelly's theory, it is important to understand exactly what they are and the method that has been used to obtain access to them. Kelly devised a method called the role construct repertory grid (sometimes called by the shorter name repertory grid), which we shall examine in detail below. There are also other ways of mapping constructs devised by Kelly and by other workers in this same tradition; these can be found in the further reading listed at the end of this chapter.

4.3 The repertory grid

Because Kelly was particularly interested in how an individual construes his or her *social world* (i.e. other people), **repertory grids** are used to explore constructs about other people in the subject's world, rather than events or aspects of the physical world, although these too could be treated in the same way. Figure 8.7 illustrates a completed repertory grid which maps the way the subject (whom I shall call Jane) construes certain people around her. These are the people who hold important social roles with respect to her. It is for this reason that the grid is often called a **role construct repertory grid** (after Kelly, 1955, p. 270).

Across the top of the grid in Figure 8.7 you will see twenty roles that other people might occupy in Jane's life and that we might expect to be important to her. You will see that 'self' is also included. Since these are the names of *role positions* rather than actual people, before filling in this grid, Jane would be asked to put the names of *individuals* who occupy these roles in her life next to each role. Obviously, for self, mother and father she need not fill in actual names, but for brother she might put 'John', for sister 'Mary', for best friend 'Lucy', for threatening person 'Dr Jamieson', and so on. She would be filling in the names of real people in her own life. These real people and the roles they occupy are called the **elements** of the grid.

The aim of a repertory grid is to discover the main constructs a person uses to understand and interpret the actions of other people. In Figure 8.7, the bipolar constructs that Jane uses when thinking about the elements (i.e. the named

	Self	Mother	Father	Brother	Sister	Spouse	Ex-flame	Best friend	Ex-friend	Rejecting person	Pitied person	Threatening person	Attractive person	Accepted teacher	Rejected teacher	Boss	Successful person	Happy person	Ethical person	Neighbour		Constructs
	1	2	3	4	5	6	7	8	9	10	11	12	13	14	15	16	17	18	19	20		
1		(X)	(X)		(O)	X		X		X			X	X			X	X	X	X	1	kind–cruel
2							X	(O)	X	(X)		(O)			X	X	X				2	frightening–gentle
3			X	X	X			X					X	X		X	(X)	(X)	O		3	carefree–conscientious
4		X		X		(X)	O	(X)					X	X		X	X	X		X	4	understanding–unsympathetic
5	O		X	X	X	(X)		(X)			X		X	X		X	X	X			5	confident–anxious
6	X	(X)	X		X	(X)	O		X		X			X	X		X			X	6	simple–intellectual

Matching scores

1–2	4	2–3	8	3–4	13	4–5	13	5–6	8
1–3	12	2–4	5	3–5	18	4–6	7		
1–4	17	2–5	8	3–6	8				
1–5	12	2–6	8						
1–6	10								

Figure 8.7 A completed role construct repertory grid

actual individuals) are listed down the right-hand side of the grid. These are unique to Jane and represent a small part of her total construct system. They were *not* entered in advance by the psychologist who explored Jane's construct system, but elicited from Jane herself.

How were these bipolar constructs arrived at? The respondent, in this case Jane, would have been asked to consider the similarities and the differences between the elements, with the elements being compared in threes or **triads**. Strictly, Jane would be asked to consider all possible triads in turn (e.g. self/mother/father; self/mother/John; self/father/John; etc.) But this is very time-consuming and rather tedious for the respondent. The procedure has been simplified by having the grid marked up to show the particular triads that psychologists have found in the past to be most likely to yield the most useful constructs. In Figure 8.7, these triads are marked with circles. Thus, for each row in the grid, Jane would have been asked to think about the three people whose names are above the squares marked with circles. In the first row, where the triad is marked as mother/father/sister, she would have been asked to think of some way in which any two of this triad are similar and the remaining one is different.

If Jane thought of her mother and father as being alike in that they are both *kind*, and her sister Mary as different in that she is *cruel*, the construct that would emerge is *kind–cruel*. This bipolar construct of kind–cruel is shown written on the right-hand side of the grid in Figure 8.7. There is a convention that the **similarity pole** of the construct (i.e. the way in which the mother and father are *similar* in being kind) is entered first, and the **contrast pole** (i.e. the *cruel* sister) is entered second, giving kind–cruel. In the second row Jane thought of a rejecting person and a threatening person as alike in being *frightening*, and her best friend Lucy as being different in that she is *gentle*. This bipolar construct is also written on the right-hand side of the grid against the second row, following the same convention for the similarity and contrast poles.

SAQ 3   In row 3

(a) Who are the three elements, i.e. the triad?

(b) Which two elements are similar and which is different?

(c) What is the construct that emerged?

(d) Which people are described by the similarity pole and which by the contrast pole?

By the time Jane had worked all the way down the rows she would have created her own, idiosyncratic repertory grid showing the particular constructs she uses. The next step is to use the bipolar constructs which have been identified to see how they apply to all the elements listed across the top of the grid. Filling in the grid involves rating each element on each of the bipolar constructs. There are several ways of doing this rating. Jane was asked to put a cross in the squares under each of the elements that she construed as matching the left-hand description of the construct (i.e. the elements that matched the similarity pole). She was asked to leave blank those squares under elements that matched the description of the contrast pole. In row 1 for instance, she put a cross under all the other elements that she construed as kind, like her father and mother; and she left a blank under the elements she construed as cruel, like her sister.

SAQ 4   In row 2:

(a) Name the individual elements Jane construed as frightening.

(b) How did she construe each of the other elements?

When a repertory grid has been completely filled in, it contains a great deal of information about a person's way of viewing the world, which can be analysed in several different ways.

ACTIVITY 4

You might like to try to analyse a small portion of Jane's grid:

1   Look at row 1 and row 4. Score 1 for each pair of squares in which there is a cross in row 1 and also a cross in row 4. For instance, under 'mother' in column 2, there is an X in row 1 and an X in row 4.

2   After counting the number of pairs of crosses in both rows, score 1 every time there is a blank in both rows (e.g. in the 'sister' column).

3   Score nothing for pairs of squares in which there is a mismatch, i.e. a cross in one row and a blank in the other (e.g. in the 'father' column).

4   Add up the scores for all cross/cross and blank/blank matches between row 1 and row 4; (answer at the end of the activity).

5   Now go through exactly the same matching process for row 1 and row 2, scoring 1 for each cross/cross and blank/blank match; (answer at the end of the activity).

6   Note that the maximum number of matches between any two rows is twenty (if all pairs of squares match). The minimum number of pair matches is zero if there are no matches at all. What is the *average* number of matches that might be expected between pairs of rows? (Answer at the end of the activity).

Answers

Row 1 and row 4: matching score = 17 (Check that you did count all the blanks)
Row 1 and row 2: matching score = 4
Average number of matches = 10 (i.e. half the possible matches)

These matching scores between pairs of rows give some indication of *overlap* between personal constructs. For instance, the relatively high number of matches between row 1 and row 4 indicates that, for Jane, the constructs *kind–cruel* and *understanding–unsympathetic* are highly correlated. She tends to use these constructs to make similar judgements about people. Another way of putting this is that Jane equates *kind* with *understanding* and *cruel* with *unsympathetic*.

If you now look at the matches between row 1 and row 2, you will see that the number of matched pairs is much lower. This means, perhaps not surprisingly, that Jane sees *kind* as the opposite of *frightening* and *cruel* as the opposite of *gentle*. These constructs are correlated but in a negative direction. People whom Jane sees as *kind* (e.g. mother) get a blank for *frightening*.

Some versions of the repertory grid use correlational techniques for identifying the major constructs which make up someone's total construct system. In Jane's case, her consistent use of the kind, gentle, understanding poles as opposed to the cruel, frightening and unsympathetic poles implies a high correlation between all three constructs. These clusters of constructs imply that there is an underlying core construct, which might perhaps be labelled, *sympathetic to me* versus *threatening to me*.

4.4 Properties of constructs and construct systems

A personal construct is simply a discrimination that an individual can make in interpreting the world. The individual may not attach a verbal label to it, although in the repertory grid technique he or she is forced to do so. According to Kelly, each individual has a finite number of such bipolar constructs. Each construct has its own **range of convenience**. This means that there are some events and objects to which it can be applied, and some to which it cannot. For example, you might distinguish people, animals, even perhaps foreign countries using the construct *friendly–unfriendly*, but you are hardly likely to use the same construct for washing machines, refrigerators or typewriters, although computers and word processors are construed as user-friendly.

Kelly also stated that people's total construct systems are hierarchical and that some constructs play a more important role in our understanding of the world that others. The constructs that are near the top of the hierarchy are considered central to that person's functioning. These are called **core constructs**.

Constructs also differ in their **permeability**. Permeable constructs can readily be applied to new elements, whereas impermeable constructs cannot. For example, *deciduous–evergreen* is a relatively impermeable construct, forming part of a rather tight construct system for construing differences between trees. In contrast, *warm–cold* is a relatively open or permeable construct in that it can be applied to many things. It is important to appreciate that permeability refers to the way we *use* a construct rather than the actual words that are used to describe it. For example, in the case of the *warm–cold* construct we might begin by using it to discriminate the physical characteristic of temperature, then use it to understand climate, and then perhaps use it to expand our understanding and discrimination between people. We might even use it to describe colours. Thus, a person's construct system can become elaborated so as to increase understanding of the world.

If every person has an idiosyncratic construct system, how are we able to understand each other or to predict each other's behaviour? As we saw earlier, Kelly used 'science' as a model for how people understand the world. Scientists are able to understand each other and communicate because they work with *shared* theories and concepts. In an analogous way, in order for people to act socially, to understand each other's viewpoint and to communicate, there has to be some overlap in construct systems. There is sufficient similarity between people for Kelly to suggest the **principle of commonality**: 'To the extent that one person employs a construction of experience which is similar to that employed by another, his/her processes are psychologically similar to those of the other person' (1955, p. 90).

Kelly also described another prerequisite for social life which he called **sociality**. In order to understand other people we have to be able to go beyond commonality or overlap. We need to be able to construe other people's construing of the world: 'To the extent that one person construes the construction processes of another she/he may play a role in a social process involving the other person' (1955, p. 95). Commonality and sociality are promoted by our upbringing and by direct pressures on us to see the world in the same way as others do; and, of course, this is greatly helped by a common language. Even if commonality is minimal to start with, as long as there is enough for a start to be made, further shared views can be *negotiated*. This process is similar to the social construction of self described by Mead, the symbolic interactionist discussed in Chapter 2, and by the Piagetian approach to the way a child gradually comes to 'think' in increasingly adult ways; see Chapter 3.

Just as it is comforting when we receive confirming evidence about the world, so too it can bolster our idea of self and identity to find support for our constructs during interaction with another person. This is how friendships and love-affairs often begin, with two people rapidly exploring similarities in their reactions to other people and events. In a more everyday sense, **consensual validation** for our constructs can be sought through more general social comparisons (see Chapter 2). The less positive and less healthy side of this is the possibility of seeking consensual validation of one's constructs from others who have been carefully chosen because they agree with us. A true scientist in Kelly's sense would risk disconfirmation by testing his or her views in situations which might lead to disagreement and even conflict.

ACTIVITY 5

Use the grid in Figure 8.8 (overleaf) to explore your own role construct repertory grid.

1   Along the top of the grid fill in the names of actual people you know who correspond to the descriptions of the elements across the top (e.g. a 'friend' 'Mary'). You can change or add to the elements if you like. For example, you might want to leave out 'spouse' and put in 'current boy/girl friend' instead.

2   For each row of the grid in turn, look at the triad of elements whose corresponding boxes contain a circle. Think of some way in which any two of the three circled elements are the same as each other and different from the third. Write this construct alongside the row using a bipolar format such as 'amusing–serious', with the similarity pole always on the left. You will notice that some of the rows have been left without circles. This is in case there are sets of three elements which you would like to use to define a particular construct. For these rows choose where to put the circles yourself and write in the constructs as before.

3   After you have filled in all the bipolar constructs, take each construct in turn and decide which pole of the bipolar construct best describes each element. For example, suppose you had the construct, 'kind–cruel'. For all those people you think are more 'kind' than 'cruel' put a cross in the box of the appropriate element; for those you think more 'cruel', leave the box blank.

4   If you wish, calculate your matching scores as outlined in Activity 4.

5   Are there any constructs that you feel you could use interchangeably? If so, are you surprised by what you have found? You might like to speculate whether any of the constructs you have used are core constructs that you typically use to judge other people.

4.5   What does Kelly mean by personality change?

You may be wondering why Kelly's theory is thought of as a personality theory? In a sense, Kelly believed that the construct systems we use to construe the world and its inhabitants *are* our personalities. Constructs come from experience and, once formed, they guide our behaviour. In a healthy personality constructs can change with experience, thus providing the basis for adaptation to the world and personal growth.

	Self	Mother	Father	Brother	Sister	Spouse	Ex-flame	Best friend	Ex-friend	Rejecting person	Pitied person	Threatening person	Attractive person	Accepted teacher	Rejected teacher	Boss	Successful person	Happy person	Ethical person	Neighbour	Constructs
	1	2	3	4	5	6	7	8	9	10	11	12	13	14	15	16	17	18	19	20	
1																	○	○	○		1
2					○	○	○														2
3	○				○		○														3
4		○			○	○															4
5											○				○	○					5
6				○	○			○													6
7														○	○			○			7
8			○									○	○								8
9	○									○								○			9
10																					10
11																					11
12																					12

Figure 8.8 Repertory grid

Elaboration and change in construct systems is a central part of Kelly's theory. In his own words: 'Man looks at his world through transparent patterns or templates which he creates and then attempts to fit over the realities of which the world is composed. The fit is not always very good. Yet without such patterns the world appears to be such an undifferentiated homogeneity that man is unable to make any sense of it. Even a poor fit is more helpful to him than nothing at all' (Kelly, 1955, p. 9). Thus construct systems are at once both enabling and restricting. The fit does not have to be perfect, but when it is very poor, something has to change. The ability to make adjustments in constructs is seen as the basis of a healthy personality.

Kelly began work as a clinical psychologist and it is from this experience that his focus on the potential for personality change derives. He had no specific training in any particular approach to clinical work. For this reason, when he began to work as a therapist he virtually started from first principles, *listening* to what his patients had to say about their distress and trying to understand *their* understanding of their worlds. It is said that he found that almost any kind of explanation he gave for their confusions and worries would work, providing only that it could account for the crucial facts *as the client saw them*, and had implications for the future which required a new way of being and behaving. This radical approach worked, Kelly thought, because it encouraged the patients to consider themselves and their situations consciously and in a new way. In other words, it prompted them into breaking out of their old belief systems and facilitated the development of new constructs.

Changes in construct systems may vary from fine adjustments to a radical overhaul. In everyone's life there are times when a dramatic change in actual circumstances (such as the loss of a job or bereavement) requires revolutionary changes in the way the individual construes those circumstances if he or she is to survive. Maintaining an outmoded construct system (e.g. believing that a shaky marriage is perfect) may lead to problems. On the other hand, finding that one's system is inadequate and *must* be changed can be terrifying.

In his personality theory, Kelly has redefined terms such as anxiety, fear, guilt and hostility as features of construct systems. For instance, he defined anxiety as the 'recognition that the events with which a man is confronted lie mostly outside the range of convenience of his construct system' (1955, p. 495). The range of convenience was defined in Section 4.4 as referring to the range of events to which a construct applies. A construct system with a limited range of convenience may appear inadequate in some situations and prevent a person from making sense of what is happening. Failure to develop adequate constructs will lead to continuing anxiety.

Kelly defined threat as the 'awareness of imminent comprehensive change in one's core structures [core constructs]. . . . We are threatened when our major beliefs about the nature of our personal, social and practical situations are invalidated and the world around us appears about to become chaotic' (ibid., p. 489). And he redefined fear thus: 'Fear is like threat, except that, in this case, it is a new incidental construct, rather than a comprehensive construct, that seems about to take over' (ibid., p. 494). Guilt is defined in terms of one's construal of one's self: 'perception of one's apparent dislodgment from his core role structure' (ibid., p. 502).

Kelly's personality theory makes strong assumptions about people and about the nature of understanding. People's relations to reality have to be good enough for survival. We have to have a working model of the world and be prepared to adjust it when it fails, but it does not necessarily have to correspond exactly with reality. Our construct systems provide each of us with a **personal reality**, a reality each of us has constructed for ourselves. Since each of us creates our own construct system and then uses it to construct our own view of the world, this version of reality can be changed, if we so choose. Kelly said 'We take the stand that there are always some alternative constructions available to choose among in dealing with the world. No one needs to paint himself into a corner; no one needs to be completely hemmed in by circumstances; no one needs to be the victim of his own biography' (ibid., p. 15). He called this aspect of his theory **constructive alternativism**.

In Kelly's theory the stress on humans as being rational 'scientists' testing constructs is largely at the expense of feelings. But, despite this emphasis on the rational model-building aspects of personality, Kelly's theory can encompass the idea that people vary considerably in the emotionality or the 'feeling tone' of their constructs. It is not difficult to imagine two people, with equivalent sets of elements, one of whom would produce constructs like angry–calm, frightening–gentle, powerful–weak, good–bad, all of which are emotive in tone. Another person might produce constructs like intellectual–non-intellectual, nice–unpleasant, reliable–unreliable. These are much cooler in emotional tone. It does seem that individual variation is implicit in all of Kelly's work.

Summary of Section 4

- Each person's behaviour and personality are a direct result of the way he or she perceives and understands (i.e. construes a model of) the world, especially other people.

- Kelly believes that we are all, in a sense, scientists. We try to understand the world in order to predict events (particularly what other people will do), and have mastery over the environment.

- The specific hypotheses people have about the world are unique and are called personal constructs. They are the building blocks of Kelly's idiographic personality theory.

- The role construct repertory grid is a technique for mapping people's construct systems.

- Constructs vary in their range of convenience and permeability.

- Communication and social life are possible because there is some commonality between people's constructions of experience and because we construe each other's construction processes (sociality).

- Change is central to Kelly's theory. Construct systems can change and thus change the way we perceive the world and behave in it.

5 | Different ways of understanding personality

This chapter began with commonsense theories of personality which are embedded in our culture and in the way we think. We use these theories about other people and ourselves to help us find our way through our social lives. But such theories are not set out formally. They have no precision and, in the ordinary course of life, they do not get tested. We use them without evaluating them. How have psychologists improved on commonsense understanding of personality? Have they provided testable theories? Have they added to the range of behaviours that can be understood in terms of personality? To what extent have they given us novel ways of explaining the consistency of behaviour that makes up what we intuitively think of as personality?

The three theories of personality that have been described in this chapter are very different (a) in the importance they assign to clear statements that can be tested, and (b) in the way they handle issues that any personality theory must address. These issues include human motivation, conscious experience and consistency in behaviour.

5.1 Testability: idiographic and nomothetic

SAQ 5 (a) What does 'nomothetic' mean?
(b) What does 'idiographic' mean?
(c) Categorize the following theories and research areas as either nomothetic or idiographic: (i) Allport's trait theory; (ii) Freud's psychodynamic approach, (iii) intelligence testing, (iv) Kelly's personal construct theory; (v) Eysenck's personality theory.

To achieve rigorous testability, theories have to be set out in a way that allows predictions about people's behaviour to be formulated and then tested using evidence that can be agreed on by everyone. For the most part, it is within the nomothetic approach that rigorous testing is possible. The nomothetic personality theorist aims at general statements about all people's personalities that can be tested against evidence from samples of these people. This approach assumes that, although people differ, they do so in the same sort of ways. For example, everyone can be classified as sociable to some degree, they can be placed somewhere on the *dimension* of sociability. This aspect of personality can be measured for a wide variety of people which allows the psychologist to assign scores to individuals, or ranks relative to others, and thus to make comparisons. In this way the nomothetic theorist builds a theory on evidence collected from many observations. He or she arrives at general rules about the nature of people and the distribution of individual differences.

Eysenck's theory of personality is nomothetic in that it states general rules about the way people differ from each other and relates these differences to basic biological characteristics. The biological explanation of personality generates hypotheses, for example, about differences in arousal, conditioning and boredom, which can be tested by experiments. This degree of testability is a particular contribution of Eysenck's work. On the other hand, experiments like those described in Box A may seem far removed from the complexities of real life. This is the cost of the nomothetic approach. It usually depends on studying particular psychological processes like learning and conditioning, rather than studying the whole person and the experience of being a person.

The testability of Allport's idiographic theory is low. In this sense, and in its use of traits, his work is closest to commonsense ideas of personality. But it goes beyond common sense in its use of evidence from observations and documentation of people's consistency, and in its potential for detailed understanding of individuals in terms of their traits, the self (proprium), and the development of functional autonomy. Fundamentally, though, this essentially idiographic theory is not testable in the sense required by the nomothetic approach.

Kelly's idiographic theory, like Allport's, is not strictly testable. This is in part because the emphasis is on individuals and their idiosyncratic views of the world. Rigorous comparisons between people are not possible because each person is unique. But Kelly's theory has gone well beyond common sense in the clarity with which it has been laid out, and in the use of repertory grid techniques to examine representations of people's construct systems. In fact there is a paradox in Kelly's work.

Kelly makes many strong statements about personality that are *general* to everyone. He assumes that everyone thinks in terms of bipolar constructs; that all cognitive processes are 'channelized' by the way people anticipate events; that everyone interprets the environment as a 'scientist'; and that everyone has hierarchical construct systems with a greater or lesser range of convenience. These claims about the *universality* of construct systems and construing cannot, in themselves, be tested outside the theory, but they give the theory a nomothetic aspect. Limited comparisons between people are possible, but ultimately the theory is idiographic.

The nomothetic aspect gives rise to one of the most serious criticisms of Kelly's personality theory. In practice it has proved difficult to think about personal construct theory in isolation from the repertory grid techniques that Kelly and his associates have developed. The very process of eliciting constructs from individuals (even when using the simple repertory grids in Activities 4 and 5) *imposes* a pattern on the way the participant structures his or her thoughts. When you are filling in a grid, like the one you did in Activity 5, it is difficult to think in any way other than in bipolar constructs. So Kelly's theory constrains the kind of data that is collected. You could say that Kelly's theory is self-validating; as long as you use the techniques he developed there is no way that evidence against the theory could possibly emerge.

There is an important point here that applies to all theories. There is no way of collecting data and analysing it which is totally objective and separate from the assumptions that underlie the work. All scientific activities are constrained by explicit or implicit assumptions and technical practices and limitations. We have already seen in the case of Eysenck's theory, that measurement techniques, statistics and computer technology for factor analysis are essential to his work. His theory depends on these technologies and the technologies, in turn, limit the evidence he can produce. However, Eysenck's theory is not self-validating in the same way as Kelly's because it is possible for factor analysis to fail to show the predicted clusters of traits, and for the experiments to produce results that run counter to the theory.

This discussion has shown that Eysenck's theory is essentially nomothetic while those of Allport and Kelly are idiographic. But it has also indicated that the nomothetic/idiographic distinction is not clear-cut. There is a limit to the testability and universality of Eysenck's theory. The theories of Allport and Kelly both inevitably include some general assumptions about the nature of all people's personalities. This tension between general laws on the one hand and attempts to explain individual differences on the other must be, by definition, a feature of all personality theories.

5.2 Personality and motivation

It is clear from the three personality theories described in this chapter and Freud's psychodynamic approach described in Chapter 4, that there is no consensus on the range of topics a personality theory should cover.

An important consideration is the underlying model of human nature that the theorist holds. One of the most important aspects of such a model is the fundamental belief held by the theorist about what motivates people. It is difficult to understand how a personality theory can avoid such a crucial question, but the theories do vary in the emphasis given to human **motivation**.

Kelly said that: 'Motivational theories can be divided into two types, push theories and pull theories. Under push theories we find such terms as drive, motive or even stimulus. Pull theories use such constructs as purpose, value or need. In terms of a well known metaphor these are the pitchfork theories on the one hand, and the carrot theories on the other. But our theory is neither of these. Since we prefer to look at the nature of the animal himself, ours is probably best called a jackass theory' (Kelly, 1958, p. 50).

Although Kelly claimed that his theory merely described 'the animal', in fact he has a very clear statement of his underlying model of the person as a scientist. The motivational base to his theory is equally clear. It is a need to predict the environment, reduce uncertainty and increase mastery over the world, ultimately in the interests of survival. Clearly, this is a very different baseline from that of, say, Freud, who saw instincts as the driving force of personality.

Eysenck's theory makes no specific statement about motivation, but his view of the person as a biological entity suggests that he sees personality as the end point of biological drives. For example, his hypothesis about extraversion–introversion and arousal levels is a motivational explanation: extraverts seek stimulation and introverts avoid it, and this affects a wide range of behaviour.

Allport's theory of personality, like Kelly's, has a creative view of the person. Allport believed in personality growth and change and was convinced that personality theories should start with healthy human beings who strive 'not so much to preserve life as to make it worth living'. Again this is a very different view of what motivates people from that of Eysenck, and perhaps even Freud.

Thus, both in motivational terms and the assumptions underlying personality, Freud and Eysenck seem closer to each other, within the old European tradition which includes abnormal with normal psychology in an essentially biological framework. Allport and Kelly, although with very different theories, are nevertheless similar in their focus on a positive view of behaviour as being motivated by a person's creative powers and choices, rather than being determined and driven by genetics and biological instincts.

5.3 **Experience and consciousness**

Kelly and Allport are also similar in their willingness to take an 'inside' perspective on personality; that is, to take account of each person's own viewpoint and inner experience. In this sense their theories are **phenomenological**. Freud, like Allport and Kelly, also uses this inner perspective, and all three of these approaches use methods that attempt to gain access to personal experience. It is probably on methodological grounds that Eysenck would reject a phenomenological approach. He would probably argue that it is not possible to understand what goes on inside another person and that only the 'outside' perspective (essentially observable behaviour) has scientific validity. For Eysenck, the use of self-report questionnaires is a way of approximating to observing behaviour. This can be contrasted with Kelly's mapping of construct systems, or Freud's explorations of the inner world through psychoanalysis. In both these cases the focus is on understanding the individual's inner world.

Personality theories also differ on the topic of conscious versus unconscious influences on behaviour, which is another crucial question for personality theorists concerning the essential nature of human beings. Eysenck's view of personality takes no account of unconscious processes. Allport, as we have seen, is strongly against the idea that the unconscious can affect what we do in a way that contradicts conscious will. Psychodynamic theories, of course, are built upon the notion of unconscious motivation. Although Kelly does not suggest that we have a dynamic unconscious whose instinctual urges have to be curbed, he does focus on 'the furniture of the mind'—the meaning structures that are built up with experience in the world. This is similar to the psychodynamic idea of internal objects.

SAQ 6   Outline at least one similarity between the personality theories of each of the following:

(a) Eysenck and Allport

(b) Freud and Eysenck

(c) Kelly and Allport

(d) Allport and Freud

(e) Eysenck and Kelly

(f) Kelly and Freud

5.4 **Consistency in behaviour**

There is one feature that all the personality theories discussed here have in common. They all assume that personality resides inside the person and that it is responsible for the consistency in a person's behaviour. For Allport, consistency in behaviour is based on traits, for Eysenck it is based on types, and for Kelly it is the result of personal construct systems. Whatever kind of inner disposition is used to account for the consistency, does it mean that a person's behaviour is *always* consistent? Consistency implies doing the same thing, or almost the same thing, irrespective of circumstances. Are people really like this?

It is easy enough to show 'inconsistency'. One example that has attracted some attention from psychologists concerns honesty. Does it make sense to describe one child as honest and another as dishonest, or might all children be honest in one situation and dishonest in another?

Between 1928 and 1930, Hartshorne and May carried out a large-scale research project on whether children would behave honestly or dishonestly under conditions where discovery seemed (to the children) impossible. Other behaviour such as self-control, persistence, impulsiveness and moral behaviour were also studied. Hartshorne and May discovered that there was very little consistency in the children's behaviour. Where it was advantageous for them to cheat, many did so, but not necessarily consistently. They concluded, and many other psychologists continue to quote this work, that traits like honesty and co-operativeness do not consistently control behaviour and that what people do is largely influenced by situational factors.

In 1968, Mischel published a book which claimed that *all* trait psychology is misconceived. Instead he argued that behaviour is under the influence of the environment and the range of situations that people encounter. The dispute between those who believe in consistent traits and those who believe that behaviour is controlled by the environment is very difficult to settle by experimental means and the argument continues to the present. The problems involved in attempting to test these alternatives by experimental studies are beyond the scope of this chapter. But common sense tells us that there are bound to be some situations in which a consistent trait of, for example, truthfulness would *not* be maintained.

Many psychologists now believe that we should be considering an *interaction* between an inner disposition and situations outside the person in order to account for behaviour. This would be rather similar to the way that we have come to think of the nature/nurture debate as neither one nor the other but a continuous interaction between the two.

It is important to have some understanding of the extent to which people's behaviour is the result of inner dispositions or of the situations in which they find themselves. This becomes strikingly clear when we consider the habits, rules, roles and skills of social behaviour. If what people do depends on the situation in which they find themselves, in what sense can we talk about 'real' personality as opposed to a social **persona** (after all, the word 'personality' is derived from the Latin *persona*, a mask)? Perhaps good manners, social conventions and behaviour in accord with the expectations of other people *is* personality. Or is social behaviour grafted on to one's real personality? This might be understandable when one thinks of a clearly prescribed piece of social behaviour—like queuing patiently at a supermarket check-out. But what about more subtle role behaviour, like that of mother, or a long lived-in occupational role, such as policeman or teacher? How might a personality theorist draw lines between the demands of the role and personality in the behaviour of these people? What is the difference between what 'we really are' and what 'we often do'?

Summary of Section 5

- Personality theories differ in the extent to which they can be tested. Nomothetic theories like Eysenck's are more open to rigorous testing. The testability of idiographic theories like Allport's is low.

- Kelly's theory is a mixture of idiographic and nomothetic approaches. Its nomothetic aspects are at odds with his stress on idiosyncratic constructions of the world.

- Personality theories vary considerably in the underlying assumptions they make about the nature of human beings and the motivation of behaviour.

- Most theorists believe that personality resides in the person but accept that behaviour is influenced to some degree by an interaction between inner dispositions and external situations.

Further reading

Textbooks on personality
These books cover many different approaches to the study of personality. There is usually one chapter devoted to each approach, and introductory and concluding chapters on theoretical and methodological issues.

HALL, C.S. and LINDZEY, G. (1978) *Theories of personality*, 3rd edition, New York: John Wiley.
This is the classic textbook on the subject; it is fairly advanced.

HERGENHAHN, B.R. (1980) *An introduction to theories of personality*, Englewood Cliffs, NJ: Prentice-Hall.
This is an excellent introductory text.

SMITH, B.D. and VETTER, H.J. (1982) *Theoretical approaches to personality*, Englewood Cliffs, NJ: Prentice-Hall.
A more advanced but very readable textbook.

HAMPSON, S.E. (1982) *The construction of personality: an introduction*, London: Routledge and Kegan Paul.
This short book presents a more coherent approach to the important issues in the study of personality.

Specialized books
LANDFIELD, A.W. and LEITNER, L.M. (eds) (1980) *Personal construct psychology, psychotherapy and personality*, London: John Wiley.

EPTING, F.R. (1984) *Personal construct counselling and psychotherapy*, London: John Wiley.

ALLPORT, G.W. (1965) *Letters from Jenny: edited and interpreted by G.W. Allport*, New York: Harcourt Brace and World.
A fascinating, easy read.

EYSENCK, H.J. and WILSON, G.D. (1975) *Know your own personality*, London: Maurice Temple Smith Ltd.
A book of self-completion questionnaires which also gives some insights into how Eysenck thinks about personality.

References

ALLPORT, G.W. (1937) *Personality: a psychological interpretation*. New York: Rinehart and Winston.

ALLPORT, G.W. (1955) *Becoming: basic considerations for a psychology of personality*, New Haven, Conn.: Yale University Press.

ALLPORT, G.W. (1960) *Personality and social encounter: selected essays*, Boston: Beacon Press.

ALLPORT, G.W. (1961) *Patterns and growth in personality*, New York: Holt, Rinehart and Winston.

ALLPORT, G.W. (1965) *Letters from Jenny*, New York: Harcourt, Brace and World.

ALLPORT, G.W. (1968) *The person in psychology: selected essays*, Boston: Beacon Press.

ALLPORT, G.W. and ODBERT, H.S. (1936) 'A psycho-lexical study', *Psychological Monographs*, 47, no. 1, whole no. 211.

BUSS, A.H. and PLOMIN, R. (1984) *Temperament: early developing personality traits*, New Jersey and London: Lawrence Erlbaum.

EYSENCK, H.J. (1953) *The structure of human personality*, London: Methuen.

EYSENCK, H.J. (1954) *The psychology of politics*, London: Routledge and Kegan Paul.

EYSENCK, H.J. (1970) *Readings in extraversion–introversion: bearings on basic psychological processes*, volume 3, New York: Wiley.

EYSENCK, H.J. and LEVEY, A.A. (1972) 'Conditioning, introversion, extraversion and the strength of the nervous system', in V.D. Nebylitsyn and J.A. Gray (eds) *Biological bases of individual behaviour*, New York: Academic Press.

EYSENCK, H.J. and WILSON, G.D. (1975) *Know your own personality*, London: Maurice Temple Smith Ltd.

EYSENCK, H.J. and WILSON, G.D. (eds) (1978) *The psychological basis of ideologies*, Lancaster: MTP Press.

HARTSHORNE, H. and MAY, M.A. (1978) *Studies in deceit*, New York: Macmillan.

HARTSHORNE, H. and MAY, M.A. (1929) *Studies in service and self control*, New York: Macmillan.

HARTSHORNE, H. and SHUTTLEWORTH, F.K. (1930) *Studies in the organization of character*, New York: Macmillan.

JUNG, C.G. (1923) 'Psychological types', *Collected Works*, volume 6, London: Routledge and Kegan Paul.

KELLY, G.A. (1955) *The psychology of personal constructs*, volumes 1 and 2, New York: W.W. Norton.

KELLY, G.A. (1958) 'Man's construction of his alternatives', in G. Lindzey (ed.) *Assessment of human motives*, New York: Holt, Rinehart and Winston.

KRETSCHMER, E. (1925) *Physique and character* (W.J.H. Sprott, trans.), New York: Harcourt Brace and World (originally published in 1921).

KRETSCHMER, E. (1948) *Körpelbau and Charakter*, Berlin: Springer.

MISCHEL, W. (1968) *Personality and assessment*, New York: Wiley.

SHELDON, W.H. (1940) *The varieties of human physique: an introduction to constitutional psychology*, New York: Harper and Row.

SHIELDS, J. (1962) *Monozygotic twins brought up apart and brought up together*, Oxford: Oxford University Press.

SPIELMAN, J. (1963) *The relation between personality and the frequency of duration of involuntary rest pauses during mass practice*, Unpublished doctoral dissertation, University of London.

Answers to SAQs

SAQ 1

We could call these dimensions 'shortness–tallness' (height); 'fatness–thinness' (weight); and 'jolliness–thoughtfulness' (perhaps the well-known extraversion-introversion dimension).

SAQ 2

Neurotic introverts, because they score highly on both the neuroticism and introversion dimensions.

SAQ 3

(a) successful person, ethical person, happy person

(b) successful person and happy person were similar, and ethical person was different

(c) carefree–conscientious

(d) successful person and happy person were both construed as being carefree (similarity pole); ethical person was construed as being conscientious (contrast pole)

SAQ 4

(a) Ex-flame; ex-friend; rejecting person; threatening person; rejected teacher; boss; successful person. All these elements have been marked with crosses indicating that they are construed using the first (similarity) pole, i.e. frightening.

(b) They have been left blank because they are construed using the second (contrast) pole, i.e. gentle.

SAQ 5

(a) The nomothetic approach to behaviour aims at explaining behaviour by general laws which apply to all human beings. In order to set up and test such laws, the nomothetic approach usually depends on some type of measurement.

(b) The idiographic approach focuses on unique individuals. It aims at understanding through describing each person's idiosyncratic behaviour and inner experience in detail.

(c) (i) idiographic; (ii) idiographic, but with some nomothetic aspects, such as general laws about dream theory or psychosexual stages; (iii) nomothetic; (iv) mostly idiographic (but see later discussion); (v) nomothetic.

SAQ 6

(a) Eysenck and Allport: neither is concerned with the unconscious, and both are anti-psychodynamic. They both make use of traits. For Allport, traits are the basis of consistency whereas, for Eysenck, traits are derived from types and it is a person's type that underlies consistency in behaviour.

(b) Freud and Eysenck: both are interested in abnormal as well as normal personality; both are essentially biological approaches.

(c) Kelly and Allport: both are idiographic and phenomenological. They take a positive view of personality as the total of a person's creative powers rather than driven by biology. There is interest in personality growth and change.

(d) Allport and Freud: both believe social learning is important. However, Freud stresses early childhood experiences whereas Allport is more interested in current experiences.

(e) Eysenck and Kelly: both aimed to produce a systematic theory that explained many aspects of personality. However, Eysenck based his theory on objective measures of personality whereas Kelly charted the internal experiences of individuals.

(f) Kelly and Freud: both are interested in personality growth and change. Freud was particularly concerned with the *dynamic* unconscious. Kelly acknowledges that many constructs may not be available to be expressed verbally, although when filling in a repertory grid, these constructs are forced into consciousness. They are both concerned with the 'meaning' the world and other people hold for the subject.

Scoring guide for Activity 3

To score your questionnaire responses, using the table overleaf, first give ½ for every 'don't know' answer. Then score 1 for 'yes' and 0 for 'no' to questions 2, 3, 5, 7, 8, 11, 12, 13, 15, 16, 18, 19 and 20. Then score 0 for 'yes' and 1 for 'no' to questions 1, 4, 6, 9, 10, 14, 17 and 21. These twenty-one questions measure the seven traits associated with extraversion–introversion as shown in Figure 8.4: questions 1–3 indicate activity (inactivity); questions 4–6 indicate sociability (unsociability); questions 7–9 indicate risk-taking (carefulness); questions 10–12 indicate impulsiveness (control); questions 13–15 indicate expressiveness (inhibition); questions 16–18 indicate practicality (reflectiveness); questions 19–21 indicate irresponsibility (responsibility).

If you wish, you can add up your scores for each trait using the scoring table below. But since this is only part of the original scale, you should note that adding up your scores will not give an accurate reflection of your position on either the traits or on extraversion–introversion.

To work out your *overall* extraversion–introversion score, add up your scores for the first five traits. For 'lack of reflection' and 'lack of responsibility' the questions were worded so that the *lower* scores indicate extraversion. So you need to add the opposite score for these two traits (i.e. if you scored 0 add 3, if you scored 1 add 2, if you scored 2 add 1, if you scored 3 add 0). The maximum score for extreme extraversion is 21; a score of 0 indicates extreme introversion. Scores of 6–12 indicate the more usual average scores at neither extreme. If you are interested in completing the whole questionnaire, you will need to read Eysenck and Wilson's book (1975).

Extraversion–introversion scoring table

	Activity	Sociability	Risk-taking	Impulsiveness	Expressiveness	Lack of reflection	Lack of responsibility
Question	1 2 3	4 5 6	7 8 9	10 11 12	13 14 15	16 17 18	19 20 21
Score							
Totals							

chapter

9

HUMANISTIC PSYCHOLOGY

Richard Stevens

Contents

1	**Introduction**	**418**
1.1	Humanistic psychology: a 'third force'	418
1.2	Assumptions of humanistic psychology	420
	Summary of Section 1	422
2	**Conscious awareness**	**423**
2.1	Stream of consciousness	423
2.2	The study of consciousness	424
2.3	Kinds of awareness	426
2.4	Altered states of consciousness	427
2.5	Peak experiences	430
	Summary of Section 2	432
3	**Creating yourself**	**433**
3.1	Existentialism	433
3.2	Self-actualization: Abraham Maslow	435
3.3	Conditions for personal growth: Carl Rogers	438
3.4	The nature of personal agency	441
	Summary of Section 3	444
4	**More methods for personal growth**	**445**
4.1	Encounter groups	445
4.2	Co-counselling	448
4.3	Gestalt therapy: Fritz Perls	449
4.4	The holistic principle: bodywork and psychosynthesis	451
	Summary of Section 4	454
5	**Humanistic psychology in everyday life**	**455**
5.1	Work	455
5.2	Relationships	457
5.3	Preparing to die	459
5.4	Experiencing joy	460
	Summary of Section 5	461
6	**Evaluation**	**461**
6.1	A psychology of the third kind	462
6.2	Limitations of humanistic psychology	463
	Personal acknowledgement	464
	Further reading	464
	References	465
	Answers to SAQs	467

1 | Introduction

If we look back over the previous chapters, we see several different approaches to psychology. Chapter 5, for example, was concerned with the *biological* bases of behaviour and mental life. It showed how some experiences, like depression, can be related to underlying physiological processes. Both evolution and genetics were regarded as having relevance to understanding behaviour. However, the chapter emphasized that, for effective understanding, it is crucial to see biological factors as interacting with environmental influences. Earlier chapters showed the importance of understanding the *development* of emotions and cognitions, and the *social context* in which this occurs.

The position presented in this *Introduction to psychology*, then, is that the study of behaviour and mental life can be approached from different perspectives and at different levels. Effective understanding depends on taking into account psychophysiology and genetic inheritance, the social context in which we live and grow up, and processes of development, each in relation to the other.

We can distinguish yet another way of looking at human behaviour and experience, in addition to biological, social and developmental perspectives. A notable feature about being human is that we possess consciousness and can both communicate and reflect on some of our conscious experience with the help of language. In other words, we are not only conscious but *self-conscious*—aware of ourselves as distinct from others. The development of this sense of self, you will remember, was the theme of Chapter 2, and its importance was emphasized by the work of Kelly and Allport, introduced in the previous chapter.

The topic of this chapter is humanistic psychology. Its focus of interest is this sense of self-awareness and the capacity to reflect, and the role that these can play in helping us to change and develop as people and in the ways we relate to each other. It argues that, if we see this as important, it has radical implications for the way we do psychology.

1.1 Humanistic psychology: a 'third force'

The humanistic tradition can be traced back to the beginning of psychology. William James, one of the fathers of modern psychology writing at the turn of the century, defined psychology as 'the science of mental life', which indicates the emphasis he placed on consciousness and experience as subject matter. His major psychological work, the fourteen-hundred page *Principles of psychology* (1890) is largely devoted to precise and careful descriptive analysis of mental states. His chosen method was introspection and his reflective mind continuously articulated his own experience. Although he acknowledged that he could not prove its existence, James was also quite emphatic in accepting the notion of 'free will', an issue of concern to the humanistic approach.

Humanistic psychology emerged as an explicit movement in the 1950s and was marked by the founding of the American Association for Humanistic Psychology (AAHP). This described humanistic psychology as:

primarily an orientation toward the whole of psychology rather than a distinct area or school. It stands for . . . respect for differences of approach, open-mindedness as to acceptable methods, and interest in exploration of new aspects of human behaviour . . . it is concerned with topics having little place in existing theories and systems: e.g. love, creativity, self, growth, . . . self-actualization, higher values, being, becoming, spontaneity, play, humor, affection, naturalness, warmth, . . . autonomy, responsibility, meaning, . . . transcendental experience, peak experience, courage and related concepts.

(American Association of Humanistic Psychology, 1962, p. 2) (Concepts such as 'self-actualization' and 'peak experience' are explained later in the chapter.)

This statement expressed the conviction of the founders (who included George Kelly, Abraham Maslow and Carl Rogers) that core aspects of human experience were being left out of account by the psychology of the time. In the USA, this consisted primarily of two distinct schools. One was an experimental psychology strongly influenced by behaviourism (see Chapter 6), which tended to disregard consciousness as a legitimate subject matter for psychology. The other was psychoanalysis (see Chapter 4), where the primary focus of interest was interpreting consciousness and behaviour in terms of unconscious determinants. The concern of humanistic psychologists was to do justice to people's *conscious* experience of themselves and their role in directing their own lives. They wanted to emphasize people's capacity for self-awareness, that they have the power to choose; and also that people are guided by purpose and meaning and are capable of responsibility and love. Because it represented essentially a reaction to the prevailing traditions of the time, humanistic psychology was sometimes termed the 'third force'.

The emergence of humanistic psychology needs to be viewed in the political and social context of the time. The late 1950s and particularly the 1960s was a period of rapid social change. The emphasis was on emancipation from tradition and exploration of new ideas and attitudes, both at a personal and a political level. The aims and assumptions of humanistic psychology suited and were encouraged by the temper of the times.

As the AAHP declaration indicates, humanistic psychologists were determined to be more open as to what constituted acceptable methods for achieving their goals. They have been open, too, about the variety of sources which have influenced their ideas and work. For example, although the movement was established explicitly as a reaction to psychoanalysis, the idea of unconscious motivation was not discarded. Several humanistic psychologists (Perls, Assagioli and Laing, for example) began their careers as psychoanalysts, and the concerns of the two perspectives quite often overlap.

In addition to its roots in both psychology and psychoanalysis, the humanistic perspective has been influenced by both European and Asian philosophies. These influences and others will become clearer in the pages which follow.

As indicated by the AAHP declaration above, humanistic psychology is essentially an *orientation* to the study of mental life rather than a 'school' of psychologists adopting a common mode of research or therapy or a coherent set of ideas and theories. There are substantial differences amongst theorists who may legitimately be regarded as humanistic, and there is not always a clear boundary between those who are humanistic and those who are not. Some humanistic psychologists are mainly theorists. Most work as psychotherapists, counsellors and group leaders. Yet others work in education and occupational psychology. They are united primarily by a set of shared assumptions about the nature of people, the aims of psychology, and the best methods to achieve these. It is as well to be explicit about what these assumptions are because they are somewhat different from those underlying other approaches in psychology.

1.2 Assumptions of humanistic psychology

Many of the approaches you have encountered in this book so far, start from a basic assumption about method: that is, that the methods of natural science are likely to be the most fruitful ones for psychologists to follow. (Not all, however: psychoanalysis is a notable exception.) They set out deliberately to study people as a natural scientist might study the physical world. This requires being objective and stepping outside one's own subjective experience. It means measuring behaviour and carefully exploring its possible causes through controlled experiments and observations in as precise and rigorous a way as possible. As you have seen, this approach has many advantages. It helps us to be clear about what it is we are studying; theories and models can be refined to help us understand the processes concerned; and in principle at least, experiments can be repeated if their findings are in dispute.

Humanistic psychologists argue, however, that there may be a price to pay. There may be a limit to how far a natural science approach can fully deal with the reality of our experience. In contrast, humanistic psychologists start with assumptions about their subject matter (i.e. the experience of being a person) rather than about the methods to be employed in investigating it. The experience of being a person has characteristics which are quite distinct from the physical world. The humanistic perspective is an approach to psychology which tries to acknowledge the particular nature of what it is like to be a human being and seeks to develop its methods and goals accordingly.

It is the distinguishing characteristics of being a person that provide the key assumptions on which humanistic psychology is based. It is assumed that, for effective understanding in psychology, we need to take into account: (1) the significance of conscious awareness; (2) the human capacity for personal agency; and that (3) each person is a whole. Let us look at each of these in turn.

Conscious awareness

An important feature of being a person is that we have conscious awareness. Rather than analysing a person from the standpoint of an external observer, the humanistic psychologist tries to work from the standpoint of the people themselves. The focus is on subjective awareness, how people *experience* their worlds and themselves: in other words, an **experiential approach**. This is also known as a **phenomenological approach** because it focuses on 'phenomena', that is, things as they appear to us.

One aspect of conscious experience is an awareness of being intrinsically involved in the process of existence. We might call this an **existential perspective**. For example, we are aware of the passage of time and that we are part of this, moving inexorably towards old age and eventual death. We are aware of being distinct individuals, of being 'inside' ourselves and separate from other people and the world around us.

Personal agency

A particular feature of this existential perspective which has interested humanistic psychologists is **personal agency**. In most situations we are aware of having some power of choice. You probably feel now that you could, if you wished, choose whether to put down this chapter or to continue reading. There may be pressures on you either to continue or to stop reading, but which you do is ultimately up to you. In other words, we often experience ourselves as *agents*, as capable of initiating both actions and thoughts. You could, if you chose, put on the kettle for a cup of tea, think about last Christmas, have your hair permed, smile at a stranger or send a picture postcard to your tutor. This can apply also to more major life decisions. For example, you are likely to have *some* choice in deciding whether or not to marry and what job to pursue. Because of fear, apathy, or because the consequences of alternative actions are too negative, we may not exercise our power of agency. There may be social constraints on our behaviour and, on occasion, such constraints may appear overwhelming. It may be that we are simply not aware of alternatives open to us. But in many if not most situations, some potential for choice is there, nevertheless.

An extension of this notion of agency is the idea that we ourselves can play a part in creating the kind of person we become. The best way to help such self-development, humanistic psychologists believe, is by becoming as aware as possible of our feelings, motivations and what influences us. This process they refer to as **personal growth**.

More detailed discussion of the problematic issues underlying the assumption of personal agency will be taken up in Section 3 below. But it is worth noting here that it could pose difficulties for the determinist assumptions of natural science, for it presupposes that human behaviour and mental life are to some extent an 'open system' and not fully explicable in terms of underlying causes.

A person is a whole

The third assumption of humanistic psychology refers to the idea that there are many aspects to our sense of self; we need to consider all of them as a whole (i.e. a **holistic approach**). We exist both in a body and in a particular social context: feelings interact with thoughts. Rather than studying specific psychological processes in isolation, humanistic psychologists tend to focus their attention on the *whole* person, 'not as a pure reason, nor as a mere mechanism, but as a unity of heart, mind, and even spleen' (Matson, 1964).

One consequence of working from such assumptions is that the emphasis has been more on personal growth than on scientific investigation. At the level of existential experience, humanistic psychologists are sceptical as to the possibility of an ultimate 'science of behaviour' in which explanation of our experience, actions and the way we conduct our lives can be made by reference to a common set of laws applying to all people. The development of humanistic psychology has involved theorizing and some research, but a major concern has been to develop ideas and methods to help people to take more responsibility for who they are and what they do, and to create new and more satisfying ways of relating to others.

Each of the three assumptions, and some of the ways in which humanistic psychologists have pursued them, will become clearer in the sections which follow. Section 2 emphasizes the phenomenological approach by discussing some of the ways in which *conscious awareness* has been studied and the problems involved. Section 3, after discussing the existential perspective, takes up *personal agency*, and shows how Maslow and Rogers have contributed to our understanding of personal growth. In Section 4, we shall see how the holistic principle, as well as the other two assumptions of an experiential approach and personal agency, are reflected in the *methods* devised for personal growth. The chapter concludes with a section on the *applications* of humanistic psychology to everyday life and an *evaluation* of its contribution.

An extension of the concern with conscious awareness is the idea of **experiential learning**: in other words, that learning is often best achieved by *experiencing* something or doing it for oneself rather than just by observing someone else or hearing about it. The aim of the activities in each section is to give you an opportunity to sample at least a flavour of some of the methods and concepts described. You do not need to do them all, but it is worth giving some effort to them if you really want to get the feel of the humanistic approach.

Summary of Section 1

- Humanistic psychology developed in the 1950s largely as a reaction to the prevailing traditions of behaviourism and psychoanalysis. It inherited a tradition earlier espoused by William James among others, and flourished as part of the wider framework of social and political emancipation of the 1960s. It is eclectic in approach and has been influenced by psychoanalysis and by both European and Asian philosophies.

- Humanistic psychology is an orientation to psychology rather than a coherent set of ideas and theories. Its starting point is the experience of being a person. The following assumptions are made:

  1 Subjective experience is primary: humanistic psychologists work from a phenomenological rather than a behaviourist perspective.

2 People possess a capacity for personal agency and personal growth: we have some choice and responsibility for what we become.

3 Each individual is a whole: a holistic approach involves trying to take into account the many aspects (feelings, thoughts and bodily awareness) which make up our experience of being a person.

● Such assumptions influence the goals and methods of humanistic psychology. There is greater emphasis on ideas and methods for personal development and experiential learning than on scientific investigation.

SAQ 1 (*SAQ answers are given at the end of the chapter*) Which statement is most likely to be endorsed by humanistic psychologists?

(a) Measurement is crucial in psychology.

(b) The best way to test ideas is by formal experiments.

(c) The most significant knowledge we can have about someone is what they are thinking and feeling.

(d) Studying animals can tell us a great deal about human behaviour.

(e) A person's later life is very largely determined by the quality of his or her childhood experience.

SAQ 2 In the context of humanistic psychology, what do the following terms mean:

(a) phenomenological

(b) existential perspective

(c) personal agency

(d) holistic

(e) experiential learning

2 | Conscious awareness

2.1 Stream of consciousness

As noted in discussing its assumption of a phenomenological approach, the central focus of humanistic psychology is on the individual's experience of being. The dominating feature of this is, in William James' phrase, our **stream of consciousness**. Flowing inexorably through time, sometimes lagging, sometimes so fleeting that we are aware of awareness only in retrospect, the ever-changing kaleidoscope of consciousness is marked by passages of changing quality—from sleep to the freshness of waking, from the grey muffled mists of depression to the excitement of expectation.

Our stream of awareness is structured into patterns of meaning. We are aware that dusk is falling; we are feeling angry; our team has won by two goals; our daughter has had a child. We construe the worlds within and without us, making what sense we can of events and situations. We are embedded in a reality which for most of us has, in fair measure, coherence, interconnectedness and predictability, though often with a sense of darkness and the unknown in the shadows beyond. Memories of childhood, nightmares, moments of tragedy or drunkenness hint at other states of awareness, unpredictable and less controlled.

The facets of our awareness cohere and have a continuity which we differentiate as our experience of *being in the world*. How far we are conscious of our 'self' at any time will vary. Sometimes we are only too aware of an 'I' who is doing and experiencing; at other times our consciousness is immersed in the activities themselves.

ACTIVITY 1 Here and now

The aim of this activity is to encourage you to focus as intensively as possible on your immediate flow of awareness—on what you experience *here and now*. It should take about ten minutes.

1   Make yourself comfortable and relax for a while, breathing slowly, steadily and deeply, but without effort.

2   Let your mind focus on whatever you can see, hear, smell and taste. You might like to focus on each sense in turn, or you may prefer to allow whichever one dominates your attention at any one time to do so. Try to be aware both of what you are experiencing (e.g. I am aware of a silky patterned blue surface; I am aware of a noise like a car engine revving up in the distance), and also of what the process of being consciously aware of focusing your attention in this way feels like (e.g. does it give you a sense of alertness or aliveness?).

3   After a while, close your eyes and shift your attention to bodily sensations and feelings. Are you aware, for example, of the sensation of your clothes against your skin and, if you are sitting, the pressure of the seat against your bottom? Can you sense any tension? Where? Or does your body feel completely relaxed?

4   Turn your focus on your feelings. What are you feeling at this particular moment? If that feeling leads to a chain of further emotions or even thoughts, let them come, all the time trying to experience fully each emotion as it arises.

5   Finally, let your mind free, following whatever fantasy or image emerges.

2.2 The study of consciousness

Investigating the contents of conscious experience itself was the main aim of **phenomenological philosophy**, a European movement very much dominated by Husserl, an Austro–German philosopher who was more or less a contemporary of Freud. This phenomenological approach has been taken up by several humanistic psychologists. Giorgi and his colleages at Duquesne University in Pennsylvania, for example, have analysed different kinds of conscious experience, including anxiety, anger, addiction, decision-making, love feelings in courting couples, and the feeling of 'being at home'. Their typical procedure is to collect individual accounts by getting people (sometimes the researcher him or herself) to reflect on and talk about a specific kind of experience. These are then analysed to find out what features they have in common. The studies (Giorgi et al., 1971) specify the nature and kinds of feeling involved in the experience (e.g. in anger), what other kinds of experience it can be distinguished from (e.g. impatience, fear, aggravation), and what kinds of situation tend to elicit it.

The major difficulty for phenomenological descriptions of psychological states is the lack of an effective method. There are several reasons for this. One problem is its dependence on asking people to introspect about their own feelings. If you introspect while you are experiencing something, it is very likely to interfere with the quality of that experience. Did you find in the 'here and now' exercise (Activity 1), for example, that 'being aware' of what you were experiencing changed the nature of what you were seeing and feeling? Introspective accounts tend, in effect, to be retrospections—a person recalling what he or she has already experienced.

Another problem is whether the words we use are a sufficient vehicle to convey the subtle, complex nuances of awareness. English is restricted in the labels it provides for psychological states. How many different kinds of relationship have to be embraced by the term 'love', for example! For this reason, phenomenological philosophers and psychologists have often invented new terms and concepts to describe aspects and kinds of experience. Another approach here is to utilize words denoting different psychological states from languages like Hindi, which reflect a traditional concern with different kinds of awareness. Thus, to extend the range of terms for describing psychological states, Taylor (1978) draws concepts from Chinese Taoist philosophy and Zen Buddhism. He distinguishes, for example, between wu-wei, to denote a sense of 'going with the flow' of thoughts or events, and wu-nien (literally 'no thought') to indicate the ability to suspend deliberately the flow of consciousness to achieve a state of awareness without conceptual thought. The problem then, of course, is that you have to find some way of communicating to other people what it is that these concepts refer to—not an easy task, and one reason why phenomenological analyses often make difficult reading. You can try to do it by description and definition as I have done above. Another method used by Taylor is to try to get you to experience the states referred to; he describes Zen techniques of meditation as a way of increasing skill in achieving them.

A third problem for phenomenological description is that conscious awareness is, as noted earlier, moving, dynamic and ever-changing. Most representative systems, such as language, are capable of rendering at any one time only a fraction of what is going on. (If you tried to express your 'here and now' experience to a partner you are likely to have encountered this problem.)

Fourth, and more problematic still, is the fact that experience is not fixed or given. To a considerable degree we are able to *create* and influence the quality of our awareness and the meanings we attribute to it. When we look back at a situation or when other people tell us how they see it, it may seem very different to us from how it seemed at the time.

> ACTIVITY 2 Experiencing the ineffable (i.e. that which cannot be expressed)
>
> Spend some time (five to fifteen minutes) listening to a piece of music you like. How far can you express accurately to someone what you experience as you listen to the music? How adequate could a verbal account of this be? If you cannot adequately express your experience in words, is there any other way you can communicate it to someone else?

Whilst acknowledging the difficulties involved, and that much of our experience may be fated to remain ineffable or unexpressed, humanistic psychologists maintain, nonetheless, that it is central to any understanding of the person. Their concern with consciousness has been pursued in various ways. A major way has been to encourage people to become as aware as they can of their feelings and inner experience. They suggest that, in appropriate settings like therapy, encounter groups and close, trusting relationships, a good way to intensify such awareness is to try to express feelings as fully as possible. This approach will be discussed in Section 4. Another way has been to develop methods for analysing how people make sense of the world. This is exemplified by Kelly's personal construct theory which you studied in Chapter 8. Other ways have been to explore different forms which awareness may take, and to study altered states of consciousness and the role these may play in facilitating personal growth. These are discussed in turn below.

2.3 Kinds of awareness

One theme of humanistic psychology is that awareness can be of different kinds and need not necessarily take a conscious or rational form. This idea has been explored by Robert Ornstein in *The psychology of consciousness* (1977). He approaches it in a typically humanistic way by integrating findings from many sources—from mythology, Eastern philosophy and phenomenological accounts, as well as from neurological and experimental studies. His central thesis is that each of us apprehends the world in two rather different though complementary ways. One mode can be described as rational, the other as intuitive. For example, although scientific work appears to involve an emphasis on rational, analytical thinking, great scientists and mathematicians like Einstein and Poincaré have recognized that research requires creative leaps of an intuitive, holistic kind, as well as the ability to work through such ideas in a rational, sequential way. The most effective ideas and research come from the integration of both modes. Ornstein applies the same argument to the process of writing a book:

In the writing of this book, I have had vague idea after idea at different times: on the beach, in the mountains, in discussion, even while writing. These intuitions are sparse images—perhaps a connection which allows a new gestalt to form—they are never fully clear, and never satisfactory by themselves. They are incomplete realizations, not a finished work. For me, it is only when the intellect has worked out these glimpses of form that the intuition becomes of any use to others. It is the very linearity [i.e. the setting out in line or sequence] of a book which enables the writer to refine his own intuitions, and clarify them, first to himself, and then if possible to the reader.

(1977, p. 38)

The idea of two modes of awareness is consistent with neurophysiological studies (see, for example, Gazzaniga, 1967) of the effects on behaviour and experience of severing the connections between the two halves (or hemispheres) of the brain, a procedure which has to be carried out occasionally for medical reasons. These studies suggest that the left hemisphere facilitates analytical thought involving sequential processing, including verbal and mathematical functions. The right hemisphere, in contrast, is mainly responsible for apprehension of wholes and patterns, and for spatial awareness.

Dualities of an analogous kind seem to occur in the mythologies of many cultures. In Chinese Taoist philosophy, for example, two complementary principles are believed to pervade nature. *Yang* represents day and the male, and is seen as active and existing through time. *Yin* is associated with darkness and the female, and is seen as receptive and existing in space. Their complementary nature is symbolized by the interlocking contours of the T'ai Chi sign (Figure 9.1).

Figure 9.1 Yin and Yang as represented in the T'ai Chi sign

The distinction between the two modes of thought, rational and intuitive, is useful if only because it sensitizes us to the possibility of different forms of awareness. There are also other kinds of awareness which have interested psychologists because they are so distinctly different from everyday consciousness.

2.4 Altered states of consciousness

Have you ever noticed that immediately after a period of intense concentration, such as studying hard for a long time, your awareness of the world takes on a different quality or feel from that of a normal, everyday waking state? This can also happen spontaneously when we are very tired, or when we are asleep in the form of dreams. Such **altered states of consciousness** (known as ASCs) have been prized by people of most, if not all, cultures, and various means sought to induce them. In western society we traditionally use alcohol or music: today, such music may quite likely be loud and rhythmic and accompanied by the flashing lights of a disco. Not only do ASCs offer stimulation, a way of loosening social inhibitions and release from the rigours of everyday worries, they may also be a source of creative inspiration. So Coleridge wrote his poem 'Kubla Khan' after smoking opium, and jazz and rock musicians sometimes seek to heighten their performance by taking drugs. In other cultures, ASCs are often treated as a source of mystical enlightenment and a variety of means are used to induce them. Incantation, meditation, and the use of special diets and sometimes sexual ecstasy, are methods favoured in eastern traditions. Many American Indian tribes attain such states through pain and physical deprivation. Similarly, in the Bible, revelation often came only after the privation and hardship of wandering in the wilderness. Exploration of heightened states of consciousness and mystical experience has fascinated a number of psychologists, one of the first major studies being William James' classic description (1902) of varieties of religious experience.

One way of inducing ASCs is by the use of drugs. Several psychologists have tried this on themselves. James, for example, sampled the effects of nitrous oxide (laughing-gas) and Freud experimented with cocaine. During the heady 1960s, some psychologists began offering psychedelic (i.e. 'mind-manifesting' or mind-changing) drugs like LSD to people in order to investigate their effects. Masters and Houston (1966) have provided detailed accounts, based on interviews, of what their subjects experienced. They assert that 'the average person may pass through new dimensions of awareness and self-knowledge to a "transforming experience" resulting in actualization of latent capacities, philosophical re-orientation [and] emotional and sensory at-homeness in the world' (p. 4).

Grof (1973) has also claimed that the experience of taking LSD can sometimes profoundly influence people's views of themselves. They are often able to get more in touch with unconscious memories and their underlying fears of physical pain, ageing and death. Such changed awareness, he believes, can provide an important basis for personal growth.

Even though only volunteers were used in such research, most psychologists regard the use of drugs in this way as unethical. It certainly carries risks. Freud's close friend Fleischl, whom he introduced to injecting cocaine, later became fatally addicted to the drug. Even if psychedelic drugs may sometimes facilitate positive experience, they can also lead to mental disturbance or psychosis. Furthermore, it is worth noting that habitual drug users often take drugs to withdraw from experience rather than to heighten it.

Other less risky ways of inducing ASCs have also been used. **Sensory flooding**, for example, is a method developed by Masters and Houston. With combinations of dissolving slides of coloured patterns and tapes of chanting and electronic music, they flooded their subjects with high levels of visual and auditory stimulation.

Another technique is **sensory deprivation**. In a series of investigations, Lilly (1977) constructed an environment to reduce sensory stimulation as much as possible. Naked, except for a specially designed respiratory mask, he immersed himself for hours in a tank of water kept at a constant 93°F. He reported 'many, many states of consciousness of being, between the usual wide-awake consciousness of participating in external reality and the unconscious state of deep sleep' (p. 103). He found that he could have 'voluntary control of these states' and reports waking dreams and vivid hallucinations: 'total events could take place in the inner realities that were so brilliant and so "real" they could possibly be mistaken for events in the outside world'. As a result of his experiences in the tank, Lilly claimed to have progressed to a deeper awareness of himself. His immersion was 'a fertile source of new ideas, new integrations' (ibid.).

Yet another means is **meditation**. Some of you may already practise this and will know of the kind of changes it can produce in consciousness. Practitioners claim to attain a harmony between emotional feeling, body state and consciousness. The capacity of experienced meditators to control body functions which are normally involuntary, like blood flow and heart rate, is certainly well documented (see, for example, Pelletier, 1978).

Differences in brain functioning as a result of meditation have been measured on *electro-encephalograms*. These record the overall pattern of minute electrical wave discharges emitted by the brain. During meditation, changes in wave pattern occur, depending on the kind of meditation engaged in. Usually, there is a tendency to produce stronger and more regular alpha rhythms (8–13 cycles per second) than in normal waking states. Although meditation is a skill which normally requires training and regular practice, Kamiya (1969), in an innovative set of experiments, found that subjects provided with immediate feedback about their brain-wave patterns could quickly learn to control these rhythms and hence their state of consciousness. If a tone sounded whenever they produced alpha rhythms, they soon learned to produce these at will and in this way to reach and maintain a meditative state.

ACTIVITY 3 Meditation

It is not easy to provide an exercise to help to induce an ASC. But if you have not done meditation before you might like to try this introductory meditation exercise. To learn skill in meditation takes time and training, but if you do the exercises below several times you may get a glimpse of the effects of meditative practice on consciousness. Try only one or two of the exercises on any one occasion, spending no more than fifteen minutes each time at first.

Find a place and position where you feel comfortable and will not be disturbed. Either lie down or sit in an easy chair. Begin by relaxing yourself. This is perhaps best done by closing your eyes, then tensing and relaxing each part of your body in turn, starting with your feet and finishing with the muscles of your face, jaw and throat. Next tense your whole body for a few moments and then relax, feeling the looseness and ease pervading your body. Breathe slowly and deeply, but without effort.

Exercise 1 Focus on your breathing. Become aware of your inhaling and exhaling without trying to change or interfere with the process. Let this awareness fill your consciousness to the exclusion of everything else. Try counting 'one' as you breathe in, 'two' as you exhale, and so on, up to 'ten' when you can start again.

Exercise 2   Select a simple object or visual stimulus like a spot on the wall or ceiling. Focus your whole attention on this stimulus, just being aware of it *without thinking about it*. Your aim is to still any thoughts or 'chatter' in your consciousness except your non-verbal awareness of the stimulus. An alternative form of this exercise is to repeat a single word over and over again, trying to focus your awareness on this experience, *not* thinking about the meaning of the word. At first you may find it tempting and easy to drift off into thinking *about* what you are doing or something else. Just keep on gently directing your attention back to the task in hand.

Exercise 3   After relaxing, try to still all thoughts in your mind. Aim at achieving the state of 'non-thought' or *wu-nien* mentioned in Section 2.2. If thoughts spontaneously emerge, then let them go or, without forcing it too much, try to block them from awareness.

You will probably find it quite difficult at first to focus your attention without distraction. But the value of achieving such ability to concentrate makes it well worth persevering.

2.5 Peak experiences

One particular quality of conscious experience which has excited the interest of humanistic psychologists is what Maslow (1973) has called the **peak experience** (PE). By this he refers to the sudden opening up of an ecstasy-like feeling, a sense of wonder and delight, of limitless horizons, a feeling of belonging and understanding. The kinds of occasion likely to spark off such an experience include listening to music, looking at a landscape or the sun setting, attaining a sense of spiritual ecstasy through prayer or meditation, working at a task which involves you totally, making love and the tranquillity which can follow this, or listening to poetry. Or it may be generated by events in the flow of everyday life, such as simply sitting with your family having a meal, or walking home after having studied intensely for several hours.

The characteristics of the peak experience seem to be:

1   A sudden shift in consciousness, so that what is being experienced is flooded with delight and fullness.

2   A sense of fusion with life with no sense of apartness or aloneness; a stilling or absence of existential anxieties about death, separation and the problem of choice; the act of being seems to have its own intrinsic meaning and wholeness.

3   The attention is completely focused and filled by the experience.

4   There is a sense of plentiful and available energy; almost anything seems possible.

Maslow found that those people he studied whom he called self-actualizers (self-actualization is discussed in the next section), and whom he regarded as particularly psychologically healthy, often reported having such peak experiences, in some cases daily. For many of us, the practical problems of everyday living suppress our capacity for such awareness. Perhaps the freshness and wonder of perceptual experience is something we tend to lose as we grow into adults. Wordsworth certainly thought so. He talked of the 'shades of the prison house closing round the growing boy', and his account of his own childhood experience in his poem *The prelude* is imbued with a sense of wonder and fusion with nature very like the description of peak experiences given by Maslow and others. As we grow older, perhaps we have to work harder at retaining the capacity to experience reality in this way.

> . . . ere the fall
> Of night, when in our pinnace we return'd
> Over the dusky Lake, and to the beach
> Of some small Island steer'd our course with one,
> The Minstrel of our troop, and left him there,
> And row'd off gently, while he blew his flute
> Alone upon the rock; Oh! then the calm
> And dead still water lay upon my mind
> Even with a weight of pleasure, and the sky
> Never before so beautiful, sank down
> Into my heart, and held me like a dream.
>
> (Wordsworth, 1805, Book II, ll. 170–80)

Maslow does not just regard peak experiences as the result of optimal psychological development but also as a means of facilitating such development. Peak experiences serve to release vital psychological energies and to stimulate a sense of purpose. The value of altered states of awareness generally is that they often reveal new perspectives on being. Creative work is often preceded by a shift in consciousness, sometimes an almost trance-like state, in which an experience or idea is reorganized and perceived in a sudden, new light. Accounts of the experiences of astronauts in space often have this quality. Seeing the Earth suspended in space in a totally new perspective, coupled perhaps with the effects of zero-gravity, have produced a sense of awe which many astronauts have acknowledged as being a new kind of awareness. Interestingly, many astronauts have subsequently dramatically changed the way they lead their lives, one becoming a preacher, another taking up meditation, and one, Edgar Mitchell, even founding the Institute for Noetic Science precisely for the purpose of exploring the nature of consciousness.

Precise description of experiential states is always difficult, as we have seen. Study of essentially *spontaneous* experiences (like PEs), and effects like the release of 'psychological energy' and a 'sense of purpose', are especially difficult to document with any precision. Much of significance in human experience is likely to remain *ineffable*. One of the problems with Maslow's assertions about the relation between peak experiences and self-actualization is that he provides little in the way of detailed analyses in support. We have, in effect, to take on trust or use our own life experience to confirm the conclusions he draws from his studies. Their value, however, is not as established facts, but lies in their capacity to stimulate us to think about our own experience, the way we live our lives and the alternatives open to us.

ACTIVITY 4 Peak experiences

1 Make a list of those occasions in your life you can remember which you consider to have been like peak experiences. In what kinds of situation did they occur? Are there any patterns? For example, did most of your peak joy moments occur when you were in the country, or listening to music, or with people you are close to?

2 Peak experiences occur spontaneously. It would be difficult if not impossible to plan them. But spend a few minutes thinking about whether there is anything you can do to make them more likely. For example, this may involve putting yourself more often in the kinds of situation where they seemed to happen in the past. Or it might involve developing an attitude of mind—being more open and alert to the possibility that they can occur.

Summary of Section 2

- Humanistic psychologists have been interested in the investigation and description of consciousness.

- Problems involved in such research include the difficulties of introspection and the limitations of language as a means of communicating private experience.

- Ways in which the study of consciousness has been pursued include:
  (a) the study of different kinds of awareness (e.g. Ornstein);
  (b) the exploration of altered states of consciousness (ASCs).

- There is particular interest in one kind of ASC—peak experiences. Maslow has claimed that these facilitate (and are facilitated by) personal development.

- The value of such concepts is their capacity to provoke reflection and self-exploration.

SAQ 3   Indicate three problems involved in producing effective accounts of phenomenological experience.

SAQ 4   Indicate three methods capable of producing an altered state of consciousness.

SAQ 5   What does Maslow consider to be the particular value of peak experiences?

3 | Creating yourself

As noted in the previous section, a significant part of our conscious awareness is a sense of ourselves as existing persons. As a person, each of us is aware of having a particular identity (albeit open to change and development), of being locked in a flow of time, of having only a limited lifespan. We are aware, too, of our power of choice and agency—our power to select one course of action rather than another and to initiate and to bring things about. Such features of our experience of being a person are what the **existential perspective** is concerned with. This, you will remember from Section 1, is the basis for the second of the assumptions at the core of humanistic psychology, *personal agency*. These features are also the concern of existential philosophy which has had a significant influence on the ideas and approach of humanistic psychology.

3.1 Existentialism

Existentialism is very much a European philosophy. It is the offspring of phenomenology (i.e. the study of our conscious awareness of the phenomena we experience). Early in this century, Martin Heidegger extended the phenomenological approach to analyse the experience of being or personal existence. Heidegger's ideas were taken up and made more widely known by French philosophers and writers like Sartre and Camus. Existentialism has also been influenced by the ideas of Nietzsche on the power of the individual to choose and to create, and of the Danish theologian and philosopher Kierkegaard who had focused on the conflict of humans facing the fact of the finiteness of life. Unlike approaches which are concerned with *essences* (i.e. which study the nature of humans and of reality from an external viewpoint), existentialism is concerned with the *process of being*. It takes the self as subject rather than as object, focusing upon the direct experience of existing. For many existentialists, this awareness of being is particularly brought home to us by consciousness of the possibility of non-being—that one day we shall cease to be. This idea is not necessarily a depressing one, and being aware of it can actually intensify your present experience of being.

Existentialists argue that it is crucial that we confront the reality of our experience of existence. They use the term **authenticity** for this. Facing the fact of the ever-changing nature of our being and our own eventual non-existence, for example, is to respond authentically; alternatively, we may attempt inauthentically to circumvent our anxiety by unrealistically seeking or assuming a false sense of permanence.

The idea that we are free to choose and create what we are is central to the existentialist approach. Existentialists acknowledge the many constraints on our lives. So much of our existence is outside our control: the fact that we will die; who our parents are; the time and place of our birth; our first language and the culture in which we have been socialized. However, within these constraints, they argue that we have freedom to choose and to create our actions and experiences. We act *authentically* if we acknowledge this freedom, accepting it and taking responsibility for our decisions and actions; we act *inauthentically* if we attempt to escape from it, ignoring the need to make choices and allowing these to be determined by events or by others. As Erich Fromm (1942) has pointed out, many people *fear* their freedom to choose and to construct themselves and their reality. Blind adherence to convention or fashion or to religious or political ideologies can often serve as a way of escaping responsibility for making choices. We may try, also, to immerse ourselves in the projects and realities created and imposed on us by our culture. But, when it comes to the central question of what we are to make of ourselves and our lives, our response, if it is to be authentic, can only be a personally constructed one. As Shaffer puts it:

Human beings realize that their relationship to the world is contingent and finite, and that the world, as experienced by them, will die with them. The more they face this ultimate aloneness, epitomized in the inevitability of their death, the more they sense that the meaningfulness of life, which might *appear* to be validated by the collective, and seemingly purposeful, activity ceaselessly taking place around them, can only be confirmed or refuted on the most personal level.

(1978, p. 20)

ACTIVITY 5 Existential awareness

This is an activity which requires some power of imagination. Find some time when you will not be disturbed for at least ten minutes. Focus on the experience of being. Become as fully aware as you can of the experience of *existing now*. Try to intensify this awareness by focusing on the prospect of non-being. Be aware that once you did not exist and at some future point you will not do so. Think of your date of birth. What was happening and what were people doing a few years before that? *Then* you did not exist. In several years time, too, other people will be alive and experiencing but you will not. *Now* you are aware and alive and others who have been or will be are not. What is this experience of 'being' like?

In Europe, existential ideas took early root in psychotherapy. A number of psychiatrists (e.g. Binswanger, Van der Berg) developed ways of working with patients from the standpoint of existential concerns. Thus, Victor Frankl, an Austrian psychiatrist, emphasized the importance for people of the **will to meaning**, that is, finding a sense of purpose and a direction in life. He quotes Nietzsche's line: 'he who has a *why* to live can bear with any *how*'. When we are in severe danger, our ability to survive may be all the point and purpose we need. Sartre describes, for example, how members of the French Resistance, under continual threat of being discovered and shot, felt a sense of freedom and excitement they rarely experienced before the war. If you have been in a situation of great danger you also may remember how good it was afterwards simply to be alive. When continued survival is not immediately at risk we seek purpose and meaning elsewhere. In traditional societies, religion typically served this need. Today, Frankl considers, most of us live in an existential vacuum. With the decline of established religion and moral orthodoxy, people have few accepted cultural values to guide them. Each person's 'why', he argues, must be constructed by him or herself. There is no one meaning or purpose to life which is shared by us all.

Frankl (1959) distinguishes four ways in which personal meaning may be sought. One way is through *actions*, in particular through *creative* activity. By building a machine, creating a garden, a poem or a painting we give value and meaning to our life. A second way is through *experience*—of beauty, nature or music, for example. A third way is through *love*, 'encountering another unique being in the very uniqueness of this human being' (p. 69). Finally, in situations of inescapable difficulty, we may find meaning through the *attitude* with which we confront this. For example, Frankl himself spent several years incarcerated in Auschwitz and Dachau. He found that one way in which some prisoners were able to give meaning to their lives, even in these awful circumstances, was by the fortitude with which they bore their suffering.

ACTIVITY 6 Purposive meaning in your life

1   List one or two ways in which meaning is given to your life. (One way of distinguishing these is to think of aspects of your life (such as a relationship or activity) which, if they were no longer possible, would significantly detract from the meaning which life has for you.) Do these come within one or other of the categories which Frankl suggests? Are there other categories you would want to add (e.g. spiritual meaning? religious belief? having children?).

2   Spend fifteen minutes listing your main life goals. Then arrange these in terms of whether they are ends in themselves or essentially means to some other end. (For example, getting a degree might be a means to getting a better job, which in turn might be a means to greater happiness.) To do this, you could ask yourself, for each goal, the question '*why* do I want that?'. Repeat the question to each of the answers you give until you can go no further. Pick out those which are primary goals (i.e. those which seem to be pretty much ends in themselves). To what extent are your 'means', 'goals' and your activities in general effectively related to achieving these primary goals?

When existential ideas were imported into the USA, they underwent something of a transformation. Much European existential writing has a somewhat gloomy quality. It is infused with a sense of the tragic nature of existence. Mortality and freedom are seen as burdens which we have to bear as best we can. We may try to construct some meaning in our life but, ultimately, existence is seen as meaningless and absurd. Transmuted by American humanistic psychology, however, the existential perspective takes on an altogether more positive air. The focus is placed firmly on our capacity to initiate and bring about events as we choose; in other words, on *personal agency*. This is apparent in the work of the two men who have been the most influential of American humanistic psychologists—Maslow and Rogers.

3.2 Self-actualization: Abraham Maslow

Maslow's ideas about peak experience were introduced in Section 2. In the late 1950s he had been one of the key figures in establishing both the Association and the Journal of Humanistic Psychology. Rather than focusing on people with neuroses and problems, Maslow's primary interest was to explore the healthy personality and the 'farther reaches of human nature'.

In his theory of motivation, originally published in 1954 (see Maslow, 1987), he argues that human needs form a hierarchy which reflects their emergence both in terms of evolution and, in most cases, the life of the individual. First come *physiological* needs necessary for human survival (both as individuals and as a species): the needs for food, drink, sleep and basic sexuality. Next come *safety* needs. People require a protected, reasonably predictable environment; a level of physical or economic security. Once physiological and safety needs have been satisfied, then comes the need for *love and belonging*. We need physical and social contact with friends and family, relationships with and acceptance by other people. The fourth level in Maslow's hierarchy refers to *esteem* needs. This involves both recognition by others of our worth and ability, and self-respect—a sense of ourselves as competent, autonomous and of value.

These four kinds of need are termed by Maslow **deficiency needs** in that they represent a drive to attain a state of satisfaction. For a while, at least, they can be satisfied. He distinguishes such deficiency needs from the fifth and highest level in the hierarchy, the need for **self-actualization**. This is a term he used to refer to the human desire for self-fulfilment, 'to become everything that one is capable of becoming' (Maslow, 1987, p. 22). This may take as many forms as there are individuals. For some, self-actualization may be in creativity, for others in discovery and understanding. It may be expressed athletically or in the desire to be an ideal mother. Maslow regards self-actualization as a need of a different order. It is not, like the others, a drive to attain an end-state where the need is assuaged. Rather expression of the need is an end in itself. Maslow has called it a 'being' need (see Figure 9.2).

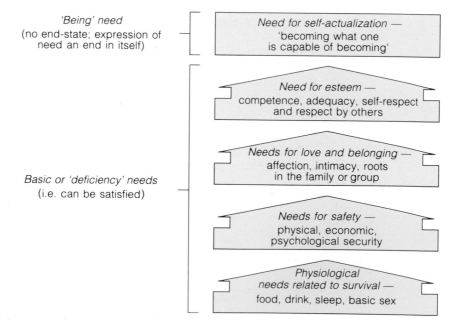

Figure 9.2 Maslow's hierarchy of needs

Maslow's original assumption was that it is necessary to satisfy deficiency needs before self-actualization can get under way. However, as Rowan (1988) has pointed out, Maslow also indicates that the distinction between them is not necessarily clear-cut. Physiological needs could be satisfied in a 'being' way, for example when aesthetic pleasure is taken in eating or sexuality. Alternatively, self-actualization could be pursued in a deficiency way if it is only aimed at achieving status.

From among personal acquaintances and public and historical figures, Maslow selected about thirty probable self-actualizers, including Thomas Jefferson, William James, Einstein and Schweitzer. On the basis of biographical material in the case of the historical figures and impressionistic analysis of the conversation and behaviour of those he knew, Maslow listed what he regarded as the typical features of a self-actualizer.

The most significant of these is being involved in a cause outside their own skin, in something outside of themselves. They are devoted, working at something, something which is very precious to them—some calling or vocation in the old sense, the priestly sense. They are working at something which fate has called them to somehow and which they work at and which they love, so that the work–joy dichotomy in them disappears.

(Maslow, 1973, p.45)

According to Maslow's analysis, self-actualizers are also creative, natural, spontaneous, prefer simplicity to artifice and see the world in unstereotyped and often original ways. Although not necessarily unconventional, they are not bound by convention. They tend to be non-evaluative and accepting, both of themselves and of others. They are capable of deep and intimate relationships and have concern for others but they are also people who can be quite happy alone. They are able to wonder at and enjoy life and, as we noted earlier, they are likely to report having had peak experiences, at least occasionally. Most of Maslow's sample were over 60 and he concludes that self-actualization is a characteristic of maturity.

Note that Maslow did not intend to imply that self-actualizers necessarily displayed these characteristics all the time. Neither were all their traits positive. They were often seen as impersonal and a little cold, and sometimes stubborn or ruthless. They could show personal vanity, guilt and anxiety (Maslow, 1987). Maslow also makes the interesting point that what are often considered to be antithetical or opposite characteristics are likely to be merged in self-actualizing people.

The dichotomy between selfishness and unselfishness disappears altogether in healthy people because in principle every act is both selfish and unselfish. Our subjects are simultaneously very spiritual and very pagan and sensual even to the point where sexuality becomes a path to the spiritual and 'religious'. . . . If the most socially identified people are themselves also the most individualistic people, of what use is it to retain the polarity? If the most mature are also childlike? And if the most ethical and moral people are also the lustiest and most animal?

(Maslow, 1987, p. 149)

Maslow's sample of self-actualizers was informal and limited, selected almost entirely from personal acquaintances and public figures. His selection criteria were (1) full use made of talents and capacities, (2) no evidence of neurosis, and (3) satisfaction of deficiency needs. All three could be regarded as culture-bound, and none of them is easy to assess. He used no comparison group and you may well feel that at least some of the features of self-actualizers he lists are circular in that they merely reflect what subjects had been selected for in the first place. Is it surprising, for example, that people selected for making full use of their talents have devoted themselves to work that they love? In spite of such criticisms though, his research is an interesting, albeit rudimentary, attempt to explore the idea of a 'healthy' personality which an individual can become.

Maslow also describes behaviour which he thinks promotes self-actualization (1973). One important basis is to try to experience fully, vividly and with total concentration. Another existential criterion is to be in touch with one's feelings, to respond as we really feel and not as we think we should do, or for effect.

At a party recently, I caught myself looking at the label on a bottle and assuring my hostess that she had indeed selected a very good Scotch. But then I stopped myself: what was I saying? I know little about Scotches. All I knew was what the advertisements said. I had no idea whether this one was good or not; yet this is the kind of thing we all do. Refusing to do it is part of the ongoing process of actualizing oneself.

(Maslow, 1973, p. 48)

Maslow considers it important when confronted with a choice to take the alternative which offers the greater possibilities for personal development and not that which is safe and defensive. He also recommends trying to open up to the possibility of peak experiences.

3.3 Conditions for personal growth: Carl Rogers

Like Maslow, Carl Rogers (who died in 1987) had a varied background in experimental and academic psychology and as a psychotherapist. He began his university studies in agriculture and science but finally majored in history. After spending time in a free-thinking theological seminary, he moved to clinical psychology with a psychoanalytic orientation. As a psychotherapist, he began working with children, only gradually turning his focus to adults. He has probably been the major figure in humanistic psychology. In a poll conducted by the American Psychological Association in 1969, he was voted third after Freud and Skinner as the theorist whose ideas have most influenced contemporary psychology.

Rogers regarded research and theory in personality as 'the persistent, disciplined effort to make sense and order out of the phenomena of subjective experience' (1959, p. 188). With his background in science and academic psychology, he considered that therapy, theory construction and research best go hand in hand. Therapy provides a rich source of hypotheses. These can then be formulated as theories and tested by more formal research methods. Research results lead in turn to modification of the theory and therapeutic procedures in a continuous on-going interaction. In this way, he viewed science as a *developing* mode of enquiry.

Rogers has set out his theory of personality as a series of formal and carefully worded propositions. There are three primary concepts: the *organism*, the *phenomenal field* and the *self*. He uses the term **organism** to refer to the totality of the individual as an organized, integrated whole (this is in line with the third humanistic assumption discussed in Section 1 about the importance of a holistic view). Like psychoanalysts, he emphasizes the dynamic, goal-directed character of the organism and behaviour. His concept of motivation is also in terms of general drive, though he postulates in place of libido, a basic tendency 'to actualize, maintain and enhance the experiencing organism'.

By **phenomenal field**, Rogers means the sum total of a person's experience. This will include experiences which are registered at an unconscious level. The phenomenal field is significant because this constitutes reality for an individual. It is the world each person experiences and to which he or she reacts. Rogers stresses that the conscious awareness of a person is the most important source of knowledge about him or her. No outside person can know this as well as the individual concerned. So clients' own internal frames of reference are the best vantage point for understanding their behaviour.

As a child grows, so a part of his or her phenomenal world becomes differentiated as 'I' and 'me', in other words, the **self**. An important feature of Rogers' theory is his assertion that there are two primary sources of the concept of self. One is the child's *experiences*—awareness of what he or she finds enjoyable, painful and exciting; awareness of what he or she can and cannot do. The other is *evaluations of self by others*—the definitions of self imposed by parents and other significant people in the child's world, and values taken over from them. Rogers again stresses the integrated, organized whole or *gestalt*-like nature of the self. Alteration of one aspect can completely change the experience of self.

The self strives for consistency. Experiences which are incongruent with the individual's concept of him or herself, are quite likely to be either misperceived or blocked from awareness. It is when significant experiences are denied awareness and cannot be properly assimilated that maladjustment arises. This can happen when a person's concept of self is heavily dependent on values and definitions assimilated from others. An example Rogers gives is of a rejecting mother who cannot admit to herself her feelings of aggression towards her child. She therefore perceives his behaviour as bad and deserving punishment. She can then be aggressive towards him without disturbing her self-concept of 'good and loving mother' because he is seen as meriting the punishment.

The origins of such incongruence between self-concept and organismic feelings often lie in childhood. Parental affection and 'positive regard' are often conditional on a child disowning his true feelings. If he really does want to hit baby brother then he is a 'bad boy', a person of no worth. So to be worthy of love, he has to mask his anger both to others and to himself. Rogers advocates that parents should not express disapproval by implying that because a child *wants* to do something undesirable, he is therefore bad.

Rather, they should indicate to the child that, although they can understand that he might feel that way, he is not permitted to *act* on those feelings because of the distress or damage such behaviour could cause. In this way a child is only required to inhibit active expression of his feelings, not to disown or distort them as a condition of his worth.

As with Maslow, the idea of self-actualization is central to Rogers' theory. He sees the basic tendency of people, both at a physiological and at a psychological level, as being to strive for growth and the expression of potential. This 'becoming a person' (the title of one of Rogers' books (1961)) is continuous and lifelong. Like Maslow, for Rogers the necessary basis for self-actualization is being fully aware of one's real or 'organismic feelings'. Only then can you distinguish a growth-enhancing move from a regressive one. The problem though is that, as we have noted above, many people have learned as children to repress their feelings.

Rogers' basic method to help his clients restore their ability to be aware of what they really feel is to provide non-evaluative, **unconditional regard**—a warmth and respect for each client regardless of what he or she thinks or does. The aim of his **non-directive, person-centred counselling** is to enable the client to admit feelings into full awareness. To facilitate this, the therapist does not attempt to direct or advise; instead, the therapist's task is to get in touch with the world of the client's inner experience and to show that this is understood and accepted. Once clients realize that they can freely express their thoughts and desires to the therapist without forfeiting his or her regard, they can begin to open themselves up to their feelings and become aware of inconsistencies between their feelings and the way they see themselves. Their concepts of self can then develop to encompass the reality of these feelings. No longer does the self depend on pleasing other people and on their definitions and values but on what the client feels. Once this happens, clients can be much less defensive. They can more easily engage with new relationships and situations which, in the past, were threatening because they risked arousing feelings incompatible with the self-image imposed by others and which had been accepted as part of the self.

Person-centred counselling is *experiential* in the sense that the client is encouraged to experience and express feelings, not just to talk about them. In line with the assumption of personal agency—that we are responsible for our own development—the counsellor can only try to help provide the *conditions* for personal growth to occur. For Rogers, therapy is a means of releasing a client's potential, and psychological maturity is where a person, by being able to integrate significant experiences into a developing self, becomes capable of self enhancement and growth.

Although it is his experience as a therapist which has been the primary source of his ideas, Rogers has also been active in research, and he has tested them out with formal procedures, including experiments. By analysing the content of psychotherapeutic interviews, for example, he showed that the number of negative self references tends to decrease and positive ones increase during the course of counselling. By using a variety of measures, Rogers has demonstrated that counselling at least generally results in greater congruence between perceived self and ideal self, and in a sense of greater freedom and autonomy. His claim is that a client in counselling moves towards 'an acceptance of the realities of the world outside and inside himself', and towards 'becoming a responsible agent in this real world' (Rogers and Stevens, 1973).

Both Maslow and Rogers, then, focus on the idea of personal growth. They stress that we are the responsible agent in the process, and that the most important condition required for personal growth to occur is being allowed to express and get more in touch with our feelings. We have seen how these ideas are embodied in person-centred counselling. But this theme underpins all humanistic therapeutic methods and some of the different ways in which they put it into practice will be explored in the next section. Before we do this, however, it is necessary to pick up on some of the thorny philosophical issues which are embedded in the idea of 'creating ourselves'.

3.4 The nature of personal agency

The assumption of personal agency stems from our *experience* of being. Although we may not always choose to exert it, we do *feel* that we have some choice in what we do. But is this sense of agency illusory? Are we *really* the agents of our own actions? Much of what you have read in this book so far has looked at the bases and determinants of action and experience: how they are influenced by our biology, social context and socialization. How is the idea of personal agency consistent with this?

Such questions touch on the issue of 'free will' and determinism (i.e. the idea that we are the product of, or determined by, factors outside our control). This is not the place to deal in detail with the extensive philosophical debates about this topic, but this seeming paradox requires some discussion. The first point I would like to make is that the nature of a problem rests on the way it is defined. Traditionally, 'free will' and determinism tend to be regarded as an either/or dichotomy. Some theorists have argued that human actions are entirely determined. Others have postulated some kind of 'free will' which is somehow exempt from the influences upon us which are outside our control. (They rarely define what this is with any precision, hence my use of inverted commas around free will.)

It would be a misconception, however, to view the concept of personal agency, as used in humanistic psychology, as in *opposition* to determinism. It arises out of determinism (i.e. the influences which shape us) but takes on 'emergent' qualities of its own, such that it is not predictable or explicable in deterministic terms alone.

Let me take the analogy of language. Clearly the language we speak is determined both biologically and socially. The capacity for speech, and the basic form which it takes, would appear to depend on the presence of certain kinds of vocal and cortical (brain) structures. The particular language we speak clearly depends also on where and how we are brought up. Nevertheless (as Chomsky has argued), anyone of us can say things which we have never before heard anyone else say. Speech then is determined, but has a quality of 'openness' in the sense that a speaker is capable of generating novel utterances.

Similarly, the notion of personal agency does not require us to posit some kind of 'free will' which somehow circumvents the biological and social influences which constrain and shape our actions. (This is one reason why our capacity to create ourselves has been referred to as 'personal agency' or 'autonomy'.) It only requires us to postulate that our actions and experience have a similar 'open' potential, in other words, that we ourselves can generate options which no one else has prescribed and laid down for us; and to accept that, in the way that we do this and the extent to which we do it, awareness and the sense of self play a crucial role.

There is no attempt then to *deny* the biological, social and developmental influences which shape us. Indeed, they are a primary source of meaningfulness in our lives. They help to make us what we are. What is asserted is the need to become ever more aware of their influence, but in an *experiential* rather than just an intellectual way. It is not only a question of knowing how, for example, a particular relationship or experience affects us but of opening up to the emotions they arouse. In this way, we move to a more integrated and autonomous self. Our actions and experience become the expression of a unique self rather than an echo of the views and assumptions of others. To take the analogy of language again: instead of speaking in clichés, we create statements which are ours.

Is this a recipe for selfishness and egocentricity? Rogers and Maslow are firm that it is not; precisely the reverse. They assume a fundamental 'goodness' in people. When people are guided by an aware and integrated sense of self, there will be a spontaneous concern for others, and this will be a concern which respects the autonomy of others rather than stifling them with care. This humanistic concept of love will be taken up in Section 5.2.

Both Maslow and Rogers, then, indicate that, given the right preconditions, self-actualization will occur spontaneously. Freedom and choice for an individual will present little problem. Growth-enhancing alternatives will be naturally chosen through 'the discovery of meaning from within oneself, meaning which comes from listening sensitively and openly to the complexities of what one is experiencing' (Rogers and Stevens, 1973, p. 52).

It might be argued that the existential problem of choice and of creating direction and meaning in one's life is not so readily soluble. Self-actualization has many possible forms for one individual and a person's life-space is inevitably limited. Even given optimum conditions, it is just not possible to become 'all that one is capable of becoming', which is what Maslow suggests that self-actualizers do. One is capable of becoming many things and these may often be mutually incompatible. There is not time or space for them all. People are confronted therefore with *choice*, not just between defensive or growthful alternatives, but between a number of alternatives, all of which may seem to represent possible destinies and offer potential for enhancing their lives.

The approach of humanistic psychology to the problem of creating ourselves has focused on finding ways to help people open up to a fuller awareness of their feelings and potentials. The aim is not just to encourage cognitive understanding but also the release of physical and emotional energies, even the development of spiritual awareness. It is also to enhance our capacity to *feel*—whether this be joy or sadness. Humanistic psychologists have developed a range of varied methods designed to facilitate personal growth in this way. Taken together they exemplify the third assumption of humanistic psychology—the need to focus on the whole person—and it is to these we now turn.

ACTIVITY 7   Creating an action

1   Think of something you would like to do but would not ordinarily do (e.g. going to a museum, taking a train instead of the car, giving a present to someone, speaking to someone you would like to get to know).
2   Imagine yourself doing this.
3   Do it.

Be aware that you have *chosen* to do it and have created an action which otherwise would not have happened.

ACTIVITY 8   Self-directed growth

This activity is designed to try to give you a feeling of your power to create self-directed change.

1   Think of one or more aspect of yourself or your life which you would like to change or develop. This may be either something *specific*—like learning to take a more light-hearted attitude in the face of problems, improving your relationship with your child or spouse or developing a latent talent like painting—or something *general* like working towards self-actualization.
2   Write down each aim and why you want it as clearly and in as much detail as possible.
3   On another piece of paper, write down, in just as much detail, all the ways in which you do *not* want this aim and do *not* want to pursue this change.
4   Put these two pieces of paper side by side and contemplate them for a while, acknowledging that there is a conflict inside you about pursuing this aim. On a third piece of paper, write an account which in some way does justice to *both* sides of the conflict, and tries to include both of them completely. This is your creative leap. Self-actualization consists in allowing these creative leaps to take place in every part of your life.

Summary of Section 3

- The existential perspective refers to our experience of being a person: it includes a sense of being part of the flow of time, a sense of agency and of having a particular identity.

- Existential philosophy emphasizes the importance of an 'authentic' response to existential issues, and, in particular, the freedom we have to choose how we act and react.

- The aspect of the existential perspective given most attention by humanistic psychologists has been personal agency and our capacity to create ourselves.

- Frankl stresses the significance of purposive meaning in people's lives.

- Maslow focused attention on the healthy personality in his study of self-actualizers and distinguished between *deficiency* needs (e.g. for physiological survival, safety, love, esteem etc.) and *self-actualization*—an on-going process of self-fulfilment not directed at an end-state where the need is satisfied.

- The aim of Rogers' *person-centred counselling* is to work towards greater congruence between the self concept and organismic feelings. The counsellor does this by (1) providing a climate of non-evaluative and unconditional regard, (2) trying to enter into the phenomenal field of his or her clients, and (3) encouraging the experiencing and expression of feelings.

- The concept of 'personal agency' is different to but not in opposition to determinism. It is best viewed as an 'emergent' property. Biology, social context and development help to construct the self, but the self can operate as an 'open system' capable of generating novel actions and ways of experiencing.

SAQ 6   Someone excuses something he has done by saying that he could not help himself. An existentialist is likely to regard this as:
(a) a lie
(b) an expression of a being need
(c) inauthentic
(d) incongruence between self-concept and organismic feelings

---

SAQ 7   Briefly define the following:
(a) self-actualization
(b) deficiency need
(c) being need
(d) unconditional regard
(e) phenomenal field

---

4 | More methods for personal growth

Humanistic psychologists like Frankl, Maslow and Rogers have practised as therapists as well as being theoreticians and/or researchers. It was this perhaps that helped develop their ideas in a humanistic direction. They needed concepts, theories and an approach which would enable them to deal with the complexities of real-life human situations. A major concern in humanistic psychology has been to find ways to help people to live their lives, relate to each other, work and love in more fulfilling ways. One of its main strengths has been the range of methods developed to facilitate personal growth.

SAQ 8   In the previous section you have already been introduced to one kind of humanistic therapy:

(a) what is it, and (b) what are its primary aims?

The diversity of methods available presents problems of selection. Those discussed here were chosen for the following reasons. Two (encounter groups and gestalt therapy) are classic approaches which are likely to feature in some way in any personal growth programme. In addition, encounter groups reflect and extend Rogers' person-centred philosophy discussed in the last section. Co-counselling is briefly mentioned because it exemplifies one of the basic principles of the humanistic approach—giving control to the individual rather than to the 'expert'. Finally, bioenergetics and psychosynthesis are introduced because, together, they most clearly demonstrate the third holistic assumption of humanistic psychology—the need to deal with the whole person. All three assumptions are represented here, though, because all the methods are experiential, encourage taking responsibility for one's own growth and try to help clients to a greater integration of feelings and bodily awareness.

4.1 Encounter groups

This is the most common form of personal growth method. About a dozen people, usually with a 'facilitator' or leader, meet either regularly or for one long intensive session, perhaps lasting over a weekend. Their interest is likely to be in personal development and/or in developing and improving their ability to communicate with and relate to others. The aim is to provide a caring environment where members of the group can feel free to share whatever thoughts and feelings they want. It is an opportunity to explore together how members feel about themselves and each other. It offers a 'laboratory' to try out new ways of behaving and relating. Also, it can often be a chance to experience the joy of intimate communion with others.

Very often, **encounter groups** are run along the lines of Rogers' person-centred approach. Acceptance and non-evaluation are emphasized. Any attempt at *explaining* and making judgements about one's own or someone else's behaviour is discouraged. Members are asked to focus on what is happening *here and now* in the groups, and not to digress from the reality of immediate experience by talking about events or people not present (though current feelings about them may be expressed). In a person-centred group, the members themselves are left to direct events, even if this means sitting in silence for minutes on end. The leader or facilitator's task is to encourage an atmosphere of trust so that members begin to feel free to express their true feelings and thoughts. This may involve some expression of his or her own feelings where this is appropriate. The idea is that when members feel non-defensive and free to express what they really feel, their ability to hear and learn from each other is increased. Each person also begins to get a clearer idea of how he or she comes over to others. The prospect of change is more likely to seem desirable rather than threatening.

The form an encounter group takes will depend on who is taking part and, particularly, on the approach and personality of the facilitator. Some leaders are more directive, intervening to question and confront and often challenging members to penetrate to a deeper realization of what they feel. 'Stranger groups' are the norm, composed of people who have not met each other before, but in some cases members come from the same environment or work setting.

Groups aim at being experiential. Following the holistic principle, they try to engage participants at an emotional and physical level rather than just in terms of words and thoughts. To foster a sense of physical and emotional freedom, people in encounter groups are encouraged to sit on the floor or on cushions rather than on chairs. If they want to, they take off their shoes. Non-verbal expression is likely to be encouraged as a way of exploring and communicating what words cannot express. Although touching, for example, can be threatening and taboo, it can also be a most powerful way to show care and to give support. Members are likely at some point to act out their feelings—shouting, crying, caressing and holding each other. A fundamental rule, though, is that members should only do what feels right for them.

Rogers has initiated extensive recording and transcribing of groups, run both by himself and colleagues. He claims there is a sequence of stages which most groups follow. (Bear in mind a group continues for at least one weekend.) In the initial stages, there is often a sense of a lack of direction, and inhibition about directly expressing feelings about what is going on in the group. Eventually, members begin to reveal their immediate feelings, both negative and positive, and to explore personally meaningful material. Rogers claims that, as a group progresses, a healing capacity begins to emerge, in that the group often seems to have a spontaneous capacity to deal in a helpful and facilitative fashion with any pain which might be experienced by its members. They begin to feel accepted for what they are, façades crack, and change becomes possible. A core feature of this phase is what Rogers calls the **basic encounter**.

Individuals come into much closer and more direct contact with each other than is customary in ordinary life. This appears to be one of the most central, intense, and change-producing aspects of group experience. To illustrate, I should like to draw an example from a recent workshop group. A man tells through his tears of the tragic loss of his child, a grief which he is experiencing *fully* for the first time, not holding back his feelings in any way. Another says to him, also with tears in his eyes, 'I've never before felt a real physical hurt in me from the pain of another. I feel completely with you.' This is a basic encounter.

(Rogers, 1970, pp. 39–40)

The later phases of a group are usually characterized by the expression of positive feelings and closeness, members becoming more spontaneous, thoughtful and helpful.

The capacity for basic encounter, to share feelings with another, may be maintained when a member returns home and, Rogers claims, this can transform existing relationships. Of course, such changes in the way feelings are expressed could prove problematic. At home or at work, openness to feelings and their expression may be neither reciprocated nor appreciated. But, for many participants, the close contact and openness they can experience in the group is sufficient satisfaction in itself.

As Rogers points out it is very difficult to *evaluate* precisely the effects of groups. Outcomes will depend on the nature of the participants, on the way the facilitator handles the sessions and on the context in which they occur. Nor is it easy to measure the kinds of changes which may happen. And, in any case, what is to be regarded as a 'positive' and what a 'negative' outcome? Rogers illustrates the last point by the story of a woman (Ellen) who wrote to him over a period of years about her experiences of participating in groups. He makes it clear that this did unsettle her and brought on deep depression. But, as he also points out, this was precisely because she learned to trust her own feelings. This brought the realization that she needed to move away from her demanding mother on whom she depended for approval and affection. Eventually, Ellen began to find satisfaction and joy in her independence and was able to meet life with new courage.

Numerous assessment and follow-up studies have been carried out, many of them instigated by Rogers and his colleagues. For example, he followed up 500 people with questionnaires three to six months after they had been in encounter groups. Eighty-two per cent replied. To ensure that this was not a biased sample, he tracked down some of the remainder, but could find no real difference in their replies. He summarizes the responses to the questionnaire as follows:

Two felt that the experience had been mostly damaging and had changed their behaviour in ways they did not like. A moderate number felt that the experience had been rather neutral or had made no perceptible change in their behaviour. Another moderate number felt that it had changed their behaviour, but that this change had largely disappeared. The overwhelming majority felt it had been constructive in its results, or had been a deeply meaningful positive experience which made a continuing positive difference in their behaviour.

(Rogers, 1970, pp. 129–30)

One may be sceptical of the value of self-report studies like Rogers' questionnaire. After all, if you have spent five days (and often money) participating in a group, it may not be easy to regard it as a waste of time. But there have also been other kinds of investigation. A well-controlled study by

Meador (1969) involved independent judges rating segments of film of an encounter group involving eight people for five sessions over one weekend. Her study reveals that the nature of the interactions in a group changes as it proceeds, all members moving from a beginning stage where communication is about externals to freer expression, acceptance and owning of feelings.

In a major study by Lieberman et al. (1973), over 200 students were allocated to seventeen different encounter groups representing ten types of approach. Evaluation included the subjects' own perceptions of their experience and various test measures taken both immediately and six months after the groups. Overall, about 60 per cent felt they had benefited. There was evidence of changes in values and some shift towards greater self-acceptance in comparison with a control group of non-participants. The effects varied quite substantially, however, depending on the particular characteristics of the group leader and the other group members.

Rogers acknowledges the possibility that participating in a group could be a negative experience. But neither he nor Gibb (1970), in his extensive study of encounter groups, found any evidence for persisting traumatic effects. Lieberman et al. considered that for 8 per cent of their subjects the experience had been 'damaging'. They concluded: 'Persons who feel essentially cut off from other people, dislike their own behaviour, and see it as less than adequate, and, in addition, believe that the encounter group experience will somehow beautifully, magically, and safely liberate them from themselves should take care' (1973, p. 440). Again, this appears to be related to specific group approaches: six groups had no 'casualties', seven had one and four had more than one. There has also been criticism of the basis for their assessment of casualties: for, as Rogers' summary of his correspondent Ellen's experience made clear, painful feelings at some stage may be necessary for subsequent personal growth. The general implication seems to be that, while there are some risks which will depend on the nature of the leader and the participants, encounter groups can be both enjoyable and valuable.

4.2 Co-counselling

I have dealt with encounter groups at some length, not just because it is here that the majority of outcome studies have been carried out, but primarily because they encapsulate the essence of the humanistic approach. I shall, of necessity, be dealing with other approaches in a more cursory fashion.

The first one I would like to make a brief mention of is **co-counselling**. This originated in the USA (Jackins, 1965), but has been refined and developed by the British psychologist John Heron (1973, 1980) and others (e.g. Southgate, 1973; Evison and Horobin, 1980).

One of the chief resources of an encounter group is the other participants. People learn from their relationships in the group and from the experiences of others as well as their own. An interesting conclusion of Gibb's (1970) review of encounter groups was that, provided members have sufficient awareness of the basic principles involved, the group process in a group without a leader is similar to a conventional group and can be useful and effective.

Co-counselling takes on board both these principles because it does away with the therapist altogether. After a few weekends training in basic listening and support skills, clients form a mutual-help network. They contract to get together in pairs, agreeing to take turns in acting as either counsellor or client for each other. This is done within a clear framework of rules and procedures, for being a co-counsellor is not the same as being a friend. The counsellor's task is to listen but *not* to interpret: in particular, he or she tries to give support and facilitate the release of emotion in his or her partner.

Co-counselling works from a set of basic concepts which have their origin in a psychodynamic model of catharsis (i.e. the release of blocked emotions; see Chapter 4). It is believed that an adult's response to a life situation may be distorted by unconscious blocks created as a result of emotional hurt in childhood. The aim of co-counselling is to release the person from such distortion by encouraging active discharge of the emotion (by sobbing, shouting etc.). By learning to express and experience such feelings rather than blocking them, a person may come to a richer, more integrated sense of self.

What is particularly interesting about co-counselling is that, while retaining the idea of the counsellor or facilitator as a 'role', it gets rid of any built-in power differential and attribution of special expertise; this would seem appropriate in an area like personal development where there may be guides but there are no scientific experts. Humanistic psychotherapists are implacably opposed to working from behind the trappings of a power role and assumed expertise. Whatever authority they might possess rests on the work they have done on themselves and their effectiveness (though, admittedly, neither is easy to assess). Co-counselling takes this a stage further, representing the most extreme example of the autonomy afforded to clients.

Heron acknowledges the political implications of co-counselling, seeing it as a model to encourage people to empower each other. He also argues that the

co-counselling method can be seen as exemplifying one form of a new research paradigm for research on persons and the human condition. I call this experiential research in which each person is both co-subject and co-researcher, refining shared ideas about persons and the human condition through the crucible of mutually interacting experiences.

(Heron, 1980, p. 105)

4.3 Gestalt therapy: Fritz Perls

Apart from Rogers, the man who has had most general influence on the techniques of humanistic psychotherapy is Fritz Perls, the originator of **gestalt therapy**. Perls uses the term *gestalt* (which means *configuration* or *whole*) to indicate his primary aim: to stimulate his client into greater awareness of his or her feelings and to acknowledge and accept these so that he or she can function as an integral whole.

Growth towards such integration is inhibited by 'unfinished business'—situations where, in the past, emotion or desire have been painfully blocked. Like Rogers, Perls maintained that the important source of such blocks is childhood. But he made no attempt to analyse the client's past. He focused very much on the present. One of the major aims of gestalt therapy is to encourage clients to full awareness of their immediate 'here and now' experience. Perls was totally against trying to explain or asking his client *why*. He distrusted reasons and interpretations of psychological states, seeing these as a way of avoiding feelings by intellectualizing. If there is something about yourself you want to change, the best strategy, Perls claimed, is to become as deeply aware of it as you can, rather than try to work out why you are that way.

Perls' focus on feelings rather than words is expressed in his exhortation to 'lose your mind and come to your senses'. He encouraged his clients to become aware and express the actual bodily and perceptual sensations they were experiencing at the time rather than talk *about* what was troubling them.

Therapist What are you aware of now?

Client   Now I am aware of talking to you. I see the others in the room. I'm aware of John squirming. I can feel the tension in my shoulders. I am aware that I get anxious as I say this.

Therapist How do you experience the anxiety?

Client   I hear my voice quiver. My mouth feels dry. I talk in a very halting way.

(Levitsky and Perls, 1970, p. 143)

Perls argued that it is important not just to be aware of feelings but to accept or *own* that they are yours. One simple technique for developing **owning** is to encourage clients to convert any expression of feeling into 'I' language:

Therapist What do you feel?

Client   My hand is trembling.

Therapist Can you take responsibility for that by saying 'I am trembling'?

One way of avoiding responsibility is to say 'I can't'. Perls tried to get the client to realize that this often means 'I won't'.

In a gestalt workshop, the therapist works with a group of clients but focuses on one individual at a time. Perls himself would start with the 'here and now' experience of that particular person and his own perception of him or her: how is he sitting, breathing; what tone of voice? There is a lot of dramatization. Posture and voice tone may be mirrored by the therapist. In turn, clients may role-play the therapist and, for example, voice the criticisms that they think may be being made of them.

Perls believed that one factor which spoils our *gestalt*—our capacity to function as a balanced, integrated, whole personality—is that, living in society we are required to play out dominant roles so that other aspects of ourselves may be suppressed. A technique which Perls often used is the **empty chair**. Clients are encouraged to explore inner conflict by voicing the different sides within them separately. One of the voices can then be 'sat' (in imagination) on the chair and the client can converse with it. A suppressed, inner voice or a character from the client's life can be conjured up in this way and spoken to or allowed to speak. Or cushions may be used to represent different aspects of a client's self and he or she may initiate a dialogue between these by taking first one part, then the other, sitting on the relevant cushions in turn.

In the safe harbour of the gestalt workshop, clients are encouraged to *act out* their blocked emotions by shouting, crying, beating a pillow or screaming at the therapist. His techniques, Perls believed, help clients to understand and accept themselves, release blocked emotions and stimulate vitality and spontaneity.

The gestalt approach flourishes. Almost all humanistic-style groups incorporate the focus on the here and now and on feelings rather than 'whys'. Most will also include a gestalt exercise (like the empty chair) or two.

ACTIVITY 9

Find someone to work with you as a partner. Get your partner carefully to guide you around the house (and even outside) while you keep your eyes tightly shut at all times. Try to be as fully aware of your sensations and feelings as possible. Afterwards discuss your experience together.

Activity 1 'Here and now' is also a good example of a basic gestalt exercise.

4.4 The holistic principle: bodywork and psychosynthesis

The core principle of gestalt therapy is to involve the whole person. This holistic approach is the third of the assumptions noted in the introduction. It is exemplified also in the range of different approaches available, from working directly with the body to fostering spiritual awareness.

Bodywork deals directly with the bodily basis of psychological experience. It stems from the idea of one of Freud's (eventually rejected) followers—Wilhelm Reich. Reich believed that unconscious conflicts and emotional blocks are often reflected in posture and in chronic muscular tensions. We are likely to tense up or flinch if attacked, for example. If a child does this often enough, it may become a physical characteristic. By using massage or physical exercise to work directly on muscular tensions or body asymmetries, such blocked energy may be released. This is the basic assumption behind **bioenergetics**. In the hands of a skilled practitioner, such body manipulations are claimed to be capable of eliciting deep emotions and memories of childhood. In fact, according to Rowan (1983), unconscious material may be brought out so quickly and unexpectedly that clients may have difficulty in dealing with it. The bioenergeticist does psychotherapy, then, but uses physical methods to open up and release emotion.

Psychosynthesis was originated by an Italian, Robert Assagioli, who, like Perls, began his career as a psychoanalyst. He gradually moved away to develop his own approach because he felt that psychoanalysis took insufficient account of a person's existential search for meaning and 'higher values' like spiritual awareness, compassion, love, wisdom and joy.

Psychosynthesis is a good example of a holistic approach. Starting from the unique existential situation of each client, it aims to increase the balance or synthesis between different aspects—intellectual, emotional and spiritual. Therapist and client co-operate in a planned and conscious reconstruction of his or her personality. They seek to explore latent potentialities, strengthen and mature underdeveloped sides of personality and activate and give direction to psychological energies.

One balance sought for is between 'eastern' (intuitive, mystical) and 'western' (rational, pragmatic) styles of dealing with experience (see Ornstein, Section 2.3). As the rational mode is dominant in western culture, psychosynthesis tends to focus on the development of *intuition*. Assagioli was particularly interested in encouraging development of the 'higher' or 'transpersonal' self, in other words, spiritual awareness. He postulated not only an unconscious but what he called a **superconscious**. In the way that the Freudian unconscious is the repository of biological drives, so the superconscious is our resource for spiritual development.

Assagioli places special emphasis on **will**. By will, Assagioli is not merely referring to will-power. He uses the term rather to refer to the conscious directing and regulating function of the personality. In his book *The act of will* (1973), he gives a useful analysis of the nature of will and suggests techniques to develop it. He does not just regard the exercise of will as a means of self-direction and control but as a way of 'realizing' one's self. It is through the exercise of choice and willing that we can create and become aware of who we are.

In psychosynthesis, each individual has to find his or her own path and life's purpose. Practitioners see themselves as guides rather than therapists. They draw on methods from various sources including psychoanalysis, eastern psychology and even athletic exercises and dance. There is particular use of meditation and techniques for directing and focusing consciousness. For example, clients learn to create vivid images in their minds so that they can visualize desired actions or specific states that they wish to attain. Symbolic imagery may be used. In one kind of **guided fantasy**, for example, a person is first relaxed and then asked to imagine in detail climbing a high mountain and, at the top, finding an old man. He can ask him any question he likes and he receives an answer. The experience is then reflected on as a way of trying to get intuitive inner guidance from the 'higher self'.

ACTIVITY 10 Guided fantasy

Relax yourself. (For a basic method for doing this see Activity 3 'Meditation'.)

Then, with your eyes closed, visualize a road which represents the path of your life. A little way along it, you come to a crossroads. Explore the alternative ways open to you. What do they look and feel like? What kind of road or pathway are they? Then choose your route forward. Follow this road and see where it takes you. Where does your life go in two years time, in five years, in ten? What is the road like? Try to become aware of any major landmarks on the way. (All this should take about twenty minutes.)

Afterwards, reflect on what possible insights this might give you about the way you are leading your life and where you want it to go. Better still, discuss your experience with a friend who has also done the exercise.

ACTIVITY 11 Spiritual psychosynthesis

Drawing on literature, history and mythology, Assagioli points out that the *rose* has often served as a symbol of the spirit. Imaging the process of growth and development of the rose, he argues, may help to stimulate the 'wonderful and mysterious action of the intrinsic vitality or livingness, both biological and psychological, that works with irresistible pressure *from within*' (Assagioli, 1965, p. 214).

Try to focus your attention and imagine vividly what is described as you read the passage below (or perhaps get a sensitive friend to read it slowly aloud for you).

Let us imagine a rosebud, closed. Let us visualize its stem and leaves, with the bud above. It appears green, because the sepals are closed, but at the very top a rose-coloured point can be seen. Let us visualize this vividly, holding the image in the centre of our consciousness.

Now begins a slow movement; the sepals start to separate little by little, turning their points outward and revealing the rose-hued petals, which are still closed. The sepals continue to open until we can see the whole of the tender bud. The petals follow suit and slowly separate, until a perfect fully-opened rose is seen. At this stage let us try to smell the perfume of this rose, inhaling its characteristic and unmistakable scent; so delicate, sweet and delicious. Let us smell it with delight (it may be recalled that religious languages frequently employed perfume as a symbol, e.g. 'the odour of sanctity'; and incense is also used in many religious ceremonies). Let us now expand our visualization to include the whole rose bush, and imagine the life force that arises from the roots to the flower and originates the process of opening. Finally, let us identify ourselves with the rose itself, or, more precisely, let us 'introject' it into ourselves. Symbolically we *are* this flower, this rose. The same life that animates the universe and has created the miracle of the rose is producing in us a like, even greater miracle—the awakening and development of our spiritual being and that which radiates from it.

(Assagioli, 1965, pp. 214–15)

By using this exercise, Assagioli claims, we can effectively foster the 'inner flowering' of spiritual growth.

In looking back over the methods of humanistic psychology introduced in this chapter, we can see that there has been some attempt to assess the effects of humanistic methods. However, there are no comparative data to suggest that any one is 'best'. Different aspects (e.g. bodywork or spiritual awareness) will appeal to people with different needs and concerns, or at different stages of self-exploration. In practice, most humanistic groups and practitioners are eclectic, using a mix of the approaches and techniques discussed above. Personal growth methods are perhaps best regarded as a form of education. As noted in the discussion of encounter groups, some assessments have been made of their effectiveness, but evaluating them is rather like evaluating a course in creative writing or a relationship. The value of the outcomes in both cases is pretty much a matter of personal experience and judgement rather than rigorously assessable. And, as with relationships, participation offers the possibility of rich rewards but demands personal investment and maybe some risk.

Like those of psychoanalysis, the concepts and methods of humanistic psychology have permeated our culture. This influence can be seen in the emergence of consciousness-raising groups, personal liberation movements, attempts to establish alternative lifestyles and the 'new age' movement. It can be seen in assertiveness training and the widespread use of experiential methods and workshops for learning skills. We go on in Section 5 to look at some of the more general applications of humanistic psychology in everyday life.

Summary of Section 4

A variety of methods have been developed to facilitate personal growth.

- *Encounter groups* provide a supportive context for participants to experience and explore feelings and the relationships within the group and to experiment with change.

- *Co-counselling* does away with the therapist as expert and helps clients to facilitate each other's personal growth.

- *Gestalt therapy* uses various techniques such as dramatization to deepen awareness of feelings and to articulate and integrate suppressed aspects of self.

- *Bodywork* uses direct physical manipulations to release blocked emotions.

- *Psychosynthesis* uses meditation and guided fantasy among other techniques to develop wholeness and balance of personality, will and spiritual awareness.

- Most humanistic work tends to be eclectic, drawing on techniques from different approaches.

SAQ 9   Indicate in which kind of personal growth session (encounter group, bioenergetics, gestalt therapy, psychosynthesis, co-counselling) the following situations are most likely to occur:

(a) Two people alone together take turns in listening to each other.

(b) A group of people sit around the floor in silence.

(c) A person talking to herself.

(d) A person jumping up and down.

(e) A group of people with eyes shut listening while another guides them in a fantasy.

SAQ 10   Give brief definitions of the following:
   (a) Basic encounter
   (b) Empty chair technique
   (c) Bioenergetics
   (d) Superconscious
   (e) Guided fantasy

5 | Humanistic psychology in everyday life

As we have seen, humanistic psychology embodies an approach to personal relations, experiencing and living. The essence of this is:

1 A commitment to *experiential* reality—an openness to feelings and awareness. This may be helped by being able to explore experience within a trusted relationship or group and trying to be as open as possible about what you are thinking and feeling, about what is really going on.

2 Taking responsibility for our own lives and actions (ie. *personal agency*) and helping others to do this.

3 A concern with the *whole person*.

The aims of this section are to show that these principles can be directly applied in everyday life not just in groups and therapy sessions. They have a particular relevance to the social situations we find ourselves in. It is perhaps as a philosophy and an approach to life wherein lies humanistic psychology's greatest potential.

5.1 Work

In the areas of interpersonal skills, management training and organizational development, humanistic ideas have exerted considerable influence. Knight (1982) has argued that there is a natural link between creative management and humanistic psychology. An ideal manager he sees as 'a *facilitator* who helps a group to *realize its potential*'; and 'like creative management, humanistic psychology starts with vision building and directs its energies to the practical means of turning visions into realities. . . . [its interest is] in enlarging the range of the possible' (pp. 2–3).

One of the first applications of humanistic ideas was a forerunner of encounter groups. **Sensitivity training** involves groups of managers and workers getting together to improve their ability to communicate and work together, and their sensitivity to how others see them. While participants in these groups often felt they gained a great deal in personal terms, there were sometimes difficulties when they returned to work and put their new awareness into action with colleagues who had not been in such groups. So, in the late 1960s, the attention of humanistic consultants turned to working with organizational structures.

For some years, Maslow himself was involved in running his family firm. In his last book *Eupsychian management* (1965), he applied his theory of motivation to the work situation. In terms of his hierarchy of needs, he argues that it is not enough for work to satisfy only 'deficiency' needs like survival or even self-esteem with good wages and working conditions. Workers need to be able to exercise autonomy in the work situation and to be given scope for exploring their potential. One expression of this shift of approach is **theories X and Y**, originally proposed by MacGregor (1960). These are representations of different sets of assumptions that managers may make about the nature of people. Theory X is the idea that people basically dislike work and need to be controlled and directed in order to get them to do it. Theory Y, in contrast, regards people as enjoying exercising their skills. If they feel personally involved, people will be committed to the work they do and seek to take responsibility for it. Most people are regarded as having considerable capacity for imagination and creativity. As Knight points out:

As managers have found, theory Y, like theory X, can be a self-fulfilling prophecy. By putting high expectations on people it often brings out the best in them. It thus shares the quality which marks out many of the theories of humanistic psychology—that by redefining the human situation it creates an opening for growth and becomes a force for change.

(Knight, 1982, p. 35)

Another attitude shift promoted by humanistically-orientated consultants has been from competitiveness to **synergy** (a term which Maslow uses and takes from the anthropologist Ruth Benedict). This is where what you do for yourself is also to the advantage of other people. By empowering others, you empower yourself. Contrast the competitive model which sees the two as mutually exclusive.

A third principle is to approach potential conflicts by trying to facilitate communication between staff members. Rogers (1970) cites an example of a large American corporation using an encounter-style approach in order to help with personnel problems posed by a merger.

1   Key staff in both companies were interviewed. They were encouraged to express any feelings, anxieties, prejudices and personal fears about the forthcoming change.

2   The facilitator then got the two sets of staff together and displayed on a board the concerns, doubts and questions of both sides.

3   This then provided the stimulus for an open discussion. The facilitator encouraged people to talk and communicate with each other as frankly as possible about what they really felt about the merger both on a personal as well as a professional level. This served the purpose, Rogers claimed, of at least clarifying what were substantial concerns and what were based on projections and misunderstandings.

In terms of *training*, the orientation of the humanistic psychologist is to encourage both the sharing of experience, and the idea that it is the individual's task rather than a supervisor's to monitor his or her own performance and to set goals for improvement. A nice example of this approach applied to professional development outside an organizational context is Heron's **peer group assessment** (1979) which he has used with dentists and doctors. A group meets for a series of sessions guided by the facilitator. First they discuss and set up their own criteria for efficient work. Each then records and evaluates his or her own performance. Later sessions focus on exploring together ways of improving their skills to meet the standards they have set, and of monitoring such improvement to ensure it is maintained.

Training in interpersonal skills and creative management is often *experiential*, i.e. the emphasis is on actually experiencing, doing and getting feedback. Thus, a group might work on a problem together. Subsequently, group members reflect on this by sharing feelings about the activity and each other's behaviour. Another example of a training procedure broadly based on humanistic principles is **assertiveness training**. This involves making one's own needs clear, while acknowledging those of the other people concerned.

The broad humanistic principles which can be applied in a work setting are also relevant, as Rogers (1983) has demonstrated, to *education*. In both cases, the shift is away from authoritarian imposition and hierarchical roles. The autonomy of workers and students is encouraged. Managers and teachers are seen as facilitators, freeing the student and worker to exercise their interest and skills. The emphasis is on learning through experience, on self-evaluation rather than evaluation by others and on taking emotional and personal needs into account. Ideally, both work and education should have some personal relevance for the people involved. And it is important to create, as far as possible, an environment of unconditional regard, where people feel comfortable about exploring and trying things out. Although the bleak realities of a profit-dominated workplace and an unruly or exam-orientated school may not always be fertile soil for such ideas, those instances where they have been applied serve as useful pointers to what might be done.

5.2 Relationships

It is not only in spheres like work and education that the principles and ideas of humanistic psychology can be directly applied but in personal life too. For example, they have considerable relevance to the way we conduct our relationships.

Jot down a few notes about the ways in which the principles and techniques you have been introduced to in this chapter could be relevant to a relationship you have.

Drawing on ideas originally put forward by Bateson and which underpin a lot of more recent work in family therapy, Ronald Laing has argued that there is a complex interaction between our relationships and the way we feel about ourselves, and that this can create problems. Our concept of self is essentially *relational*. To be a mother you require a child. You cannot be a husband without a wife, nor a lover without a beloved. How others see us and relate to us therefore affirms (or denies) what we feel ourselves to be. The process may be circular. The reactions of significant others determine how we regard ourselves. Their reactions may then seem justified in the light of this identity we have assumed. This process is particularly powerful in childhood.

Our sense of self then, is critically dependent on our relationships with others, particularly on how we *assume* they regard us. Not only do we have to infer what others think of us, but we know that they know that we are capable of doing this. They, in turn, are aware of the same in relation to us. These perspectives on perspectives can create complex webs in the pattern of relationships. Laing has attempted to portray some of the tangles that can arise.

For example, in several poems from his book *Knots* (1972), he shows how people need each other to validate their sense of worth. This may lead them to present themselves in such a way (even when this is not what they feel) as to get the reaction they desire.

> She wants him to want her
> He wants her to want him
> To get him to want her
> she pretends she wants him
> To get her to want him
> he pretends he wants her

Jack wants	Jill wants
Jill's want of Jack	Jack's want of Jill
so	so
Jack tells Jill	Jill tells Jack
Jack wants Jill	Jill wants Jack

> a perfect contract

(Laing, 1972, p.48)

This may not work, however. If a person was not valued enough as a child, he may have such low self-esteem, that whatever the other person says or does may not be enough to convince him of his own worth. The problem is that we know that what people say may be different from what they really feel.

Jill   You think I am stupid

Jack   I don't think you're stupid

Jill   I must be stupid to think you think I'm
        stupid if you don't: or you must be lying.
        I am stupid every way:
        to think I'm stupid, if I am stupid
        to think I'm stupid, If I'm not stupid
        to think you think I'm stupid, if you don't.

(Laing, 1972, p. 22)

Humanistic psychology's answer to such tangles is to try to break the spiral of inference and demand. What is regarded as vital for this is that each partner be allowed to express what he or she is feeling, and to listen to what the other is saying without evaluating or inhibiting the person speaking. Each should then in turn have the opportunity to express the feelings which the other partner's statement arouses. Principles like Rogers' *unconditional regard* and Perls' *owning* (i.e. expressing your views not as statements about what the other person is like but as expression of your own feelings) are directly relevant here.

While effective communication requires openness and caring, partners are encouraged to take responsibility for themselves and not for the other person. Two important principles of humanistic psychology about relationships are:

1   To accept other people's right to be themselves: to avoid imposing your expectations and judgements on other persons about what they should do and be like.

2   The idea of love being, in Fromm's words, 'the union of two individuals without loss of their individuality'.

From an existential perspective, love can be regarded as a means for overcoming existential isolation. A relationship is not a 'given' but, like other aspects of our lives, can be consciously created. In this case, however, such creation is a *mutual* process to be negotiated together by the people involved. In this process, the capacity for open and unrestricted communication is a tremendous asset.

Yet another function of humanistic psychology is to open people up to alternatives, for, like paintings and novels, relationships can be created in different forms. It may help the creative process to extend the creator's repertoire of what is possible. In this respect it is worth comparing the different approaches to research on relationships of experimental social psychology and humanistic psychology. Whereas the primary aim of the former is to establish general laws to explain, say, love (what makes one person attracted to another etc.), humanistic research is more concerned with opening people up to different ways in which it is possible to love. Thus Rogers' book *Becoming partners: marriage and its alternatives* (1973), as its title suggests, explores the experience of people in widely different kinds of intimate relationships.

5.3 Preparing to die

The principles of humanistic psychology have application also to the darker sides of life. Just before his death in 1987 Rogers wrote, for example, of his own experience of growing old.

One of the areas which is most taboo in industrialized western societies is dying. Death is removed from us. Few of us ever see a dead person. Relatives and medical staff may conspire not to inform a dying person of the reality of his or her condition. Even if they do, they may deny its reality by bland assurances that everything will be 'all right'. In many cases, of course, such denial merely forces the dying person into a state of greater isolation. His or her deepest anxieties and fears cannot be expressed or discussed. Death has to be faced alone.

In contrast, the humanistic approach emphasizes openness, there is an effort to break through the crust of inhibitions and conventions which lead us to hide our feelings from each other and even from ourselves, and which can often distort our experiences. Elizabeth Kubler-Ross (1970) and others have argued that the same approach can be applied to dying. She encourages friends, helpers and relatives to be much more open. Dying people can thus prepare for and experience their fate ('the final stage of growth', as she calls it) in a more authentic and probably more psychologically comfortable way.

Encounter-type groups have been used to prepare people for their eventual death, sometimes involving role-playing of gradual deterioration and dying. Some psychologists (e.g. Grof and Halifax, 1978) have advocated the use of drugs such as marijuana or even LSD to help people come to terms with and enjoy their last moments of life, without needing to deny the fact that they are soon to die.

5.4 Experiencing joy

Finally, I want to mention what is, in my view, an integral feature of humanistic psychology—an active concern with fostering *joy*. This is not just a question of pleasure; rather, it is a joy which takes many forms but which above all asserts a oneness with the life of which we are a part. There are four particular avenues which humanistic psychologists use as ways of facilitating the experience of joy. One is *meditation*. Another is the sense of deep and close *community* which comes from sharing intimate feelings and thoughts with a group of trusted people. The third is heightening our capacity for *awareness* through the senses; by massage, for example. Fourth is the experience of *celebration*. This may come by gathering together with dance and ritual, or it may be by consciously promoting an appreciation of life in all its rich and varied forms.

In the view of many humanistic psychologists, one of the most important sources of joy comes from working through painful experiences. The essential point of humanistic methods like encounter groups is to acknowledge the reality of the experience we feel—whether this be a deep sense of fear, conflict, laughter, longing or grief. Joy comes, they would argue, from opening oneself up to this reality with the support and resources of other caring people; in this way, one can begin to come to terms with whatever darkness lies within.

In the earlier sections, we have considered the basic assumptions of humanistic psychology and how these have been given shape in theory and technique. In this section we have also seen something of how these can be applied in both personal life and society. Some evaluative comments have already been made. To conclude, the final section will draw the threads together and assess what humanistic psychology has to offer.

Summary of Section 5

The principles of humanistic psychology can be applied in everyday life:

- *At work*: by encouraging personal involvement, synergy and communication: in training, through peer group assessment, experiential groups, assertiveness and sensitivity training.

- *In education*: by encouraging experiential learning, self-evaluation and freedom to explore.

- *In relationships*: by encouraging mutual openness through unconditional regard, the owning and expression of feelings, and acknowledgement of each other's autonomy. Existentially a relationship can be viewed as an on-going mutual creation for overcoming aloneness.

- *Dying*: as Kubler-Ross has shown, the humanistic principles of openness and bringing hidden feelings to the surface may be helpfully applied with dying people.

- *Joy*: humanistic psychology is concerned with ways to foster our experience of joy.

SAQ 11   You are a teacher. If you are following humanistic principles in your classroom, which of the following are likely to be particularly important to you?

(a) Trying to be aware, as far as possible, of what your students are thinking.

(b) Trying to get them actively involved in their work.

(c) Keeping control by ignoring undesirable behaviour.

(d) Rewarding students by paying particular attention to them when they are well behaved.

(e) Making sure they pass their exams.

SAQ 12   Briefly define: (a) sensitivity training; (b) synergy; (c) 'owning'.

6 | Evaluation

List what you consider to be some of (a) the strengths of humanistic psychology, and (b) its weaknesses.

What then is humanistic psychology? Essentially, it represents a perspective—a way of approaching psychology which works from core assumptions about the nature of the person rather than about methods. It assumes that conscious awareness is central to our experience of being a person, that we are not fixed by the influences upon us but have some capacity for personal agency, and that personal growth is most likely to come about if we try to open up to our feelings and integrate the different aspects of ourselves. This has resulted in a collection of theories, ideas and concepts about the nature of being a person and a variety of techniques for facilitating personal growth, many of which are applicable in everyday life.

6.1 A psychology of the third kind

Evaluation inevitably involves assumptions about what *evaluative criteria* are to be employed. As we have seen, humanistic psychology differs in several important respects from other approaches in psychology. Because its assumptions, goals and subject matter are different, it is not necessarily appropriate to apply the evaluative criteria which have been adopted by, say, behaviourist or experimental psychology. It can be argued, for example, that meanings, awareness and feelings (the central subject matter of humanistic psychology) are difficult to measure without losing much of their richness. Nor can many of the phenomena which interest humanistic psychologists, such as peak experiences, be easily created in a laboratory (though it's a nice idea!). Experimental evidence no longer has the same relevance when personal growth rather than explanation is your goal. You cannot demonstrate experimentally that self-actualization is a desirable aim.

As the assumptions and goals of different approaches to psychology are different, so too are the kinds of understanding which they yield. Much of psychology is experimental, adopting the approach of natural science. But areas which focus on a person's experience and relation with others introduce a different style (see, for example psychoanalysis, Chapter 4; some personality theories, Chapter 8; and some social psychology, Chapter 3). The understanding they offer often consists of concepts and interpretations of the meaning of actions rather than explanations in terms of causes. Humanistic psychology introduces a third aspect. For, with its assumptions about personal agency—the 'open system' nature of being a person and the role of the self in bringing about change—it is concerned not just with the causes and meaning of behaviour, but with how people *might* behave and experience. In this sense, it becomes to some extent what we might call a 'moral science', using that term in its broadest sense. The notions of personal growth, self-actualization and Maslow's criteria for a 'healthy personality' would all seem to be of this order. Such issues have been, in western thought, traditionally the province of religious faith and the reasoning of moral philosophers. In humanistic psychology, they are approached not from a basis of faith or by reasoning alone, but by exploring and reflecting on the experience of being a person.

6.2 Limitations of humanistic psychology

Even if we accept the humanistic perspective in terms of its own goals and assumptions however, there are still a number of criticisms which can be made.

1 *Insufficient concern with social context?* One criticism is that humanistic psychology, because of its focus on the individual, largely ignores the power of social and cultural forces. Sufficient emphasis is rarely given to the social origins of meaning and awareness. It is possible, for example, that what seem to be 'existential realities', like the experience of individual autonomy, may be merely one outcome of a specific form of social organization rather than fundamental experiences universal to mankind. Thus, perhaps the desire for personal growth derives from our experience of living in a technological society where the idea of 'progress' and change is the norm.

This raises the question of how far humanistic psychology, with its focus on the self, reflects the values of the society in which it was conceived—the individualism and achievement orientation of western capitalism. Maslow's ideas of a healthy personality and self-actualization might well carry some resonance of upwardly mobile achievement. The focus on personal growth may seem self-centred. As Maslow, Rogers, Fromm and others have argued, though, it is only if you understand and accept yourself that healthy love (i.e. one that acknowledges the autonomy of the other person) becomes possible. Their particular concern has been to encourage openness, trust and care in relations between people. Any approach, particularly one concerned with human possibilities, is bound to be influenced by the society of which it is a part. One reason why humanistic psychology has tried to take on board some eastern ideas is an attempt to broaden its conception of the person to what is more universally human. It has also been argued that humanistic psychology is only for the élite few; that it has little relevance to the 'person in the street'. It is true, of course, that taking part in encounter groups is more accessible to some than others. But, as the last section demonstrates, the basic philosophy and principles of humanistic psychology are applicable in areas of life in which all of us engage, and can be relevant, as the experience of Frankl in concentration camps illustrates, even where resources and freedom are at a minimum.

2 *Overemphasis on personal agency?* Another criticism made of humanistic psychology is that too much faith is placed in the power of personal agency. We may believe that we are capable of self-direction but this may merely be a delusion which masks our control by unconscious forces rooted in biology, culture and our own personal past. As we have seen, though, humanistic psychologists such as Rogers have been influenced by psychoanalytic ideas. There is no attempt to *deny* the unconscious, even though it is not given as much weight. In many group and individual techniques, attention is paid to becoming aware of and harnessing unconscious and biological processes. Although the phenomenal world is the point of access to them, personal growth and agency can be regarded, as suggested in Section 3.4, as emerging from the integrated self. It is by opening oneself up to feelings and accepting what one is which makes growth possible. It is a matter of discovery as much as decision.

3   *Insufficient evaluation of methods and ideas?* Perhaps the most trenchant criticism is that directed at the status of humanistic psychology as a body of knowledge. It is true that Rogers has made great efforts to formulate his theory in terms of precise propositions and to relate them to research findings. However, as we have seen with the writings of Maslow, there is often a tendency for theories and concepts to be formulated in a rather vague and imprecise way. Statements are often just assertions supported only by anecdotal observation or loose argument. Even given the nature of their aims and subject matter, there is room for tighter conceptualization and more precise expression of ideas. The development of understanding requires both creating ideas *and* evaluating them. It is the latter in which humanistic psychology is lacking; there has been insufficient refinement of ideas and assessment of methods.

Such weaknesses of humanistic psychology should not preclude acknowledgement of the innovations which it has attempted to make both in terms of the approach and the 'politics' of psychology. The radical shift in assumptions which it represents makes it a fundamentally different way of approaching psychology (which is one reason why, like psychoanalysis, it does not always sit easily in academic psychology). In psychotherapy, it has shifted power to the client away from the 'expert' therapist. For this reason alone, as Gendlin (1988) has put it, Rogers 'faced down the hatred of most of the profession because in the work place, classroom, therapist's office and all around him, he turned the social system upside down'. There is some evidence that some of its methods can provide positive change and are often found intrinsically worthwhile. In particular, humanistic psychology offers conceptual tools to stimulate thinking about ourselves and methods for exploring our experience. Many people have found that these have alerted them to new ways of looking at themselves and others. You can judge its value in this respect by your own experience of the ideas presented here. I hope you have at least been stimulated to explore one or two of them a little further.

Personal acknowledgement

I would like to thank John Rowan for his helpful comments on this chapter.

Further reading

HUXLEY, A. (1976) *Island*, St. Albans: Panther. An absorbing account of a fictional society where childrearing, education, work, relationships and dying are structured and run along humanistic lines.

SCHUTZ, W. (1971) *Joy: expanding human awareness*, London: Souvenir Press. One of the pioneers of humanistic psychology provides illustration and discussion of some methods used in his groups.

ORNSTEIN, R.E. (1977) *The psychology of consciousness*, 2nd edn, New York: Harcourt Brace Jovanovich. A wide-ranging and readable study of different kinds of awareness.

PAYNE, B. (1973) *Getting there without drugs*, New York: Viking Press. A selection of exercises for changing awareness.

ROWAN, J. (1988) *Ordinary ecstasy: humanistic psychology in action*, 2nd edn, London: Kegan Paul. A comprehensive account of psychotherapy methods and applications of humanistic psychology.

ROGERS, C. (1973) *Encounter groups*, Harmondsworth: Penguin. Readable, classic description and evaluation of encounter groups.

SCHAFFER, J. (1978) *Humanistic psychology*, Englewood Cliffs, NJ: Prentice Hall. A concise account of the philosophy and theory of humanistic psychology.

HUXLEY, A. (1967) *The doors of perception*, London: Panther. This provides a brief, vivid account of his experiences of ASCs induced by the drug mescalin.

ST. JOHN, J. (1977) *Travels in inner space*, London: Gollancz. A readable account of one man's experience of different kinds of humanistic group.

REASON, P. and ROWAN, J. (1981) *Human enquiry: a source book of new paradigm research*, Chichester: Wiley. A collection of research studies along humanistic lines.

References

AMERICAN ASSOCIATION OF HUMANISTIC PSYCHOLOGY (1962) *Articles of association*, AAHP.

ASSAGIOLI, R. (1965) *Psychosynthesis*, New York: Dorman and Co.

ASSAGIOLI, R. (1973) *The act of will*, New York: Viking Press.

EVISON, R. and HOROBIN, R. (1980) *How to change yourself and your world*, Sheffield: Co-counselling Phoenix.

FRANKL, V.E. (1959) *Man's search for meaning: an introduction to logotherapy*, Boston, Mass.: Beacon Press.

FROMM, E. (1942) *Fear of freedom*, London: Routledge and Kegan Paul.

FROMM, E. (1948) *The art of loving*, London: Routledge and Kegan Paul.

GAZZANIGA, M.S. (1967) 'The split brain in man', *Scientific American*, August, pp. 24–9.

GENDLIN, E. (1988) 'Obituary on Carl Rogers', *American Psychologist*.

GIBB, J.R. (1970) 'The effects of human relations training', in Bergin, A.E. and Garfield, S. (eds) *Handbook of psychotherapy and behaviour change*, New York: Wiley, pp. 820–62.

GIORGI, A., FISCHER, W.F. and VON ECKARTSBERG, R. (1971) *Duquesne studies in phenomenological psychology*, vol. 1, Duquesne, Penn.: Duquesne University Press.

GROF, S. (1973) *Realms of the human unconscious: observations from LSD research*. New York: Dutton.

GROF, S. and HALIFAX, J. (1978) *The human encounter with death*, London: Souvenir Press.

HERON, J. (1973) 'Re-evaluation and co-counselling: personal growth through mutual aid', *British Journal of Guidance and Co-counselling*, no. 1.

HERON, J. (1979) 'Peer review audit', unpublished paper, British Postgraduate Medical Foundation: University of London.

HERON, J. (1980) 'History and development of co-counselling', *Self and Society*, vol. 8, no. 4.

JACKINS, H. (1965) *The human side of human beings: the theory of re-evaluation counselling*, Seattle, Wash.: Rational Island Press.

JAMES, W. (1890) *Principles of psychology*, London: Macmillan.

JAMES, W. (1902) *Varieties of religious experience*, London: Longman.

JAMES, W. (1943) *Essays on faith and morals*, London: Longman.

KAMIYA, J. (1969) 'Trained self-control of the EEG alpha rhythm', in Tart, C. (ed.) *States of consciousness*, New York: Wiley.

KNIGHT, K. (1982) *Humanistic psychology in management education*, Brunel Institute of Organisation and Social Studies.

KUBLER-ROSS, E. (1970) *On death and dying*, London: Tavistock.

LAING, R.D. (1972) *Knots*, Harmondsworth: Penguin.

LEVITSKY, A. and PERLS, F.S. (1970) 'The rules and games of gestalt therapy', in Fagan, J. and Shepherd, I.C. (eds) *Gestalt therapy now: theory, techniques, applications*, Palo Alto, Calif.: Science and Behaviour.

LIEBERMAN, M.A., YALOM, I.D. and MILES, B. (1973) *Encounter groups: first facts*, New York: Basic Books.

LILLY, J.C. (1977) *The deep self*, New York: Simon and Schuster.

MACGREGOR, D. (1960) *The human side of enterprise*, New York: McGraw Hill.

MASLOW, A.H. (1965) *Eupsychian management—a journal*, Homewood, Ill.: Irwin.

MASLOW, A.H. (1973) *The farther reaches of human nature*, Harmondsworth: Penguin.

MASLOW, A.H. (1987) *Motivation and personality*, 3rd edn, New York: Harper and Row (first published 1954).

MASTERS, R.E. and HOUSTON, J. (1966) *Varieties of psychedelic experience*, New York: Holt, Rinehart and Winston.

MATSON, F. (1964) *The broken image*, New York: George Braziller.

MEADOR, B. (1969) 'An analysis of process movement in a basic encounter group', Ph.D. dissertation; cited in Rogers, 1970.

MONTE, C.F. (1980) *Beneath the mask: an introduction to theories of personality*, 2nd edn, New York: Holt, Rinehart and Winston.

ORNSTEIN, R.E. (1977) *The psychology of consciousness*, 2nd edn, New York: Viking Press.

PELLETIER, K.R. (1978) *Towards a science of consciousness*, New York: Delacorte Press.

PERLS, F.S. (1969) *Gestalt theory verbatim*, Moab, Utah: Real People Press.

REASON, P. and ROWAN, J. (1981) *Human enquiry: a source book of new paradigm research*, Chichester: Wiley.

ROGERS, C.R. (1951) *Client-centered therapy*, New York: Houghton.

Rogers, C.R. (1959) 'A theory of therapy, personality and interpersonal relationships as developed in the client-centered framework', in Koch, S. (ed.) *Psychology: a study of a science*, vol. 3, pp. 184–256, New York: McGraw Hill.

Rogers, C.R. (1961) *On becoming a person: a therapist's view of psychotherapy*, London: Constable.

Rogers, C.R. (1970) *Encounter groups*, Harmondsworth: Penguin.

Rogers, C.R. (1973) *Becoming partners: marriage and its alternatives*, London: Constable.

Rogers, C.R. (1983) *Freedom to learn for the 80s*, Columbus, OH: Charles E. Merrill.

Rogers, C.R. (1987) 'On growing older', *Journal of Humanistic Psychology*.

Rogers, C.R. and Stevens, B. (1973) *Person to person*, London: Souvenir Press.

Rowan, J. (1983) *The reality game: a guide to humanistic counselling and therapy*, London: Routledge and Kegan Paul.

Rowan, J. (1988) Personal communication.

Shaffer, J.B.P. (1978) *Humanistic psychology*, Englewood Cliffs, NJ: Prentice Hall.

Southgate, J. (1973) *Dialectical peer counselling*, London: Polytechnic of North London.

Taylor, E. (1978) 'Asian interpretations: transcending the stream of consciousness', in Pope, K. and Singer, J.L. (eds) *The stream of consciousness*, New York: Plenum Press.

Wordsworth, W. (1805) *The prelude*, 2nd edition in de Selincourt, E. and Gill, S. (eds) (1970) *Wordsworth: the prelude*, Oxford: Oxford University Press.

Answers to SAQs

SAQ 1

Humanistic psychologists focus on the thinking and feeling (i.e. experience) of individuals (c). They believe that the complexities of everyday experience cannot be adequately measured (a) and experimented upon (b). The capacity for language and symbolic awareness makes humans unique, so studies of animals (d) have only very limited relevance. Although they accept that childhood experience does influence personality, they still regard adults as open to change and development (e). Thus (c) is the best choice.

SAQ 2

(a) *Phenomenological*—based on subjective experience.

(b) *Existential perspective*—from the standpoint of the experience of being an existing person.

(c) *Personal agency*—a person's capacity to initiate actions and thoughts.

(d) *Holistic*—concern with the whole person—thought, feelings and body.

(e) *Experiential learning*—experiencing something or doing it yourself rather than just hearing about or watching someone else do it.

SAQ 3

Any three from:

- Introspection is necessarily involved and this can interfere with what is being experienced.
- Language is not adequate to capture and communicate the nuances of experiences.
- Experience is dynamic and ever-changing—only a small part can be recorded.
- Experience is not fixed; we can, to some extent, construct it.

SAQ 4

Any three of: alcohol, drugs, music, rhythm, intense concentration, sensory flooding, sensory deprivation, meditation. (Also, possibly, hypnosis, inducing sleep and therefore dreaming.)

SAQ 5

They can facilitate personal growth by releasing psychological energies and stimulating a sense of purpose.

SAQ 6

Existentialists regard everyone as having the capacity to choose. Excusing an action by saying he could not help himself is a way of avoiding choice and this would be regarded as inauthentic (c). It is not a lie (a) as he may well believe it to be true. A 'being need' (b) is from Maslow's theory and refers to self-actualization, and this is not applicable here. 'Incongruence between self-concept and organismic feelings' (d) is from Rogers' theory and it refers to a disparity between what is felt and the kind of person one thinks one is. It does not especially fit the statement given. This, though, is the next best choice, for such incongruence *might* underlie the situation described.

SAQ 7

(a) *Self-actualization*—self-fulfilment, 'to become everything that one is capable of becoming'.

(b) *Deficiency need*—basic needs such as that for food, sex, safety, or esteem, which stem from a drive to attain a state of satisfaction.

(c) *Being need*—a need whose expression is sufficient end in itself as, for example, self-actualization.

(d) *Unconditional regard*—warmth and respect for a person regardless of what he or she thinks or does.

(e) *Phenomenal field*—a term used by Rogers to refer to the sum total of a person's experience.

SAQ 8

(a) Rogers' non-directive, person-centred counselling.

(b) Its primary aims are to try to help clients towards a fuller awareness and integration of their feelings and thus towards greater congruence between organismic feelings and self concept. This is achieved by (1) providing a climate of non-evaluative and unconditional regard, (2) trying to enter the phenomenal world of clients and expressing this understanding to them, and (3) encouraging the experiencing and expression of feelings.

SAQ 9

(a) Co-counselling.

(b) Encounter group.

(c) Gestalt therapy.

(d) Bioenergetics.

(e) Psychosynthesis.

SAQ 10

(a) *Basic encounter*—a term used by Rogers for when individuals come into much closer and more direct contact with each other than is usual in ordinary life.

(b) *Empty chair technique*—the method used in gestalt groups where a person explores a suppressed part of themselves or a conflict between two 'inner voices' by placing in imagination each one on a cushion or empty chair (or on separate cushions or chairs) and then having a conversation between them, playing first one and then the other.

(c) *Bioenergetics*—the use of massage or physical exercise to work on muscular tensions to release blocked energy.

(d) *Superconscious*—Assagioli's concept of the unconscious resource within each of us for spiritual development.

(e) *Guided fantasy*—a technique used in psychosynthesis where a person creates his or her own sequence of visualization according to a broadly presented scenario, as a means of getting in touch with unconscious resources.

SAQ 11

The answers are (a) and (b).

SAQ 12

(a) *Sensitivity training*—an early form of encounter group used in a work context where people get together to give each other feedback about the impressions they create when working on a task together.

(b) *Synergy*—a situation where what is good for you is also good for other people.

(c) *'Owning'*—accepting one's own feelings rather than expressing them as statements or judgements about other people or events.

Overview of Part IV

Now that you have been introduced to several theories about intelligence and personality, several points may have struck you. You may have noticed that, although intelligence, and particularly the cognitive styles discussed in Chapter 7, Section 5, have obvious implications for the type of person you become, there has been little convergence between research studies on intelligence and personality. Quite a lot of research in these two fields uses the same psychometric method of measuring differences in performance and analysing correlations between test scores, using factor analysis. Despite the similarity in methods, Hans Eysenck is one of the few psychologists to have put forward theories about the genetic roots of both intelligence and personality (see Chapter 7, Section 3 and Chapter 8, Section 3). Yet even Eysenck does not fully amalgamate these two areas into one overall description of how an individual's intellect and personality interact.

There is an equally striking gulf between most personality research studies and the work of humanistic psychologists. The theories and therapies propounded by humanistic psychologists like Rogers and Maslow have obvious implications for personality. Yet there have been few contacts between researchers in the humanistic tradition and those working on personality and intelligence. An exception was Kelly, a co-founder of the American Association of Humanistic Psychology, as described in Chapter 9, Section 1. Kelly studied the constructs people use to structure their personal experiences, particularly their judgements about other people. The implication is that people's personalities are reflected in the way they approach the world and their ability to react flexibly when faced with new circumstances. Finally, it is interesting to note that there have been traditional 'resistances' to incorporating Freud's writings on personality into the mainstream of personality research, despite the many 'unconscious' influences of Freudian ideas.

Nature versus nurture

The possibility that differences in intelligence are due to genetic factors is fully discussed in Sections 3 and 4 of Chapter 7. Chapter 8, Section 3, examines Eysenck's theory that personality is inherited (and, of course, he applies the same theory to intelligence). He believes the main personality types, as defined by the dimensions of introversion–extraversion, neuroticism–stability and psychotism, are rooted in differences in the nervous system, which are genetically determined. If one is born with both a high level of arousal and a labile autonomic nervous system, the result is a tendency towards introverted behaviour and an emotionally neurotic personality (see Section 3.4 of Chapter 8).

Other personality theorists emphasize the importance of social learning. Allport (Chapter 8, Section 2) stresses the here and now, at the expense of past experience, but nevertheless implies that personality traits have arisen through social learning in the past. Similarly, Kelly's personal constructs arise from interactions with the environment in which the person 'as scientist' constructs and tests theories (Chapter 8, Section 4). Yet neither Allport nor Kelly really spell out the kinds of experiences which might lead to the great variety of personalities we see around us.

The weight that should be given to inborn and situational factors in explaining intellectual and personal differences is still a matter of debate. The balance of the evidence quoted in Chapter 7 indicates that genetic factors may play a role but that they are not likely to have a very strong influence in explaining individual differences in intelligence. Equally important are the social and cultural factors which affect people's lives. In any case, as is made abundantly clear in Chapter 7, Section 3, because inherited tendencies interact with a progressively changing environment, it is impossible to make a hard and fast estimate of heritability which applies in all situations.

Consistency and change

Problems about consistency and potential for change also form an important theme in Chapter 8. To what extent is a person's personality type fixed, as suggested by Eysenck? Are Allport's personality traits and Kelly's constructs relatively fixed aspects of a person's personality? As indicated in Chapter 8, Section 5.4, this is not a simple issue. One of the main aims of a personality theory is to provide an explanation for *consistency* in behaviour. For example, a trait of sociability describes the tendency for a person to act sociably in a variety of situations. On the other hand, most personality theories allow for development through life. Even Eysenck talks about physiological dimensions which constrain but do not completely determine behaviour. Allport and Kelly both stress possibilities for personality development.

An extreme version of the potential for change lies at the heart of the humanistic perspective. Because people can become more aware of their own conscious experiences, they are able to make decisions to adopt ways of being which will release their potential. A client of Rogers, or someone exposed to gestalt therapy, will be encouraged to open themselves up to their own feelings. According to Maslow (Chapter 9, Section 3.2), once basic needs are fulfilled, people are able to become self-actualizers, choosing whether to develop their full potential. How does this humanistic control of one's own destiny, and the infinite possibilities for change, fit in with the other approaches? Are there any constraints which might set boundaries to self-determinism?

One set of constraints is *biological*. These include both the general functioning of the nervous system, and genetic factors which contribute, to a greater or lesser extent, to each person's intelligence and personality. A second strand concerns *unconscious* motivations and frustrations, based on early experience, which may constrain behaviour into patterns and habits despite every conscious wish to change for the better. Thirdly, there are the effects of *experience*. Each individual has a set of personal experiences which may be emotionally and intellectually rich or poor, financially advantaged or disadvantaged. We all also have contacts with people and institutions which may be constricting or liberating. In addition to all these individual experiences, strong cultural influences operate in every society, determining social roles and expectations.

If behaviour is determined, and changes are at the mercy of reinforcement by the environment, are humans capable of personal choice at all? This is a philosophical question which has been debated for well over two thousand years. Here it has been emphasized that human beings are a species noted for their flexibility and adaptiveness to change. The mix of heredity, the ability to learn from experience, the capacity to reflect consciously about some, if not all, of our experiences and feelings and to respond in different ways to the demands of other people and to society itself: all these factors are responsible for the enormous, and exciting, diversity of human beings.

Acknowledgements for Volume 1

Grateful acknowledgement is made to the following sources for permission to reproduce material in these chapters:

Text

Box A, p. 20: The British Psychological Society (1978) 'Ethical principles for research with human subjects', *Bulletin of The British Psychological Society*, vol. 31; *Extracts C and D, pp. 90–91 and 104–5:* J. Piaget (1962) 'The stages of intellectual development of the child', *Bulletin of the Menninger Clinic*, vol. 26, ©Menninger Foundation; *Extracts, chapter 4:* Sigmund Freud Copyrights Ltd., The Institute of Psycho-Analysis and The Hogarth Press for permission to include extracts from *The Standard Edition of The Complete Psychological Works of Sigmund Freud*, translated and edited by James Strachey; *Box B, p. 335:* adapted from *Wechsler Intelligence Scale for Children– Revised*. Copyright © 1974 by the Psychological Corporation. Reproduced by permission. All rights reserved; *Extract, p. 431:* from W. Wordsworth (1805) 'The Prelude', in E. de Selincourt and S. Gill (eds.) (1970) *Wordsworth: The Prelude*, Oxford University Press; *Extract, p. 458:* from R. D. Laing (1972) *Knots*, Tavistock Publications.

Figures

Figure 2.1: adapted from R. L. Fantz (1961) 'The origin of form perception', *Scientific American*, vol. 204; *Figure 2.2:* reproduced from *The Social Foundations of Language and Thought: Essays in Honour of Jerome S. Bruner*, edited by David R. Olson, by permission of W. W. Norton & Company, Inc. Copyright © 1980 by David R. Olson; *Figure 2.3:* adapted from M. Lewis and J. Brooks-Gunn (1979) *Social Cognition and the Acquisition of Self*, Plenum Publishing Corp.; *Figure 2.4:* originally from G. G. Gordon, 'Self-recognition in chimpanzees', *American Psychologist*, vol. 32, pp. 329–38, 1977. Copyright 1977 by the American Psychological Association. Reprinted by permission; *Figure 3.1:* M. V. Cox (1980) 'Visual perspective-taking in children', M. V. Cox (ed.) *Are Young Children Egocentric?*, B. T. Batsford Ltd.; *Figure 3.5:* from R. M. Krauss and S. Glucksberg (1969) 'The development of communication: competence as a function of age', *Child Development*, vol. 40, The University of Chicago Press, copyright © The Society of Research on Child Development, Inc.; *Figure 3.6:* from M. Donaldson (1978) *Children's Minds*, William Collins, Sons & Company Ltd.; *Figure 5.1:* adapted from *Motivation: The Organisation of Action*, by Douglas G. Mook, by permission of W. W. Norton & Company, Inc. Copyright © 1987 by W. W. Norton & Company, Inc.; *Figure 5.18:* adapted from F. Toates (1986) *Motivational Systems*, Cambridge University Press; *Figure 6.1:* from F. A. Geldard (1963) *Fundamentals of Psychology*, John Wiley & Sons Inc.; *Figure 7.3:* figure A5 from J. C. Raven et al. (1983) *Standard Progressive Matrices*, reprinted by permission of J. C. Raven Limited; *Figure 7.5:* reprinted with the permission of the publisher from *Journal of Personality*, 19 (September 1950): 1–15. Copyright 1951, renewed 1979, by Duke University Press; *Figure 8.1:* from W. Mischel (1987) *Introduction to Personality*, Holt, Rinehart & Winston, Inc.; *Figure 8.3:* from H. J. Eysenck (1953) *The Structure of Human Personality*, Methuen; *Figures 8.4 and 8.5:* adapted from H. J. Eysenck and G. D. Wilson (1975) *Know Your Own Personality*, reprinted with the permission of the authors and Gower Publishing Co. Ltd.; *Figure 8.6:* from H. J. Eysenck (1954) *The Psychology of Politics*, Routledge & Kegan Paul. Reprinted by permission of Curtis Brown Ltd.

Tables

Table 7.1: adapted from *Wechsler Adult Intelligence Scale-Revised*. Copyright © 1981, 1955 by the Psychological Corporation. Reproduced by permission. All rights reserved; *Table 7.4:* from L. Erlenmeyer-Kimling and L. F. Jarvik, 'Genetics & Intelligence: A Review', *Science*, vol. 142, pp. 1477–9, 1963, copyright © American Association for the Advancement of Science.

Name index for Volume 1

Allport, G. W., 323, 377, 378ff., 397, 407ff., 413, 418, 470ff.
Anderson, J. R., 370
Anisman, H., 234
Ashby, B. 359
Assagioli, R., 419, 451ff.

Back, K., 64
Barker, L. M., 309
Barker, W. B., 357
Barnes, P., 127
Bates, P. B., 343
Bateson, G., 457
Beck, A., 230
Belkin, B., 230
Benedict, R., 456
Berg, K., 346
Bergin, A. E., 176, 465
Bernstein, M., 324
Best, M. R., 309
Bettelheim, B., 133
Bindra, D., 286, 305
Binet, A., 83, 327f., 333
Binswanger, L., 434
Blackman, D., 24
Blackman, S., 367
Blatt, S. J., 363
Blau, Z. S., 70, 360
Bloom, F. E., 245
Blumer, H., 58, 74
Boakes, R. A., 246, 307
Bocock, R., 180
Bolles, R. C., 285, 294ff., 297, 299, 307f.
Bolton, W., 233
Booth, D. A., 226
Borke, H., 109
Bourne, B., 182
Bowlby, J., 37
Brazelton, T. B., 34, 37
Breland, K., 298f., 305
Breland, M., 298f., 305
Breslow, R., 230
Breuer, J., 159
Broadbent, D., 6
Brooks-Gunn, J., 38ff., 44
Brown, G., 234
Bruch, H., 227
Bruner, J., 114f., 122ff.
Bryson, G. E., 44
Bruckingham, N., 117, 120
Burke, P. J., 70
Burkhard, B., 308
Burks, B. S., 351
Burns, R. B., 75
Burt, C., 5, 83, 345, 347ff.
Buss, A. H., 376, 384, 392

Butcher, H. J., 359

Campbell, B. A., 309
Camus, A., 433
Cardinal, M., 180
Carkhuff, R., 176
Carpenter, F., 275, 307
Catania, A. C., 275, 307
Chandler, M. J., 108, 113
Chapman, J., 127
Charcot, J. M., 159
Chomsky, N., 441
Church, R. M., 309
Code, C. F., 247
Cohen, D., 307
Coleridge, S. T., 428
Colman, A. M., 345, 350, 367
Colvin, S. S., 324
Conway, B. E., 324
Cook, M., 128
Cooley, C. H., 42, 47, 48, 50, 61, 64
Cooperman, O., 357f.
Corey, L., 346
Corsaro, W. A., 58ff., 74
Court, J. H., 337, 342
Cox, M. V., 99
Cuff, E. C., 74
Czernicwska, P., 127

Damon, W., 46, 47, 52f.
Darwin, C., 33, 80ff., 210, 267, 296f., 326
Dawes, R. M., 176
Dawkins, R., 215ff., 246
Deakin, J. F. W., 247
Dearborn, W. F., 324
DeCasper, A. J., 34f.
Denzin, N., 52, 58, 74
Descartes, R., 46
DeVries, R., 108
Dickinson, A., 287, 294, 307
Dinnage, R., 180
Domjan, M., 308, 309
Donaldson, M., 114ff., 126
Dukes, W. F., 173
Dyk, R. B., 361

Eaves, L., 346
Ebbinghaus, H., 8
Eckartsburg, R. von, 425
Edwards, D., 123
Eichler, U., 182
Eikelboom, R., 304
Einstein, A., 365, 426, 437
Elliott, C. D., 336
Epstein, A. N., 226

Epting, F. R., 412
Erikson, E., 60, 177
Erlenmeyer-Kimling, L., 350f.
Evison, R., 448
Eyferth, K., 357f.
Eysenck, H. J., 3, 172, 173, 176, 180, 237, 307, 350f., 354f., 360, 366, 377, 383ff., 398, 407ff., 413, 470ff.

Fagan, J., 466
Fancher, R. E., 345, 366
Fantz, R. L., 34
Farr, R., 7
Faterson, H. F., 361
Festinger, L., 64, 66
Fiedler, F. E., 176
Fifer, W. P., 34f.
Fischer, W. F., 425
Fisher, E., 127
Fitzsimons, J. T., 220
Flavell, J. H., 49, 108
Flynn, J. R., 343
Foss, B. M., 78
Frankl, V. E., 434f., 445, 463
Freeman, F. N., 348
Freud, S., 3, 4f., 8, 28f., 32, 132ff., 185ff., 253, 320, 376, 381f., 407, 409f., 424, 428, 438, 451, 470
Friedman, R. J., 309
Fries, E. D., 231
Fromm, E., 177, 434, 459, 463

Gabain, M., 128
Gabain, R., 128
Galen, 383, 386
Gallup, G., 41ff., 45
Galton, F., 323, 326ff., 346f.
Garcia, J., 300ff.
Gardner, B. T., 306, 308
Gardner, R. A., 306, 308
Garfield, S. L., 181, 465
Garvey, C., 52
Gay, P., 180
Gazzaniga, M. S., 427
Geldard, F. A., 256
Gellner, E., 180
Gelman, R., 112
Gendlin, E., 464
Gergen, K., 62, 65
Getzels, J. W., 364
Gibb, J. R., 448
Giorgi, A., 425
Glass, C. V., 176
Gleitman, H., 175
Glucksberg, S., 111

Goddard, H. H., 344f.
Goffman, E., 71, 75
Goldstein, K. M., 367
Goodenough, D. R., 361
Gottman, J., 58
Gould, S. J., 345, 366
Gray, J. A., 17, 285, 295, 413
Grof, S., 428, 460
Gruber, S., 108
Guilford, J. P., 364
Gustavson, C. R., 302
Guttman, N., 277

Halifax, J., 460
Hall, C. S., 171f., 412
Hall, D., 70
Hall, G. S., 83
Halliday, T., 247
Hampson, S. E., 343, 362f., 365, 412
Harbart, J. F., 136
Harlow, H., 43
Harlow, M. K., 43
Harnad, S., 307, 310
Harris, T., 234
Hartman, G., 182
Hartshorne, H., 411
Hearnshaw, L. S., 348
Heath, A., 346
Heidegger, M., 433
Henderson, N., 351
Henmon, V. A. C., 324
Hergenhahn, B. R., 412
Herman, D., 182
Herman, N., 180
Heron, J., 448, 449, 457
Herrnstein, R. J., 277, 296
Hershenson, M., 34
Hertzman, M., 361
Hinson, R. E., 304
Hippocrates, 383
Hogan, J. A., 213
Holzinger, K. J., 348
Horn, J. M., 352
Horney, K., 177
Horobin, R., 448
Houston, J., 428
Hudson, L., 364
Hughes, H., 228
Hume, D., 45, 50
Husserl, E., 424
Huxley, A., 464, 465

Ignatieff, M., 182
Inhelder, B., 115

Jackins, H., 448
Jackson, P. W., 364
James, W., 45, 46, 50, 64, 67, 136, 418, 423, 428, 437

Jarvik, L. F., 350f.
Jefferson, T., 437
Jenkins, M. D., 356f.
Jensen, A. R., 342, 350, 354f., 359f., 366
Jolly, A., 77
Joseph, A., 357f.
Juel-Nielsen, N., 349
Jung, C. G., 156, 165, 174, 175, 177, 386f.

Kalat, J. W., 226, 245
Kalish, D., 282
Kamin, L. J., 290ff., 348ff., 366
Kamiya, J., 429
Karp, S. A., 361
Katz, M. M., 309
Katz, R., 235
Katz, S. H., 357
Kelley, H., 64
Kelly, G. A., 377, 397ff., 407ff., 418, 419, 426, 470ff.
Kierkegaard, S., 433
Klein, M., 151, 155f., 174, 175, 177f.
Kline, P., 171ff.
Knight, I., 336
Knight, K., 455, 456
Koch, S., 467
Kocis, J., 230
Koelling, R. A., 300f.
Kogan, N., 364
Koslowski, B., 37
Kosslyn, S. M., 370
Krank, M. D., 304
Krauss, R. M., 111
Kretschmer, E., 384
Kubler-Ross, E., 460
Kuhn, M. H., 67

Laing, R. D., 419, 457f.
Landfield, A. W., 412
Landman, J. T. L., 176
Lazerson, A., 245
Leahy, A. M., 351
Lee, V., 127
Leitner, L. M., 412
LeMagnen, J., 225
Levey, A. A., 393
Levine, S., 295
Levitsky, A., 450
Lewin, K., 64
Lewis, H. B., 361
Lewis, M., 38ff., 44, 75
Lewontin, R. C., 355f.
Lieberman, M. A., 448
Light, P. H., 109f., 117, 120
Lilly, J. C., 428f.
Lindzey, G., 412
Lock, A., 127

Loehlin, J. C., 352
Logue, A. W., 246
Lomas, P., 176
Luborsky, L., 176
Lynn, R., 343

Maccoby, E. E., 43
Macfarlane, D. A., 280
Machover, K., 361
Mackenzie, B., 360
MacKinnon, D. W., 173
Mackintosh, N. J., 287, 308, 342, 355, 359, 360
MacLean, C., 43
Magus, P., 346
Mahler, M. S., 32f., 44, 151
Main, M., 37
Maratsos, M., 112
Mascie-Taylor, C. G. N., 342, 355, 359, 360
Maslow, A. H., 419, 422, 430f., 435ff., 440ff., 445, 456, 462ff., 470ff.
Masson, J. M., 154, 159
Masters, R. E., 428
Matson, F., 421
May, M. A., 411
McCall, G. J., 68, 71
McCarthy Gallagher, T., 127
McGregor, D., 456
McGuffin, P., 235
McKinney, W. T., 240
McPartland, T. S., 67
Mead, G. H., 28f., 42, 45ff., 57, 58ff., 61, 64, 68f., 72, 73f., 146, 185ff., 320, 382, 402
Meador, B., 448
Meissner, P. B., 361
Mercer, N., 123
Messick, S., 361, 367
Meyer, A., 136
Middleton, D., 123ff.
Miles, B., 448
Miles, T. R., 324
Milgram, S., 19f.
Miller, A., 159
Mischel, W., 411
Mitchell, E., 431
Moberg, G. P., 309
Monte, C. F., 436
Mook, D. G., 308
Morrison, A., 359
Morrison, D. L., 361, 365
Morse, S., 65
Moss, H. A., 33
Mowrer, O. H., 286
Mulford, H., 69
Munsinger, H., 128
Mutran, E., 70

Nance, W., 346
Nebylitsyn, V. D., 413
Newman, H. H., 348f.
Nietzsche, F., 433, 434
Nightingale, F., 380

Oates, J., 127
Oatley, K., 233
Odbert, H. S., 323, 379
Olsen, D. R., 36
Oltman, P. K., 361
Orbach, S., 228
Ornstein, R. E., 426f., 452, 464
Osborne, S. R., 306
Overton, W., 127

Packer, C., 215
Pakstis, A. J., 357
Palmer, R. L., 228, 246
Park, R. E., 70
Parkhurst, J., 58
Paul, D. B., 350
Pavlov, I. V., 255ff., 266, 270,
    279, 284, 285f., 288f., 296,
    303, 393
Payne, B., 465
Payne, G. C. F., 74
Pelletier, K. R., 429
Perls, F. S., 419, 449ff., 459
Perner, J., 108
Pfaff, D. W., 247
Phillips, A., 180
Piaget, J., 3, 5, 28f., 56, 58f., 82ff.,
    138, 146, 156, 177, 185ff., 320,
    402
Pinter, R., 324
Plomin, R., 376, 384, 392
Poincaré, H., 426
Pope, K., 467

Quinlan, D. M., 363

Rachman, S. J., 175
Raskin, E., 361
Raven, J., 337, 342
Raven, J. C., 337, 342
Reason, P., 465
Reed, T. E., 355
Reich, W., 451
Rescorla, R. A., 292f., 306, 308
Richards, M. P. M., 35
Richardson, K., 127
Ridley, M., 245
Rieff, P., 182
Ripple, R., 121
Ritchie, B. F., 282
Robbins, H., 117, 120
Robins, A. H., 232
Robinson, E., 112, 114
Robinson, W., 112, 114

Rockastle, V., 121
Rogers, C. R., 175, 419, 422, 435,
    438ff., 445ff., 456f., 459,
    463ff., 470ff.
Rolls, B. T., 220
Rolls, E. T., 220
Rose, A. M., 77
Rose, H., 277
Rose, S., 277, 355
Rosenblum, L., 75
Rosenzweig, S., 173
Rowan, J., 437, 451, 465
Rowland, N., 246, 247
Rozin, P., 226
Rycroft, C., 179

Salisbury, W., 69
Sartre, J. P., 433, 434
Scarr, S., 352, 355, 357f.
Schachter, S., 64
Schaffer, H. R., 37
Schaffer, J., 465
Schaie, K. W., 343
Schlenker, B., 67, 71
Schutz, W., 464
Schwartz, B., 307
Schweitzer, A., 437
Segal, H., 180
Seligman, M. E. P., 226, 302, 305,
    306
Selman, R. L., 49, 55ff., 60f., 107
Shaffer, J. B. P., 434
Sharma, R., 359
Shatz, M., 112
Sheldon, S., 127
Sheldon, W. H., 384f.
Shepherd, I. C., 466
Sherif, M., 64
Shields, J., 348f., 392
Shotter, J., 53
Shuey, A. M., 355
Shuttleworth, F. K., 413
Siegel, S., 304
Simmons, J. L., 68, 71
Simon, T., 327
Singer, B., 176
Singer, J. L., 467
Skeels, H. M., 352
Skinner, B. F., 3, 5, 219, 268ff.,
    279, 294, 296, 303ff., 307, 438
Skodak, M., 352
Sluckin, A., 75
Smith, A., 45, 50
Smith, B. D., 412
Smith, M. L., 176
Smith, P. K., 75
Solaas, M., 346
Southgate, J., 448
Spearman, C., 339
Spielman, J., 393

Sprott, W. J. H., 414
St. John, J., 465
Statham, A., 44
Stern, W., 328
Sternberg, R. J., 324f., 366
Stevens, B., 441, 442
Stewart, J., 304
Storr, A., 180
Strachey, J., 133, 179
Stryker, S., 44
Sundet, J., 346
Sutherland, N. S., 230, 246
Sylva, K., 77
Szeminska, N., 104

Tamarin, R. H., 351
Tart, C., 466
Taylor, E., 425
Terman, L. M., 324, 328, 333,
    344f.
Thibaut, D., 64
Thorndike, E. L., 263ff., 279, 283,
    294, 296, 324
Thurstone, L. L., 324, 339f.
Tinklepaugh, O. L., 283, 294
Tizard, B., 357f.
Tizard, J., 357f.
Toates, F., 219, 220, 221, 224,
    225, 226, 233, 245, 246, 286,
    305, 306, 308
Tolman, E. C., 277, 279, 280ff.,
    286, 294f., 304f.
Tomlinson, A., 128
Tomlinson, J., 128
Truax, C., 176
Turkle, S., 132
Turner, R., 68

Van Adrichem, P. W. M., 310
Van der Berg, C. J., 434
Vaughan, V. C., 75
Vega, L. de, 286
Vernon, P. E., 363
Vetter, H. J., 412
Videbeck, R., 62f.
Vygotsky, L. S., 53f. 114, 122ff.

Wallach, M. A., 364
Wapner, S., 361
Watson, J. B., 252ff., 259ff., 266,
    267, 277, 279, 280, 296, 303f.,
    307
Wechsler, D., 329, 332, 333ff.,
    340
Weinberg, R. A., 352, 357f.
Wiepkema, P. R., 306
Willerman, L., 352
Willner, P., 229, 230, 232, 241f.,
    246
Wilson, G. D., 172, 388, 396, 413

Wilson, G. T., 175
Wimmer, H., 108
Winnicott, D. W., 32, 151, 155, 177f., 180
Wise, R. A., 240
Wissler, C., 326

Wit, H. de, 304
Witkin, H. A., 361ff.
Witty, P. A., 356f.
Wolff, P. H., 33
Wood, D., 123ff.
Woodrow, H., 324

Wordsworth, W., 431
Wundt, W., 252, 386

Yalom, I. D., 448
Youniss, J., 54f., 58, 60

Zacharko, R. M., 234

Concept index for Volume 1

Page numbers in bold indicate where a concept is defined.

Accommodation, **92**
Acting out, **169**
Action potential, **197**
Afferent neurons, **201**
Age cohort, **343**
Aggression, 9ff.
Altercasting, **71**
Altered states of consciousness
  (ASCs), **427f.**
Anal stage, **148**
Animal models, **194**, 240
Animism, **96**
Anorexia nervosa, **227**
Anxiety, **144**
ARAS, **391**
Arousal level, **391**
Ascending reticular activating
  system (ARAS), **391**
Assertiveness training, **457**
Assimilation, **91, 92**
Authenticity, 72, **433**
Autism, 47, 48
Autonomic nervous system, **391**

Basic encounter, **446**
Behaviour, **3**, 253
Behaviourism, 251, **253ff.**
Behaviourists, **3**
Bioenergetics, **451**
Bipolar constructs, **398**
Bodywork, **451**
British Ability Scales, 336, 358
British Psychological Society
  Guidelines, 19f.

Cardinal traits, **379**
Castration anxiety, **154**
Catharsis, **159**, 449
Cathexis, **143**
Causal explanation, **213**
Causal texture, **294**
Causes, **8**
Cell, **196**
Central nervous system (CNS),
  196
Central traits, **380**
Centration, **85, 87**, 98
Chemical messenger, **202**
Chemical synapse, 201
Chemical transmitter, **202**
Choleric, 323, **384**
Chromosome, **208**
Circular reactions, **88**
Classical conditioning, **257ff.**,
  272f., **284ff.**, 393
Classical contingency, **258**, 261

Clinical psychologist, **4**
Co-counselling, **448f.**
Cognition, **84, 281**, 294
Cognitive approach, **281ff.**, 287,
  294ff.
Cognitive map, **281**
Cognitive shift, 279, 304
Cognitive styles, **361**, 365, 470
Commonality, principle of, **402**
Communication, 111ff.
Components of intelligence, **325**
Concordance, **237**
Concrete operations, **94f.**
Conditional reflex, **256**
Conditional response (CR), **256**,
  260
Conditional stimulus (CS), **256ff.**
Conditioning, **257**, 393
Confederate, **63**
Conformity, **65**
Congruent validation, **341**
Conscience, **140**
Conscious, **139**, 253, 420, 426
Consensual validation, **403**
Consequences, 272
Conservation, **101ff.**, 117ff.
Consistency (of personality), 410,
  471
Consistency (of test), **341**
Construct system, **397**
Constructive alternativism, **405**
Contingency, **123f.**, **258**, 266f.
Continuous reinforcement, **271**
Contraprepared (for association),
  300
Contrast pole, **399**
Control group, **14**
Convergent thinking, **363**
Core constructs, **402**
Correlation, **62**, **325**, **390**
Correlation matrix, **334**
Counter-transference, **169**
CR, **256**, 260
Criterion, **12**
Criterion validation, **341**
Cross-sectional studies, **343**
CS, **256ff.**
Culture-fair tests, **359**
Culture-free, **359**

Darwin's theory of evolution by
  natural selection, **210**
Data, **12**, 252
Death instinct (Thanatos), **147**
Defence mechanisms, **144**

Deficiency needs, **436**
Deoxyribonucleic acid, **208**
Discrimination, **274**
Discriminative stimulus, **275**
Disembed, **114**
Disposition, **376**
Distribution (of test scores), **330**
Divergent thinking, **363**
Dramaturgical theory, **71**
Dream symbolism, **165**
Dream-work, **163**
Drive, **219**
Dynamic unconscious, **136**
Dynamic, **134**, 137

Economic view, **143**
Efferent neuron, **201**
Ego, **139**, 141, 149, 156
Ego ideal, **140**
Ego psychology, **144**
Egocentrism, **85, 87**, 100, 107ff.,
  116
Elements of repertory grid, **398**
Elicited response, **273**
Embedded figures test, **362**
Emitted response, **273**
Emotion, **3**
Empirical evidence, **171**
Empty chair, **450**
Encounter groups, **445f.**
Endogenous, **233**
Eros, **147**
Erotogenic zones, **148**
Ethical problems, **18**, 62, 344f.
Evidence, **7**
Evolution, 209ff., 240
Existential perspective, **421, 433**
Exogenous, **233**
Expectancy, **280**, 283, 284, 287ff.
Experiential approach, 186,
  420f., 471
Experiential learning, **422**, 442
Experimental method, **14**
Explanation, **7**, 241
External danger, **144**
Extinction, **259**, 270
Extraversion–introversion
  dimension, **285**, 393

Face validity, **390**
Factor analysis, 324, **339**, **390**
Fecundity, **211**
Field dependent, **362**
Field independent, **362**
Fitness, **211**, 240
Fixation, **151**, 173

Flexible behaviour, 280, 285f.
Formal operations, **95**
Free association, **160**
Free will, 418, 441
Friendship, 54ff.
Friendship development,
    Selman's stages of, 56ff.
Functional autonomy, **383**
Functional explanation, **213**

Game stage, **49**
Garcia effect, **300**
Gene, **208**, 214ff.
General intelligence, (g), 338,
    339
Generalized other, **49**, 51
Genetic epistemology, 83f.
Genital stage, **148**
Gestalt therapy, **449**f.
Goal-directed dynamics, 137
Group tests, **338**
Guided fantasy, **452**

Heritability, 235, 320, **345**f., 353
Hierarchy (in organization of
    personality), **386**
Holistic approach, **421**, 451
Homeostasis, **219**
Hormones, **197**
Human sense, 114, **116**
Hydraulic model, **143**
Hypnosis, **159**
Hypothesis, **11**, 158
Hysteria, **157**

I, **46**, 50, 68, 72, 73, 424, 439
Id, **139**, 140, 144, 148, 156
Identical twins, **347**
Identification, **154**
Idiographic approach, **377**, 407ff.
Implicit personality theories, **374**
Implicit theories, **8**, 374
Incentive, **224**
Index of correlation, **325**
Index of learning, 253, 257f.
Individual differences, 320, **323**
Inherited, **8**, 235
Inhibitory synapse, **204**
Innate, **33**
Instinct theory, **144**
Instinctive drift, **299**
Instrumental conditioning, **266**
Instrumental contingency, **266**
Intelligence, 320, **324**ff., 354
Intelligence quotient (IQ), 320,
    324, **328**ff.
Interactional age, **48**
Internal danger, **144**
Internal objects, **147**
Interneuron, **201**
Inter-role conflict, **69**

Intra-role conflict, **69**
Intrinsic motivation, **92**
Introjection, **154**
Introspection, **18**, 252
IQ, 320, 324, **328**ff.
Item on a personality rating
    scale, **389**

Lability, 391, **392**
Latency period, **148**
Latent content, **163**
Law of effect, **265**
Learning curve, 263f.
Levels of analysis, **22**
Libido, **143**
Life instinct, **147**
Light receptor, **200**
Longitudinal studies, **343**

Manifest content, **163**
Me, **46**, 50, 72, 73, 439
Measure, **12**, 18, 253, 326, 333,
    377, 470
Meditation, **429**, 460
Melancholic, 323, **384**
Membrane, **196**
Mental age, **327**
Mental processes, **4**
Mill Hill Vocabulary Scale, 338,
    359
Models, **397**
Moral anxiety, **144**
Motivation, **4**, 92, 137f., **218**ff.,
    409, 471
Motor neuron, **201**
Movement contingency cues, **40**
Mutant, **212**
Mutation, **212**

Nature, **344**, 470
Negative cognitive set, **230**
Negative correlation, **325**
Negative feedback system, **220**
Negative reinforcement, **271**
Negative transference, **169**
Nerve cell, **196**
Nervous system, **196**
Neural pathway, **198**
Neuron, **196**ff.
Neurosis, **158**
Neurotic anxiety, **144**
Neuroticism–stability dimension,
    385
Neurotransmitter, **202**
Neutral stimulus (NS), **256**, 262
Nociceptor, **199**
Nomothetic approach, **377**, 407ff.
Non-directive, person-centred
    counselling, **440**
Normal distribution (of test
    scores), **330**

NS, **256**, 262
Nucleus, **207**
Nurture, **344**, 470

Object permanence, **85, 87**
Object relations, **147**, 155f., 177
Objective anxiety, **144**
Objective measure, **12**, 320
Objectivity, **17, 171,** 174
Observational method, **13, 58**
Oedipus complex, 5, 149, **152**ff.,
    171ff.
One-way mirror, **38**, 59
Operant, **271**
Operant conditioning, 270f.,
    284ff.
Oral stage, **148**
Organ, **195**
Organism, 298, **439**
Overdetermination, **136**
Owning, **450,** 459

Palatability, **224**
Parallel-form reliability, **341**
Parapraxes, **132**ff., 160
Partial reinforcement, **271**
Participant observation, **18, 59**
Pavlovian conditioning, **257**
Peak experience (PE), **430**ff.
Peer group assessment, **457**
Penis envy, **154**
Performance measures, **394**
Permeability, **402**
Person-centred counselling, **440,**
    445
Persona, **411**
Personal agency, **421,** 441f., 463
Personal construct, **397,** 470
Personal growth, 320, **421,** 438
Personal reality, **405**
Personality, 320, 376, 470
Personality dimension, **384**
Personality rating scale item, **389**
Personality traits, **374, 379**
Phallic stage, **148,** 152f.
Phenomenal field, **439**
Phenomenological approach,
    410, 421, 425f.
Phenomenological philosophy,
    424f.
Phlegmatic, 323, **384**
Plasma, **196**
Play stage, **48,** 51ff.
Pleasure principle, **144**
Positive correlation, **325**
Positive feedback, **233**
Positive reinforcement, **271,** 276
Positive transference, **168**
Practical intelligence, **325**
Preconscious, **139**
Prediction, **9,** 287

Pre-Oedipal stage, **155**
Pre-operational, **94**, 96ff., 104f.
Preparatory stage, **48**
Prepared (for association), **300**
Primary mental abilities, **339**
Primary process thinking, **163**
Primary socialization, **48**, 51
Principle of commonality, **402**
Problem solving, **325**
Proprium, **382**
Psyche, **138**
Psychic secretions, **255**
Psychoanalysis, **134**
Psychoanalytic psychotherapy, 157ff., 166ff., **169**ff.
Psychodynamics, **134**ff., 449
Psychological determinism, **135**f.
Psychometrics, 320, **333**, 365, **377**, 388, 470
Psychosexual stages, 146, 148ff., 156
Psychosynthesis, **451**, 453
Punishment, **271**
Purposive (behaviour), **280**f., 285ff.

Racial admixture studies, **356**f.
Racial crossing studies, **357**f.
Radical–conservative dimension, **395**
Range of convenience, **401**
Raven's Progressive Matrices, 337
Reaction formation, **152**
Reaction times, **326**
Reality principle, **144**
Receptor, **202**
Reductionism, **241**
Reflexes, **88**
Regression, **151**
Reinforcement, **266**, 270ff., 295
Reinforcer, **266**
Reliability (of test), **341**
Repertory grid, **398**
Replication, **208**
Representation, **54**, 86f., 93
Repression, **144**
Reproduction, **208**
Resistance, **160**, 167f.
Response, **252**f.
Rod and frame test, **362**
Role, 47, **67**ff.
Role construct repertory grid, **398**
Role-take, **47**
Rotating room test, **362**

Salivation reflex, **255**f.
Sample, **12**

Sanguine, 323, **384**
Scaffolding, **123**
Schedule of reinforcement, **271**
Schema/schemata, **91**, 92
Scientific method, 17f., 173ff., 253ff., 397
Scientist (as used by Kelly), **397**, 402, 409, 470
Screen memories, **161**ff.
SD, **330**
Secondary dispositions, **380**
Secondary process thinking, **163**
Secondary socialization, **48**, 51
Selective placement, **352**
Self, **31**, 67ff., 424, **439**
Self-actualization, **436**, 440
Self-concept, **42**, 46, 50, 61ff.
Self-esteem, **65**
Self-reflexiveness, **47**
Sensitivity training, **455**
Sensori-motor stage, **88**, 90f., 94
Sensory deprivation, **428**
Sensory discrimination, **326**
Sensory flooding, **428**
Serotonergic, **203**
Serotonin, **203**
Shaping, **270**
Similarity pole, **399**
Skinner box, **219**, **269**ff., 294ff.
Social behaviour, **4**, 31, 48, 106ff., 114ff., 272
Social comparison theory, **64**ff.
Social feedback, **61**ff.
Social identity, **71**
Social perspective taking, 56ff., 107, 115f.
Sociality, **402**, 407
Socialization, **31**, 48, 68
Split-half reliability, **341**
Spontaneous remission, **176**
S–R psychology, **260**ff., 272ff.
Stability (of test), **341**
Stage of development, 95, 148, 185
Standard deviation (SD), **330**
Stanford–Binet scale, 83, **333**, 349, 358
Statistical analysis, **13**
Stereotype, **374**
Stimulus, **252**f.
Stimulus–response psychology (S–R), **260**ff., 272ff.
Stream of consciousness, **423**f.
Structure, **94**
Subjects, **19**
Successive approximations, **270**
Superconscious, **452**
Super-ego, **140**, 142, 148, 156
Symbolic dialogue, **50**
Symbolic function, **87**

Symbolic interactionism, **44**, 50, 74
Synapse, **201**
Synaptic cleft, **202**
Synergy, **456**

T-dimension, **395**
Television violence, 9ff.
Temperament, **323**, **384**
Temporal contiguity, **258**
Test norm, **327**
Testing, **7**, 119f., 158, 341f., 407f., 470
Test–retest reliability, **341**
Theories X and Y, **456**
Theory, **7**
Therapeutic alliance, **169**
Topographical model, **138**
Tough-mindedness–tender-mindedness dimension, **395**
Trait, **323**, **379**
Trait labels, **379**
Transference, **168**
Trauma, **144**, 158
Triad in repertory grid, **399**
Type theory, **384**

UCR, **256**, 260
UCS, **255**ff., 263
Unconditional reflex, **256**ff.
Unconditional regard, **440**, 459
Unconditional response (UCR or UR), **256**, 260
Unconditional stimulus (UCS or US), **255**ff., 263, 393
Unconscious conflict, **136**
Unconscious, 136, **139**ff., 452, 471
UR, **256**
US, **255**

Validity (of test), **341**
Verbal intelligence, **325**
Viability, **211**

WAIS-R, **334**, 335
Wechsler Adult Intelligence Scale (revised), **333**f., 335, 349, 358
Wechsler Intelligence Scale for Children (revised), **334**, 335
Wechsler Preschool and Primary Scale of Intelligence, **334**
Will, **452**
Will to meaning, **434**
WISC-R, **334**, 335
Working through, **167**f.
WPPSI, **334**

Zone of proximal development, **122**